REVIEW OF RESEARCH IN EDUCATION

Review of Research in Education is published on behalf of the American Educational Research Association by SAGE Publications, Thousand Oaks, CA 91320. Copyright © 2010 by the American Educational Research Association. All rights reserved. No portion of the contents may be reproduced in any form without written permission from the publisher. POSTMASTER: Send address changes to AERA Membership Department, 1430 K St., NW, Suite 1200, Washington, DC 20005.

Member Information: American Educational Research Association (AERA) member inquiries, member renewal requests, changes of address, and membership subscription inquiries should be addressed to the AERA Membership Department, 1430 K St., NW, Suite 1200, Washington, DC 20005; fax 202-238-3250. AERA annual membership dues are $120 (Regular and Affiliate Members), $100 (International Affiliates), and $35 (Graduate and Undergraduate Student Affiliates). **Claims:** Claims for undelivered copies must be made no later than six months following month of publication. Beyond six months and at the request of the American Educational Research Association, the publisher will supply missing copies when losses have been sustained in transit and when the reserve stock permits.

Subscription Information: All non-member subscription inquiries, orders, back-issue requests, claims, and renewals should be addressed to SAGE Publications, 2455 Teller Road, Thousand Oaks, CA 91320; telephone (800) 818-SAGE (7243) and (805) 499-0721; fax: (805) 375-1700; e-mail: journals@sagepub.com; http://www.sagepublications.com. **Subscription Price:** Institutions: $148; Individuals: $52. For all customers outside the Americas, please visit http://www.sagepub.co.uk/customercare.nav for information. **Claims:** Claims for undelivered copies must be made no later than six months following month of publication. The publisher will supply missing copies when losses have been sustained in transit and when the reserve stock will permit.

Abstracting and Indexing: Please visit http://rre.aera.net and click on the Abstracting/Indexing link on the left-hand side to view a full list of databases in which this journal is indexed.

Copyright Permission: Permission requests to photocopy or otherwise reproduce copyrighted material owned by the American Educational Research Association should be submitted by accessing the Copyright Clearance Center's Rightslink® service through the journal's website at http://rre.aera.net. Permission may also be requested by contacting the Copyright Clearance Center via its website at http://www.copyright.com, or via e-mail at info@copyright.com.

Advertising and Reprints: Current advertising rates and specifications may be obtained by contacting the advertising coordinator in the Thousand Oaks office at (805) 410-7763 or by sending an e-mail to advertising@sagepub.com. To order reprints, please e-mail reprint@sagepub.com. Acceptance of advertising in this journal in no way implies endorsement of the advertised product or service by SAGE or the journal's affiliated society(ies). No endorsement is intended or implied. SAGE reserves the right to reject any advertising it deems as inappropriate for this journal.

Change of Address: Six weeks' advance notice must be given when notifying of change of address. Please send old address label along with the new address to ensure proper identification. Please specify name of journal.

International Standard Serial Number ISSN 0091-732X
International Standard Book Number ISBN 978-1-4129-8191-0 (Vol. 34, 2010, paper)
Manufactured in the United States of America. First printing, March 2010.
Copyright © 2010 by the American Educational Research Association. All rights reserved.

Printed on acid-free paper

REVIEW OF RESEARCH IN EDUCATION

What Counts as Evidence
in Educational Settings?
Rethinking Equity, Diversity,
and Reform in the 21st
Century

Volume 34, 2010

Allan Luke, Editor
Queensland University of Technology

Judith Green, Editor
University of California, Santa Barbara

Gregory J. Kelly, Editor
Pennsylvania State University

American Educational
Research Association

Ⓢ SAGE

Review of Research in Education
What Counts as Evidence in Educational Settings? Rethinking Equity, Diversity, and Reform in the 21st Century
Volume 34

EDITORS

ALLAN LUKE
Queensland University of Technology, Australia

JUDITH GREEN
University of California, Santa Barbara

GREGORY J. KELLY
Pennsylvania State University

CONTRIBUTORS

LORA BARTLETT
University of California, Santa Cruz

KEVIN M. LEANDER
Vanderbilt University

GAIL L. SUNDERMAN
George Washington University

LAUREN BERESFORD
University of California, Berkeley

JUDITH WARREN LITTLE
University of California, Berkeley

MARK WARSCHAUER
University of California, Irvine

KATHERINE HEADRICK TAYLOR
Vanderbilt University

SAMUEL R. LUCAS
University of California, Berkeley

KEVIN WELNER
University of Colorado, Boulder

WILL J. JORDAN
Temple University

DYLAN WILIAM
Institute of Education, University of London

TINA MATUCHNIAK
University of California, Irvine

JAMES G. LADWIG
University of Newcastle, New South Wales, Australia

NATHAN C. PHILLIPS
Vanderbilt University

ALEXANDER W. WISEMAN
Lehigh University

EDITORIAL BOARD

ALFREDO ARTILES
Arizona State University

RICHARD DUSCHL
Pennsylvania State University

JOSEPH TOBIN
Arizona State University

DAVID BAKER
Pennsylvania State University

VIVIAN GADSDEN
University of Pennsylvania

AMY TSUI
University of Hong Kong, China

DAVID BLOOME
Ohio State University

CAROL LEE
Northwestern University

GEOFF WHITTY
Institute of Education, University of London

BRYAN BROWN
Stanford University

PAMELA MOSS
University of Michigan

JOHN YUN
University of California, Santa Barbara

MARIA LUCIA CASTANHEIRA
Federal University of Minas Gerais, Brazil

JAMES PELLEGRINO
University of Illinois, Chicago

AMERICAN EDUCATIONAL RESEARCH ASSOCIATION
TEL: 202-238-3200   FAX: 202-238-3250
http://www.aera.net/pubs

FELICE J. LEVINE
Executive Director

TODD REITZEL
Director of Publications

BARBARA LEITHAM
Publications Coordinator

Contents

Cover image © 2009 Jupiterimages Corporation.

Introduction

What Counts as Evidence and Equity?

ALLAN LUKE
Queensland University of Technology

JUDITH GREEN
University of California, Santa Barbara

GREGORY J. KELLY
Pennsylvania State University

The most durable and robust problem facing education research since mid–20th century is the persistence of educational inequality. Under new economic, technological, and cultural conditions, increasingly diverse populations and communities are facing persistent and emergent patterns of educational inclusion and exclusion. How we name and describe, document and understand educational equality and inequality, inclusion and exclusion, centrality and marginality, then, is *the* issue facing educational systems in economically hard times. In this volume, we bring together reviews on different approaches to the formation and use of evidence in educational policy and reform. We asked the authors to examine different approaches to evidence and to focus on how each reflects particular ways of defining, explaining, and framing inequality and equality in educational policy and practice. They also provide critical analyses of evidence-based policies to date, discussing policy assumptions about and impacts on educational equity.

This volume is a companion to the last four volumes of *Review of Research in Education*. In our two previous edited volumes, we focused on "what counts as learning" (Vol. 30), and "what counts as knowledge" (Vol. 32). There we and our editorial boards and authors attempted to broaden and expand debates over policy and practice that were becoming narrowly circumscribed in the transnational push for accountability-driven, evidence-based policy. Our goal in these volumes was to bring state-of-the-art research and theoretical perspectives across traditions and disciplines

Review of Research in Education
March 2010, Vol. 34, pp. vii-xvi
DOI: 10.3102/0091732X09359038
© 2010 AERA. http://rre.aera.net

in order to bear on factors that support and constrain what is possible educationally in and out of classrooms, school, community, and regional policy contexts. In these volumes, we recognized the roles of qualitative, mixed-method, action, and practitioner-based research in generating valuable, local and situated issues and opportunities around learning in reform contexts. Adjacent volumes of *Review of Research in Education* have focused on reviews of critical research and development work on race, difference, and diversity (Parker, 2007), and on "at risk" student and youth communities (Gadsden, Artiles, & Davis, 2009). These have expanded our engagement with standpoints and perspectives of those student communities that have experienced educational exclusion and marginalization.

In this volume, authors engage with different angles, frames, and levels for discussing matters of the analytic scale and scope of educational reform (see Bryk & Gomez, 2007): a key response to problems of equity in a two-decade-long push for "evidence-based" social and educational policy in advanced industrial nations and economies. Following the lead of transnational organizations such as the Organization of Economic Cooperation and Development (OECD) and the World Bank, the press for accountability-driven educational policy has extended to emergent economies and countries still building basic school and postsecondary educational infrastructure (see Wiseman, Chapter 1). One result has been the driving of the reform of school and classroom practice on the basis of a single major performance indicator: student achievement on high stakes standardized testing. The laudable goal of many of these policies has been closure of what is now termed *the equity gap*—the differential between general population norms and the performance of identified equity groups: for example, African Americans, Latinos, migrants, second language speakers, and students from low socioeconomic backgrounds (see Lucas & Beresford, Chapter 2; Jordan, Chapter 5).

Not surprisingly, the demand for evidence has opened a Pandora's Box of arguments over the appropriate grounds for documenting and analyzing student socioeconomic, cultural and linguistic background, student performance and achievement, systemic delivery of resources, school-type and structure, and school and teacher practices. It is axiomatic that any policy "fix" or strategic approach is contingent on how the problems, target populations, variable contexts, and factors are defined and parceled out and observed, represented and measured, and analyzed. How we define and describe the contexts and impacts of difference and diversity, then, remains on the policy table. In the United States, Canada, the United Kingdom, Australia and New Zealand, European, and Asian systems, there are robust debates over what kinds of evidence can and should be enlisted to analyze systems' equity performance and to shape and implement innovation and reform.

Since its inception more than a century ago, modern educational research has been based on distinctive and, at times, contending conceptions of evidence and, indeed, educational science. These range across descriptive and interpretive, quantitative and qualitative, empirical and hermeneutic approaches that draw from varied theoretical models of education and schooling, knowledge and culture, the learner and society (Green, Camilli, & Elmore, 2006). As the sciences *and* arts of education have evolved, differing research paradigms have defined educational phenomena in distinctive terms and provided contending forms of evidence for policymakers, educational system bureaucrats, curriculum developers, teachers, students, and parents.[1] But this cannot be attributed solely to academic paradigm wars, contending sociocultural value systems, or, in some cases, media and public misrepresentation of research. It raises foundational questions of what kinds of science and philosophy can and should inform educational practice.

On its face, it is a simple, straightforward idea: that educational and social policy should be based on scientific evidence rather than specific political view, philosophy, religious belief, or social ideology. The use of science to inform the formation of laws, institutions, and governance of the secular state has a long and, at times, undistinguished history. It featured prominently in 17th- and 18th-century debates over the rational foundations of the modern nation state, with varied bids for governance to be based on the logics and evidence of the sciences of economics, eugenics, psychology, sociology, medicine, and so forth (e.g., Gould, 1981). Appeals to a "gold standard" of scientific evidence were central to the work of the British Royal Society in the 18th and 19th centuries (Kenner, 1985), with "scientific" evidence subsequently applied to the social problems such as population control and migration, sexuality, birth, marriage and the family, race and gender relations, illness, poverty and crime, and industrial and ecological regulation (Rose, 1999). We find further appeals for the "scientific" management of the state and its institutions across the political spectrum in the 20th century, with heated disputes in the inter- and postwar period between logical positivists and pragmatists, socialists, liberal humanists, and conservatives about what kinds of science should count in the regulation of everyday life. Many contemporary research organizations have their roots in Cold War government funding of the intelligence and research and development sectors (Reich, 2005).

The implications of the scientific, quasi-scientific, and pseudo-scientific control of institutions and everyday life is a prominent theme across millennia of utopian and dystopian fiction from the works of Swift to Orwell and Huxley to recent novels by William Gibson and Margaret Atwood. And we encounter it again in ongoing disputes over the contentious use of "evidence-based policy" and "policy-based evidence" as the rationale for geopolitics, war, and invasion (Haas, 2009) and, most obviously, in current debates over the evidence of human agency in climate change. In a democratic state, making decisions about institutions, communities, environment and place, and people based on rationally argued and supported grounds is a clear imperative—but which scientific evidence, whose sciences, and whose interpretations will count is a far tougher call.

The use of evidence and science to address issues of educational equity and social justice is not straightforward. Educational systems have been profoundly troubled by complexity, diversity, and difference. Some of these matters arise in an era of cultural and economic globalization: emergent forms of cultural and ethnic identity and affiliation, large- and medium-scale migration, refugees from warfare and cultural conflict, employment-driven population shift and movement within countries and regions, and, for many, new and difficult conditions of poverty. In other instances, it is because of the official and local recognition of the unresolved issues of cultural and linguistic diversity: where communities' voices, rights, and very existence are "named" for recognition where they might have been written over or silenced before. All contemporary educational systems are dealing with increasingly heterogeneous populations. What were previously referred to as *nonmainstream* and *minority* populations are frequently the norm rather than the exception.

The task at hand also involves addressing the powerfully articulated educational rights of those communities that historically have sat at the margins—often unnamed in curriculum, policy, and practice (see Welner, Chapter 3; Sunderman, Chapter 7; Jordan, Chapter 5). This includes, but is not limited to, cultural and linguistic "minorities" that, in some jurisdictions, have become majorities: For example, Indigenous peoples whose histories, cultures, and languages were excribed from models of curriculum and pedagogy, the specific educational needs and aspirations of girls and women, students of diverse sexual orientations, and those students whose specialized learning needs hitherto have escaped "naming," recognition, and equitable provision.

This is not to invoke the specter of what the media refers to as "political correctness"—nor to sideline the broad goals of just and equitable schooling built around concepts of intergenerational transmission of common and shared knowledge, social skill, and economic capacity, laudable goals at the heart of democratic education. But it is a practical matter of how school systems can best build on and from the complex forms of what we could broadly term the increasing *epistemological diversity* that teachers, curriculum planners, teacher educators, and, indeed, educational policymakers face on a daily basis.

On its surface, evidence-based policy is the new common sense of government secretaries, ministers and advisors, senior civil servants, local school board members, and principals. But it calls into question two issues: (a) what might count as "scientific" evidence sufficient to shape rational, normative defensible policy decisions and (b) the interpretive and contextual work of policy formation (see Sunderman, Chapter 7; Wiseman, Chapter 1). Claims that this is a simple, self-evident, or straightforward matter that can be taken without reflection and interpretation, robust dialogue and debate, due consideration of history and theory, narrative as well as expository knowledge, and an understanding of the disciplinary bases and assumptions of different educational sciences are naïve and risky. Our authors here provide catalytic reviews and analyses, which, hopefully, will have the effect of unsettling elements of prevailing common sense and provide a broad map of possible research and policy directions.

Alexander Wiseman (Chapter 1) begins the volume with a comparative national and international review of approaches to evidence and equity. He attributes the move toward evidence-based policy to the ongoing demand for political legitimacy, with variable normative goals tending to focus on "quality," "equity," and "control." Wiseman goes on to track how these different goals have been realized in U.S. states' moves toward evidence-based policy, then contrasts these with other national and transnational strategies around gender equity. He concludes that the effects of evidence-based policies have tended to reflect specific systems' normative goals, but notes the tendency of systems to adopt a technical bureaucratic approach to the definition, collection, and interpretation of evidence rather than the "evidence in context" approach advocated by Whitty (2006) and others.

The push toward evidence-based policy has indeed raised major issues around the actual locus of control in educational governance and around the institutional restructuring of state education. Focusing on policy and court cases in the U.S. context, Gail Sunderman (Chapter 7) shows current approaches to equity have evolved over the past century and a half. This evolution is linked to two broader, contradictory movements: first, toward increased federal control over education, and second, toward the promotion of models of privatization and marketization. Sunderman concludes that the byproduct of school reform has been increased centralized bureaucratic control over education. This is predicated on the assumption, she argues, that "standards, assessments and accountability reforms" can address problems that are rooted in persistent social and economic conditions.

As Sam Lucas and Lauren Beresford (Chapter 2) argue, policies and evidence work from a priori definitions of human populations, target groups, and sociological assumptions about what might constitute equitable outcomes. Governance and the modern state works through the establishment of specific grids of specification, classificatory schemes, and taxonomies for the definition, categorization, and surveillance of human subjects. These categories are far from "natural" or "transparent." What and whom we include in what may appear a common sense category of "race," "language," or "social class" are elementary problems of social science. Lucas and Beresford review the last half-century of empirical approaches to describing and measuring equity. They then map the foundational assumptions of different categories and definitions and affiliated measurement approaches. Their point is that all classificatory schemes of equity cohorts and approaches to the measurement of their performance align themselves with particular models of society and culture.

Although specific kinds of evidence have been used as rationale and legitimation for policy, the evidentiary bases for legal claims about equality of educational opportunity and equity of outcomes are a neglected area of consideration. Court decisions shape the "bottom line" for debates around public accountability, systemic risk and liability, and issues of social and economic justice. Kevin Welner (Chapter 3) shifts our attention to how we might legally demonstrate equal and unequal provision and outcomes. Reviewing legal and judicial decisions around educational equity, Welner focuses on the variable evidence on equality and inequality in "opportunities to learn." He focuses on the legal precedents in cases where plaintiffs have contested placements and effects of streaming and tracking systems. He concludes that the push for accountability with explicit equity targets has opened the way for "classroom-based litigation," which may provide communities and individuals with leverage in defining what might count as equitable learning opportunities and, indeed, outcomes.

Beginning from the *Brown* decision, Will Jordan (Chapter 5) examines whether and how test-based accountability strategies such as *No Child Left Behind* have explained and addressed inequitable patterns of achievement for "people-of-color." Beginning from recognition of the complexity of definition, Jordan questions whether test-driven accountability policy has engaged with a rich and diverse research literature on effective practices for minority learners. Jordan reviews the qualitative, ethnographic, and longitudinal pathway research on the schooling of cultural minorities that is often excluded as evidence from policy debates. On this basis, he asks whether test-driven policy has the capacity to enhance authentic learning, to address longstanding issues of social access and mobility facing minority students, and to ameliorate the systemic causes and challenges of economic and cultural exclusion.

As several chapters have indicated—much of the dispute over "evidence" has been based on the strengths and limits of standardized testing. Major U.S., U.K., Canadian, Australian, and New Zealand policymaking has relied principally on an evidence base of standardized test results, despite what we know about the strengths and limits of standardized testing as an assessment technology (e.g., Klenowski, 2009; Moss, Girard, & Hanniford, 2006). What are the alternatives? James Ladwig (Chapter 4) here reviews curriculum research on "social outcomes." He begins by acknowledging a public and educational consensus that traditional academic measures do not address broader goals and outcomes of schooling: ranging from the moral and cultural, to the social and dispositional. He reviews claims on social outcomes from curriculum fields such as multicultural, citizenship, and ecological/environmental education. Ladwig concludes with a troubling caveat: Although technologies to assess a broader range of educational capacities and performance are available, would we want to bring this host of "other" educational outcomes under the umbrella of high-stakes accountability systems? With what educational consequences and in whose interests?

Dylan Wiliam (Chapter 8) further examines technical issues of equity in assessment. Wiliam begins with an historical review on foundational and operational definitions of "construct" and "validity." Examining three specific cases—higher education admission assessment, the movement toward portfolio-based authentic assessment and assessment-for-learning models, and finally, the impacts of high-stakes testing systems on special needs students—Wiliam makes the case that there has been an incremental conflation of construct and validity. This, in turn, has confounded the interpretation of patterns of gender, cultural/linguistic minority, and special needs achievement, with more attention needed to "construct interpretation" in the analysis of achievement. He argues that conventional and alternative assessment systems need to begin from and rigorously maintain a careful separation of definition of constructs from the test construction process.

The foregoing debates around evidence and equity raise questions about the nature of evidence, the defining and classification of populations, the technical limits of current assessment practices, and the particular political, socioeconomic, cultural, and legal contexts for policy formation and school reform. Yet they focus principally on equitable access to traditional print-based skills and knowledge. The impact of digital technologies on dominant modes of information, everyday expression, and creativity complicates the picture further. The emergence of new technologies challenges the mandate and responsibility of educational systems—raising issues of equitable access and engagement that extend beyond print basics and access to traditional curriculum knowledge. One of the principal contradictions of the current curriculum settlement is that it extols the necessity of new capacities for what are variously termed *information societies* and *knowledge economies* (e.g., creativity, collaboration, critical thinking, intercultural communication), while judging and assessing the efficacy of schools, teachers, and instructional approaches at delivering performance via print-based behaviors on standardized tests. Mark Warschauer and Tina Matuchniak (Chapter 6) review the issues around equity raised by the emergence of digital technology. They examine the evidence on home, community, and school technological access and use and they critically reappraise the literature on differential educational outcomes. There is, indeed, evidence of a significant and persistent divide in access and achievement, but as importantly, Warschauer and Matuchniak describe an emergent literature on the possibilities of enlisting new technologies to engage marginalized learners and build from their out-of-school engagement with digital culture. They also raise questions about how to assess the overall impacts of new technologies on the achievement of linguistic and cultural minorities, and students from low socio-economic communities and families.

The first wave of evidence-based policy in the United States and the United Kingdom had a strong concentration on the measurement of student outcomes— often to the exclusion of systematic evidence on teachers' work and career pathways, teacher education, changing workforce demographics, and variable school/community contexts. This is ironic, given the tendency of public debate to define and position teachers as the problem, and, with an emergent policy focus on "teacher quality," to reposition them as the solution. Judith Warren Little and Laura Bartlett (Chapter 9) review the extensive qualitative and quantitative evidence on teachers' work and its relationship to educational equity. Their argument is that much of the policy literature approaches teacher capacity from an "individualistic frame of reference," which tends to seek "human capital" and "market solutions" to the issue of teacher quality. These obscure the equity implications of the organizational and institutional structures of teachers' work. As a result, the prevailing policy logic tends to stress academic preparedness, workforce diversity, and capacity to engage with cultural diversity, for example, independent of issues of the reform of structural and organizational contexts of schooling. Warren Little and Bartlett conclude by proposing a more comprehensive, contextual model of teacher quality and teaching effectiveness that duly considers the complex institutional ecologies of school organization, teachers' work, and community contexts.

A second key omission in current debates over evidence is a focus on schools and communities as social and geographic spaces: Teachers and learners do not work in universal, neutral, and generalizable cultural and social environments (Ercikan &

Roth, 2008). Beginning from social geographic research that documents the spatialized character of poverty, social, and cultural marginalization, Kevin Leander, Nathan Phillips, and Katherine Taylor (Chapter 10) shift the lens to another neglected area of policy focus: the social organization of space in learning. Educational administration and policy entails, inter alia, the designing and allocation of space and the assignment, organization, and movement of bodies across that space. Much educational policy, Leander, Phillips, and Taylor argue, has been dominated by a "classroom as container" metaphor—working with the confines of space–time organization established with the founding of the industrial school, and taking for granted the generalizability of the classroom as a unit of description and analysis. Reviewing education research over the past decade that has adopted a social geographic perspective, they raise questions about the impacts of the shaping, structuring, and organization of "schools" and "classrooms" on learning and cultural identity. Like Warschauer and Matuchniak (Chapter 6), they also comment on how minority and lower socioeconomic students are actively using the virtual spaces of new technologies for learning and identity work.

Taken together, these chapters open a broad canvas of what might count as evidence: qualitative and quantitative, empirical and interpretive, synchronic and diachronic, transnational and national, systemic and local. Though none would purport to provide a comprehensive map of the field, each leads us to evidence that has been neglected in current educational debates—including legal, sociodemographic, political economic, sociological, linguistic, anthropological, and social geographic research. The argument here is that the guidance of educational policy and practice committed to equity and social justice requires something more than approaches to accountability reliant on narrow measurement and performance indicators.

Educational policy cannot and does not entail the unmediated, direct translation of factual, empirical claims into direct actions. Even in an idealized moment without overt political pressures and influences—the translation of the empirical, expository claims about "what is" in terms of student outcomes, teacher capacity, school-level operations into the normative, prescriptive moves of legislation, centralized or local intervention in policy and practice is a contingent process. Policy formation requires the building and testing of narrative scenarios (Luke & Woods, 2008). It is contingent on our understandings of how, regionally and locally, something might be seen to be "working," for whom and in whose interests. It is contingent on how one names, identifies, and defines different human subjects. It is contingent on the validity and, indeed, reliability of available evidence. In this context, the diversity of kinds and levels of research that are admitted as "evidence" to the policy bar is a crucial matter. As our contributors here note, the evolution of evidence-based educational policy over the past two decades has been marked by a narrowing, rather than widening, of that bar.

At the same time, the translation of "facts to norms" is an interpretive, hermeneutic, and, ultimately, speculative and risky process (Habermas, 1996)—no matter how convinced one is of the social facts. There is always a range of plausible interpretations of factual claims and their textual representations, explanations of how they configure and explain each other. And there is no policy handbook or checklist on how to then translate evidence into complex narrative scenarios that might enable or disenable more equitable, just, and democratic education. These translations, the authors consistently remind us, are utterly dependent on the system's normative goals underlying the use of evidence. And even then they depend upon another neglected matter in a policy and media environment that tends to freely assign blame to principals, teachers, students, parents, families and communities, academics, and teacher educators: the actual technical and professional capacities of complex and often unwieldy bureaucracies to lead, resource, and implement reform for equity.

There are other lessons in this volume. To address matters of scalability of reform requires due consideration of the complex mediations involved in the formation and implementation of policy. The bridge between policy and more equitable educational outcomes, broadly construed, are the message systems of curriculum, pedagogy, and assessment. These by definition require detailed, careful consideration for any centrally mandated reform that expects to make a difference. Across this volume, our contributors call for expanded consideration of studies of community cultural and economic contexts, staffrooms, and classrooms as mediating "spaces" for more equitable educational practice. By definition, teaching and learning, equity and inequity are situated, historically dynamic, and local phenomena.

Evidence matters in the ongoing struggle for more equitable and just education. But there is no direct link between "fact" and norm, between science and policy. To address questions of equity requires rich, interpretive, and evolving sciences, not a narrow technical approach that invites capture by particular doctrinal and generic approaches to systems reform, public policy, and institutional governance.

ACKNOWLEDGMENTS

The editors thank our authors, editorial board, and developmental reviewers, who grappled throughout the development, planning, and editorial process with the complex relationships between evidence and equity. Gaye Bear, Queensland University of Technology, provided expert editorial support to authors and editors. We thank Felice Levine, Todd Reitzel, and the AERA publications committee for support across three volumes. Megan Toomey of SAGE provided us with patient support in the production process.

NOTES

[1]See AERA's *Standards for Reporting Empirical Social Science Research in AERA Publications* and *Standards for Reporting Humanities-Oriented Research in AERA Publications*, http://www.aera.net/publications/Default.aspx?menu_id=32&id=1850.

REFERENCES

Bryk, A. S., & Gomez, L. (2007, October). *Ruminations on reinventing an R&D capacity for educational improvement.* Paper presented at the American Enterprise Institute Conference: The Supply Side of School Reform and the Future of Educational Entrepreneurship, Washington, DC. Retrieved December 7, 2009, from www.aei.org/event1522

Ercikan, K., & Roth, W. (Eds.). (2008). *Generalizing from educational research.* New York: Routledge.

Gadsden, V., Artiles, A. J., & Davis, J. E. (Eds.) (2009). Risk, equity and schooling. *Review of Research in Education, 33,* vii-xi.

Green, J., Camilli, G., & Elmore, P. B. (Eds.) (2006). *Handbook of complementary methods in education research.* Mahwah, NJ/Washington, DC: Lawrence Erlbaum/American Educational Research Association.

Gould, S. J. (1981). *The mismeasure of man.* New York: W. W. Norton.

Haas, R. (2009). *War of necessity, war of choice: A memoir of two Iraq wars.* New York: Simon & Schuster.

Habermas, J. (1996). *Between facts and norms* (W. Rehg, Trans.). Cambridge: MIT Press.

Kenner, H. (1985). *The counterfeiters.* Baltimore: Johns Hopkins University Press.

Klenowski, V. (2009). *Raising the stakes: The challenges for teacher assessment.* Paper presented at the annual meetings of the Australian Association for Research in Education, Canberra.

Luke, A., & Woods, A. (2008). Policy and adolescent literacy. In L. Christianbury, R. Bomer, & P. Smagorinsky (Eds.), *Handbook of adolescent literacy research* (pp. 197-215). New York: Guilford Press.

Moss, P., Girard, B. J., & Hanniford, L. C. (2006). Validity in educational assessment. *Review of Research in Education 30,* 109-162.

Parker, L. (Ed.) (2007). Difference, diversity and distinctiveness in education and learning. *Review of Research in Education, 31,* xi-xv.

Reich, G. A. (2005). *How the Cold War transformed the philosophy of science.* Cambridge, UK: Cambridge University Press.

Rose, N. (1999). *Powers of freedom.* Cambridge, UK: Cambridge University Press.

Whitty, G. (2006). Education(al) research and educational policy making: Is conflict inevitable? *British Educational Research Journal, 32,* 159-176.

Chapter 1

The Uses of Evidence for Educational Policymaking: Global Contexts and International Trends

ALEXANDER W. WISEMAN
Lehigh University

In the past 150 years, educational systems have expanded and become integrally linked with economic, political, and social status in modern nation-states (see Kamens, Meyer, & Benavot, 1996). As the stakes for education have risen, so has the call for more and improved use of scientific evidence as a basis for educational policymaking (Luke, 2003; Slavin, 2002). The rise in the use of scientific evidence for educational policymaking rests on two common beliefs: One is the belief that school knowledge is abstract and universal, and the other is the belief that empirical evidence is an efficient indicator of knowledge and learning. As a result, there are serious educational policymaking consequences for individuals and schools tied to evidence (Olson, 2006).

Evidence from averaged scores on international assessments of math and science achievement in particular have become important indicators of national political and economic strength, but there are many different kinds of evidence to consider (LeTendre, Baker, Akiba, & Wiseman, 2001; Wiseman & Baker, 2005). For example, high-stakes consequences resulting from averaged academic achievement scores exist for students and schools in the United States but even more so in other countries, such as Japan (LeTendre, 1999; E. Smith, 2005). However, how and why evidence is used for educational policymaking both in the United States and around the world are the larger questions this chapter addresses.

To investigate the uses of evidence for educational policymaking, this volume and this chapter ask two fundamental orienting questions: Why use evidence in educational policymaking? And why is evidence-based educational policymaking a global phenomenon? The answer to the first orienting question serves as a foundation for introducing relevant macrotheoretical perspectives and exploring the motivations and agendas that drive educational policy and decision making. The answer to the

Review of Research in Education
March 2010, Vol. 34, pp. 1-24
DOI: 10.3102/0091732X09350472
© 2010 AERA. http://rre.aera.net

second orienting question provides a snapshot of the scope of the evidence-based decision-making phenomenon and some reasons why it has gained significance among educational policymakers around the world.

COMPONENTS OF EVIDENCE-BASED DECISION MAKING

Educational policymaking around the world has been permeated by a tendency to validate and legitimize educational processes and products as "evidence based" (Oakley, 2002). It is increasingly taken for granted that policymakers will make decisions that are evidence based rather than based on intuition or belief. Evidence-based educational decision making and policy implementation often depend on assessments of "what works." "What works" is a pseudonym for "best practices"—another evidence-based policymaking rationale that is an interesting mix of both individualized and agenda-driven educational policy decisions and reforms (Slavin, 2008). These policymaking efforts are frequently based on exceptional cases that represent success (often measured as student achievement gains) in unusual contexts or difficult situations (e.g., Herz & Sperling, 2004).

Best practices and "what works" approaches to educational policymaking typically prescribe the type of educational research done to inform policymaking—namely, using empirical, quantitatively based methodologies (Chatterji, 2004; Whitty, 2007). One criticism of this approach is that it can be tautological. In other words, educational policymaking based on "best practices" often focuses only on what works in specific situations or with unique communities. Sometimes this approach does not address the intervening variables that may prevent what works in one context from having the same positive effect in other particularly difficult or inappropriate contexts.

The best-practices approach in educational policymaking is far from the original evidence-based research tradition, which began in the field of medical research. Some argue that the overlap between what is fundamentally organizational or sociological "science" cannot be evidence based the same way that the natural sciences are (Biesta, 2007). In this era of educational accountability and evidence-based evaluation, others have suggested that although basing educational policymaking on scientific evidence may be a good idea, its implementation and rigor are lacking (Weiss, Murphy-Graham, Petrosino, & Gandhi, 2008). These accusations call for a further examination of the rationale and goals of evidence-based educational policymaking. Regardless of the criticisms, "evidence-based" educational policymaking is the most frequently reported method used by politicians and policymakers (i.e., those who have educational policy decision-making authority). But frequency of reporting does not necessarily mean that this is actually the method being used to make decisions about education and policy.

The reason certain educational policies are made often has as much to do with legitimacy seeking as it does the actual evidence policymakers are provided. Legitimacy seeking means that policymakers are doing what is expected of them by their individual and institutional peers (e.g., Benveniste, 2002). In fact, some argue that in spite of recent emphases on evidence-based, scientific research on education, the consumers of educational research results (namely, policymakers) demand research not so much for its scientific rigor but for the legitimacy that it provides (Brewer & Goldhaber, 2008). As a result, decision-making methods that garner legitimacy for both the individual policymaker and institutions that they act on behalf of are commonly introduced by policymakers and implemented in schools.

Another key factor in the approach to evidence-based policymaking is the nature of the evidence being used. As in educational research, the merits and disadvantages of quantitative and qualitative methods and data are central to the debate among policymakers and scholars about what constitutes valid and reliable evidence. Quantitative research evidence is often the most legitimate among politicians and policymakers because it is perceived to be more accurate and trustworthy. The word *scientific* for international or national educational agencies often means "based in empirical research"—typically quantitative (Center for Education, 2004; Towne & Shavelson, 2001). Useful qualitative data are not often considered "scientific" enough for national or international educational funding (e.g., Ravitch, 2005).

The measurability of achievement scores, for example, seems clearer and more direct than that of learning potential or the transferability of ideas that may be measured with less quantitative instruments or methods. And more specifically "scientific" evidence has been de facto interpreted as randomized field trials, as evidenced by the U.S. Department of Education's grant funding policies (Henig, 2008). Ironically, however, experts have observed that even when quantitatively measurable trends or evidence are reported, they do not always significantly affect educational policymaking (Saunders, 2007). In fact, isolated personal experiences and vocal testimonies can often have as much or more of an impact on educational policymakers than evidence from "scientific" research does (Milton, 2007).

Evidence-based educational policymaking has become a global phenomenon. This is true in part because of the rise of new public management and particular accountability policies spreading through educational systems around the world (Hall, 2005; Wittman, 2008). These policies frequently devolve responsibility for educational reform and implementation to the local schools and districts while centralizing regulatory authority farther up in the educational organizational hierarchy (Astiz, Wiseman, & Baker, 2002). Part of the new public management and educational accountability trends are attributable to increased awareness of national and international educational achievements (Wiseman & Baker, 2005). Published reports of educational performance comparing nations have become increasingly relevant to educational decision making and policymaking as international competition in science, technology, and politics increases (T. M. Smith & Baker, 2001).

One reason that the concept of "evidence" has become increasingly important in international (as well as national and subnational) educational policy is the role it plays in national educational agendas (e.g., No Child Left Behind [NCLB] in the United States). In fact, evidence-based decision making has become a staple of educational reform and funding requirements worldwide. Significant multinational organizations, such as the Organisation for Economic Co-operation and Development (OECD) and the World Bank, have made evidence-based policymaking a priority both in their own work as influential research and policy organizations as well as for their member or client nations (OECD, 2007). In a surprising number of cases, educational researchers and policymakers alike believe that empirical research evidence (specifically defined as randomized field trials) is a legitimate method for determining causal relationships between educational phenomena—and that after the evidence suggests causality, then a "solution" can be prescribed (Mosteller & Boruch, 2002; Schneider, Carnoy, Kilpatrick, Schmidt, & Shavelson, 2007).

There are advantages to quantitative information from randomized field trial–based research for policymakers, but there are also many reasons to criticize this approach. Criticisms include the potential oversimplification of more complex contexts and issues as well as the de facto mandate for "scientific" evidence, which limits the scope and type of research that will eventually inform educational policymakers (Lather, 2004). For example, quantitative evidence is useful for many types of educational policymaking and decision making, but its usefulness or relevance is often one-dimensional. In other words, there are rich contextual elements that quantitative analysis cannot capture the same way that qualitative data do. It is also not quite clear where educational research differentiates from more scientific and more sociological usefulness. Indeed, scientific educational research is often used to make social policy decisions, and sociologically oriented educational research is sometimes presented as scientific findings (Huston, 2008).

Contextualization of findings is frequently the main element lacking in educational research evidence and the resultant policymaking (Carnoy, 1999; Zajda, 2005). This means that evidence for educational policymaking often consists of unsubstantiated findings or one-shot phenomena that may take precedence over long-term trends and cultural characteristics (Ball, 1998). Indeed, making educational policy exclusively on the basis of empirical research evidence is neither possible nor preferred in many cases because of the importance of considering the evidence within context (Whitty, 2006).

EXPLAINING EVIDENCE FOR EDUCATIONAL POLICYMAKING

There are three fundamental macrotheoretical approaches that explain why evidence either is or should be used to inform or guide educational policymaking: (a) the technical-functional perspective, (b) the sociopolitical perspective, and (c) the institutional or organizational perspective. The first perspective suggests that educational policymakers use evidence to find the most effective and successful ways to address important educational issues and problems, the goal most often being increased student learning and effective classroom teaching at the least possible expense. This is a straightforward approach to educational decision making. It is technically and functionally efficient and the most frequently and most publicly expressed perspective among policymakers (Rogers, 2003; Wiseman, 2005).

The second perspective is more complex. Social and political agendas often shape policymakers' decisions and approaches to educational issues or problems (Whitty,

2002). It should not be surprising, then, that the use of "evidence" in educational policymaking may be a way to advance these agendas. This can have positive, negative, or mixed consequences for education and, by proxy, the economic, political, or social system within countries. The third perspective suggests that rationally legitimized models for policymaking exist and become slowly institutionalized as part of many organizational systems (Jepperson, 2002; Meyer & Baker, 1996), which includes educational systems. The legitimacy of certain perspectives (such as the technical-functional approach) in some cases becomes the public face of educational policymaking, whereas the specific process of educational policymaking may depend more on political agendas or some other more specific purpose.

The rationalized belief that legitimizes evidence-based educational policymaking is very simple: It is the taken-for-granted belief that education favorably affects social, economic, and political progress (Meyer, 1977). As a result, both schooling and educational policymaking frequently become entwined with testing because test results are a way to provide measurable evidence of the impact that education has or is going to have on an economy, political system, or society (Broadfoot, 1996; LeTendre, 1999). This interpretation assumes that the impact of education on each is inherently good, positive, or desirable. There are three main explanations for the goals of evidence-based policymaking that are tied to this belief. One is that educational policymakers seek evidence related to student and school performance to measure and ensure quality of education. Another reason for the prominence of evidence is to maintain equality in schooling. And finally, a more cynical but no less true goal of evidence-based policymaking is to control education (and the economy, political system, and society by proxy).

Evidence-Based Policymaking for Quality

There is little doubt that the most popular reason for using evidence as a basis for policymaking is that evidence provides an indicator of how much someone has learned or how much impact a certain educational technique has on students. But the reason policymakers talk about evidence goes much deeper. There is a chain of assumptions attached to individual student learning and performance. It goes something like this: The more students learn, the more they know. The more students know, the better their test performance (a key form of evidence) will be. The better students' test performance is, the better the teacher or school is. And, so the chain of association continues. The bottom line of this chain of reasoning is quality (Irons & Harris, 2006; United Nations Educational, Scientific, and Cultural Organization [UNESCO], 2004). Quality of students, schooling, or both is given most often as the reason education professionals assess performance with tests, homework, or other written work and consequently is why policymakers rely on "evidence."

Assessment used to estimate and provide evidence of quality is sometimes called *summative assessment* because it is a way to summarize how well an individual or an organization is doing (Nitko & Brookhart, 2006). Summative assessment is, therefore, a tool for making judgments or decisions about educational quality. It is usually a one-way and one-shot assessment. In classrooms, summative assessments aimed at gauging the quality of a student are end-of-unit tests, midterm examinations, and final exams. These sorts of evidence-producing assessments are one-shot because they are given only once per course. They represent the final sum of knowledge that a student has been taught or has learned up until that point.

Summative assessments are usually one-way because after these assessments, there is often no opportunity for teachers to adjust instruction for that particular group of individual students or to revisit the content in the hopes that students will better or differently learn whatever they might have missed the first time around. In other words, the evidence that comes from summative assessment flows from student to teacher to policymaker. There is neither provision nor opportunity for teachers to provide feedback or further instruction to students. Likewise for students, these sorts of summative assessments are one-shot because there are no second chances. Students either do well on these tests or not. Either way, the evidence based on their test performance informs policymakers about the perceived quality of education.

Even more-absolute forms of summative assessment that gauge educational quality and provide evidence for policymakers are state, national, and international tests. These types of tests are given in every state in the United States as well as in many countries worldwide. They are known by different names and boast varied content in different states. For example, in Texas, students take the Texas Assessment of Knowledge and Skills throughout their school careers and the Texas Assessment of Academic Skills at the exit level. In Pennsylvania, students take the Pennsylvania System of School Assessment every year. And in Oklahoma, students take the Oklahoma Core Curriculum Tests every year. National tests, such as the National Assessment of Educational Progress in the United States and the National Test in the Kingdom of Saudi Arabia, provide nationally representative achievement information in core subjects. International assessments that are widely taken by students in approximately 70 countries (including the USA) are part of larger international educational studies like the Trends in International Mathematics and Science Study (TIMSS) and the Programme for International Student Assessment.

Although the results of these sorts of assessments usually do not directly affect individual students (Doig, 2006), the average student scores for schools, districts, states, and nations as a whole are widely accepted indicators of educational quality and have a big impact on educational policymaking (LeTendre et al., 2001). Even though these tests are typically offered to each grade cohort once a year at the most, the results from state, national, and international assessments are often used to make important decisions about crucial issues, such as next year's funding for schools and districts. This can have important indirect effects on students because the response of the state- or district-level department of education can change available resources, required curriculum, and in-class teaching methods using the "evidence" from these assessments. In short, the dominant rationale for testing in the United States' and other nations' schools is to assess how close to "excellence" the quality of students, schools, and (by association) communities comes. However, excellence as an indicator of quality is only half of the evidence-based educational policymaking equation. Quality is necessarily partnered with equality.

Evidence-Based Policymaking for Equality

Obtaining evidence that indicates the degree of equality attained in an educational system is another reason often given for assessing the performance of students and schools (Hursh, 2005; Meyer, 2001). By seeing who performs highly and who does not, it is possible for teachers, principals, and policymakers to see where disparity exists between individual students, classrooms, and schools (Mehrens, 1998). By being able to see these differences in performance, decision makers can plan or make policy about how to remedy low performance in particular students, classrooms, and communities. For example, if a teacher gives a quiz on poetry to fifth graders, and she notices that many of her students are missing questions on idioms or hyperbole, she can then review these concepts and requiz until her students all seem to understand the concept. When assessment is used in this way, it is sometimes called *formative assessment* because the results of assessment are used to form a person's, classroom's, or school's body of knowledge in a back-and-forth process (Elwood, 2006).

Evidence from formative assessment usually comes from classroom-based tests, quizzes, and homework because it allows educators the flexibility to decide how to assess, when to assess, and what to do with the class or students after the assessment (McMillan, 2001). Most importantly, formative assessment has multiple assessment opportunities so that educators can see change or spot problem areas, adjust instruction or teaching, and then reassess the students to see whether performance improves. The key is that formative assessment leads to changes in the way content is taught or that education happens in the classroom—it rarely makes it to the educational policymaking level in its formative state. Its goal is to locally improve learning and consequently performance on tests as a result of active intervention and instruction. Quite frankly, formative assessment is the stated goal of most testing programs—even the state and national testing programs—although stated goals such as these are often political rhetoric (Irons & Harris, 2006).

Given the one-shot, one-way nature of many state and national tests that provide evidence for educational policymakers, it is reasonable to ask how statewide or national tests can be equity driven and formative. They can be formative if they lead to change or revision in the way education occurs either now or in the future—through adjusting either curriculum content, the way teachers teach, or something else related to excellence and equity in schooling (Taras, 2005). It is extremely rare for these large-scale tests to be formative with the same cohort of students that was tested, but the intent is instead for policymakers to use the evidence from those test results to make policies that will help next year's cohort of students on the basis of what this year's test results suggest. For example, most school district and state testing programs are part of larger "accountability" systems for schools.

In California, the Standardized Testing and Reporting (STAR) results are used by the state superintendent of schools as well as local district policymakers (a) to gauge the progress that students in California are making from year to year as well as (b) to pinpoint where problems exist that might hinder students from making academic progress ("A Look at the New STAR," 2003). California, like most other states, has a wide achievement gap between students from various social and economic groups (Jacobson, Olsen, Rice, & Sweetland, 2001). Since the STAR results show that this gap exists, that it is wide, and which content areas have the largest gap, educational policymakers can use this evidence to make policies for schools and teachers in communities that scored on the low end to shift their curricular and classroom focus to close these gap areas (California Department of Education, 2005). Of course, in the United States, if the average scores for students in California or any other state do not show adequate yearly progress, then the U.S. Department of Education may withhold federal funding from the state or districts within the state (Irons & Harris, 2006; McDermott & Jensen, 2005).

Large-scale assessments can also be formative and aimed at producing equity in education if they are part of a larger social agenda (Doig, 2006). Equity goals often target race, class, or gender and, as Welner's (2010) chapter in this volume suggests, are often represented by students' opportunity to learn. One of the best-known examples of this in recent history is the Coleman Report from the late 1960s. With little fanfare, President Lyndon B. Johnson's administration released a two-volume report on July 2, 1966. That report, *Equality of Educational Opportunity* (Coleman, 1966), is now widely regarded as one of the most important education studies of the 20th century. The findings of the well-known Coleman Report suggest that family and peer influences, not school resources, are the important determinants of student performance (Baker & LeTendre, 2005; Cohen, 1982). This "evidence" changed the course of equity-driven educational policymaking both in the United States and abroad.

The background for the Coleman Report is in President Lyndon Johnson's Great Society program, which has historical roots in Franklin D. Roosevelt's New Deal and the civil rights era (Ravitch, 1983, 2000). Inequality in American society drove public policy during this administration. In particular, inequalities related to race, social class, urbanization, and long-term poverty were hotbed issues. The Coleman Report was part of Johnson's strategy to level the playing field by identifying evidence of inequality in schooling. He wanted to find which inequalities most affected achievement. With a team of researchers, Coleman administered surveys to approximately 569,000 students, which was quite a logistic feat at the time. Modern social scientists might ask why Coleman's team did not just look at school records. The answer is simple. In the 1960s, there were no central records in the United States because the administration of education was (and still is) so decentralized. As a result, Coleman was the first to bring large-scale social science into public policy as a way of providing data-based "scientific" evidence for use in educational policymaking. And this evidence-based educational policymaking aimed to aid education as a formative tool for changing the fundamental structure of society in the United States.

Johnson and his administration thought that fixing school inequality would be relatively straightforward because the government could just pour more resources (i.e., money) into low-socioeconomic-status or poorer-performing schools (Stein, 2004; Ravitch, 1983, 2000). This prediction did not develop as originally thought. Coleman's team found evidence for some of the things they expected about unequal resources by class and race, but they also found that these equity indicators did not predict achievement as consistently as they expected. In other words, the evidence was messy; resources alone were not the problem with educational inequality. The real finding from the Coleman study was that variations in family background and outside-of-school environment affected achievement at least as much as variations in school resources and quality did. Instead of providing formative evidence that the quality of schools is the most important factor for a student's academic success—as its sponsors had expected—the report showed evidence that a child's family background and a school community's socioeconomic makeup are the best predictors of student achievement. These are equity variables that are much harder (or impossible) to control through educational policy than how much money a school receives or the qualification levels of teachers. In other words, evidence-based policy would be much more understandable if policy impacts could be controlled by the policymakers.

Evidence-Based Policymaking for Control

Control is yet another reason for evidence-based educational policymaking. This usually means control by whichever person or group has responsibility for evaluating the results of assessment. So in the classroom, a teacher can control both what students learn and whether they advance through their class and through the school system. At the state and national levels, test results are increasingly tied to funding (McDermott & Jensen, 2005). This was especially true in the United States during the era of NCLB because of the adequate yearly progress (AYP) requirement. AYP is tied to both federal funding and schools' reputations. Because the U.S. Department of Education has the responsibility for evaluating schools' and states' performance, it can and does use test performance as evidence and a means to control the curriculum schools adopt, the content teachers teach, and other components of schooling.

Although only a small percentage of schools' budgets comes from the U.S. federal government, this small percentage is still a significant amount. Without a supply of federal funding, most schools would not be able to operate because they would fall short of their budgetary requirements. Because AYP is tied to federal funding among other things, it became vital policymaking evidence for school systems in every state (Irons & Harris, 2006). When the federal NCLB legislation came into action, several states' school systems were caught off guard. For example, one state, Virginia, had many of its best schools declared as failing schools because students in those schools did not show a significant rise in scores on the state test during 1 year (National Education Association, 2006).

In some of these schools, the reason that they were declared "failing" was flawed evidence. For example, many schools were already performing highly, and it was difficult to improve scores when students are already performing at high levels (Million, 2004). Another reason was that many schools in the state served large groups of special-needs students who could not perform on the state test as well as their mainstream peers because of their special needs (Irons & Harris, 2006). Regardless of the reason, many of these schools lost significant federal funding because of their inability to show AYP (McDermott & Jensen, 2005). Afterward, many states wised up and began to adjust their testing programs so that AYP could be shown (Porter, Linn, & Trimble, 2005). This manipulation of the evidence for educational policymaking was unfortunately not the solution that most reformers who backed NCLB had hoped for and undermined the control that national-level educational policymakers had.

In reality, it is impossible to separate the goals of quality, equality, and control from one another, and in fact, each relies in part on the other two. The fact that evidence-based educational policymaking serves each of these three goals is important to answering the question about why evidence is used in educational policymaking. For example, the quality of schooling is affected by the equality of education that is available in a classroom, school, or community. And quality is a large part of the official reason certain individuals and groups can officially use assessment to directly or indirectly control or guide education. An evidence base provides the rationale or justification for decision making and serves to scientize or rationalize the policies that are made by couching the decisions in terms of quality, equality, or control (Drori, Jang, & Meyer, 2006). But is the evidence frequently used to make educational policy related to quality, equality, or control valid and reliable?

CRITICISMS OF EVIDENCE-BASED EDUCATIONAL POLICYMAKING

Scholars and policymakers began arguing that comparisons of student achievement guide policymakers to model their nation's or school's policies on potentially incomparable systems of education in frequently misguided efforts to attain systemic legitimization (Atkin & Black, 1997; Baker, 1997). This argument was based on the observation that little secondary or in-depth analysis of these data took place beyond the initial descriptions. The impact that the context of schooling has on what and how well students learn and teachers teach is still relatively unexplored (LeTendre et al., 2001). Instead, frequently premature policy recommendations based on straightforward comparisons of average student achievement scores are common (e.g., Schmidt & Prawat, 1999).

So is comparison of means of student achievement a valid comparison of educational systems or school outcomes and, therefore, adequate evidence for educational policymaking? The most frequent criticism of comparisons of student achievement is that they compare apples and oranges. This criticism is leveled because of the obvious differences researchers, policymakers, and even the lay public see in national-level contexts and educational systems. For example, the governance and curriculum in the U.S. educational system is extremely localized and variable, whereas in Japan the opposite is true. Given that American educational policymakers and researchers have historically made so many comparisons between the United States and Japan, this fundamental difference between systems should be an important part of the evidence forming the foundation of these policy and research discussions. Unfortunately, it rarely is.

Another argument suggests that the instruments of evaluation and assessment that provide the evidence policymakers use are themselves unreliable (Beaton, 1998; Bracey, 2004; Ercikan, 1998; Foy, 2005). Reliability of instruments is an issue from the local level all the way up to the global level. Yet there have not been any or many research studies done on the reliability of these instruments at either the local or the broader level. For example, in each international education study, many efforts have been made to make the assessments and background questionnaires comparable across nations (Martin, Mullis, & Chrostowski, 2004; Schulz & Sibberns, 2004). Although there is certainly always room for improvement and these are not infallible instruments, many of these studies provide relatively good data if researchers and policymakers consider each nation's unique situation and context and use these considerations as filters when drawing conclusions from or suggesting policy based on "evidence" from cross-national assessments and surveys. Still, the nature of schooling and culture vary dramatically between nations. This means that the possibility that international educational data are unreliable is more a question of degrees than anything else.

The results of internationally comparative tests of student performance are frequently interpreted as evidence indirectly representing the economic status of a nation as well (Ramirez, Luo, Schofer, & Meyer, 2006). The criticism can be made that schools are perceived as indicators of modernization and economic productivity and that, consequently, student achievement is inappropriately used in these cross-national comparisons as evidence of each nation's level of development and economic output. For example, data from UNESCO and TIMSS suggest that public expenditure on education per capita and GNP per capita closely associate with student achievement but that public expenditure on education as a percentage of GNP, GDP growth, and gross domestic investment are not significant correlates of student achievement (Wiseman, 2007a). This means that direct spending on education and the overall strength of the economy may positively associate with student achievement, but this relationship is tenuous and not supported by other measures of economic development and productivity (Ramirez et al., 2006). This is indeed bad news for those developing nations that are contributing up to twice as much of their government funds to education as economically strong nations, such as the United States, do. And it suggests that perhaps education itself is not the best indicator of or contributor to national economic development.

Another criticism arising from cross-national comparisons of student achievement as evidence for educational policymaking is that some nations' educational environment and curricular exposure, in particular, make cross-national comparison inappropriate.

In the United States, some have argued that schools' curricula are "a mile wide and an inch deep," leading students, teachers, and classrooms to be unfocused and lack vision (Schmidt, McKnight, & Raizen, 1997). These critics suggest that characteristics of the educational system itself, such as curricular content and coverage, make educational policy resulting from comparisons of achievement in these fundamentally different systems misguided at best.

Comparativist Keith Watson argues that the context of schooling is often as important as or more important than the content. Watson (1999, p. 238) makes the argument that the research data from internationally comparative studies of education are too superficial to be "really meaningful." Consequently, another critical point is that cultural, contextual, and organizational characteristics prevent straightforward cross-national comparison of student achievement. Cultural contexts uniquely shape educational and economic communities and learners. Scholars, such as Hoffman (1999) and Crossley (1999), have argued that cultural context is increasingly important in an era devoted to measuring trends in globalization and isomorphism.

Important to a cultural criticism of policymaking evidence from cross-national comparisons of student achievement are historical and traditional characteristics of educational systems (Crossley, 2000). Attention to local conditions and classroom pedagogy have been topics for consideration in studies estimating the effectiveness of schools (Fuller & Clarke, 1994). One of the most interesting debates along the line of educational context and the developmental stage of education took place between David Baker and Ian Westbury in the early 1990s (Baker, 1993; Westbury, 1992, 1993). Their debate concentrated on the interpretation of student achievement rankings in the United States and Japan given the instructional opportunity and curricular exposure in each nation.

Baker (1993) argued that in spite of the fact that Japanese and American students were exposed to different math curricula at the same age or grade, American students really were scoring below Japanese students. Westbury (1992, 1993) argued that the different exposure to curricula in Japan and the United States meant that the differences in students' performance were not because American students were really doing worse; they were instead because Japanese students had learned something more than what most American students had. Either way, the use of internationally comparative evidence for educational policymaking is a complex dilemma to unravel but a topic that is of major global importance.

COMPARATIVE EXAMPLES OF EVIDENCE-BASED
EDUCATIONAL POLICYMAKING

Gender equity in education is one of the most researched, discussed, and politicized issues in educational policy. It has become an issue of such prominence because the impact of gender either in or on education has come to represent the same struggles and issues of gender that exist in the larger economic, political, and social arena. In other words, this is a globally relevant example of how educational policymaking based on evidence has the potential to affect society beyond the schools.

Gender-egalitarian standards are increasingly becoming institutionalized components of formal political, social, and economic policies (Wiseman, 2007b). For example, women have the right to vote in most developed and many developing nations around the world, the civil liberties of women are recognized and even enforced in many nations, and women technically have the opportunity to hold the same positions in the labor market (Ramirez, Soysal, & Shanahan, 1997)—although it is also well documented that girls and women are still often denied these rights and opportunities even in communities where they are law. Still, this recent emphasis on gender egalitarianism can have a double effect because as gender-egalitarian standards become institutionalized components of school policy and structure, the definition and scope of gendered inequality expands, which means that more and more, gendered differences are both observed and identified as inequality (Young, Fort, & Danner, 1994).

Since the World Conference on Education for All (EFA) in Jomtien, Thailand, in 1990, the push for girls' universal participation in modern mass schooling has become a primary focus of national education policymakers and researchers around the world (UNESCO, 2003, 2004). This push has made the international community painfully aware of (a) widespread and specific gendered inequality in schooling around the world as well as (b) the benefits to individuals and communities that result from educating girls and women that many nations and communities were missing because of these gendered inequalities (e.g., Abu-Ghaida & Klasen, 2004). As a result, half of the EFA goals given in the declaration that came out of this world conference in Thailand address the global importance of improving and equalizing education between boys and girls.

The widespread "girls' education" movement has become central to most global education policies and multilateral agencies participating in or directing the development of nations around the world (UNESCO, 2004; Wiseman & Baker, 2007). International organizations, such as the World Bank, United Nations International Children's Emergency Fund, UNESCO, and others, have helped establish and maintain the girls' education movement, which significantly overlaps with the larger women's rights movement and most nations' formal educational policies (Berkovitch, 1999; Chabbott, 2003; Chabbott & Ramirez, 2000). The far-reaching (some say overreaching) efforts of the 1990 EFA conference and subsequent initiatives have focused on improving access to and the quality of education for girls and women. As a result, there is increased emphasis on evidence-based policymaking on girls' education even in nations that have maintained separate educational systems for girls and boys for social and cultural reasons. For example, Saudi Arabia, which has one of the most rigidly divided educational systems along gender lines, carefully documents evidence on gender parity in education and has the equal and increasing participation of girls and women in the public educational system as one of its core educational aims (Saudi Arabia Ministry of Education, 2005).

In a recent EFA report from UNESCO, gender parity in access to education was identified as one of the key indicators of achieving education for all (UNESCO,

2003). In fact, this report listed evidence from 40 countries that had achieved gender parity in primary and secondary education enrollment and 34 that were likely to achieve gender parity in the next few years (UNESCO, 2003, p. 109). Yet the persistent question of gender inequality in education continues to focus most intensely on evidence in terms of academic achievement, especially in math and science.

One of the most recent cross-national studies of math and science achievement is TIMSS, administered by the International Association for the Evaluation of Educational Achievement. The evidence from this study suggests that eighth-grade girls and boys do not perform at significantly different levels in mathematics in most nations nor, in many nations, in science. Across the 46 nations that participated in TIMSS in 2003, for example, the average gender difference in eighth-grade mathematics achievement was nonsignificant. In fact, in 28 of the 46 countries (61%), there was no significant gender difference in math achievement. There were, however, significant differences in 18 countries (39%).

Of the 18 countries showing a significant math achievement gender difference, girls—not boys—had significantly higher achievement in half of these countries. Interestingly, there were also 9 countries that showed boys scoring significantly higher than girls in math. So in 37 of the 46 nations (80%) that participated in TIMSS in 2003, either there was no significant difference in math achievement by gender or there was a significant girls' advantage compared to boys in math achievement. This quantitative evidence does not suggest widespread male dominance in math achievement—at least not at the eighth-grade level in these countries.

The TIMSS 2003 results for eighth-grade science achievement are somewhat different. In 28 of the 46 countries (61%) participating in TIMSS in 2003, boys scored significantly higher than girls on the eighth-grade science test. There were still 11 countries where there was no significant gender difference in eighth-grade science achievement and 7 countries where girls scored significantly higher than boys in eighth-grade science. More than one third (39%) of the nations either showed no significant gender difference or showed a significant girls' advantage in science achievement compared to boys.

Even though the science achievement story is not as positive as the math achievement one, the fact that there is as much parity or girls' advantage in math and science achievement as there is suggests that some improvements have been made in the schooling of girls worldwide. For example, in both math and science, girls outperformed boys in countries where, according to some studies, they should not have. In particular, there have been studies and reports that have demonstrated the subordination of women and girls in traditionally Muslim nations (Fish, 2002; Mehran, 1997; Winter, 2001), yet the TIMSS 2003 results either show no significant difference in girls' and boys' performance or show girls outperforming boys by a significant margin in several predominantly Muslim nations.

Yet there is still a marked difference in achievement by gender in the later years of secondary school and in postsecondary schooling in most nations. This is troubling evidence for educational policymakers. In sharp contrast to the good news outlined above, gender inequality in achievement often worsens in the secondary and post-secondary school years, especially in math and science. This is not a positive story at all, and the obvious question policymakers ask when confronted with this evidence is, Why is there such a dramatic shift in the small but positive trends in gender differences in achievement when students in the final year of secondary school are sampled? There are no easy answers to this question, so policymakers use the evidence they have to the degree with which they are able to understand and interpret it. This has led to some interesting evidence-based, gender-related educational policies, such as those dealing with single-sex schooling. This is when context is needed to supplement the quantitative "evidence" that TIMSS provides.

Single-sex schooling in the United States and in the United Kingdom has been discussed by policymakers first in terms of pedagogical or educational importance and secondarily in relation to society or culture (Harker, 2000; Spielhofer, Benton, & Schagen, 2004). In general, the single-sex schooling movement in the United States and in the United Kingdom is related to the growing concern for girls' and boys' education relative to their interaction with the other gender. Some of the quantitative evidence suggests that girls benefit from single-sex schooling to a greater degree than boys (Daly, 1996), so many girls' and women's advocacy groups have supported single-sex education for those reasons. The more recent emphasis on the "crisis" in boys' education suggests that there are reasons why single-sex schooling may (or may not) be detrimental to boys' educational opportunities and performance (Salomone, 2006). Again, the evidence that influences policymaking the most is largely quantitative: Girls' achievement on performance tests tends to be higher relative to boys in single-sex schooling situations.

In stark contrast to the United States and the United Kingdom, Saudi Arabia is the only country in the world with a 100% single-sex schooling system (Wiseman, 2008). The reasons for this separation are first social, cultural, and religious. The reasons are secondarily pedagogical or educational. There is, however, interesting evidence from both the qualitative and the quantitative traditions on single-sex schooling in Saudi Arabia. From the more quantitative perspective, single-sex schooling is advantageous to girls and women in the educational system because enrollment parity and even achievement advantages for girls and women have been demonstrated. Yet more qualitative evidence is much less common and, when it does occur, much more critical of the single-sex schooling system in Saudi Arabia. The research-based evidence that is used for official policymaking and educational agenda-setting is more quantitative in nature and, therefore, provides a more positive perspective on the single-sex practices of Saudi Arabian schooling.

Additionally, the Saudi Arabian educational system is a good example of the way that gender equality in education can be established as a legitimate norm for education policymakers even in more traditional societies that are in many ways reluctant to establish some rights leading to the full equality of girls and women (Baki, 2004; Calvert & Al-Shetaiwi, 2002; Somers & Caram, 1998). Public schooling (apart from

Qur'anic schools) is a relatively recent phenomenon in Saudi Arabia. The first public primary schools in Saudi Arabia began around 1930, and girls were not formally enrolled in public schools until approximately 30 years later, in 1960. Yet in spite of this early differentiation, rapid progress toward gender parity in schooling has occurred. The obvious question is, Why?

Evidence that policymakers both in the Kingdom of Saudi Arabia and at international development organizations, such as UNESCO or the World Bank, might use shows that gender parity in Saudi Arabia may be nearly achieved—in spite of the actual situation on the ground in Saudi Arabia. For example, girls' enrollment has risen dramatically, from only 25% of the total Saudi student population in 1970 to approximately 50% of the student population in 2000. Furthermore, the Saudi Arabian Ministry of Education declares that girls' education was developed to fulfill the social and economic requirements of the state (Saudi Arabia Ministry of Education, 2005).

In addition to enrollment equity, quantitative evidence suggests that Saudi Arabia has also made important advances in achievement equity among boys and girls. For example, Saudi Arabia is one of the countries participating in TIMSS that posted either significant girls' achievement advantages compared to boys (in science) or no significant difference between girls' and boys' average achievement (in math). The Saudi example illustrates the impact that "scientific" evidence can have on the decisions made by educational policymakers. All of the quantitative indicators (enrollment, achievement, and opportunity to learn) used by international organizations to evaluate and assess gender equality in education show relative parity between boys and girls in Saudi schools. So how does a discussion about gender equality in one of the most publicly segregated systems in the world converge with educational policies and policymaking norms in other countries? And what does "evidence" have to do with this phenomenon?

EVIDENCE-BASED POLICY CONVERGENCE

Policy convergence highlights the effects of a process of policy development over time toward a common purpose (Leuze et al., 2007). One way to achieve policy convergence is to base educational policy on "scientific" evidence. There are several variations on policy convergence, including diffusion and transfer, but convergence is unique (Pilton, 2009). Policy convergence is different from policy diffusion because the emphasis of diffusion is on processes rather than on effects or outcomes. Policy diffusion is particularly interested in the spreading process or mechanism. Policy convergence is different from policy borrowing or transfer because of, again, the focus that transfer has on processes (not outcomes) and because policy transfer assumes agency (Phillips & Ochs, 2003; Steiner-Khamsi, 2004).

Although all of these are overlapping and share critical criteria, policy convergence is the most appropriate for discussing the phenomenon of evidence-based policymaking because of its emphasis on the effects of a process of policy change over time toward a common point (Pilton, 2009). Therefore, discussions of policy convergence in the use of scientific evidence in educational policymaking investigate an increase in similarity during a specified period of a set of certain policymaking phenomena across a predetermined set of jurisdictions.

There are several ways that policy convergence in the use of evidence for educational policymaking can occur (Pilton, 2009). One way is through imposition. Imposition is typically a result of political demand or pressure (e.g., OECD agenda or World Bank or International Monetary Fund loan conditions). Independent problem solving occurs when separate entities arrive independently at similar solutions that involve the use or requirement of evidence for policymaking—often coincidentally. This, however, is difficult to observe because it is random. International harmonization involves compliance with international or supranational law, which often includes international institutional arrangements. For example, the OECD is a voluntary membership organization that has no legal powers, so there is no legal obligation to comply from member nations, yet member nations do encourage evidence-based policymaking as a result of OECD urging. Regulatory competition suggests that the integration or interdependence of markets leads national systems to adopt domestic regulations intended to make them more globally competitive. Again, OECD serves as support for this mechanism.

But the key mechanism for policy convergence, especially regarding evidence-based educational policymaking, is transnational communication, as synthesized by Humphreys (2002). In particular, the stimuli for international policy convergence are often,

> [n]on-binding international agreements or propositions on . . . goals and standards that national policies should aim to achieve, institutionalized peer review and identification of best practice (benchmarking) as well as the construction of league tables ranking national policies in terms of performance to previously agreed criteria. (p. 54)

What Humphrey suggests is that transnational problem solving typically occurs within transnational communities, defined as networks of policymakers who share common principled beliefs about ends, causal beliefs about means, and common standards of accruing and testing new knowledge. In the case of gender equality in education, these networks of policymakers share a common idea about which evidence suggests gender parity and how this evidence can be interpreted to make policy decisions about girls' education in Saudi Arabia or other countries. Interestingly, common educational and normative backgrounds typically facilitate joint development of common policy models (Holzinger & Knill, 2005, p. 784). Although it may not appear obvious that Saudi Arabia and the United States have much in common, their educational systems and the norms associated with expectations for education and schooling in these countries are surprisingly similar because of their common adherence to a modern mass schooling system.

The importance of evidence-based policymaking regarding gender and education in countries around the world is largely attributable to the shared mass education experience. Mass education systems are flexible enough to accommodate culturally specific discourses of education but are rationalized to the point that they share common themes or characteristics (Meyer & Ramirez, 2000). For example, they all share an emphasis on scientific rational inquiry through empirical evidence and research. One important construction of education is as a "technical" science that can be studied, rationalized, and quantified. This happens in the production of schooling, in the training of teachers, and in the study of educational phenomena—in ways that privilege technological, scientific, and quantitative knowledge. So if the evidence that shows gender equality is parity in enrollment, achievement, and opportunity to learn, then that is what policymakers will emphasize when they make policy.

Now policies and pedagogies in national education systems around the world rely on the (largely quantitative) results of the scientific assessments and empirical evidence. In fact, as discussed earlier, the policymaking discourse is increasingly framed in international or global terms because of the availability of international data on education (Baker & Wiseman, 2005). This global discourse and international data lead to extensive policy convergence across countries, which is a much more complex process than simply transferring or borrowing of one policy, method, or model from one country to another. But what widely available international data on education has done is create an intellectual space where educational policymaking is not geographically or politically bounded but is instead bounded by the extent of the legitimated evidence used to support one decision or policy versus another.

CONCLUSIONS

This chapter began by asking two fundamental orienting questions: Why use evidence in educational policymaking? And why is evidence-based educational policymaking a global phenomenon? The goals of using evidence for policymaking both in the United States and around the world are to gauge quality, create equality, and establish control over schooling. The goal of using evidence to make policy for a particular school, district, or nation largely determines who benefits and how. When the point of evidence for policymaking is quality, then students directly benefit and the larger community benefits indirectly. When the point of evidence for policymaking is to create equality, then the students and communities both benefit directly, because there is, hopefully, a more even distribution of knowledge and power throughout the schooled society. When the point of evidence for policymaking is to control schooling, then the people, organizations, or groups who administer assessments and evaluate their results are the beneficiaries, because they are the ones who can then dictate what goes on in schools on the basis of the evidence and their own agenda.

A great example of how this works now is the growing push worldwide by central educational governing agents to make all educational policy and decision making "evidence based." By making an evidence base a mandatory condition of educational policymaking, particularly through the requirement that randomized field trials be the basis for evidence, educational governance has simply become a new version of a rational bureaucratic authority (Ioannidou, 2007). But instead of centralizing and focusing on evidence-based decision making, the tendency of central governing bodies has been to bureaucratize the ways that evidence is collected, presented, and interpreted (as Sunderman's [2010] chapter in the volume suggests). In spite of the bureaucratic jungle that central governing bodies in educational systems often become, there is a trend in educational governance that suggests that those who control which knowledge or policy is legitimate are those who govern. And if legitimacy is in reference to evidence-based educational policy exclusively, then perhaps educators should be thinking about challenging what they take for granted to make changes and improvements to the way educational policymaking occurs worldwide.

REFERENCES

A look at the new star. (2003). *Leadership, 32*(3), 12-15, 29.

Abu-Ghaida, D., & Klasen, S. (2004). *The economic and human development costs of missing the millennium development goal on gender equity.* Washington, DC: World Bank Education Advisory Service.

Astiz, M. F., Wiseman, A. W., & Baker, D. P. (2002). Slouching towards decentralization: Consequences of globalization for curricular control in national education systems. *Comparative Education Review, 46*(1), 66–88.

Atkin, J. M., & Black, P. (1997). Policy perils of international comparisons: The TIMSS case. *Phi Delta Kappan, 79*(1), 22–28.

Baker, D. P. (1993). Compared to Japan, the U.S. is a low achiever . . . really: New evidence and commentary on Westbury. *Educational Researcher, 22*(3), 18–20.

Baker, D. P. (1997). Surviving TIMSS: Or, everything you blissfully forgot about international comparisons. *Phi Delta Kappan, 79*(4), 295–300.

Baker, D. P., & LeTendre, G. K. (2005). *National differences, global similarities: Current and future world institutional trends in schooling.* Stanford: Stanford University Press.

Baker, D. P., & Wiseman, A. W. (Eds.). (2005). *Global trends in educational policy* (Vol. 6, International Perspectives on Education and Society Series). Oxford, UK: Elsevier Science.

Baki, R. (2004). Gender-segregated education in Saudi Arabia: Its impact on social norms and the Saudi labor market [Electronic version]. *Education Policy Analysis Archives, 12*. Retrieved June 1, 2008, from http://epaa.asu.edu/epaa/v12n28/

Ball, S. J. (1998). Big policies/small world: An introduction to international perspectives in education policy. *Comparative Education, 34*(2), 119–130.

Beaton, A. E. (1998). Comparing cross-national student performance on TIMSS using different test items. *International Journal of Educational Research, 29*, 529–542.

Benveniste, L. (2002). The political structuration of assessment: Negotiating state power and legitimacy. *Comparative Education Review, 46*(1), 89–118.

Berkovitch, N. (1999). *From motherhood to citizenship: Women's rights and international organizations.* Baltimore: Johns Hopkins University Press.

Biesta, G. (2007). Why "what works" won't work: Evidence-based practice and the democratic deficit in educational research. *Educational Theory, 57*(1), 1–22.

Bracey, G. W. (2004). International comparisons: Less than meets the eye? *Phi Delta Kappan, 85*(6), 477–478.

Brewer, D., & Goldhaber, D. (2008). Examining the incentives in educational research. *Phi Delta Kappan, 89*(5), 361–364.

Broadfoot, P. (1996). *Education, assessment and society.* Buckingham, UK: Open University Press.

California Department of Education. (2005). *Star 2005 test results*. Retrieved May 15, 2007, from http://star.cde.ca.gov/star2005/viewreport.asp

Calvert, J. R., & Al-Shetaiwi, A. S. (2002). Exploring the mismatch between skills and jobs for women in Saudi Arabia in technical and vocational areas: The views of Saudi Arabian private sector business managers. *International Journal of Training and Development, 6*(2), 112–124.

Carnoy, M. (1999). *Globalization and educational reform: What planners need to know*. Paris: United Nations Educational, Scientific, and Cultural Organization.

Center for Education. (2004). *Advancing scientific research in education*. Washington, DC: National Academies Press.

Chabbott, C. (2003). *Constructing education for development*. New York: RoutledgeFalmer.

Chabbott, C., & Ramirez, F. O. (2000). Development and education. In M. Hallinan (Ed.), *Handbook of sociology of education* (pp. 163–187). New York: Plenum.

Chatterji, M. (2004). Evidence on "what works": An argument for extended-term mixed method (ETMM) evaluation designs. *Educational Researcher, 33*(9), 3–13.

Cohen, M. (1982). Effective schools: Accumulating research findings. *American Education, 18*(1), 13–16.

Coleman, J. S. (1966). *Equality of educational opportunity*. Washington, DC: U.S. Department of Education, National Center for Education Statistics.

Crossley, M. (1999). Reconceptualising comparative and international education. *Compare, 29*(3), 249–267.

Crossley, M. (2000). Bridging cultures and traditions in the reconceptualisation of comparative and international education. *Comparative Education, 36*(3), 319–332.

Daly, P. (1996). The effects of single-sex and coeducational secondary schooling on girls' achievement. *Research Papers in Education, 11*(3), 289–306.

Doig, B. (2006). Large-scale mathematics assessment: Looking globally to act locally. *Assessment in Education: Principles, Policy and Practice, 13*(3), 265–288.

Drori, G. S., Jang, Y. S., & Meyer, J. W. (2006). Sources of rationalized governance: Cross-national longitudinal analysis, 1985–2002. *Administrative Science Quarterly, 51*, 205–229.

Elwood, J. (2006). Formative assessment: Possibilities, boundaries and limitations. *Assessment in Education: Principles, Policy and Practice, 13*(2), 215–232.

Ercikan, K. (1998). Methodological issues in international assessment. *International Journal of Educational Research, 29*(6), 487–489.

Fish, M. S. (2002). Islam and authoritarianism. *World Politics, 55*(1), 4–37.

Foy, P. (2005). Estimating and interpreting variance components in international comparative studies in education. *Studies in Educational Evaluation, 31*(2/3), 173–191.

Fuller, B., & Clarke, P. (1994). Raising school effects while ignoring culture? Local conditions and the influence of classroom tools, rules, and pedagogy. *Review of Educational Research, 64*, 119–157.

Hall, K. D. (2005). Science, globalization, and educational governance: The political rationalities of the new managerialism. *Indiana Journal of Global Legal Studies, 12*(1), 153–182.

Harker, R. (2000). Achievement, gender and the single-sex/coed debate. *British Journal of Sociology of Education, 21*(2), 203–218.

Henig, J. R. (2008). The evolving relationship between researchers and public policy. *Phi Delta Kappan, 89*(5), 357–360.

Herz, B., & Sperling, G. B. (2004). *What works in girls' education: Evidence and policies from the developing world*. New York: Council on Foreign Relations.

Hoffman, D. M. (1999). Culture and comparative education: Toward decentering and recentering the discourse. *Comparative Education Review, 43*, 464–488.

Holzinger, K., & Knill, C. (2005). Causes and conditions of cross-national policy convergence. *Journal of European Public Policy, 12*(5), 775–796.

Humphreys, P. (2002). Europeanisation, globalisation and policy transfer in the European Union. *Convergence, 8*(2), 52–79.

Hursh, D. (2005). The growth of high-stakes testing in the USA: Accountability, markets and the decline in educational equality. *British Educational Research Journal, 31*(5), 605–622.

Huston, A. C. (2008). From research to policy and back. *Child Development, 79*(1), 1–12.

Ioannidou, A. (2007). A comparative analysis of new governance instruments in the transnational educational space: A shift to knowledge-based instruments. *European Educational Research Journal, 6*(4), 336–347.

Irons, E. J., & Harris, S. (2006). *The challenges of No Child Left Behind: Understanding the issues of excellence, accountability, and choice.* Lanham, MD: Rowman and Littlefield Education.

Jacobson, J., Olsen, C., Rice, J. K., & Sweetland, S. (2001). *Educational achievement and Black-White inequality: Statistical analysis report.* Washington, DC: U.S. Department of Education, National Center for Education Statistics.

Jepperson, R. L. (2002). The development and application of sociological neoinstitutionalism. In J. Berger & M. Zelditch Jr. (Eds.), *New directions in contemporary sociological theory* (pp. 229–266). Lanham, MD: Rowman and Littlefield.

Kamens, D. H., Meyer, J. W., & Benavot, A. (1996). Worldwide patterns in academic secondary education curricula. *Comparative Education Review, 40,* 116–138.

Lather, P. (2004). Scientific research in education: A critical perspective. *British Educational Research Journal, 30*(6), 759–772.

LeTendre, G. K. (1999). *Competitor or ally? Japan's role in American educational debates.* New York: RoutledgeFalmer.

LeTendre, G. K., Baker, D. P., Akiba, M., & Wiseman, A. W. (2001). The policy trap: National educational policy and the third international math and science study. *International Journal of Educational Policy, Research and Practice, 2*(1), 45–64.

Leuze, K., Brand, T., Jakobi, A. P., Martens, K., Nagel, A., & Rusconi, A. et al. (2007). *Analysing the two-level game: International and national determinants of change in education policy making.* Bremen, Germany: University of Bremen.

Luke, A. (2003). After the marketplace: Evidence, social science and educational research. *Australian Educational Researcher, 30*(2), 87–107.

Martin, M. O., Mullis, I. V. S., & Chrostowski, S. J. (Eds.). (2004). *TIMSS 2003 technical report.* Chestnut Hill, MA: Boston College, TIMSS and PIRLS International Study Center.

McDermott, K. A., & Jensen, L. S. (2005). Dubious sovereignty: Federal conditions of aid and the No Child Left Behind Act. *Peabody Journal of Education, 80*(2), 39–56.

McMillan, J. H. (2001). Secondary teachers' classroom assessment and grading practices. *Educational Measurement: Issues and Practice, 20*(1), 20–32.

Mehran, G. (1997). A study of girls' lack of access to primary education in the Islamic Republic of Iran. *Compare, 27*(3), 263–277.

Mehrens, W. A. (1998). Consequences of assessment: What is the evidence? *Education Policy Analysis Archives, 6*(13). Retrieved June 15, 2009, from http://epaa.asu.edu/epaa/v6n13.html

Meyer, J. W. (1977). The effects of education as an institution. *American Journal of Sociology, 83,* 55–77.

Meyer, J. W. (2001). The evolution of modern stratification systems. In D. B. Grusky (Ed.), *Social stratification: Class, race, and gender in sociological perspective* (Vol. 2, pp. 881–890). Oxford, UK: Westview.

Meyer, J. W., & Baker, D. P. (1996). Forming American educational policy with international data: Lessons from the sociology of education. *Sociology of Education, 69*(Suppl.), 123–130.

Meyer, J. W., & Ramirez, F. O. (2000). The world institutionalization of education. In J. Schriewer (Ed.), *Discourse formation in comparative education* (pp. 111–132). Frankfurt, Germany: Peter Lang.

Million, J. (2004). Been AYP'd yet? *Education Digest: Essential Readings Condensed for Quick Review, 69*(6), 32–33.

Milton, P. (2007). Opening minds to change: The role of research in education. *Education Canada, 47*(1), 39–42.

Mosteller, F., & Boruch, R. F. (2002). *Evidence matters: Randomized trials in education research.* Washington, DC: Brookings Institution Press.

National Education Association. (2006). *More schools are failing NCLB law's "adequate yearly progress" requirements.* Retrieved May 15, 2007, from http://www.nea.org/esea/ayptrends0106.html

Nitko, A. J., & Brookhart, S. M. (2006). *Educational assessment of students* (5th ed.). New York: Prentice Hall.

Oakley, A. (2002). Social science and evidence-based everything: The case of education. *Educational Review, 54*(3), 277–286.

Organisation for Economic Co-operation and Development. (2007). *Evidence in education: Linking research and policy.* Paris: Author.

Olson, L. (2006). As AYP bar rises, more schools fail: Percent missing NCLB goals climbs amid greater testing. *Education Week, 26*(4), 1.

Phillips, D., & Ochs, K. (2003). Processes of policy borrowing in education: Some explanatory and analytical devices. *Comparative Education, 39*, 451–461.

Pilton, J. (2009). *Policy convergence in education.* Unpublished manuscript, Lehigh University, Bethlehem, PA.

Porter, A. C., Linn, R. L., & Trimble, C. S. (2005). The effects of state decisions about NCLB adequate yearly progress targets. *Educational Measurement: Issues and Practice, 24*(4), 32–39.

Ramirez, F. O., Luo, X., Schofer, E., & Meyer, J. W. (2006). Student achievement and national economic growth. *American Journal of Education, 113*(1), 1–30.

Ramirez, F. O., Soysal, Y. N., & Shanahan, S. (1997). The changing logic of political citizenship: Cross-national acquisition of women's suffrage rights, 1890 to 1990. *American Sociological Review, 62*, 735–745.

Ravitch, D. (1983). *The troubled crusade: American education, 1945–1980.* New York: Basic Books.

Ravitch, D. (2000). *Left back: A century of failed school reforms.* New York: Simon & Schuster.

Ravitch, D. (Ed.). (2005). *Brookings papers on education policy.* Washington, DC: Brookings Institution.

Rogers, B. (2003). Educational research for professional practice: More than providing evidence for doing "X rather than Y" or finding the "size of the effect of A on B." *Australian Educational Researcher, 30*(2), 65–85.

Salomone, R. C. (2006). Single-sex programs: Resolving the research conundrum. *Teachers College Record, 108*(4), 778–802.

Saudi Arabia Ministry of Education. (2005). *Education for girls* [Electronic version]. Retrieved November 14, 2009, from http://www.moe.gov.sa/openshare/EnglishCon/About-Saud/Education6.htm_cvt.htm

Saunders, L. (Ed.). (2007). *Educational research and policy-making: Exploring the border country between research and policy.* London: Routledge.

Schmidt, W. H., McKnight, C. C., & Raizen, S. A. (1997). *A splintered vision: An investigation of U.S. science and mathematics education.* Dordrecht, Netherlands: Kluwer.

Schmidt, W. H., & Prawat, R. S. (1999). What does the third international mathematics and science study tell us about where to draw the line in the top-down versus bottom-up debate? *Educational Evaluation and Policy Analysis, 21*(1), 85–91.

Schneider, B., Carnoy, M., Kilpatrick, J., Schmidt, W. H., & Shavelson, R. J. (2007). *Estimating causal effects using experimental and observational designs.* Washington, DC: American Educational Research Association.

Schulz, W., & Sibberns, H. (Eds.). (2004). *IEA Civic Education Study technical report.* Amsterdam: International Association for the Evaluation of Educational Achievement.

Slavin, R. E. (2002). Evidence-based education policies: Transforming educational practice and research. *Educational Researcher, 31*(7), 15–21.

Slavin, R. E. (2008). Perspectives on evidence-based research in education: What works? Issues in synthesizing educational program evaluations. *Educational Researcher, 37*(1), 5–14.

Smith, E. (2005). Raising standards in American schools: The case of "No Child Left Behind." *Journal of Education Policy, 20*(4), 507–524.

Smith, T. M., & Baker, D. P. (2001). Worldwide growth and institutionalization of statistical indicators for education policy-making. *Peabody Journal of Education, 76*(3/4), 141–152.

Somers, P., & Caram, C. A. (1998). Veiled delusions: Gender, education, and employment in Saudi Arabia. *Initiatives, 58*(4), 49–58.

Spielhofer, T., Benton, T., & Schagen, S. (2004). A study of the effects of school size and single-sex education in English schools. *Research Papers in Education, 19*(2), 133–159.

Stein, S. (2004). *The culture of education policy.* New York: TC.

Steiner-Khamsi, G. (Ed.). (2004). *The global politics of educational borrowing and lending.* New York: Teachers College Press.

Sunderman, G. L. (2010). Evidence of the impact of school reform on systems governance and educational bureaucracies in the United States. *Review of Research in Education, 34*(1), 226–253.

Taras, M. (2005). Assessment: Summative and formative. Some theoretical reflections. *British Journal of Educational Studies, 53*(4), 466–478.

Towne, L., & Shavelson, R. J. (2001). *Scientific research in education.* Washington, DC: National Academies Press.

United Nations Educational, Scientific, and Cultural Organization. (2003). *Gender and education for all: The leap to equality.* Paris: Author.

United Nations Educational, Scientific, and Cultural Organization. (2004). *EFA global monitoring report 2004: Education for all. The quality imperative.* Paris: Author.

Watson, K. (1999). Comparative educational research: The need for reconceptualisation and fresh insights. *Compare, 29*(3), 233–248.

Weiss, C. H., Murphy-Graham, E., Petrosino, A., & Gandhi, A. G. (2008). The fairy godmother—and her warts: Making the dream of evidence-based policy come true. *American Journal of Evaluation, 29*(1), 29–47.

Welner, K. G. (2010). Education rights and classroom-based litigation: Shifting the boundaries of evidence. *Review of Research in Education, 34*(1), 85–112.

Westbury, I. (1992). Comparing American and Japanese achievement: Is the United States really a low achiever? *Educational Researcher, 21*(5), 18–24.

Westbury, I. (1993). American and Japanese achievement . . . again: A response to Baker. *Educational Researcher, 22*(3), 18–20.

Whitty, G. (2002). *Making sense of education policy: Studies in the sociology and politics of education.* London: Sage.

Whitty, G. (2006). Education(al) research and education policy making: Is conflict inevitable? *British Educational Research Journal, 32*(2), 159–176.

Whitty, G. (2007, June). *Education research under New Labour: Some lessons.* Keynote address presented at the Australian Association for Research in Education Annual Conference, Canberra, Australia.

Winter, B. (2001). Fundamental misunderstandings: Issues in feminist approaches to Islamism. *Journal of Women's History, 13*(1), 9–41.

Wiseman, A. W. (2005). *Principals under pressure: The growing crisis.* Lanham, MD: ScarecrowEducation.

Wiseman, A. W. (2007a). National school systems. In B. J. Bank (Ed.), *Gender and education: An encyclopedia* (pp. 201–208). Westport, CT: Greenwood.

Wiseman, A. W. (2007b). A world culture of equality? The institutional structure of schools and cross-national gender differences in academic achievement. In M. A. Maslak (Ed.), *The structure and agency of women's education* (pp. 179–199). Albany: State University of New York Press.

Wiseman, A. W. (2008). A culture of (in)equality? A cross-national study of gender parity and gender segregation in national school systems. *Research in Comparative and International Education, 3* (2), 179–201.

Wiseman, A. W., & Baker, D. P. (2005). The worldwide explosion of internationalized education policy. In D. P. Baker & A. W. Wiseman (Eds.), *Global trends in educational policy* (Vol. 6, pp. 1–21). London: Elsevier Science.

Wiseman, A. W., & Baker, D. P. (2007). Educational achievements in international context. In B. J. Bank (Ed.), *Gender and education: An encyclopedia* (pp. 407–414). Westport, CT: Greenwood.

Wittman, E. (2008). Align, don't necessarily follow. *Educational Management Administration and Leadership, 36*(1), 33–54.

Young, G., Fort, L., & Danner, M. (1994). Moving from "the status of women" to "gender inequality": Conceptualisation, social indicators and an empirical application. *International Sociology, 9*(1), 55–85.

Zajda, J. (Ed.). (2005). *International handbook on globalisation, education and policy research.* Dordrecht: Springer.

Chapter 2

Naming and Classifying: Theory, Evidence, and Equity in Education

Samuel R. Lucas
Lauren Beresford

University of California, Berkeley

Education names and classifies individuals (Meyer, 1977). This result seems unavoidable. For example, some students will graduate, and some will not. Those who graduate will be *graduates*; those who do not graduate will be labeled otherwise. The only way to avoid such labeling is to fail to make distinctions of any kind. Yet education is rife with distinctions, and as long as there is any nontrivial knowledge involved, labels for the more and less knowledgeable seem inherent to the enterprise. Thus, analysts and policymakers seem to have accepted the inevitability of at least some inequality in education.

However, analysts and policymakers demonstrate some concern with the extent to which success or failure in education is associated with other sociodemographic factors. Multiple analysts have documented such a relation (e.g., Becker & Tomes, 1986; Blau & Duncan, 1967; Bourdieu & Passeron, 1977; Bowles & Gintis, 1976; Sewell & Hauser, 1980), and multiple anthologies echo those findings of sustained inequality (e.g., Karabel & Halsey, 1977; Jencks & Phillips, 1998). As analysts document and explain such an association, they may facilitate policy responses to improve the education and educational outcomes for the disadvantaged.

Yet many factors stand in the way of successful policy response. First, the nominal categories that constitute the sociodemographic dimensions are not simply given. Accordingly, prior to documenting sociodemographic inequality in education, analysts need attend to the theoretical bases of the categories in use. As the theoretical bases of the categories can be replete with contention and controversy, analysts may receive conflicting guidance as they proceed.

Setting aside such debate, the very measurement of educational inequality itself is also not a given. Consequently, analysts must draw on the many debates within the literature as they seek to appropriately measure the phenomena of interest.

Review of Research in Education
March 2010, Vol. 34, pp. 25-84
DOI: 10.3102/0091732X09353578
© 2010 AERA. http://rre.aera.net

In addition, by itself, empirical research offers little to social analysts and policymakers; theory is essential for drawing proper inferences from the research. Yet the wide set of plausible theories, and strategies of analysis that are not designed to eliminate nonviable theories, can ultimately render social science evidence of little value to policy.

These problems, and others, pose serious challenges to the effort to bring social science evidence into the policy discussion on education and inequality. In the pages that follow, we outline the major aspects of these problems and offer some next steps for analysts' effort to bridge the divide between social science research on one hand and policy construction on the other. We draw on the sociological literature that has attended closely to the definition and measurement of social location. A key theme of our assessment is that empirical analyses need become more theory laden (Horan, 1978) if any progress on informing policy is to be realized.

To that end, we first critically consider the conceptualization and measurement of various sociodemographic dimensions, including class, race, and gender. Then we turn briefly to the other side of the inequality equation to relate the existing evidence on the connection between those sociodemographic dimensions and each of several dimensions of education. Next, we turn to theory, first by noting four different metatheoretical dimensions along which theories may be located and then by discussing 11 theories involved in the cross-disciplinary contemporary debate on the basis of sociodemographic inequality in education. Using these theories as resources, we then outline the challenge of moving from theory and evidence to social policy. In response, we offer suggestions for improving the ability of social science research to inform egalitarian policy development around education. To reach those suggestions, however, we must begin by considering the ways in which analysts have theorized the sociodemographic dimensions within which students and other key actors in education are categorized. To that task we now turn.

CONCEPTUALIZATION AND MEASUREMENT OF MULTIPLE SOCIODEMOGRAPHIC DIMENSIONS

The institution of education wields great predictive power over the social and economic outcomes of both individuals and groups (e.g., Card, 1999). At the same time, prominent sociodemographic dimensions are associated with educational outcomes. Thus, class, race, ethnicity, gender, and language status stratify both U.S. society at large and the U.S. educational system in particular.

Underlying each of these sociodemographic dimensions is the concept of power. Social scientists have articulated a vast array of definitions and perspectives on power (Lukes, 1986). For example, some definitions reference intentionality (e.g., Russell, 1938), whereas others suggest that power may be exercised both intentionally and unintentionally (e.g., Lukes, 1986). Some definitions emphasize coercion (e.g., Blau, 1967), whereas others see power in more subtle efforts to influence outcomes or in the structure of relations (e.g., Poulantzas, 1973). Weber (1946) classically defines power as the chance one or more persons "realize their own will in a communal action even against the resistance of others who are participating in the action" (p. 180), but some definitions do not require triumph over resistance for one to observe the operation of power (e.g., Parsons, 1963).

These are but a few of the many dimensions along which analysts' definitions of power disagree. Power, it turns out, is elusive both at the conceptual and empirical level, even as analysts are aware of power in microinteraction and macrostructural arrangements. In this context, therefore, the phenomena of class, race, ethnicity, gender, and language status can be conceived both as manifestations of power and as pathways through which power operates. Seen in this way, measured disparities that align with these sociodemographic dimensions can provide valuable indicators of who holds and who lacks power.

Although easier to define and measure than power, class, race, ethnicity, gender, and language status are also contested concepts and, thus, often defy the presumption of stolid classificatory schemes. Social scientists have debated throughout the 20th century and into the 21st the underlying basis and the malleability of these sociodemographic dimensions as well as the extent to which observed inequality associated with those dimensions may vary. In what follows, we address the complexity of defining and classifying persons along assumed equity-relevant dimensions by outlining competing definitions of these dimensions.

Socioeconomic Status and Class

Sociological definitions of socioeconomic location and class are contested. Although numerous sociologists have put forth a plethora of definitions, most definitions can be categorized along two dimensions. One dimension concerns whether the measure is based on self-assessment or, instead, on researchers' classification of persons according to some stated systematic theory. A second dimension concerns whether the measure is gradational or relational. A gradational phenomenon arrays units throughout a continuum from low to high. A relational phenomenon is defined by the connections, contradictions, and oppositions of different statuses or locations.

Taking the second dimension first, a relational theory of class, best exemplified by the Marxist tradition, specifies a structure of positions in relational opposition to one another. Wright (1979) defines class as one's position in the process of production or the "social relations of production" (p. 20). Positions in production are inherently relational and, in fact, likely in conflict. For example, all positions do not have equal authority—some positions entail authority over the occupants of other positions. As another example, some positions entail autonomy, the power to control some or all aspects of one's own work, and some do not. Furthermore, only some positions control organizational resources. Conflict is inherent in these oppositions; for example, supervisors may order subordinates to do something the subordinates do not want to do (e.g., follow a particular procedure for accomplishing a task). The supervisor is seen as legitimate when directing subordinates; because this legitimacy reflects the institutionalization of the power of the supervisor to rule over and against the wishes of subordinates, this legitimacy ensconces conflict in the very structure of class. Because a relational analysis focuses on the oppositions inherent in structural relations of positions, a relational analysis is fundamentally an analysis of "empty places" and not of individuals (Wright, 1979, p. 21).

Seen in this way, class arrangements are a product of ongoing historic contestation. Any given arrangement, therefore, is a product of class struggles concerning the class relations at the time (Wright, 1979, p. 23). The intrinsic and extrinsic rewards that accrue to control of the labor process motivate this struggle. Struggles occur in regard to at least three interdependent dimensions within the social relations of production: (a) control of financial capital, that is, investment and accumulation, which can influence how much and what is produced; (b) control of physical capital, which determines how commodities are produced; and (c) the relations of authority entailing supervision. The latter two dimensions concern the direct possession and management of the means of production.

The modern era has seen an expansion of industrial production, which has led to the expansion of management as well as other white-collar positions, creating a "new middle class" composed of social categories that occupy contradictory or liminal relations within the class structure. For instance, middle managers and supervisors lack autonomy but have authority. Are they capitalists, proletarians, or something else? At the same time, small proprietors may lack authority (they may have no employees) but have autonomy. Are they capitalists, proletarians, or something else? Different analysts offer different answers to these questions, answers that have implications at both the conceptual and the empirical level. Wright, however, was the first to attempt to integrate these positions in a Marxist analysis without treating them as epiphenomenal and without implicitly rejecting the more structural aspects of Marxist thought. Through additional efforts, he has elaborated his position to more deeply historicize it as well as to integrate additional dimensions, all while remaining within a Marxist framework (e.g., Wright, 1985, 1994). Multiple analysts have critiqued Wright's perspective (e.g., Brenner, 1988; Burawoy, 1987), and vigorous debate continues (e.g., Sørenson, 2000; Wright, 2000). Throughout the debates, however, a definitive aspect of Marxist definitions is that they focus on structural positions in society and their relationship to one another in the organization of production (Wright, 1979, p. 4).

Alternatively, analysts have used an approach based on gradational perspectives on socioeconomic class, typically measuring the economic resources, economic status (e.g., impoverished or not), occupational location, and educational attainment of individuals or members of their family (e.g., parents, grandparents, siblings). Although earnings, poverty, and educational attainment are intrinsically gradational and interval-like in their measure, occupations are nominal and not easily transformed into gradational scales. Yet many analysts see occupations as fundamental markers of socioeconomic class, and therefore, analysts have sought to use persons' occupations to measure class or socioeconomic position.

The aim of transforming occupations into a gradational measure of class is sometimes seen as connected to a Weberian tradition (e.g., Grusky & Sørenson, 1998). Although Weber (1946) sees class as existing when

(1) a number of people have in common a specific causal component of their life chances, in so far as (2) this component is represented exclusively by economic interests in the possession of goods and opportunities for income, and (3) is represented under the conditions of the commodity or labor markets, (p. 181)

many analysts who construct or use gradational measures do not explicitly reference Weber or, indeed, any overarching theory of class. Even so, the connection between occupations and education and earnings provide a pragmatic foundation for the measurement strategy.

Duncan's (1961) socioeconomic index (SEI) used occupational education and occupational income to measure socioeconomic status (SES) and thus provided a way to transform nominal occupations into an interval-level indicator for widespread use. This breakthrough was followed with many updates (e.g., Featherman & Stevens, 1982; Stevens & Cho, 1985) to keep the measure current as the list of occupations changed owing to technological change and changes in economic structure. More recently, Hauser and Warren (1997) found that constructing a summary SEI of occupations was of less utility than simply using occupational income and occupational educational attainment (measures of the central tendency of occupational incumbents' income and educational attainment, respectively).

The socioeconomic tradition does not theorize socioeconomic locations as consisting of empty places in the occupational structure. In fact, the ordering of the places is a function of the characteristics of the persons who occupy the occupation. Still, the gradational view of class directly implicates a vertical hierarchy, allowing analysts to coherently investigate inequality.

Returning to the first dimension—class as an economic phenomenon, or class as a personal subjective phenomenon—Jackman (1979) studied the way in which Americans classify persons into the categories of poor, working class, middle class, upper middle class, and upper class. She found that they relied on socioeconomic cues (e.g., income, job authority) as well as personal factors (e.g., a person's lifestyle). Jackman and Jackman (1983) provided further evidence that persons' subjective reports are not grounded in an exclusively economic sociotheoretic logic, in contrast to stratification researchers, who attempt to base their classification of persons into classes or socioeconomic strata in an explicit sociotheoretic claim concerning economic phenomena. It is not a matter of right or wrong, but it is important to note the differences in the basis of the classification depending on the source of the classification.

One response to the disparity between academics and their respondents is to claim that the site of production is no longer the basis for a coherent understanding of class;

instead, subjective experience, based on cleavages of cultural meaning, are required (e.g., Eyerman, 1994; Laraña, Johnston, & Gusfield, 1994). An alternative approach calls for analysts to stop aggregating persons into overarching classes; claiming that occupations are the basis of much social action and the site of economic relations (e.g., licensing, capital investment, authority), they call for analysts to basically treat occupations as classes (Grusky & Sørenson, 1998; Weeden & Grusky, 2005). The subjective-objective distinction, and how to understand and respond to the difference analytically, remains contentious.

Returning to the gradational-relational dimension, these two views of class have spawned two arguably divergent analyses of stratification in society. Despite their differences, both concern an unequal distribution of power, denoted in relation to factors of production. And despite their similar interests, Marxist measures of class location have been used relatively rarely in the study of inequality in education. Although the empirical association between Marxist class position and SEI suggests that the findings produced through use of a Marxist-inspired measure of class in the study of educational outcomes would generally agree with findings analysts have produced using SEI, it is also true that if there are inherent conflicts consistent with a Marxist definition of class, the "smoothed" correlations between educational outcomes and SEI measures may obscure rather than reveal those conflicts. For this very reason, Wright, Costello, Hachen, and Sprague (1982) collected their own nationally representative data using survey questions designed to allow persons to be placed in Marxist class categories. When they did so, they found the inherent conflicts visible in their empirical analysis. Notably, they found that when one considers the social relations of work rather than the occupational titles of persons' jobs, the working class is "by far the largest class" (Wright et al., 1982, p. 709).

Gender

On the face of it, gender may appear to be biologically fixed. Yet the social concept of gender is also socially defined and determined by taken-for-granted assumptions surrounding what it means to be feminine or masculine. Indeed, even the putatively fixed biological reality of sex is less fixed than lay belief suggests (Diamond & Sigmundson, 1997; Dreger, 2001).

Disagreeing with the biological evidence, some social scientists have defined gender as biologically based sexual differentiation of behaviors (Udry, 1994, p. 561). In this view, sex-typed behaviors cause gendered social structures that humans are predisposed to create owing to sexual dimorphism (Urdy, 1994). In this model, biology trumps the effects of any socialization that might seek to diminish the behavioral differences between men and women (Udry, 1994).

In contrast, other social theorists see social structure as a determinant of gendered behaviors and roles (Dunn, Almquist, & Chafetz, 1993; Ferree & Hall, 1996; Risman, 1998). Larger structures, such as labor markets, nations, and communities, determine access to scarce resources, such as jobs, legal rights, and child care, that reflect the allocation of life chances to males and females (Dunn et al., 1993). Social structural theories of gender examine the contours of family, work, politics, and the household as predictors of gender inequality. The question of gender rests on who receives what and how much and the features of the social structure that facilitate this distribution. Access to education as a resource is a dimension along which social structuralists assess gender inequality. In this view, gendered behaviors are taken for granted, deeply engrained, and consistent over time.

Social interactionist models focus on the reproduction of gendered behavior and the enforcement of societal gender norms through a myriad of everyday social interactions (Ridgeway & Smith-Lovin, 1999). Social interactionists more readily tease apart measurements of gendered behavior. By focusing on how expected gendered behaviors are activated under certain circumstances (e.g., in mixed-gender settings, while performing stereotypical tasks, or in situations where one sex dominates as authority figures), social interactionists demonstrate the mutability of gender (Ridgeway & Smith-Lovin, 1999). Gender is not constant but is asserted, produced, reproduced, and altered within the context of social interactions.

In a similar vein, cultural theorists argue that gender is actively constructed through books, magazines, television, and other vehicles of mass culture (McRobbie, 1999; Walkerdine, 1984). These media-conveyed conceptualizations of gender appear to be widely shared, institutionalized, and embedded within social structures. Cultural discourses of femininity emphasize a gendered hierarchy in which men dominate women.

These discourses are produced and reproduced within schools. For example, parents, teachers, and school administrators encourage girls to take "feminine" subjects, steering them away from "masculine" ones, such as math and science (Blackmore & Kenway, 1993). Furthermore, schools encourage gender inequality and reinforce power relations through curricula that emphasize the accomplishments of White men, hidden curricula in which authority figures enact disparate gendered behaviors through staffing relations and authority patterns, unequal treatment of students by teachers whereby teachers interact more with boys, and negative interactions between male and female students (often involving attention to the female body) that are left without reprimand by school authority figures (Weis, 1997). Research finds such disparate treatment in coed schools, all-boys schools, and all-girls schools (V. E. Lee, Marks, & Byrd, 1994).

The solidification of the gendered hierarchy need not occur passively or in the same manner between social groups. Jean Anyon (1984) points out that what is considered appropriate female behavior differs by class. Lower- and working-class women are often expected to take on more feminized roles in the family by staying at home and taking care of children, whereas middle-class and professional women are expected to achieve in the labor market. Yet in contradiction with these expectations, working-class women are often faced with the obligation to work to augment their family's income, and professional women are expected to fulfill their domestic roles and be feminine. Women struggle with these contradictions through a process of accommodation and resistance that begins at a young age and plays itself out in the school setting. Yet even resistance often does not aim to dismantle patriarchal social structures; rather, its goal is to seek protection within the gendered hierarchy, thereby granting gendered power arrangements further legitimacy. Cultural scholars argue that promoting oppositional cultural discourses in curricula and pedagogy that emphasize a nontraditional, expansive view of femininity can mitigate cultural discourses that marginalize girls' education (Blackmore & Kenway, 1993).

The conceptual disagreements about what gender "is" are consequential. Alas, rarely do these disagreements, or coherent positions within the debate, become reflected in the assessment of the relation between gender and student outcomes. The disagreements are not irrelevant; instead, they have little traction in most cases because the measurement of sex and gender does not draw in a direct or coherent fashion on these different frames. Furthermore, it is unclear what feasible measurement strategies would allow analysts to draw on those different frames, especially for studying minors, who are appropriately protected from invasive study designs by federal authorities. Thus, data on student achievement record students' self-reported sex or the sex to which they are assigned by their parents and/or school authorities. Consequently, although these disagreements bear directly on the sociological implications of any sex or gender differences in achievement, the data are not of sufficient theoretical sophistication to allow the typical analysis to use the resources the debate makes visible or even to address the debate at issue, at least with nationally representative data.

Race

Much the same could be said of some of the pivotal debates concerning race—many perspectives call for genetic indicators of race, but there appear to be no nationally representative data sources on educational outcomes that use gene-based indicators of race.

Race has and continues to be a particularly forceful means by which persons phenotypically categorize individuals on the basis of a supposed genotype. Although persons place great weight on such visible characteristics (Loury, 2002), and those characteristics have a genetic basis, in actuality, there is no clear sociologically relevant genetic difference between people of purportedly different races (Correll & Hartmann, 1998; Long, 2004; Yu et al., 2002). If biological definitions of race do not hold scientific water, then how can race be defined?

Sociological theory has emphasized a socially constructed definition of race in which members of society, not principles of biology, define who belongs to what race and what such a membership means in terms of power and access to social resources (e.g., Omi & Winant, 1994, p. 65). Indeed, the very origin of race as a divisive concept in the American context is based in power relations at the inception of the union (C. I. Harris, 1993; Lucas, 2008b).

Omi and Winant (1994) maintain that racial categories and categorization schemes are produced through a sociohistorical process they term *racial formation*. This process is the result of contending projects—efforts at meaning making, institution building, and policy adoption—that may be haphazard and certainly are not cross-coordinated. A result of this process is a particular understanding and instantiation of race that for many of those living within it, may take on the character of common sense. Yet its historicized nature, its sensitivity to the clash of interests, and its difference from other periods signify that any particular common sense about racial categorization has a nondeterministic relation to biological factors, despite the way in which racial categorization may be understood, in any particular epoch, to be so based.

Affirmation of the social basis of race creates an oft-unrecognized challenge for commentators on race. On one hand, one argument pits those claiming a biological basis for race against those intoning the mantra that race is socially constructed. On the other hand, a different argument places many of those who claim that race is socially constructed in opposition to those claiming that the only way to move beyond race is to stop recording or referencing race. Consequently, many of those claiming that race is socially constructed are caught in a crossfire between two opponents, one rejecting the claim that race is socially constructed, one embracing the claim that race is socially constructed. Only a nuanced reading of the phenomenon of race can produce a coherent position that rejects both a biological basis for race and the facile call to ignore race.

Race is, indeed, a powerful marker owing to the social meanings with which we imbue these socially fabricated designations. Being a product of historical circumstances and the operation of power in context, racial demarcations and categories can change over time and differ across space. This mutability is evidenced in the changing racial categories of the U.S. census as well as in legal definitions such as the "one-drop" rule, which historically fixed notions of African American racial descent (Correll & Hartmann, 1998, p. 24). Although some may regard these rules as immutable, such rules of exclusion have changed over time.

However, mutability can be easily overstated. Although the categories have changed over time, the categories have meaning in persons' lives, based in a history of racialized exclusion. Historic racial exclusion has created a structural social relation that has outlived the moment of its construction (Lucas, 2008b). Because of that structure, transcending the racialized history of the United States requires more than deciding to eschew race; one must, also, both decide to and act to dismantle the structural social relation that flows from the racial formations of the past and present. Thus, socially constructed race is structurally erected race and, as such, is as solid in its reality as it would be if it were truly based in biology alone (Loury, 2002).

As for measurement, analysts have not routinely obtained blood samples for race-typing students for nationally representative investigations of educational outcomes.

Thus, even though multiple measurement strategies have been used, adherents of the view that race is fundamentally a biological phenomenon have never confined their attention to genetic evidence as the only appropriate measurement strategy. The multiple strategies of measurement have turned not on acceptance of biology but instead on how to phrase the race question and of whom the race question should be asked.

Prior to the 1960 census, enumerators reported on persons' racial characteristics; for the 1960 census, however, a self-report was obtained (Hirschman, Alba, & Farley, 2000; Taeuber & Hansen, 1966). This subtle change from enumerator reports to self-reports opens the door to framing measures of race in terms of racial identity, with momentous implications for the meaning of the data obtained. Indeed, the current federal guidelines for the collection of race data state,

Self-identification is the preferred means of obtaining information about an individual's race and ethnicity, except in instances where observer identification is more practical (e.g., completing a death certificate). (Office of Management and Budget, 1997, p. 57875)

Note that if one is interested in power or in effects of discrimination, the key question concerns not one's racial identity but, instead, the categories in which one is placed by others. Prior to the use of self-reports, the measures of race categorized persons according to this more directly relevant phenomenon. Even so, early on, the move to the self-report was of little consequence, as enumerator reports likely matched the consciousnesses of the categorized owing to understandings of race and in-group solidarity under oppressive circumstances. However, more recently, consistency across various reports has become less complete, a feature reflected in and amplified by the move to allow persons to select multiple racial categories in the 2000 census; notably, the resulting classificatory scheme enumerated 126 different racial combinations (Fischer & Hout, 2006, p. 23). Yet it is doubtful that persons act on 126 different racial categories during social interactions or decision making. Thus, the current official classificatory approach likely clouds the coherent observation of race relations.

Notably, adoption of the Census 2000 categories and data collection strategy was greatly affected by explicit appeals to politics as sociotheoretic coherence was deemphasized, as representatives of various groups vied for recognition (Honneth, 2003) and, ultimately, for rights and benefits from the state. This was not necessarily a new development, as racial classification has always been politicized (Skrentny, 2002). However, the debates concerning Census 2000 seemed to intensify the politicization.

The results of the 2000 census have produced a cottage industry, allowing many researchers to investigate racial patterns to a degree hitherto impossible (e.g., J. Lee & Bean, 2004), while at the same time, scholars have returned to other data sources that, by fortuitous design, allow them to investigate self-reporting patterns under different conditions (e.g., Doyle & Kao, 2007; D. R. Harris & Sim, 2002) as well as the connection between the reports provided by different sources (e.g., Saperstein, 2006). Although the research highlights the existence of inconsistency, in actuality, the consistency between various sources still far exceeds the consistency researchers find when they investigate the reliability of measures of other important sociodemographic factors (e.g., educational attainment, occupation, earnings). For example, D. R. Harris and Sim (2002) report that approximately 87% of adolescents classify themselves in the same monoracial group when asked to state their race at school versus when asked the same question in a home interview. This high level of consistency was obtained even though D. R. Harris and Sim deleted from their analysis those with missing data on parent characteristics. As missing data on parent characteristics are associated with race (Looker, 1989), we cannot confidently regard the sample as representative of race in the United States. Furthermore, D. R. Harris and Sim (2002) find that they are more likely to delete students from southern states; southern states have less racial intermarriage than other regions for all groups except Asians (Qian, 1999), and thus, the overrepresentation of southern children in the deletions may increase the incidence of discrepant race reports in the remaining sample for non-Asian groups. Even so, it should also be noted that even the discrepancy level of 13% that D. R. Harris and Sim (2002) report reflects a Pearson correlation across the two contexts of approximately .74, hardly a low level of reliability when compared to error rates for other sociodemographic variables. For example, Looker (1989) finds correlations as low as .33 for adolescent reports of parents' education when compared to parents' reports of their own (or partner's) education.

Despite such high levels of reliability, the discrepant responses are the object of focus for many analysts. For example, Saperstein (2006, p. 61, Table 1) shows that 94.3% of adult respondents classify themselves in the same category as do observers. Yet the bulk of the article focuses on the 163 out of 2,869 respondents for whom there is a discrepancy. Moreover, 109 of the 163 discrepant categorizations concern persons who call themselves non-Black/non-White whereas observers call them White. Thus, 99% of self-reported Whites are called White by observers, and 97% of self-reported Blacks are called Black by observers—an extremely high degree of interrater agreement.

Indeed, the finding of interrater reliability concerning race seems robust, for after all the debate concerning the multiracial census options, J. Lee and Bean (2004) find that only 2.4% of persons were classified as multiracial in the 2000 census. For any other sociodemographic factor (e.g., occupation, class, income, earnings, parental education), such low levels of disagreement and high levels of coverage would be regarded as a major measurement triumph, given that missing classifications and other inaccuracies are unavoidable in any measurement effort involving 300 million study participants. Yet even though the measurement of race is incredibly more successful than the measurement of virtually any other sociodemographic dimension, the measurement of race has become a focus of intense attention and critique (e.g., D. R. Harris & Sim, 2002; Saperstein, 2006).

In light of the unmatched success of the measurement of race, we believe that this intense focus on the reporting of race is intriguing. Were similar levels of attention paid to assessing measurement complexities of any of the other sociodemographic dimensions (e.g., institution quality to improve the measurement of educational attainment), analysts would produce far more dividends in understanding than they produce by continued probing of the various possible ways of placing people into what is, when conceived in essentializing biological terms, an inherently infinite categorical scheme owing to the genesis of schoolchildren in the mating patterns of current generations, the concomitant lack of a biological basis for any classificatory demarcations, and the necessary yet largely unpredictable social basis of any categorization scheme one may adopt (but see Morning, 2008, for an intriguing discussion of multiple dimensions of racial classification systems). This is not to suggest that *nothing* can be learned from further research on racial classification, but it is to state emphatically that the marginal gain is low compared to that available for bringing the same intensity of scrutiny to other sociodemographic dimensions that reveal far larger discrepancies and problems of measurement.

The focus on race is, actually, a reflection of the transformation of the concept as used by sociologists, from one rooted in a history of ancestry-based power relations in a particular country (e.g., C. I. Harris, 1993; Loury, 2002; Lucas, 2008b) into one of ancestry-based identity (e.g., Doyle & Kao, 2007; Saperstein, 2006). The shift to identity is often poignantly expressed by advocates for various proposals for official racial classification. Funderberg (1996) writes,

People say I can't have it both ways. Yes, I'm part black and part white, but every day I am forced to choose one or the other. On mortgage applications, school forms and on the decennial United States census, I've been asked to pick from four exclusive categories: black, white, American Indian, and Asian and Pacific Islander. (Funderberg, 1996, p. A15)

After noting the press for a *multiracial* category, Funderberg disagrees, claiming to "fear that this proposal simply creates another category which multiracial people must force themselves into" (Funderberg, 1996, p. A15). She continues,

I don't think of myself as multiracial; I think of myself as black and white.

A multiracial identity should not be exclusive, but inclusive. People of mixed heritage (which includes up to 75 percent of African Americans) should be able to check any boxes that apply. Let all Americans speak truthfully about who they are. (Funderberg, 1996, p. A15)

Funderberg captures in words the experience of many. It is important to acknowledge that experience. However, one may affirm persons' subjective experience, including the anguish, confusion, and anger that may accompany it without thereby accepting that subjective experience provides a theoretically coherent basis for understanding the phenomenon at issue.

The excerpts' emphasis on subjective understanding of one's experience, as well as the social scientific embrace of identity as a basis of racial classification, reflects a critical yet often unacknowledged proposed transformation in the understanding of race.

This transformation raises serious questions for policy, not least of which is whether policy can be justified around identity-based race; that is, it is uncertain that concern with inequality can be justified or sustained for a phenomenon defined primarily in terms of identity. In other words, shorn of its basis in historic and contemporary power relations, as has occurred implicitly in many studies of the empirical classification of persons into burgeoning racial categories, concern with identity-defined racial inequality becomes no easier to maintain than might concern with inequality between those who identify as right-handed and those who identify as left-handed. Ironically, in offering itself as a response to the mutability of racial categorization schemes, a response that would seem to be exceedingly aware of history, the race-as-identity advocates implicitly deemphasize a race-as-power perspective and thus implicitly dehistoricize race. In doing so, the race-as-identity advocates raise yet fail to address a central question their position necessarily poses: Why, after all, should state actors address disparate outcomes for individuals who merely feel they belong to a particular (racial) group or be concerned with patterns of disadvantage afflicting self-proclaimed groups whose existence flows, ultimately, only from their members self-avowedly chosen identity?

Ethnicity

Ethnicity provides a nice test case of this question, for ethnicity differs from race on the very issue of choice. As Waters (1990) argues, ethnicity in the United States is far more a matter of choice than is race. Ethnicity denotes the common ancestral bonds that demarcate a people through blood and descent as well as rituals and traditions. Weber (1956) defines ethnic groups as "human groups that entertain a subjective belief in their common descent because of similarities of physical type or of customs or both, or because of memories of colonization and migration" (p. 389). In more common sociological parlance, ethnicity is strongly associated with culture, in which group members share common customs, beliefs, language, and modes of living. In this context, Skrentny (2002) shows that the failure of White ethnic groups to make an analogy with Blacks harmed their efforts to racialize their group and thus become eligible for affirmative action. The intriguing implication is that efforts to base race on identity may ultimately reclassify Blacks and other disadvantaged racialized groups as ethnic groups in the public understanding of the concept of race. If Skrentny is any guide, this move may ultimately facilitate the erosion of any remaining efforts to address racial inequality. Consequently, the race-as-identity advocates appear to, perhaps inadvertently, be setting the stage for the ethnicization of race, to the detriment of any understanding of race that draws on relations of power to render the concept coherent in historic and contemporary perspective.

Returning to ethnicity as a concept, in the U.S. context, sociologists examine ethnicity mainly in terms of immigration. Robert Park's (1914) theory of assimilation has often provided a point of departure for discussions of ethnicity. Assimilation occurs when ethnic groups encounter each other and reduce socially distinct boundaries to the extent that the knowledge of their ethnic descent "in no way gives a better predic-tion or estimation of their relevant social characteristics than does knowledge of the behavior of the total population of the community or nation involved" (Lieberson, 1963, p. 10). Early waves of European immigration fit the mold of assimilating ethnic identities into mainstream American culture. It is around this phenomenon that Park (1926/1950, p. 149) developed his thesis of assimilation, in which immigrants made contact with different groups, competed over scarce resources, became accustomed to one another's presence, and gradually assimilated into the mainstream society.

Cultural pluralism provides a contrary view of ethnicity in American society. Ethnic groups in society are viewed not as "melting" into the dominant culture but as retaining distinct ethnic identities, even if these identities become reconstituted in a new land (N. Glazer & Moynihan, 1970, p. 17). In this paradigm, ethnic identities are maintained via political interests. Even though some modicum of assimilation occurs among ethnic transplants to the United States, many groups retain and main-tain their ethnic identities.

Notably, even though the measurement of ethnicity is straightforward, persons' self-reports of ethnicity are considerably more mutable than their self-reports of race (Waters, 1990). Yet no major effort to nail down the measurement of ethnicity for all ethnic groups has ensued. Indeed, there are few sustained research efforts to continu-ally chronicle the relative educational attainments of different White ethnic groups. Consequently, attention to ethnic inequality is often a way of attending to the achieve-ment of Latino/as, a group whose status as a racial category is contested. Indeed, as Hayes-Bautista and Chapa (1987) note, the countries of Latin America share neither language nor race nor culture. Hayes-Bautista and Chapa note that the most salient feature the countries of the region share is a political relationship with a dominating northern neighbor, the United States, a country whose efforts to dominate the region were codified in U.S. policy as early as 1823. According to Hayes-Bautista and Chapa, the relationship between Latin American nations and the United States has affected the immigrant incorporation of those who hail from Latin America.

These observations are consistent with what we believe is a peculiar and uneven emphasis on ethnicity that stems from the de facto racialization of Latino/a ethnicity. Behaviors and appearances, including, but not limited to, cultural practices, physi-cal appearance, and language are taken by others to be markers of (trans-)Latino/a ethnicity and are thus generalized to a variegated mix of peoples of many nation-alities with disparate historical circumstances of incorporation in the United States. Although various Latino/a groups have diverse histories, some highly oppressive and others more favorable, Latino/a claims to a cohesive ethnic identity stem from a common stake in political issues surrounding low standards of living and language status barriers (Calderon, 1992). Power is implicated in this specific arrangement, and because it is contested as a racial category, ethnicity serves as a placeholder for a group of people that may be similar to a racial group because of histories of exclusion, deprivation, stigma, and racism.

Language Status

Inequality based on language status often brings together class, race, and ethnic inequalities. Paramount to understanding language-minority status is an acute comprehension of immigration patterns in the United States. At the turn to the 21st century, approximately 20% of school-age children came from immigrant families (Kao & Thompson, 2003, p. 418). As a country composed predominantly of ancestors of immigrants and those the immigrants enslaved, most U.S. residents have family members that were required to learn English to succeed (immigrants) or survive (the enslaved) in the new nation. Today the pivotal issue in educating new immigrants has centered on competency in the English language, because a purported lack thereof has been cited as a causal factor in lower achievement (Rumberger & Larson, 1998, p. 68).

The issue of language status is particularly salient when discussing Latino/a immigrants, because they compose a majority of non-English-speaking immigrants (Rumberger & Larson, 1998, p. 69). Nearly half of Latino/a youths are immigrants or children of immigrants (Kao & Thompson, 2003, p. 418). Furthermore, among U.S.-born students, 64% of Latino/as, in contrast to 4% of other ethnic groups, self-reported the use of a non-English language at home (McArthur, 1993, as cited in Rumberger & Larson, 1998, p. 69).

Language status is often measured by determining the language of students' parents. However, a more comprehensive approach determines persons' facility with four central tasks of language: reading, writing, hearing, and speaking. Fluency in one modality is not necessarily a sign of fluency in another. Such comprehensive measures are rare, but there is some research that explores multiple dimensions of language proficiency (e.g., Stolzenberg, 1990) or that combines multiple dimensions in one measure (e.g., Espinosa & Massey, 1997).

Sociodemographic Dimensions: A Summary

All social demographic dimensions pose both theoretical and epistemological challenges. For class, race, and gender, a fundamental division exists between those who highlight persons' subjective experience and those who privilege measurement strategies that reflect particular sociotheoretic understandings of phenomena. Analysts also disagree about whether some phenomena of interest are better conceived in relational or gradational terms and whether phenomena have or lack a biological basis.

Of course, at least for the subjective experience–sociotheoretic coherence distinction, it would be possible to split the difference and use both perspectives. However, the result of such an alleged compromise could be even more confusion, as such a compromise simply postpones the effort to address the key question: What do the findings on inequality mean? Do they primarily reflect differences traceable to different selections people make from among the virtually infinite possible identities they might adopt, in which case respect for persons' autonomy might imply a small and limited role for policy? Or, instead, are differences primarily the result of different opportunities people obtain, in which case respect for persons' autonomy might mean a large and broad role for policy? If both, what is the balance of forces, and therefore, how best should one proceed in an effort to operationalize the phenomenon for empirical investigation?

The lack of a resolution to such disagreements has not prevented continued research on inequality. And substantively, there is a great deal of evidence of inequality along the lines erected by and reflected through the sociodemographic dimensions discussed earlier. Considering that evidence occupies the section that follows.

MEASUREMENT IN EDUCATION AND EQUITY: MULTIPLE DIMENSIONS OF IN-SCHOOL EXPERIENCE, ATTAINMENT, AND ACHIEVEMENT

One important question is whether one observes educational inequality along the above described sociodemographic dimensions. One could investigate many education outcomes and experiences, but we consider curriculum differentiation, discipline, measured achievement, and educational attainment because they cover students' positional placement, treatment, and achievement, all of which are important aspects of education. The following will evaluate controversies of measurement and assess overall and group-specific patterns for each dimension.

Curriculum Differentiation: Conceptualization, Measurement, and Inequality

Students' curricular placement in the school is analogous to adults' occupational placement in the economy—both are nominal designations, both constrain the tasks to which persons will orient, and thus both dramatically differentiate persons' experiences. These similarities make the measurement of curricular placement as important and challenging as the measurement of occupational placement.

The challenge of measuring curriculum placement flows from the complexity of *curriculum differentiation*. The concept of curriculum differentiation refers to the division of a domain of study into segments and/or the division of students into groups. Tracking, "ability grouping," special education placement, gifted and talented education (GATE) programs, and English language-learning (ELL) programs (e.g., bilingual education) are all phenomena that either require or produce curriculum differentiation.

Enrollment in ELL, special education, and GATE are straightforward to ascertain. In contrast, students' track placement is much more complex to measure. Complexities follow from the multiple dimensions of curriculum differentiation, the lack of consensus concerning the priority to give various dimensions, and variation in the source of a report for persons' placement. Navigating this challenge is aided by formal consideration of the multiple dimensions along which systems and forms of curriculum differentiation may vary.

Sørenson (1970) identified key dimensions of curriculum differentiation. Two dimensions, *horizontal* differentiation and *vertical* differentiation, concern the grounds for the differentiation. Horizontal differentiation divides the curriculum into domains of study. For example, the division of foreign language study into German, French, and Spanish is horizontal differentiation. Vertical differentiation, however, reflects a division of students along lines relevant for learning, such as prior knowledge, for example, the division of French into introductory (French I), intermediate (French II), and advanced (French III). Students' mastery of the material of one horizontally differentiated course can be irrelevant for their placement in some other horizontally differentiated course; however, for vertical differentiation, students' placement in one course depends on their mastery of the material covered in the previous course.

Other key dimensions of curriculum differentiation are *scope, electivity, mobility*, and *selectivity*. Scope reflects the extent to which students share the same peers throughout the school day. If scope is high, groups are segregated. Electivity refers to the degree to which students play a role in determining their curricular placement. Mobility concerns the amount of movement across curricular positions, and selectivity measures the degree of homogeneity within the curricular positions.

These dimensions allow analysts to see how programs that may differ conceptually and empirically still share a fundamental basis in the need to somehow divide students into groups for instruction (in that all students of a given age or grade cannot be taught effectively by one teacher in one large auditorium). For example, special education, a form of curriculum differentiation, has changed over time. Originally, special education was a high-scope program with low electivity, low mobility, and relatively high selectivity (i.e., relatively high degrees of homogeneity in the program). However, efforts to mainstream students, as well as changes in program administration (e.g., allowing special education resource specialists to work with other students as well) have transformed special education to a moderate-scope program.

Special education is not unique, as both GATE and ELL programs share a similar set of values for the various dimensions of curriculum differentiation. Both GATE and ELL are low-electivity, moderate-scope programs; for example, neither need cover all subjects, and thus neither need determine students' course taking in subjects not covered by the program. Although GATE is a low-mobility program, the mobility of ELL students is unclear. ELL programs project an eventual transition out of the program for participants. Thus, even if one finds low yearly mobility rates out of ELL, this may be by design (e.g., a 4-year Transitional Bilingual Education program). Seen another way, however, ELL programs have high mobility, in that virtually all students are expected to eventually leave the program. Notably, historic change in the values, and the similarity in the values for special education, GATE, and ELL, suggest that the values for the various dimensions of curriculum differentiation have more to do with societal understandings of how to arrange education than with fundamental limitations of education, just as cross-national research on persons' understandings of tracking suggests (e.g., LeTendre, Hofer, & Shimizu, 2003).

Table 1 contains information on the proportion of different groups of students categorized in GATE and special education based on either nationally representative data or censuses of students. Unfortunately, national-level reporting of placement in many programs is not required, and even those that are required need break down the reports only by race and/or gender.

Even the special education data are not standardized, for special education policies vary dramatically across states. Students with the same exact conditions could be placed in entirely different categories for special education or, in fact, not be categorized as eligible for special education, depending on the jurisdiction (Donovan & Cross, 2002). Analysts have long criticized the national reporting requirements as well as the arbitrary nature of an assignment process that can assign the same student to disparate categories in different geographic locales (e.g., Francis et al., 2005; Macmann, Barnett, Lombard, Belton-Kocher, & Sharpe, 1989; Magliocca & Stephens, 1980; Mehan, Hertweck, & Meihls, 1986; Reschly, 1987).

For all these reasons, there is no national census of placement for many programs or many sociodemographic dimensions (e.g., parents' occupations). Still, Table 1 indicates some association between race and gender and special education and GATE. Furthermore, research on more targeted samples shows an important association between SES and GATE placement that benefits the socioeconomically advantaged (e.g., McKenzie, 1986).

From Curriculum Differentiation to Tracking: Measurement and Inequality

GATE, special education, and ELL programs historically have involved a minority of students. Prior to GATE, special education, and ELL, however, tracking existed and played a role in determining students' experience of school. Indeed, one can interpret GATE, special education, and ELL programs as simple elaborations of broad-based tracking.

Tracking at the elementary school level is often called ability grouping, suggesting that students are assigned to their placements owing to their ability. This appellation implies that group assignment is somehow based on student potential. Alas, it is impossible to measure potential with sufficient precision to make such assignments, as we show in the following discussion of measured achievement.

Elementary school tracking tends to occur inside classrooms and to be fairly flexible in the number of groups and students' assignments during the course of a school year. Only a few subjects are typically involved. Analysts typically obtain information on students' assignments from teachers or other school personnel. Research indicates that tracking matters for student achievement. Gamoran (1989) found that high-track elementary school students learned more material than their low-track peers and explained the difference owing to some extent to instructional differences between the tracks, most notably, the provision of more information to high-track students. Pallas, Entwisle, Alexander, and Stluka (1994) also found high-track elementary school students to learn more than their lower-track peers and clear evidence of instructional effects.

Secondary school tracking, defined in various ways, is enacted in more complex ways than is elementary school tracking, and the differences greatly complicate

TABLE 1

Group-Specific Incidence of Placement in Gifted and Talented Education and Various Special Education Categories

		Special Education		
Sociodemographic Category	Gifted and Talented	Mental Retardation	Learning Disability	Emotional Disturbance
Race				
White	7.5[a]	1.2[b]	6.0[c]	0.9[d]
Black	3.0[a]	2.6[b]	6.5[c]	1.5[d]
Asian	10.0[a]	0.6[b]	2.2[c]	0.3[d]
Latino/a	3.6[a]	0.9[b]	6.4[c]	0.6[d]
Native American	4.9[a]	1.3[b]	7.5[c]	1.0[d]
Gender				
Male	6.3[e]	—	—	—
Female	7.0[e]	—	—	—

[a]Donovan and Cross (2002, p. 55). [b]Donovan and Cross (2002, p. 41). [c]Donovan and Cross (2002, p. 48). [d]Donovan and Cross (2002, p. 50). [e]Snyder, Dillow, and Hoffman (2007, Table 51).

measurement. One restrictive view might regard tracking as existing only when a formal process assigns students to explicit, overarching programs encompassing multiple subjects and years. Alternatively, tracking can be defined as an association across disparate subjects, regardless of whether a formal program assignment process exists (Lucas, 1999), or as an association of course taking across time (Lucas, 1999). And the least restrictive definition sees curriculum differentiation *itself* as tracking (Wheelock, 1992).

Historically, the definitions would likely have led to the same assessment of whether a school was tracked, because *classical tracking*—a system in which students are formally assigned to overarching programs that allow virtually no mobility across programs and that determine the level of all of their academic courses—satisfies all the criteria. Classical tracking was the aim of original tracking advocates, who argued that the vast majority of students should be taught "followership," which would lead those students to uncritically parrot the views of their ostensible betters (Finney, 1928). Furthermore, these advocates contended that some students should be taught leadership, so that they could eventually, unapologetically, take power. In other words, these advocates sought *disparate socialization*, an aim that, they argued, required students to be consistently segregated.

Classical tracking took root in the United States during a period of high immigration and rising nativist fears. Evidence suggests that prior to 1965, most high schools assigned students to explicit, overarching programs that determined their academic course taking and thus governed the socialization to which they would be exposed.

Classically, there were three broad tracks: (a) college preparatory, (b) general, and (c) vocational. Students appear to have been assigned to one such program when entering high school (e.g., Alexander, Cook, & McDill, 1978; Hollingshead, 1949), and students in a school spent most of their time with students in the same track. However, evidence suggests that the system of classical tracking began to erode in the late 1960s, such that by the turn of the 21st century, very few schools practiced classical tracking (Carey, Farris, & Carpenter, 1994; Moore & Davenport, 1988; Oakes, 1981).

Although it has long been apparent that most secondary schools lack formal processes of overarching track assignment, Lucas (1999) contends that an unremarked revolution in tracking had occurred, unremarked in that even though analysts acknowledged the change in school practice, analytic approaches had not been altered to respond to the new situation. Prior to the end of classical tracking, the self-report was eminently useful as a measure of students' placement in the curricular structure, because the formal assignment procedure made tracking visible and salient (Gamoran & Berends, 1987). However, the end of formal program assignment transformed students' self-reports into a largely social-psychological measure (Lucas & Gamoran, 2002) and rendered the referent of school personnel reports even more opaque. This suggests that analysts may continue to use the self-report but not as an indicator of structural placement.

The problem with the self-report as a measure of students' structural track location is made visible by considering the analogy with class as measured through occupations. One might ask adults to report their social class, but their self-report would be an indicator of their consciousness, not of their structural location, because as research shows (e.g., Jackman, 1979; Jackman & Jackman, 1983), respondents may or may not base their reports exclusively on information about the dimensions of occupations that have sociotheoretic relevance for various conceptions and traditions of class analysis. If adults can provide social-psychologically accurate yet structurally questionable measures of their socioeconomic category, so may students provide social-psychologically accurate yet structurally questionable measures of their curricular category. In such a situation, for all its empiricist accuracy, noting the empirical association between the two reports cannot justify the conflation of one by the other, for they reflect different theoretical claims and concerns and different social phenomena.

However, one might directly contest the claim that the self-report is not a structural indicator. Indeed, analysts that implicitly maintain that curriculum differentiation *is* tracking might specifically do so. The view that curriculum differentiation is tracking has been the basis of proposals to end curriculum differentiation and instruct all students in heterogeneous classrooms. This policy proposal has often been called *detracking*, implying thereby that curriculum differentiation is tracking (e.g., Wheelock, 1992). The claim that curriculum differentiation is tracking could also be based in a view that as long as there is curriculum differentiation, students in the same school may be exposed to vastly different levels of rigor and types of socialization.

Under this view, measurement is considerably easier; if curriculum differentiation is tracking, the formal course enrollment process coupled with the salience of courses means students may report on the courses they are taking and thus provide a measure of structural placement. Although researchers have studied students' level of placement in individual subjects (e.g., Catsambis, 1994), this research seems to be based on an assumption of the inherent importance of those subjects, not on an explicit claim that curriculum differentiation is tracking.

However, if one accepts the critique of the self-report, the question is raised— What other sources can be used to ascertain students' curricular placements? Analysts have used school personnel reports, although such reports have also been criticized for nationally representative studies (e.g., Lucas, 1999, pp. 156–159). Alternatively, one may use students' transcripts to obtain information on their course taking and use information on their course taking to assign students to different tracks. Two distinct ways of using transcripts have been developed. In some respects, these two different approaches reflect the two broad classes of ways analysts have studied occupations.

One measurement approach, similar in some ways to the SEI tradition discussed earlier, is to use transcript data to assign students to tracks based on a network analysis (Friedkin & Thomas, 1997). In this approach, students who share the same courses form a track. In their analysis of High School and Beyond data, Friedkin and Thomas (1997) delineated eight different tracks and found an association between network-defined track placement and parents' SES, students' race, students' ethnicity, and students' gender. Because the approach defines tracks on the basis of the characteristics of persons in the tracks (i.e., the other courses they are taking), the approach is similar in some respects to the SEI tradition. One criticism of this approach, however, is that unlike the SEI tradition, it is more purely empiricist. The SEI tradition uses a theory of what about occupations is important to select characteristics of occupations to consider and posits a relationship between empirical observables and latent, more fundamental, social phenomena.[1] By selecting observables, the SEI tradition explicitly identifies some factors as relevant and treats an infinity of other factors as irrelevant. In contrast, the network approach defines tracks by the extent to which students share courses and thus is based on the intercorrelation of observed phenomena only. However, focused only on the questions of whether and how courses hang together, the network approach is unable to identify what underlies the sharing of courses—for example, it could be that preexisting friendship networks, ethnic cleavages, (social) class closure, or some other nonacademic factor actually underlies some or all of what appear to the network analysis as distinct tracks. Thus, the network approach is agnostic concerning pedagogic content or hierarchy, allowing tracks to be anything from incredibly rigid, overarching instructional arrangements to epiphenomenal associations driven by extra-academic, preexisting cleavages.

Another measurement approach eschews empiricism using, instead, a theory of school organization to assign students to tracks (Lucas, 1990, 1999; Lucas & Gamoran, 1991). Using information about the content, level, and rigor of courses drawn from the course catalog descriptions, the approach draws directly on Sørenson's (1970) delineation of the dimensions of curriculum differentiation. The Course-Based Indicator resembles the Hauser, Sewell, and Alwin (1976) measure of track location, which used transcript data to assign Wisconsin students to tracks based on whether their courses satisfied the requirements to enter the state's flagship university in Madison. Also, by using a theory to classify courses, the approach also resembles Marxists' efforts to categorize adults according to a theoretically informed system of occupations. Of course, if one disagrees with the theory or with how Lucas (1990, 1999) translated the theory into measures, then one may reject the measure as well.

However track placement is measured, evidence indicates that high-track students obtain higher test scores (e.g., Gamoran & Mare, 1989), are more likely to enter college (e.g., Rosenbaum, 1980), and exert more effort in academic pursuits (e.g., Carbonaro, 2005). These effect estimates are based on assessing the outcomes of persons in different tracks. However, when *systems* with and without tracking are compared, findings are more complicated. Hoffer (1992) reported that high-track students do better compared to low-track students in tracked schools, but overall achievement is not higher in tracked than in untracked middle schools. Furthermore, research indicates that the structure of tracking in the school affects the impact of track location on achievement (Gamoran, 1992), suggesting that not only whether one tracks, but also how one tracks, matters for achievement.

Analysts have also found tracking to matter for persons' experience of school. Oakes (1982) found that students had more positive experiences of affirmation in high-track classes and more negative, self-esteem lowering experiences in low-track classes. Ethnographic research documented different conditions in different track levels, with more supportive arrangements in the high-track (e.g., Page, 1990). The differences of experience in the different levels touch teachers as well, as Finley (1984) found in one school. Finley further found that although teachers regarded as less able were assigned low-track classes, even a teacher regarded as able became less able after being assigned to such classes. And Kelly (2004) documented the assignment of less experienced teachers to low-track classes on a nationally representative sample, a feature likely to systematically reduce the quality of instruction in low-track classes compared to high-track classes.

Analysts have also studied the correlates of student placement. That evidence indicates that Asian students and students of higher SES are clearly more likely to be assigned to more demanding placements (e.g., Gamoran & Mare, 1989; Garet & DeLany, 1988). However, the evidence for Blacks, Whites, and Latino/as is considerably more mixed. When no variables are controlled, Blacks and Latino/as lag behind Whites in placement (e.g., Oakes, 1985). However, when controls for socioeconomic location and achievement are included, findings vary appreciably, with some researchers finding Blacks to be disadvantaged (e.g., Mickelson, 2001), some finding Blacks to be advantaged (e.g., Garet & DeLany, 1988), and still others finding Black, White, and Latino/a parity (e.g., Lucas & Gamoran, 2002). Notably, some research suggests that all these analyses are correct, because racial-ethnic differences in track placement vary across schools, and the variation is connected to region and school-level racial diversity (Lucas & Berends, 2002). Indeed, Lucas and Berends (2007) used multi-level models to find that the more diverse the school, the more likely White students are to be in advanced programs; whereas for Blacks of equivalent social background and prior achievement, the more diverse the school, the less likely they are to be in advanced programs. Graphing the results showed a crossover in college-prep course-taking probabilities and slopes that appear equal sized and opposite signed (Lucas & Berends, 2007, p. 180). Kelly (2009) replicated these findings on the National Education Longitudinal Study (NELS) high school students, although data problems that make NELS inappropriate for multilevel modeling of high schools and high school students renders the replication insecure.

However, research also indicates that the sociodemographic composition of the school matters for the structure of tracking. Hallinan (1994a, 1994b) argued that tracking was primarily a technical pedagogical device. Oakes (1994a, 1994b) countered that tracking is also a politicized policy used to resegregate desegregated schools along lines of class and race. Research has found that the more racially diverse the school, the more rigid the system of tracking (Braddock, 1990). This result was replicated for race and extended to socioeconomic class, even after analysts controlled for the achievement distribution in the school (Lucas & Berends, 2007). Overall, the evidence is consistent with Oakes's thesis of tracking as a politicized mechanism of segregation.

These findings suggest that tracking as a system is the school-level analog to occupational structure in the wider society. The use of tracking is associated with sociodemographic diversity above and beyond its association with the preexisting distribution of achievement such that tracking appears more rigid in socioeconomically and sociodemographically diverse schools. Tracking as a system matters for the distribution of achievement growth, raising it for high-track students, lowering it for low-track students, even as overall growth is equal in tracked and untracked schools. At the individual level, sociodemographic factors matter for students' placements in complex ways. And teachers are also assigned in systematic ways that can exacerbate the differences in student achievement across tracks. Thus, despite considerable change over time in the processes of tracking, tracking remains an extremely important manifestation of curriculum differentiation.

Discipline

Although the connection between discipline and education may seem so elementary as to be taken for granted, sociologists have wrestled with the connection between a well-ordered school environment and academic performance. Although it is evident from empirical research that students' behavior is highly correlated with their academic performance, the causal order remains unclear. Some may contend that treatment in school and school discipline produces alienation and delinquency, whereas others may argue that delinquency provokes discipline. In the latter view, students behave well or poorly, and the poorly behaving are punished. Alternatively, students are treated differently on the basis of their sociodemographic categories, with males, the socioeconomically disadvantaged, and students of African descent being treated poorly. This differential treatment then produces alienation on the part of the students receiving poor treatment, alienation that eventually becomes delinquency. Owing to data limitations, disentangling the causal order to discern which of these narratives is most accurate is a serious challenge (Berends, 1995).

Researchers measure discipline in many ways, from calculating the ratio of discipline to misbehavior to examining enforcement of certain rules related to dress codes, hall passes, smoking, vandalism, and closed-campus lunches (DiPrete, 1981). Most measures of discipline are directly related to reports of misbehavior that can vary in severity from tardiness to assault.

Measures of misbehavior may range from more behavioral definitions, including the number of assaults, to more affective definitions, such as students' perceived safety (Gaddy, 1988). Thus, once again, we see analysts grappling with whether to base their measures on the attitudinal, subjective experience of the research subjects or, rather, to measure the phenomenon using some other approach or referent. For instance, DiPrete (1981, p. 26) attempted to test hypotheses concerning the causal relationship between misbehavior and grades, measuring misbehavior using students' self-reported personal behavior related to the number of days absent for reasons not related to illness, number of days tardy, whether they cut class every once in a while, whether they refused to regularly complete homework, and whether they experienced trouble with the law. These queries measured reported misbehavior across a circumscribed amount of time.

Others have measured misbehavior in a cumulative manner rather than across a single time period. Myers, Milne, Baker, and Ginsburg (1987) measured student misbehavior over time using a Guttman scale based on the three following questions, coded 0 or 1: (a) Do you cut class? (b) Are you perceived as a troublemaker? (c) Have you ever been in serious trouble with the law?

The use of bounded and unbounded approaches follows from the existence of an abiding temporal dimension that requires attention. Both bounded and unbounded approaches present challenges. If the measure is bounded, at whatever end the measure is bounded, students may err by *telescoping*, that is, by reporting an event that occurred outside the interval of interest as if it occurred within the interval of interest (Gaskell, Wright, & O'Muircheartaigh, 2000). Analysts have devised ways of reducing such errors, such as obtaining reports of landmark events (e.g., Loftus & Marburger, 1983), but they come with their own complexities (Gaskell, Wright, & O'Muircheartaigh, 2000). The alternative, an unbounded measure that cumulates across long time periods, may also lead to underreporting if persons simply forget incidents. Or the behavior several years ago may no longer reflect the students' orientation to school. Consequently, both measurement approaches pose conceptual and logistical challenges the analyst must surmount.

Multiple measures of misconduct also represent the continuum of severity along which sociologists tend to operationalize discipline. For example, Jenkins (1995) examined the relationship between school commitment and delinquency, measuring delinquency with three indices, including school crime, misconduct, and nonattendance. Crime was measured using a 14-item index composed of use of illegal drugs, alcohol, and/or cigarettes; the sale of drugs; stealing at school; assault of a teacher or student; vandalism and property damage; and weapons possession. Misconduct was measured by the propensity to talk in class, use foul language, plagiarize or fail to do homework, throw objects in class, deface walls or desks, cheat, refuse to do in-class assignments, wear inappropriate clothing, and loiter in the halls without permission or a hall pass and the tendency to be suspended, to be deprived of bus-riding privileges, and to be dismissed from the classroom by the teacher. Class cutting, tardiness, and absence without an appropriate reason measured nonattendance. This information was gleaned from a questionnaire administered to seventh- and eighth-grade students.

On their face, comprehensive measurements may seem relatively solid. Yet the meaning of even simple measures of discipline, for example, tardiness, may change as the definition of what counts as tardiness may differ from location to location and change over time. Other measures, such as the number of expulsions or suspensions, may also be context and time specific (Gaddy, 1988). Self-reported measures of discipline also suffer from the drawbacks of self-report data, because students may under- or overreport their behaviors.

Related, although separate from such individual accounts of behavior and achievement, is the connection between the larger school environment and an individual's behavior and performance. Individual instances of misbehavior may cumulate to produce an environment that affects not only those misbehaving but also the students with whom they share the school environment (Gaddy, 1988, p. 500).

Discipline in schools is not meted out equally among all races, classes, and genders, and in fact, disparity in punishment exists along all of these lines (Skiba, Michael, Carroll Nardo, & Peterson, 2002, p. 318). Students of lower SES, such as those who receive a free lunch or have unemployed fathers, are more likely to receive suspension (Skiba et al., 2002, p. 319). Severity of punishment also differs by socioeconomic status, with higher-SES groups receiving lighter punishments than those of lower SES (Skiba et al., 2002, p. 319). African American youths are statistically overrepresented in expulsions and suspensions (Skiba et al., 2002, p. 320), and evidence indicates that White teachers rate Black students' behaviors differently than do Black teachers (Downey & Pribesh, 2004). Furthermore, African Americans experience a high rate of severe punishment, such as corporeal punishment (Skiba et al., 2002, p. 320). Evidence also supports the finding that the proportion of school suspension of African Americans increases following desegregation, with a propensity for a sharper increase in higher-SES school sites (Skiba et al., 2002, p. 320).

Along gender lines, boys are punished more readily than girls (Skiba et al., 2002, p. 320). Evidence suggests that boys are 4 times as likely to be suspended or physically punished (Skiba et al., 2002, p. 320). Race, gender, and SES intersect to exacerbate this disparity for African American males. Wu, Pink, Crain, and Moles (1982, p. 322) found that minority students continue to experience higher levels of suspension when controlling for SES.

Discrimination is one explanation for the persistent disparity in discipline. Although this explanation is difficult to prove, it is likely that this disparate treatment produces and reinforces the stratification of American society (Bowditch, 1993).

Some research places discipline in a larger context of the policies that affect its operation. Arum (2000) contends that since 1970, coercive forms of disciplinary practices, such as corporeal punishment, have waned, as student rights to due process are now applicable to public school students. Arum (2003) argues that courts increasingly inserted themselves into the operation of schools, second-guessing administrators and supporting students' rights versus the authority of school personnel. Arum maintains that this climate of court support for students dissolved the legitimacy of school personnel authority and has thus led school personnel to become wary of exercising authority. Thus, Arum argues, school discipline has waned, leaving many students vulnerable to delinquent peers. In this context, Arum suggests that students' perceptions of fairness and strictness matter for outcomes of interest, such as test scores and classroom behavior, and on this basis, Arum proposes that policymakers and the courts work to restore legitimacy to school personnel. One major policy prescription is that courts rescind due-process rights for all punishments except those that involve extended removal from school; this proposal is accompanied by the contention that such protections are actually not even in place at present, only that school site actors *believe* they are in place. On the basis of this contention, Arum argues that rescinding these nonprotections will not usher in greater racial bias or negative effects of harsh school discipline. Instead, he asserts, removing these protections will be simply symbolic, restoring the moral authority of school personnel.

In Arum's view, student, teacher, and administrator perceptions are key. However, if perceptions are the pathway through which court action matters, then changing those perceptions, even with merely symbolic actions, will facilitate school personnel abusing their authority. Reasonable people can disagree about the policy choice, but this is a real policy dilemma that cannot be finessed. Reduce actual or perceived protections for those in one's charge—as, for example, a Secretary of Defense might do by abrogating his or her country's historic commitment to the Geneva Conventions—and one opens the door to abuse. That does not mean any particular authority figure will abuse others, but it does mean the likelihood of abuse will increase.

This observation implies that the Arum (2003) analysis of discipline, although placed in a broader institutional context, has been shorn of historical context. Misunderstanding is the result. For example, Arum fails to acknowledge an easily identified alternative understanding of the alleged delegitimation of school personnel authority, an alternative based in reading a longer history of court intervention. The alternative story is that the courts began to intervene in the schools' treatment of children because the schools were discriminating against Blacks under the rubric of separate but equal. This intervention was the result of a change in elite policy preferences owing to changing U.S. geopolitical opportunities and constraints (Dudziak, 2000). Had southern school officials and their political leaders acquiesced to federal authority, the story might have ended there, with teachers' and principals' legitimacy intact.

However, instead of complying with federal orders, school personnel and others engaged in several strategies to violate the law. Variously, schools were closed, school districts were dissolved, private schools were opened, and a governor even stood in the schoolhouse door to prevent Black students from entering all-White educational institutions. Those efforts were faced down by federalized National Guardsmen. This was a constitutional crisis in the making with a seriousness that, prior to that time, had not been seen since the end of Reconstruction.

The approach southern school officials and their political representatives followed was based not on accepting due process but, instead, on a commitment to violate due process, a thorough-going effort to substitute brazen power for accepted adjudicatory procedures. People all over the world, notably in Africa and Asia, watched this drama, as the U.S. federal government attempted to end (or at least ameliorate) the second-class citizenship of African Americans (Borstelmann, 2001; Dudziak, 2000). Schools were often center stage in that battle, and thus, schoolchildren across the nation were also numbered in the audience.

This was not the way it had to be. Had school personnel (and constituted state authority) decided to protest the decision through the legitimate means available—voting, marching, and so on—but followed the law of the land when they entered the schoolhouse door, they might have escaped any delegitimation of their authority. But by refusing to acknowledge the authority of the Supreme Court, school personnel inadvertently demonstrated that authorities can be resisted, even by extralegal means, if they attempt to force you to do what you do not want to do, even when those authorities have been legitimately vested with just those responsibilities. This demonstration is unlikely to have reduced student delinquency and is also unlikely to have increased student willingness to accede to the authority of the persons who happened to be in charge of the schools they attended.

Most parents either know intellectually, or come to face in reality, or both, that children watch what adults do and are quick to ferret out discrepancies between what adults ask of children and what adults ask of themselves. The broader story Arum's (2003) analysis misses is that owing to children's attentiveness, the ultimate source of any delegitimation of school personnel authority that may have occurred is likely owing to highly visible actions of school personnel themselves who refused to accept legitimate authority when it led in directions they were unwilling to go. And when their actions demonstrated that even school personnel, despite being charged with demonstrating respect to impressionable youths, resist constituted authority (perhaps through illegal means) when their desires are stifled, school personnel as a class lost the moral basis for maintaining that one should accept constituted authority. And that moral basis of respect, once lost, is very difficult if not impossible to restore. This is, at least, one plausible reading of how the history of the late 20th century matters for contemporary discipline policies in U.S. schools.

Measured Achievement

The sociological literature measures achievement in terms of grades and test scores. Test scores are often preferred because grading standards can vary by schools and curriculum. Grades also retain a subjective element because teachers may hold different students or groups to different standards when assigning grades. Some regard standardized tests as an accurate depiction of a student's potential and aptitude rather than their concrete achievements (Herrnstein & Murray, 1994), but other research finds that performance is bound up with context (e.g., Aronson et al., 1999; Spencer, Steele, & Quinn, 1999; Steele, 1997; Steele & Aronson, 1995), strongly suggesting that measures of potential are impossible unless performance is measured in all possible contexts.

However interpreted, standardized tests have been charged with various kinds of biases against disadvantaged groups, even though the psychometric evidence for racial bias is weak (e.g., Schmidt & Hunter, 1999). However, others charge that standardized tests do not so much reflect unequal achievement as reproduce and legitimate power relations by design (Lucas, 2000). The best evidence for such arguments comes not from well-known disparities in test scores along the lines of gender, race, and socioeconomic status but, instead, from evidence on the construction, scoring, and use of standardized tests (e.g., Kidder & Rosner, 2002; Lucas, 2000, 2008b). The evidence seriously problematizes the alleged logic of testing, undermining the claim that existing tests are neutral measures of achievement.

In regard to the statistics on test scores, however, mean standardized test scores demonstrate that Asian students outperform all other races on standardized reading and math tests. White students' test scores rank second to Asians, followed by those of Hispanic and African American students (Grodsky, Warren, & Felts, 2008). These testing patterns persist from kindergarten through college entry (e.g., Phillips, Crouse, & Ralph, 1998).

Individuals from varying socioeconomic backgrounds, measured by parental education and household income, also fare disparately. Children of college-educated parents routinely outscore children of high school dropouts (e.g., Perie, Moran, & Lutkus, 2005).

Test scores show consistent, although less remarkable, indications of disparity between the sexes. It has been demonstrated that girls modestly outperform boys on standardized reading tests in the early grades (Fryer & Levitt, 2005). Yet boys outperform girls on standardized math tests, although the performance gap on math tests has declined over time (Grodsky et al., 2008). Girls, however, have historically received better grades than boys (Buchmann, DiPrete, & McDaniel, 2008). At present, girls outperform boys in terms of grades in math and science, even though boys perform better on standardized tests in these subjects. Furthermore, boys and girls take equally difficult math courses, and girls continue to receive better grades than boys in these classes (Buchmann et al., 2008).

Some scholars, such as Herrnstein and Murray (1994), have argued that such differences reflect disparate, innate abilities of various groups in society. Others doubt this inference, because it is difficult to ignore the unequal distribution of resources and opportunities among socioeconomic and racial groupings (e.g., Fischer et al., 1996).

Educational Attainment

Educational attainment has been measured in two broadly different ways. Traditionally, analysts measured educational attainment by years of schooling completed or by the highest grade completed. However, because of concerns that different persons could spend the same amount of time in school yet attain different levels of credentials owing to grade retention and the proliferation of different kinds of degrees, coupled with concern that the credential might matter more than the time to attain it, analysts shifted to measuring the highest degree attained directly.

The measurement of the credential obtained varies greatly. For example, the measurement of high school graduation rates is notoriously contentious. Some reports of dropout rates claim national dropout rates as high as 32% (e.g., Swanson, 2004), state dropout rates as high as 49% (Swanson, 2004, for South Carolina), and district dropout rates as high as 50% (e.g., Fine, 1986). However, these results are based on using administrative data to calculate either the ratio of graduates in a given year and the number of freshman entrants 4 years earlier (Fine, 1986) or the ratio of matriculants in each grade and the total number of completers of the previous grade, multiplied together across multiple years to calculate what is purported to be a measure of cohort-specific graduation incidence. The 4-year approach ignores that students enter throughout the 4 years, making the denominator clearly incorrect. Furthermore, students leave throughout the 4 years, some moving to other districts or private schools. Hence, the numerator is also incorrect. The multiple-year calculation is also flawed for similar reasons—the denominators are not secure because persons who leave a district could enter another district or a private school. However, fixing these problems in administrative data requires recording, categorizing, and counting the different entrances and exits according to their source and destination. That task is prone to difficulty because record keeping is not at a high enough level at many schools to assure the categorization and count will be correct. Swanson (2004) uses the Common Core of Data (CCD), but such data are simply a set of data collected from administrator reports and, as such, simply pass through any weaknesses in school- and district-level record keeping.

It turns out that demographic analyses of nationally representative data reveal much lower dropout counts. Indeed, using Current Population Survey (CPS) data, Kominski (1990) found a national yearly dropout rate for the mid-1980s that was in the low single digits. These rates cumulate to closely match the dropout incidence estimated on the basis of longitudinal data of individual students' trajectories. For example, using High School Effectiveness Study (HSES) data, Rumberger and Thomas (2000, p. 48), although finding substantial school-to-school differences in dropout incidence, also report an overall high school dropout rate of 7%. The HSES is weighted toward the schools in the 30 largest metropolitan areas, such that it is not a nationally representative sample of high schools (Ingels, Scott, Taylor, Owings, & Quinn, 1998). However, Warren and Lee (2002, p. 107), using the full nationally representative sample of the NELS, found a national dropout rate of 6%.

Even though dropout incidence appears far lower than some of the estimates based on weak measures suggest, a widespread literature indicates that sociodemographic factors are associated with various education transitions. Disparity in educational attainment is visible in differences in both high school graduation rates and college entry rates.

One finding is that although dropout is associated with lower levels of prior achievement, a nontrivial number of low-income, high-achieving youth do drop out (Renzulli & Park, 2000). For example, Renzulli and Park (2000) show that 48% of gifted dropout students were in the lowest SES quartile, whereas only 3.6% of gifted dropouts were in the highest SES quartile. This suggests that a substantial pool of untapped talent may be lost owing to SES disadvantage.

Concerning race, rates of high school completion have become more equal between racial groups in the United States over time. However, racial-ethnic disparity remains. As of 2007, 93.4% of White 25- to 29-year-olds had completed high school, whereas for Blacks and Latino/as, only 86.3% and 63.2% had completed high school, respectively (Snyder, Dillow, & Hoffman, 2007). Many complexities attend these findings, however. For example, owing to high levels of Latino/a immigration, many Latino/as ages 25 to 29 may not have obtained their schooling in the United States. Consequently, it is unclear to what extent the completion rate reflects the operation of education systems in the United States. Driscoll (1999) may shed some light on the question; using NELS data, she finds that first-, second-, and third-generation Latino/a immigrants all have a dropout incidence of approximately 20%, suggesting time in the country is not directly relevant. However, after other factors are controlled, first- and second-generation Latino/as have lower dropout rates than their third-generation peers, suggesting again a more complex story.

A similar complexity concerns Black students. When researchers control for socioeconomic factors, the Black-White high school completion gap disappears (Bauman, 1998; Lucas, 1996, p. 526). Consequently, the lower high school completion probability for Blacks seems completely explained by socioeconomic differences between Blacks and Whites.

Further complexities are revealed when one disaggregates large ethnic groups. Differences within ethnic groups tell a more complicated story, because some immigrant subgroups often have much lower rates of high school completion (Kao & Thompson, 2003, p. 427). Those ethnic groups that exhibit low rates of high school completion are often from lower socioeconomic backgrounds. Findings suggest that family background and structure have salient effects on the propensity of students to complete high school (Kao & Thompson, 2003, p. 428).

Although some research indicates that Latino/as, Native Americans, and African Americans are also more likely to drop out of school than their White or other ethnic minority counterparts (Kao & Thompson, 2003, p. 425), other research finds that race-ethnicity differences in dropping out are explained by other factors (White & Kaufman, 1997). Mare and Winship (1988) found that family background explains the majority of the attainment differences between Whites and these disadvantaged ethnic groups. Ethnicity and language status intersect in rates of high school graduation, severely disadvantaging groups with lower rates of English proficiency.

Women also experience a lower high school dropout rate than men (Buchmann et al., 2008). Data show that as of 2005, approximately 11% of males (ages 16 to 24) dropped out of high school, compared to 8% of females (Buchmann et al., 2008). Furthermore, the male disadvantage is sustained for all major racial and ethnic groups (Buchmann et al., 2008). More males also obtained a general equivalency diploma. These statistics support the long-running trend (since 1870) of larger high school completion rates for women (Jacobs, 1996, p.156).

The women's advantage in school enrollment continues in college. Women's entry and enrollment in college have not only increased in the ensuing decades but have surpassed those of men. Women composed approximately 53% of students enrolled in college in 1992 (Jacobs, 1996, p. 155), surpassing men in the number of bachelor's degrees earned in 1982 (Jacobs, 1996, p. 155). Women earn a majority of bachelor's degrees (58%) and compose 57% of all students enrolled in college (Buchmann et al., 2008). Men are also more likely to delay entrance into college after graduation from high school (60% of men vs. 66% of women enrolled directly after high school in 2000).

As in the case of gender, so in the case of race: College enrollments of racial and ethnic minorities have increased over time. Data from 1996 show that 45% of Whites, 36% of African Americans, and 35% of Hispanics were enrolled in college as a percentage of high school graduates (Kao & Thompson, 2003, p. 429). Nonetheless, Hauser and Anderson (1991) found evidence that college entry for African Americans, after rising in the early 1970s, decreased in the late 1970s and early 1980s. In the more recent period, African Americans continue to be less likely than Whites to make an immediate transition from high school to college. And a low rate of college attendance among Latino/as follows from this group's low rate of high school completion (Kao & Thompson, 2003, p. 430).

SES matters not only for whether persons continue in school but also for the characteristics of the institution in which their schooling continues. Evidence indicates an association between SES and entry into more selective American institutions of higher education (Karabel & Astin, 1975; Kao & Thompson, 2003, p. 430). Students from poorer, lower-class backgrounds remain underrepresented within elite institutions; a 1995 study of 19 elite institutions found that only 3% of admissions came from poor, less educated parents (Bowen, Kurzweil, & Tobin, 2005, p. 99).

Unequal admission by SES is a result in part of processes that occur long before the university admission decision. Bowen et al. (2005) show that if a student is from a lower-class background, he or she is less likely to take the SAT and more likely to perform poorly on it. Students take different paths because of child rearing, the quality of primary and secondary schools (which depends in part on spatial location), and the inequality of resources between and within schools. Curriculum and tracking also enter the equation because the propensity to take advanced courses is linked to residential area and family background.

When socioeconomically disadvantaged students enter elite institutions, they often do very well, and family income and parental education has little effect (Bowen et al., 2005, pp. 124, 135), but they do not fare as well in the long run compared to their classmates, often receiving lower earnings and experiencing lower likelihood of pursuing advanced degrees. This and similar forms of evidence have led some academics (e.g., Kahlenberg, 1996) and policymakers (e.g., Williams, 1996) to propose class-based affirmative action, yet evidence indicates that class-based affirmative action, for all its possible value for addressing class inequities, would not produce racial diversity (Kane, 1998).

A great deal of research studies one educational credential at a time. Interestingly, analysts have long used information on the number of years of schooling to infer (with some error) the highest degree attained. Using this approach, analysts developed the Mare model (Mare, 1980, 1981) of education transitions. The Mare model essentially estimates the effect of each variable on persons' probability of completing each transition.

The Mare model illuminates educational attainment as a process, allowing analysts to investigate the role of sociodemographic factors in students' completion of different levels of schooling. In this educational transitions tradition, progression through the education system is viewed as a concatenated series of decisions in which an individual chooses either to remain in school by continuing on to the next grade level or degree or to cease attending school altogether. When sociologists have investigated the effect of social background on multiple transitions, they have found that social background matters less as one proceeds through educational transitions (e.g., Hauser & Andrew, 2006; Mare, 1980).

Multiple theories have been proposed to explain the pattern. Two theories, the life course perspective of Müller and Karle (1993) and the theory of selective attrition of Mare (1980), have been rejected on the basis of extensive research (e.g., Mare, 1993; Shavit & Blossfeld, 1993). Remaining theories under discussion include maximally maintained inequality (MMI; Raftery & Hout, 1993), relative risk aversion (RRA; Breen & Goldthorpe, 1997), and effectively maintained inequality (EMI; Lucas, 2001). Some of these theories have implications for outcomes beyond educational attainment. We describe these theories, but first we turn to a series of overarching theories of inequality in education.

Substantive Findings on Inequality

Multiple sociodemographic factors determine the quantity and quality of persons' educational outcomes. As an individual transitions through the educational system, different dimensions appear connected to the structural locations in which any education he or she obtains will occur as well as whether he or she will continue or exit the education system altogether. Evidence indicates that gatekeepers may respond to students, at least in part, on the basis of their sociodemographic characteristics, and students of different sociodemographic categories bring different resources to the educational enterprise. Either or both phenomena may be implicated in patterns of placement, discipline, measured achievement, and educational attainment. Given this dual meaning of sociodemographic categories, theoretical perspectives are required to make sense of the multiplicity of findings and possibilities.

SOCIODEMOGRAPHIC STATUS AND EDUCATION: DIMENSIONAL DICHOTOMIES AND GENERAL THEORIES

Multiple theories have been proposed to make sense of the association between sociodemographic dimensions and education outcomes. Before turning to some of the broader theories, it is helpful to identify five key dichotomies or trichotomies in relation to which theories may be placed: (a) the relational-gradational binary, (b) the social-nonsocial dichotomy, (c) the queueing-nonqueueing binary, (d) the static-dynamic trichotomy, and (e) the specificity-generality binary.

We have already discussed the relational-gradational binary because of its centrality for measurement. The social-nonsocial dichotomy exists because some theories interpret sociodemographic factors as social phenomena and thus craft explanations that highlight social processes that involve the social construction, maintenance, or operation of those sociodemographic factors in social space. Other theories interpret sociodemographic factors as nonsocial phenomena, perhaps as presocial, or as constructed by nonsocial phenomena (e.g., biology). Interestingly, as we show later, a cutting-edge area of research in biology—epigenetics—raises serious questions about the validity of this dichotomy (Pray, 2004).

Some theories see social-demographic factors and/or education in terms of a queue. For example, a queueing theory of education would regard the content attached to different degrees, or the size of the difference (in preparation, test scores, years of school, or any other scaleable measure) between those with bachelor's degrees and those with associate's degrees, as irrelevant. What *is* relevant to queueing theories is the ordinal position of different persons; queueing theories, therefore, claim that those with BA degrees stand ahead of those with AA degrees in the job queue, the earnings queue, and possibly other queues. In contrast, nonqueueing theories are more likely to highlight the content they believe attends different levels of schooling and/or the gap in some scalable characteristic. In such theories, reducing the gap between those with, say, AA and BA degrees in certain characteristics (e.g., test scores) can raise the economic prospects of those with less lucrative training, whereas queueing theories are less confident that reducing the gap will make a difference, because queueing theories see ordinal position as key.

The static-dynamic dimension refers to the extent theories are meant to address differences in the cross-section or, instead, meant to explain change over time. All theories of causal effects have implicit implications for both the cross-section and change over time (Lieberson, 1985), but many theories highlight one or the other. Some theories, however, do explicitly address both static conditions and dynamics of change. Because these are not mutually exclusive, it is not quite accurate to pose these possibilities as if they are dichotomous alternatives.

Finally, several focused theories have been proposed to explain the associations between sociodemographic factors and educational outcomes. Many of these theories explain a single outcome or association. At the other extreme are widely encompassing theories that seek to explain a broad set of outcomes and/or the connection between education and a broad set of sociodemographic dimensions. Although focused theories are of value, they pose two challenges: (a) aggregating several specific theories into a larger, coherent whole and (b) distinguishing them from the substantive claims or observations from which they flow. The second challenge is more serious because a theory that merely restates the substantive claim may lack generalizability, raising the question of whether it is a theory or, instead, simply a summary. Summaries are of value, but they are not necessarily theories. Consequently, accepting the possible utility of specific theories, in what follows, we highlight broader theories relevant for inequality in multiple education outcomes.

Meritocratic Theory

Meritocracy, a term coined by Michael Young (1958/1994), provides a functional account of inequality in society that justifies occupational outcomes by educational attainment. Meritocratic theory posits that education rather than inheritance should be the basis of the stratification system. Such a stratified society will spur economic competition. Inequality will not cease to exist but will be restructured as the unintelligent offspring of the upper classes experience downward mobility and the intelligent offspring of the socioeconomically disadvantaged classes move upward. In such a society, people advance on the basis of intelligence and effort. For instance, in such a society, employers promote employees on the basis of measured intelligence and test scores.

Antecedents to this notion of a meritocratic society can be found in K. Davis and Moore's (1945) functionalist account of social stratification. K. Davis and Moore argue that society must induce individuals to assume certain positions in society. All positions are not created equal; some are more important to the proper functioning or even the survival of society (e.g., the military in times of external threat, medical scientists in times of pestilence, foodstuffs deliverers in times of famine). To induce persons to perform these jobs well, these jobs are highly rewarded in money and/or prestige. Other jobs require special talents and training. K. Davis and Moore claim,

"Social inequality is thus an unconsciously evolved device by which societies insure that the most important positions are conscientiously filled by the most qualified persons" (p. 243). Education fulfills the role of training elites to assume these positions in the economy. Social inequality is thereby justified as important to the functional operation of society.

Although empirical evidence suggests that the United States is not a meritocracy, meritocratic theory plays a large role within national debates about educational policy (Krauze & Slomczynski, 1985; Weakliem, McQuillan, & Schauer, 1995). Reliance on testing, a focus on education as a vehicle for placing persons into jobs, the global competition and international hierarchy of educational prowess, mechanisms of standardization in education exemplified by the No Child Left Behind Act, and an ideology of an undeserving poor in which individuals end up where they should on the basis of merit pervade our discussions of education.

Although educational attainment has increased across all groups and at all levels among the U.S. population, merit has yet to supplant seniority or experience. And although education appears to sort people into various jobs with unequal rewards, inherited social attributes, such as class, race and ethnicity, and gender, continue to undermine a causal relationship between education and labor market outcomes. Inequality of access to opportunity persists as a distinguishing heritable attribute among disparate social groups across U.S. society.

Wisconsin Social-Psychological Model of Status Attainment

The Wisconsin Social-Psychological Model of Status Attainment (aka the Wisconsin model) offers a social-psychological causal chain to explain differences in educational attainment (Hauser, Tsai, & Sewell, 1983; Sewell & Hauser, 1980). The theory is broad because it identifies social-psychological connections that link parental sociodemographic characteristics to children's educational and occupational expectations and outcomes as well as to their ultimate earnings. The model provides an encompassing perspective within which more recent developments in social psychology, such as stereotype threat (e.g., Steele, 1997) and an asymmetry of (race and gender) experience (Lucas, 2008b, pp. 23–52), may be placed.

The original work used Wisconsin Longitudinal Study (WLS) data on Wisconsin high school graduates of 1957, but replications have extended the model nationwide (e.g., Alexander, Eckland, & Griffin, 1975) and beyond (e.g., Nachmias, 1977, on Israel; Hansen & Haller, 1973, on Costa Rica; Naoi & Fujita, 1978, on Tokyo, Japan).

The key factor in the Wisconsin model is significant others' influence—the encouragement of parents, teachers, and peers the child perceives. The higher SES or academic performance, the greater the encouragement children perceive. Significant others' influence directly affects the child's educational aspiration and occupational aspiration, and educational aspiration affects educational attainment.

The Wisconsin model offers a powerful explanation of observed variation in attainments. The model explains 45% of the variation in significant others' influence,

74% of the variation in educational aspirations, and 68% of the variation in educational attainment. Furthermore, the model explains 73% of the variation in early career occupational status and 69% of the variance in occupational status at midlife (Hauser et al., 1983). By any estimation, this theoretical model provides a robust explanation of the process of educational attainment.

Biogenetic Theory

The Wisconsin model contrasts sharply with the biogenetic explanation of variation in educational attainment. Biogenetic theorists see ability as the driver in educational attainment and see ability as largely determined by genes, which are determined by one's parents. And to complete the circle, assortative mating on educational attainment and other markers of social class reinforce distinctions of ability (Herrnstein & Murray, 1994).

This theory has been refuted on scientific grounds. In *Inequality by Design: Cracking the Bell Curve Myth*, published in 1996, Claude Fischer and colleagues provide a thorough refutation of the biogenetic explanation of social inequality, including inequality in educational attainment. Additional authors, motivated perhaps by the apparent staying power of the biogenetic thesis in the popular imagination, have provided additional refutations (Devlin, Fienberg, Resnick, & Roeder, 1997; Jencks & Phillips, 1998).

None of these social analyses drew deeply on new developments in genetic research. Geneticists have long seen DNA as the basic building block of life. However, how DNA is expressed, and what determines its expression, is a cutting-edge area of research. Notably, epigenetics research has found that the determinant of the expression of DNA is directly affected by the environment. An important, crucial finding of this research is that organisms pass the proclivity for expression on to the next generation. So, in other words, epigenetics is reintroducing the formerly discredited idea of Lamarckism and, at the same time, destroying the assumption that DNA is sufficient to clone a particular living organism.

Lamarck (1873/1914) claimed that parents acquire certain traits in life and then pass those traits on to their progeny. The classic example is that giraffes stretch their necks to reach higher leaves, and they pass their longer necks on to their offspring. The arrival of Darwinian natural selection sentenced Lamarckism to disrepute. However, epigeneticists are finding that humans, other mammals, and insects experience certain environments that, through identifiable hormonal pathways, affect DNA expression. The resulting phenotypes are then visible in multiple later generations even after the environment changes (e.g., Lumey, 1992).

This epigenetics research means that the nature-nurture dichotomy at the center of the effort to emphasize biological factors rather than social factors is even more unsustainable than critics have usually maintained. Analysts have already established that the statistical separation of outcomes into that owing to genes and that owing to environment is impossible because genes and environment intertwine to produce observed outcomes (e.g., Daniels, Devlin, & Roeder, 1997). New findings from epigenetics go farther, suggesting that the very expression of the DNA of an organism is affected by environment, and thus the environment fundamentally produces the way in which the very genetic code of the organism is translated into material existence and, in this way, produces the biological endowment of the progeny of that organism. If the research on these links is confirmed, the claim that genes set a limit on the power of social factors will finally be revealed to have been as fundamentally mistaken as opponents of that view have oft maintained. Indeed, it appears that social factors, including education, not only may nurture native ability, but they may cause the very native ability they later nurture. Seen in this way, either the biogenetic position should be abandoned, or the relation it describes entirely reversed.

Human Capital Theory

Analysts find more support for human capital theory, a theory sharing some affinities with the Wisconsin model. According to human capital theory, adults' productivity is a function of ability and investment. In this view, individuals invest in their productivity, and all else equal, the more able invest more. Yet ability is not completely unfettered, as many individuals face credit constraints and thus cannot make investments they would otherwise make (Becker, 1962). Hence, the socioeconomic gradient in education is partly attributable to the role of credit constraints in preventing the poor from obtaining optimal levels of education given their ability (Becker & Tomes, 1986; Tomes, 1981). Thus, human capital theory suggests and explains a high association between parent and child educational attainment.

Human capital theory accounts for a wide variety of observed patterns, including concave age-earnings profiles, the lower unemployment rates of more highly educated persons, and the greater likelihood of school attendance by younger persons. Notably, human capital theory does not imply high mobility. Because investment requires capital, and poor (and middle-class) youth face credit constraints, poor (and middle-class) youth may not be able to make optimal investments. Thus, lack of access to credit explains, in part, the intergenerational association of status. Unlike the Wisconsin model, which highlights social-psychological processes, human capital theory highlights varying access to financial capital.

Cultural Capital Theory

In *Reproduction in Education, Society, and Culture*, Pierre Bourdieu and Jean-Claude Passeron (1977) provided another theoretical explanation for the association between parental status and educational outcomes. They contend that schools reward behavior that complies with the norms and standards of the dominant group in a society, yet those authors also note that one's core, one's *habitus*, develops in the family, is difficult or impossible to change, and directly affects one's likelihood of educational success. Bourdieu (1986) allows one to interpret the association between parental status and educational attainment as resulting from at least three factors:

gatekeeper exclusion, arbitrarily selected criteria of evaluation that advantage the previously advantaged, and parent-child interaction.

One reading of the Bourdieu position asserts also that markers of success are selected *because* of their ability to legitimate social closure for the advantaged. In this view, much that schools value is of no intrinsic utility. Some analysts have contested the claim that schools value irrelevancies (e.g., Kingston, 2001), yet others claim Bourdieu is incoherent on this and several other points (e.g., Elster, 1981). Still others, however, maintain that exclusion is the key theoretical content of the concept of cultural capital (Lamont & Lareau, 1988) or that the social construction of merit is its essential referent (Lareau & Weininger, 2003).

Marxist Theory

Bowles and Gintis (1976) articulate a Marxist explanation for educational inequality. They highlight the role of educational attainment in slotting students into the economy. Notably, Bowles and Gintis claim that education socializes students for particular roles, with skill acquisition being a secondary aspect. In this way, education selects for advancement and educational success those who have internalized the appropriate personalities. In this view, persons who are more conformist are more likely to be selected for advanced training. They present evidence showing that personality factors, not test scores, are more important predictors of supervisors' ratings of job performance.

Bowles and Gintis (1976) maintain that the reason personality matters is that to sustain the capitalist economy, children must exit the school in ways that place them on trajectories that will not destabilize the status quo, and those trajectories generally have more to do with the affective ease of transition into specific labor market positions than with cognitive skill. Consequently, students are sorted into different slots in the school, and students' length of time in school is associated with different kinds of socialization tuned to different levels of jobs in the capitalist economy. Those destined for lower occupations will be exposed to stringent external discipline in school to prepare their expectations for what they will encounter at work. In contrast, those destined for higher occupational levels will be socialized in ways that motivate an internalization of the rules, so their support for the status quo will be sufficient enough that constant monitoring will be unnecessary. This is important because the jobs for which they qualify can be difficult to monitor and because their acceptance of the status quo will check their ability or willingness to mobilize against it. Hence, Bowles and Gintis see education as an important support for capitalist economies, even as they claim that economic relations determine the educational system and that skill is not the key content of education.

The Marxist perspective makes sense of inequality in multiple education outcomes. Discipline is unequal because of the role of discipline in molding students for different positions in the workforce. Educational attainment is unequal because different levels of schooling are associated with different kinds of training. Tracking exists to produce differential socialization, thus, students are supposed to be placed in tracks and courses that treat them differently, and mobility across tracks is expected to be low. One result of these processes is lower test scores for those placed at the bottom, and low test scores legitimate their lowly placement.

Reproduction Theory

Amid allegations that the Marxist perspective articulated by Bowles and Gintis (1976) allowed no room for agency and thus seemed to suggest no room for transformative action, analysts began to offer an alternative, which came to be called either reproduction theory or resistance theory. *Learning to Labour: How Working Class Kids Get Working Class Jobs* (Willis, 1977) is a foundational work in this perspective. Willis (1977) provided ethnographic observations of selected male students acting out both inside and outside the school. Willis saw the students as partially comprehending the system in which they were embedded, a system that claimed to offer the opportunity for upward mobility. Willis concluded that the students saw the offer as a lie and thus rejected school through their resistant delinquency. However, Willis found that in resisting, the students end up reproducing the trajectory of their parents and find themselves in the same occupational positions after leaving the school. Thus, the students' ultimate destination was a product not only of top-down socialization but also of student agency.

Willis (1977) provides a theory of class reproduction. One could interpret Ogbu's theory of oppositional culture (Fordham & Ogbu, 1986; Ogbu, 1987) as a theory of the reproduction of racial disadvantage. In this way, one can see the possibility of exploring reproduction processes for any sociodemographic dimension.

The class reproduction perspective does not necessarily reject the Marxist analysis, as far as it goes. It may only supplement the Marxist analysis with deeper information about how actors on the ground reproduce the structure as well as their location within the structure. On the other hand, several criticisms of Willis's (1977) conclusion and approach have been described. Some research suggests that reproduction or resistance theory strongly resembles culture-of-poverty theory, with the major difference being the researcher's affective posture toward the acts in which the youths engage (Davies, 1995). Other analysts contend that the evidentiary basis for resistance theory claims has been identified and that resistance reproduces capitalist domination; for example, Bhavnani (1991) contends that Willis often failed to fully investigate students' interpretations, leading to a weak empirical basis for the claims. Analysts have also questioned the claim of having identified a phenomenon of working-class cultural resistance when only males were studied (e.g., Bhavnani, 1991, pp. 32–33) and only a nonrepresentative set of those (e.g., Hammack, 1980, pp. 515–516).

Credentialing Theory

Credentialing theory is seen as standing in stark contrast to human capital, Marxist, and meritocratic theories of education. Proponents of credentialing theory argue that educational attainment is most plainly defined by possession of a credential, a normative symbol or marker of certified skills, ability, and aptitude conferred by legitimate educational institutions and professional associations that screen access to labor market positions (Weeden, 2002).

Following in the footsteps of Weber, Randall Collins (1971) proposes a credential theory of educational stratification in which status groups compete for "wealth, power, and prestige" in society (p. 1009). In this competition, credentials confer status rather than mark skills, and it is status that translates into increased productivity (Boylan, 1993).

In this view, the function of schools is to "teach particular status cultures, both in and outside the classroom" (Collins, 1971, p. 1010). Employers select job applicants with credentials not because of any skill conferred by credentialing institutions but because the credentialed have internalized the norms and values of the dominant culture (Collins, 1971). In fact, job skills, if definable, are most readily acquired on the job and not within an educational institution (Collins, 1979). In sum, employers hire credentialed workers on the basis of a normative assumption that highly educated workers should assume specific jobs (Bills, 2003). If a particular status group wields power over the educational enterprise, it may exert control as a gatekeeper specifying educational requirements for various jobs, leading to differential earnings and prestige (Collins, 1971). Social inequality is perpetuated not through a functionalist account or class conflict but through the power plays of distinct status cultures that lay claim to education as a legitimate marker of labor market skills and abilities.

Empirical evidence for credentialing theory is demonstrated by the "sheepskin effect" (Bills, 2003), which refers to the finding that diploma years produce larger financial returns than other years of education (Belman & Heywood, 1991). In this sense, college degrees serve as a signal of status, and the returns to this signal are greater than the attainment of an equivalent 4 years of undergraduate schooling (Pascarella & Terenzini, 2005). The finding that unobserved differences between degree holders and others do not explain the additional returns to degree procurement, when family background effects are held constant, further strengthens the finding (Frazis, 1993).

Preliminary Concluding Remarks

These broader theories highlight the ways individuals navigate systems of education by using their personal resources as well as those provided by their families. Each purports to explain multiple education outcomes and to account for a wide range of inequalities. More recent research highlighting cross-national comparisons has moved toward integrating macrolevel considerations into the understanding of the production of educational attainment. Some of these theories are also applicable beyond the single outcome of educational attainment. We turn now to briefly describe three more recent theories that bear on educational inequality.

THEORIZING SOCIODEMOGRAPHIC STATUS AND EDUCATION: ILLUSTRATIVE CONTEMPORARY DEVELOPMENTS

The larger overarching theories are indispensable resources. Yet analysts have continued to theorize the production of educational inequality. By way of illustration, consider these efforts to explain the role of socioeconomic background on students' transition through the system of education. This research has been motivated by many factors, including the nearly ubiquitous finding in cross-national research of waning associations between socioeconomic background and education transitions across transitions, a pattern some have interpreted as indicating that education systems are egalitarian at higher levels (e.g., Stolzenberg, 1994).

MMI

Raftery and Hout (1993) and Hout, Raftery, and Bell (1993) postulate MMI, a proposal composed of four tenets to explain the pattern of social background effects on educational attainment. The first tenet is that expansion of secondary and higher education reflects increased demand generated by population increase and the rising level of parents' education caused by *earlier* education expansion and other factors. Second, if enrollment rises faster than demand, then the socioeconomically disadvantaged obtain more schooling. Even so, the socioeconomic association is unchanged. Third, if completion of a level of education becomes universal for upper-class persons, then the effect of social background on *that* transition declines but only if educational expansion cannot be otherwise maintained. And fourth, falling socioeconomic effects can reverse and become rising effects; for example, if government support for educational attainment is reduced, socioeconomic effects will increase.

MMI implies that perhaps the only route to reducing the effect of social background is to expand schools. Even so, effects of social background will always be as large as possible. Multiple studies have found patterns consistent with MMI in multiple countries (e.g., Gerber & Hout, 1995; Tolsma, Coenders, & Lubbers, 2007).

RRA

Breen and Goldthorpe (1997) offer a model of RRA to explain stable class differentials across cohorts, declining class effects across transitions, and rapidly changing gender effects. RRA has affinities with the Wisconsin model owing to its focus on perceptions of the likelihood of educational success, perceptions driven in part by ability. RRA also may draw on human capital theory by highlighting cost constraints. Seen in this way, RRA can be conceived as a synthesis of the Wisconsin model and human capital theory. However, Breen and Goldthorpe add the proviso that persons are risk averse and seek to attain a social class at least equal to that of their parents.

RRA interprets MMI as a special case in which costs decline across the board for all classes. RRA claims that if costs decline differentially for different classes, the patterns highlighted by MMI will not occur. For examples RRA can explain and MMI cannot, Breen and Goldthorpe point to rapid decline in the gender effect owing to changes in perceptions of appropriate roles, and thus likely levels of educational success, and to Sweden, a rare case in which class effects did decline with expansion owing to compensatory support for the education of disadvantaged children.

Whereas RRA is generally applicable to any choice set, MMI explicitly concerns attainment only. This is important because MMI thus ignores potentially important qualitative differences in schooling. Breen and Jonsson (2000) found that the power of socioeconomic background varied with the path students took to their completed educational attainment. They concluded that suppressing qualitative distinctions weakens the understanding of the role of social background in educational transitions (Breen & Jonsson, 2000).

EMI

Consistent with that insight, Lucas (2001) proposed the theory of EMI, which considers both qualitative and quantitative dimensions of inequality. Lucas contends that socioeconomically advantaged actors secure for themselves and their children advantage wherever advantages are commonly possible. If quantitative differences are common, the socioeconomically advantaged obtain quantitative advantage. If qualitative differences are common, the socioeconomically advantaged obtain qualitative advantage.

Articulated as a general theory of inequality, EMI explained socioeconomic effects on education in one of at least two ways. When some attain a particular level of schooling whereas many others do not (e.g., high school completion throughout the first half of the 20th century in the United States), the socioeconomically advantaged use their advantages to secure that level of schooling. However, if that level of schooling becomes widely or perhaps even universally attained, the socioeconomically advantaged seek out whatever qualitative differences there are at that level, using their advantages to secure quantitatively similar but qualitatively better education (e.g., qualitatively better, more challenging curricular tracks). Thus, EMI notes that actors' foci may shift as qualitative differences supplant quantitative differences in importance. Alternatively, actors may reference qualitative differences even when quantitative differences are common. Either way, EMI claims that the socioeconomically advantaged will use their advantages to secure both quantitatively and qualitatively better outcomes.

Notably, EMI differs from both MMI and RRA in specifying a role for class-based action to maintain advantage. In contrast, both MMI and RRA are articulated as individual rational choice models; both deny a role for collective action. Lucas (2001), however, points to empirical, ethnographic observation of collective action (e.g., Useem, 1992) as warrant for the supposition of an important role for collective action. Analysts have found evidence of EMI in multiple nations (e.g., Ayalon & Shavit, 2004, and Ayalon & Yogev, 2005, for Israel; Tolsma et al., 2007, for the Netherlands).

THE CHALLENGE OF MOVING FROM THEORY
AND EVIDENCE TO SOCIAL POLICY

The vast majority of research reveals the substantive fact of inequality in a multiplicity of educational processes and outcomes as well as linkages between inequality and sociodemographic dimensions. With such a store of largely uncontested facts, how is it that these facts have not provided the basis for policy responses that will mute or eliminate consequential inequality?

There are two noteworthy classes of answers to this question. One class focuses on what social scientists might supply in the way of policy advice, and the other highlights what policymakers or sectors of the wider public might demand in the way of policy advice. The focus on demand risks imputing disinterest to policymakers, even though the rigorous research base for such a claim may not be evident. Although we believe that exploring that thesis may produce useful insights, we prefer to consider supply for one very important reason: Social scientists can immediately affect what they supply. Thus, to the extent that what social scientists supply underlies the gap between how education operates and how education might operate were social science knowledge to more deeply inform education, social scientists can act immediately to alter their impact on education. Were social scientists interested in gaining policy influence, what might they do? Many analysts have begun to weigh in on this question, inspired in part by and reacting in part against Burawoy's (2005) call for a public sociology that is engaged beyond the academy. Partly in response, one can consider two key contributions social science might make: empirical research and theoretical perspective.

On Empirical Research

To consider what social scientists might do to supply better empirical research, we need turn to theory. Theories serve many purposes, and one purpose they serve is to render a cacophony of disconnected findings coherent. In doing so, they may facilitate the task of both policymaker and social analyst. For example, consider the evidence showing that children of socioeconomically advantaged parents are more likely to continue school. Absent theory, this empirical fact simply is. With theory, this empirical fact has a causal basis—the higher educational attainment of socioeconomically advantaged children is a result of parents' ability to make greater financial investments in their educational success; is a result of greater levels of parental, peer, and school personnel encouragement; is based in biological advantages the wealthy possess; or some other cause. The key conclusion is that absent theory, all one may obtain is a collection of disconnected empirical observations. With theory, the different empirical observations coalesce into more or less coherent narratives. Those narratives form the justifiable basis of various policy options as well as a viable point of departure for additional research.

When considering why it is that decades of research showing sociodemographic inequality in education has not led to successful policy responses, one part of the basic answer is that the facts of inequality provide little policy guidance by themselves. Theory is required. Policymakers need theory, but, alas, when too many theories vie for supremacy, policymakers are likely to follow one of two unproductive strategies. Many policymakers may become paralyzed, unable to support any policy intervention. Just as many may become frenzied, supporting a large set of possibly contradictory policy interventions, with each intervention perhaps receiving insufficient funds and vigor to succeed. Either approach is likely to lead to failure, and with each policy failure, the ability to implement new policies that might succeed is diminished as the public's willingness to act is dissipated.

This is a general phenomenon, yet earlier, we outlined several theories of the patterns of educational inequality. Our ability to provide multiple, conflicting, plausible frameworks for interpreting inequality in education suggests that the general phenomenon *is* manifest in the realm of education, with paralyzing or dissipating implications. For example, faced with the evidence of socioeconomic advantages in college entry as well as the connection between college attendance and later economic success, what might one propose? (a) Do nothing, as meritocratic theory might advocate; (b) provide more counseling and encouragement to promising disadvantaged students, as the Wisconsin model might imply; (c) offer financial aid targeted toward high-performing poor and middle-class students, as human capital theory might suggest; (d) repeal the tax-exempt status of private colleges and use the funds to expand public collegiate institutions, as a Marxist theory might contend; (e) elaborate alternative pathways to certification, as credentialing theory might suggest; or (f) do nothing, as biogenetic theory might maintain? It is clear that the policy prescription depends more on the theoretical perspective one adopts than on the social fact one is considering, even when the social fact is not in dispute.

Many of the illustrative policy prescriptions are contradictory. For example, two theories imply that the policymaker should do nothing. The counsel to do nothing is not, really, a counsel to do nothing, for "doing nothing" is to actively maintain the existing structure, such that even "doing nothing" is to do something. Thus, one contrast is between theories that suggest policymakers should maintain matters as they are and other theories that suggest policymakers should make adjustments.

Some adjustments are complementary. For example, the Wisconsin model suggestion of increasing the encouragement to students, depending on the content of the encouragement, is likely consistent with many perspectives. However, some adjustments are not necessarily complementary. For example, the human capital theory proposal leaves institutions largely intact while supplementing students' finances. In this view, public and private tuitions are set by other dynamics, and the policymaker can help by cushioning the cost for poor students. In contrast, the Marxist solution described here ends public subsidies to private institutions and expands the public sector to meet demand. The two proposals are not necessarily complementary because the human capital proposal basically provides more subsidies to private institutions, whereas the Marxist proposal does not.

The implication of the illustration is that faced with the same empirical finding, the policy counsel is dependent on the theoretical frame into which the finding is placed. Two implications follow and suggest great difficulty for research to inform policy. First, it seems that one challenge of moving from evidence to policy is posed by the embarrassment of theoretical riches analysts have produced for understanding inequality in education.

Second, this conclusion suggests that continued documentation of educational inequality, for all its admitted utility in maintaining an up-to-date awareness of the facts on the ground, will likely be of little value for moving from evidence and theory to social policy. With each study that shows, yet again, that African Americans, Mexican Americans, and Puerto Ricans are disadvantaged compared to Whites, or that the poor obtain less schooling than the wealthy, little marginal gain is produced. Empirical research is of potential value, but to realize that value, two features must pertain. First, although it is clear that most empirical research cites one or a few theoretical works, often the empirical research has a hazy, vague, or loose relationship even to the theories on which it draws. Often the theory supplies little more than a label under which one or more variables are placed. Thus, human capital serves as a second-level label for mother's and father's education, or cultural capital serves as a second-level label for mother's and father's education—neither study usually offers anything other than a few anecdotal observations or pro forma citations in support of the second-level label, if that, suggesting that the connection between theory and empirical data is loose. For empirical research to inform policy, a tighter connection between measures and theories is required.

Second, empirical research must be directly, explicitly, in dialogue with *multiple* theories. The example above is telling—it is common to see two papers, with two different authors, using the same data set, the same variables, yet labeling the variables differently and doing so simply by fiat. Such work is unable to adjudicate between the various plausible larger theories that have been offered. Yet if the aim is to bridge the divide between evidence and theory, on one hand, and social policy, on the other, a thorough-going effort to adjudicate between the proposed theories is exactly what is required.

Of course, classic, productive empirical work has been conducted mainly to demonstrate the plausibility of a preferred theory (e.g., Bourdieu & Passeron, 1977). Yet even the more recent proposed theories under discussion have usually been investigated in isolation (e.g., Hout et al., 1993). But given that analysts regard multiple theories as plausible, further progress requires that analysts move from further empirical demonstration of the plausibility of one theory to empirical studies designed to test multiple theories rather than to champion only one (e.g., Ayalon & Shavit, 2004; Hauser et al., 1983).

Admittedly, no one empirical study may provide a crucial experiment that forever eliminates a given theory from consideration, as our earlier recognition of the resurgence of Lamarckism affirms. Yet multiple studies designed to test multiple alternatives could cumulate to a consensus that some theories just do not remain viable when considered in comparison to others. Even if this did not occur, other outcomes could be equally useful. For example, multiple comparative analyses might reveal the extent to which different theories apply under different conditions or might lead analysts to see fundamental points of agreement across ostensibly conflicting theories.

Conducting cross-theory comparative analyses would be a step forward, but the task of relating theory and evidence to social policy will remain a challenge, because the theoretical indeterminancy owing to a bounty of viable theories is only one problem, although it is perhaps the largest. But other problems exist as well. We think that these other problems would initially become more challenging if analysts more tightly connected empirical research to theory but that, over time, they would become easier to navigate. For example, one problem policymakers encounter is in determining whether a given study remains relevant for their concerns. Analysts are always studying the past, whereas policymakers are always seeking to intervene in the present. Temporal distance can undermine the validity of the conclusions, as conditions may have changed. For example, a locality with only Blacks and Whites may have become a locality with Blacks, Asians, and Latino/as. Is the research still relevant? Or perhaps the research has concerned Latino/as, but the context for which the policymaker is responsible has Guatemalans. Is the research relevant? Guatemalans are Latino/as, but did the study's Latino/as include Guatemalans or Latino/as who resemble Guatemalans culturally, socioeconomically, and more? More generally, are the research categories consistent with legal or policy categories, or is there some degree of mismatch?

These challenges exist in any effort to move between empirical research and policy. However, we contend that if empirical research were more tightly connected to theory, the very tightness of that connection would aid policymakers in ascertaining the relevance of any given study or set of studies for their policy question. A tight connection between theory and empirical research renders the people—women or men, different racial groups, different language groups—as actors beset by and acting within more fundamental sociological dynamics. Policymakers could then use the empirical research to grasp those fundamental dynamics, facilitating policy construction.

On Theoretical Research

A neglected way of bridging the divide between social policy and sociological evidence is to conduct purely theoretical research. In this approach, the analyst traces the theoretical implications of various claims, *without* simultaneously attempting to conduct an empirical analysis of the claims. In many fields, such work is essential, yet in the study of education and inequality, such work is rarely pursued. The vitality of such work comes from its ability to allow analysts to investigate the logical coherence of different theories without requiring the same analysis to contain an empirical investigation. As noted previously, a great deal of empirical work is hazily related to theories. Even were the connection tight, many reasons other than the strength or

weakness of a given theory can produce empirical results that lend support to errone-
ous theories and undercut more accurate ones (Lieberson, 1998). Consequently, a
field that confines the effort to adjudicate theories to empirical work alone is almost
certain to fail in the adjudication project.

Purely theoretical work could pay major dividends. In the first instance, purely theoretical work can save a great deal of time by warning scholars away from what might
actually be nonfalsifiable theories. For example, analysts have used empirical research
methods to assess the Raftery and Hout (1993) theory of MMI in multiple countries
(e.g., Raftery & Hout, 1993, for Ireland; Hout et al., 1993, for the United States; Gerber
& Hout, 1995, for Soviet-period Russia; Tolsma et al., 2007, for the Netherlands), but
recent purely theoretical research reveals that MMI is not falsifiable and thus is not a
scientific theory (Lucas, 2009). This example suggests that purely theoretical work can
eliminate theories where empirical research might never be able to do so.

In the second instance, purely theoretical work can crystallize similarities in and
differences between theories to sharpen empirical analysts' efforts to adjudicate
between different theoretical positions. For example, one might view the RRA theory
of Breen and Goldthorpe (1997) and the EMI theory of Lucas (2001) as having different views of students, but recent purely theoretical research shows some intriguing
connections between the theories (Lucas, 2009). For example, Lucas (2009) finds
that both theories—EMI directly but RRA implicitly—posit the existence of myopia
on the part of students. This is an intriguing result because to the extent that RRA
draws on human capital theory, one would expect RRA to deny myopia. Yet hiding
within the equations that constitute RRA is an implication of myopia, making RRA
have some affinity with EMI and, thus, making the discovery of myopic agents in
empirical research fail to provide an adjudicatory test of the two theories.

Finally, such work might reveal that two ostensibly disparate theories are, actually,
the same. If so, any differences in the policy proposals the two theories may seem to
imply can be revealed as likely having some other basis—perhaps value commitments
of the scholars working in the two different traditions.

Of course, there are many kinds of theoretical works, but from a cursory survey
of the broader social science literature, two genres emerge. One approach articulates
multiple, complex concepts and their interrelationship on the basis of words alone.
Classic examples of this genre include the work of Bourdieu (e.g., 1986), Coleman
(e.g., 1988), and Collins (e.g., 1979). A different approach articulates multiple, complex concepts and their interrelationship through precisely defined mathematical
equations. Classic examples of this genre include the work of Becker (e.g., 1962),
Roemer (e.g., 1988), and Breen and Goldthorpe (e.g., 1997).

Bourdieu (1986) and Becker (1962) both present theories of the development
of human capital, but one uses words whereas the other uses theoretical equations.
Roemer (1988) and Coleman (1988) articulate Marxist and non-Marxist theories
of the social basis of investment and the generation of surplus, but one uses equations whereas the other uses words alone. Collins (1979) and Breen and Goldthorpe

(1997) both describe theoretical explanations for educational attainment, but Collins uses words alone whereas Breen and Goldthorpe use words and equations. These observations suggest that the means of expression and the specific phenomena conceptualized are orthogonal, implying that one should be able to articulate any theory both with and without equations. Consequently, there is no reason to embrace one mode of presentation and dismiss another. Analysts need probe multiple theories without regard to the language through which they originally found articulation. Thus, the counsel is to conduct more purely theoretical, cross-comparative analyses of existing theoretical traditions; the way in which that work is conveyed can be through equations (e.g., Lucas, 2009) or words alone (e.g., Lucas, 2008b).

On the Indeterminancy of Evidence

It cannot go unremarked that evidence and theory are not the only legitimate sources of policy. Policymaking is a political process, and in a society in which office-holders govern with the consent of the governed, the values and commitments of the wider polity may play a legitimate role in policy development, selection, and implementation.

However, most of the polity is uninvolved in any given policy realm. A vast literature has explored the reasons policymaking is often left to interested parties (e.g., A. Glazer, 1993; Rowley, Tollison, & Tullock, 1983). It is beyond the scope of our work to do more than point to that literature; our aim, here, is simply to convey the conclusion that even in a matter of such wide interest as education, it is often the case that much of the public is not directly involved in policymaking.

When the public is involved, the involved are often parents who have concerns about the education of their own child. The presence of parents in educational policymaking can greatly hinder the development and adoption of egalitarian policies, as socioeconomically advantaged parents use legitimate and illegitimate means and resources to preserve their advantages (Lucas, 2001), posing a major challenge for analysts and policymakers who seek to reduce socioeconomic inequality (Lucas, 2008a). In such situations, evidence may be virtually irrelevant to antagonists of egalitarian policies (Lucas, 2008a). It is important to acknowledge this possibility, for otherwise, a major potential determinant of how education is arranged will go unrecognized, making it likely that other factors that are not necessarily detrimental to the process of education may be blamed. And it should be obvious that only failure is likely to ensue from misdiagnosing the basis of the apparent intransigence of sociodemographic inequality in education.

CONCLUDING REMARKS: BEST-CASE SCENARIOS FOR INFORMING REFORM WITH SOCIAL SCIENCE EVIDENCE

Two key sources of the interest in sociodemographic educational inequality are the socioeconomic consequences of educational disadvantage and the understanding of sociodemographic dimensions as demarcating the allocation of power. Even so, social scientists engage in various debates concerning the content of sociodemographic categories as well as the phenomena those categories collectively reference. Sometimes, as in the case of race and class, those debates may involve an implicit proposal to reject power as the basis for classification in favor of persons' subjectively understood experience. Such a subtle change could have large implications, for the very basis of policymaker attention to sociodemographic inequality might be undermined to the extent that identity, rather than power, is understood to be the basis of any observed inequality.

These debates as to how to conceive sociodemographic dimensions and categories occur amid repeated documentation of sociodemographic-linked inequality in education. Even in areas of low overall inequality, such as the incidence of high school graduation, analysts find noteworthy differences in rates of success attached to various sociodemographic dimensions. The ubiquity of such findings encourages a turn to theory, a turn that reveals multiple plausible explanations for the existence and maintenance of inequality. Intransigent inequality raises the question as to why policy has not been marshaled to address the well-documented disparities.

We contend that the multiplicity of theories is one key factor that undermines the ability of social science to aid policy development. Many plausible theories point to different, perhaps contradictory, policy options. Although we, too, have our preferred theories, and we expect they hold promise for continued research and possible policy guidance, our larger and more important general point in this context is that unless scholars set about adjudicating between existing theories, either to eliminate some nontrivial number (but not necessarily all but one), and/or to produce coherent syntheses, it is unlikely that social science as such will be available to counsel any political actor who sought diagnostic and prescriptive guidance from the various disciplines.

But we believe there are simple, next-step responses that may greatly improve matters. In the best immediate case, scholars will tie their empirical studies tightly to theoretical frameworks, such that their empirical analysis will convey not only substantive facts, but also shed light on multiple contending theories. At the same time, analysts will conduct purely theoretical analyses of phenomena, the better to sharpen the logical implications of the various theories. Working together, these two approaches will greatly illuminate existing theories, revealing their fundamental points of contention and perhaps unseen points of agreement. As this happens, social science research will become better positioned to provide helpful guidance for policymakers interested in reducing sociodemographic inequality in education.

A closing word of caution is in order, however. We convey this counsel in perhaps deceptively straightforward terms. It is also true that the institutional structure of academia, especially as reflected in the journal reviewing process, is not necessarily arranged to support the changes we propose. Most social science journals are more likely to publish an empirical research paper than to publish a theoretical investigation. Moreover, cross-theory comparative analyses are likely to be longer than the typical paper, and some journals enforce rigid word count limitations, placing every submission on a Procrustean bed difficult to justify in a time of burgeoning electronic media. At the same time, any truly comparative paper—that is, any paper that conveys the limitations of *every* theory it treats in an honest and respectful manner—is likely to find itself in a crossfire between adherents of the different theoretical perspectives it treats or ignores when it enters the reviewing process. Few papers are likely to survive that process unless editors are willing to publish papers even though reviewers may advise otherwise (perhaps offering to publish the reviewers' unvarnished comments to facilitate dialogue and to motivate reviewers to ground their appraisals in the text under review and the conversation it seeks to engage).

Taken together, these institutional features make adoption of our counsel more difficult than it might at first appear. After all, who can contend that analysts should vaguely draw on theory or that analyses should consistently fail to adjudicate between theories? Yet the plethora of plausible theories, coupled with the massive empirical literature amid a dearth of studies that eliminate theoretical approaches, suggests that despite the obvious desirability of the proposal, its adoption is not yet in evidence.

But times change, and new commitments can be forged. If editors open their volumes to work that directly compares alternatives and, most important, close their pages to work that is not cross-theory comparative, analysts will follow. And if analysts follow, it is unlikely that one theory will eventually emerge as the consensus one. However, it is also likely many of the vast theories currently under consideration *will* be eliminated, and many others will be merged together when their consistency is made visible through painstaking theoretical analysis. When that happens, social science will be effectively poised to provide policymakers with both substantive knowledge and, it is hoped, wise counsel on how to proceed to reduce hitherto intransigent sociodemographic inequality in education.

NOTES

[1]In this sense, the socioeconomic index tradition is based on a theory that, although distinguishable, shares some features with Abend's (2008) seven-category typology of the meanings of the term *theory* in sociological research.

ACKNOWLEDGMENTS

We thank Kate Senger for providing citations to epigenetics and comments on an earlier draft.

REFERENCES

Abend, G. (2008). The meaning of "theory." *Sociological Theory, 26,* 173–199.

Alexander, K. L., Cook, M., & McDill, E. L. (1978). Curriculum tracking and educational stratification: Some further evidence. *American Sociological Review, 43,* 47–66.

Alexander, K. L., Eckland, B. K., & Griffin, L. J. (1975). The Wisconsin model of socioeconomic achievement: A replication. *American Journal of Sociology, 81,* 324–342.

Anyon, J. (1984). Intersections of gender and class: Accommodation and resistance by working-class and affluent females to contradictory sex-role ideologies. *Journal of Education, 166,* 25–48.

Aronson, J., Lustina, M. J., Good, C., Keough, K., Steele, C. M., & Brown, J. (1999). When White men can't do math: Necessary and sufficient factors in stereotype threat. *Journal of Experimental Social Psychology, 35,* 29–46.

Arum, R. (2000). Schools and communities: Ecological and institutional dimensions. *Annual Review of Sociology, 26,* 395–418.

Arum, R. (2003). *Judging school discipline: The crisis of moral authority.* Cambridge, MA: Harvard University Press.

Ayalon, H., & Shavit, Y. (2004). Educational reforms and inequalities in Israel: The MMI hypothesis revisited. *Sociology of Education, 77,* 103–120.

Ayalon, H., & Yogev, A. (2005). Field of study and students' stratification in an expanded system of higher education: The case of Israel. *European Sociological Review, 21,* 227–241.

Bauman, K. (1998). Schools, markets, and family in the history of African-American education. *American Journal of Education, 106,* 500–531.

Becker, G. (1962). Investment in human capital: A theoretical analysis. *Journal of Political Economy, 70* (Suppl.), 9–49.

Becker, G., & Tomes, N. (1986). Human capital and the rise and fall of families. *Journal of Labor Economics, 4,* S1–S39.

Belman, D., & Heywood, J. S. (1991). Sheepskin effects in the returns to education: An examination of women and minorities. *Review of Economics and Statistics, 73,* 720–724.

Berends, M. (1995). Educational stratification and students' social bonding to school. *British Journal of Sociology of Education, 16,* 327–351.

Bhavnani, K.-K. (1991). *Talking politics: A psychological framing for views from youth in Britain.* New York: Cambridge University Press.

Bills, D. B. (2003). Credentials, signals, and screens: Explaining the relationship between schooling and job assignment. *Review of Educational Research, 73,* 441–469.

Blackmore, J., & Kenway, J. (1993). *Gender matters in educational administration and policy: A feminist introduction.* Bristol, PA: Falmer.

Blau, P. M. (1967). *Exchange and power in social life.* New York: Wiley.

Blau, P. M., & Duncan, O. D., with Tyree, A. (1967). *The American occupational structure.* New York: Free Press.

Borstelmann, T. (2001). *The Cold War and the color line: American race relations in the global arena.* Cambridge, MA: Harvard University Press.

Bourdieu, P. (1986). The forms of capital. In J. Richardson (Ed.), *Handbook of theory and research for the sociology of education* (pp. 241–258). New York: Greenwood.

Bourdieu, P., & Passeron, J. C. (1977). *Reproduction in education, society, and culture* (2nd ed.). London: Sage.

Bowditch, C. (1993). Getting rid of troublemakers: High school disciplinary procedures and the production of dropouts. *Social Problems, 40,* 493–509.

Bowen, W. G., Kurzweil, M. A., & Tobin, E. M. (2005). *Equality and excellence in American higher education.* Charlottesville, VA: University of Virginia Press.

Bowles, S., & Gintis, H. (1976). *Schooling in capitalist America: Educational reform and the contradictions of economic life.* New York: Basic Books.

Boylan, R. D. (1993). The effect of the number of diplomas on their value. *Sociology of Education, 66,* 206–221.

Braddock, J. H., II. (1990). Tracking the middle grades: National patterns of grouping for instruction. *Phi Delta Kappan, 71,* 445–449.

Breen, R., & Goldthorpe, J. H. (1997). Explaining educational differentials: Towards a formal rational action theory. *Rationality and Society, 9,* 275–305.

Breen, R., & Jonsson, J. O. (2000). Analyzing educational careers: A multinomial transition model. *American Sociological Review, 65,* 754–772.

Brenner, J. (1988). Work relations and the formation of class consciousness. *Critical Sociology,* *15,* 83–89.

Buchmann, C., DiPrete, T. A., & McDaniel, A. (2008). Gender inequalities in education. *Annual Review of Sociology, 34,* 319–337.

Burawoy, M. (1987). The limits of Wright's analytical Marxism and an alternative. *Berkeley Journal of Sociology, 32,* 51–72.

Burawoy, M. (2005). 2004 presidential address: For public sociology. *American Sociological Review, 70,* 4–28.

Calderon, J. (1992). "Hispanic" and "Latino": The viability of categories for panethnic unity. *Latin American Perspectives, 19,* 37–44.

Carbonaro, W. (2005). Tracking, students' effort, and academic achievement. *Sociology of Education, 78,* 27–49.

Card, D. (1999). The causal effect of education on earnings. In O. C. Ashenfelter, & D. Card (Eds.), *Handbook of labor economics* (Vol. 3, pp. 1801–1863). Amsterdam, Netherlands: Elsevier Science B.V.

Carey, N., Farris, E., & Carpenter, J. (1994). *Curricular differentiation in public high schools: Fast response survey system E.D. tabs.* Rockville, MD: Westat.

Catsambis, S. (1994). The path to math: Gender and racial-ethnic differences in mathematics participation from middle school to high school. *Sociology of Education, 67,* 199–215.

Coleman, J. S. (1988). Social capital in the creation of human capital. *American Journal of Sociology, 94,* S95–S120.

Collins, R. (1971). Functional and conflict theories of educational stratification. *American Sociological Review, 36,* 1002–1019.

Collins, R. (1979). *The credential society: An historical sociology of education and stratification.* New York: Academic Press.

Correll, S., & Hartmann, D. (1998). *Ethnicity and race: Making identities in a changing world.* Thousand Oaks, CA: Pine Forge.

Daniels, M., Devlin, B., & Roeder, K. (1997). Of genes and IQ. In B. Devlin, S. E. Fienberg, D. P. Resnick, & K. Roeder (Eds.), *Intelligence, genes, and success: Scientists respond to the bell curve* (pp. 45–70). New York: Springer-Verlag.

Davies, S. (1995). Leaps of faith: Shifting currents in critical sociology of education. *American Journal of Sociology, 100,* 1448–1478.

Davis, K., & Moore, W. E. (1945). Some principles of stratification. *American Sociological Review, 10,* 242–249.

Devlin, B., Fienberg, S. E., Resnick, D. P., & Roeder, K. (1997). *Intelligence, genes, and success: Scientists respond to the bell curve.* New York: Springer.

Diamond, M. H., & Sigmundson, K. (1997). Management of intersexuality: Guidelines for dealing with individuals with ambiguous genitalia. *Archives of Pediatric and Adolescent Medicine, 151,* 1046–1050.

DiPrete, T. A., with Muller, C., & Shaeffer, N. (1981). *Discipline and order in American high schools.* Washington, DC: National Center for Education Statistics.

Donovan, M. S., & Cross, C. T. (2002). *Minority students in special and gifted education.* Washington, DC: National Academies Press.

Downey, D. B., & Pribesh, S. (2004). When race matters: Teachers' evaluations of students' classroom behavior. *Sociology of Education, 77,* 267–282.

Doyle, J. M., & Kao, G. (2007). Are racial identities of multiracials stable? Changing self-identification among single and multiple race individuals. *Social Psychology Quarterly, 70,* 405–423.

Dreger, A. D. (2001). *Hermaphrodites and the medical invention of sex.* Cambridge, MA: Harvard University Press.

Driscoll, A. K. (1999). Risk of high school dropout among immigrant and native Hispanic youth. *International Migration Review, 33*, 857–875.

Dudziak, M. L. (2000). *Cold War civil rights: Race and the image of American democracy.* Princeton, NJ: Princeton University Press.

Duncan, O. D. (1961). A socioeconomic index for all occupations. In A. J. Reiss, Jr., (Ed.), *Occupations and social status* (pp. 109–138). New York: Free Press.

Dunn, D., Almquist, E. M., & Chafetz, J. S. (1993). Macrostructural perspectives on gender inequality. In P. England (Ed.), *Theory on gender/feminism on theory* (pp. 69–90). New York: Aldine de Gruyter.

Elster, J. (1981). Snobs. *London Review of Books, 3*(20), 10–12.

Espinosa, K. E., & Massey, D. S. (1997). Determinants of English proficiency among Mexican migrants to the United States. *International Migration Review, 31*, 28–50.

Eyerman, R. (1994). Modernity and social movements. In D. B. Grusky (Ed.), *Social stratification: Class, race, and gender in sociological perspective* (pp. 707–710). Boulder, CO: Westview.

Featherman, D. L., & Stevens, G. (1982). A revised socioeconomic index of occupational status: Application in analysis of sex differences in attainment. In M. G. Powers (Ed.), *Measures of socioeconomic status: Current issues* (pp. 93–129). Boulder, CO: Westview.

Ferree, M. M., & Hall, E. J. (1996). Rethinking stratification from a feminist perspective: Gender, race, and class in mainstream textbooks. *American Sociological Review, 61*, 929–950.

Fine, M. (1986). Why urban adolescents drop into and out of public high school. *Teachers College Record, 87*, 393–409.

Finley, M. K. (1984). Teachers and tracking in a comprehensive high school. *Sociology of Education, 57*, 233–243.

Finney, R. L. (1928). *A sociological philosophy of education.* New York: Macmillan.

Fischer, C., & Hout, M. (2006). *Century of difference: How America changed in the last one hundred years.* New York: Russell Sage.

Fischer, C., Hout, M., Jankowski, M. S., Lucas, S. R., Swidler, A., & Voss, K. (1996). *Inequality by design: Cracking the bell curve myth.* Princeton, NJ: Princeton University Press.

Fordham, S., & Ogbu, J. U. (1986). Black students' school success: Coping with the "burden of 'acting White.'" *Urban Review, 18*, 176–206.

Francis, D. J., Fletcher, J. M., Stuebing, K. K., Lyon, G. R., Shaywitz, B. A., & Shaywitz, S. E. (2005). Psychometric approaches to the identification of LD: IQ and achievement scores are not sufficient. *Journal of Learning Disabilities, 38*, 98–108.

Frazis, H. (1993). Selection bias and the degree effect. *Journal of Human Resources, 28*, 538–554.

Friedkin, N. E., & Thomas, S. L. (1997). Social positions in schooling. *Sociology of Education, 70*, 239–255.

Fryer, R. G., & Levitt, S. D. (2005). *The Black-White test score gap through third grade* (NBER Working Paper 11049). Washington, DC: National Bureau of Economic Research.

Funderberg, L. (1996, July 10). Boxed in. *The New York Times*, p. A15.

Gaddy, G. D. (1988). High school order and academic achievement. *American Journal of Education, 96*, 496–518.

Gamoran, A. (1989). Rank, performance, and mobility in elementary school grouping. *Sociological Quarterly, 30*, 109–123.

Gamoran, A. (1992). The variable effects of high school tracking. *American Sociological Review, 57*, 812–828.

Gamoran, A., & Berends, M. (1987). The effects of stratification in secondary schools: Synthesis of survey and ethnographic research. *Review of Educational Research, 57*, 415–435.

Gamoran, A., & Mare, R. D. (1989). Secondary school tracking and educational equality: Compensation, reinforcement, or neutrality? *American Journal of Sociology, 94*, 1146–1183.

Garet, M. S., & DeLany, B. (1988). Students, courses, and stratification. *Sociology of Education, 61*, 61–77.

Gaskell, G. D., Wright, D. B., & O'Muircheartaigh, C. A. (2000). Telescoping of landmark events: Implications for survey research. *Public Opinion Quarterly, 64*, 77–89.

Gerber, T., & Hout, M. (1995). Educational stratification in Russia during the Soviet period. *American Journal of Sociology, 101*, 611–660.

Glazer, A. (1993). On the incentives to establish and play political rent-seeking games. *Public Choice, 75*, 139–148.

Glazer, N., & Moynihan, D. P. (1970). *Beyond the melting pot.* Cambridge, MA: MIT Press.

Grodsky, E., Warren, J. R., & Felts, E. (2008). Testing and social stratification in American education. *Annual Review of Sociology, 34*, 385–404.

Grusky, D. B., & Sørenson, J. B. (1998). Can class analysis be salvaged? *American Journal of Sociology, 103*, 1187–1234.

Hallinan, M. (1994a). Further thoughts on tracking. *Sociology of Education, 67*, 89–91.

Hallinan, M. (1994b). Tracking: From theory to practice. *Sociology of Education, 67*, 79–84.

Hammack, F. M. (1980). Review of *Learning to labour: How working class kids get working class jobs. American Journal of Education, 88*, 510–518.

Hansen, D. O., & Haller, A. O. (1973). Status attainment of Costa Rican males: A cross-cultural test of a model. *Rural Sociology, 38*, 269–282.

Harris, C. I. (1993). Whiteness as property. *Harvard Law Review, 106*, 1707–1791.

Harris, D. R., & Sim, J. J. (2002). Who is multiracial? Assessing the complexity of lived race. *American Sociological Review, 67*, 614–627.

Hauser, R. M., & Anderson, D. K. (1991). Post-high school plans and aspirations of Black and White high school seniors: 1976–86. *Sociology of Education, 64*, 263–277.

Hauser, R. M., & Andrew, M. (2006). Another look at the stratification of educational transitions: The logistic response model with partial proportionality constraints. *Sociological Methodology, 36*, 1–26.

Hauser, R. M., Sewell, W., & Alwin, D. (1976). High school effects on achievement. In W. Sewell, R. M. Hauser, & D. Featherman (Eds.), *Schooling and achievement in American society* (pp. 309–341). New York: Academic Press.

Hauser, R. M., Tsai, S.-L., & Sewell, W. H. (1983). A model of stratification with response error in social and psychological variables. *Sociology of Education, 56*, 20–46.

Hauser, R. M., & Warren, J. R. (1997). Socioeconomic indexes for all occupations: A review, update, and critique. *Sociological Methodology, 27*, 177–298.

Hayes-Bautista, D., & Chapa, J. (1987). Latino terminology: Conceptual bases for standardized terminology. *American Journal of Public Health, 77*, 61–68.

Herrnstein, R. J., & Charles, M. (1994). *The bell curve: Intelligence and class structure in American life.* New York: Free Press.

Hirschman, C., Alba, R., & Farley, R. (2000). The meaning and measurement of race in the U.S. census: Glimpses into the future. *Demography, 37*, 381–393.

Hoffer, T. B. (1992). Middle school ability grouping and student achievement in science and mathematics. *Educational Evaluation and Policy Analysis, 14*, 205–227.

Hollingshead, A. B. (1949). *Elmtown's youth: The impact of social classes on adolescents.* New York: Wiley.

Honneth, A. (2003). Redistribution as recognition: A response to Nancy Fraser. In N. Fraser, & A. Honneth (Eds.), *Redistribution or recognition: A political-philosophical exchange* (pp. 110–197). New York: Verso.

Horan, P. M. (1978). Is status attainment research atheoretical? *American Sociological Review, 43*, 534–541.

Hout, M., Raftery, A. E., & Bell, E. O. (1993). Making the grade: Educational stratification in the United States, 1925–1989. In Y. Shavit & H.-P. Blossfeld (Eds.), *Persistent inequality: Changing educational attainment in thirteen countries* (pp. 25–49). Boulder, CO: Westview.

Ingels, S. J., Scott, L. A., Taylor, J. R., Owings, J., & Quinn, P. (1998). *National Education Longitudinal Study of 1988 (NELS, 88) base year through second follow-up: Final methodology report* (Working Paper 98-06). Washington, DC: U.S. Department of Education.

Jackman, M. (1979). The subjective meaning of social class identification in the United States. *Public Opinion Quarterly, 43,* 443–462.

Jackman, M. R., & Jackman, R. W. (1983). *Class awareness in the United States.* Berkeley: University of California Press.

Jacobs, J. A. (1996). Gender inequality and higher education. *Annual Review of Sociology, 22,* 153–185.

Jencks, C., & Phillips, M. (1998). *The Black-White test score gap.* Washington, DC: Brookings Institution.

Jenkins, P. H. (1995). School delinquency and school commitment. *Sociology of Education, 68,* 221–239.

Kahlenberg, R. D. (1996). *The remedy: Class, race, and affirmative action.* New York: Basic Books.

Kane, T. J. (1998). Racial and ethnic preferences in college admissions. In C. Jencks & M. Phillips (Eds.), *The Black-White test score gap* (pp. 431–456). Washington, DC: Brookings Institution.

Kao, G., & Thompson, J. S. (2003). Racial and ethnic stratification in educational achievement and attainment. *Annual Review of Sociology, 29,* 417–442.

Karabel, J., & Astin, A. W. (1975). Social class, academic ability, and college entry. *Social Forces, 53,* 381–398.

Karabel, J., & Halsey, A. H. (1977). *Power and ideology in education.* New York: Oxford University Press.

Kelly, S. (2004). Are teachers tracked? On what basis and with what consequences? *Social Psychology of Education, 7,* 55–72.

Kelly, S. (2009). The Black-White gap in mathematics course taking. *Sociology of Education, 82,* 47–69.

Kidder, W. C., & Rosner, J. (2002). How the SAT creates "built-in headwinds": An educational and legal analysis of disparate impact. *Santa Clara Law Review, 43,* 131–211.

Kingston, P. W. (2001). The unfulfilled promise of cultural capital theory. *Sociology of Education, 74*(Extra Issue), 88–99.

Kominski, R. (1990). Estimating the national high school dropout rate. *Demography, 27,* 303–311.

Krauze, T., & Slomczynski, K. M. (1985). How far to meritocracy? Empirical tests of a controversial thesis. *Social Forces, 63,* 623–642.

Lamarck, J. B. (1914). *Zoological philosophy.* London: Macmillan. (Original work published 1873)

Lamont, M., & Lareau, A. (1988). Cultural capital: Allusions, gaps, and glissandos in recent theoretical developments. *Sociological Theory, 6,* 153–168.

Laraña, E., Johnston, H., & Gusfield, J. R. (1994). *New social movements: From ideology to identity.* Philadelphia: Temple University Press.

Lareau, A., & Weininger, E. B. (2003). Cultural capital in educational research: A critical assessment. *Theory and Society, 32,* 567–606.

Lee, J., & Bean, F. D. (2004). America's changing color lines: Immigration, race/ethnicity, and multiracial identification. *Annual Review of Sociology, 30,* 221–242.

Lee, V. E., Marks, H. M., & Byrd, T. (1994). Sexism in single-sex and coeducational independent secondary school classrooms. *Sociology of Education, 67,* 92–120.

LeTendre, G. K., Hofer, B. K., & Shimizu, H. (2003). What is tracking? Cultural expectations in the United States, Germany, and Japan. *American Educational Research Journal, 40,* 43–89.

Lieberson, S. (1963). *Ethnic patterns in American cities.* New York: Free Press of Glencoe.

Lieberson, S. (1985). *Making it count: The improvement of social research and theory.* Berkeley: University of California Press.

Lieberson, S. (1998). Examples, submerged statements, and the neglected application of philosophy to social theory. In A. Sica (Ed.), *What is social theory? The philosophical debates* (pp. 177–191). Malden, MA: Blackwell.

Loftus, E. F., & Marburger, W. (1983). Since the eruption of Mount St. Helens, has anyone beaten you up? Improving the accuracy of retrospective reports with landmark events. *Memory and Cognition, 11,*114–120.

Long, J. C. (2004). *Human genetic variation: The mechanisms and results of microevolution.* Understanding Race and Human Variation Project, American Anthropological Association. Retrieved March 7, 2009, from http://www.understandingrace.org

Looker, E. D. (1989). Accuracy of proxy reports of parental status characteristics. *Sociology of Education, 62,* 257–276.

Loury, G. C. (2002). *The anatomy of racial inequality.* Cambridge, MA: Harvard University Press.

Lucas, S. R. (1990). *Course-based indicators of curricular track location.* Unpublished master's thesis, University of Wisconsin-Madison.

Lucas, S. R. (1996). Selective attrition in a newly hostile regime: The case of 1980 sophomores. *Social Forces, 75,* 511–533.

Lucas, S. R. (1999). *Tracking inequality: Stratification and mobility in American high schools.* New York: Teachers College Press.

Lucas, S. R. (2000). Hope, anguish, and the problem of our time: An essay on publication of *The Black-White Test Score Gap. Teachers College Record, 102,* 463–475.

Lucas, S. R. (2001). Effectively maintained inequality: Education transitions, track mobility, and social background effects. *American Journal of Sociology, 106,* 1642–1690.

Lucas, S. R. (2008a). Constructing equal pathways in an effectively maintained inequality society. In J. Oakes & M. Saunders (Eds.), *Beyond tracking: Multiple pathways to college, career, and civic participation* (pp. 233–250). Cambridge, MA: Harvard Education Press.

Lucas, S. R. (2008b). *Theorizing discrimination in an era of contested prejudice: Discrimination in the United States.* Philadelphia: Temple University Press.

Lucas, S. R. (2009). Stratification theory, socioeconomic background, and educational attainment: A formal analysis. *Rationality and Society, 21,* 459–511.

Lucas, S. R., & Berends, M. (2002). Sociodemographic diversity, correlated achievement, and de facto tracking. *Sociology of Education, 75,* 328–348.

Lucas, S. R., & Berends, M. (2007). Race and track location in U.S. public schools. *Research in Social Stratification and Mobility, 25,* 169–187.

Lucas, S. R., & Gamoran, A. (1991, August). *Race and track assignment: A reconsideration with course-based indicators of track locations.* Presentation at the annual meeting of the American Sociological Association, Cincinnati, OH.

Lucas, S. R., & Gamoran, A. (2002). Tracking and the achievement gap. In J. E. Chubb & T. Loveless (Eds.), in *Bridging the achievement gap* (pp. 171–198). Washington, DC: Brookings Institution.

Lukes, S. (1986). Introduction. In S. Lukes (Ed.), *Power* (pp. 1–18). New York: New York University Press.

Lumey, L. H. (1992). Decreased birthweights in infants after maternal in utero exposure to the Dutch famine of 1944–1945. *Paediatric and Perinatal Epidemiology, 6,* 240–253.

Macmann, G. M., Barnett, D. W., Lombard, T. J., Belton-Kocher, E., & Sharpe, M. N. (1989). On the actuarial classification of children: Fundamental studies of classification agreement. *Journal of Special Education, 23,* 127–149.

Magliocca, L. A., & Stephens, T. M. (1980). Child identification or child inventory? A critique of the federal design of child-identification systems implemented under P.L. 94–142. *Journal of Special Education, 14,* 23–36.

Mare, R. D. (1980). Socioeconomic background and school continuation decisions. *Journal of the American Statistical Association, 75,* 295–305.

Mare, R. D. (1981). Change and stability in educational stratification. *American Sociological Review, 46,* 72–87.

Mare, R. D. (1993). Educational stratification on observed and unobserved components of family background. In Y. Shavit & H.-P. Blossfeld (Eds.), *Persistent inequality: Changing educational attainment in thirteen countries* (pp. 351–376). Boulder, CO: Westview.

Mare, R. D., & Winship, C. (1988). Ethnic and racial patterns of educational attainment and school enrollment. In G. P. Sandfeur, & M. Tienda (Eds.), *Divided opportunities: Minorities, poverty, and social policy* (pp. 173–203). New York: Plenum.

McArthur, E. K. (1993). *Language characteristics and schooling in the United States, a changing picture: 1979 and 1989.* Washington, DC: National Center for Education Statistics.

McKenzie, J. A. (1986). The influence of identification practices, race and SES on the identification of gifted students. *Gifted Child Quarterly, 30,* 93–95.

McRobbie, A. (1999). *In the culture society: Art, fashion, and popular music.* New York: Routledge.

Mehan, H., Hertweck, A., & Meihls, J. L. (1986). *Handicapping the handicapped: Decision making in students' educational careers.* Stanford, CA: Stanford University Press.

Meyer, J. W. (1977). The effects of education as an institution. *American Journal of Sociology, 83,* 55–77.

Mickelson, R. A. (2001). Subverting Swann: First- and second-generation segregation in Charlotte-Mecklenburg schools. *American Educational Research Journal, 38,* 215–252.

Moore, D. R., & Davenport S. (1988). *The new improved sorting machine.* Madison: University of Wisconsin-Madison, School of Education, National Center on Effective Secondary Schools.

Morning, A. (2008). Ethnic classification in global perspective: A cross-national survey of the 2000 census round. *Population Research and Policy Review, 27,* 239–272.

Müller, W., & Karle, W. (1993). Social selection in educational systems in Europe. *European Sociological Review, 9,* 1–23.

Myers, D. E., Milne, A. M., Baker, K., & Ginsburg, A. (1987). Student discipline and high school performance. *Sociology of Education, 60,* 18–33.

Nachmias, C. (1977). The status attainment process: A test of a model in two stratification systems. *Sociological Quarterly, 18,* 589–607.

Naoi, A., & Fujita, H. (1978). Kyoiku tatsusei katei to sono chii keisei kouka [The process of educational achievement and its effects on the formation of status]. *Kyoiku Shakaigaku Kenkyu, 33,* 91–105.

Oakes, J. (1981). *Tracking policies and practices: School by school summaries: A study of schooling in the United States* (Tech. Rep. Series No. 25). Los Angeles: University of California at Los Angeles, Graduate School of Education. (ERIC Document Reproduction Service No. ED214893).

Oakes, J. (1982). Classroom social relationships: Exploring the Bowles and Gintis hypothesis. *Sociology of Education, 55,* 197–212.

Oakes, J. (1985). *Keeping track: How schools structure inequality.* New Haven, CT: Yale University Press.

Oakes, J. (1994a). More than misapplied technology: A normative and political response to Hallinan on tracking. *Sociology of Education, 67,* 84–89.

Oakes, J. (1994b). One more thought. *Sociology of Education, 67,* 91.

Office of Management and Budget. (1997). Revisions to the standards for the classification of federal data on race and ethnicity. *Federal Register, 62,* 58782–58790.

Ogbu, J. U. (1987). Variability in minority school performance: A problem in search of an explanation. *Anthropology and Education Quarterly, 18,* 312–334.

Omi, M., & Winant, H. (1994). *Racial formation in the United States: From the 1960s to the 1990s*. New York: Routledge.

Page, R. (1990). Games of chance: The lower-track curriculum in a college-preparatory high school. *Curriculum Inquiry, 20,* 249–281.

Pallas, A. M., Entwisle, D. R., Alexander, K. L., & Stluka, M. F. (1994). Ability-group effects: Instructional, social, or institutional? *Sociology of Education, 67,* 27–46.

Park, R. E. (1914). Racial assimilation in secondary groups with particular reference to the Negro. *American Journal of Sociology, 19,* 606–623.

Park, R. E. (1950). *Race and culture*. Glencoe, IL: Free Press. (Original work published 1926).

Parsons, T. (1963). On the concept of political power. *Proceedings of the American Philosophical Society, 107,* 232–262.

Pascarella, E. T., & Terenzini, P. T. (2005). *How college affects students: A third decade of research*. San Francisco: Jossey-Bass.

Perie, M., Moran, R., & Lutkus, A. D. (2005). *NAEP 2004 trends in academic progress: Three decades of student performance in reading and mathematics* (Rep. NCES 2005-464). Washington, DC: U.S. Department of Education.

Phillips, M., Crouse, J., & Ralph, J. (1998). Does the Black-White test score gap widen after children enter school? In Jencks, C., & Phillips, M. (Eds.), *The Black-White test score gap* (pp. 229–272). Washington, DC: Brookings Institution.

Poulantzas, N. (1973). *Political power and social class* (T. O'Hagan, Trans.). London: New Left Books.

Pray, L. A. (2004). Epigenetics: Genome, meet your environment. *Scientist*. Retrieved March 7, 2009, from https://notes.utk.edu/bio/greenberg.nsf/0/b360905554fdb7d985256ec5006 a7755?OpenDocument

Qian, Z. (1999). Who intermarries? Education, nativity, region, and interracial marriage, 1980 and 1990. *Journal of Comparative Family Studies, 30,* 579–597.

Raftery, A. E., & Hout, M. (1993). Maximally maintained inequality: Expansion, reform, and opportunity in Irish education, 1921–75. *Sociology of Education, 66,* 41–62.

Renzulli, J. S., & Park, S. (2000). Gifted dropouts: The who and the why. *Gifted Child Quarterly, 44,* 261–271.

Reschly, D. (1987). Assessing educational handicaps. In A. K. Hess & I. B. Weiner (Eds.), *The handbook of forensic psychology* (pp. 155–187). New York: Wiley.

Ridgeway, C., & Smith-Lovin, L. (1999). The gender system and interaction. *Annual Review of Sociology, 25,* 191–216.

Risman, B. (1998). *Gender vertigo: American families in transition*. New Haven, CT: Yale University Press.

Roemer, J. E. (1988). *Free to lose: An introduction to Marxist economic philosophy*. Cambridge, MA: Harvard University Press.

Rosenbaum, J. E. (1980). Track misperceptions and frustrated college plans: An analysis of the effects of tracks and track perceptions in the National Longitudinal Survey. *Sociology of Education, 53,* 74–88.

Rowley, C. K., Tollison, R. D., & Tullock, G. (1988). *The political economy of rent-seeking*. Boston: Kluwer Academic.

Rumberger, R. W., & Larson, K. A. (1998). Toward explaining differences in educational achievement among Mexican American language-minority students. *Sociology of Education, 71,* 68–92.

Rumberger, R. W., & Thomas, S. L. (2000). The distribution of dropout and turnover rates among urban and suburban high schools. *Sociology of Education, 73,* 39–67.

Russell, B. (1938). *Power: A new social analysis*. London: Allan and Unwin.

Saperstein, A. (2006). Double-checking the race box: Examining inconsistency between survey measures of observed and self-reported race. *Social Forces, 85,* 57–74.

Schmidt, F. L., & Hunter, J. E. (1999). Bias in standardized educational and employment tests as justification for racial preferences in affirmative action programs. *Research in Social Stratification and Mobility, 17,* 285–302.

Sewell, W. H., & Hauser, R. M. (1980). The Wisconsin longitudinal study of social and psychological factors in aspirations and achievement. *Research in Sociology of Education and Socialization, 1,* 59–99.

Shavit, Y., & Blossfeld, H.-P (1993). *Persistent inequality: Changing educational attainment in thirteen countries.* Boulder, CO: Westview.

Skiba, R. J., Michael, R. S., Nardo, A. C., & Peterson, R. L. (2002). The color of discipline: Sources of racial and gender disproportionality in school punishment. *Urban Review, 34,* 317–342.

Skrentny, J. D. (2002). *The minority rights revolution.* Cambridge, MA: Belknap Press of Harvard University Press.

Snyder, T. D., Dillow, S. A., & Hoffman, C. M. (2007). *Digest of education statistics, 2007* (NCES 2007017). Washington, DC: National Center for Education Statistics. Available from http://nces.ed.gov/pubsearch/pubsinfo.asp?pubid=2007017

Sørenson, A. (1970). Organizational differentiation of students and educational opportunity. *Sociology of Education, 43,* 355–376.

Sørenson, A. B. (2000). Toward a sounder basis for class analysis. *American Journal of Sociology, 105,* 1523–1558.

Spencer, S. J., Steele, C. M., & Quinn, D. M. (1999). Stereotype threat and women's math performance. *Journal of Experimental Social Psychology, 35,* 4–28.

Steele, C. M. (1997). A threat in the air: How stereotypes shape intellectual identity and performance. *American Psychologist, 52,* 613–629.

Steele, C. M., & Aronson, J. (1995). Stereotype threat and the intellectual test performance of African-Americans. *Journal of Personality and Social Psychology, 69,* 797–811.

Stevens, G., & Cho, J. H. (1985). Socioeconomic indexes and the new 1980 Census Occupational Classification Scheme. *Social Science Research, 14,* 142–168.

Stolzenberg, R. M. (1990). Ethnicity, geography, and occupational achievement of Hispanic men in the United States. *American Sociological Review, 55,* 143–154.

Stolzenberg, R. M. (1994). Educational continuation by college graduates. *American Journal of Sociology, 99,* 1042–1077.

Swanson, C. B. (2004). *Who graduates? Who doesn't? A statistical portrait of public high school graduation, class of 2001.* Washington, DC: Urban Institute. Retrieved June 9, 2009, from http://www.urban.org/UploadedPDF/410934_WhoGraduates.pdf

Taeuber, C., & Hansen, M. S. (1966). Self-enumeration as a census method. *Demography, 3,* 289–295.

Tolsma, J., Coenders, M., & Lubbers, M. (2007). Trends in educational inequalities in the Netherlands: A cohort design. *European Sociological Review, 23,* 325–339.

Tomes, N. (1981). The family, inheritance, and the intergenerational transmission of inequality. *Journal of Political Economy, 89,* 928–958.

Udry, R. (1994). The nature of gender. *Demography, 31,* 561–573.

Useem, E. (1992). Middle schools and math groups: Parents' involvement in children's placement. *Sociology of Education, 65,* 263–279.

Walkerdine, V. (1984). Some day my prince will come: Young girls and the preparation for adolescent sexuality. In A. McRobbie, & M. Nava (Eds.), *Gender and generation* (pp. 162–184). London: Macmillan Education.

Warren, J. R., & Lee, J. C. (2002). The impact of adolescent employment on high school dropout: Differences by individual and labor-market characteristics. *Social Science Research, 32,* 98–128.

Waters, M. C. (1990). *Ethnic options: Choosing identities in America.* Berkeley: University of California Press.

Weakliem, D., McQuillan, J., & Schauer, T. (1995). Toward meritocracy? Changing social-class differences in intellectual ability. *Sociology of Education, 68,* 271–286.

Weber, M. (1946). Class, status, party. In H. H. Gerth & C. W. Mills (Eds.), *From Max Weber: Essays in sociology* (pp. 180–195). New York: Oxford University Press.

Weber, M. (1956). The belief in common ethnicity. In G. Roth & C. Wittich (Eds.), *Max Weber: Economy and society* (pp. 387–393). Berkeley: University of California Press.

Weeden, K. A. (2002). Why do some occupations pay more than others? Social closure and earnings inequality in the United States. *American Journal of Sociology, 108,* 55–101.

Weeden, K. A., & Grusky, D. B. (2005). The case for a new class map. *American Journal of Sociology, 111,* 141–212.

Weis, L. (1997). Gender and the reports: The case of the missing piece. In C. Marshall (Ed.), *Feminist critical policy analysis I: A perspective from primary and secondary schooling* (pp. 73–90). London: Falmer.

Wheelock, A. (1992). *Crossing the tracks: How "untracking" can save America's schools.* New York: Norton.

White, M. J., & Kaufman, G. (1997). Language usage, social capital, and school completion among immigrants and native-born ethnic groups. *Social Science Quarterly, 78,* 385–398.

Williams, M. L. (1996, November 15). Racial diversity without racial preferences. *Chronicle of Higher Education,* p. A64.

Willis, P. E. (1977). *Learning to labour: How working class kids get working class jobs.* Farnborough, UK: Saxon House.

Wright, E. O. (1979). *Class structure and income determination.* New York: Academic Press.

Wright, E. O. (1985). *Classes.* London, UK: Verso.

Wright, E. O. (1994). *Interrogating inequality: Essays on class analysis, socialism, and Marxism.* London, UK: Verso.

Wright, E. O. (2000). Class, exploitation, and economic rents: Reflections on Sørensen's "sounder basis." *American Journal of Sociology, 105,* 1559–1571.

Wright, E. O., Costello, C., Hachen, D., & Sprague, J. (1982). The American class structure. *American Sociological Review, 47,* 709–726.

Wu, S.-C., Pink, W., Crain, R., & Moles, O. (1982). Student suspension: A critical reappraisal. *Urban Review, 14,* 245–303.

Young, M. (1994). *The rise of the meritocracy.* New Brunswick, NJ: Transaction Publishers. (Original work published 1958).

Yu, N., Chen, F.-C., Ota, S., Jorde, L. B., Pamilo, P., & Patthy, L. et al. (2002). Larger genetic differences within Africans than between Africans and Eurasians. *Genetics, 161,* 269–274.

Chapter 3

Education Rights and Classroom-Based Litigation: Shifting the Boundaries of Evidence

KEVIN WELNER

University of Colorado, Boulder

The majestic equality of the laws, which forbid rich and poor alike to sleep under bridges, to beg in the streets, and to steal their bread. . . .[1]

Anatole France, 1930

Inequality in American schools is multidimensional. Educational and social researchers have identified elements of children's lives taking place before, within, and after school with disheartening potential to intensify these inequalities. Within schools, harm is inflicted by unequal distributions of key resources, including teachers and buildings, as well as curricular and pedagogical approaches that are often ill suited for low-income students of color (Darling-Hammond, 2000; Delpit, 1996). Earlier in childhood, even before the onset of formal education, these children suffer from unequal distributions of resources, such as health care, nutrition, safe environment, preschool, and within-home learning resources (Barton & Coley, 2009; Berliner, 2009; Rothstein, 2004). All along, social capital—particularly family efficacy in the manipulation of the educational system to gain access to better resources—is unequally distributed for children (Fine, 1993; Lareau, 1989; Wells & Serna, 1996).

Even this short list illustrates that many key sources of inequality are not directly attributable to schools. Yet school policies can either amplify or minimize the inequalities that arise outside of school. Consider the epigraph from Anatole France and imagine a hypothetical policy that allocates a school's best teachers to only those students who are able to document the highest number of volumes in their parents' home libraries. Such a policy would tend to discriminate against students from less-wealthy families—even if such a policy could be described as facially neutral and nondiscriminatory.

Review of Research in Education
March 2010, Vol. 34, pp. 85-112
DOI: 10.3102/0091732X09349795
© 2010 AERA. http://rre.aera.net

Each such governmental decision about how to allocate educational resources has alarming potential to advantage some students at the expense of others. It is true that some of these policies may claim an inherent logic. Consider, for instance, school choice policies, which appeal to our sense of liberty—of wanting to give families as much freedom as possible (see Berkowitz, 2003). Unfortunately, empirical research documents that these policies, if unconstrained, tend to increase segregation by characteristics and factors such as race, family income, special education status, and students' test scores (Hsieh & Urquiola, 2003; Mickelson, Bottia, & Southworth, 2008; Saporito & Sohoni, 2006; Welner & Howe, 2005). At what point does the inherent logic—the acknowledged value of greater parental freedom, in the case of school choice—no longer justify the foreseeable and documented harm of a policy? By analogy, could the hypothetical policy assigning better teachers to students with larger home libraries be defended if its rationale were to encourage and reward the beneficial parental practice of having more books in the home?

Similarly, ability grouping (often called "tracking") can claim an inherent logic: efficiently meeting the diverse educational needs of a wide range of students. A heterogeneous student body must be provided with schooling appropriate to each individual's academic capacity as well as his or her future job (see discussion in Oakes, 2005). Yet as discussed in detail later in this chapter, the well-established effects of tracking are anathema to core goals of American schooling. Lower-tracked students, who are disproportionately low-income students of color, are provided with watered-down opportunities and suffer substantially diminished life chances (see later discussion; see also Heubert & Hauser, 1999; Oakes, 2005). This leads to a comparable question to the one asked earlier regarding school choice: At what point does the inherent logic—the common-sense appeal to meaningful and efficient sorting, in the case of tracking—no longer justify the foreseeable and documented harm of a policy?

This chapter explores that question, examining some fundamental policy issues through a legal lens. There are, it should be noted, substantial barriers standing in the way of the litigation explored in this article. As a legal matter, neither the empirical reality nor the foreseeability of inequality is likely to provide a sufficient foundation for a successful court challenge (*Washington v. Davis*, 1976). But it is to those policies—the ones that appear to be facially neutral but that in reality stratify students and opportunities—that we as researchers ascribe the lion's share of unequal educational opportunities. Whatever daunting obstacles face legal advocates for the educational rights of disadvantaged students, litigation cannot meaningfully succeed without attacking this problem—and broader success is unlikely to be found without litigation. Courts are given the constitutional role of protecting the rights of political minorities, and courts have at crucial moments in American history played that role with considerable effectiveness.

THE CLASSROOM AND COMPREHENSIVE LITIGATION

Potential plaintiffs in education rights litigation face the basic legal hurdle of bringing before the courts a comprehensive set of allegations. A court faced with only piecemeal allegations that narrowly frame a small part of systemic inequality is neither in a practical position to understand the systemic issues nor in a legal position to remedy them. With regard to the systemic nature of issue framing, consider the *Brown v. Board of Education* (1954) Court's declaration that "separate educational facilities are inherently unequal" (p. 495). The statement implicitly raises the question of what is an educational facility. In that case, the unit of analysis was the school; a separate school is inherently unequal. Also, on the basis of the Court's logic, it would be difficult to argue that larger units, such as school districts, could be equal if they were racially segregated. Segregated school districts and schools have the direct effect of ensuring that students are educated separately.

But in the United States, the primary unit of instruction is not the district or the school—it is the classroom (see discussion in Ladwig [2010], chap. 4 of this volume). Integrated schools that are nonetheless segregated at the classroom level educate students separately just as surely and harmfully as do segregated schools. As Gary Orfield has noted, "The benefits of school desegregation are not known to penetrate concrete walls" (quoted in Heubert, 1999, p. 17). We know empirically that this describes a real problem in the United States. In racially diverse schools, tracked classrooms do tend to be racially segregated, and these separate educational facilities (classrooms) do tend to be unequal (Welner, 2001b; see also the discussion of tracking later in this chapter). This presents a textbook case of inequity: When White students are educated in high-track, well-resourced classes, they are given disproportionate benefits—higher expectations and greater educational opportunities—as compared to students of color in low-track classes. In fact, such tracking results in an inequitable distribution of opportunities notwithstanding race; as discussed later in this chapter, there is arguably no rational basis for enrolling *any* group of studies in a track that provides watered-down, less-engaging instruction and curriculum. (These inequities are discussed as "opportunity-to-learn" issues later in this chapter.)

Classroom-level obstacles to learning are inextricably linked to barriers at higher levels of the educational system, and this has implications in the legal arena. Past legal challenges to inequitable educational opportunities have usually—but, as discussed later, not always—focused on the school or the school district as the primary unit of analysis. These challenges and the policy reforms that they engendered thus left open escape routes at subordinate levels of the educational system, allowing inequities to elude court interventions. For instance, a finance reform addressing between-district inequities leaves open the possibility of intradistrict (between-school) inequities. And reforms at the district and school levels often leave open the possibility of inequities at the classroom level.

Responding to the existence and nature of these escape routes, this chapter contends that those contemplating education rights litigation should consider a foundational focus on the classroom. That is, analyses should begin at the classroom level and then move up as appropriate to the school level, the district level, and the state level. By making the classroom the primary unit of analysis within a multilevel framework, advocates are better able to bring before courts a systemic portrait of educational inequities. Actual educational opportunities can be more directly matched to actual educational needs. It is in the classroom where accumulated inequalities are most clearly evident and often most in need of remediation. Understanding and addressing those needs will usually implicate needed reforms at higher levels, but those higher-level reforms will be informed by, and responsive to, needs in the classroom.

To illustrate this broad contention, this chapter considers legal challenges to ability grouping in the context of state laws mandating high school exit exams. These exit exam policies require all students, notwithstanding the opportunities given them or denied them throughout schooling, to demonstrate that they have cleared a given threshold of learning. As such, they frame an equity issue that is, as a matter of policy and of law, focused on classroom learning opportunities. The racially identifiable tracking noted earlier points to one such equity issue, but legal and equity implications arguably attach even if the tracking is taking place in an already-segregated school with an all-White, all-Black, or all-Latino student body. That is, this chapter explores—in the context of exit exams that hold all students to the same learning standard—the legal bases for challenging a practice that targets inferior educational opportunities to a subsection of the student body. In doing so, the chapter draws on legal constructs of equity and adequacy developed primarily through school finance litigation. Most broadly, the chapter describes the need for education rights litigation to be comprehensive and systemic, and it contends that doing so requires attention to classroom-level inequality.

UNITS OF ANALYSIS

As noted, past legal challenges to inequitable educational opportunities have usually focused on the school or the school district as the primary unit of analysis. Oftentimes, however, the named defendant is one level up from the unit of analysis—the level of comparative inequity. For instance, the Topeka, Kansas, school district was the defendant in *Brown v. Board of Education* (1954), but each individual school—school-level segregation—was the unit of analysis. Similarly, the unit of analysis in school finance litigation, which generally names state-level defendants, has often been at the school district level, challenging the defendant state's policies for allocating resources among those districts.

The appropriate unit of analysis for a given lawsuit depends on the policy domain. If quality teaching is the policy domain, then classroom-based (or student-based) litigation is most appropriate, even though the suit would likely implicate school- and district-level allocation policies as well. If quality principals or facilities are the domain, then the school is clearly the unit of analysis. If equal and adequate operational funding is the domain, then the school is the likely unit of analysis. If extracurricular opportunities, school overcrowding, or transportation resources are the domain, the school and district again appear to be the most appropriate units of analysis.

Yet even in the domains where the school or district ultimately becomes the primary focus, insights about equity can often be gained by starting with a close look at the classroom level. Starting with the finer grain and then backing up and considering other levels of the educational hierarchy can aid in constructing a coherent, systemic, multilevel analysis.

These litigation decisions are generally linked to important areas of research. For instance, the initial wave of challenges to property tax–based school finance systems was prompted by research from John Coons and his colleagues and from Art Wise, among others (Coons, Clune, & Sugarman, 1970; Wise, 1968). Present-day research could do the same. For instance, Marguerite Roza and Paul Hill have presented scholarly analyses of school district budgeting practice that appear to disadvantage certain schools (Roza & Hill, 2004). These authors describe how, in the four districts they studied, budgeting practices assign to each school the average teacher cost (salary plus benefits), which hides substantial inequalities between schools. High-poverty and low-performing schools have lower teacher salaries, effectively meaning that they have less experienced teachers. Accordingly, students in these disadvantaged schools are effectively subsidizing students in more advantaged schools, because the districts could not otherwise afford to pay those teachers in these advantaged schools more (unless it shifted salary costs away from the less advantaged schools). Roza and Hill (2004) also note that job openings in these more advantaged schools tend to elicit many more applicants, giving the principal a larger talent pool to choose from. Finally, they point out that this salary averaging changes the allocations of Title I funds, minimizing the assistance provided to the neediest schools.[2]

Litigators may use such research as a basis for school-level finance litigation (see *Rodriguez v. Los Angeles Unified School District*, described in Roos, 1998, for an example of such litigation). More generally, research can point to the most appropriate domain on which litigation should focus. In that regard, it is worth emphasizing that this chapter does not advocate a classroom focus on all education rights litigation; a complaint that is truly systemic might most appropriately involve issues far removed from the classroom. What this chapter does contend is that key policy domains—such as ability grouping and teacher quality—do exist at the level of the classroom. Furthermore, this chapter contends that the classroom should often be the foundational unit of analysis—that is, the finest grain of analysis—even when litigation ultimately focuses on a policy domain at a level of the educational hierarchy above the classroom.

EXIT EXAM POLICIES

High-stakes accountability policies provide a legal hook on which to hang systemic allegations describing accumulated inequalities. Although it is true that when a student receives an inferior set of educational opportunities, he or she is disadvantaged in many facets of life (including higher education, employment, and civic participation), these disadvantages often have only minimal legal salience because they are insufficiently direct and concrete. More direct and concrete are the laws conditioning receipt of a high school diploma on passing an exit exam—laws that exist in half of all states in the United States.[3]

On the surface, these exams equally affect all students in a given state. But this facial neutrality of exit exam statutes again brings us back to Anatole France: Any practical meaning of neutrality evaporates given the systemic and accumulated inequalities in U.S. schools. Policies and practices in schools are terribly effective at identifying students who are most disadvantaged and then adding to that disadvantage through the discriminatory allocation of educational opportunities. This statement may seem harsh and unfair; after all, Title I and other compensatory programs demonstrate a societal interest in helping disadvantaged children. But consider the empirical effects of policies such as tracking, unregulated school choice, teacher distribution (between schools and between classrooms), and access to high-quality facilities and materials. In each case, otherwise advantaged children tend to gain the additional advantage of richer opportunities in their formal schooling.

Placing an exit exam at the end of this process adds insult (and injury) to injury. For any given state, it might be true that the exit exam is set at a basic level, and it might also be true that the exam tests only knowledge, ideas, and skills that every high school graduate should know and be able to do. At this measurement level, exit exams merely evidence the larger problem of unequal schooling opportunities. But at the applied level, the exams exact a callous punishment on many students who have already been victimized in fundamental ways throughout their schooling. The patent nature of an exit exam administered in the context of stark inequality is that it punishes the victim for not knowing what their schools have never taught them (or about which their schools provided only watered-down opportunities to learn)—and low-socioeconomic-status (SES) students rely on schools for academic knowledge and skills far more than do high-SES students.

INEQUITABLE RESPONSES TO INEQUALITY

Test passage rates should be understood in terms of probabilities across a population distribution. For any given population subgroup (e.g., White students, Latino students, or students from low-wealth families), student exit exam scores will generally fall into an approximately normal distribution. The so-called test score gap between different groups shows up as shifts in these distributions, with the curves for White and wealthier populations shifted toward higher scores. The distribution of White students includes some very low-scoring students, but it also includes a relatively large number of high-scoring students (compared to the overall population). Correspondingly, the distribution of Latino students includes some very high-scoring students, but it also includes a relatively large number of low-scoring students (compared to the overall population).

With this in mind, consider the educational pathways awaiting two hypothetical groups of 100 four-year-old children. Group A children have wealthy parents with high educational levels; Group B children have low-wealth parents with little or no college education. These two groups of children will probably arrive at school with disparate average levels of academic preparation (and other important factors, such as health care and nutrition; see Berliner, 2009; Karoly, 2009). If a state administers age-appropriate exams at this point, the Group B children would be more likely to fail the exam.

Faced with this reality, schools could recognize and respond to the initial differences, channeling additional resources to these needier students, such as is done by some compensatory programs. This intervention could shift the Group B distribution toward equality with the Group A distribution. Or schools could zealously work to ensure that all children are given equal opportunities, no matter how prepared they are when entering school. This policy might narrow the gap between the two groups, or it might result in a fairly steady gap. But the majority of American schools have effectively chosen a third approach: Using mechanisms that are often based—implicitly or explicitly—on meritocracy and choice, they generally respond to initial differences with policies (albeit overload on compensatory programs) that channel additional resources to the most advantaged students. In common terminology, the first choice is an example of "vertical equity," and the second choice evidences "horizontal equity" (Koski & Reich, 2007). The third choice can be considered only inequity.

"EQUAL OPPORTUNITY TO HAVE AN ADEQUATE EDUCATION"

One could reasonably expect that after 13 years of schooling within such a system, the Group B children would be even more likely to fail an exit exam. Researchers, lawyers, and others can straightforwardly denounce this system as unfair, but does it violate any statutes or constitutional provisions? The Kentucky Supreme Court's seminal decision in *Rose v. Council for Better Education* (1989) includes the following passage:

> The system of common schools must be substantially uniform throughout the state. Each child, every child, in this Commonwealth must be provided with an equal opportunity to have an adequate education. Equality is the key word here. The children of the poor and the children of the rich, the children who live in the poor districts and the children who live in the rich districts must be given the same opportunity and access to an adequate education. (p. 211)

An "equal opportunity to have an adequate education" is not the same thing as equal access to all educational opportunities. It bases legal protection on a simple threshold of adequacy and is thus a watered-down version of the vertical or horizontal equity policies described earlier. Imagine a state that defines an adequate science education merely as "every child must know that there are more than four elements." This standard would have no bearing on the education of the vast majority of high school students, who have moved far beyond the earth, fire, air, water categorization of the ancient Greeks. Therefore, schools in the state would be largely free to distribute the best science education opportunities to the most advanced students without fear that more unprepared students would receive an "inadequate" science education. Although the particulars of this hypothetical are farfetched, consider the 2002 decision of the appellate division in New York's adequacy case,[4] which held that eighth- or ninth-grade-level skills would prepare students for menial employment and to read basic information in a newspaper—a level of education that the court deemed sufficient to meet the state constitution's requirements (*Campaign for Fiscal Equity, Inc. v. State*, 2002). This general idea of sufficiency or adequacy set at a relatively low level is part of the American mind-set. In fact, the Texas federal court in *GI Forum v. Texas Education Agency* (2000) upheld that state's accountability system using essentially this same reasoning (see also *Board of Education v. Walter*, 1979).

These examples also point to the need for a brief digression because they illustrate reasonable concerns about a "race to the bottom" that might ensue if standards and accountability laws are given teeth as applied to the responsibilities and obligations of states. In response to pressures associated with failure to meet NCLB targets, states have apparently opted for low standards of proficiency (Bandeira de Mello, Blankenship, & McLaughlin, 2009). Similarly, policymakers might lower standards and lower cut scores if fiscal repercussions for taxpayers are attached to student failure. Such buyers' remorse seems likely if states are asked to pay the bill for the extensive resources that would be needed to help all students demonstrate learning at high levels (see Silberman, 2000). The possibility of this type of litigation leading to weakened standards and tests and to narrowed curriculum—schools focusing instruction on only material included in the exit exam—is explored elsewhere (see Koski & Reich, 2007; Liu, 2006a); their absence here should not be understood as minimizing their importance.[5]

Returning to the court's language in *Rose v. Council for Better Education*, if that opinion were issued in a state with a rigorous high school exit exam (Kentucky does not administer an exit exam), the wording might change from "every child . . . must be provided with an equal opportunity to have an adequate education" to "every child must be provided with an equal opportunity to pass the exit exam." Consider again the 100 children in Groups A and B, each with an approximately normal distribution. Providing lesser opportunities to the children in Group B through tracking or other mechanisms denies them an equal opportunity to pass the exam. If the threshold (the exit exam cut score) is placed anywhere within the range from basic to advanced, the straightforward result of a set of practices that provides uniformly lesser opportunities to students in Group B is more children in that group being denied a high school diploma (see Figure 1).

This example also highlights the hybrid nature of the *Rose v. Council for Better Education* court's rule. It combines notions of both equity and adequacy—an idea returned to later in this chapter.

OPPORTUNITY TO LEARN

Back in the late 1980s, advocates of equal educational opportunity developed the concept of "opportunity to learn" (OTL). OTL focused on resources—on inputs. Students provided with OTL would have access to high-level schooling opportunities, allowing them to meet performance and content standards and providing them with good career opportunities (Oakes, 1989; see also Darling-Hammond, 1994; Stevens & Grymes, 1993). One of the natural corollaries to this argument was that students should not be held to high performance standards unless their schools have met equally high OTL standards. Or, offering another variant on the *Rose v. Council*

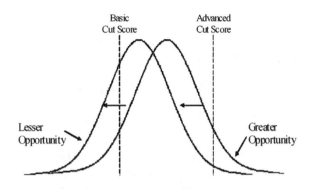

FIGURE 1   Educational and Test-Passing Opportunities

for Better Education (1989) court's wording, every child must be provided with an equal opportunity to have a rich set of opportunities to learn.

But the focus on inputs—the OTL approach—never gained enough favor among political leaders, who opted instead to put their faith in the idea that the process of measuring outcomes and holding schools accountable for meeting certain outcome objectives will itself drive improved practices. (For a recent illustration of this mindset, see *Horne v. Flores*, 2009.) Instead of providing better resources, the outcome approach was intended to drive better use of existing resources. These standards-accountability reforms, ultimately epitomized by the No Child Left Behind Act (NCLB, 2002), rely on content and performance standards plus high-stakes testing. In theory, such standards and tests (aligned with inputs such as teacher preparation and textbooks) will drive the educational establishment to ensure a quality education for every child (Smith & O'Day, 1991). In practice, schools have indeed mustered available resources toward the goal of reporting higher test scores, and sometimes this entails enhanced student learning, but many children are nonetheless falling through the cracks.[6]

For those who still perceive wisdom in the old OTL framework, there may be a silver lining to the high-stakes-assessment cloud. Although policymakers chose outcome standards in lieu of OTL standards, courts may insist on linking the two. In the context of so-called adequacy litigation, this means that courts may turn to state standards and accountability laws as strong evidence of what a given legislature has determined to be necessary to comply with the education clause in that state's constitution (Koski, 2001; Rebell, 2005; see also Rebell & Wolff, 2008). Although this approach may hold promise, the approach I am taking here is, as explained later, more focused on equity than on adequacy and more focused on due process and equal protection concerns than on education clauses.

The analyses that follow speak generally of "opportunity to learn," "resources," and "inputs." But unpacking these OTL ideas yields specific, concrete factors, such as credentialed, experienced teachers; safe environments and well-maintained buildings;

adequate heating and air conditioning; relatively small school and class size; challenging and engaging coursework with high expectations; available and current textbooks; and computer and Internet access. In educational facilities with high OTL, a court is not likely to find a legal impediment to the denial of diplomas to students failing to achieve above a threshold on a high-stakes test. However, in schools or classrooms with low OTL, basic fairness and equality issues may prompt court intervention.

Challenges Based on High-Stakes Testing

Past challenges to high-stakes testing have usually arisen in the context of high school graduation and have sought the remedy of a diploma being awarded (see *Debra P. v. Turlington*, 1981; *GI Forum v. Texas Education Agency*, 2000). Plaintiffs in these cases challenged the "fundamental fairness" of exit exams when the underlying schooling provided insufficient preparation for the assessment. The Supreme Court has held that the 14th Amendment prohibits the government from depriving a person of life, liberty, or property without procedural protections, such as the right to a hearing (*Cleveland Board of Education v. Loudermill*, 1985); the government also cannot take away these things without appropriate justification, protecting "substantive" due process regardless of any procedural protections (*Griswold v. Connecticut*, 1965). The notion of fundamental fairness in the application of exit exams focuses on the "property" interest in a diploma and bridges the gap between procedural and substantive due process, although courts veer toward characterizing it as procedural (*Brookhart v. Illinois*, 1983, p. 186; *Debra P. v. Turlington*, 1981, p. 404).

In contrast to these earlier cases, future exit exam challenges might contend that a plaintiff's inferior schooling itself gives rise to the legal wrong. Most likely such plaintiffs (the plaintiff class) would be young students looking perspectively at the set of structures and opportunities awaiting them in school district, seeking injunctive relief. Instead of twelfth graders focusing on the immediate deprivation (the diploma denial), these younger students' legal attacks might challenge the state's impending failure to fulfill its duty to provide each student with a fair opportunity to learn the material covered by the high-stakes exam. As explained below, such an action would likely continue to build on fundamental fairness and due process arguments but would be primarily grounded in the equal protection clause.

These shifts in focus have the potential to accomplish four goals: (a) putting the judge in the position of enforcing, rather than overturning, the state's exit exam policy;[7] (b) suggesting the remedy of increased educational resources for students (i.e., OTL); (c) allowing for claims either grounded in racial discrimination or independent of the students' race; and (d) allowing for a broad framing of the complaint, encompassing allegations of governmental actions and inactions that systemically combine to deny educational opportunities, including those focused at the classroom level (see Koski, 2001; Rebell, 2005; Welner, 2001c). Such lawsuits would concede each state's authority to adopt learning standards and to make diplomas contingent on certain learning as demonstrated by a given assessment. But the plaintiffs would argue that the state must implement its policy decision in a fair manner.

Several courts have already taken note of state-adopted standards, using them as indicators of adequacy from the perspective of the legislature (see Superfine, 2008, pp. 131–162; see also *Campaign for Fiscal Equity v. State*, 2003 [New York]; *Columbia Falls Elementary School District No. 6 v. State*, 2005 [Montana]; *Leandro v. State*, 1997 [North Carolina]; *Montoy v. State*, 2005 [Kansas]). Legislatively adopted standards can provide only guidance—not a definitive understanding—regarding constitutional adequacy, given that a state's courts must take ultimate responsibility for interpreting constitutional protections. But these courts have welcomed the guidance.

Alternatively, an action might focus on express statutory provisions regarding standards and accountability, which offer explicit or implicit determinations of schools' obligations to prepare students for the state tests. This latter type of lawsuit would allege that the state is in violation of its own standards-based reform legislation (see Koski, 2001). Koski (2001) also discusses the possibility of equal protection actions, which he argues could be grounded in any of the following three arguments:

1. the failure to apply the same high content and performance standards to schools in poor or minority communities as those applied in middle-class communities;
2. the failure to hold accountable schools in poor or minority communities for the same performance standards as schools in middle-class communities; and
3. the failure to provide to students in poor or minority communities the same standards-driven educational inputs, such as curricula linked to the standards, as are provided in middle-class communities. (Koski, 2001, p. 311)

As described in the following section, Koski's (2001) third argument is akin to the approach set forth herein.

Leveraging Outcome Standards

In the past, education rights litigation has heavily relied on the U.S. Constitution's equal protection clause (14th Amendment) as well as on Title VI of the 1964 Civil Rights Act and its implementing regulations (see Welner & Oakes, 1996). These authorities have provided the legal foundation for a great deal of progress, but they also tend to encounter difficult evidentiary barriers, including the requirement that plaintiffs prove intentional discrimination (Welner, 2001a; Welner & Oakes, 1996). Education clauses and equal protection clauses in state constitutions have accordingly become increasingly important, particularly in driving greater equity in school finance structures.

State outcome standards can now be added to this mix of key legal authorities. Simply put, a state that sets forth standards attached to accountability mechanisms should be held responsible for providing corresponding learning opportunities. Although this contention is strongest as regards exit exams, a standards-based challenge might also be based on end-of-course exams or the threat of retention in grade.[8] Keeping in mind that the remedy contemplated here is educational opportunity (rather than course passage or grade promotion), the theory underlying any such action is simply that the state has an obligation—grounded in due process, equal protection, and education clauses and possibly also in the accountability statutes themselves[9]—to provide equitable learning opportunities that correspond to standards for which students are held accountable.

These opportunities can be considered at the level of the school, as reflected in much past litigation, or at the level of the classroom. In fact, arguments focused on school-level equity are logically extended to require similar quality at every level within an academic tracking structure. Inequalities attributable to classroom stratification within a larger (presumably adequate) system are just as unfair and inadequate as are inequalities branching out at other levels of the educational hierarchy (Welner, 2001c).

TRACKING LITIGATION: PAST AND FUTURE

Given the context of state and federal accountability regimes, what possible justification—or, using the wording of our courts, what possible "rational basis"—might exist for providing watered-down opportunities to some students when those students are ultimately held to the same standards as their colleagues who get the richer curriculum and instruction? The basic cause of action explored in this chapter implicates the equal protection clause of the 14th amendment and is suggested by the preceding question.

Research on Tracking

Research on tracking has, for decades, conclusively established several findings. Student enrollment differences are associated with race, family income, and parent education level (Hallinan, 1992; Lucas, 1999; Oakes, Ormseth, Bell, & Camp, 1990; Vanfossen, Jones, & Spade, 1987). Children are more likely to be enrolled in lower-track classes if their parents have less formal education and are lower income, and they are also more likely to be enrolled in these classes if they are Latino or African American (Heubert & Hauser, 1999; Oakes, 2005). These enrollment patterns have direct educational consequences, linked to observed differences between high- and low-track classrooms. The curriculum and instruction in higher-track classes tend to be more rigorous; lower-track classes use more worksheets and focus more on rudimentary skills, whereas higher-track classes use more constructivist, project-based approaches focused on developing critical thinking skills (Oakes, 2005). Teachers themselves are similarly "tracked," with lower-track classes more often staffed by emergency-credentialed teachers, long-term substitutes, and generally, teachers who are less accomplished and experienced (Darling-Hammond, 1987; Oakes, 2005; Oakes et al., 1990).

Recent tracking research has now demonstrated certain outcomes that follow from these differences between high- and low-track classes. When students are placed in lower-track classes, their subsequent achievement tends to decrease (Gamoran & Mare,

1. Learning opportunities in lower-track classes are almost always inferior in terms of resources, curriculum, expectations, and instruction;
2. A school's decision to enroll a student in a lower-track class will likely provide that student with an inferior education;
3. No defensible educational purpose generally exists for a school to provide some students with an inferior education;
4. A decision by a state, district, or school to attach negative consequences (such as diploma denial) to a student's failure to learn adds a direct punishment to this inferior education, thus increasing the indefensibility of the decision to enroll students in classes with lesser opportunities to learn;
5. Course placement in a low-track class is equally indefensible whether made by school recommendation or by student choice, since the school's job is to challenge each student academically even if that student volunteers for a lesser education or if that student performed poorly in earlier classes or on earlier tests; and
6. None of the above contentions are minimized by equity at other levels of the schooling system; a perfectly equitable system can break down at the level of classroom tracking.

FIGURE 2   A Rationale for Finding No Rational Basis for Low-Track Classes

1989; Heubert & Hauser, 1999; Oakes et al., 1990; Welner, 2001b). Correspondingly, positive effects on student achievement have been associated with reforming the tracking system and universally accelerating all students in rigorous classes (Boaler & Staples, 2006; Burris, Heubert, & Levin, 2006; Burris & Welner, 2005; Levin, 1997). This is consistent with a great deal of educational research showing a strong association between student achievement and learning opportunities (Adelman, 2006; American Educational Research Association, 2004; Singham, 2003). Joining other authoritative voices, a recent report from the National Research Council and the Institute of Medicine (2004) has recommended "that both formal and informal tracking by ability be eliminated. Alternative strategies should be used to ensure appropriately challenging instruction for students who vary widely in their skill levels" (p. 219; see also Burris & Garrity, 2008). Although not a panacea, a high-track classroom environment—one with skilled, supported teachers and challenged, supported, and engaged students—is more likely to result in student success on exit exams and other outcome measures.

Rationale for Exit Exam Legal Challenge

Building on this research, the six-point argument set forth in Figure 2—which is grounded in both equity and adequacy frameworks—asks the fundamental question, *Even if some threshold of adequacy is met, what is the rationale for providing some students with lesser educational opportunities?*

Near the heart of this legal argument about exit exams and tracking lies a determination of the extent of a given state's voluntarily assumed affirmative duty (see *DeShaney v. Winnebago County Department of Social Services*, 1989). This is illustrated by the reasoning of the federal court in *Debra P. v. Turlington* (1981), which stressed that the state of Florida, when it opted to implement an exit exam, took on an obligation to teach the material that would be tested: "The test was probably a good test of what the students should know but not necessarily of what they had an opportunity to learn" (p. 405, n. 11). When a state adopts an exit exam policy, it assumes an affirmative duty to provide each student with an opportunity to learn the tested content.

Moreover, this duty may be heightened in cases, such as *Debra P. v. Turlington*, that allege inequalities strongly correlated with students' race. This is reflected in the approach taken by the plaintiffs in California's *Williams v. State of California* (2000) case, which was primarily grounded in the state constitution's equal protection and education clauses and which cited racial disparities in asserting the state's obligation to intervene and address OTL problems in schools throughout the state. The *Williams v. State of California* case was also based on the scholarship of University of California, Los Angeles, law professor Gary Blasi, who had argued that accountability should be understood in a broader sense than is typical in standards-based accountability regimes (Blasi, 2002). Among other things, he advocated for "universal accountability:"[10]

Once one reframes accountability in terms of the delivery of the tools for learning to individual classrooms and the responsibility for insuring their delivery, it becomes even more obvious that the exclusive focus on teachers and principals [in many accountability laws] is misguided. With each role in the vast bureaucracies and organizations that deliver public education, from the school custodian to the Governor and Superintendent of Public Instruction, there are only two possibilities: either the person in that role is accountable in some way for the delivery of one or more significant inputs to education, or that role should be abolished and its funding transferred elsewhere. (Blasi, 2002, p. 76)

This broader, universal notion of accountability imposes on higher levels of the bureaucracy a responsibility for providing or ensuring OTL.[11]

Yet opportunities guaranteed by the state are best measured on relative scales as well as absolute scales—that is, as both equity and adequacy. Due process litigation generally focuses on clearing a threshold, asking questions such as whether the student has been taught what is being tested. But this should be only the first inquiry. The next question should concern equality of opportunities. Consider a student in School X who has had 2 days of exposure to the Pythagorean theorem, sharing a textbook with two other students, taught by an inexperienced, emergency-credentialed teacher in an overheated, overcrowded classroom. This student has been taught the material, but his or her OTL was negligible compared to the student in School Y who has all the advantages denied the first student. To the extent that these inequalities are attributable to governmental policies, they should be subject to legal challenge—of denial of "an equal opportunity to have an adequate education" (*Rose v. Council for Better Education*, 1989).

Overcoming the Limited Success of Past Tracking Litigation

To some extent, legal challenges to tracking, such as those described here, have been tried in the past, with a mixed record of success (see Welner & Oakes, 1996). Equal protection challenges to tracking, if they are to be reviewed with so-called heightened judicial scrutiny, require showing either that school officials are engaged in intentional discrimination on the basis of race (or another protected classification) or that racially disparate tracking is the present result of past intentional discrimination (*McNeal v. Tate County School District*, 1975). Otherwise, the standard applied will likely be merely "rational basis" scrutiny, pursuant to which the policy will be found constitutional as long as it is a reasonable (or "rational") way to achieve a legitimate goal.

The rationale set forth earlier, in Figure 2, presents the argument that tracking policies fail to meet even this lesser, rational-basis standard of review. As a policy argument, it holds up well; but as a legal argument, it faces considerable obstacles. After all, courts generally defer to the discretionary judgment of educators and policymakers. Moreover, the litigation approach set forth in this chapter suggests a remedial order that would effectively require an influx of resources—something else that courts hesitate to include in their orders.

In a nutshell, past challenges to tracking have come up against a powerful three-part argument: (a) Tracking is a widespread practice, evidencing its acceptance by the public, educators, and policymakers; (b) the plaintiffs (in any given case) have failed to show that the racial imbalances in tracking are the result of intentional discrimination; and (c) courts are ill equipped to question the judgment of local educators and policymakers (see Welner & Oakes, 1996, and cases cited therein). Here, for instance, is language from an influential 1981 federal court of appeals decision:

The merits of a program which places students in classrooms with others perceived to have similar abilities are hotly debated by educators; nevertheless, it is educators, rather than courts, who are in a better position ultimately to resolve the question whether such a practice is, on the whole, more beneficial than detrimental to the students involved. Thus, as a general rule, school systems are free to employ ability grouping, even when such a policy has a segregative effect, so long, of course, as such a practice is genuinely motivated by educational concerns and not discriminatory motives. (*Castañeda v. Pickard*, 1981, pp. 996–997)

Sixteen years later, similar reasoning was used by another federal appellate court:

Tracking is a controversial educational policy [and] lawyers and judges are not competent to resolve the controversy. The conceit that they are belongs to a myth of the legal profession's omnicompetence that was exploded long ago. To abolish tracking is to say to bright kids, whether white or black, that they have to go at a slower pace than they're capable of; it is to say to the parents of the brighter kids that their children don't really belong in the public school system; and it is to say to the slower kids, of whatever race, that they may have difficulty keeping up, because the brighter kids may force the pace of the class. The vast majority of public school students in the United States are tested, ranked, and segregated into separate ability groups and classes based on standardized test performance. This may be deplorable, . . . but as the consensus of the nation's educational authorities, it deserves some consideration by a federal court. (*People Who Care v. Rockford Board of Education School District*, 1997, p. 536; internal citations omitted)

These cases outline the rational-basis argument that would likely be successfully asserted to defend a tracking system in the absence of an exit exam. The *People*

Who Care v. Rockford Board of Education School District opinion is an extreme case of inappropriate appellate fact finding (see Welner, 2001b, for a full critique). But it does reflect some familiar judicial thinking in tracking litigation and therefore illustrates the sort of roadblocks that may face the type of litigation outlined in this chapter. Tracking, district officials might explain, furthers the interests of student choice and systemic efficiency. Students who envision a life and career without college, for instance, should be entitled to choose non-college-preparatory courses. And schools should be given the discretion to separate students into different tracks on the basis of such plans and aptitude.

But this argument largely falls apart when all students face the same exit exam. Although only a subgroup of students might be seen to benefit from preparation for college, all students benefit from a high school diploma (Murnane, Willett, & Tyler, 2000). Even a tracking system based solely on student choice is suspect, given the lack of a clear, rational basis for facilitating students' choices for a less challenging set of courses that will increase the likelihood of their not receiving diplomas. The fundamental-fairness arguments underlying the due process concerns of *Debra P. v. Turlington* (1981) thus highlight the irrationality of providing stratified opportunities, with school officials essentially placing their thumbs on the exit exam scale, decreasing the likelihood that those in lower tracks will ever receive their diplomas.[12]

That said, rational-basis challenges in court only rarely succeed. The most frequently applied standard of rational-basis review allows a classification (such as the distinction between low- and high-track students) to withstand a challenge "if there is any reasonably conceivable state of facts that could provide a rational basis for the classification" (*FCC v. Beach Communications*, 1993, p. 313; see also *Heller v. Doe*, 1993). But a more rigorous rational-basis review has also been applied in some cases involving discrimination against commonly oppressed groups, such as undocumented children, persons with mental disabilities, and most prominently, the gay and lesbian community (*Lawrence v. Texas*, 2003, p. 580, O'Connor, J., concurring; see also *City of Cleburne v. Cleburne Living Center, Inc.*, 1985; *Plyler v. Doe*, 1982; *Romer v. Evans*, 1996). This more rigorous review more closely examines the law's actual effects. The litigation contemplated here, challenging a tracking system in an exit exam state, might prompt this more thorough form of rational-basis scrutiny given the due process concerns, the importance of education (see *Plyler v. Doe*, 1982), and the disadvantages correlated to race and class.

In an exit exam system, the best theoretical rationale for tracking is that it does in fact help teachers remediate struggling students. Pursuant to this reasoning, separate, low-track classrooms allow schools to concentrate increased resources and the most useful curriculum and instruction at these students, catching them up to their more advanced peers (Hallinan, 1994). Were there any significant research support for this strategy, it would certainly constitute a rational basis for the policy. But the research is very strong in pointing to the opposite effect: Students in lower-tracked classes regularly fall further behind (see Oakes, 2005).

Put in terms of the rationale presented earlier (in Figure 2), this new type of action is set apart from the earlier tracking cases by the fourth step: the direct consequences introduced by exit exams. In legal terms, these exams introduce due process issues of fundamental fairness (*Debra P. v. Turlington*, 1981). Widespread practices are no longer acceptable if they are harmful when combined with a new practice. This message, along with the well-developed social science research base concerning tracking and detracking—which directly contradicts key factual conclusions set forth in the earlier-quoted 1981 and 1997 opinions[13]—can help frame the litigation in ways that more urgently and indisputably point to the need to question the discretion of local educational policymakers to merely assert rational-basis contentions about choice and efficiency. Ultimately, of course, the success of this (and other) education rights litigation will depend on the values embraced by judges. But as described in the following section of this chapter, the systemic, classroom-based approach outlined here changes the potential value of such success, giving judges the tools and information they would need to craft a meaningful remedy.

CRAFTING SYSTEMIC ACTIONS

As noted, individuals who are denied a diploma pursuant to a high-stakes testing system can—under certain circumstances—seek the granting of the diploma as a direct remedy for that harm. However, such a remedial approach focuses on only the most superficial symptoms of what are often serious, endemic problems. If substantial numbers of students are being denied diplomas after 13 or more years of schooling, this is an indication of systemic flaws. If these failures are strongly correlated with race, class, gender, language minority, or special education status, the need to identify and correct those systemic flaws becomes crucial for those interested in equity. As explained in this section, systemic legal challenges can play a critical role in bringing about these more comprehensive remedies.

The diploma denial systems that will, by 2012, exist in more than half of all U.S. states and cover 74% of all students are built on an interesting series of beliefs and assumptions. Most directly and defensibly, the system affirms a belief among policymakers that the granting of a diploma should be a meaningful, affirmative confirmation of a state determination that the student has achieved at a certain threshold level (Chudowsky, Kober, Gayler, & Hamilton, 2002). In addition, many policymakers believe that the accountability system will prompt higher levels of achievement among students, who will recognize the necessity of learning the material on which they will be tested (see Hamilton, Stecher, & Klein, 2002). As a side benefit, having high stakes for students increases the likelihood that they will take the tests seriously, giving their best efforts, and thus avoiding the internal validity problem faced in states where standardized tests suffer as a measurement instrument because of lack of student buy-in (see Wheelock, Bebell, & Haney, 2000).

But policymakers in exit exam states include a second component in their accountability systems: accountability of schools and school districts, and sometimes teachers, for students' test scores. Imagine, then, a high school enrolling 100 students in its 12th-grade class. If 40 of these students fail to achieve a passing score on the state test, they will be denied diplomas. In addition, the school itself will likely face repercussions, such as being publicly identified as a failing school and perhaps being put on a state watch list for reconstitution, meaning that all teachers could lose their jobs (Carnoy, 2005).[14]

In such a hypothetical scenario, the state is faced with a logical dilemma in allocating responsibility. If the policy allocates responsibility to the teachers and the school, determining that they have failed, then the student responsibility should be reduced or eliminated. That is, the school and teachers are being held accountable because they have presumably denied or substantially impaired the students' OTL. As a legal matter and as a matter of fairness, the students should not be held responsible if their OTL was denied. On the other hand, if the policy allocates responsibility to the students themselves—if they are to blame—then the working assumption is that the school and teachers have indeed provided the students with a fair OTL. In that case, the school and teachers should not be criticized or sanctioned.

A reasonable assumption may be that low test scores are the result of combined failures on the part of students, teachers, and schools. Yet this is certainly not always the case, and accountability systems are built on the fiction that the state can correctly and precisely allocate causal responsibility among these multiple parties—or, more accurately, that all the parties are always at fault (Welner, 2005). In truth, standardized tests serving as measurements of educational outcomes are limited in their capacity to capture all that schools teach and students learn (Linn, 2000).

More importantly, for purposes of the present analysis, we know that educational outcomes are the result of various factors, many of which are beyond the control of a given school (Barton & Coley, 2009; Berliner, 2009; Rothstein, 2004). The 40 students who failed the exit exam in this hypothetical high school might blame flaws in the exam. Or they might take personal responsibility for their own failure to learn. Or they could point to schooling-related causes attributable to any or all of the following: their current teachers; unchallenging classes or poor curriculum; untrained, inexperienced, or otherwise weak teachers in earlier grades (perhaps in private schools or in schools in other school districts, other states, or other countries); poor resources provided by the schools, district, and state (e.g., outdated textbooks, overcrowded schools and classrooms, or decrepit facilities); or distractions in the educational environment (e.g., safety issues, noise, or temperature). They may also be justified in pointing to causes that have little to do with their formal schooling. Do they have good nutritional and exercise habits? Do they have access to good health care, and did their mothers have good prenatal health care? Do they have considerable responsibilities other than school work? Do they have strong parental involvement and educational expectations? Did their parents provide a good preparation through early childhood education (something, like many items on this list, very highly correlated to the parents' own educational level)? Can their parents afford, and have they supplied, educational resources, such as books, tutors, and computers? Accordingly, and notwithstanding the implicit assumption of standards-based accountability policies, poor educational outcomes cannot be confidently tied to any particular input.

Because this insight undermines the rationality of diploma denial, it carries straightforward policy import, but its indirect import is also noteworthy. It helps to build an understanding that although any given policy issue—such as tracking or teacher quality—may play a key role in student outcomes, a single reform will not directly address the vast majority of other factors, as listed previously, that will continue to disadvantage some students. Poor outcomes are usually caused by comprehensive problems, requiring comprehensive remedies or, at least, targeted remedies of sufficient intensity as to overcome the comprehensive problems. Although today's courts should not be expected to remedy out-of-school disadvantages that are beyond the direct control of the government (e.g., few books in home library), they can and should remedy state action that attaches negative consequences to those disadvantages (e.g., placement in a low track). But courts can be expected to design such remedies only if plaintiffs are able to present a complete evidentiary picture.

Moving toward such comprehensiveness requires legal approaches that focus a court's inquiry and remediation at deeper layers of schooling problems (Losen & Welner, 2001). Lawsuits hold this potential when they leverage accountability laws and challenge the overall fairness of OTLs. As noted, judges in typical education rights cases will generally craft a narrow remedy for the specific wrong placed before them. Most of these judges probably know that their remedy will carry few, if any, benefits as an educational policy matter. Yet even the most conscientious judge is usually not in a position to address the key causal policies, because the case before him or her is too narrowly drawn—either in its original form or after successful defense motions on the pleadings.[15] A benefit of broader education rights litigation is that it captures realities of schooling, placing before the court a fuller view of those realities and giving the judge the opportunity to craft more responsive remedies.

For students who fail an exit exam, diploma denial is a real harm, but this immediate harm represents only the last of a long series of injuries concerning (or masked by) such factors as inappropriate special education placement, grade retention, and placement in dead-end tracks. Denial of educational opportunity for such students likely has resided in policies and practices—in areas such as tracking, teacher assignment, textbooks, buildings and maintenance, overcrowding, curriculum and instruction, counseling, computers and science labs—that, time after time, offered them substandard resources and facilities. When such disadvantaged students repeatedly fail an exit exam, it probably does mean that they have not learned curriculum. It also means that the state's inequitable policies had the foreseeable effect of denying those students an equal educational opportunity.

Recent litigation concerning the California High School Exit Exam (CAHSEE) provides a nice illustration of these issues. The plaintiffs had claimed that the diploma denial violated the state constitution's equal protection clause as applied to students who had passed all the course requirements for graduation but who had not been provided with adequate educational resources to pass the CAHSEE. An appellate court ordered that a preliminary injunction against the diploma denial law be vacated (thus allowing for the denials). But the court also implicitly distinguished between the right to a diploma and the right to an education, cautioning that requiring the state to award diplomas to students who did not pass exit exams would "[ensure] that the state would never live up to its pedagogical responsibility to these students" (*O'Connell v. Valenzuela*, 2006, p. 1497). Eventually, the case was settled (see California's AB 347, signed into law on October 12, 2007), with the state agreeing to—among other things—provide these students with 2 years of additional instruction beyond Grade 12 (or until students pass the CAHSEE). Importantly, the settlement focused on providing supplemental opportunities to learn (in bandaid form), even though the remedy sought in the lawsuit was the granting of a diploma.

LIMITATIONS ON JUDICIAL RELIEF

The tendency of policymakers to promote quick fixes to engrained, complex problems is no less prevalent for judges than for legislators. In fact, judges in the United States are required to circumscribe remedial orders, addressing only the specific legal wrong or wrongs proven in the particular case—to "make the plaintiff whole" and no more (*Randall v. Loftsgaarden*, 1986, p. 663). This requirement serves to limit judicial overreaching, but it also presents a fundamental limitation on the likelihood that court orders will effect meaningful change in education rights cases. The Supreme Court's decision in *Milliken v. Bradley* (1974), for instance, effectively bound judicial relief in desegregation cases around only those school districts shown to have intentionally discriminated, thus paving the way for White flight to new districts in the suburbs.

A second limitation is even more fundamental: Most courts are tremendously hesitant to question the decisions of educational policymakers serving in coequal governmental branches. As a general rule, judges feel unprepared and unqualified to engage in educational policymaking. This is particularly true if the court sees no manageable standards to apply (see, e.g., *Baker v. Carr*, 1962). Accordingly, judges tend to defer to other authorities, whether elected or appointed, bending over backwards to avoid substituting their own judgment for the judgment of policymaker defendants. Such decorum, when observed, helps to keep courts safely outside realms best left to other governmental (and private) authorities. Yet a result of this hesitancy can be the denial of justice to those children who are ill served by pervasive inequalities in the present political system (see Fraser, 1992). When a plaintiff proves that the political system has yielded a violation of constitutional rights, a judge's deferral to that system is simply an abdication of his or her responsibilities to protect those rights.

Neither of these limitations on judicial relief disappears with the approach outlined here. However, as discussed earlier, both are minimized. The foundational focus on classroom-level wrongs and systemic challenges carries the potential for more comprehensive cases and remedies. In particular, the focus on exit exams and therefore on each state's standards-based reform legislation provides courts with guidelines concerning the level of academic preparation that elected representatives have resolved to be necessary, thus obviating the need for judges to make such determinations without clear guidance. Deference to elected legislators regarding resources and opportunities is less appropriate when that same legislator has created a system of standards and consequences that are logically linked to those inputs.

GUIDANCE FOR FUTURE EDUCATIONAL RESEARCH

This chapter presents what are essentially policy arguments couched in legal terms. A key to making these policy arguments salient in court is for researchers to identify and empirically establish whatever links exist between state actions, resource inequalities at the classroom level, and student achievement. In addition to the discussion regarding tracking, consider for instance the state action of facilitating teacher transfers between schools. Under the present system, many teachers begin their careers at schools serving disadvantaged populations. As they gain experience and seniority, however, they tend to move to more well-off neighborhoods (Carroll, Reichardt, & Guarino, 2000; Lankford, Loeb, & Wyckoff, 2002). These teachers are following a clear set of incentives, and the patterns are known to state and district officials (Jacobson, 2006). Yet the incentives and the patterns remain in place year after year.[16] A legal challenge to state and district policies would best be built on research connecting the governmental actions to teacher hiring and transfer patterns and also connecting those patterns to student achievement.

To be most helpful, this research would be both general and specific. That is, attorneys representing plaintiffs in classroom-based, systemic litigation could turn to research showing general patterns but would also be aided by research detailing the effects of the challenged policy or policies on these particular plaintiffs. Using tracking as an example, scholarly research generally describing the effects of tracking would be combined with research showing the effects of the tracking policy on the plaintiffs' opportunities vis-à-vis their jurisdiction's exit exam (e.g., showing lower results for comparable students enrolled in lower-tracked classes).

CONCLUSION

The call for American students to meet world-class standards in the federal Goals 2000: Education America Act (1994) and No Child Left Behind legislation, as well as state standards and accountability legislation, has been explicitly inclusive: *All* students must be held to these high standards. The same objective underlies the demand that students served under the Individuals with Disabilities Education Act be included in state testing and reporting regimens. Yet the performance standards tied to this objective need a functional mechanism for improving educational outcomes. They provide rhetorical and punitive accountability but, in most states, little pedagogical assistance.

Litigation offers the potential to leverage standards-based accountability laws in ways that refocus attention on opportunities to learn. Moreover, the lens of systemic, classroom-based litigation offers new insights into how evidence can be conceived in ways to advance equity-minded challenges to current policies. Some of these approaches have been tried in the past, with mixed success. More often, education rights litigation has narrowly focused the court on a specific state or district offense and thus seeks an equally narrow remedy. The result is what Lucas (2001) calls effectively maintained inequality—the litigation may force changes to specific practices, but the overall allocation of opportunities is maintained through alternative practices. The type of classroom-based litigation described in this chapter is unquestionably more difficult. It represents an ambitious strategy, fraught with obstacles. But it holds the potential for real change.

ACKNOWLEDGMENTS

I owe a debt of thanks to Bill Koski and to the chapter's developmental reviewers, Jay Heubert and Jeanne Powers, as well as to the editors of this volume, Allan Luke, Judith Green, and Gregory Kelly, for very helpful and supportive comments.

NOTES

[1]This observation was made by novelist Anatole France, describing late-19th-century Paris (France, 1930, p. 95).

[2]For another example of research that may support litigation, see Goodwin Liu's (2006b) scholarly argument highlighting financial disparities across states, linked to federal Title I policy, that he concludes disproportionately burden low-income children of color. However, others have countered that Title I distributions are less problematic than asserted by Liu, because higher aid levels, which appear to go to wealthier states, happen to go to states where labor costs are generally higher (see Baker & Green, 2007).

[3]Twenty-four states had mandatory exit exams in 2008: Alabama, Alaska, Arizona, California, Florida, Georgia, Idaho, Indiana, Louisiana, Maryland, Massachusetts, Minnesota, Mississippi, Nevada, New Jersey, New Mexico, New York, North Carolina, Ohio, South Carolina, Tennessee, Texas, Virginia, and Washington. Two additional states, Arkansas and Oklahoma, plan to add exit exams over the next several years. These 26 states include 74% of all students and 84% of all students of color. In addition, end-of-course exams, which assess mastery of specific course content, are also gaining popularity. Fifteen states plan to use end-of-course exams by 2015: Arkansas, Indiana, Maryland, Massachusetts, Mississippi, North Carolina, New Jersey, New York, Oklahoma, Pennsylvannia South Carolina, Tennessee, Texas, Virginia, and Washington (Zabala, Minnici, McMurrer, & Briggs, 2008).

[4]This decision was reversed by the state's highest court (CFE, 2003).

[5]Similarly, Nichols and Berliner (2006) describe the extreme level of goal displacement and even corruption that inevitably follows from high-stakes testing.

[6]For example, nearly 2 million students in 2005 were not counted when schools reported yearly progress by racial groups (Feller & Bass, 2006). It is far beyond this chapter to explore the ultimate set of outcomes, both intended and unintended, that have followed from No Child Left Behind (NCLB). However, the website of Education Trust (http://www2.edtrust. org/edtrust) is a good place to find a defense of the law. For more skeptical analyses, see Ryan (2004) and Welner (2005).

[7]Courts have been hesitant to require the awarding of a diploma, finding that instructional remediation and additional opportunities to take the exit exam satisfy due process requirements (see *Rene v. Reed*, 2001). As noted earlier, meaningful relief in these exit exam cases is difficult because of (among other obstacles) low thresholds of necessary exposure to tested content. It is also true, however, that the equal protection approach suggested in this chapter,

which is aimed at addressing the denial of rich instructional opportunities, comes with its own set of difficulties. Courts are hesitant to question educator discretion or require additional resources. These obstacles are explored in greater detail later.

[8]In this regard, consider the conclusion of a National Research Council report that high-stakes tests should not be used to retain students if those students are not given adequate supports: "Research shows that students are typically hurt by simple retention and repetition of a grade in school without remedial and other instructional supports" (Heubert & Hauser, 1999, p. 3; see also Heubert, 2005). However, most courts will probably find that a student does not have a protected property interest that is denied by grade retention (*Bester v. Tuscaloosa Board of Education*, 1984; *Erik v. Causby*, 1997; Quigley, 2001).

[9]For instance, Section 22-7-401 of the Colorado Education Code provides, in part, that "it is the obligation of the general assembly, the department of education, school districts, educators, and parents to provide children with schools that reflect high expectations and create conditions where these expectations can be met."

[10]Blasi's (2002) argument cites the California Supreme Court's *Butt v. State* (1992) decision, holding that the state "bears the ultimate authority and responsibility to ensure that its district-based system of common schools provides basic equality of educational opportunity" (Butt v. State, p. 1251).

[11]Governor Schwarzenegger settled the *Williams v. State of California* (2000) lawsuit at the outset of his first term in office. The settlement included nearly $1 billion set aside to correct the most egregious resource shortages in the state's lowest-performing schools, and it also included significant new accountability requirements for monitoring students' access to basic education resources that make state and county governments more accountable to students and parents. The settlement also created a new complaint process as a tool for engaging parents and students in improving schools (Renee, Welner, & Oakes, in press). But early results from this new process have been disappointing (Newman, 2009).

[12]Although the litigation contemplated here is probably best pursued as a class action (because among other reasons, any given plaintiff could not prove that tracking caused a decrease in the student's exit exam score), the process of getting certified as a class will not likely be straightforward. Of particular note is the importance of showing the cohesiveness of the aggregate unit—the common wrong across all similarly situated (low-track) students in the exit exam state (see Nagareda, 2009). The tracking system of one school will be different from that of another, as might tracking systems in different grade levels of the same school. This issue is well beyond the scope of the present article, but worth noting here is simply that courts faced with this decision will likely turn to experts on the nature of the import of differences associated with this type of variance across schools and grades.

[13]This article does not address issues of causation. A student's exit exam results are, as noted in the main text, the result of many different factors, only some of which are, like tracking, within the control of the school. Plaintiffs could not sensibly contend that a student's score is "because" of low-track enrollment. Rather, the causal case will have to be made on the basis of widespread research findings concerning tracking's harm of detracking's potential benefit. That is, the court would have to make a causal finding that the practice of tracking generally decreased the likelihood of exit exam failure. Put another way, the court would have to accept the argument implicit in Figure 1, set forth earlier.

[14]Under NCLB, a Title I school that fails to make adequate yearly progress for 5 consecutive years faces mandatory reconstitution or major governance restructuring.

[15]The pretrial stages of litigation often involve motions to strike individual causes of action or to otherwise narrow the scope of the litigation.

[16]Some districts have recently initiated efforts to try to changes the incentives (see Gonring, Teske, & Jupp, 2007).

REFERENCES

Adelman, C. (2006). *The toolbox revisited: Paths to degree completion from high school to college.* Washington, DC: U.S. Department of Education.

American Educational Research Association. (2004). Closing the gap: High achievement for students of color. *Research Points, 2*(3). Retrieved July 27, 2007, from http://www.aera.net/uploadedFiles/Journals_and_Publications/Research_Points/RP_Fall-04.pdf

Baker v. Carr, 369 U.S. 186 (1962).

Baker, B. D., & Green, P. C. (2007, January). *Financing schools to meet educational needs.* Paper presented at the National Title I Conference, Nashville, TN.

Bandeira de Mello, V., Blankenship, C., & McLaughlin, D. H. (2009). *Mapping state proficiency standards onto NAEP scales: 2005-2007.* Washington DC: NCES.

Barton, P., & Coley, R. (2009). *Parsing the achievement gap II.* Princeton, NJ: Educational Testing Service. Retrieved June 26, 2009, from http://www.ets.org/Media/Research/pdf/PICPARSINGII.pdf

Berkowitz, P. (2003). Liberalism and school choice. In P. Peterson (Ed.), *The future of school choice* (pp. 107–131). Palo Alto, CA: Hoover Institution.

Berliner, D. C. (2009). *The effects of out-of-school factors on student behavior and academic achievement.* Boulder, CO, and Tempe, AZ: Education and the Public Interest Center and Education Policy Research Unit. Retrieved February 28, 2009, from http://epicpolicy.org/publication/effects-of-out-of-school-factors

Bester v. Tuscaloosa Board of Education, 722 F.2d 1514 (11th Cir. 1984).

Blasi, G. (2002). *Five: Reforming educational accountability* (California Policy Options, Paper 942). Los Angeles: University of California, Los Angeles, School of Public Affairs. Retrieved July 29, 2009, from http://repositories.cdlib.org/cgi/viewcontent.cgi?article=1057&context=uclaspa

Boaler, J., & Staples, M. (2006). Creating mathematical futures through an equitable teaching approach: The case of Railside School. *Teachers College Record, 110*(3), 608–645.

Board of Education v. Walter, 390 N.E.2d 813 (Ohio, 1979).

Brookhart v. Illinois, 697 F.2d 179 (7th Cir. 1983).

Brown v. Board of Education, 347 U.S. 473 (1954).

Burris, C. C., & Garrity, D. T. (2008). *Detracking for excellence and equity.* Alexandria, VA: ASCD.

Burris, C. C., Heubert, J., & Levin, H. (2006). Accelerating mathematics achievement using heterogeneous grouping. *American Educational Research Journal, 43*(1), 103–134.

Burris, C. C., & Welner, K. G. (2005). Closing the achievement gap by detracking. *Phi Delta Kappan, 86*(8), 594–598.

Butt v. State, 842 P.2d 1240 (Cal. 1992).

Campaign for Fiscal Equity, Inc. (CFE) v. State, 295 A.D.2d 1 (1st Dep't, N.Y., 2002).

Campaign for Fiscal Equity, Inc. (CFE) v. State, 801 N.E.2d 326 (N.Y., 2003).

Carnoy, M. (2005). Have state accountability and high-stakes tests influenced student progression rates in high school? *Educational Measurement: Issues and Practice, 24*(4), 19.

Carroll, S., Reichardt, R., & Guarino, C. (2000). The distribution of teachers among California's school districts and schools (MR-1298.0-JIF). Santa Monica, CA: RAND.

Castañeda v. Pickard, 648 F.2d 989 (5th Cir. 1981).

Chudowsky, N., Kober, N., Gayler, K., & Hamilton, M. (2002). *State high school exit exams: A baseline report.* Washington, DC: Center on Education Policy.

City of Cleburne v. Cleburne Living Center, Inc., 473 U.S. 432 (1985).

Cleveland Board of Education v Loudermill, 470 U.S. 532 (1985).

Columbia Falls Elementary School District No. 6 v. State, 109 P.3d 257 (Mont., 2005).

Coons, J. E., Clune, W. H., & Sugarman, S. D. (1970). *Private wealth and public education.* Cambridge, MA: Harvard University Press.

Darling-Hammond, L. (1987). Teacher quality and equality. In P. Keating, & J. I. Goodlad (Eds.), *Access to knowledge* (pp. 237–258). New York: College Entrance Exam Board.

Darling-Hammond, L. (1994). National standards and assessments: Will they improve education? *American Journal of Education, 102*(4), 478–510.

Darling-Hammond, L. (2000). New standards and old inequalities: School reform and the education of African American students. *Journal of Negro Education, 61*(3), 237–249.

Debra P. v. Turlington, 644 F.2d 397 (5th Cir. 1981).

Delpit, L. (1996). *Other people's children: Cultural conflict in the classroom.* New York: New Press.

DeShaney v. Winnebago County Department of Social Services, 489 U.S. 189 (1989).

Erik V. v. Causby, 977 F. Supp. 384 (E.D.N.C, 1997).

FCC v. Beach Communications Inc., 508 U.S. 307 (1993).

Feller, B., & Bass, F. (2006, April 22). Spellings to examine "No Child" loophole. *The Washington Post.*

Fine, M. (1993). (Ap)parent involvement: Reflections on parents, power, and urban schools. *Teachers College Record, 94*(4), 26–43.

France, A. (1930) *The red lily* (W. Stephens, Trans.). London: John Lane.

Fraser, N. (1992). Rethinking the public sphere: A contribution to the critique of actually existing democracy. In C. Calhoun (Ed.), *Habermas and the public sphere* (pp. 109–142). Cambridge, MA: MIT Press.

Gamoran, A., & Mare, R. D. (1989). Secondary school tracking and educational inequality: Compensation, reinforcement or neutrality? *American Journal of Sociology, 94*, 1146–1183.

Goals 2000: Educate America Act (1994). P.L. 103-227 [H.R. 1804], 20 U.S.C. § 5801.

GI Forum v. Texas Education Agency, 87 F.Supp.2d 667 (W.D.Tex. 2000).

Gonring, P., Teske, P., & Jupp, B. (2007). *Pay for performance teacher compensation: An inside view of Denver's ProComp Plan.* Cambridge, MA: Harvard Education Press.

Griswold v. Connecticut, 381 U.S. 479 (1965).

Hallinan, M. T. (1992). The organization of students for instruction in the middle school. *Sociology of Education, 65*(2), 114–127.

Hallinan, M. T. (1994). Tracking: From theory to practice. *Sociology of Education, 67*(2), 79–91.

Hamilton, L., Stecher, B., & Klein, S. (2002). *Making sense of test-based accountability in education.* Retrieved June 26, 2009, from http://www.rand.org/pubs/monograph_reports/MR1554/

Heller v. Doe, 509 U.S. 312 (1993).

Heubert, J. P. (1999). Six law-driven school reforms: Developments, lessons, and prospects. In J. Heubert (Ed.), *Law and school reform: Six strategies for promoting educational equity* (pp. 1–38). New Haven, CT: Yale University Press.

Heubert, J. P. (2005). High-stakes testing, nationally and in the South. In C. Edley, G. Orfield, & J. Boger (Eds.), *School resegregation: Must the South turn back?* (pp. 221–238). Chapel Hill: University of North Carolina Press.

Heubert, J. P., & Hauser, R. M. (Eds.) (1999). *High stakes: Testing for tracking, promotion and graduation.* Washington, DC: National Research Council.

Horne v. Flores, U.S. LEXIS 4733 (2009).

Hsieh, C.-T., & Urquiola, M. (2003). *When schools compete, how do they compete? An assessment of Chile's Nationwide School Voucher Program* (NBER Working Paper No. 10008). Washington DC: National Bureau of Economic Research.

Individuals with Disabilities Education Act, 20 U.S.C. §§ 1400 et seq.

Jacobson, L. (2006). Teacher-pay incentives popular but unproven. *Education Week, 26*(5), 1-20.

Karoly, L. A. (2009). *Preschool adequacy and efficiency in California: Issues, policy options, and recommendations.* Santa Monica, CA: RAND.

Koski, W. S. (2001). Educational opportunity and accountability in an era of standards-based school reform. *Stanford Law and Policy Review, 12,* 301.

Koski, W. S., & Reich, R. (2007). When "adequate" isn't: The retreat from equity in educational law and policy and why it matters. *Emory Law Journal, 56*(3), 543–615.

Ladwig, J. G. (2010). Beyond academic outcomes. *Review of Research in Education, 34*(1), 113–141.

Lankford, H., Loeb, S., & Wyckoff, J. (2002). Teacher sorting and the plight of urban schools. A descriptive analysis. *Educational Evaluation and Policy Analysis, 24*(1), 37–62.

Lareau, A. (1989). *Home advantage: Social class and parental intervention in elementary education.* New York: Falmer.

Lawrence v. Texas, 539 U.S. 558 (2003).

Leandro v. State, 346 N.C. 336, 488 S.E.2d 249 (1997).

Levin, H. M. (1997). Raising school productivity: An x-efficiency approach. *Economics of Education Review, 16*(3), 303–312.

Linn, R. (2000). Assessment and accountability. *Educational Researcher, 29*(2), 4–16.

Liu, G. (2006a). Education, equality, and national citizenship. *Yale Law Journal, 116,* 330.

Liu, G. (2006b). Interstate inequality in educational opportunity. *New York University Law Review, 81,* 2044.

Losen, D., & Welner, K. G. (2001). Disabling discrimination in our public schools: Comprehensive legal challenges to inappropriate and inadequate special education services for minority children. *Harvard Civil Rights-Civil Liberties Law Review, 36*(2), 407–460.

Lucas, S. R. (1999). *Tracking inequality: Stratification and mobility in American high schools.* New York: Teachers College Press.

Lucas, S. R. (2001). Effectively maintained inequality: Education transitions, track mobility, and social background effects. *American Journal of Sociology, 106*(6), 1642–1690.

McNeal v. Tate County School District, 508 F.2d 1017 (5th Cir. 1975).

Mickelson, R. A., Bottia, M., & Southworth, S. (2008). *School choice and segregation by race, class, and achievement.* Boulder, CO, and Tempe, AZ: Education and the Public Interest Center and Education Policy Research Unit. Retrieved June 26, 2009, from http://epicpolicy.org/files/CHOICE-08-Mickelson-FINAL-EG043008.pdf

Milliken v. Bradley, 418 U.S. 717 (1974).

Montoy v. State, 278 Kan. 769, 102 P.3d 1160 (2005).

Murnane, R. J., Willett, J. B., & Tyler, J. H. (2000). Who benefits from obtaining a GED? Evidence from high school and beyond. *Review of Economics and Statistics, 82*(1), 23–37.

Nagareda, R. A. (2009). Aggregate Litigation Across the Atlantic and the Future of American Exceptionalism. *Vanderbilt Law Review, 62,* 1-52.

National Research Council & the Institute of Medicine. (2004). *Engaging schools: Fostering high school students' motivation to learn.* Washington, DC: National Academy Press.

Newman, A. (2009, April 15). *The role of moral claims in education litigation: An examination of Williams v. California.* Paper presented at the annual meeting of the American Educational Research Association, San Diego, CA

Nichols, S. L., & Berliner, D. (2006). *Collateral damage: How high-stakes testing corrupts schools.* Cambridge, MA: Harvard Education Press.

No Child Left Behind Act of 2001. (2002). Pub.L. No. 107–110, 115 Stat. 1425, 20 U.S.C. §§6301 et seq. reauthorizing the Elementary and Secondary Education Act of 1965.

Oakes, J. (1989, Summer). What educational indicators? The case for assessing the school context. *Educational Evaluation and Policy Analysis, 11*(2), 181–199.

Oakes, J. (2005). *Keeping track: How schools structure inequality* (2nd ed.). New Haven, CT: Yale University Press.

Oakes, J., Ormseth, T., Bell, R., & Camp, P. (1990). *Multiplying inequalities: The effects of race, social class, and tracking on opportunities to learn mathematics and science.* Santa Monica, CA: Rand.

O'Connell v. Valenzuela, 141 Cal.App.4th 1452 (2006).

People Who Care v. Rockford Board of Education School District No. 205, 111 F.3d 528 (7th Cir. 1997).

Quigley, W. P. (2001). Due process rights of grade school students subjected to high-stakes testing. *Boston Public Interest Law Journal, 10,* 284.

Plyler v. Doe, 457 U.S. 202 (1982).

Randall v. Loftsgaarden, 478 U.S. 647 (1986).

Rebell, M. A. (2005). Adequacy litigations: A new path to equity? In A. S. Wells, & J. Petrovich (Eds.), *Bringing equity back: Research for a new era in American educational policy* (pp. 291–323). New York: Teachers College Press.

Rebell, M. A., & Wolff, J. R. (2008). *Moving every child ahead: From NCLB hype to meaningful educational opportunity.* New York: Teachers College Press.

Rene v. Reed, 751 N.E. 2d 736 (Ind. Ct. App. 2001).

Renee, M. A., Welner, K. G., & Oakes, J. (in press). Social movement organizing and equity-focused educational change: Shifting the "zone of mediation." In A. Hargreaves, M. Fullan, D. Hopkins, & A. Lieberman (Eds.), *International handbook of educational change* (2nd ed.). New York: Springer International Handbooks.

Romer v. Evans, 517 U.S. 620 (1996).

Roos, P. (1998). Intradistrict resource disparities: A problem crying out for a solution. In M. Gittell (Ed.), *Strategies for school equity: Creating productive schools in a just society* (pp. 40–52). New Haven, CT: Yale University Press.

Rose v. Council for Better Educ., 790 S.W.2d 186 (Ky. 1989).

Rothstein, R. (2004). *Class and schools: Using social, economic, and educational reform to close the Black-White achievement gap.* Washington, DC: Economic Policy Institute.

Roza, M., & Hill, P. (2004). How within-district spending inequities help some schools to fail. In D. Ravitch (Ed.), *Brookings papers on education policy 2004* (pp. 201–227). Washington, DC: Brookings Institute.

Ryan, J. E. (2004). The perverse incentives of the No Child Left Behind Act. *New York University Law Review, 79,* 932–988.

Saporito, S., & Sohoni, D. (2006). Coloring outside the lines: Racial segregation in public schools and their attendance boundaries. *Sociology of Education, 79,* 81–105.

Silberman, T. (2000, October 23). State might have to ante up for standards. *North Carolina News and Observer.*

Singham, M. (2003). The achievement gap: Myths and reality. *Phi Delta Kappan, 84*(8), 586–591.

Smith, M., & O'Day, J. (1991). Systemic school reform. In S. Fuhrman, & B. Malen (Eds.), *The politics of curriculum and testing* (pp. 233–268). Bristol, UK: Falmer.

Stevens, F. I., & Grymes, J. (1993). *Opportunity to learn: Issues of equity for poor and minority students.* Washington, DC: U.S. Department of Education, National Center for Education Statistics.

Superfine, B. M. (2008). *The courts and standards-based education reform.* New York: Oxford University Press.

Vanfossen, B. E., Jones, J. D., & Spade, J. Z. (1987). Curriculum tracking and status maintenance. *Sociology of Education, 60,* 104–122.

Washington v. Davis, 426 U.S. 229 (1976).

Wells, A. S., & Serna, I. (1996). The politics of culture: Understanding local political resistance to detracking in racially mixed schools. *Harvard Educational Review, 66*(1), 93–118.

Welner, K. G. (2001a). *Alexander v. Sandoval: A setback for civil rights. Education Policy Analysis Archives, 9*(24). Retrieved July 29, 2009, from http://epaa.asu.edu/epaa/v9n24.html

Welner, K. G. (2001b). *Legal rights, local wrongs: When community control collides with educational equity.* Albany: State University of New York Press.

Welner, K. G. (2001c). Tracking in an era of standards: Low-expectation classes meet high-expectation laws. *Hastings Constitutional Law Quarterly, 28*(3), 699–738.

Welner, K. G. (2005). Can irrational become unconstitutional? NCLB's 100% presuppositions. *Excellence and Equity in Education, 38*, 171–179.

Welner, K. G., & Howe, K. R. (2005). Steering toward separation: The policy and legal implications of "counseling" special education students away from choice schools. In J. Scott (Ed.), *School choice and student diversity: What the evidence says* (pp. 93–111). New York: Teachers College Press.

Welner, K. G., & Oakes, J. (1996). (Li)Ability grouping: The new susceptibility of school tracking systems to legal challenges. *Harvard Educational Review, 66*(3), 451–470.

Wheelock, A., Bebell, D. J., & Haney, W. (2000). Student self-portraits as test-takers: Variations, contextual differences, and assumptions about motivation. *Teachers College Record.* Retrieved July 29, 2009, from http://www.tcrecord.org (ID No. 10635)

Williams v. State of California, San Francisco Superior Court, Case No. 312236 (filed in May, 2000).

Wise, A. E. (1968). *Rich schools, poor schools: The promise of equal educational opportunity.* Chicago: University of Chicago Press.

Zabala, D., Minnici, A., McMurrer, J., & Briggs, L. (2008). *State high school exit exams: Moving toward end-of-course exams.* Washington, DC: Center on Education Policy.

Chapter 4

Beyond Academic Outcomes

JAMES G. LADWIG

University of Newcastle, New South Wales, Australia

The common wisdom [is] that measureable outcomes may be the least significant results of learning.

—McNeil (1986, p. xviii)

Many debates about schooling are often very predictable. Perhaps one of the most predictable debates comes up around the question of the outcomes of schooling: in public policy debates about school accountability, in private lounge room conversations among parents about what they want from schools for their children. Very quickly in these conversations someone will point out that schooling is meant to provide many more things than just "academic" outcomes. Politicians, like President Obama (and George W. Bush before him), will make the case that schooling needs to promote the kind of innovative thinking and spirit needed to advance the nation, economically and socially. Parents are likely to have some sense of the kind of values and character they hope their children might garner from schools (even if that is an antiauthoritarian, resistant disposition). No one really expects to settle these debates, and many debaters are likely to accept Linda McNeil's view (noted above) that significant results of learning are not measurable. But even with that common wisdom in mind, somewhere along the track education researchers may well be asked just what we know about schooling for outcomes beyond the traditional measured academic outcomes.

This chapter attempts to survey contemporary debates and research on outcomes of schooling that have been grouped together under the convenient label *nonacademic*. This is not an affirmative labeling. As the nomenclature indicates, it is not a label that groups together things that share like properties. Rather, this is a label of distinction, a naming of what lies on the outside. At the outset, it is very important to be clear that this chapter cannot, nor will it even attempt to, provide a comprehensive survey of all

Review of Research in Education
March 2010, Vol. 34, pp. 113–141
DOI: 10.3102/0091732X09353062
© 2010 AERA. http://rre.aera.net

research on student outcomes that are nonacademic outcomes. The potential set of that research is literally infinite. By way of providing some useful analysis, however, in what follows, I will attempt to identify some of the central educational tensions that will be confronted by any analysis of, and advocacy for, educational programs designed to promote student outcomes other than academic outcomes in schools. Although the focus on school outcomes does not limit the still infinite, it does allow us to identify a set of exemplars to use as heuristic devices to examine the underlying logic at play here.

I will argue that contemporary calls for nonacademic outcomes face a conundrum. On one hand, most programs that seek to promote these outcomes are not in a position to declare definitive success in defining educational programs that produce substantial effect in school outcomes, despite the fact that many calls for nonacademic outcomes seek to promote social effects with which few would disagree (like promoting a more fully democratic citizenry). Furthermore, very few have even attempted to link school programs with later effects beyond schooling, even though these broader social effects are their *raisons d'être*. There is clearly much more research to be done as we attempt to find ways to better know if nonacademic educational programs "work" both in producing schooling outcomes and in the intended subsequent social effect.

On the other hand, many calls for nonacademic outcomes seek to promote behaviors and dispositions that defy, or lie outside of, the logic of measurement and accountability available to schooling in the first place. There is truth in what McNeil (1986) called common wisdom, but the line between what is measurable and what is not measurable is not as clear as that which common wisdom suggests. The examples offered below do provide an indication that the frontiers of the measurable lie well beyond conventional testing and academic outcome measures.

But pushing the frontiers of promoting nonacademic outcomes, applying the technology of measurement to more and more aspects of learning comes at a price. Applying the logic of school outcomes to learning means opening that learning to the logic of governance and control embedded in schooling. As we pursue these goals, as an educational community, I hope this chapter prompts us to keep in mind the question of just how much do we really want schools to do and how much do we really need to measure?

To ground this discussion, after some initial analytical and historical framing of the academic tradition, I present four examples of research on nonacademic outcomes in schooling and comment on the current state of affairs in each: values education, nonacademic outcomes in multicultural education, civics and democratic education, and environmental education. I address the final two examples in detail to highlight my central arguments. I focus on civics and democratic education as an example of one call for nonacademic outcomes that is quite compatible with the academic tradition and which is currently well placed to extend studies of effects beyond schooling itself. Environmental education provides an example that includes some calls for nonacademic outcomes that are contradictory to schooling itself. I focus more specifically on the research literature in environmental education to illustrate this archetypical condition in contemporary nonacademic outcomes research.

From that point I attempt to place the call for nonacademic outcomes in the context of the logic of schooling and show how that placement carries significant implications for how we understand "outcomes." Finally, I will outline the limits of our current knowledge about nonacademic school outcomes and suggest a line of theoretical and empirical research that would be needed if we are ever going to open our debates about the multiple purposes of schooling to a more systematic and rationalized level, if we ever agree that this is something we really want, or need, to do. As the examples I present below will illustrate, no attempt to research or advocate for a systematic knowledge about outcomes of schooling is without its consequences. If anything, this chapter will highlight just what some of the consequences are and give pause to those who eagerly seek to have others comply with their own version of what counts as the outcomes schools ought to produce.

ON THE TRADITION OF COMPETING NORMATIVE ENDS FOR SCHOOLING AND THE PLACE OF THE "ACADEMIC"

Current debates on the outcomes of schooling in the United States often build from critique of a focus on testing and schooling accountability mechanisms that are themselves banked on standardized achievement tests—primarily in numeracy and literacy. Although the strength of the interest in testing is probably not as strong in other countries, the focus on testing "academic" outcomes is worldwide, although some exceptions in national testing regimes are notable (with some countries expanding this to include technology, computing, science, etc., and others employing tests more diagnostically for systems based on sampling procedures). Some prominent examples of challenges to strict testing of "academic" outcomes can be found even within international testing programs such as the OECD Programme for International Student Assessment (PISA), with PISA advocating a lifelong learning framework and adopting very general notions of "mathematical and scientific literacy" as the bases of their measuring endeavors. Similar challenges can be found beyond conventional testing regimes, with the general push for "outcomes-based education" standing as an obvious example (the 1989 NCTM Standards and the 1990s search for "alternative assessments" are specific cases in point here).

This debate, however important and of current concern, is merely an extension of the long-standing historical reality that schools have always served multiple purposes. The history of education, the philosophy of education, and the more specific history of mass schooling are all replete with literature that is essentially advocacy of multiple aims, goals, and purposes for schooling. There are even many historical accounts in which the main argument is to characterize this reality, with differing metaphors used to describe it. For example, Herb Kleibard's (1986) historical analysis of U.S. curriculum, *The Struggle for the American Curriculum*, uses the metaphor of archaeological strata to describe the way different curricular movements accumulated but never fully supplanted each other over the 20th century. The turn of the 20th century dispute between Dewey and Snedden on vocational education stands as another classic example of this debate (see Wirth, 1983).

Whatever the outcome advocated in this tradition of debate is ultimately based on a normative argument about what schools should do. The normative basis of this debate is sometimes well articulated, sometimes muted or embedded within observations about reality, and sometimes forgotten (confused with claims about reality). The need to recognize the normative basis of all calls for outcomes from schooling is paramount if any move to research, estimate, or measure those outcomes can be pursued meaningfully.

One distinction that needs to be made very clear differentiates between the outcomes of schooling per se and the broader individual and social effects of the measurement regimes of those outcomes. Current debates on the validity and meaning of the PISA measurements illustrate this distinction. Where some of the debate about PISA is concerned with what the testing itself measures (see, e.g., Bautier & Rayou, 2007), this question is focused on the outcomes of schooling per se. There are also, however, very big questions about the sociopolitical and systemic effects of PISA that are not unlike many of the concerns about the uses of testing in America's No Child Left Behind Act (see, e.g., McGaw, 2008; Nichols & Berliner, 2007; Spring, 2008). Although there is clearly going to be a strong relationship between the outcomes of schooling and the effects of the systems designed to measure those outcomes, the purpose of this chapter will be to focus specifically on the outcomes themselves.

The history of the dominance of the so-called academic outcomes is well known in curriculum history, linked to the development of secondary schooling built in the shadow of already well-articulated university curriculum, developed from the Middle Ages University's foci on the Trivium and Quadrivium carried forward. The major benchmarks in U.S. curriculum history include the Committee of Ten reports from 1892, among many other subject-based defenses over the 20th century.

Volumes have been written on this history, of course. In the U.S. context, two continuing dynamics of this history can be noted from very early in the 20th century. First, then as now, the call to break away from the influence academic disciplines impel on school subjects has been a consistent feature of school curricular debates. Second, then as now, the hegemony of institutionalized, "means–ends," rationality has continued essentially unscathed. In fact, these two features of contemporary debates can be seen in the early replies to the 1918 NEA's Cardinal Principals of Secondary Education from their Commission on the Reorganization of Secondary Education (see Bobbitt, 1920). It is worth recalling that the Cardinal Principles called for a focus on seven broad aims for secondary education in which traditional subjects were barely featured. These seven, now well known in curricular literature, included the following:

1. Health
2. Command of fundamental processes
3. Worthy home membership
4. Vocation
5. Citizenship

6. Worthy use of leisure
7. Ethical character

From this simple listing of aims, it is clear that the call to focus secondary schooling on things other than academic outcomes was well articulated, and well cited, long ago. Any casual read of the history of Progressive Education in the United States, and its subsequent lack of impact, would find the critique of focusing schooling only on academic outcomes was a prominent feature of what is now at least a century-old debate.

At the same time, it was clear that the force of schooling as an institution was also paramount. However much there might have been a broad agreement that breaking away from academic outcomes was desirable, whatever the outcomes of schooling might be, they needed to be subjected to the what we would now call "technical rationality" or "means–ends" reasoning (what the German sociologist Max Weber termed *zweck-rational*, sometimes translated as "instrumental reasoning"). In the words of Franklin Bobbitt himself, that now iconic father-figure of technical curricular reasoning,

There is a growing realization within the educational profession that we must particularize the objectives of education. We, too, must institutionalize foresight, and, so far as the conditions of our work will permit, develop a technique of predetermination of the particularized results to be aimed at. We are awakening to the obvious truth that when a long journey is to be taken, one of the most necessary things to know before setting out is the destination. (Bobbitt, 1920, p. 738)

Here it is important to recognize that Bobbitt's concern for specifying objectives (in very specific terms) was part of a larger movement to "scientifically" study the effects of school practices and their relative success or failure to meet the intended aims of schooling. As Bobbitt's contemporary, David Snedden put it 4 years earlier,

All education is tending to become scientific, to become a field of applied science, as are already medicine, war, navigation, agriculture, metal-working, and the like. But efficiency of action in any field of applied science is possible only on the basis of clearly defined aims. Right methods and sound testing of results are practicable only as they are consciously and specifically based upon clearly defined and carefully tested aims. To prove itself capable of developing in accordance with scientific standards and principles education must in all its phases formulate and study its new problems of aim. (Snedden, 1916, p. 187)

So it is that the dominance of academic outcomes as the main focus of schooling in the United States can be seen in light of its institutionalized context. Roughly speaking, the continuing dominance of academic outcomes was given a big push in the 20th-century development of testing and the growing sophistication of measurement, but the institutionalization of testing as a mechanism for selection embedded this focus. Counterexamples of this dominant trend make the point. Alternative university entry programs that rely on broad evidence and criteria remain the exception, alternative entry processes into professional schools (such as medical schools) remain exceptions, and the home of performance-based assessments, the arts, is still largely not typically included in lists of "core" subjects. The fact these are counterexamples simply provide an indication of the general rule, that traditional academic outcomes remain hegemonic.

Several curricular schools have suggested that the internal dominance of the "core" subjects is directly linked to university selections. So the historical case for the dominance of academic outcomes can be readily linked to matriculation requirements.

Among these views, one perspective that tends not to be heard all that much comes from institutional analyses of power. This view points out a clear paradox in relation to the value of many standardized tests (including tests such as the SAT). On one hand, it is clear that the predictive capacity of the standardized tests for attainment is unquestionable (because these scores are what often determine entry into higher levels of attainment). On the other hand, there is also a fairly well-known lack of predictive capacity for later achievement. This paradox is taken, in an institutional view, as a clear sign of decoupling (Meyer, Ramirez, & Soysal, 1992; Meyer & Rowan, 1977), or from a Weberian view, as a sign of the technological fallacy that supports public understandings of school (Collins, 1979). In many ways, the work of historians of education such as David Labaree can be seen as an extension of this institutional analysis of schooling, and his institutional interpretation of how academic subject disciplines remain securely in place is backed by substantial historical evidence (see Labaree, 1991, for an example of this line of reasoning from Labaree's early work).

The basic skills focus on numeracy and literacy, and standardized testing is something of a least common denominator corollary. Accounts of why the focus on standardized testing has become dominant are by no means new (Apple, 1971, 1979, 1980; Apple & King, 1977), and the rationale by which these have become the dominant force in policy are by now well known and have been rehearsed recently on the global stage in McGaw's (2008) defense of the PISA testing agenda.

When juxtaposed with this broad historical backdrop, the current concerns of developing scientific research methods and quasi-experimental evaluations of teaching and curriculum are clearly mimicry of long-standing debates in schooling and curriculum. This is especially true in the United States, where the push for developing "scientific curriculum" was perhaps most strong among the international educational scene, for at least 100 years, if not longer.

This historical backdrop is crucial when considering the current state of research on "nonacademic" outcomes, because, as we will see below, programs intended to promote "nonacademic" outcomes remain as open to the criticisms of old as ever, and the push to measure and assess the effectiveness of these programs (if only as a response to criticisms) continues to this day. What is distinctly different, however, is that we are now in a position to question just how much of this trajectory is wise to follow. The consequences of applying technical rationality to ever more aims of schooling, of embedding normative ends underneath a façade of "objective," dispassionate science, are perhaps more clear now than a century ago. As the dynamics of globalization are now well embedded in the mindset of educators, the illustrations discussed below are designed to illuminate some of the consequences and to allow a more reflective questioning of them.

FOUR CASES OF THE STRUCTURE OF LOGIC IN THE ADVOCACY AND STUDY OF NONACADEMIC OUTCOMES

Clearly, the history of official curricula has long included many specific calls for outcomes that would now be considered "nonacademic." From calls for schooling to promote health (physical and mental), "character," and the arts, to vocational education, schools have long served many ends. Equally so, individual research traditions trace each of these specific curricular areas. Although it is not possible to review all these areas of nonacademic interests, it is important to note that each body of research on them includes some degree of advocacy. This advocacy often takes the form of straight and open calls for school education to recognize a need to focus on one of these alternative nonacademic ends. But it is also important to recognize that even the most distanced, empirical, "objective," or evaluative research implies some degree of advocacy, if only in dedicating the necessary resources to conduct research on a given area. (Even direct counterarguments imply a recognition that advocacy of alternatives is sufficiently worthy to require response, thereby acknowledging that at least some important educators see a legitimate case for nonacademic outcomes.)

This blending of advocacy and research is part and parcel of the educational enterprise of course, but in the context of a globalized field of educational policy, this dynamic carries a peculiar twist. That is, the use of research (in a variety of forms) to leverage policy calls for nonacademic outcomes lends itself to a perception of such calls being new. Part of the point of recalling the history of curriculum symbolized by the Cardinal Principles, however, was to signal that even the most radical of calls for nonacademic outcomes usually is a manifestation of a longer history, even as current policy calls claim to be responding to new societal or global issues.

In the United States, the current education research interest in nonacademic outcomes for schooling has a more recent history, of course. At the turn of the 21st century, two special issues of *The Elementary School Journal* presented several cases of interest at the time (both issues, May 1999 and May 2000, were edited by Thomas Good). Included in those volumes were articles dedicated to the promotion of physical activity, service learning, self-regulation (for democratic education and for academic success), tolerance, social–emotional development, and the reduction of "high-risk" behavior. In his proposed alternative index of school performance, Richard Rothstein included three specific indexes of nonacademic outcomes: (a) responsible democratic citizenship, (b) sound wellness practices, and (c) teamwork and social ethics (Rothstein, 2000).

Although subsequent years of educational politics may have diverted the end of the century interest in nonacademic outcomes in the United States, there have been several lines of education research within the United States and international settings that have pushed ahead since that survey. To provide a range of examples of this work (apart from research in subject areas typically taken to be nonacademic), four areas of research directly related to nonacademic outcomes are outlined below: (a) a current international interest in "values education," (b) multicultural education, (c) civics and democratic education, and (d) environmental education. These areas are not taken to be definitive, but have been selected to illustrate the broader argument of this chapter, on the ambivalent tension that underscores all calls for nonacademic outcomes.

To provide a full illustration of the logic behind calls for nonacademic outcomes, I elaborate on the last two examples: civics and democratic education and environmental education. Although many calls for nonacademic outcomes would be motivated by normative frameworks that are socially quite contested, both these examples have been chosen because they hold a relatively neutral position in contemporary debates. Few (in the main readership of this journal) would question the reasons for saying we need civics and democratic education. Similarly, with the growing recognition of human-induced climate change, relatively few would argue that a decent environmental education should go astray. However, these two examples differ in two important ways. First, calls for democratic education have been around for a very long time (at least since Dewey and Kilpatrick) and attempts to develop measures of student outcomes for them are well advanced. Environmental education has really only developed measures of related outcomes in the past few decades. Second, civics and democratic education can be seen as quite consistent with more conventional academic traditions, in terms of the knowledge, skills, and dispositions for which they call. However, the most organic and environmentally sensitive forms of environmental education are actually quite contradictory to the culture of schooling itself (and schooling is itself seen as part of the problem). Thus, these two examples offer two relatively accepted normative positions with very different relationships to the culture of schooling (and research that builds claims about "outcomes" of schooling). I turn first to brief outlines of values education and nonacademic outcomes in multicultural education.

The Current Rendition of Values Education

Within the United Kingdom, Europe, and Australia, there is currently a distinct interest in the development of "values education." Clearly, the area of "values education" or "moral education" is a field in its own right, with entire journals dedicated to research and scholarship in the area (e.g., *The Journal of Values Education, The Journal of Moral Education*). In the current work, the call for curricular programs specifically designed to promote a given set of values has the backing of several national governments (Australia and the United Kingdom are notable in this respect), as well as international organizations such as the OECD (Aspin & Chapman, 2007). In one sense, the current policy interest in values education is directly built on the Cardinal Principles' call for character education. In the United Kingdom, in fact, the very terms of the near century statements have not changed much at all, with calls for character education still carrying currency (Revell & Arthur, 2007).

In other ways, the trajectory of research in values education in the United Kingdom follows a more recent implementation logic, with earlier reviews (Halstead & Taylor, 2000) and advocacy research (Silcock & Duncan, 2001) being followed by studies of program effects (Arweck, Nesbitt, & Jackson, 2005). The connection between values education and academic outcomes has also been a steady concern. From demonstrations that values are embedded in the international measurements of mathematics (MacNab, 2000) to later demonstrations of this occurring in mathematics classrooms (Bills & Husbands, 2005), the relationship between academic outcomes and values education has clearly been a concern, at least in the United Kingdom.

Perhaps predictably, the recent U.K. interest in values education can be traced to other parts of the world. With many of these connections, the adoption of the international interest to concerns of more local national interest is evident, for example, in the Swedish concern to embed values in the daily rules and life of schooling (Thornberg, 2008) and the Australian welding of values education with Australia's interest in promoting quality teaching (Lovat & Toomey, 2009). This juxtaposition highlights a central tension in the field between those who advocate schooling that follows the values ostensibly promoted as opposed to those teaching about them.

Although the U.K. and European interest in values education is clearly a political response of broad social concerns for social order and social integration, for U.S. educators, the similarity between this research and that sparked more than 30 years ago in the United States following Kohlberg's early work and the then fashionable values clarification initiatives will be apparent. Few researchers are now in a position that is any less qualified than that of U.S. scholars who, when reviewing the effects of those earlier U.S. programs 30 years ago, noted limited implementations and marginal effects, at best (Lockwood, 1978).

The Place of Nonacademic Outcomes in Multicultural Education

Although advocacy for dedicating school to "nonacademic" outcomes comes from many different educational interests that are arguably of universal appeal (does anyone argue against values per se?), the call for nonacademic outcomes becomes particularly ambiguous for educators concerned about social and educational equity. That is, in the long tradition of research on educational inequalities relating to class, gender, and race, the relationship of nonacademic and academic outcomes take three different tacks. For the purposes of this analysis, consider the field of multicultural education as an illustrative example.

As with values education, multicultural education is an area of education research rightfully considered a field in its own right, with its own journals (e.g., *The International Journal of Multicultural Education*, *The Journal of Multiculturalism in Education*). One tack taken in multicultural education research is to analyze the sources and social origins of cultural inequities and the well-documented inequities of educational provision. For example, in her review on multicultural education policy, Darling-Hammond (2004) focused on unequal distribution of funding, teachers, curriculum, and resources and policies that allow these inequities of provision to continue. Whereas authors of research such as this are often critical of policies that focus solely on academic outcomes, the concern for unequal distribution of educational provision in itself does not question what outcomes are the results of such inequities. In fact, much of this research accepts measures of participation, retention, and credentialing at face (or market) value.

The second tack taken in multicultural education research is to take nonacademic outcomes such as student engagement as a means to better conventional outcomes (including academic outcomes). Much of the current interest in understanding the complexity of student identities, for example, essentially focuses on identity as a medium through which schooling works to increase engagement in schooling (Nieto, Bode, Kang, & Raible, 2008; Rogers & Mosley, 2006; Trofanenko, 2006). Arguably, this is very much the logic behind much of the now prominent push for preparing teachers for diverse student populations and improving multicultural programs in teacher education (Grant, Elsbree, & Fondrie, 2004; Ladson-Billings, 1999).

The third tack taken in multicultural education is to make direct appeals to alternative programs that produce outcomes that are quite distinct from academic outcomes and clearly ends in their own right. Perhaps the most developed body of research in this vein is the growing interest in the promotion of "intergroup relations" in school (Schofield, 2004; Stephan & Stephan, 2004), with programs demonstrating moderate effects.

Civics and Democratic Education

One of the central normative pillars of mass education, perhaps especially in the United States, has been the long-standing belief that schooling should contribute to, and is essential for, civic life in a democratic society. In this line of reasoning, from among the variety of ways schooling might promote a democratic civil society, its core function rests on schooling's capacity to produce engaged and competent citizens. Although this general argument is so pervasive as to be considered common sense (in the United States), there is a very large body of research that specifically focuses on questions of citizenship, and which would arguably date back to the political foundations of the Unites States and the push for mass schooling itself.

Without needing to survey the entirety of this literature, for the purposes of this chapter, one example of recent research can provide a glimpse into the larger field at the same time as outlining the general logic of most pushes to advance nonacademic outcomes from schooling. It is important to note, though, that this subfield of education research has a very long tradition and is well advanced. The literature relating to any one of the specific areas of nonacademic outcomes will include philosophical and theoretical articulations of the concern at hand, with a strong focus on establishing the normative basis for that concern, as well as a plethora of specific case-based qualitative studies that describe the intended curricular and pedagogical programs. As we know from the relatively recent interest in quantitative meta-analyses, the number of studies that develop and apply measures of alternative outcomes is typically relatively few, as a portion of the studies in any one area. Developing and testing measures in themselves usually constitutes the focus of several studies, without necessarily studying those measures as outcomes of specific programs. It is usually only a very advanced area of study that has moved through these necessary stages of research where it is possible to find studies that examine the effects of programs on measured outcomes (in a variety of research designs).

Because studies in civics and democratic education have been accumulating for more than a century, it is readily possible to identify studies based on measures of intended outcomes. The recent works of Joseph Kahne and coworkers (Kahne, Chi, & Middaugh, 2006; Kahne & Sporte, 2008; Kahne & Westheimer, 2003) provide such an example. Assuredly, this is but one example among many. Recent other comparable examples in this line of research would include, for example, the work of Feldman, Pasek, Romer, and Jamieson (2007), who link larger questions of democratic education and civics to the use of discussions in classrooms. Kahne's work has been used as an example here because it clearly links specific curricular practices with a relatively specifically identified set of nonacademic school outcomes, which are then linked to larger societal "needs" in a relatively concise manner (within one article, Kahne & Sporte, 2008).

Drawing on the larger historical literature supporting the normative case for civics education, Kahne and Sporte's (2008) recent analysis of the impact of civic learning opportunities is particularly notable. In the rationale and background to their recent research, Kahne and Sporte provide a concise and well-formed snapshot of the logic behind this particular nonacademic outcome argument and the current state of the field. First, the argument establishes that there is a broad agreement to the normative goals of civics education for schools, which adopts a functional logic that banks the value of what schooling does on the basis of what society needs. In this case, the logic would suggest that a "democratic" society needs particular kinds of citizens; therefore, schools should do things that develop democratic citizenship. Second, the argument points out that we actually know very little about how and how well schooling delivers on this function. Third, the argument translates the larger societal need (competent and engaged citizens) into its schooling outcome counterpart. Fourth, the question is turned to asking which schooling practices best promote the specified nonacademic schooling outcome. This fourth step in the argument's logic is the point of departure for beginning research.

For Kahne and Sporte (2008), the first, second, and fourth steps of this argument are established in the first two paragraphs of their recent article and reinforced throughout the article. The overall logic of the argument, however, falls into place in their third paragraph:

Some reformers, scholars, and foundation leaders are now looking for ways to reassert the democratic purposes of schooling (Gibson & Levine, 2003). Those promoting democratic priorities want schools to develop the skills and commitments that students need in order to be concerned for the well-being of others. They also want schools to teach students how government works and how they can work with others on solutions to community problems. This focus reflects concern for the health of American democracy. Numerous studies have found that levels of civic engagement in the United States are lower than desirable, particularly among youth (Galston, 2001; Macedo et al., 2005; Putnam, 2000). Indeed, as a panel of experts convened by the American Political Science Association recently found, "Citizens participate in public affairs less frequently, with less knowledge and enthusiasm, in fewer venues, and less equitably than is healthy for a vibrant democratic polity" (Macedo et al., 2005, p. 1). (Kahne & Sporte, 2008, p. 739)

Here, we can see the translation of the larger societal need for democratic citizens being translated into more specific "outcomes." "Skills and commitments" needed to be "concerned for the well-being of others" and knowledge about how government works and how students can "work with others" to solve community problems are all identified individual attributes that could serve as schooling outcomes. The explicit naming of social concern and individual capacities to engage in the collective endeavor to solve community problems clearly identifies the desired student outcomes from this particular example of civics education. Feldman et al.'s (2007) focus on outcomes was slightly more specific, with measures of the extent to which individual students follow politics, their sense of political efficacy, and their knowledge of political events and issues.

Although each set of outcomes is distinct, the link between them is relatively clear: (a) the extent to which individual students follow politics can be understood as a manifestation of their commitment to societal concerns (even if their politics are ultra-individualistic, placing that in the political arena by definitions makes it social), (b) an individual sense of efficacy would be necessary for these commitments, and (c) both sets of outcomes share background knowledge of government and civics. Thus, although each set is distinct, they are also driven from a similar point of reference: They share some generalized sense of what it takes to be a good democratic citizen.

So it is that research in civics and citizenship offers a prime example of one path toward a focus on "nonacademic" outcomes. There is a clear overt commitment to (a) a normative ideal for individuals, schools, and society; (b) a clear articulation of how that normative ideal translates into curricular designs and pedagogical practices; (c) a reasonably clear set of student outcomes linked to that normative train of thought; and (d) to a lesser extent, an examination of the degree to which those nonacademic outcomes translate into behaviors beyond schooling itself, as active democratic citizens. Arguably, each of these four steps can be found in most, if not all, calls for schooling that promotes nonacademic outcomes.

Even versions of democratic education that eschew predetermined articulations of desired outcomes (as can be found in some versions of the most Deweyian of curriculum, or in that hallmark of progressive pedagogy A. S. Neil's *Summerhill*) still have some notion of each of these logical steps—they just refuse to name the outcomes ahead of time, leaving that up to the students to experience and determine. In these less-predetermined versions of pedagogy, there still is a commitment to having outcomes, it is just that those outcomes are meant to be maximally influenced by the students themselves. And that commitment is based on a normative notion of how society should be.

The question for this chapter, however, is just what is the relationship between these desired outcomes and those traditionally taken to be "academic" outcomes? Or, in other words, just how "nonacademic" are these nonacademic outcomes? Here the reason for highlighting the work of Kahne should become clearer.

If we are going to argue for schools to develop curricular programs that promote nonacademic outcomes, let us also be clear about just what the relationship is between these desired other outcomes and those already found within the academic tradition of schooling. Using the work on democratic education noted above as our first example, consider three dimensions of student outcomes articulated in that work: students' knowledge, skills, and dispositions. In relation to the knowledge and skills desired in these democratic education programs, it is clear that a large portion of the knowledge desired is already precisely the same as that found in conventional academic programs in the social sciences and civics. There might be some shifts in the specific knowledge and skills included on this topic, depending on the relative political slant of the selector, but even the most radical call for democratic education would include much of the same material on the formal functions of government and the like. The main points of difference among the desired dispositional outcomes of different democratic education programs would lie in the degree to which collective or communal problem solving would be valued; but, even in relation to dispositional outcomes, all democratic programs would carry some degree of both individual and collective responsibility claims (as the politically logical counterparts to individual and collective rights). Overall, then, the outcomes desired in most calls for democratic education are quite compatible for the knowledge, skills, and dispositions needed for academic outcomes, particularly considering the need for individual capacities in public reasoning and debate.

Environmental Education[1]

Environmental education offers a counterpoint example of a subfield of education research based on an advocacy of nonacademic outcomes that is quite different from civics and democratic education. Before discussing research in environmental education, note how the literature in environmental education differs from that in civics and democratic education. First, although there are historical legacies in environmental education dating at least as far back as calls for civics and democratic education, the formal push to develop programs for environmental education reported in education research literature has a much more recent history. The growth of research in environmental education clearly matches the growing public recognition of human impacts on the global environment over the past few decades. Second, because its history is more recent than civics and democratic education, it is possible to examine research in environmental education more comprehensively by focusing on the past decade alone. Because of this, a comprehensive search of literature in environmental education research was conducted for this analysis.

Although there are several debates about how best to understand and theoretically frame education in this area, for this analysis the review of literature in environmental education encompassed research that included the self-descriptive terms *environment*, *environmental*, *ecological*, or *sustainability*, including named foci such as *environmental education*, *education for the environment*, *education for sustainability*, and *ecological literacy*. Ten well-known electronic databases were included in this search (in order of most cited for this search): Informaworld, EBSCOhost Mega File Premier, Proquest

5000, Informit, Scopus, JSTOR, ERIC, Sage Journals online, ScienceDirect, and Ovid Databases). Limiting the search to the period 1998 to March 2009 produced a collection of 583 published articles from all around the world. This sample of literature was then analyzed to provide an overall characterization of the field with some relatively simple categorization of whether or not

1. the research reported some empirical findings,
2. the research addressed questions of outcomes directly (some focused purely on establishing the normative case),
3. the outcomes discussed were student outcomes (some focused on teachers' environmental understanding and knowledge),
4. the student outcomes were analyzed using some quantitative measure, and
5. the measured student outcomes were studies in the context (as an effect) of a specific curricular program.

Although these are not all mutually exclusive distinctions, they do allow some important observations about the overall state of research in environmental education.[2]

First, it is important to note that a focus on student outcomes was not a concern for a majority of these studies. Of the 583 articles, 354 had no focus on student outcomes. Eighty-eight of the 583 articles did focus on teacher outcomes, being studies of teachers or trainee teachers. In all, 225 articles did have a focus on student outcomes (38.5%, inclusive of a few with a focus on both student and teacher outcomes). This general landscape is not entirely unexpected because, as noted above, a large portion of the interest in environmental education necessarily is focused on raising educators' awareness of the need to do something about the climatic and environmental concerns facing all humans today. Thus, a fair bit of attention has been given rightly to establishing the normative basis for the area and in developing theoretical frameworks needed to design curricular programs matching that normative desire.

Of the 225 articles with a focus on student outcomes, 200 contained observed outcomes. That is, some of the focus on student outcomes did not necessarily mean empirically observed student outcomes were reported. Furthermore, of the 200 reports of observed student outcomes, 121 measured those student outcomes for some form of quantitative analysis (about 60% of the observed student outcomes reported, 20.7% of the total). This includes studies that quantified qualitative student outcomes (using quasi-quantification techniques). Thus, it is clear that at least some researchers focusing on environmental education have begun the task of developing measures for student outcomes.

Of the 121 articles with measured student outcomes there were approximately 60 articles with outcomes attained from specific environmental programs/initiatives. Most of the other 61 with measured student outcomes were reporting the development of instruments or reporting baseline data. Thus, of the 583 articles identified in this analysis, 10.3% of the studies reported quantitative measures of student outcomes linked to curricular programs designed to produce those outcomes.

So it is that the current literature on environmental education reveals a very broad range of research, in terms of its theory and methodology. This literature also reveals the degree to which measuring student outcomes is not necessarily the main game in environmental education. Some of the reasons why measuring student outcomes is not a main concern of this literature would be consistent across most research relating to nonacademic outcomes. Clearly, a great deal of attention has been given to what we might understand to be preliminary work that is necessary in all areas of science— in the development of interest and theoretical tools for researching new frontiers of educational knowledge. This would be true of any new area of interest and in many ways is how education researchers as a community sift and winnow through the ongoing cascade of educational fads and policy chimera.

But there also is a more fundamental reason some environmental education research does not measure students' nonacademic outcomes. That is, because much of the push in environmental education directly argues against applying technical rationality, input–output models of education, it is not surprising to see researchers taking the stance not to engage in research based on accepting an institutionalized rationality. This would be true of any call for nonacademic outcomes that carries a similar rejection of technical rationality. In the case of environmental education, the technical rationality of schooling can be seen as one of the central problems in attempts to get whole populations to shift away from what might best be character-ized as an individualistic, consumerist, culture of material accumulation. In this view, schooling as we know it, based on a rationality that is consistent with an ecologically problematic culture, is part of the problem in the first place.

Whether or not other areas of nonacademic outcomes share this rejection of the hegemonic culture of schooling would depend on which call for nonacademic out-comes we consider. This is a point to which we will return, but the area of environmental education was selected to illustrate this point in greater depth. That illus-tration could come straight from a review of the theoretical positions taken within environmental education (see Gruenewald & Manteaw, 2007), but it is also evident by specifically considering just what is measured as student outcomes in environmen-tal education.

Taking the 60 studies with identified measures of student outcomes, the list of just what is taken to be an outcome of environmental education is quite long, and includes (in alphabetical order)

- Achievement motivation
- Action competence
- Awareness of social activism and activism itself
- Comfort levels within the environment
- Conceptions of environment
- Critical thinking skills
- Decision-making skills
- Engagement

- Environmental attitude
- Environmental behavior
- Environmental concern
- Environmental intensions
- Environmental interest
- Environmental knowledge
- Environmental motivation
- Environmental perceptions
- Environmental values
- Influence on environmental sensitivity
- Locus of control
- Problem-solving skills
- Skill improvement through environmental education
- Student–parent environmental communication
- Systems reasoning

Although the most frequently measured outcomes among this list are environmental knowledge and attitudes, it is clear that outcomes that extend well beyond what might be typically considered "academic" outcomes are of interest to these environmental education researchers. That is, the concern for seeing impacts on the degree of student–parent environmental communication increases in the awareness of and involvement in social activism, environmental values, action competence, and even comfort levels in "the environment," and all represent outcomes that extend beyond conventional academic outcomes.

Two distinctions illustrate the ways in which these student outcomes are in fact nonacademic. First, it is clear that the purpose of environmental education is to motivate actions and behaviors that take place outside the realm of the school—in families and communities in addition to behaviors within schools. In this sense, student outcomes of some environmental education programs do not rely on an indirect causal path from some school certification to later efficacy but are directed toward more direct and immediate impact beyond schooling. Second, the specific environmental attitudes measured are often reflective of the theoretical stance that opposes the hegemonic culture of schooling itself. Advocates of many of the other outcomes listed (locus of control, systems reasoning) also establish the need for these outcomes on the basis of a critique of academic outcomes as not including and in fact oppositional to these important aspects of developing environmentally responsive populations.

It is important to note that these nonacademic outcomes of environmental education are really just the tip of the oppositional iceberg. As Robert Stevenson (2007) makes clear, in an article recently reprinted from its earlier 1987 publication, there are a host of curricular and pedagogical implications to be drawn from environmental education research that are in many ways anathema to conventional schooling. The list of practices identified as contradictory to conventional, academic-based, schooling offers a lens through which we can characterize the nature of the culture of schooling against which some nonacademic outcome advocates struggle.

For Stevenson (2007), environmental education calls for a degree of collective problem solving on current environmental problems, in the "real" world, ideally including taking direct social action to address those problems. Teaching for this is meant to be cooperative and requires a very high degree of students' construction of knowledge, where knowledge itself is seen as problematic. Furthermore, because students would be developing and undertaking their own actions, it is needless to say that this form of curriculum would be flexible to the point of not really allowing predetermined outcomes to be established that would directly reflect the action students decide to take. Clearly, the degree of social activism advocated here is not common in academic schooling (to say the least) but it should also be recognized that even this is not the most "nonacademic" environmental education can be.

In the view of many other environmental educators (David Orr and Steven Van Matre might stand as well-known examples here), a sense of spiritual connectedness with the environment is required that would be absent from social activism that accepts conventional means of societal governance. In its most connected form, environmental education speaks of a sense of wholeness and interconnectedness with "the land" where its (at least partial) compatibility and interaction with Indigenous cultures of the world become obvious. Less obvious are the political implications of this turn, because there is a measure of environmental conservatism that is related to some forms of social conservatism (after all, many Indigenous cultures of the "New Worlds" are not exactly perfectly aligned with "progressive" politics). This political ambiguity is evident in the history of the conservation movements of the United States and Europe (and elsewhere) and rests behind the well-rehearsed political ambiguities of Green Party politics around the globe. In its more spiritual edge, however, we have a wonderful example of a way in which the calls for nonacademic outcomes come face to face with cultural explanations of educational inequality.

WHEN ADVOCACY OF NONACADEMIC OUTCOMES CONFRONTS THE LOGIC OF SCHOOLING

The last two examples of specific subfields of education research that advocate nonacademic "outcomes" provided above illustrate a fundamental tension that rests underneath any attempt to apply the logic of schooling to many forms of curriculum and pedagogy. This tension is embedded both in the attempts to institutionalize practice in these areas (e.g., in trying to get schools to adopt the most environmentally connected forms of pedagogy) and in the attempt to research these areas in conventional "outcomes-based" research paradigms.

Taking research in the first instance, consider what it means to ask what evidence alternative educational programs can produce to demonstrate they are successful in meeting the outcomes they desire. Here, we are applying a logic that seeks to establish several steps in a roughly linear causal chain (recursive feedback loops not withstanding). In civics and democratic education, for example, these logical steps worked from a perceived social need providing a normative case for schooling (a democratic citizenry) that has a readily translatable student counterpart (students who exhibit the qualities of that democratic citizenry). From this point, clearly articulated educational theories meeting this demand are required for the development of curricular and pedagogical programs designed to develop those student qualities and to decide just what those outcomes should be and how we might have evidence of them. From there the question becomes whether or not programs that are implemented in the name of civics and democratic education are in fact faithfully implemented, and if so, how effective they are in producing the desired student outcome. Finally, we are left with the question of whether or not those student outcomes actually translate into behaviors and practices beyond schooling that are consistent with the originally identified social need.

Summarizing this logic in sequential steps, we can characterize this causal chain in six steps:

1. Perceived normative social need and its translation into desired student outcome
2. Development of educational theory for that normative requirement
3. Development of programs of curriculum and pedagogy
4. Implementation of programs
5. Production (and measurement) of student outcomes
6. Student outcomes transported beyond the school

Applying this logic clearly imposes the sort of input–output model or logic many educators criticize. There are several theoretical positions in the curriculum field that would take this sort of framework to be a theoretical imposition of technical rationality, confusing a means-ends rationality with what is more rightly seen as a more human/humane synthesis. The rejections of imposing a "technical–rational" framing can come from, inter alia, Deweyian recognition that the world created within schooling is as important as any world outside, to existentialist rejections of *techné*, to studies of the ontology of education, to Buddhist commitment to experiencing the path rather than fixating on the object of the destination.

However theoretically true these rejections of an analysis that separates educational philosophy, pedagogic actions, and outcome, there are both pragmatic and political reasons not to presume the philosophic intent of an educational program actually translates into pedagogic action that is consistent with that intent nor that the outcome of those actions actually are what was wanted in the first place. The feminist and poststructural critique of Critical Pedagogy stands as a firm reminder that presuming too much may well be unwise (see Gore, 1993; Luke & Gore, 1992). From the environmental example given above, we can readily see that whatever the philosophical intentions of an environmental education program or theory, it would be a mistake to presume student outcomes are actually produced by alternative programs. In addition to the obvious outcomes question (did it work?), the six steps of our causal chain highlight the many other often asked empirical questions: Is an educational theory reasonably faithfully implemented in practice? Do measures of student outcomes validly and reliably measure what was intended? Do those student outcomes translate into behaviors and practices beyond schooling? and so on.

However much we can agree with educational theories that stand in opposition to conventional schooling, there is still good reason to accept some form of a casual chain logic. In terms of how education is experienced by school students in a given moment, on a given day, the social and systemic reality of schooling means their experience will not always be consistent with the various educational theories that lie behind whatever they do experience. The distinctions made in separating pedagogical programs from their theories and student outcomes from the implementation of those programs are not just analytical distinction. They also represent very different lived realities.

Synthetic theories calling for wholeness and connectedness are certainly appealing; however, the distinctions made following the casual chain, *zweckrational* (means–ends reasoning), can not be washed away with a premature Hegelian synthesis. Here, the reference to Hegel is intentional, because many forms of radical pedagogies (including positions influenced by poststructural and postmodern theories as well as their Marxist and feminist predecessors) all rely on some form of rejection of Hegelian idealism. But when alternative education programs or pedagogic philosophies (including the most radical) fail to make the distinctions implied in the causal chain logic or overtly reject them, they cover over distinct social phenomena under singular umbrellas of good intent. This failure to open one's eyes to experiences other than one intends occurs at the risk of recreating dogma, reinvigorating power structures the authors intend, often, to change. From the example given above, just because a teacher works from a very holistic environmental theory does not mean student experience is consistent with that theory, or that they eventually exhibit the intended outcomes.

Synthetic theories that disallow distinguishing philosophical rationale, pedagogic action, and outcomes fundamentally ignore that there are specific people with particular educational rationale, which in these cases is clearly intentional. Furthermore, there is a range of specific pedagogic action made more probable when following specific philosophies; and the experience of these pedagogic actions has consequences that are distinct *in the lived experience of students*. Separated by time, place, social context, and bodies, examining these phenomena separately does not violate their conjunction in given moments; it simply acknowledges that schooling is composed of several moments linked but not determined by the pedagogic intent of teachers.

The forced conjunction of realities can be taken to be a premature Hegelian synthesis in as much as the Hegelian impulse to bring together theory and antithesis is clear. In the case of environmental education where the intent is to get students to take action they themselves determine, it might appear impossible to measure empirically whether or not the programs produced their desired outcomes. However, if we assume the theoretical intent is what actually happens, that would prematurely prevent researchers from more honestly opening up our collective educational hopes to sincere examination. The analytical impositions that ask us to examine outcomes as being distinct from intent, and the practices that make them more likely, simply accepts that there is a valid social point to distinguishing empirical reality from philosophical proclamation.

This position is similar to that advocated for sociology by Pierre Bourdieu and his colleagues (Bourdieu, 1993; Bourdieu, Chamboredon, & Passeron, 1991). This position also implies a critique of the critiques of calls for empirical analyses of effects (Biesta, 2007). Because the debates caused by the current push for a "scientific" basis of education research and research on school reform have already rehearsed many of these criticisms, and can be found within the literature supporting many of the areas of nonacademic outcomes in their own right (see, e.g., Gruenewald & Manteaw, 2007), we do not need to rehearse them here. What this position does imply, though, is that whatever the theoretical position behind a given area of nonacademic outcome, the causal chain logic outlined above identifies six distinct moments that can be open to critical analysis, and all of them involve some degree of empirical claim.

The degree to which these steps require a social analysis may not be apparent but can be readily seen from the first step of articulating a normative agenda and its translation into some desired student outcome. Taking these steps requires some sociological analysis of how schools and society currently operate. If the advocate is arguing for something not currently done, there must be some normative societal case as well, because even a strictly psychological case carries sociological implications once that is placed in the context of schooling. Although some alternative outcome arguments are largely articulated in psychological form (such as calls for promoting self-esteem or self-concept), once placed in the realm of schools they must take some measure of sociological theory with them. This necessary link between theories of learning and teaching and broader sociological understanding has long been recognized by many educational psychologists. As Jerome Bruner once put it:

A theory of instruction is a political theory in the proper sense that it derives from consensus concerning the distribution of power within the society—who will be educated to fulfil what roles? In the very same sense, . . . pedagogical theory must surely derive from a conception of economics, for where there is division of labor within the society and exchange of goods and services for wealth and prestige then how people are educated and in what number and with what constraints on the use of resources are all relevant issues. The psychologist or educator who formulates pedagogical theory without regard to the political, economic, and social setting of the educational process courts triviality and merits being ignored in the community of the classroom. (Bruner, 1968, p. 69)

So it is that calls for nonacademic outcomes, no matter how fundamental the critique of schooling, become subjected to the same technical, means–ends social rationality on which schooling has been historically based. This confrontation is never more apparent than in the realities of schooling experienced by Indigenous people around the world. In contexts where the culture of Indigenous students' families are so different from that of schooling such that the difference can rightfully be best described as incommensurate, nontranslatable, the culture of schooling is literally imposed. Bourdieu and Passeron's (1977) theory of pedagogy as symbolic violence based on the imposition of "the cultural arbitrary" is apparent here. Many scholars in the industrialized world may have once taken the language of symbolic violence as being at least overstated, but the confrontation between any call for nonacademic outcomes that align with cultures that are incommensurate with schooling, and the logic of student outcomes embedded within schooling is clearly based on the legitimated imposition of a culture specific to schooling itself.

Any of the current calls for educational innovations designed to promote nonacademic outcomes will become subject to the same logic outlined above once they are brought to bear on the school systems of the world. As Sam Wineburg (1989) once noted of the heightened interest in situated cognition,

> The theory of learning put forth by the authors has generated great excitement, deservedly so. But to survive in the marketplace of ideas, a theory of learning has to be situated in a theory of schooling. Otherwise, it may leave its mark on archival journals, but leave the world of classrooms virtually untouched. (p. 9)

Whether we consider the long-standing interests in multicultural education that are designed to promote the recognition and valuing of cultural differences, or current interest in programs that promote well-being, or the now international interest in values education, once any of these initiatives to promote nonacademic outcomes are placed in the context of schooling, it becomes possible to query each in terms of the normative social theories driving them, the educational theoretical counterpart to that normative case, curricular designs and implementation, the desired student outcomes, and the final question of whether or not those programs actually do deliver the social consequences sought in the normative case in the first place.[3]

Herein lies the general cautionary note that applies to all promoters of nonacademic outcomes, in the form of a question: How much do we really know about whether or not any of these programs has the desired effect beyond schooling? Where civics and citizenship pushes can rely on a handful of studies that link outcomes of their programs with later civic behaviors beyond schooling, other new areas of alternative programs (such as environmental education) would be hard pressed to find any evidence in support of their programs having impacts beyond schooling.

In their review of transfer from schooling to out-of-school experience, Pugh and Bergin (2005) were quite strong in coming to a similar conclusion. In their words, "We have identified a few areas of inquiry that hold potential for addressing the question of whether subject matter learned in school makes a difference in out-of-school experience, *but the question remains largely unanswered*" (p. 20, italics added). Whereas Pugh and Bergin are not entirely dismissive of the possibility of finding evidence for transfer to out-of-school experience under certain (as yet unknown) circumstances, they are careful to point out that we know very little about this and that the methodological implications of this gap in our knowledge are substantial. It is very important to note that this is a question that has been raised in relation to academic outcomes as well, in the context of the PISA agenda (Hopmann, 2008).

ON THE CONSEQUENCES OF THE
OUTCOMES OF SCHOOLING

The relative lack of understanding of the consequences of the outcomes of schooling needs to be compared with our knowledge about the effects of the "academic" outcomes identified as attainment and achievement. From numerous sociological and demographic studies we actually know quite a lot about the social consequence of academic outcomes (even though much of what is known in research does not always fit the common sense of public understandings). Given this, and given the public faith in conventional measures of academic achievement, whatever the differences in norms and values that underlie debates about the relative virtue of nonacademic outcomes, there seems little likelihood that a shift in the public reliance on academic outcomes will be forthcoming until we know a lot more than we do about nonacademic outcomes. The contemporary approach is essentially to allow specialization and social differentiation at some later point in schooling, such as we find in specialist magnet high schools, schools of the arts, and so on. This situation may well work for the specific students involved, but it does little to challenge the strong focus on requisite common curriculum.

The main problem for advocates of nonacademic outcomes is that we do not know much about which schooling outcomes, apart from academic outcomes, matter "in the long haul." To understand this issue, we need to begin a more systematic and serious analysis of the effects of alternative school outcomes in a broader sociology of schooling outcomes, or what Bruner termed a political economy of pedagogy. To the extent that these alternative outcomes may be the effect of specific curricular programs and/or instructional regimes, we would then be fulfilling the as yet unmet promise originally identified in the sociology of curriculum (Bernstein, 1990). We also would have a much stronger basis on which to have public debate on the purposes and effects of schooling.

Michael Young (2008) has recently recast his understanding of this problematic with a specific focus on knowledge, and there is much merit in this formulation. However, because many of the outcomes of schooling are inclusive of much more than knowledge specifically, it would be a mistake to impose such a limit on a broader sociology of school outcomes. Current sociological analyses of the effects of schooling and specific subfields of education give some insight into what a broader theoretical framework might look like (Albright & Luke, 2008). Here the attempt is to link specific forms of knowledge, skills, and dispositions (as differing forms of economic, social, and cultural capitals) to both their social origins and their currency in fields beyond schooling.

Taking environmental education as an example, we can understand the knowledge, skills, and dispositions found in scientific understandings of climate change as being consistent with the culture of schooling and having a relatively direct potential payoff beyond schooling in fields where those forms of cultural capital (and the social and economic capitals associated with them) are valued, such as in university-based programs taking a similar approach to climate change or government departments or industries reliant on that science. But the nonscientific or more spiritual, nonanthropomorphic, or holistic forms of knowledge, skills, and dispositions found in some environmental education programs would probably not carry a huge payoff in the same social destinations. Looking backward, so to speak, we could also speculate as to which students are more and less likely to find developing scientific forms of environmental knowledge skills and dispositions readily accessible and achievable. We could also hypothesize which students are more likely to espouse strong nonscientific sensitivities to the environment while at the same time their behavior exhibits a lack of that sensitivity. (We might also make the same hypotheses about ourselves, irrespective of our own educational experiences.)

In terms drawn from the sociological theories of Bourdieu, we could hypothesize that the degree of nonscientific empathy with the environment and the dispositions to act accordingly would be stronger among those for whom more expensive alternative behaviors are a real economic option and among those whose background more closely connected them to the land (in concrete terms of lived experience). In more colloquial terms, it is easier to be environmentally friendly when you can afford it, and it is more likely you will understand the impact of climate change more if you "live on the land."

But the payoff of adopting these forms of cultural capital would differ sharply, dependent on the constellation of economic, social, and cultural capitals each person holds, relative to where that payoff is sought. In crude terms, if you did not do all that well in schooling and did not have much money, being environmentally sensitive alone would not get you into an Ivy League university; but, if you had the required academic achievements and the money to pay tuition (or a scholarship), being environmentally sensitive might give you an edge in trying to gain access to elite institutions who see themselves as open and forward thinking.

This form of theorizing about the outcomes of schooling does much more than simply trace the social paths of students beyond schooling; it calls for a larger mapping of the flows of power in society. If we are going to make claims about the benefits of nonacademic outcomes and make normative social appeals for their inclusion within schooling, we would do much better if we actually knew which of these mattered for whom, to do what, where, and when. Broadening Young's terms beyond knowledge per se, we need to better know just which outcomes of schooling are in fact powerful outcomes.

CONCLUSION

In December 2005, there were a series of incidents on the southern beaches of Sydney, Australia, now infamously known as "The Cronulla Riots" (Cronulla being a suburb of Sydney and the name of a beach where the incidents began). The riots are widely recognized as being based on ethnic rivalry and racist intolerance; between some mostly White "Australian" youth and Australians of Middle Eastern descent (among many others). Over the subsequent days, thousands of people were involved in a combination of nonviolent but antagonistic protests and violent exchanges. Eventually, with a fair amount of heavy policing, and public debate and calls for peace, things settled down. In a sense, this was an Australian version of the now semi-regular flashpoints of racial tensions in my homeland, the United States.[4]

One of the interesting things about the Cronulla riots is that any of the youth involved who attended schools in the Sydney region would have gone to schools in which there have long been official policies and some curricular practices designed to promote racial and ethnic harmony, with strong advocacy from teachers' unions and departmental bureaucrats. Whatever those policies and curricula achieved, however, they clearly were not sufficient to prevent the deeply embedded forms of human mutual self-destruction based on racism that we have all inherited. Although it would be foolhardy to rest the responsibility for preventing justifiable social unrest entirely on schooling, it would be nice if we knew whether any form of education could provide some predictive capacity in the attempt to rid our societies of such ignorance-based acts of hatred, and if so, which forms of education those were. The election of the first African American president not withstanding, the need for better understanding of the social consequences of programs promoting nonacademic outcomes has never been clearer.

But as Max Weber and Jürgen Habermas have long warned, the imposition of the means–ends rationality required in schooling, and in research that attempts to trace causal chains, is a double-edged sword. That is, whenever the more we attempt to gain a better grasp and instrumental control over forms of human life that currently escape the controls of our institutions, our bureaucracies, the more we colonize more of our "life world" within a restrictive logic of systemic input–output prediction. Understanding the call for nonacademic outcomes and the need to know more about the calls for schooling to promote nonacademic outcomes within this sociophilosophical view allows us to query which programs have what effect for whom. From this view we can also reflectively question just how much measurement we want, of what.

It is clear that some of the "species-being" reproductive functions of schooling (the purposes of schooling related to reproducing human societies) rest on attempts to alleviate or prevent modes of self-destruction that face humanity as a whole. On the surface of it, there are clear threats to humanity that lie within, forms of self-destruction facing humanity that have been brought to consciousness at least since Auschwitz. In the current world, the most obvious of these threats include our own contributions to potentially irreparable destruction of the global environment and the seemingly never-ending mutual destructions based on religious and ethnic differences. Each of these links clearly and quite directly with the concerns addressed in environmental education and education for sustainability, on one hand, and multicultural and antiracist education, inter alia. (A similar logic would apply to many other nonacademically focused educational programs such those focused on well-being or mental health, physical and health education, democratic citizenship education, peace education, etc.)

Conceiving educational programs as contributions of humanity as such, however, entails more than a purely totalizing and individualizing logic. That is, once we recognize the species-being functions of schooling (how we promote growth as a species), and see schools as historical institutions serving this broadest function (the means by which we humans reproduce our societies), the Foucauldian view of modern institutions is evident. Here we can understand Foucault's demonstration that modern institutions deploy techniques of power that not only individualize but also apply to any who lives within those institutions, thereby also being universal. If Foucault and Foucauldian analyses of education have taught us nothing else, isn't it that modern institutions like schools always use and create power? The question is not whether or not schools will use and make power but in what ways and for whom.

However, this totalizing logic leaves unaddressed the unequal social distribution of *primary goods*, to use Rawls's term, produced in schooling. That is, where Foucauldian analyses teach us the details of how schools use and produce power, they tell us little about whether or not that distribution is just or justified. To understand these questions requires some moral philosophical framework, such as found in the philosophical debates sparked by Rawls's notions of distributive justice.

Bringing together these conceptual frameworks results in a manifold logic. Where schooling is clearly both individualizing and universalizing, it is also socially differentiating—with social differentiation occurring on multiple, historically contingent dimensions of social inequality. (For the current discussion, I leave aside the question of how different forms of social inequality interrelate or which are "primary.")

The importance of this theoretical background cannot be overstated, however abstract it may seem, because it lies behind many of the contemporary debates that circulate around and within either side of the academic–nonacademic outcomes discussions. For example, when critics within multicultural education argue that a reliance on programs that focus mostly on celebrations of difference and the recognition and valuing of nondominant cultures leaves unaddressed issues of structural transformation and the redistribution of power, they are building from the fundamental recognition that the institution of schooling functions as both a universal and differential mechanism of recognition and (re)distribution. Herein rests the reason it is possible to find variants of race theory, or multicultural education, that self-identify as "critical race theory" or "critical multiculturalism." The critical impulse to understand and work with the differentiating functions of schooling, as part of the larger societal apparatuses of structural inequality, will apply in any debate about what outcomes schooling does, could, or should produce. Herein lies the reason skepticism remains about the ultimate efficacy of programs that focus on celebrations and recognition of difference or identity in the critical pursuit of structural transformation (Badiou, 2008).

Ultimately, however, such debates are not going to be settled by theoretical fiat or analytical nuance. The questions about what outcomes schools might produce and what their effects may be in the larger distributions of primary goods beyond schooling can be advanced beyond irreconcilable theoretical debate only if they are understood as questions of lived experience, empirical effects, and social collective experience.

In 1981, Harold Berlak and Ann Berlak pointed out a paradox facing progressive educators who are concerned with "educating the whole child." That is, as one of their dilemmas of schooling, Berlak and Berlak named a tension that lies between understanding the child as a person versus the child as a client. Applied to our current discussion, teachers focusing on the child as a client might be more inclined to focus on academic outcomes, whereas those concerned about the child as a person might lean toward focusing on nonacademic outcomes. However, as tempting as it is, as Berlak and Berlak pointed out, the more sides of a child's life we address as teachers, the more we open the whole child to our surveillance and control. Herein lies one of the paradoxes faced in debates about nonacademic outcomes. At the same time, though, it is very hard to know which outcomes to promote (or choose not to promote) without much more research into which nonacademic programs actually do "work" and which have lasting, powerful outcomes.

ACKNOWLEDGMENTS

In addition to the *RRE* series editors, I would like to thank my consulting editors Hannu Simola and Mark Berends whose work and thoughts continue to challenge and teach me. I would also like to thank the members of my local *Principia Methodologica* seminar group, and in particular Anne Ross for her outstanding assistance in the preparation of this chapter.

NOTES

[1]The term *environmental education* is used here to generically refer to both the longer history of like studies and to be inclusive of the more contemporary notion of "education for sustainability." I acknowledge there is substantial debate about the meaning and implication of these terms and labels within the field. The descriptive terms used in our search convey the generic perspective taken for this chapter.

[2]Articles for this review were drawn from more than 100 journals including general education research journals such as the *American Educational Research Journal, Anthropology & Education Quarterly, Asia Pacific Journal of Education, British Educational Research Journal, Cambridge Journal of Education, Canadian Journal of Education, Curriculum Inquiry, Curriculum Journal, Educational Leadership, Educational Philosophy & Theory, Educational Researcher, European Journal of Psychology of Education, Journal of Curriculum Studies, Journal of Philosophy of Education, Oxford Review of Education, Phi Delta Kappan, Review of Educational Research and Theory into Practice.* More specialist journals represented include *Applied Environmental Education & Communication, Australian Environment Review, Australian Journal of Environmental Education, Australian Journal of Outdoor Education, Canadian Journal of Environmental Education, Environment and Behaviour, Environmental Education & Information, Environmental Education and Information, Environmental Education Research, Environmental Management Environmentalist, International Journal of Environmental Education and Information, International Journal of Environmental Studies, International Journal of Leadership in Education, International Journal of Science Education, Journal of Research in Science Teaching, Science Education, The International Journal of Environmental, Cultural, Economic & Social Sustainability,* and *The Journal of Environmental Education.*

[3]A soon to be published study (Jennings & DiPrete, in press) offers another interesting angle on this, by examining the effects of teachers on what they term *social skill.* Where other areas build from an overt advocacy of specific nonacademic outcomes, this research simply takes social skill development as an already existing phenomenon. There is a very sound empirical logic in this approach but ultimately does not avoid the implied normative advocacy for what gets defined as social skills.

[4]The resonance between the Cronulla riots and Mike Davis's (1990) analysis of urban America is noteworthy.

REFERENCES

Albright, J., & Luke, A. (Eds.). (2008). *Pierre Bourdieu and literacy education*. Mahwah, NJ: Lawrence Erlbaum.

Apple, M. W. (1971). The hidden curriculum and the nature of conflict. *Interchange*, *2*(4), 29–40.

Apple, M. W. (1979). *Ideology and curriculum*. London: Routledge/Kegan Paul.

Apple, M. W. (1980). Analyzing determinations: Understanding and evaluating the production of social outcomes in schools. *Curriculum Inquiry*, *10*, 55–76.

Apple, M. W., & King, N. R. (1977). What do schools teach? *Curriculum Inquiry*, *6*, 341–358.

Arweck, E., Nesbitt, E., & Jackson, R. (2005). Common values for the common school? Using two values education programmes to promote "spiritual and moral development." *Journal of Moral Education*, *34*, 325–342.

Aspin, D. N., & Chapman, J. D. (2007). *Values education and lifelong learning: Principles, policies, programmes*. Dordrecht, Netherlands: Springer.

Badiou, A. (2008, January/February). The Communist hypothesis. *New Left Review*, *49*, 29–42.

Bautier, E., & Rayou, P. (2007). What PISA really evaluates: Literacy or students' universes of reference? *Journal of Educational Change*, *8*, 359–364.

Berlak, A., & Berlak, H. (1981). *The dilemmas of school*. London: Methuen.

Bernstein, B. (1990). *The structuring of pedagogic discourse: Class code and control* (Vol. IV). London: Routledge.

Biesta, G. (2007).Why "what works" won't work: Evidence-based practice and the democratic deficit in educational research. *Educational Theory*, *57*, 1–22.

Bills, L., & Husbands, C. (2005). Values education in the mathematics classroom: Subject values, educational values and one teacher's articulation of her practice. *Cambridge Journal of Education*, *35*(1), 7–18.

Bobbitt, F. (1920). The objectives of secondary education. *The School Review*, *28*, 738–749.

Bourdieu, P. (1993). *Sociology in question* (R. Nice, Trans.). Thousand Oaks, CA: Sage.

Bourdieu, P., Chamboredon, J.-C., & Passeron, J.-C. (1991). *The craft of sociology: Epistemological preliminaries* (R. Nice, Trans.). New York: Walter de Gruyter.

Bourdieu, P., & Passeron, J. C. (1977). *Reproduction in education, society and culture* (R. Nice, Trans.). London: Sage.

Bruner, J. S. (1968). Culture, politics and pedagogy. *Saturday Review*, p. 69.

Collins, R. (1979). *The credential society: An historical sociology of education and stratification*. London: Academic Press.

Darling-Hammond, L. (2004). What happens to a dream deferred? The continuing quest for equal educational opportunity. In J. A. Banks & C. A. M. Banks (Eds.), *The handbook of research on multlicultural education* (2nd ed., pp. 609–630). San Francisco: Jossey-Bass.

Davis, M. (1990). *City of quartz: Excavating the future in Los Angeles*. London: Verso.

Feldman, L., Pasek, J., Romer, D., & Jamieson, K. H. (2007). Identifying best practices in civic education: Lessons from the student voices program. *American Journal of Education*, *114*, 75–100.

Galston, W. (2001). Political knowledge, political engagement, and civic education. *Annual Review of Political Science*, *4*, 217–234.

Gibson, C., & Levine, P. (2003). *The civic mission of schools*. New York: Carnegie Corporation of New York and the Center for Information and Research on Civic Learning.

Gore, J. M. (1993). *The struggle for pedagogies*. London: Routledge.

Grant, C. A., Elsbree, A. R., & Fondrie, S. (2004). A decade of research in the changing terrain of multicultural education research. In J. A. Banks & C. A. M. Banks (Eds.), *The handbook of research on multicultural education* (pp. 184–207). San Francisco: Jossey-Bass.

Gruenewald, D. A., & Manteaw, B. O. (2007). Oil and water still: how No Child Left Behind limits and distorts environmental education in US schools. *Environmental Education Research*, *13*, 171–188.

Halstead, J. M., & Taylor, M. J. (2000). Learning and teaching about values: A review of recent research. *Cambridge Journal of Education, 30,* 169–202.

Hopmann, S. T. (2008). No child, no school, no state left behind: Schooling in the age of acountability. *Journal of Curriculum Studies, 40,* 417–456.

Jennings, J. L., & DiPrete, T. A. (in press). Teacher effects on social/behavioral skills in early elementary school. *Sociology of Education.*

Kahne, J. E., Chi, B., & Middaugh, E. (2006). Building social capital for civic political engagement: The potential of high school government courses. *Canadian Journal of Education, 29,* 387–409.

Kahne, J. E., & Sporte, S. E. (2008). Developing citizens: The impact of civic learning opportunities on students' commitment to civic participation. *American Educational Research Journal, 45,* 738–766.

Kahne, J. E., & Westheimer, J. (2003). Teaching democracy: What schools need to do. *Phi Delta Kappan, 85*(1), 34–40, 57–66.

Kleibard, H. M. (1986). *The struggle for the American curriculum 1893–1958.* New York: Routledge.

Labaree, D. F. (1991). Does the subject matter? Dewey, democracy and the history of curriculum. *History of Education Quarterly, 31,* 513–521.

Ladson-Billings, G. J. (1999). Preparing teachers for diverse student populations: A critical race theory perspective. *Review of Research in Education, 24,* 211–247.

Lockwood, A. L. (1978). The effects of values clarification and moral development curricula on school-age subjects: A critical review of recent research. *Review of Educational Research, 48,* 325–364.

Lovat, T., & Toomey, R. (2009). *Values education and quality teaching: The double helix effect.* Dordrecht, Netherlands: Springer.

Luke, C., & Gore, J. M. (Eds.). (1992). *Feminisms and critical pedagogy.* London: Routledge.

Macedo, S., Alex-Assensoh, Y., Berry, J. M., Brintnall, M., Campbell, D. E., & Fraga, L. R. (2005). *Democracy at risk: How political choices undermine citizen participation and what we can do about it.* Washington, DC: Brookings Institution.

MacNab, D. (2000). Raising standards in mathematics education: Values, vision, and TIMSS. *Educational Studies in Mathematics, 42*(1), 61–80.

McGaw, B. (2008). The role of the OECD in international comparative studies of achievement. *Assessment in Education, 15,* 223–243.

McNeil, L. M. (1986). *Contradictions of control: School structure and school knowledge.* London: Routledge/Kegan Paul.

Meyer, J. W., Ramirez, F. O., & Soysal, Y. (1992). World expansion of mass education, 1870–1980. *Sociology of Education, 65,* 128–149.

Meyer, J. W., & Rowan, B. (1977). Institutionalized organizations: Formal structures as myth and ceremony. *American Journal of Sociology, 83,* 340–363.

Nichols, S. L., & Berliner, D. C. (2007). *Collateral damage: How high-stakes testing corrupts America's schools.* Cambridge, MA: Harvard Education Press.

Nieto, S., Bode, P., Kang, E., & Raible, J. (2008). Identity, community, and diversity: Retheorizing multicultural curriculum for the postmodern era. In F. M. Connelly, M. F. He, & J. I. Phillion (Eds.), *The Sage handbook of curriculum and instruction* (pp. 176–197). London: Sage.

Pugh, K. J., & Bergin, D. A. (2005). The effect of schooling on students' out-of-school experience. *Educational Researcher, 34*(9), 15–23.

Putnam, R. (2000). *Bowling alone: The collapse and revival of American community.* New York: Simon & Schuster.

Revell, L., & Arthur, J. (2007). Character education in schools and the education of teachers. *Journal of Moral Education, 36*(1), 79–92.

Rogers, R., & Mosley, M. (2006). Racial literacy in a second-grade classroom: Critical race theory, whiteness studies, and literacy research. *Reading Research Quarterly, 41,* 462–495.

Rothstein, R. (2000). Toward a composite index of school performance. *The Elementary School Journal, 100,* 409–441.

Schofield, J. W. (2004). Fostering positive intergroup relations in schools. In A. J. Banks & A. M. C. Banks (Eds.), *The handbook of research on multicultural education* (pp. 799–812). San Francisco: Jossey-Bass.

Silcock, P., & Duncan, D. (2001). Values acquisition and values education: Some proposals. *British Journal of Educational Studies, 49,* 242–259.

Snedden, D. (1916). New problems in secondary education. *The School Review, 24,* 177–187.

Spring, J. (2008). Research on globalization and education. *Review of Educational Research, 78,* 330–363.

Stephan, W. G., & Stephan, C. W. (2004). Intergroup relations in multicultural education programs. In J. A. Banks & C. A. M. Banks (Eds.), *The handbook of research on multicultural education* (pp. 782–798). San Francisco: Jossey-Bass.

Stevenson, R. B. (2007). Schooling and environmental education: Contradictions in purpose and practice. *Environmental Education Research, 13,* 139–153.

Thornberg, R. (2008). Values education as the daily fostering of school rules. *Research in Education, 80,* 52–62.

Trofanenko, B. (2006). Displayed objects, indigenous identities, and public pedagogy. *Anthropology and Education Quarterly, 37,* 309–327.

Wineburg, S. S. (1989). Remembrance of theories past. *Educational Researcher, 18*(4), 7–10.

Wirth, A. G. (1983). *Productive work in industry and schools: Becoming persons again.* Lanham, MD: University Press of America.

Young, M. F. D. (2008). From constructivism to realism in the sociology of curriculum. *Review of Research in Education, 32,* 1–28.

Chapter 5

Defining Equity: Multiple Perspectives to Analyzing the Performance of Diverse Learners

WILL J. JORDAN
Temple University

Defining equity within the context of a diverse, multiracial, multiethnic, multilingual, and multicultural society, and one where social class strongly influences one's life chances is problematic. This chapter reexamines equity in an attempt to advance the discourse beyond the debate about strategies to close the achievement gap between White students and students of color. I situated the issue of equity within an analysis of broader social forces that cultivate inequality throughout society—in employment, housing, criminal justice, and so forth—so that educational inequality is part and parcel of overarching social ills. The notion of equity will be unpacked by asking a more basic and fundamental question about the ultimate purpose of education. If we assume the end game of education is producing student learning, then we should ask whether learning outcomes are distributed randomly across race, ethnicity, and social class. Moreover, I will explore whether No Child Left Behind (NCLB)-like assessments or high-stakes tests measure real learning necessary for social and economic success, or do they measure something else. The role of increased accountability via state-based systems as an approach to obtaining equity is hotly debated. Although advocates are many, several studies have found the consequences of high-stakes testing, which are nonobvious and perhaps unintended, have not helped advance the nation toward equitable schooling.

The pursuit of educational equity has long been a goal of reform efforts in the United States. Yet creating a system of education where all children have equal access to quality instruction and widely available opportunities to learn to their fullest human potential has been elusive. More than half a century ago, the *Brown v. Board of Education* decision settled persistent concerns about the degree to which access to quality schooling was based on race (Ball, 2006; Ball & Samy, 2006; Gutiérrez

Review of Research in Education
March 2010, Vol. 34, pp. 142-178
DOI: 10.3102/0091732X09352898
© 2010 AERA. http://rre.aera.net

& Jaramillo, 2006). However, structural inequality in education based on race and class, which was overt and legally sanctioned prior to *Brown*, has become murkier since then and the demographic landscape in the public schools has become more complex. In fact, the work of several scholars document how we have come full circle in the segregation of American schools—a complete cycle from segregation, to integration, and back again to segregation (Darling-Hammond, 2000; Levine, Cooper, & Hilliard, 2000; Orfield & Lee, 2005). Indeed, some scholars argue that integration was never actually achieved, but instead new forms of segregation emerged. Increasing cultural, linguistic, racial, and ethnic diversity among learners makes it timely to reexamine the current discourse and debates about equity and to formulate a clearer definition of equity.

Drawing on the extant research literature, this chapter examines multiple perspectives and approaches for analyzing educational outcomes among diverse learners. Particular attention will be paid to the ways in which learning is studied as a primary outcome of schooling. I focus on learning as the key dependent variable, rather than student achievement, because the latter is a narrower concept and driven to a large extent by dominant policy discourse. This chapter also examines how definitions of educational equity have changed meaning over the years as the discourse on inequality has evolved.

Before advancing a working definition of equity, it is important to provide a brief historical overview of the discourse on educational achievement of students of color in American schools. It is not possible to describe the evolution of the educational system in the United States adequately without addressing the role of race relations and the legacy of segregation (Gadsden, Smith, & Jordan, 1996). In *Brown*, the Supreme Court settled the debate that racially isolated schools were "inherently unequal" and laid the legal groundwork for building a more equitable education system. Yet, as we continue to celebrate this landmark victory over structured inequality, schools nationwide are challenged by increasing racial, ethnic, and social class segregation (Roscigno, 2000).

According to Orfield and Lee (2005), current and rising levels of segregation should be considered in light of the strong empirical relationship between race and poverty, suggesting that unequal access to a quality education continues to play a role in opportunities for social and economic mobility. Orfield and Lee's study reviewed the wide sweep of segregation changes nationally, regionally, and by state since *Brown*. Their analysis included a decade of resegregation since the Dowell decision in 1991, which the authors contend relaxed desegregation regulations and authorized a return to neighborhood schools. Orfield and Lee (2005) asserted that children in racially and ethnically segregated schools often experience "conditions of concentrated disadvantage, including less experienced or unqualified teachers, fewer demanding pre-collegiate courses and more remedial courses, and higher teacher turnover" (p. 4). Overall, evidence presented in this study suggests that many Black and Latino students attend schools of concentrated poverty, and that many White students experience high levels of racial isolation as well.

However, the extant literature on equity offers insights on diversity and school segregation, which encompasses thoughtful analysis of cross-cultural and multiracial experiences that go beyond Black/White conceptions of schooling inequality. In analyzing data from the 2000 U.S. Census, Zhou (2003) provides a profile of racial and ethnic demography of the United States and explores challenges that children and their families face at a time of rapid change. She examines intragroup diversity, residential segregation, immigration, intergenerational issues, and highlights challenges of schooling in an urban context. Focusing on Asian American and Hispanic communities in California, Zhou raises the question of the roles communities play in helping diverse children do well in school and finds they do matter.

Notwithstanding Zhou's (2003) work, increasing cultural diversity has shifted but not eliminated lingering traditional race relations as the Black/White and Hispanic/White gaps in achievement have been largely stable over the past decade (a point I will elaborate below). The work of Orfield and Lee (2005), along with those of numerous other scholars (Bali & Alvarez, 2004; Gadsden et al., 1996; Gamoran, 2007; Roscigno, 2000), suggests that while the *Brown* decision helped America stumble forward in reconciling a major social injustice, there remains considerable work to be done to establish a fair and equitable system of education, where opportunities to learn and the ability to reach high standards are uncorrelated to race, ethnicity, and class. After essentially ignoring the demands of *Brown* for more than a decade, school districts nationwide began gradually integrating Black and White children, primarily via busing strategies and the creation of magnet schools. Put simply, school desegregation was an affirmative action policy assuring some Black and Latino students access to schools that previous generations could not attend.

In *Stepping Over the Color Line: African American Students in White Suburban Schools*, Wells and Crain (1997) examine the implementation and impact of a federal court order that imposed an interdistrict desegregation intervention on a highly segregated St. Louis, Missouri metropolitan area. The program linked the predominately poor and Black St. Louis City to its Whiter and more affluent suburbs by allowing city students to transfer to suburban schools. The 5-year case study of the St. Louis urban–suburban desegregation program involved interviewing more than 300 educators, policymakers, parents, students, lawyers, and judges. The authors state "we learned through their eyes [the interviewees] just how entrenched the color line is and why people on both sides of that line lack the will to erase it" (p. 18). According to Wells and Crain, during the postdesegregation era, policies focused on race-based allocations of resources are now seen as largely out of sync with core American values, and perhaps they are. However, they assert,

> Most civil rights legislation and court cases focused on giving African Americans the same opportunities as whites to achieve in a white-dominated society. Under such policies, blacks were suddenly unshackled and then expected to compete in a contest in which whites had a 200-year head start—a contest for which whites had written the rules and constructed the meaning of "merit" on their own terms. (p. 2)

The present chapter does not dwell on the *Brown* decision and its impact on equity, race relations, and schooling, as this topic is thoroughly described elsewhere (Fruchter, 2007; Ladson-Billings, 2004). Instead, the 1954 *Brown* decision can be viewed as a baseline for a discourse on equality of educational opportunity, or the lack thereof. Moreover, as a result of ongoing demographic shifts resulting from immigration, expansion and contraction of cities, internal geographic mobility, and general population growth, the American cultural tapestry has evolved over the years so that racial politics are no longer simply Black and White, or Black, Hispanic, and White. For example, Akom's (2008) work on Black metropolis and mental life focuses in part on the centrality of race and racism and their intersectionality with other forms of oppression. This theoretical paper was based on a 4-year comparative ethnographic research project on forms of racial domination in the San Francisco Bay Area. Building on the work of Collins (2000), Akom suggests that race can be viewed from the "intersection of other forms of oppression such as class, gender, religion, nationality, sexual orientation, immigration status, surname, phenotype, accent, and special needs, by illustrating how these forms of oppression interlock creating a system of oppression" (p. 257).

This is not to say, however, that race and ethnicity no longer play a role in social interactions and social mobility—because it does indeed. Still, many studies of student achievement often use these racial/ethnic categorizations to illuminate differences between subgroups. This chapter integrates this language (e.g., Black/White achievement differences) along with more progressive language on race, diversity, and learning. I sometimes use the overly broad term *people of color* to refer to several racial and ethnic groups, including Blacks, Latinos, American Indians, Asian Americans, and people of Far East and Middle Eastern decent (Suyemoto & Fox Tree, 2006). I recognize this diverse group of children and families is not monolithic, to be sure. In an essay to community psychologists, Suyemoto and Fox Tree, an Asian American and Native American scholar (self-described), use the phrase "people of color" to contextualize experiences and conflicts in relation to race hierarchies. Their aim was to attack the "divide and conquer strategy" to construct bridges across racial and cultural differences and to critique the maintenance of White privilege.

There is considerable variability on cultural dimensions, school outcome measures, and broader structural factors both within and between these groups. For example, some studies have found similar patterns and distribution of standardized achievement among Asian Americans and Whites (Bempechat, Graham, & Jimenez, 1999; Lew, 2006; Paik & Walberg, 2007). However, these and other studies reject the notion of Asian American students as a "model minority" on the grounds that test scores do not tell the full story and many Asian American students continue to be at risk of school failure and encounter structural barriers in many facets of American society. Lew (2006), for example, in his paper on the "burden of acting neither white nor black: Asian American identities and achievement in urban schools" asserts that "the stereotype of Asian 'success' much like black 'failure' cannot be explained solely on their cultural orientation" (p. 350). He concludes that although culture and race influence students' general outlook on life and how they negotiate their opportunity structures, the process is fluid and changes and adapts within specific social and school contexts.

Lew's (2006) study compared educational and cultural experiences of two groups of Korean American students, one attending a competitive New York City magnet high school, and the other dropouts attending a community-based GED program. The purpose of the study was to extend the "acting White" debate beyond a Black-and-White discourse. His research focused on how Asian American students, in two different social and economic contexts, negotiate their race and ethnic identities. Using a model minority stereotype that conflates Asian Americans with whiteness, this study describes how the two groups of Korean American adolescents adopt different racial strategies depending on their socioeconomic backgrounds, peer networks, and school contexts. The findings of this case study research problematize current understandings of the role of culture in school achievement and illustrate how culture intersects with class, race, and schools. To be sure, Lew's work and the research of others point to stark sociocultural differences among people of color (in this case Asian Americans) and between people of color and Whites that manifest in school. At the aggregate level, Asian American students appear to achieve parity or exceed school achievement of White students (Zhou, 2003), yet many continue to struggle in school. Among those who are academically successful, obtaining social justice in mainstream society is an ongoing battle (Zia, 2000).

Black and Latino students frequently share common status as the low achievers in American schools; however, there are critical cultural and linguistic differences between the groups. Bali and Alvarez (2004) investigated when and how the Black–White and Hispanic–White achievement gaps develop in the elementary grades. Evidence for their analysis was drawn from a rich database, containing reading and math test scores, along with a variety of background and school context variables for students attending the Pasadena Unified School District (PUSD), California from 1999 through 2002. PUSD is a district with a large population of students of color, where more than 80% of the students are Black or Hispanic. The methodology of the study employed multivariate analysis to predict the annual reading and math test scores of a student cohort from first through fourth grade, controlling for school context and family background factors. The authors' findings affirm that in this racially diverse school district achievement gaps develop in elementary school for both Black and Hispanic students. The Hispanic–White gaps develop later, however, especially in math, and they were considerably smaller than the Black–White achievement gaps. The authors further conclude that the eventual widening of the gaps for both Hispanic and Black students does not seem to be attributable to attending schools of less quality.

To complicate matters further, Blacks, Latinos, and indeed all racial and ethnic groups, present considerable intragroup variability as mentioned above (Bhatti, 2006; Noguera, 2003). These factors make it difficult to generalize research findings to whole categories of students. For example, the classification of "African American" sometimes includes voluntary immigrants of African descent (Ogbu, 1978), for instance, second-generation African students and students from the Caribbean who often perform quite well academically, better than American Blacks who are just a few generations removed from slavery. By contrast, Lee's (2008) historical analysis of the "de-minoritization" of Asian American students suggests that Southeast Asians from Cambodia and Vietnam demonstrate some of the oppositional positions and underperformances of African American and Hispanic students. Such a contrast is important because they are often placed in the same category as Chinese, Japanese, and Korean students.

Lee's (2008) historical study examines the process whereby Asian American students have been gradually removed from minority status, or deminoritized in the University of California (UC) system. The UC system provided the platform for this study because California is home to large numbers of Asian Americans. More higher education in California has also been the site of significant affirmative action developments and controversies about Asian American admissions in past decades. Findings from Lee's study revealed policy shifts at UC reflecting how Asian Americans have been "racialized" over time, "through an unstable and contested process that began with the establishment of Asian Americans' minority status in the 1960s and its removal in the 1980s" (p. 130).

Several themes recur throughout this chapter. First, that the promises of *Brown*—to create a racially and ethnically integrated educational system with equal opportunity and access for all students—were never kept, although progress has been made. Second, there is a tremendous amount of diversity in American public schools that exists mostly in large cities and metropolitan areas that leave many kids behind. I believe urban education should be the frontline on increasingly redressing equity. Third, equity is a complex social phenomenon and equalizing opportunities and equalizing outcomes are vastly different enterprises. What is equitable and fair can be better understood in relationship to other things and from within a given context. In other words, perspectives of equity may vary among diverse groups and may be linked to culture. Fourth, problems in measuring and defining learning using "objective" standards versus cultural knowledge or multiple ways of knowing complicates attempts to define equity. Because it is difficult, if at all possible, to measure learning using a common yardstick in a diverse environment, it is similarly problematical to define equity using a unitary metric.

The No Child Left Behind Act (NCLB) represents perhaps the most recent and significant policy initiative to redress inequity at a national level. Indeed, a major goal of NCLB is to educate all children to proficiency or above by 2014. A primary mechanism for fostering improvement is a series of carrots and sticks, but mostly the latter, aimed at identifying "evidence-based" instructional practices or those activities and experiences that are empirically linked to state accountability systems (high-stakes, standardized tests). The theory of action undergirding NCLB is that increasing accountability for states, districts, and schools—or allocating blame for subpar test scores—will apply positive pressure on educators, motivate the use of effective practices, and ultimately improve achievement. However, a problem with this argument is that obtaining equity is not as simple as eliminating or reducing variability in test scores. In fact, there is a broad literature that describes how overemphasis on high-stakes testing can create perverse incentives for educators (Lipman, 2004; McNeil, 2000), which cause them to teach to the test and falsely inflate depictions of student learning. Thus, I argue that standardized testing has only limited utility in helping to understand learning and equity. I further contend in this chapter that learning is complex, dynamic, linked to human development, and embedded with a specific cultural context. A definition of equity should take into account these factors.

Equity is not about providing the same education to all students regardless of race, social class, or gender. In fact, because of increasing cultural and linguistic diversity it is advantageous to define educational equity in terms of providing knowledge, skills, and worldviews which would enable social mobility. Therefore, contexts shape our views of equity, and it takes on different meanings among different populations.

Accountability

The accountability policy framework (Diamond & Spillane, 2004; Mazzeo, 2001) holds that the purpose of schooling should be to educate every student to the same high standards of performance. Mazzeo's historical study examined the early history of academic assessment in the United States. He argued that, while it is generally accepted that school accountability is the raison d'être of educational policymaking, between 1865 and 1965 an accountability framework for state-based assessment failed to take hold, despite numerous attempts. According to Mazzeo (2001),

> [I]nstitutionalized clusters of normative and causal ideas play in educational policymaking. These idea structures—called policy frameworks—define the core principle or principles that animate state action, the legitimate aims served by intervention, and the manner in which these ends are to be achieved. (p. 367)

He further asserts that since the late 19th century, three dominant policy frameworks (examination, guidance, and accountability) have shaped discourse and action in the United States. Mazzeo's (2001) work is important because it suggests the current culture of accountability, which drives reform at all levels, is a fairly recent policy phenomenon. State accountability systems based on standardized testing, according to Mazzeo, first appeared in the early 1970s and have persisted to the present day. The initial theory of action undergirding the accountability framework was that "objective" information about student performance would help educators detect educational problems. Reforms could then be implemented, using knowledge from state tests, to improve academic performance for all students. Mazzeo contends that by the 1980s, states began modifying the focus of their testing strategies from identifying achievement problems of individual students, to evaluating whole institutions, that is, districts and schools. Since NCLB, emphasis on creating bigger and better accountability systems has steadily increased.

With the exception of the military, each year more resources are devoted to elementary and secondary education than any other common good in the United States, and Americans depend heavily on public schools to narrow social and economic inequalities in society (Rothstein, Jacobsen, & Wilder, 2008). The American public wants schools to produce graduates who will contribute to the stability and health of our democracy and to advance strategic competitiveness in a global economy, and an educational system where past inequities are ameliorated (Goyette, 2008; Sunderman, Kim, & Orfield, 2005). High-stakes standardized tests often are put forward as the primary yardstick against which schools are measured to these ends (Gamoran, 2007; Lee, 2007; Lee & Wong, 2004; Smith & Garrison, 2005; Wolf, 2007; Wong & Rutledge, 2006; Yeh, 2006). The ubiquitous and persistent gap in standardized achievement between students of color and white students is regarded as evidence of lingering inequity in education (Gold, 2007). Although it is probably true that the race gap reflects ongoing inequality, traditional studies of achievement, which compare subgroups of students (typically Black, White, and Hispanic) by selecting quantitative outcomes, fall short of telling the whole story of educational equity (Conchas & Noguera, 2006; Rousseau & Powell, 2005). Rothstein et al. (2008) argue that standardized tests currently in use within many state-based accountability systems can provide necessary information about student performance and equity, but not all traits for which schools should be held accountable can or should be measured by pencil-and-paper exams. Noncognitive or affective outcomes such as motivation (Jungert, 2008; Kozminsky & Kozminsky, 2003; Martin, 2005; Tuan, Chin, Tsai, & Cheng 2005; Zoldosova & Prokop, 2006) and aspirations (Akos, Lambie, Milsom, & Gilbert, 2007; Anderman, 2002; Bandura, Barbaranelli, Caprara, & Pastorelli 2001; Hanson, 1994; Mickelson, 1990) are also important in influencing educational and economic success.

However, in traditional studies of accountability and achievement, such affective variables are seldom captured or investigated. Steele and Aronson's (1995) work on "stereotype threat" is an example of often neglected affective characteristics. According to the authors, stereotype threat is the state of being at risk of confirming a negative stereotype about one's racial or ethnic group. Their research examined stereotype vulnerability of African American college students taking a challenging verbal test by varying whether or not their performance put them at risk of fulfilling the racial stereotype about their intellectual ability. Steele and Aronson suggest, reflecting the pressure of this vulnerability, Blacks underperformed in relation to Whites in what they refer to as ability-diagnostic conditions, but not in the nondiagnostic condition where aptitude is controlled. Their research further suggests that mere salience of the stereotype could impair Blacks' performance even when the test was not ability diagnostic.

There are other often unmeasured factors in studies of achievement and accountability. For example, teacher quality plays an important role in increasing equity and excellence in schools (Jacob & Lefgren, 2004), which is often not accurately measured in existing accountability systems. Nevertheless, there has been a clear preference for quantitative factors within educational accountability systems. Perhaps the allure of quantitative factors is the perception of objectivity and precision they contain. However, a nonobvious limitation is that subjectivity is often embedded at the front end of quantitative analysis, as researchers and evaluators operationalize concepts, formulate constructs, and decide how to numerically express meaning. In other words, selecting or creating test items is an attempt to validate what counts as knowledge and to place selective value on learning. Still, quantitative factors are not useless as they provide specific information about what happens in school. Problems arise mainly in educators' and researchers' misuse and misinterpretation of the data.

Standards-based reform and state-based accountability policies, which are ostensibly culturally neutral, are central to current wisdom of educational policy and educational improvement efforts (Diamond & Spillane, 2004; Gamoran, 2007). However, as elsewhere, the accountability debate is seldom placed within its proper historical context (see Mazzeo, 2001), and often neglects the importance of race, class, and culture in measuring student outcomes. As Ladson-Billings (2009) argued, children of color are often viewed as White students who simply need extra help to succeed in school. Rousseau and Tate (2003), in an essay to educational practitioners, argue that efforts to neutralize cultural differences or to view children through a lens of color-blindness can have undesirable effects on the quality of teaching and learning in a classroom. Such notions of colorblindness of race miss how race, culture, and learning are conflated and shortchange the potential cultural assets of students of color. This is why I reject the position of cultural neutrality and argue that schools and school systems must do a better job of incorporating and building on the cultural knowledge children possess.

Learning

Learning always occurs within a cultural context (Bransford, Brown, & Cocking, 1999; Bruner, 1996) and it is fundamentally a socially mediated process. Although cognitive functioning is essential for learning, other psychological mechanisms involved in learning are shaped by socialization and sociocultural factors (Nieto, 1999). As mentioned above, traditional quantitative studies of student achievement approach equity by demonstrating how the amount of knowledge acquired by a certain time differs across diverse groups of students (Bempechat et al., 1999; Bishop, 1998; de Valenzuela, Copeland, Huaqing Qi, & Park, 2006; Griffith, 2002; Zhou, 2003; and others). Bempechat et al.'s (1999) study offers an example of how a traditional quantitative study handles equity and achievement. Their data included roughly 600 White, Black, Hispanic, and Asian American fifth and sixth graders enrolled in public and catholic schools in the Boston area. The purpose of the study was to examine differences in school performance of poor students and students of color, by focusing on cognitive socialization, or ways in which parents influence the basic intellectual development of their children, and academic socialization, or ways in which parents influence students' attitudes and motivations that are critical for student success. The analysis involved a series of nested regression models where math achievement is predicted by ethnicity, attributions, and educational socialization, along with a battery of interactions-terms between controls.

But the aim of traditional studies of student achievement is primarily to discover whether or not a given group of students has gained specific knowledge taught in school, ignoring the learning that occurs at home in the communities (Rothstein et al., 2008). Seldom do such studies seek to provide evidence on the varied ways in which students are able to demonstrate cultural knowledge or multiple ways of knowing (Gardner, 1993; Harris, 2007; Nieto, 1999). Conceivably, school knowledge from the enacted curriculum can be viewed as the result of an interaction of home/community language/knowledge with the official curriculum. This interaction is nuanced and often exclusionary, but it is an interaction nonetheless. Still, I believe understanding the teaching and learning of authentic knowledge is essential to defining equity. My definition of authentic knowledge borrows from Darling-Hammond and Snyder's (2000) work on authentic assessment. Darling-Hammond and Snyder's analysis suggests that a growing number of teacher education programs using authentic assessments of teaching as a set of tools to beginning teachers build bridges from generalizations about practice to contextualized instances of learning. According to the authors, authentic assessment includes opportunities for developing teachers' thinking and practices in situations that are experience-based and that include or simulate actual teaching. They argue that the demands of teaching rigorous academic content to diverse students suggest a need for teacher training that enables practitioners to become more sophisticated in their understanding of the effects of context and learner variability on teaching and learning. Effectively teaching diverse learners, Darling-Hammond and Snyder posit, involves attending to distinctive assets each brings to the table, including prior experiences and knowledge, cultural, and linguistic capital, different dispositions, and sources of potential identification and opposition. Thus, authentic knowledge is defined in relationship to human diversity and aims for cognitive flexibility.

Equity is not about educating all kids to the same high standards of achievement (Noguera 2003; Rousseau & Tate, 2003); if so, it would be an unattainable and perhaps an undesirable goal within the context of a diverse, multiracial, multiethnic, and multilingual society. Additionally, a case can be made that schools by definition stratify knowledge. Instead, educational equity in a global society is about providing transformative learning experiences for students who require such experiences for social mobility, as well as social and cultural reproduction for students already on top. Given the educational stratification of diverse students, the implications for equity would suggest the allocation of resources relative to needs of children and families. In other words, to be transformative, schools serving poor students and students of color might require more resources to obtain the desired results. Moreover, rather than imposing a definition of equity that denotes fairness and respect for humanity, a nuanced definition should be co-constructed by all stakeholders of public education, incorporating a wide variety of voices, particularly with the aid of poor families and families of color.

Definitions of educational equity have changed meaning over the years as the discourse on inequality has evolved (Milem, Umbach, & Ting, 2004; Mohr & Lee, 2000). At least two distinct views have emerged, which represent different world-views or deep-seated values about the nature of inequality in society and the purpose of policy responses to it. One view holds that there is an assumption that inequality preexists and is inevitable, and that policy and practice are trying to ameliorate it. This view includes proponents of affirmative action policies, which support the notion of assessing groups by using different standards, to fix existing and prior discrimination. Conversely, the counter-perspective holds there are few or no embedded inequalities, thus everyone deserves equal treatment, without regard background characteristics such as race or ethnicity.

PERSPECTIVES OF DIVERSE LEARNERS

Bourdieu and Passeron's (1977) theory of cultural and social reproduction affords guidance in understanding differential educational outcomes for students and problematizing the issue of educational equity. They examine the dynamic relationship between "pedagogic action," which they define holistically as more than teaching but as the work of the educational system, and the reproduction of social class stratification in society. Social reproduction is premised on a fundamental principle of the theory of sociological knowledge, that "every power which manages to impose meanings and to impose them as legitimate by concealing the power relations that are the basis of its force, adds its own specifically symbolic force to those power relations" (p. 4). Like Bowles and Gintis (1976), Bourdieu and Passeron provide a critique of education within a capitalist society. However, Bourdieu and Passeron's analysis of macro-sociological forces challenges us to consider the fundamental purpose and social functions of public education. In so doing, we should also consider what counts as evidence of student learning, which is a necessary precursor to defining equity. Who ultimately decides what the learning objectives or academic standards should be—what a student must know and be able to do—and how achieving such standards relate to life chances (higher education, employment, decent housing, etc.)?

In many respects, poor students and students of colors face inequality at the starting gate (Lee & Burkam, 2002) and, to be successful in school and society, they must rapidly obtain cultural capital that emanates primarily from the dominant groups. Affluent and White students, on the other hand, have ready access to cultural capital, and navigating between the worlds of family, peers, and schools (Phelan, Davidson, & Yu, 1998) is comparatively less daunting.

Knowledge for Teaching

Learning, or acquiring and applying knowledge of the world, and educational equity, the fair and just distribution of learning opportunities and outcomes, can be understood only within a specific cultural context. If the ultimate aim of educational reform is to improve learning for all children and to reduce or eliminate between-group gaps, then a sophisticated understanding of theories of learning (Bransford et al., 1999) and human development (Santrock, 2005) should be employed. Providing an exhaustive look at learning theories here is beyond the scope of this chapter. However, minimally, we should be wary of studies that attempt to measure learning and achievement too narrowly (Rothstein et al., 2008). Bourdieu and Passeron (1977) underscored the futility of focusing on any one variable as a determinant of educational success. Instead, they suggested the continual, cumulative interaction between the "objective" measures (test scores) of learning themselves, along with the internalization of objective measures in the form of subjective evaluations (Bali & Alvarez, 2004), along with a variety of explanatory variables (Bishop, 1998; Cooper, 2007; Kim & Crasco, 2006; Nettles & Herrington, 2007; and others).

At a micro-sociological level, identity, family background, and socialization influence children's perceptions, motivations and experiences in schools (Nieto, 1999; 2000), which, in turn influence learning and engagement. In recognition of the "symbolic violence" embedded in pedagogic action, as suggested by Bourdieu and Passeron, the pursuit of equity should involve consciously building on the cultural strengths and human potentials of diverse learners. Educating children, or teaching, then can be seen as a political act and it is never simply about imparting knowledge into empty vessels. According to Nieto (1999),

> If we understand teaching as consisting primarily of social relationships and as a political commitment rather than a technical activity, then it is unquestionable that what educators need to pay most attention to are their own growth and transformation and the lives, realities and dreams of their students. (p. 131)

There are controversial aspects of Nieto's analysis. First, current efforts to reform teaching tend to favor technicist or behaviorist approaches, rather than strategies centered on student thinking, ways to build on students' understandings, or on the political nature of teaching (Kincheloe & Hayes, 2007; Matsumura, Garnier, Pascal, & Valdés, 2002). For example, the discourse around defining what it means to be a "highly qualified teacher" heavily weighs subject matter content knowledge (e.g., in mathematics, science, social studies, and reading) at the expense of pedagogical content knowledge or generalized pedagogical skills. In other words, within the context of current policy debates, having knowledge of a subject trumps having the ability as a practitioner to meaningfully engage children in the learning process. Arguments in favor of building knowledge content in academic subjects are compelling; however, knowledge for teaching is different than knowledge in its own right (Shulman, 1987). In the process of teaching, mathematics teachers apply conceptual and computational knowledge of the subject differently than do carpenters, engineers, or pilots, who also use math in executing their work, yet the level of content knowledge might not be dissimilar among each group. In addition to focusing heavily on content, the view of teaching as a technicist activity is evident in numerous reforms aimed at improving teacher behaviors, such as preparation of lesson plans, writing

lesson objectives on the chalkboard, posting the state's learning standards in designated areas, wait-time, use of praise, and so on, rather than also informing and challenging teachers' epistemological beliefs about teaching and learning. The other
controversy embedded in Nieto's (1999) analysis is that "lives, realities and dreams
of their students" are as diverse as the students themselves and can push educators to
identifying different outcomes for students. If some poor students and students of
color who represent a continuation of generations of unrealized dreams develop low
expectancies for self-mobility, should educators accept and sanction their wishes, or
should we force them to want more?

To be sure, finding a proper balance between imposing dominant values of educational and career aspiration on students, versus allowing them to find their own way
is difficult. Beyond policy discussions around school choice, the field has not yielded
evidence of effective strategies for incorporating voices of the students and families
served into ideas for improvement. Regarding poor students and students of color,
education is something done *to* them, rather than *with* or *for* them, an idea which is
asserted in recent research on cogenerative dialogic instruction (Emdin, 2007; Tobin,
2006). The absence of a clear consensus on the purpose and goals of education within
a diverse society further problematizes the notion of pursuing the goals of having all
students reach the same high standards of achievement, despite widespread inequality
in the system and uneven access to quality schooling.

Student Worlds

An ethnography study conducted at four desegregated schools in California by
Phelan et al. (1998) illuminated ways in which diverse adolescents negotiate or fail
to negotiate social borders and boundaries between family, school, and community.
The 3-year investigation involved 55 adolescents and hundreds of hours of shadow-
ing, interviews, and observations. This study examined what the authors referred to
as students' multiple worlds, and theorized about factors that enhance or inhibit the
conversion of borders into boundaries. Drawing on cultural compatibility theory
(Spindler & Spindler, 1992), the authors investigated the congruence of sociocultural components of adolescent worlds to explicate factors affecting learning and
engagement. Phelan and her colleagues use the term *worlds* to reflect "cultural knowledge and behaviors found within the boundaries of students' particular families, peer
groups and school; we presume that each world contains values and beliefs, expectations, actions, and emotional responses familiar to insiders" (p. 7). This research
underscores the writings of Nieto (1999) and other scholars who suggest teaching
and learning, and by extension assessment and equity, occur within a specific cultural
context.

Findings from Rousseau and Tate's (2003) study of teacher beliefs around race
and the cultural context of learning suggest a lack of attention among educators to
issues of race, culture, and equity, which also extends to teacher reflection within
mathematics education. That is, although there was recognition that inequality

exists, teachers often viewed themselves as being "color-blind," and interacting with students in a racially and culturally neutral manner. According to Rousseau and Tate, because the teachers conceived of equity as a process (e.g., equal treatment), different learning outcomes among students was not a catalyst for thoughtful reflection on pedagogical practices or relationships with students. Teachers in the study allowed students to fail without treating them differentially based on race, and this pattern of failure was not interpreted as problematical from the teachers' perspective. Teachers had no reason to question their own pedagogy, according to the authors, as long as they believed equal treatment was given to all students, regardless of race and culture. For example, giving each student the same opportunity for instructional help when they believed the students took responsibility for their own learning was seen as a marker for color-blindness. The authors conclude,

> In contrast, an overt reflective process linked to justice and race-consciousness would call into question any situation in which the results for students of color are disproportionately negative. Thus, we argue that it was, at least in part, the teachers' views of justice as simply an equalization process that allowed this pattern of disproportionate failure to go unaddressed. From their viewpoint, the pattern of failure was just. Therefore, it did not trigger any sustained teacher reflection. (p. 215)

Phelan et al.'s (1998) research revealed that school personnel often dwell wholly within the realm of the school, in classrooms and corridors, and as a result, they are frequently ignorant about the broader social milieu that students inhabit. Teachers and administrators are frequently uninformed about deep-seated values, beliefs, and ideals that hold sway in students' "real" world, as well as experiences and events that take place among families and communities outside of the reach of schools. The lack of cultural knowledge of students directly or indirectly affects the teaching and learning of academic subjects. The social context of students' lives that manifests in families and among peers shapes educational motivations, or the lack thereof, but educators are frequently out of position to help students navigate the social and psychological terrain. This research, similar to Luke's (2009), incorporates Bourdieu and Passeron's notion of *habitus*, where cultural capital, created by hegemonic forces, is the primary currency in schools and classrooms. As just mentioned, cultural capital, or the absence of it, offers a useful theoretical framework for explaining school success and the life chances of people of color. However, Phelan and colleagues, rather than accepting the inevitability of structural and sociocultural barriers, which disenfranchise some students, offer suggestions for pedagogical approaches to ameliorate inequities and to bridge boundaries between family, peers, and school.

Culture, Race, and Class

The discourse on the cultural context of learning unveils nuances and variability in the experiences and backgrounds of schoolchildren and challenges our ability to define equity in a straightforward, uncomplicated manner. In other words, given the full range of human interests, motivation, values, and ability, expecting education to produce the same outcomes for all students is simplistic, unfeasible, and likely unattainable. Moreover, if equal achievement in American schools was doable, framed as educating all students to the same high standards (where high standards are measured as test scores), I would ask whether it was desirable in light of the required diversity of knowledge, skills, and interest needed to maintain democracy and global competitiveness. However, the extensive body of literature on the persistent race gap in student achievement, like desegregation research which preceded it, points to ongoing non-nuanced, striking, and severe inequality in education (Altshuler & Schmautz, 2006; Gold, 2007; Horvat & O'Connor, 2006; Jencks & Phillips, 1998; Kaplan, 2007; Roscigno, 2000). Research on the race gap broadens the lens allowing us to consider how structural barriers influence equity and learning. Specifically, studies of the race gap in education analyze how race, social class, and culture are often conflated. Nationally, the existence of race gaps in test scores is a largely undisputed fact as evidenced in many studies where achievement is examined after controlling for individual, family, and school factors, and substantial racial gaps still remain (Bali & Alvarez, 2004).

In a study of race and the social reproduction of educational disadvantage, Roscigno (1998) examined several significant factors in the Black–White achievement gap; paramount among them were family background and social class. Merging data from the National Educational Longitudinal Survey (NELS, p. 88) and the Common Core of Data, Roscigno used hierarchical modeling to analyze the influence of family/peer and educational institutional processes simultaneously on the Black–White gap in achievement. The analytic procedures elucidated a more comprehensive understanding of the reproductive interinstitutional dynamics at play, which provided evidence of linkages between family/peer group attributes and access to educational resources. He concludes by suggesting the need for further inquiry leading to the development of theoretically driven contextual and spatial understanding of educational opportunity and achievement. Like Orfield (2001), Roscigno's analysis yielded a strong correlation between race and poverty. Roscigno asserted that socioeconomic status of the student's household—often operationalized as family income, parents' educational attainment, and parents' occupation status—was consistently influential for achievement. This relationship is critical to understanding the racial educational gap for Black and Latino students who continue to be disproportionately from lower socioeconomic households (Zhou, 2003). He adds that family structural differences between Blacks and Whites are likewise important, having implications for the availability of resources, parental time and supervision, and socialization. Using multivariate analysis, this study also contributed to the line of research underscoring the ways in which the educational system itself "perpetuates, rather than reduces, already existent societal inequalities" (p. 1034).

The implication of this research, along with cultural reproduction theory described earlier, is that it directly and indirectly connects equity in education to race relations, class struggle, and broader social stratification in society. The observed race and social class gaps are not just educational problems but a widespread social ill (Anyon, 2005; Lipman, 2004). Black, Latino and poor students lag behind affluent and White students, not only in academic achievement but also in access to quality health care, employment opportunities, quality housing, and fair treatment in the criminal justice system, indeed, in virtually all aspects of social life. As Anyon (1997) suggested in her landmark book, *Ghetto Schooling*, core problems faced by schools serving poor students and students of color did not emerge overnight. Anyon's research was centered on a 6-year case study of an elementary school, called Marcy, in Newark, New Jersey that was struggling to improve. This case study was conducted in tandem with a historical analysis of the political economy of New Jersey. Her analysis suggested the core problems of the Marcy School, which served mostly poor Black urban students, were not manifested or originated at the school. Instead, Anyon found that the chronic ineffectiveness and academic failure of Marcy and by extension, many similar city schools and districts, resulted from a perfect storm lasting more than a century. In it, schools suffered willful neglect, municipal mismanagement, incompetent leadership, graft, and institutionalized racism, from which they could not recover. While schools themselves did not have a hand in creating such problems, they were nevertheless manifested in schools.

Given overlapping and intersecting social policy arenas that affect education (housing, transportation, public health, criminal justice, employment, tax law, etc.), Anyon (1997) argues the educational system cannot be "fixed" from within. Instead, broad-based solutions encompassing several policy arenas are warranted. Inequities encountered by diverse students are experienced in many facets of social life, above and beyond education, so that closing the educational achievement gap cannot be adequately pursued without closing gaps in health, housing, employment, equal justice under the law, and so forth. Anyon thus concludes that public will to improve school quality is a necessary precursor, along with bold thinking which combine educational policymaking with social policy reform.

In *Urban Schools, Public Will*, Fruchter (2007) also points to a generalized inability to marshal support for resources to better meet the educational and social needs of urban poor students and students of color as problematic. However, this optimistic piece makes two key arguments: That city schools can be improved to effectively educate students who attend them, and that school districts can be levers to spark the transformation. Fruchter's position suggests the reasons inadequate urban schools continue to exist in the post-NCLB era do not include an absence of understanding about how to create equitable and efficient educational programs. Indeed, the United States has numerous exemplary schools, most serving affluent students. Instead, one of the reasons ineffective schooling persists is because of the challenges involved in marshalling public support to provide meaningful educational opportunities for students who are darker and different (Delpit, 1998).

I believe demystifying and clarifying what educational equity means involves joining competing discourses. On the one hand, much has been written about variations in standardized student achievement, a hallmark of high-stakes tests (Diamond & Spillane), as alluded to in the above passage. In policy circles, empirical studies of achievement and technical aspects of teaching and learning have been viewed as the dominate discourse (McNeil, 2000). At the same time, I have argued thus far that considerable research has looked more broadly at learning as primary outcomes, rather than achievement, and connects learning to culture (Bransford et al., 1999; Bruner, 1996; Nieto, 1999; Ladson-Billings, 2009; and others). There is tension between the kinds of knowledge commonly assessed on standardized tests and the kinds of knowledge students of color develop as a result of lived experiences, language use, social networks, and within the total sociocultural milieu of their daily existence. How this is resolved has implications for equity.

HIGH-STAKES TESTING

Several authors have questioned the utility of standardized test scores in advance policy and practice for educational improvement. For example, Abedi (2002) illustrated how standardized achievement measures are less stable indicators for English Language Learners (ELL) than for the non-ELL students. According to Abedi, ELL students at the lower end of the English proficiency distribution suffered from low reliability, and their language background may add another dimension to the assessment outcome, which serves as a source of measurement error in the assessment for English language learners. Additionally, the correlation between test scores and external criterion measures was significantly higher for the non-ELL students than for the ELL students. Abedi concluded,

> [T]he results of this study suggest that ELL test performance may be explained partly by language factors. That is, linguistic complexity of test items unrelated to the content being assessed may at least be partly responsible for the performance gap between ELL and non-ELL students. (p. 255)

In viewing the functionality of standardized testing from a Vygotskian perspective, it is conceivable they measure what students know and can do without assistance or cultural cues, or knowledge within students' zone of proximal development (Nieto, 1999; Vygotski, 1929, 1986). Yet I believe such tests cannot measure a child's full learning potential within a rich sociocultural context (Rothstein et al., 2008); or what students can do in learning ecologies that are saturated with cognitive tools and multiple forms of supports.

The end game of NCLB is said to be the pursuit of equity by raising standards of performance for all students (Downs & Strand, 2006). However, there is an intense debate about the impact, usefulness, and sustainability of accountability policies anchored by a program of state-regulated standardized achievement testing. Some scholars argue that one of the reasons why NCLB has failed to deliver on its promise is because of its narrow and inadequate characterization of learning and equity and overreliance on quantitative measures (Rothstein et al., 2008) that form the basis of assessment. According to Rothstein and his colleagues, perhaps the most important reason NCLB and advocates for increasing state-based testing got accountability wrong is because

> We've wanted to do accountability on the cheap. Standardized test that assess only low-level skills and that can be scored electronically cost very little to administer—although their hidden costs are enormous in the lost opportunities to develop young people's broader knowledge, traits and skills. (p. 7)

Low-level skills and knowledge that are tested are often what count as achievement, at the expense of true learning.

Rothstein et al. (2008) instead argue in support of developing more sophisticated and dynamic approaches to measure educational outcomes, for the purpose of both accountability and equity. There are many different ways that equitability might be defined when applied to educational assessments (Brennan, Kim, & Wenz-Gross, 2001). Because we cannot know, or precisely measure, the true intellectual abilities of students, we attempt to approach equity by using proxy measures of achievement on high-stakes tests. However, equating equity and test scores have been fraught with problems.

Since the passage of NCLB, educators and policymakers have used a variety of policy instruments in an attempt to ensure that all children receive high-quality education (Diamond & Spillane, 2004). An increasingly popular but controversial strategy relies on external accountability systems, including high-stakes testing, to improve teaching and learning, and hold teachers and students accountable for student performance outcomes. Critics of high-stakes testing argue that such policies exacerbate inequalities by leading teachers to marginalize low-performing students (McNeil, 2000; Lipman, 2004; and others) by tailoring instruction to tested areas. Further, in the process, teachers themselves become deskilled, according to McNeil (2000), as they focus instructional energies on solely or disproportionately on tested subject areas. Because teachers and administrations are placed in a system where they are forced to equate learning with higher test scores, authentic knowledge of how the world works, or relevant insights which can spark interest among students, seldom enters into the classroom. However, proponents of high-stakes testing assert that such assessments have several advantages, such as removing unreliable and subjective assessments of learning, reducing curriculum differentiation processes such as tracking and ability-grouping, and, hopefully, raising teacher expectations of the learning potential of diverse students. According to Diamond and Spillane (2004), proponents contend that external assessments provide objective information for school-based decision making and therefore work against more subjective judgments that contribute to unfair stratification. Furthermore, they argue, that to understand the implications of high-stakes testing it is important to examine how such policies are understood and implemented in particular school contexts.

I use a working definition of "high-stakes" established by professional organizations in education research, psychology, and measurement and evaluation. According to this definition,

> When significant educational paths or choices of an individual are directly affected by test performance, such as whether a student is promoted or retained at a grade level, graduated, or admitted or placed into a desired program, the test is said to have "high-stakes." (American Educational Research Association, American Psychological Association, & National Council on Measurement in Education, 1999, p. 139)

Because educational success is connected to social mobility and social stratification, high-stakes testing has broad implications for students' life chances. In other words, affecting educational paths such as grade retention and program admissions could have dramatic effects on future higher education and job opportunities, or the absence thereof.

According to Lee and Wong (2004) the policy debate about accountability and high-stakes testing tends to be polarized and suffers from a lack of generalizable empirical evidence. Paradoxically, in order to marshal evidence for or against the merits of high-stakes testing in a policy context it is first necessary to engage in the accountability debate and use accepted conventions for its discourse. Attempts to change or shift the discourse from the outside, by reliance on disconfirming evidence and using language not found within the accountability lexicon have been largely futile (McNeil, 2000). Regardless of whether high-stakes testing improves or hinders educational quality, Lee and Wong suggest the actual impact of accountability policies on learning and equity might be contingent on the level of support available to schools, teachers, and students. There is a lack of research evidence illustrating benefits from accountability policies, with or without adequate support for schooling conditions and resources.

McNeil's (2000) study of educational accountability, *Contradictions of School Reform*, which predates NCLB and is based on seminal reform efforts conducted in Houston and throughout Texas, represent the hidden consequences of reliance on accountability systems to produce equity and excellence. She argues that standardized testing, as currently implemented, is harmful and has deleterious effects on teaching and learning. McNeil's research is based on case studies of magnet schools in Houston, along with policy analysis just prior to NCLB. Situating this work in Houston was significant because, according to McNeil, Texas was a seedbed for the most rigid forms of standardization in education. In fact, the Superintendent of Schools in Houston during the period of her study, Rod Paige, went on to become the U.S. Secretary of Education after the publication of *Contradictions of School Reform*. Capturing the voices of educators, McNeil's work chronicles and provides rich descriptions of the impact of state-based accountability on three urban magnet schools, which emerged as part of a desegregation plan, MedIC Pathfinder and Science, Engineering, and Technology. McNeil maintains that prior to the policy shift toward increased standardization, teachers in these schools were empowered to innovate and encouraged to improve their pedagogical practices by focusing on the authentic learning needs of students. According to McNeil, the result was functional, nurturing and effective urban schools that served not only students of color, but the City of Houston.

Market Metaphor

McNeil's (2000) work also illuminates how the discourse of business, as asserted by the Texas power elite, helped to dismantle authentic school improvement efforts that were being cultivated in Houston public schools. According to McNeil, promising school reform efforts were ultimately replaced with tight bureaucratic control and accountability systems which demoralized students, "deskilled" teachers, and contributed to the downward spiral of the overall quality and conditions of education. Her study describes how many talented educators fled the Houston district under tightly controlled conditions and some left the profession altogether.

Lipman (2004) contributes to the discourse on the potential perils of market inspired, NCLB-like accountability by connecting globalization and deindustrialization to urban school reform. Lipman's methodology is similar to Anyon's in that she highlights case studies of schools in a large urban city, in this case Chicago, while providing a critical analysis of policy reforms. Like Anyon, Lipman analyzes the implications of policy shifts in relationship to the political economy and the cultural politics of the city. Both authors foreground race and ethnicity and view these factors as instrumental in understanding the conditions of education in American cities.

Neoliberal school policies, such as choice and high-stakes testing, Lipman (2004) contends, are ostensibly aimed at preparing students for the global economy. She argues "education policy has been explicitly tied to global economic competitiveness as the fluidity of investment capital and global competition for investments and markets have dominated more and more aspects of social life in cities and nations" (p. 8). The consequence of such social forces is a fundamental shift toward competence-based skills at the expense of critical thinking skills and cultural competencies that are necessary for autonomous learning, and development and participation as citizens in a democracy. Focusing her analysis on an American global city, Chicago, Lipman stresses how educational policy has become conceptualized as a central component of national economic planning and comprehensive urban renewal. Specifically, the national discourse about economic and educational policy is directly linked in numerous ways, including the proliferation of career academies, school-to-work programs, the development of "new" basic skills, and via a host of market-based reforms. Within this framework, where accountability for achievement and learning resembles corporate accountability for productivity and profit, there is precious little room for multiple ways of knowing, co-constructed knowledge, situated learning, or learning as building on children's own understandings.

In view of the current literature on the market metaphor for redesigning educational practice, I share many of the concerns raised by Lipman (2004) and McNeil (2000), but I also see possible benefits. For example, issues such as differentiated salaries for teachers are cornerstones in highly regarded professions outside of teaching (e.g., law and medicine) but have been largely resisted from within. However, presently, there is little empirical evidence suggesting whether rethinking the way in which teachers are compensated can improve the culture and climate within a school in a positive way. Ultimately, the challenge for policymakers, educators, and researchers is to determine which market-based strategies have appropriate application to education, which are benign, and which constitute an unwelcome intrusion and hijacking of the school reform. More often, critics of the market metaphor typically focus on the latter. Combined, Lipman and McNeil's analyses offer a cogent argument against increasing accountability in education and other popular market-based strategies, which have had nonobvious but significant effects on the profession.

In many respects, the accountability policy framework or culture of testing that predominates in educational discourse is centered on addressing social justice and equity issues. That a student's opportunity structure and his or her life chances continue to be linked to race, class and gender contradicts mainstream American values and ideals. However, policy efforts to operationalize equity by defining it strictly in terms of standardized test scores seems reasonable on the surface but harbors many contradictions. Such policies continue because there is tremendous power and persuasion in their appearance as simple truths. Despite credible critiques of high-stakes testing, that they reproduce inequality and exacerbate failure among poor students and students of color, only courageous scholars have argued to outright dismantle the educational accountability system. Educational policy is seldom nuanced, so that critics of high-stakes testing are seen as anti-accountability or as if we are arguing that schools and students should not be accountable for outcomes. However, this type-casting misses the larger point—that for accountability to work, it is essential to identify the most critical outcomes, which are often difficult to measure. Learning, as defined within a cultural context, rather than achievement, should be among the core outcomes.

Proponents of high-stakes testing assert that standardized assessment of students can and does improve academic performance in elementary and secondary schools. In a conceptual paper on improving student achievement through frequent assessments, Wolf (2007) rejects the notion that students are overtested and argues instead that testing provides educators with critical intelligence about the abilities and needs of students and they are essential for evaluating the performance of academic programs. While this paper provides no new evidence to support the claims of the benefits of testing, it references the author's previous work in support of vouchers, school choice, and urban educational reform. Although the evidence is thin, the view that testing is good, I believe, reigns in the current policy environment despite notable critiques. According to Wolf, regularly assessing students, using standardized and diagnostic tests, focuses the efforts of both teachers and students on important material that needs to be mastered and fosters higher achievement. He further asserts that standardized testing provides educators with a wealth of information about the learning needs and abilities of individual students as well as whether a specific academic program or instructional strategy is effective for them. This point underscores the link between achievement and accountability. Results of standardized exams are said to give students and parents timely and useful feedback regarding how well or poorly the student is acquiring essential academic skills and knowledge. Further, as the argument goes, standardized testing allows for the identification of motivational and learning problems with individual students at an early stage, when interventions have the greatest prospects for success. This, Wolf (2007) asserts, is particularly important in the areas of early reading and literacy. Moreover, he posits that standardized and diagnostic tests are beneficial in their own right. "In and of themselves (standardized tests) provide students with an important skill—test taking experience and facility—that will benefit them as they engage in a world that regularly 'tests' their abilities, concentration, and willingness to follow directions." He concludes that "testing generally is good for kids. America's students would be smarter, more self-confident, and better prepared to be productive contributors to society if teachers and schools did more of it" (p. 691).

Although this view is compelling in many policy circles, it neglects the unintended consequences of using a narrow accountability system to drive teaching and learning, as I have argued above. Yet, Wolf's (2007) paper illustrates how market-based strategies carry over into the field of education and can morph into commonplace, often unchallenged, policies and procedures. To maintain their competitiveness, businesses continually collect and analyze data on a variety of indicators such as staffing, operating procedures, sales, distribution, and cash flow. In this business paradigm, perhaps the most important data elements appear on balance sheets. However, the metaphor comparing student achievement (or learning) and corporate profits is problematic.

In an extensive review of the literature on the impact of high-stakes testing, Nichols (2007) found the number of valid studies highlighting the negative effects of standardized tests overwhelmingly outweighed papers such as Wolf's. Nichols reports dissatisfaction with the existing body of research because of limitations in their approaches for measuring high-stakes testing policy, within the context of a rapidly changing political climate. According to Nichols, states rapidly transform and adapt their accountability systems making it difficult to isolate their effects. Her study created an empirical rating scale capturing a differentiated version of testing pressure embedded in 25 states' accountability systems. The scales were based on data from the National Assessment of Educational Progress (NAEP) and only states with complete or almost complete NAEP participation since 1990 were included. Nichols' scales were termed the Assessment Pressure Rating (APR), which relied on a set of portfolios designed to describe in as much detail as possible the past and current characteristics of accountability practices state by state. Specifically, the portfolios included documents describing the legislative activity, politics, and effects of a state's high-stakes testing program as well as print media serving as a proxy for legislative implementation and impact.

Using a method of "comparative judgments" for scaling study states along a hypothetical continuum of high-stakes testing pressure, Nichols (2007) concludes,

> The findings from the most rigorous studies on high-stakes testing do not provide convincing evidence that high-stakes testing has the intended effect of increasing student learning.

> Moreover, the modest gains found in some studies should be viewed with caution since the findings indicate that increases in achievement could be the result of teaching to the test. (p. 57)

Interestingly, what Wolf (2007) calls instruction, which focuses teachers and students on important material that needs to be mastered, Nichols (2007) regards as teaching to the test. In preparing students for an assessment, it is reasonable to align curriculum and instruction with the objectives and competencies that will be covered on the test. However, pedagogy is compromised and becomes counterproductive when instructional activities are carried out specifically for students to perform better on a test. According to Nichols,

> This is especially true when it comes at the cost of other kinds of instruction or subject matter coverage. Studies that consider performance on NAEP suggest that by and large, high-stakes testing does not lead to "real" learning gains, but rather manufactured ones that are more likely the result of greater attention to the material that will be tested. (p. 57)

In addition to Nichols' review, other scholars have found little support for the idea that high-stakes testing improves achievement and equity. In a study of the impact of state-level accountability policy on racial and socioeconomic equity, Lee and Wong (2004) found no evidence that accountability yields "significant progress or setback toward equity in educational resources and student outcomes, the policy's long-term effect remains to be examined" (p. 821).

Combining data from state policy surveys, F-33, SASS, and NAEP, Lee and Wong (2004) investigated the degree to which performance-driven educational accountability policy enhances or hinders racial and socioeconomic equity. Their analysis suggests that during the 1990s, states largely did not address racial and socioeconomic resource disparities between school resources and failed to narrow the achievement gaps. Although the accountability policies of the 1990s had no adverse effects on equity, Lee and Wong's research suggests equity was not at the center of accountability reforms. Performance-driven accountability policies alone, they assert, cannot move the nation forward toward equity. However, they argue that long- and short-term impacts might be different. Although state-run accountability systems do not hurt adequacy or equity in education according to Lee and Wong, there is very limited evidence that they yield progress. Further, states' actions in developing accountability policy did not bring significant improvement in the distribution of student achievement outcomes.

Race Gap

Many empirical studies have verified the existence of a persistent race gap (Gamoran, 2007; Jencks & Phillips, 1998; Lee, 2007; and others). As mentioned above, equity is typically investigated and discussed through the discourse of accountability. Before continuing and diving more deeply into issues of equity, learning, and diversity, it is necessary to return to the discussion of achievement gaps to provide an overview of national trends in mathematics and readings by race. The figures in this chapter illustrate the NAEP achievement trends for Black, White, and Hispanic fourth grade students in mathematics and reading from 1990 to 2007.

NAEP is often referred to as a common yardstick because it is the only nationally representative and continuing assessment, sponsored by the U.S. Department of Education designed to measure what students know and can do in various academic subject areas. Although not a high-stakes test, NAEP is a standardized exam conducted periodically in mathematics, reading, science, writing, the arts, civics, economics, geography, and U.S. history. Assessments are administered uniformly throughout the United States, using the same sets of test booklets and similar testing conditions. According to its website, NAEP results serve as a common metric for all states and selected urban districts so that national comparisons can be made. Additionally, NAEP instruments remain essentially the same from year to year, which is a designed feature that permits a clear picture of student academic progress over time, both nationally and state by state.

Figure 1 presents the Black/White race gap in mathematics in NAEP. As shown in this figure, there was a 32-point difference in scale scores between Black and White children in 1990, which rose to a 35-point difference by 1992. Since then, the gap has slowly contracted after remaining stuck on a 26-point difference between 2005 and 2007. It is also important to point out that all scores, for both White and Black fourth graders, have increased over time. But Black children continue to lag behind. In fact, scores for Black children in 2007 were roughly equivalent to scores for White children in 1991 (scale score = 222, as compared with 220).

Reading achievement during the same period is presented in Figure 2. Compared with the results for mathematics, scores for White students have remained flat, with modest growth between 1990 and 2007, and a small (1 point) dip in 2000. The Black/White race gap expanded and contracted during this period but it was widest in 1994. Although the smallest gap was evidenced in 2007, there was a 27-point difference in scale scores between Black and White fourth graders at that time.

The pattern of results for the Hispanic/White mathematics achievement gap in NAEP somewhat resembles the Black/White gap; however, there are notable differences. Figure 3 shows the Hispanic/White trends. Perhaps the biggest difference is that the gap was slightly smaller for Hispanic fourth graders, or in other words, Hispanic students scored higher than Blacks throughout this period. For example, in 1990 the average scale score for Black students in mathematics was 188 points (Figure 1), as compared with 200 points for Hispanic students. Because scale scores for Whites were 220, the gap between Black students was 32 points, as mentioned above, but 20 points for Hispanics. However, by 2007, Hispanic students gained no ground as the mathematics gap increased 1 point to 21.

Finally, the results for Hispanic/White students on fourth grade reading are presented in Figure 4. Again, the trend appears similar to the Black/White gap, with the same exception. That is, NAEP scores for Hispanic students are slightly higher, which means the gap was somewhat smaller. Again, Hispanic schoolchildren gained no ground in reading between 1990 and 2007.

FIGURE 1
Black/White Achievement Gap in Fourth Grade Mathematics

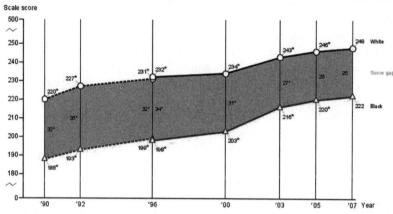

Source. The Nation's Report Card, National Assessment of Educational Progress. Institute of Education Sciences, U.S. Department of Education (http://nationsreportcard.gov/).

Taken together, these figures summarize a blatant and disturbing gap between White students and students of color, which has been well documented in the literature (Paik & Walberg, 2007; and others). While the differences between groups are stark, a question remains about whether NAEP and other standardized assessments actually measure learning as opposed to other sources of inequality in society, such as cultural capital, affluence, and middle class advantages, which are suggested thus far. Moreover, analysis of achievement trends by subgroups, such as the above, has been sometimes misused in applying empirical evidence to policy and practice. Categorization of individuals into specific cultural or racial/ethnic groups has been treated causally (i.e., as if being Black affects outcomes), yielding explanations of achievement or learning outcomes on the basis of category membership, assuming that all group members share the same experiences, skills, and interests (Gutiérrez & Rogoff, 2003). This reasoning led to the increasing support for one-size-fits-all policymaking, or an approach to equity that involves providing equal treatment and resources to all, rather than balancing resources to fit individual and group needs.

Brennan et al. (2001) examined race and ethnic variability in the Massachusetts Comprehensive Assessment System (MCAS) compared with student report card grading. The authors sought to discover whether high-stakes tests were more equitable than teacher-assigned grades. Similar to the studies described above (Orfield & Lee, 2005), they identified a methodological problem in trying to make sense of raw data on high-stakes testing in that socioeconomic status and other important characteristics of students are unevenly distributed across schools and districts. In other

FIGURE 2
Black/White Achievement Gap in Fourth Grade Reading

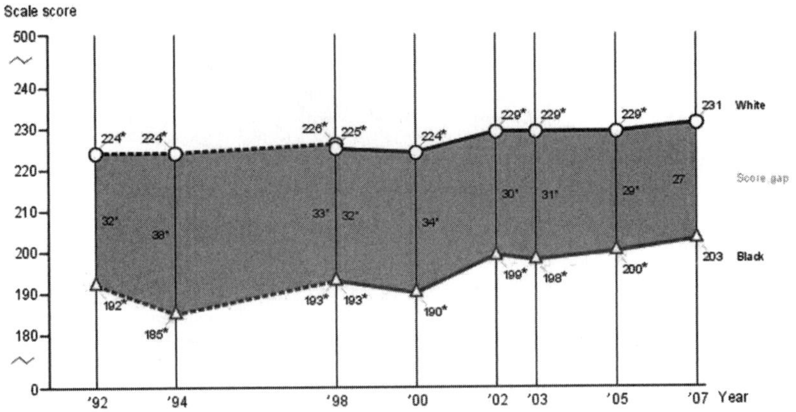

Source. The Nation's Report Card, National Assessment of Educational Progress. Institute of Education Sciences, U.S. Department of Education (http://nationsreportcard.gov/).

words, differences between racial groups on MCAS may be attributable partly to the fact that the Black, Latino, and White students attend different schools. The authors found that in comparison to teacher-assigned grades, standardized testing appears to hurt the average competitive position of Black students in mathematics and science. Furthermore, there was suggestive evidence that MCAS may also have a differential impact on Latinas/Latinos in math. Based on their analysis, Brennan et al. conclude that Black and Latino students lag further behind White and Asian students when measured against a standardized test. However, they add,

> In arguing that the equitability gaps are maintained or increased under high-stakes testing, we explicitly do not assert that this demonstrates that high-stakes tests are more biased than grades or even biased at all. Bias would exist if we knew that one or both of the assessments resulted in an evaluation of students that differed from their true abilities, but, as Supovitz and Brennan (1997) noted, "to judge which assessment is closer to real student performance, we must know each child's true ability." (p. 496)

A common multivariate model used to measure what affects student achievement includes an array of factors such as prior achievement, family background, school characteristics, and program or teacher characteristics. Such models tend to be hierarchical because student-level factors are nested over time, and these effects are nested within the classroom, which are nested within schools, and so forth (Stewart, 2008; Wong & Rutledge, 2006). This chapter suggests, however, that even sophisticated statistical models of student achievement fail to take culture into account in

FIGURE 3
Hispanic/White Achievement Gap in Fourth Grade Mathematics

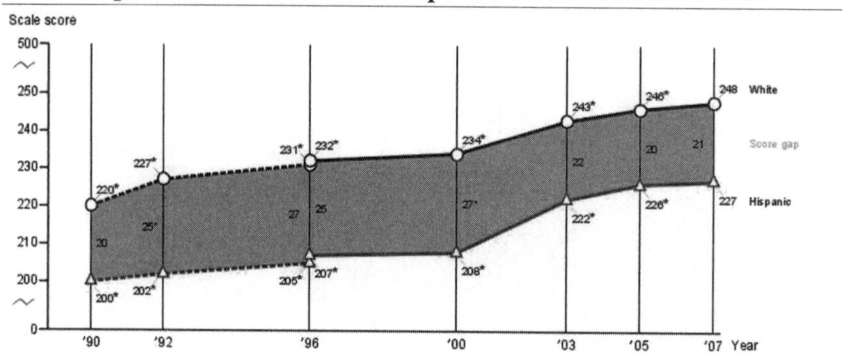

Source. The Nation's Report Card, National Assessment of Educational Progress. Institute of Education Sciences, U.S. Department of Education (http://nationsreportcard.gov/).

the way put forward by the theories of learning (Bransford et al., 1999; Cole, Engeström, & Vasquez, 1997).

The evidence to date suggests that under NCLB there has been a narrowing of perspectives of strategies to measure the complexities of learning, which affects the ways in which equity is defined. Rather than focusing teaching, learning and assessment on understanding big ideas in mathematics or theoretical foundations of literacy, for example, we hold schools and students accountable for only a narrow band of knowledge contained on a statewide test (Rothstein et al., 2008). Several scholars, including the author, believe students' scores on standardized tests and acquisition of knowledge are equated in ways that they should not be (McNeil, 2000), at the expense of helping students to be autonomous thinkers and learners (Nichols, 2007).

Learning: The End Game of Reform

Learning is an often used but complex concept that is challenging to assess and evaluate. It is not simply memorizing and recalling facts, although memory plays a role in learning. Of course learning involves thinking, but measuring "quality" thinking empirically is daunting for researchers and practitioners. Moreover, reasonable people can disagree about what constitutes quality thinking within the context of a classroom. For these reasons, learning is perhaps a phenomenon that is too nuanced and dynamic to form a basis for policy to improve schools, teaching, and learning. Instead, as argued earlier, the term achievement, which is a simpler concept, is often used as a primary outcome. However, learning, in the elaborated sense of the term, should be the ultimate objective of a quality education and the end game of school reform.

Although it is mediated through cultural and social context, learning is above all a mental process and the science of learning is evolving. According to Bransford

FIGURE 4
Hispanic/White Achievement Gap in Fourth Grade Reading

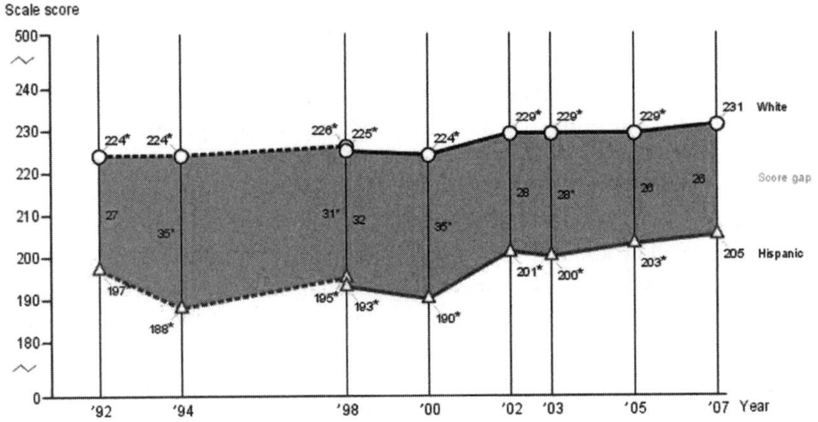

Scale score

Source. The Nation's Report Card, National Assessment of Educational Progress. Institute of Education Sciences, U.S. Department of Education (http://nationsreportcard.gov/).

et al. (1999) there are five key characteristics of learning: (a) memory and the structure of knowledge, (b) problem solving and reasoning, (c) the early foundations, (d) regulatory processes that govern learning, and (e) how symbolic thinking emerges from the culture and community of the learner. In a sense, learning can be viewed as mastering knowledge of how the world works while employing these dimensions of mental life. Learning includes not only mastering academic subjects but also the essence of the human mind. Bransford and his colleagues assert, "understanding the mind—and the thinking and learning that the mind makes possible—has remained an elusive quest" (p. 3). However, learning theory has evolved in recent years.

Achievement, as measured by standardized testing, is far less difficult to discern and manipulate in a policy context (Rothstein et al., 2008). Many performance assessments address only the first two or three of Branford et al.'s (1999) key characteristics of learning, memory, problem solving, and early foundations. Few standardized tests are designed to capture information of how knowledge is applied within a cultural context. In essence, standardized and diagnostic tests are crafted in efforts to figure out "whether" students are smart or have learned some aspect of the curriculum, rather than asking "how" are students smart, how do they know what they know, and how can teaching build on their existing knowledge. This raises the question of validity of performance assessments. In a thorough and exhaustive review of the literature on conceptions of validity in testing, Moss (1992) suggests that assessing student performance via standardized assessment presents a number of validity problems not easily handled with traditional methodology and criteria for validity research. She further argues that assessments often allow students considerable latitude in interpreting and responding to tasks; however, they result in fewer independent responses. Student responses to assessment items are complex, "reflecting integration of multiple skills and knowledge" and as a result, "they require expert judgment for evaluation" (p. 229). Moss concludes that satisfactorily meeting validity criteria as well as reliability, generalizability and comparability of assessments is problematic. Still, she appears somewhat optimistic that validity research on student performance research will evolve and improve over time, and I share this optimism.

Moreover, as quantitative researchers, we often attempt to measure learning linearly, by default, when we know pragmatically that it is sometimes circuitous, interrupted, or can follow a range of patterns based on the cultural context in which it occurs. Nevertheless, within the current accountability system, the success of school improvement is measured by year to year gains, and we call a teacher "effective" when her students, on average, gain a year's worth of knowledge in a year's time.

Is it possible to obtain high standards without standardization? The short answer, I believe, is yes, but the explanation is not simple within the context of an increasing diverse educational system. The difficulty, or infeasibility, of objectively measuring multiple ways of learning and of knowing, and cross-cultural meaning making complicates this discussion. The longer answer will involve using authentic assessments, along with numerous indicators, quantitative and qualitative, or multiple ways of measuring academic standards, and linking this discussion to the current standards movement. The next section expands the discussion of learning and equity, drawing on research in the field. Such a discussion is a necessary precursor to examining whether learning is equitable.

LEARNING AND EQUITY

I have argued thus far that learning is a complex phenomenon; however, in a policy context, learning and student achievement are often viewed as one and the same. Frequently, test scores are perceived as objective indicators of the amount of knowledge students have acquired, or not, in a subject area taught at school. However, this is an overly simplistic view of learning. Learning happens in the mind and it is shaped within a cultural context (Bruner, 1996; Cole et al., 1997). From a cultural–historical perspective, learning happens first on the interpersonal/social plane and then becomes intrapersonal/individual; culture (and cultural context) is not separate or a container; from this perspective, culture mediates learning. Learning has to be understood in its context of development. Moreover, an emerging theory of learning is coming into focus, which could lead to different approaches to the design of curriculum, teaching, and assessment than those in use in schools today (Bransford et al., 1999). According to Bransford and his colleagues, one of the hallmarks of new theories of learning is an emphasis on teaching and learning for understanding. Although understanding is a desired outcome of a quality education, the authors assert, "students often have limited opportunities to understand or make sense of topics because many curricula have emphasized memory rather than understanding. Textbooks are filled with facts that students are expected to memorize, and most tests assess students' abilities to remember the facts," (pp. 9–10) rather than understand underlying concepts and ideas on which the facts are premised.

Additionally, the new science of learning described by Bransford et al. (1999) highlights the importance of prior knowledge in the acquisition of new knowledge. Children begin their schooling with a wide range of prior knowledge, skills, and beliefs about how the world works and these inputs can exert heavy influence on what interests and engage them, they attend to and ignore in schools and classrooms, and how they organize and interpret it. This preexisting knowledge, in turn, affects students' ability to remember, reason, solve problems, and acquire new knowledge—which ultimately affects both real learning and standardized achievement.

> A logical extension of the view that new knowledge must be constructed from existing knowledge is that teachers need to pay attention to the incomplete understandings, the false beliefs, and the naive renditions of concepts that learners bring with them to a given subject. Teachers then need to build on these ideas in ways that help each student achieve a more mature understanding. If students' initial ideas and beliefs are ignored, the understandings that they develop can be very different from what the teacher intends. (Bransford et al., 1999, p. 10)

The research of Bransford and his colleagues suggests there may be better, more effective, ways of introducing academic content to students, and similar to scholars cited above, it points to limitations of overreliance on test scores to assess real learning. But schools are more adept at selecting talent than developing it. Notwithstanding its shortcomings, in studying equity, standardized testing cannot be ignored because there is absence of viable alternatives. Paradoxically, although standardized testing may harm teaching and learning (Nichols, 2007), common valid measures of learning and achievement are needed to unveil and correct educational inequity. Numerous studies have attempted to investigate what is learned in school by conducting multivariate analysis of effects on achievement (Lee & Wong, 2004; Lew, 2006; Matsumura et al., 2002; Nichols, 2007; Rumberger & Gándara, 2004; and others).

EQUAL OPPORTUNITY AND EQUITABLE OUTCOMES

Equity in education can be framed in terms of either equality of opportunity or equal outcomes (Nieto, 1999), including the contexts in which students participate in educational experiences and the extent to which those experiences enable their academic growth (de Valenzuela et al., 2006). From a historical perspective, the language of *Brown* situated the equity discourse as a mandate to provide educational opportunities to all students, with the unstated aim to help all children, regardless of racial or ethnic background, to reach the similar educational and career goals. However, NCLB-like assessment systems frame the debate fully in terms of outcomes. But the question remains about whether outcomes and opportunities can be equalized in the same way.

Let us consider access to high-quality health care as a point of departure, and hospitals as an analog for educational equity. The policy drive toward universal health care is about providing the same access (opportunities) to health care for all citizens, regardless of an individual or family's ability to pay. As in education, the health gap between affluent and poor and between people of color and Whites has persisted for some time. To simplify this complex issue, advocates for health care reform argue that if the American health care system was modified so that costs for the insured were kept low, waste and abuses of the system were removed, new regulations and policies were put in place, and every citizen has access to first-rate care, then social justice in the health care system would be achieved. Further, because health costs drain a staggering amount of capital from corporate interests, if implemented correctly, a reformed health care system would aid our competitiveness in the global economy. Money otherwise spent on health care could be directed to improve efficiency, productivity, and profits. However, health care reform advocates do not suggest strategies for directly equalizing outcomes because health outcomes, such as low mortality and reduced chronic disease, are only partially influenced by health care institutions themselves. Health outcomes, like educational outcomes, are influenced by cultural and family background, and psychosocial forces. For example, regular exercise, diet, rest and mental health, along with a decent health care plan, contribute to a person's overall health status. To obtain equal health outcomes, inputs must first be controlled, but in reality they cannot be. From the vantage point of the health care industry, many important variables are not malleable. Thus, health care providers have greater success in treating patients who already lead generally healthy lives, while they struggle to improve the lives of patients who, because of poverty or other circumstances, have preexisting poor conditions. Similarly, schools have greater success educating students with cultural capital and resource advantages at the starting gate.

In this context, it is not feasible to argue in favor of equalizing health outcomes for all, when there is tremendous diversity of inputs, an uneven playing field. Imagine two hypothetical patients, Patient A and Patient B. Patient A is an African American, middle-aged, diabetic male with hypertension and poor diet and exercise habits. Patient B is a White male of the same age, but he has no preexisting ailments and, in fact, he is an avid jogger and perennial marathoner. To be sure, Patient A poses special challenges for health care providers, and he is likely to have a markedly different outcome from a hospital visit than Patient B, who has a different and higher health baseline. Of course both patients deserve high-quality care. Creating a system that allows access to a high-quality standard of care for each patient is a responsible and attainable goal. However, creating a system where health care outcomes, as measured by quantitative indicators such as the presence of disease, blood pressure, cholesterol levels, and life expectancy for Patient A and Patient B are equalized, is not viable and perhaps not desirable.

These hypothetical patients depict the relationship between health and hospitals and help to draw comparisons between learning and schooling, with the goal of problematizing the definition of equity in the latter. The health profession, to reconcile quality and equity in service delivery, focuses on "standards of care," rather than promising equal outcomes for all patients, regardless of preexisting conditions and overall health. The phrase "standards of care" describes a set of treatments or actions that would be expected by a consensus of practitioners in the medical community in a given situation, or reflects how a knowledgeable colleague would act in a certain circumstance (Empey, Carpenter, Jain, & Atzema, 2004). However, according to Empey and his colleagues, precisely defining standards of care in the medical profession is frequently difficult and controversial, and in many cases, no clear predetermined standard will exist. Furthermore, the authors contend involvement in ongoing research activities will help advance the scientific foundation of effective practice, thereby helping to establish clearer practice quality standards and their application in a variety of settings.

"Standards of care" help guide the medical profession by providing general guidelines and rules about quality practice for practitioners. However, because every person has a unique medical history and different baselines of general health condition, "standards" vary from patient to patient. Reasonable practitioners can disagree on a course of action, and both could be right. The main objective of the profession is to improve the quality of health among individuals who are served by the system. Health, like learning, is a dynamic dependent variable that is influenced by numerous factors, both within and beyond organizational control.

TOWARD AN EQUITABLE APPROACH TO MEASURING LEARNING IN DIVERSE EDUCATIONAL SETTINGS

This chapter began by suggesting that the quest for equity has been long, and rooted in a desire to fulfill the promises of *Brown*. Race relations in the United States have evolved to a point where diversity, in many respects, is far more complicated than half a century ago and its implications for educational policy are less clear. Discovering whether an educational system is equitable within the context of a diverse, multiracial, multiethnic, multilingual, and multicultural society, and one where social class powerfully influences one's life chances is problematic. I set out to reexamine equity in education in an effort to push the discourse beyond the debate about strategies to close the achievement gap between White students and students of color. In this regard, I situated the issue of equity within an analysis of broader social forces that cultivate inequality throughout society—in employment, housing, criminal justice, and so forth—so that educational inequality is part and parcel of overarching social ills. Equity was unpacked by first asking a more basic and fundamental question about the ultimate purpose of education. From a policy perspective, if we assume the end game of education is producing student learning, then we should ask whether learning outcomes are distributed randomly across race, ethnicity, and social class. We should question whether NCLB-like assessments or high-stakes tests measure the kind of knowledge necessary for social and economic success, or whether they assess something else, partially related to one's life chances. As I have argued, the role of increased accountability via state-based systems as an approach to obtaining equity is hotly debated. Although advocates are many, several of the consequences of high-stakes testing, which are nonobvious and perhaps unintended, have not helped advance the nation toward more equitable schooling.

Without diminishing the need to refine standards of educational equity and excellence within a diverse society, I believe the more important aim is creating a context within which students are nurtured socially and intellectually and given real opportunities to learn high-content, standards-based material. Equity then, could be measured in terms of "quality of care" and rigor, as well as via individual achievement indicators. Perhaps ongoing work to create standards-based assessments in diverse educational settings may hopefully lead to an evolution of the current accountability policy framework.

REFERENCES

Abedi, J. (2002). Measuring instructional quality in accountability systems: Classroom assignments and student achievement. *Educational Assessment, 8,* 231–257.

Akom, A. A. (2008). Black metropolis and mental life: Beyond the "burden of 'acting white'" toward a third wave of critical racial studies. *Anthropology & Education Quarterly, 39,* 247–265.

Akos, P., Lambie, G. W., Milsom, A., & Gilbert, K. (2007). Early adolescents' aspirations and academic tracking: An exploratory investigation. *Professional School Counseling, 11,* 57–64.

Altshuler, S. J., & Schmautz, T. (2006). No Hispanic student left behind: The consequences of "high-stakes" testing. *Children & Schools, 28,* 5–14.

American Educational Research Association, American Psychological Association, &; National Council on Measurement in Education. (1999). *Standards for educational and psychological testing.* Washington, DC: American Educational Research Association.

Anderman, E. M. (2002). School effects on psychological outcomes during adolescence. *Journal of Educational Psychology, 94,* 795–808.

Anyon, J. (1997). *Ghetto schooling: A political economy of urban educational reform.* New York: Teachers College Press.

Anyon, J. (2005). *Radical possibilities: Public policy, urban education, and a new social movement.* New York: Routledge.

Bali, V. A., & Alvarez, R. M. (2004). The race gap in student achievement scores: Longitudinal evidence from a racially diverse school district. *Policy Studies Journal, 32,* 393–415.

Ball, A. F. (Ed.). (2006). *With more deliberate speed: Achieving equity and excellence in education—Realizing the full potential of Brown v. Board of Education: Part II* (2006 Yearbook of the National Society for the Study of Education: Vol. 105, Issue 2). Malden, MA: Blackwell.

Ball, A. F., & Samy, A. H. (2006). Preparation, pedagogy, policy, and power: Brown, the King case, and the struggle for equal language rights. In A. F. Ball (Ed.), *With more deliberate speed: Achieving equity and excellence in education—Realizing the full potential of Brown v. Board of Education: Part II* (2006 Yearbook of the National Society for the Study of Education: Vol. 105, Issue 2, pp. 104–124). Malden, MA: Blackwell.

Bandura, A., Barbaranelli, C., Caprara, G., & Pastorelli, C. (2001). Self-efficacy beliefs as shapers of children's aspirations and career trajectories. *Child Development, 72,* 187–207.

Bempechat, J., Graham, S. E., & Jimenez, N. V. (1999). The socialization of achievement in poor and minority students: A comparative study. *Journal of Cross-Cultural Psychology, 30,* 139–158.

Bhatti, G. (2006). Ogbu and the debate on educational achievement: An exploration of the links between education, migration, identity and belonging. *Intercultural Education, 17,* 133–146.

Bishop, J. H. (1998). The effect of curriculum-based external exit exam systems on student achievement. *Journal of Economic Education, 29,* 171–182.

Bourdieu, P., & Passeron, J. C. (1977). *Reproduction in education, society and culture.* Beverly Hills, CA: Sage.

Bowles, S. & Gintis, H. (1976). *Schooling in Capitalist America: Educational reform and the contradictions of economic life.* New York: Basic Books.

Bransford, J. D., Brown, A. L., & Cocking, R. R. (1999). *How people learn: Brain, mind, experience, and school.* Committee on Developments in the Science of Learning, Commission on Behavioral and Social Sciences and Education, National Research Council. Washington, DC: National Academies Press.

Brennan, R. T., Kim, J., & Wenz-Gross, M. (2001). The relative equitability of high-stakes testing versus teacher-assigned grades: Analysis of the Massachusetts Comprehensive Assessment System (MCAS). *Harvard Educational Review, 71,* 173–216.

Bruner, J. (1996). *The culture of education.* Cambridge, MA: Harvard University Press.

Cole, M., Engeström, Y., & Vasquez, O. (1997). *Mind, culture, and activity: Seminal papers from the Laboratory of Comparative Human Cognition.* Cambridge, UK: Cambridge University Press.

Collins, P. H. (2000). *Black feminist thought.* New York: Routledge.

Conchas, G. Q., & Noguera, P. A. (2006.). *The color of success: Race and high-achieving urban youth.* New York: Teachers College Press.

Cooper, L. A. (2007). Why closing the research-practice gap is critical to closing student achievement gaps. *Theory Into Practice, 46,* 317–324.

Darling-Hammond, L. (2000). New standards and old inequalities: School reform and the education of African American students. *Journal of Negro Education, 69,* 263–287.

Darling-Hammond, L., & Snyder, J. (2000). Authentic assessment of teaching in context. *Teaching and Teacher Education, 16,* 523–545.

Delpit, L. (1998). *Other people's children: Cultural conflict in the classroom.* New York: New Press.

de Valenzuela, J. S., Copeland, S. R., Huaqing Qi, C., & Park, M. (2006). Examining educational equity: Revisiting the disproportionate representation of minority students in special education. *Exceptional Children, 72,* 425–441.

Diamond, J. B., & Spillane, J. P. (2004). High-stakes accountability in urban elementary schools: Challenging or reproducing inequality? *Teachers College Record, 106,* 1145–1176.

Downs, A., & Strand, P. S. (2006). *Using assessment to improve the effectiveness of early childhood education.* Berlin: Springer Science & Business Media.

Emdin, C. (2007). *Exploring the contexts of urban science classrooms: Cogenerative dialogues, coteaching and cosmopolitanism.* Unpublished doctoral dissertation, Graduate Center of the City University of New York.

Empey, M., Carpenter, C., Jain, P., & Atzema, C. (2004). What constitutes the standard of care? *Annals of Emergency Medicine. 44,* 527–531.

Fruchter, N. (2007). *Urban schools, public will: Making education work for all our children.* New York: Teachers College Press.

Gadsden, V. L., Smith, R. R., & Jordan, W. J. (1996). The promise of desegregation: Tendering expectations and reality in achieving quality schools. *Urban Education, 31,* 381–402.

Gamoran, A. (2007). *Standards-based reform and the poverty gap: Lessons for No Child Left Behind.* Washington, DC: Brookings Institution Press.

Gardner, H. (1993). *Multiple intelligences: The theory in practice.* New York: Basic Books.

Gold, B. A. (2007). *Still separate and unequal: Segregation and the future of urban school reform.* New York: Teachers College Press.

Goyette, K. A. (2008). College for some to college for all: Social background, occupational expectations, and educational expectations over time. *Social Science Research, 37,* 461–484.

Griffith, J. (2002). A multilevel analysis of the relation of school learning and social environments to minority achievement in public elementary schools. *Elementary School Journal, 102,* 349–366.

Gutiérrez, K. D., & Jaramillo, N. E. (2006). Looking for educational equity: The consequences of relying on Brown. In A. F. Ball (Ed.), *With more deliberate speed: Achieving equity and excellence in education—Realizing the full potential of Brown v. Board of Education: Part II* (2006 Yearbook of the National Society for the Study of Education: Vol. 105, Issue 2, pp. 173–189). Malden, MA: Blackwell.

Gutiérrez, K. D., & Rogoff, B. (2003). Cultural ways of learning: Individual traits or repertoires of practice. *Educational Researcher, 32*(5), 19–25.

Hanson, S. (1994). Lost talent: Unrealized educational aspirations and expectations among U.S. youths. *Sociology of Education, 67,* 159–183.

Harris, M. (2007). *Ways of knowing: Anthropological approaches to crafting experience and knowledge.* New York: Berghahn Books.

Horvat, E. M., & O'Connor, C. (2006). *Beyond acting white: Reframing the debate on black student achievement.* Lanham, MD: Rowman & Littlefield.

Jacob, B. A., & Lefgren, L. (2004). The impact of teacher training on student achievement: Quasi-experimental evidence from school reform efforts in Chicago. *Journal of Human Resources, 39,* 50–79.

Jencks, C., & Phillips, M. (1998). *The black–white test score gap.* Washington, DC: Brookings Institution Press.

Jungert, T. (2008). Opportunities of student influence as a context for the development of engineering students' study motivation. *Social Psychology of Education, 11,* 79–94.

Kaplan, H. R. (2007). *Failing grades: The quest for equity in America's schools* (2nd ed.). Lanham, MD: Rowman & Littlefield.

Kim, J. J., & Crasco, L. M. (2006). Best policies and practices in urban educational reform: A summary of empirical analysis focusing on student achievements and equity. *Journal of Education for Students Placed at Risk, 11,* 19–37.

Kincheloe, J. L., & Hayes, K. (2007). *Teaching city kids: Understanding and appreciating them.* New York : Peter Lang.

Kozminsky, E., & Kozminsky, L. (2003). Improving motivation through dialogue. *Educational Leadership, 61,* 50–54.

Ladson-Billings, G. (2004). Landing on the wrong note: The price we paid for Brown. *Educational Researcher, 33*(7), 3–13.

Ladson-Billings, G. (2009). *The dreamkeepers: Successful teachers of African American children* (2nd ed.). New York: Wiley.

Lee, J. (2007). *The testing gap: Scientific trials of test-driven school accountability systems for excellence and equity.* Charlotte, NC: Information Age.

Lee, J., & Wong, K. K. (2004). The impact of accountability on racial and socioeconomic equity: Considering both school resources and achievement outcomes. *American Educational Research Journal, 41,* 797–832.

Lee, S. S. (2008). The de-minoritization of Asian Americans: A historical examination of the representations of Asian Americans in affirmative action admissions policies at the University of California. *Asian American Law Journal, 15,* 129–175.

Lee, V. E., & Burkam, D. T. (2002). *Inequality at the starting gate: Social background differences in achievement as children begin school.* Washington, DC: Economic Policy Institute.

Levine, D. U, Cooper, E. J., & Hilliard, A. (2000). National Urban Alliance Professional Development Model for improving achievement in the context of effective schools research. *Journal of Negro Education, 69,* 305–322.

Lew, J. (2006). Burden of acting neither white nor black: Asian American identities and achievement in urban schools. *Urban Review, 38,* 335–352.

Lipman, P. (2004). *High-stakes education: Inequality, globalization and urban school reform.* New York: Taylor & Francis.

Luke, A. (2009). Race and language as capital in school: A sociological template for language education reform. In R. Kubota & A. Lin (Eds.), *Race, culture and identities in second language education* (pp. 286–309). London: Routledge.

Martin, A. J. (2005). Exploring the effects of a youth enrichment program on academic motivation and engagement. *Social Psychology of Education, 8,* 179–206.

Matsumura, L. C., Garnier, H., Pascal, J., & Valdés, R. (2002). Measuring instructional quality in accountability systems: Classroom assignments and student achievement. *Educational Assessment, 8,* 207–229.

Mazzeo, C. (2001). Frameworks of state: Assessment policy in historical perspective. *Teachers College Record, 103,* 367–397.

McNeil, L. M. (2000). *Contradictions of school reform: Educational costs of standardized testing.* New York: Routledge.

Mickelson, R. (1990). The attitude-achievement paradox among Black adolescents. *Sociology of Education, 63,* 44–61.

Milem, J. F., Umbach, P. D., & Ting, M. P. (2004). Educating citizens for a diverse democracy: How students learn from diversity in college. In R. L. Hampton & T. P. Gullotta (Eds.), *Promoting racial, ethnic, and religious understanding in America* (pp. 87–108). Washington, DC: Child Welfare League Press.

Mohr, J. W., & Lee, H. K. (2000). From affirmative action to outreach: Discourse shifts at the University of California. *Poetics: Journal of Empirical Research on Literature, the Media, and the Arts, 28,* 47–71.

Moss, P. A. (1992). Shifting conceptions of validity in educational measurement: Implications for performance assessment. *Review of Educational Research, 62,* 229–258.

Nettles, S. M., & Herrington, C. (2007). Revisiting the importance of the direct effects of school leadership on student achievement: The implications for school improvement policy. *Peabody Journal of Education, 82,* 724–736.

Nichols, S. L. (2007). High-stakes testing: Does it increase achievement? *Journal of Applied School Psychology, 23,* 47–64.

Nieto, S. (1999). *The light in their eyes: Creating multicultural learning communities.* New York: Teachers College Press.

Nieto, S. (2000). *Affirming diversity: The sociopolitical context of multicultural education* (3rd ed.). New York: Longman.

Noguera, P. (2003). *City schools and the American dream: Reclaiming the promise of public education.* New York: Teachers College Press.

Ogbu, J. U. (1978). *Minority education and caste: The American system in cross-cultural perspective.* New York: Academic Press.

Orfield, G. (2001). *Schools more separate: Consequences of a decade of re-segregation.* Cambridge, MA: Harvard University, The Civil Rights Project.

Orfield, G., & Lee, C. (2005). *Why segregation matters: Poverty and educational inequality.* Cambridge, MA: Harvard University, The Civil Rights Project.

Paik, S. J., & Walberg, H. J. (2007). *Narrowing the achievement gap: Strategies for educating Latino, Black and Asian students.* Berlin: Springer.

Phelan, P., Davidson, A. L., & Yu, H.C. (1998). *Adolescents' worlds: Negotiating family, peers, and school.* New York: Teachers College Press.

Roscigno, V. J. (1998). Race and the reproduction of educational disadvantage. *Social Forces, 76*, 1033–1061.

Roscigno, V. J. (2000). Family/school inequality and African-American/Hispanic achievement. *Social Problems, 47*, 266–290.

Rothstein, R., Jacobsen, R., & Wilder, T. (2008). *Grading education: Getting accountability right*. Washington, DC: Economic Policy Institute.

Rousseau, C., & Tate, W. F. (2003). No time like the present: Reflecting on equity in school mathematics. *Theory Into Practice, 42*, 210–216.

Rousseau, C. K., & Powell, A. (2005). Understanding the significance of context: A framework to examine equity and reform in secondary mathematics. *High School Journal, 88*(4), 19–31.

Rumberger, R. W., & Gándara, P. (2004). Seeking equity in the education of California's English learners. *Teachers College Record, 106*, 2032–2056.

Santrock, J. W. (2005). *Life-span development*. New York: McGraw-Hill.

Shulman, L. S. (1987). Knowledge and teaching: Foundations of the new reform. *Harvard Educational Review, 57*, 1–22.

Smith, D. G., & Garrison, G. (2005). The impending loss of talent: An exploratory study challenging assumptions about testing and merit. *Teachers College Record, 107*, 629–653.

Spindler, G. D., & Spindler, L. (1992). Cultural process and ethnography: An anthropological perspective. In M. D. LeCompte, W. L. Millroy, & J. Preissle (Eds.), *Handbook of qualitative research in education* (pp. 53–92). San Diego, CA: Academic Press.

Steele, C. M., & Aronson, J. (1995). Stereotype threat and the intellectual test performance of African Americans. *Journal of Personality and Social Psychology, 69*, 797–811.

Stewart, E. B. (2008). Individual and school structural effects on African American high school students' academic achievement. *High School Journal, 91*(2), 16–34.

Sunderman, G. L., Kim, J. S., & Orfield, G. (2005). *NCLB meets school realities: Lessons from the field*. Thousand Oaks, CA: Corwin Press.

Suyemoto, K. L., & Fox Tree, C. A. (2006). Building bridges across differences to meet social action goals: Being and creating allies among people of color. *American Journal of Community Psychology, 37*, 237–246.

Tobin, K. (2006). *Uses of cogenerative dialogue to create socially and culturally adaptive classrooms and distributed responsibility for teaching and learning*. Paper presented at the Taiwan Teacher Education Conference, Taipei, Taiwan.

Tuan, H. L., Chin, C. C., Tsai, C. C., & Cheng, S. F. (2005). Investigating the effectiveness of inquiry instruction on the motivation of different learning styles students. *International Journal of Science and Mathematics Education, 3*, 541–566.

Vygotski, L. S. (1929). The problem of the cultural development of the child. *Pedagogical Seminary and Journal of Genetic Psychology, 36*, 415–434.

Vygotski, L. S. (1986). *Thought and language* (A. Kozulin, Ed., revised edition) Cambridge: MIT Press.

Wells, A. S., & Crain, R. L. (1997). *Stepping over the color line: African American students in white suburban schools*. New Haven, CT: Yale University Press.

Wolf, P. J. (2007). Academic improvement through regular assessment. *Peabody Journal of Education, 82*, 690–702.

Wong, K. K., & Rutledge, S. A. (2006). *Systemwide efforts to improve student achievement*. Greenwich, CT: Information Age.

Yeh, S. S. (2006). *Raising student achievement through rapid assessment and test reform*. New York: Teachers College Press.

Zhou, M. (2003). Urban education: Challenges in educating culturally diverse children. *Teachers College Record, 105*, 208–225.

Zia, H. (2000). *Asian American dreams: The emergence of an American people*. New York: Farrar, Straus, & Giroux.

Zoldosova, K., & Prokop, P. (2006). Analysis of motivational orientations in science education. *International Journal of Science and Mathematics Education, 4*, 669–688.

Chapter 6

New Technology and Digital Worlds: Analyzing Evidence of Equity in Access, Use, and Outcomes

MARK WARSCHAUER
TINA MATUCHNIAK
University of California, Irvine

There is broad consensus among educators, communication scholars, sociologists, and economists that the development and diffusion of information and communication technologies (ICT) are having a profound effect on modern life. This is due to the affordances of new digital media, which bridge the interactive features of speech and the archival characteristics of writing; allow many-to-many communication among people without regard to time and space, including mass collaborative editing of texts; facilitate the creation of a global hyper-indexed multimodal information structure; and enable content production and distribution in both writing and multimedia on a scale previously unimaginable (Jewitt, 2008; Warschauer, 1999). For all these reasons, computer-mediated communication can be considered a new *mode of information* (Poster, 1990), or a "fourth revolution in the means of production of knowledge" (Harnad, 1991, p. 39), following the three prior revolutions of language, writing, and print.

The previous revolution, brought about through the development and diffusion of printing, took centuries to unfold, as its full impact depended on the industrial revolution that Gutenberg's printing press preceded by several centuries (Eisenstein, 1979). Today, though, the development and diffusion of computers and the Internet occur simultaneously with a new economic revolution, based on transition from an industrial to an informational economy (Castells, 1996). This helps explain both why new media have spread so fast and also why they are so crucial to enabling full social and economic participation. As Castells (1998) concludes, based on his exhaustive socioeconomic analysis of this postindustrial stage of capitalism, "information technology,

Review of Research in Education
March 2010, Vol. 34, pp. 179-225
DOI: 10.3102/0091732X09349791
© 2010 AERA. http://rre.aera.net

and the ability to use it and adapt it, is the critical factor in generating and accessing wealth, power, and knowledge in our time" (p. 92).

To emphasize this point, the U.S. Department of Labor's most recent *Occupational Outlook Handbook* lists "Network systems and data communication," "computer software engineers, applications," "computer systems analysts," "database administrators," and "computer software engineers, systems software" among the fastest growing occupations in the United States (U.S. Bureau of Labor Statistics, 2007). Looking more broadly, in the informationalist economy, high-paid blue-collar jobs based on manual labor are, for the most part, a thing of the past, with the previous split between blue- and white-collar workers now replaced by a three-way division among *routine-production workers* (e.g., data processors, payroll clerks, factory workers), *in-person service workers* (e.g., janitors, hospital attendants, taxi drivers), and *symbolic analysts* (e.g., scientists, engineers, executives, lawyers, management consultants, professors; Reich, 1991). The income, status, and opportunities for workers in the first two categories are continually diminishing, whereas symbolic analysts command a disproportionate and rising share of the wealth in the United States and other countries. And although some types of symbolic analysts might be considered as technology specialists, virtually all of them make extensive use of new digital media on a daily basis to identify, solve, and broker problems and to communicate complex concepts. Thus, access to new technologies, whether at home or at school, is critical to the development of symbolic analysts, but how such technologies are put to use is even more important, with a high premium placed on abstraction, system thinking, experimentation, and collaboration (Reich, 1991; Warschauer, 1999).

Levy and Murnane's (2004, 2005) detailed study of occupational patterns in the United States provides empirical support for the above analysis. Their examination of census data shows that from 1969 to 1999 the demand for jobs requiring complex communication rose nearly 14%, and the demand for jobs requiring expert thinking rose about 8%. In the same period, the demand for jobs requiring manual or routine cognitive tasks fell by 2% to 8% (see Figure 1). These numbers actually downplay the real changes, because they only reflect shifts *among* different occupations, not changes in skills required *within* the same occupation. Overall, the demand for jobs in which a computer can substitute for human thought has steadily declined, whereas the demand for jobs in which computers can complement and amplify the creativity and expert thinking of humans has steadily expanded.

The large and growing role of new media in the economy and society serves to highlight their important role in education, and especially in promoting educational equity. On the one hand, differential access to new media, broadly defined, can help further amplify the already too-large educational inequities in American society. On the other hand, it is widely believed that effective deployment and use of technology in schools can help compensate for unequal access to technologies in the home environment and thus help bridge educational and social gaps.

For these reasons, accurately assessing diverse demographic groups' experiences with technology, both in and out of school, has been an important priority for

FIGURE 1
U.S. Job Skill Demand, 1969–1999 (1969 = 0)

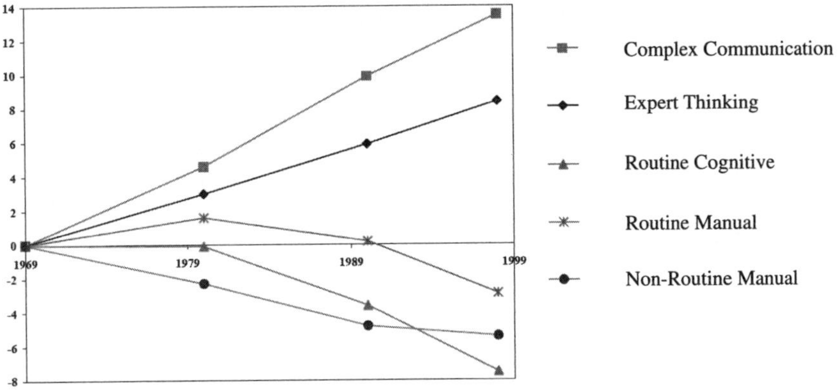

Source. Levy and Murnane (2005; based on data from Autor, Levy, & Murnane, 2003).

advocates of social and economic equality in the United States and elsewhere. Early efforts to do so focused on a narrowly defined *digital divide* of differential access to computers (see, e.g., National Telecommunications and Information Administration [NTIA], 1998). However, a danger to this approach is that it overly fetishizes technical matters. As Kling explains,

[The] big problem with "the digital divide" framing is that it tends to connote "digital solutions," i.e., computers and telecommunications, without engaging the important set of complementary resources and complex interventions to support social inclusion, of which informational technology applications may be enabling elements, but are certainly insufficient when simply added to the status quo mix of resources and relationships. (Warschauer, 2003, pp. 7–8)

In this review, we take a much broader perspective on how to analyze issues of technology and equity for youth in the United States.[1] We begin with *access* as a starting point, but consider not only whether diverse groups of youth have digital media available to them but also how that access is supported or constrained by technological and social factors. From there we go on to the question of *use*, analyzing the ways in which diverse youth deploy new media for education, social interaction, and entertainment. We then move to the question of *outcomes*, considering the gains achieved by diverse groups through use of new media as measured by academic achievement, acquisition of 21st century learning skills, and participation in technology-related careers. Finally, we include one example—the disparities of involvement in computer science study— to illustrate how issues of access, use, and outcome are intertwined.

Conducting such a broad review is theoretically and methodologically challenging. The very concept of ICT or digital media is difficult to define, and could potentially include anything from a cell phone to a global positioning system. In this review, we not only focus on computers and the Internet but also consider other related media, such as video game consoles, if evidence suggests their use may be related to differential educational or social outcomes. In addition, the diverse ways that people use new media and the outcomes they might achieve are neither well understood nor easily gauged. For example, the value of *21st century learning skills* is broadly recognized (see, e.g., North Central Regional Educational Laboratory & the Metiri Group, 2003; Partnership for 21st Century Skills, 2009), but few studies have tried to operationalize those skills or measure their achievement. In spite of these limitations, we offer this review in the spirit of American statistician John Tukey (1962), who declared that "far better an approximate answer to the right question, which is often vague, than an exact answer to the wrong question, which can always be made more precise" (p. 62).

ACCESS

Notions of technology access have steadily shifted over the past 15 years from a narrow focus on the physical availability of digital media to a broader focus on the sociotechnical factors that influence whether and how people access technology (see, e.g., Warschauer, 2003). We adopt that broader perspective in this analysis, examining first the physical availability of Internet-connected computers and then the factors that support or constrain access, both in the home and school environments.

Home

Although people access the Internet from a variety of locations, home access allows a degree of flexibility and autonomy difficult to replicate elsewhere (see discussion in Dimaggio, Hargittai, Celeste, & Shafer, 2004; Fairlie & London, 2009). The degree of home access to computers by diverse demographic groups has been well documented in the United States through seven reports issued over the past 15 years by the NTIA (1995, 1998, 1999, 2000, 2002, 2004, 2008a). All seven NTIA reports were based on the Current Population Surveys (CPS) of about 50,000 U.S. households conducted by the U.S. Bureau of Labor Statistics and the U.S. Census Bureau. The CPS surveys collect general demographic data on a monthly basis and supplement those with specialized data at different times. Supplemental data on computer and Internet access were collected on seven occasions between 1994 and 2007 and formed the basis of the NTIA analyses.

The NTIA reports provide an excellent basis for evaluating the overall digital divide in the United States and how it has evolved over time. The CPS data they are based on are superior to other sources of data, such as those from the widely cited telephone surveys of the Pew Internet & American Life Project (see discussion below), because of the large CPS sample size; the methodological rigor in sampling; the in-person survey procedures by the U.S. Census Bureau, which achieves a response rate of more than 90%; and the consistency of questions asked over multiple years, thus allowing longitudinal analysis (U.S. Census Bureau, 2006). Taken as a whole, the reports suggest that steady progress has been made in extending home Internet access to low-income and minority households, but that gaps based on income and race still remain substantial and that there is a long way to go to achieve universal access.

The most recent NTIA study reports that a total of 61.7% of U.S. households have some type of Internet access at home. The largest gaps in home Internet access are observed between groups with differential income and educational attainment (see Table 1). Home Internet access by income varies from 95.5% for households earning more than $150,000 per year to 24.6% for households earning between $5,000 and $10,000 per year. (Households earning less than $5,000 per year have a slightly higher rate at 31.9%, perhaps because of the number of students at this income level.) Home Internet access by educational attainment of head of household varies from 18.5% for those with an elementary education to 84.1% for those with at least a bachelor's degree. These gaps by income and education are further exacerbated by the fact that it is precisely those households with little economic or human capital that are least able to provide other advantages for youth in the development of technological or academic skills.

Differences by race/ethnicity are not as large as by education or income but are still troubling. Rates of home Internet access by race vary from 75.5% for Asians to 41.5% for Native Americans. Figure 2, which shows home Internet access for Whites, African Americans, and Latinos over a 10-year period, indicates the persistence of a racial gap over time.

The low rate of Internet access by Latinos is caused to a large extent by a language divide. Based on his analysis of the CPS 2003 data, which included language as a variable, Fairlie (2007) reports that at that time only 13.1% of "Spanish only" Mexican or Mexican American families in the United States (i.e., those families in which all adults spoke only Spanish) had home Internet access, as compared with a home Internet access rate of 40.1% among English-speaking Mexican or Mexican American families in the United States, and that much of this gap held true even when controlling for education, family income, immigrant status, and other factors. Fairlie concluded that the digital divide between White, English-speaking non-Hispanics, and Spanish-speaking Hispanics in the United States was "on par with the Digital Divide between the United States and many developing countries" (p. 287). More recent data suggest that non-English-speaking Latinos remain a group with alarmingly low rates of Internet access and use (Fox & Livingston, 2007).

In considering all of the above, it is important to keep in mind that households with children tend to have greater access to computers and the Internet than the general population. According to the CPS data, 70.3% of family households with children younger than 18 years have Internet access at home, as compared with 57.4% of households without children. A study with children rather than households as the unit of analysis, conducted by the Kaiser Family Foundation, interviewed a nationally representative sample of 2,032 8- to 18-year-old children at school and found

TABLE 1
Percentage of U.S. Households With Internet Access

	Percentage of Households With Internet Access			Broadband as Percentage of Those With Access
	Total With Access	Broadband	Dial-up	
Total households	61.7	50.8	10.7	82.3
Family income ($)				
<5,000	31.9	26.7	5.3	83.6
5,000-9,999	24.6	18.4	6.1	74.5
10,000-14,999	26.1	18.9	7.1	72.2
15,000-19,999	35.5	26.9	8.5	75.9
20,000-24,999	40.7	28.8	11.8	70.9
25,000-34,999	50.9	39.7	11.2	77.9
35,000-49,999	65.7	51.0	14.4	77.7
50,000-74,999	80.1	66.0	13.8	82.3
75,000-99,999	88.6	76.8	11.3	86.8
100,000-149,999	92.1	83.7	8.0	90.9
≥$150,000	95.5	90.3	5.0	94.6
Educational attainment of head of household				
Elementary	18.5	13.1	5.4	70.8
Some secondary	28.2	20.5	7.4	72.7
High school graduate	49.1	36.8	12.1	74.9
Some college	68.9	56.5	12.1	82.0
BA+	84.1	74.2	9.7	88.2
Race of head of household				
White	67.0	54.9	11.8	82.0
Black	44.9	36.4	8.4	80.9
Native American	41.5	29.8	11.2	71.9
Asian	75.5	69.1	6.1	91.5
Hispanic	43.4	35.2	8.0	81.1
Household type				
With child <18 years	70.3	59.5	10.6	84.7
No children	57.4	46.4	10.7	80.9

Source. National Telecommunication and Information Administration (2008b).

that 74% of them reported living in houses with Internet access, with the number rising to 78% of 11- to 14-year-olds and 80% of 15- to 18-year-olds (Roberts, Foehr, & Rideout, 2005).

FIGURE 2
Home Internet Access by Race/Ethnicity, 1997–2007

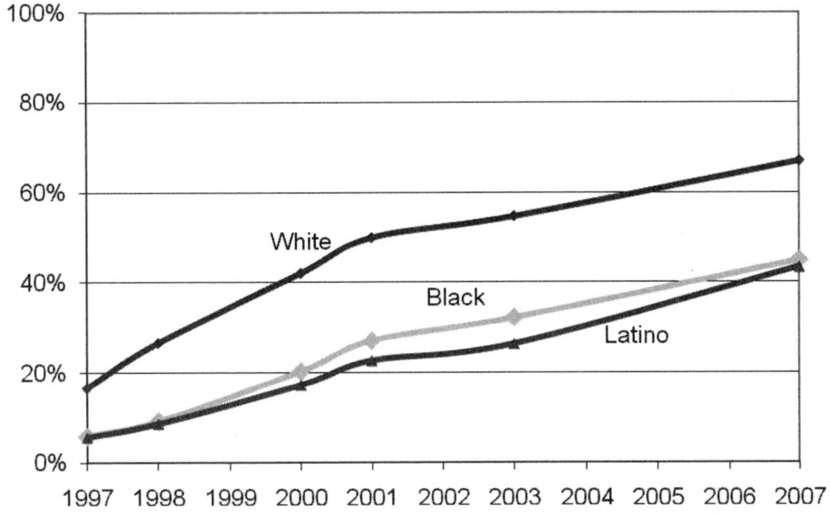

Source. Fairlie (2008).

Conditions of Access

Access to technology is not a binary division between information haves and have-nots; rather, there are differing degrees and types of access (see discussion in Warschauer, 2003). People without access at home may use the Internet at libraries, community centers, friends' houses, or schools, as will be discussed throughout this chapter. And people who have access to the Internet at home do so under widely varying technical and social conditions.

One of the most important technical conditions is type of Internet connection. Overall, 82.3% of the households with home Internet access have a broadband connection (i.e., via cable or DSL [digital subscriber line]), with the remaining 17.7% connecting via a dial-up connection (see Table 1). Not surprisingly, though, type of connection varies by household income, educational level, and other factors. For example, among Native Americans, 71.9% of Internet households have a broadband connection, whereas among Asian Americans, 92% of Internet households use broadband. Combining the differential percentage of diverse households with Internet connections with the differential percentage of broadband use among Internet-connected households yields even starker disparities of total broadband access. Only 29.8% of Native Americans have broadband access compared with 69.1% of Asian Americans; only 18.4% of households with incomes between $5,000 and $10,000 have broadband access compared with 90.3% of families with incomes more than

TABLE 2
Percentage of U.S. Broadband Versus Dial-up Users Engaging in Online
Activities in a Typical Day (and Who Have Ever Done the Activity)

	Typical Day (Ever)		
Usage Categories	All Internet Users	Broadband at Home Users	Dial-up at Home Users
Use a search engine	49 (89)	57 (94)	26 (80)
Check weather reports and forecasts	30 (80)	36 (84)	14 (75)
Get news online	39 (73)	47 (80)	18 (61)
Visit a state or local government website	13 (66)	16 (72)	4 (55)
Look online for information about the 2008 election	23 (55)	27 (62)	10 (37)
Watch a video on a video-sharing site	16 (52)	20 (60)	5 (29)
Look online for job information	6 (47)	6 (50)	4 (36)
Send instant messages	13 (40)	16 (44)	6 (38)
Read someone else's blog	11 (33)	15 (40)	3 (15)
Use a social networking site	13 (29)	16 (33)	7 (21)
Make a donation to charity online	1 (20)	2 (23)	0 (9)
Downloaded a podcast	3 (19)	4 (22)	1 (8)
Download or share files using peer-to-peer networks	3 (15)	3 (17)	2 (15)
Create or work on your own blog	5 (12)	6 (15)	3 (8)

Source. Horrigan (2008).

$150,000; and only 13.1% of households headed up by someone with an elementary school education have broadband access compared with 74.2% of those headed up by someone with a bachelor's degree.

Furthermore, research suggests that people who have home broadband connections use the Internet in markedly different ways than people who have home dial-up accounts (Horrigan, 2008; see Table 2). For example, 62% of adults with broadband access looked online for information about the 2008 election, whereas only 37% of those with home dial-up access did so. Although no similar comparative data are available for youth, one would imagine that the types of bandwidth-intensive applications that are considered especially valuable for young people, such as development and distribution of sophisticated multimedia content (Ito et al., in press), would be rarely carried out on a dial-up account, both because of the slower download and

TABLE 3
Number of Household Members Per Home Computer for Students in a California School District

	African Americans	Hispanics	Asians	Whites
Mean number of computers per household	1.56	1.22	2.48	2.27
Mean household size	2.63	4.61	3.46	2.18
Mean home user/computer ratio	1.68/1	3.78/1	1.40/1	0.96/1

upload times as well as the need to tie up a household telephone line for Internet use.

Although not as thoroughly investigated, other technical conditions surely shape home access to the Internet. For example, students per computer ratio was identified a decade ago as a key factor influencing how well computers are deployed for teaching and learning at schools (Becker, 2000a), yet household members per computer ratio has not yet been seriously analyzed as a factor affecting home computer use. Unpublished data from Grimes and Warschauer's (2008) recent study of a laptop program in an urban California district, combined with U.S. census reports of average family household size by race/ethnicity in the school district's county, indicate dramatic differences in household members per computer by racial/ethnic group, with White families having roughly one household member per computer and Hispanic families having nearly four people per computer (see Table 3). Such disparities will likely affect youth's opportunities to enjoy unpressured time to explore learning opportunities with computers.

According to analysis of CPS data by Fairlie (2007), African Americans and Latinos tend to own computers that are no older than those of Whites, yet they are more likely to report that their computers are not capable of Internet access. This could perhaps be explained by computers falling into disrepair or their owners simply lacking the means to purchase Internet access. As for other technical factors that likely affect computer use, such as differential access to software or peripherals, there are little data available.

Social factors are equally important as technical factors in shaping access. Influence from family members and friends can be critical in deciding whether and how to make use of computers and the Internet. A study of 1,000 people in San Diego found that social contact with other computer users was a key factor correlated with computer access (Regional Technology Alliance, 2001). As the study reports,

Although most respondents stated that they know people who used computers, the digitally detached (those who do not have home personal computers, Internet access, or access to the Internet outside of the home) did not. And when compared with the impact of ethnicity, income, and education level, this sentiment—that they did not know others who used computers—is far more significant. (p. 12)

Youth today are not likely to be "digitally detached"; indeed, as will be discussed below, almost all youth use computers. However, with computer mastery depending heavily on social support, both from peers (see, e.g., Margolis, Estrella, Goode, Holme, & Nao, 2008) and family members (see, e.g., Barron, Martin, Takeuchi, & Fithian, 2009), many low-income or immigrant youth will have few friends or relatives who are sophisticated users of digital media. Conditions in the household (and neighborhood) such as relatively few computers, lesser degrees of broadband Internet access, fewer people with a college education, and fewer English speakers are likely to shape the kinds of experience youth have with digital media. We will return to this issue later in the chapter when we examine the diverse ways that youth use technology.

School Access

Given the ongoing discrepancies in home access to digital media, achieving equity of access at school takes on greater priority. There have been steady gains in this area, as more public schools of all types get more Internet-connected computers, but, once again, gaps persist.

The National Center for Educational Statistics gathered data on school access through surveys of about 85,000 schools administered nine times from 1994 to 2005, and presented these data in two issue briefs and five reports published between 1999 and 2006, each titled "Internet Access in U.S. Public Schools and Classrooms." The number of public school students per Internet-connected instructional computer in diverse types of schools was calculated for each year from 1998 to 2005, except for 2005 (Wells, Lewis, & Greene, 2006; see Table 4). In 1998, schools with 50% or more minority enrollment had 70.3% more students per Internet-connected computer than did schools with less than 6% minority enrollment (with ratios of 17.2:1 in high minority schools and 10.1:1 in low-minority schools). By 2005, that gap had fallen to 36.7% (with ratios of 4.1:1 in high-minority schools and 3.0:1 in low-minority schools). When examining access by rate of poverty, as defined by percent of students eligible for free or reduced-price lunch, the gap has almost closed. In 1998, schools with 75% or more of their students eligible for free or reduced-price lunch had 58.5% more students per Internet-connected computer than did schools with less than 35% of their students so eligible (with ratios of 16.8:1 in high-poverty schools and 10.1:1 in low-poverty schools), but in 2005 the gap was reduced to 5.3% (with ratios of 4.0:1 in high-poverty schools and 3.8:1 in low-poverty schools). The narrowing of these gaps is due in large part to government funding, with the federal e-Rate program providing about $2 billion per year for telecommunications and Internet access in schools, and many schools in low-income communities using Title I funding to purchase educational computers.

As in home environments, though, sociotechnical factors support or constrain use of computers and the Internet in schools, often in ways that heighten educational inequity. A comparative study of school technology use in high– and low–socioeconomic status (SES) communities found that the low-SES neighborhood

TABLE 4
Ratio of Public School Students to Instructional Computers With Internet Access, 1998–2005

	Years						
	1998	1999	2000	2001	2002	2003	2005
All public schools	12.1	9.1	6.6	5.4	4.8	4.4	3.8
Instructional level							
Elementary	13.6	10.6	7.8	6.1	5.2	4.9	4.1
Secondary	9.9	7.0	5.2	4.3	4.1	3.8	3.3
Locale							
City	14.1	11.4	8.2	5.9	5.5	5.0	4.2
Urban fringe	12.4	9.1	6.6	5.7	4.9	4.6	4.1
Town	12.2	8.2	6.2	5.0	4.4	4.1	3.4
Rural	8.6	6.6	5.0	4.6	4.0	3.8	3.0
Percentage minority enrollment							
<6	10.1	7.0	5.7	4.7	4.0	4.1	3.0
6–20	10.4	7.8	5.9	4.9	4.6	4.1	3.9
21–49	12.1	9.5	7.2	5.5	5.2	4.1	4.0
≥50	17.2	13.3	8.1	6.4	5.1	5.1	4.1
Percentage of students eligible for free or reduced-price lunch							
<35	10.6	7.6	6.0	4.9	4.6	4.2	3.8
35–49	10.9	9.0	6.3	5.2	4.5	4.4	3.4
50–74	15.8	10.0	7.2	5.6	4.7	4.4	3.6
≥75	16.8	16.8	9.1	6.8	5.5	5.1	4.0

Source. Wells, Lewis, and Greene (2006).

schools tended to have less stable teaching staff, administrative staff, and IT support staff, which made planning for technology use more difficult (Warschauer, Knobel, & Stone, 2004). As the study reported, the high-SES schools "tended to invest more in professional development, hiring full-time technical support staff and developing lines of communication among teachers, office staff, media specialists, technical staff, and administration that promoted robust digital networks." This, in turn, "encouraged more widespread teacher use of new technologies." In comparison, "the low-SES schools had achieved less success in creating the kinds of support networks that made technology workable" (p. 581). Because teachers in low-SES schools were less confident that the equipment they signed up for would actually work, and that if it did not work, they would have available timely technical support, they were more reluctant to rely on technology in their lesson plans.

In addition, even when teachers in low-SES schools had confidence in the hardware and software they were using, the sheer complexity of their instructional environments made it more difficult to use technology well. Challenges they faced included larger numbers of English language learners and at-risk students, larger numbers of students with limited computer experience, and greater pressure to increase test scores and adhere to policy mandates. As a teacher in a low-SES California high school said,

Time is probably the biggest [problem]. Now it's even worse. Now that we're changing our curriculum big time to make it a standards-based curriculum . . . we really have to be efficient to cover the stuff that's in the standards in one academic quarter. There's not much time for other stuff . . . Before, if somebody pushed the computer lab, great. I could drop something that we were doing. It's not that critical, you know, it's an assignment we like, but, okay, let's drop it and let's go into the computer lab. And now we're dropping something that's on the [state] exam at the end of the year and our API score that goes in the [news] paper then could go down because of having more emphasis on computers. So, that is, to me, time is an even bigger obstacle now than it was the first couple of years. (Warschauer, Knobel, et al., 2004, p. 582)

Access From Other Locations

More than half of U.S. teenagers say they have accessed the Internet from libraries and at friends' houses (Lenhart, Arafeh, Smith, & Macgill, 2008; Lenhart, Madden, & Hitlin, 2005), though there is scant research documenting what teens do in these locations. In contrast, there is a wide body of research reporting youth's rich experiences with the Internet and other digital media at community centers (see, e.g., Hull & Katz, 2006; Kafai, Peppler, & Chapman, 2009), yet studies suggest that fewer than 1 in 10 youth report using the Internet at such centers, and almost no youth report such centers as the main place they go online (Lenhart et al., 2005). More discussion of how youth make use of technology at community centers and the role of such centers in addressing equity issues with technology will be discussed later in this paper.

USE

The most recent data on number of youth who use the Internet is provided by the Pew Internet & American Life Project, which interviewed 700 parent–child pairs by telephone and found that 89% of youth aged 12–17 years use the Internet at home and 94% use it from any location (Lenhart, Arafeh, et al., 2008; see Table 5). The 89% figure is considerably higher than the 70.3% Internet access rate for households with children reported by CPS (NTIA, 2008b) as well as the 78-80% rate of home Internet use for teenagers reported by the Kaiser Family Foundation (Roberts et al., 2005). The differences may be because of the later date of the Pew survey compared with the Kaiser Family Foundation survey, as well as due to differences in the methodology of the Pew survey compared with the CPS. Pew reports a 25% rate of response to its telephone survey, and although the responses are weighted for race and education, they are not weighted for income, and are thus likely to underrepresent low-income families who either lack a working telephone line or do not wish to be

TABLE 5
Percentage of U.S. Teenagers Who Use the Internet at Different Locations

	Anywhere	At Home	At School	At a Library
All teens	94	89	77	60
Gender				
Girls	95	91	76	59
Boys	93	86	78	60
Age (years)				
12–14	92	89	71	58
15–17	96	89	82	61
Race/ethnicity				
White	96	91	78	59
Black	92	80	83	69
Hispanic	87	85	69	53
Annual household income ($)				
<30,000	86	70	75	72
30,000–49,000	93	86	88	63
50,000–74,000	96	87	72	55
≥75,000	97	99	74	57

Source. Lenhart, Arafeh, Smith, and Macgill (2008).

interviewed for a research project. Most important, the parent–child pair interviews were only conducted in English, thus leaving out Spanish-speaking Latino families who are known to have markedly lower rates of Internet access than do English-speaking Latinos (Fairlie, 2007). Finally, the Pew survey reports on teenagers, whereas the NTIA discusses households with any age children younger than 18 years.

That being said, there is little disagreement that the strong majority of youth find a way to get online somewhere. Because African American and low-income youth use the Internet in public libraries at significantly higher rates than their White or higher income counterparts (see Table 5), it appears that the library serves, at least to some extent, as an alternative outlet for those without home Internet access.

It is also the case that youth spend a considerable amount of time online or otherwise using computers. The Kaiser Family Foundation reported the average amount of time spent on computers by age group as 37 minutes per day for 8- to 10-year-olds, 1 hour and 2 minutes per day for 11- to 14-year-olds, and 1 hour and 22 minutes per day for 15- to 18-year-olds. Their data, however, were collected in 2004, thus before the rapid growth of social network sites that have proven so popular among youth.

What, then, do youth do online? We will consider both out-of-school and in-school practices.

Out-of-School Use of Digital Media

A recent report, based on interviews and observations with hundreds of middle school– and high school–aged youth, provides an in-depth view of how young people in the United States use digital media today (Ito et al., in press). Ito and her colleagues identified two primary categories of online practices, which they label *friendship-driven* and *interest-driven*. Friendship-driven practices essentially involve hanging out with their peers online and either take the place of or complement other forms of youth socializing, such as hanging out at the mall. Youth usually hang out online with peers from school, but also occasionally with friends they meet through participation in sports, religious groups, or other offline activities. Hanging out rarely involves people that youth do not already know from their "real life," except in the case of groups who are especially marginalized, such as gays and lesbians, who may venture out more broadly online to seek social contacts. The principal tools for hanging out are social networks sites (specifically MySpace and Facebook), Instant Messaging, and computer and video games. Typical friendship-driven activities include chatting or flirting; uploading, downloading, or discussing music, images, and video; updating profiles and writing on friends' walls; and playing or discussing games.

The majority of youth do not move beyond friendship-driven activities, but the more creative and adventurous venture into interest-driven genres. As with friendship-driven activities, interest-driven activities typically involve communicating, game playing, and sharing of media. But in interest-driven genres, it is the specialized activity, interest, or niche identity that is the driving motivation, rather than merely socializing with local peers. This results in a much deeper and more sophisticated engagement with new media, and also brings participants into communication and collaboration with people of diverse ages and backgrounds around the world, rather than principally with their own local peers. As Ito et al. (in press) explain,

Interest-driven practices are what youth describe as the domain of the geeks, freaks, musicians, artists, and dorks, the kids who are identified as smart, different, or creative, who generally exist at the margins of teen social worlds. Kids find a different network of peers and develop deep friendships through these interest-driven engagements, but in these cases the interests come first, and they structure the peer network and friendships, rather than vice versa. These are contexts where kids find relationships that center on their interests, hobbies, and career aspirations.

The Digital Youth Project identified two stages of interest-driven participation, which they label *messing around* and *geeking out*. Messing around involves early exploration of personal interests, wherein young people "begin to take an interest in and focus on the workings and content of the technology and media themselves, tinkering, exploring, and extending their understanding" (Ito et al., 2008, p. 20). Activities in this regard include searching for information online and experimenting with digital media production or more complex forms of gaming. Geeking out is the next stage, and involves "an intense commitment to or engagement with media or technology, often one particular media property, genre, or type of technology" and "learning to navigate esoteric domains of knowledge and practice and participating in communities that traffic in these forms of expertise" (Ito et al., 2008, p. 28). Examples of geeking out include creation and sharing of animated films that use computer game engines and footage (machinima); posting and critiquing of creative writing related to popular culture (fan fiction); development and publishing videos based on clips from anime series set to songs (anime music videos); writing and distribution of subtitles of foreign films or television programs, especially anime, within hours after the films or programs are released (fansubbing); and creation and posting of short dramatic or humorous films on YouTube (video production).

Learning and media theorists such as Gee (2003, 2004) and Jenkins (2009) make a compelling case that youth's engagement with new media provides vital learning experiences. However, their writings principally focus on youth who are engaged in interest-driven activities, and especially those who "geek out." Yet the Ito et al. (2008) study reports that only a small minority of youth move on to this geeking out stage, and also makes evident that access to additional technological and social resources, beyond a simple computer and Internet account, are critical to determining who moves on to these more sophisticated forms of media participation. Given the nature of geeking out activities, technological resources presumably include broadband access, relatively new computers with graphics and multimedia capacity, digital production software, and equipment such as digital cameras and camcorders. Social resources include a community that values and enables the sharing of media knowledge and interests, which can be found among family, friends, interest groups, or educational programs such as computer clubs and youth media centers.

Ito et al.'s (2008) study does not attempt to identify who, with the help of these resources, typically moves on to the geeking out stage, and who does not, but other studies have addressed this issue. One of the most compelling accounts is provided by Attewell and Winston (2003), who spent several months observing and interviewing two groups of computer users at home and school. The first group consisted of African American and Latino children aged 11 to 14 years who attended public middle school; most came from poor and working-class families, and all scored below grade level in reading. The second group consisted of school children from more affluent families who attended private schools.

The wealthier youths studied by Attewell and Winston (2003) were frequently engaged in interest-driven activities. For example, a White fourth-grade private school student named Zeke was a "political junky at ten years old" (p. 124). He spent his online time reading up on the Presidential inauguration, downloading video clips of politicians, and reading candidates' speeches. To assist his candidacy for class president—an office that was not sanctioned officially by the teachers at his school—Zeke found a free website that allowed visitors to construct quizzes and modified it to develop an online voting system. With the cooperation of his rival for office, he told each child in his class to visit the Web page for the voting system both to read the campaign speeches that he and his opponent posted and eventually to vote.

The low-SES group also pursued their interests, but in very different ways. Typical was Kadesha, a 13-year-old African American girl. Kadesha and her friends spent much of their online time checking out rappers and wrestlers (whom they referred to as their "husbands"), downloading their pictures as screensavers and pasting images into reports (Attewell & Winston, 2003, p. 117). They also went cyber-window shopping together, checking out everything from hot new sneakers to skateboards to Barbie dolls. The authors explained how Kadesha's ability to exploit the Internet was greatly restricted by her limited reading and writing skills:

As image after image flashes by, . . . it becomes noticeable how rarely, how lightly, Kadesha settles on printed text. Like many of her friends, she reads far below grade level. So she energetically pursues images and sounds on the Web, but foregoes even news of her love interest if that requires her to read. (p. 117)

Of course working, with images and sounds can be an important part of geeking out, but Attewell and Winston's description makes clear that, in the case of Kadesha and many of her friends, engagement with multimedia was limited to consumption, not creation.

A study analyzing the 2003 CPS data provides statistical evidence of a home use divide (DeBell & Chapman, 2006). Among children in grades pre-K to 12 who used a computer at home, Whites were more likely than Blacks or Hispanics to use word processing, e-mail, multimedia, and spreadsheets or databases. These applications were also more widely used by children who lived in high-income families, those with well-educated parents, and those with English-speaking parents, as compared with children from low-income families or whose parents did not graduate high school or did not speak English. Further statistical evidence comes from a recent study of creative computing participation in two California middle schools, one in a high-SES community and one in a nearby low-SES community. Students at the high-SES school had greater access to diverse digital tools (including computers, the Internet, printers, scanners, handheld devices, digital cameras, and video cameras) and were much more likely to have both depth and breadth of experience in digital media production (Barron, Walter, Martin, & Schatz, in press).

Games

In the realm of games, research suggests that there are also important differences associated with SES and with gender as well. Andrews (2007, 2008a, 2008b) compared the game-playing practices of 133 students living in high-income neighborhoods and attending a private college preparatory school with those of 95 students living in low-income neighborhoods and attending a public Title I school (i.e., a school with more than 40% of its students qualifying for subsidized lunches). Methods included surveys, interviews, and *pile sorts*; the latter involved handing students game boxes and asking them to sort them into various categories, such as whether the students had seen or heard of them before, whether the games made sense to them, what categories of games they thought they were, and what kind of

TABLE 6

Types of Video Games Played by Students in Two U.S. High Schools

	Socioeconomic Status		Gender (%)	
	High (%)	Low (%)	Male (%)	Female (%)
Casual games	22.6	10	4.5	29.7
Computer games (noncasual)	19.4	4.5	14.3	7.7
Fantasy games	16.1	7.3	16.1	5.5
Sports games	19.4	44.5	47.3	15.4

Source. Andrews (2008b).

people they thought played them. Based on the pile sorts and interviews, Andrews developed four categories of games, which she called *casual* (e.g., puzzle, word, card games), *computer noncasual* (e.g., simulation and strategy games such as The Sims or Grand Theft Auto), *fantasy* (involving mythological or mystical characters, including both individual role-playing games for videogame consoles such as the Playstation and massively multiplayer role-playing games [MMORPG] for computers such as World of Warcraft), and *sports* (e.g., NBA Live).

When asking students to identify the top three games that students had played over the past year, Andrews found major differences both by SES and gender (see Table 6). High-SES students were more likely than their low-SES counterparts to play every genre of game except for sports. The difference was particularly pronounced in the noncasual computer games, which include strategy and simulation games believed to be important for learning purposes (see discussion in Gee, 2003). In the pile sorts and interviews, low-income students explained that these more involved computer games were "too complicated" or "too confusing" (Andrews, 2008b, p. 207). Boys were more likely than girls to play every kind of genre except casual games. And combined survey and interview data reported by Andrews suggests that by the end of her study, a large number of high-SES students were playing World of Warcraft, but that very few females or low-SES males were playing this or any other MMORPGs—an important finding given that the complex and highly collaborative nature of MMORPGs makes them ideal for advanced learning and literacy practices (see, e.g., Steinkuehler, 2007).

This last finding is associated with a broader trend identified by Andrews: high-SES students were far more likely than low-SES students to play games with other people, and males were similarly more likely than females to do so (see Table 7). For example, high-SES students were nearly five times as likely to play games with strangers online as low-SES students, and boys were more than eight times as likely as girls to do so. Boys were also more than six times as likely as girls to play with friends online. Finally, disparities were also noted in regards to students' related literacy practices outside the games. For example, males and high-SES students were more likely

TABLE 7

**Differences in Social Patterns of Gaming Between
Students in Two U.S. High Schools**

	Socioeconomic Status		Gender	
	High (%)	Low (%)	Male (%)	Female (%)
With one friend online	37.0	16.2	24.6	4.1
With many friends online	39.1	17.6	26.3	4.1
With strangers online	50.0	10.3	26.3	3.1
With strangers in person (net café, etc.)	15.2	4.3	6.1	1.0
With one friend in person			57.9	6.7
With many friends in person			57.9	28.6
At a friend's house			58.6	37.8
At a relative's house			40.5	23.5
At a game store			17.2	2.0

Source. Andrews (2008b).

than girls or low-SES students to read magazines about games or access online *walk-throughs* (i.e., sites that provide written or illustrated instructions on optimal ways to beat a game or level).

Andrews's (2008b) findings are supported by other research on youth's experiences with game playing. The 2003 CPS data indicate that, among students who have home computers, boys, Whites, children from high-SES families, children with well-educated parents, and children whose parents speak English are all more likely to use computers for game playing than are girls, Blacks and Hispanics, children from low-SES families, or children whose parents did not graduate high school or do not speak English (DeBell & Chapman, 2006). The Pew Internet & American Life Project surveyed 1,102 12- to 17-year-olds in the United States from November 2007 through February 2008, and found that, compared with girls, boys were more likely to play videogames, play more game genres, play online games, and, by a nearly three to one margin, play massively multiplayer online games (Lenhart, Kahne, et al., 2008). The Pew study also found that of those who played games, Whites were slightly more likely than Blacks, and more than twice as likely as Hispanics, to play as part of a guild or group, and that Whites are much more likely than Blacks to play massively multiplayer online games. Other studies suggest that when males and females or high-SES and low-SES youth or Blacks and Whites play the same game, they may experience the game differently because of their background knowledge, belief systems, or sensitivity to racially or sexually charged material (see, e.g., Kafai, Heeter, Denner, & Sun, 2008; DeVane & Squire, 2008).

Community Centers and Libraries

A number of studies suggest that community technology centers and other informal digital media programs directed at youth can help overcome many of these disadvantages regarding access and use of technology. Center programs typically feature up-to-date equipment, high-speed Internet access, and access to digital peripherals such as printers or camcorders. Equally important, they provide a social context for learning with and through technology, whether in courses, workshops, drop-in clubhouse hours with mentors, or informal interaction with peers. A range of studies have reported the positive experiences for youth in such centers, whether working on digital storytelling (Hull & Katz, 2006; Hull & Nelson, 2005), media creation through use of programming languages (Peppler & Kafai, 2007), or digital documentaries on the social reality in local communities (Warschauer, 2003). Yet only 9% of youth indicate that they have ever gone online at a community center, youth center, or house of worship (Lenhart et al., 2005). There is thus much room to grow in giving youth opportunities for these media-rich experiences in informal settings.

Public libraries are much more widespread than community technology centers and are a much more common point of Internet access for youth (Lenhart, Kahne, et al., 2008). However, they usually lack the extensive technology instruction or expert mentorship available in community centers, and thus use of computers and the Internet in libraries is more differentiated by SES, as users must rely on their own unequal social resources for support. For example, a study in Philadelphia found that introduction of new technology in the city's libraries actually widened a divide in the quality of library use (Neuman & Celano, 2006). Children in low-income communities received little parent mentoring in libraries and, after technology was introduced, spent considerable time either waiting for computers to be free or playing computer-based games with little textual content; technology thus displaced reading for these children. In contrast, parents in middle-income communities "carefully orchestrated children's activities on the computer, much as they did with books" (Neuman & Celano, 2006, p. 193). Children in those communities thus spent more time on print-based computer applications, averaging 11 lines of print per application compared to 3.9 lines of print for the children in low-income communities. As a result, children in middle-income communities doubled the amount of time spent on reading following the introduction of technology, and the literacy gap between low- and high-income youth increased.

In-School Use

Discrepancies in whether youth use computers and the Internet at school are narrower than at home. This is seen in both the Pew study discussed above (Table 5) as well as in DeBell and Chapman's (2006) analysis of CPS data, which showed that 85% of Whites in grades pre-K to 12 in 2003 reported using a computer at school, compared with 80% of Hispanics and 82% of Blacks. However, the most important technology discrepancies in U.S. schools are not in whether computers and the

Internet are used, but for what purpose. The two widest U.S. studies (Becker, 2000c; Wenglinsky, 1998) on this topic were conducted in the 1990s. Both showed sharp disparities by race and SES in how new technologies were deployed for education.

Wenglinsky (1998) analyzed data from the 1996 National Assessment of Educational Progress (NAEP) to describe technology use patterns of 6,627 fourth graders and 7,146 eighth graders across the United States. Of all racial groups, African Americans were more likely to use computers at least once a week for mathematics at both the fourth grade and eighth grade level, likely because of the frequent use of remedial computer-based drills in math. Yet, paradoxically, a smaller percentage of African American students than any other racial group was taught math by teachers who had had professional development in technology use in the previous 5 years.

Wenglinsky (1998) divided up computer use into two broad categories. The first involved applying concepts or developing simulations to use them, activities that are both thought of as teaching higher order skills. The second involved drill and practice activities, which by nature focus on lower order skills. The study found that substantial differences by race/ethnicity, school lunch eligibility and/or type of school exist with regard to whether students reported their teachers primarily using these activities (see Table 8). Most notably, more than three times as many Asian students as Black students reported their teachers as primarily using simulations and applications in eighth grade mathematics instruction, whereas only about half as many Asians as Blacks reported their teachers primarily using drill and practice. Wenglinsky does not report how much of this differential was related to Asians and Blacks taking different types of math classes in eighth grade, and how much, if any, may have been independent of that.

In the second national study, Becker surveyed a representative sample of 4,000 teachers across the United States. His study confirmed the differences found by Wenglinsky, and found that they applied more generally rather than just in mathematics (Becker, 2000b, 2000c). He summarized the findings thus

Computer use in low-SES schools often involved traditional practices and beliefs about student learning, whereas computer use in high-SES schools often reflected more constructivist and innovative teaching strategies. For example, teachers in low-SES schools were more likely than those in high-SES schools to use computers for "remediation of skills" and "mastering skills just taught" and to view computers as valuable for teaching students to work independently. In contrast, teachers in high-SES schools were more likely to use computers to teach students skills such as written expression, making presentations to an audience, and analyzing information. (Becker, 2000c, p. 55)

Becker also found that amount of usage by school SES differed by subject area. In mathematics and English—subjects in which, at least at that time, drill and practice software predominated—computers were used more frequently in low-SES schools than in high-SES schools. However, in science instruction, which tended to involve more simulations and applications, computers were used more frequently in high-SES schools.

Much has changed in computer capacity and usage in the time since these two national studies were conducted. Unfortunately, there have been no similar

TABLE 8
Percentage of U.S. Eighth Graders Whose Teachers Report Simulations/
Applications and Drill/Practices as Primary Computer Uses

	Simulations/Applications	Drill/Practice
Total	27	34
Race/ethnicity		
Asian	43	27
Hispanic	31	30
White	25	34
Black	14	52
Family income		
School lunch ineligible	33	31
School lunch eligible	22	34
Type of school		
Private schools	30	10
Public schools	27	36

Source. Wenglinsky (1998).

large-scale quantitative studies done since to confirm or challenge these findings. However, a number of smaller case studies conducted by the first author of this chapter have examined the same issue with a narrower lens. These include a comparison of a high-SES private and low-SES public school in Hawaii, both known for good uses of educational technology (Warschauer, 2000); a study of 20 mathematics, science, English, and social studies teachers at three high-SES and five low-SES secondary schools in Southern California (Warschauer et al., 2004); and a multisite case study of 10 diverse schools in Maine and California with one-to-one laptop programs, in which all students in one or more classrooms were provided an individual computer (Warschauer, 2006). Taken as a whole, these studies have confirmed important discrepancies by student and school SES, while also suggesting that the specific nature of these discrepancies may be evolving over time. For example, Warschauer's studies have found differences not only in constructivist versus rote applications of technology, as suggested by Becker, but rather in different types of constructivist activity, with those occurring in low-SES schools more typically focused on what Scardamalia and Bereiter (2003) called *shallow* as opposed to *deep constructivism.* In these instances, individual or collaborative student-centered work, such as writing newsletters or finding information on Web pages, was often carried out with very limited goals, such as the development of most basic computer skills, rather than the achievement of deeper knowledge, understanding, or analysis through critical inquiry, as more frequently occurred in high-SES schools.

The California study carried out by Warschauer et al. (2004) illustrated in part why teachers in low-SES schools feel a need to emphasize computer skills. Surveys in the schools indicated that 99% of high-SES students had computers at home and 97% had Internet access, whereas in the low-SES schools, the rates were 84% for computer access and 72% for Internet access. In interviews, teachers made clear that they were keenly aware of these differences, and indeed, they tended to exaggerate them; while teachers in high-SES schools knew that almost all their students had computers and Internet access, teachers in low-SES schools believed that only a minority of their students had such access. However, whether their views were exaggerated or not, the teachers in low-SES schools were correct to assume that substantial numbers of their students did not come to school with the requisite access to have developed basic computer literacy. They thus used a disproportionate amount of time to teach hardware and software operations, and they were reluctant to assign homework, such as research papers or projects, that required out-of-school access to the Internet. In high-SES schools, teachers correctly assumed that they could forego instruction in basic hardware and software operations, because students had likely learned these at home—and that assigning more in-depth research that required out-of-school computer and Internet access would not unduly burden their students.

Finally, the more recent laptop study (Warschauer, 2006) carried with it both bad and good news as to the potential of these programs for alleviating inequity. On the one hand, laptop programs were more challenging to implement in low-SES schools for many of the reasons cited throughout this chapter. Students in low-SES schools had less home computer experience, and thus took more time to adapt to using laptops. Teachers in low-SES schools tended to be less experienced, and technical support infrastructures were not always as good. Parents were less able to guide their children on effective use of technology. Many low-SES schools were in high-crime neighborhoods, and there was thus more concern about laptops being stolen when taken home. And teachers had difficulty figuring out the best way to integrate laptops in situations where there were larger numbers of English language learners and students at below-basic reading levels. However, on the positive side, there were a number of schools and programs identified in the study that carried out exemplary technology-enhanced instruction with culturally and linguistically diverse low-SES students. In these programs, well-trained and highly committed teachers were able to use laptops to help raise low-SES students' test scores while simultaneously engaging students in more opportunities for critical inquiry and in-depth learning. Finally, because low-SES students were also less likely to have a computer at home, having take-home laptops allowed them to gain opportunities to learn technological skills that they might not have otherwise had.

One example given is Castle Middle School (pseudonym) in Maine, where about half the students are highly impoverished Whites from nearby housing projects, a quarter of the students are refugees and immigrants, and many of the remaining students are from middle-class and upper-middle-class suburbs. Previously, the school had been highly stratified, with seven distinct educational tracks, including one for the highly gifted, one for the accelerated (but not gifted), one for special education, one for non-English speakers, and several others calibrated by ability. In the 1990s, the school had rejected the tracking approach and developed an integrated program, with students of all abilities (including as many special education and ESL students as possible) grouped together into "houses" of about 60 learners with 4 main teachers. The entire curriculum for each house was organized into three 8- to 12-week theme-based learning expeditions, where students worked collaboratively on authentic projects. Though the reform had predated the school's one-to-one laptop program, the development of the laptop program amplified the success of the reform, by providing the best possible tool for students to collaboratively carry out research; present findings; and reflect on, critique, and document their work, while allowing for individual differences in knowledge and skills. As a result, Castle's combined test scores in writing, mathematics, and science have exceeded the state average, in spite of the school's large numbers of English learners and low-income students, and all students at the school are given a more equitable opportunity to excel than would be typical in such a stratified population.

OUTCOMES

Measuring outcomes is the most complex aspect of analyzing technology-enhanced learning, in part because the goals of teaching with technology are so diverse, and in part because many of those goals do not have clearly operationalized outcome measures. We begin by discussing academic outcomes, which are somewhat easier to measure, and then move on to examining 21st century learning skills.

Academic Outcomes

In testimony before a Congressional hearing on educational technology, Chris Dede (1995) wisely pointed out the problems with what he termed the "fire" metaphor of information technology. Just as a fire radiates heat, many people expect a computer to radiate learning. Unfortunately, that's not the case. Rather, as Dede noted, "information technologies are more like clothes; to get a benefit, you must make them a part of your personal space, tailored to your needs" (p. 10).

The most persuasive evidence that access to computers raises standard academic outcomes, such as grades, test scores, and graduation rates, comes from home rather than school settings. It may be the case that at home people are more able to make computers part of their personal space and tailor them to their needs.

One of the largest and most rigorous studies of the relationship of home computer use to test score outcomes in the United States was conducted by Beltran, Das, and Fairlie (in press). They used information from two national data sets to explore the causal relationship between computer ownership and high school graduation rates. The data sets were the Computer and Internet Use Supplements of the CPS for 2000–2003 (discussed above), and the National Longitudinal Survey of Youth 1997 (NLSY97). The latter involved hour-long interviews of a representative sample of 9,000 U.S. youth and their parents annually from 1997 to 2002, and also included the gathering of educational data such as youths' schooling history, performance on standardized tests, course of study, and the timing and types of degrees earned.

They found a dramatic relationship between home ownership of computers and high school graduation rate, with a differential in graduation between computer owners and nonowners of 24.3 percentage points according to the NLSY97 data and 16.6 percentage points according to the CPS data. They note that the 16.6 point difference attributed to owning a computer found in the CPS data is larger than the White/black difference (13.4 points) and comparable with the differences between teenagers who have college-educated and high school dropout fathers (19.7 percentage points), who have college-educated and high school dropout mothers (20.7 percentage points), and who live in families with incomes of $75,000–$100,000 versus $20,000–30,000 (19.2 percentage points) found in the same data.

Part of the reason this differential is so high is that computer ownership correlates with a number of other factors associated with youth's educational achievement, such as family income, race, or parents' education. However, when controlling for these and other individual, parental, and family characteristics, it was found that teenagers who have access to home computers are 6 to 8 percentage points more likely to graduate from high school than teenagers who do not have home computers. They noted that this implies a larger difference in graduation probability than the difference from having a college graduate parent relative to a high school dropout parent. Using similar controls as above, the study found that having a computer was associated with a 0.22 point positive difference in grade point average (based on a 4-point grade scale, thus roughly 2/3 the value of a + or – grade), and a decline of 2.8 percentage points in the likelihood of being suspended from school. The study does not reveal the reasons for all these benefits, but the authors speculate that use of a home computer for schoolwork is a principal one, citing data from the CPS that 93.4% of youth with home computers use them for school assignments.

One question that Beltran et al. (in press) did not investigate was the possible differential effect of home technology access by SES or gender. Simply put—do the benefits of home computer use accrue equally across demographic groups? Using a previous iteration of the National Longitudinal Youth Survey (NLYS88), and based, this time, on standardized tests, Attewell and Battle (1999) found that, without other controls, having a home computer was correlated with about a 12% increase in both reading and math test scores. When SES and other factors were controlled for, having a home computer raised test scores by 3% to 5% of the average score. Most interestingly, they also studied the differential effect by SES, and found that, controlling for other possible factors, low-SES students who had home computers received much less benefit from them in raising their test scores than did high-SES students who had home computers. Table 9 shows the effect size on math and reading scores for high-SES students (1 standard deviation [SD] above the SES average), average-SES students, and low-SES students (1 SD below the SES average.) The numbers in the table indicate the changes in reading or math score measured in standard deviation units associated with 1 SD increase in home computer ownership by families at that SES level. They indicate that among families with home computers and controlling

TABLE 9
Size of Home Computer Effect by Socioeconomic Status (SES)

	Effect on Math Scores	Effect on Reading Scores
High SES	2.77	1.55
Average SES	1.69	1.08
Low SES	0.60	0.61

Source. Attewell and Battle (1999).

for all other possible variables, children from high-SES families compared with low-SES families receive more than four and a half times the benefit in increased math scores and more than two and a half times the benefit in increased reading scores. Substantial discrepancies further exist when comparing males versus females, Whites versus Hispanics, and Whites versus Blacks; in each case the former group achieved greater benefit on school test scores from having a home computer than did the latter group when controlling for other variables.

In sum, according to this study, not only were African Americans, Hispanics, and low-SES students less likely to have a home computer, but even when they *did* have a computer in this study, they, as well as females, received less academic benefit from having one compared to White, high-SES, and male students. Attewell and Battle's (1999) study provides no data as to why this may be the case. They speculate that it may be due to the *social envelope* (Giacquinta, Bauer, & Levin, 1993) that surrounds children's home use of computers and includes the kinds of technology resources (e.g., educational software) and social resources (scaffolding, modeling, and support from parents) that we have discussed earlier. They conclude that

> Home computing may generate another "Sesame Street effect" whereby an innovation that held great promise for poorer children to catch up educationally with more affluent children is in practice increasing the educational gap between affluent and poor, between boys and girls, and between ethnic minorities and Whites, even among those with access to the technology. (Attewell & Battle, 1999, p. 1)

Attewell and Battle's study is based on data that are some 20 years old, and the amount of home computers and the ways they are used have expanded dramatically during this time. However, a recent colloquium paper by three Duke economists reports similar results from a study in North Carolina, with race and SES strongly mediating the effect on academic achievement of home computer and Internet access (Clotfelter, Ladd, & Vigdor, 2008). If the Duke findings hold up under scrutiny of peer review, they are even more disheartening, as the study indicates an overall negative effect on math and reading test scores for low-SES and African American students with computer and Internet access, presumably because of "unproductive uses" of technology that "may not only crowd out productive computer time, but may also crowd out offline studying" (p. 37). As with the Philadelphia library study discussed above, such findings support the notion that the "social envelope" surrounding computer use is more important than computer access itself.

Academic Outcomes From School Use

Studies of academic outcomes from school use of technology are mixed (see, e.g., discussion in Kulik, 2003). Many studies are based on very small sample sizes and take place in schools or classrooms where individual educators are highly expert in particular uses of technology, and thus these studies may not be generalizable to other contexts.

Larger studies, though, suggest that the drill and practice activities favored in low-SES schools tend to be ineffective, whereas the uses of technology disproportionately used in high-SES schools achieve positive results. The best evidence of this discrepancy comes from Wenglinsky (2005), who analyzed data from the NAEP in 1996, 1998, and 2000. Overall, Wenglinsky found a consistently negative interaction between frequency of technology use and test score outcomes in mathematics (at both the fourth and eighth grade), science (at both the fourth and eighth grade), and reading (at the eighth grade; see Table 10). This appears to be because of the negative effects of drill and practice activities that are used predominately with low-SES students. In contrast, the more constructivist educational technology activities typically used with high-SES students were correlated with higher test score outcomes.

For example, in mathematics, Wenglinsky found that the use of simulations/applications in eighth grade and games in the fourth grade positively affected test scores, whereas drill and practice at the eighth grade negatively affected the scores. In science, games (fourth grade), word processing (fourth grade), simulations (fourth and eighth grade) and data analysis (fourth grade) all positively affected test scores. And in eighth grade reading, use of computers for writing activities positively affected test scores, but use of computers for grammar/punctuation or for reading activities (which usually involve drill or tutorials) negatively affected test scores. In each of the three subject areas, student SES was the strongest factor predicting whether technology use would be positively or negatively associated with test score outcomes.

More recent large-scale studies offer support for Wenglinsky's findings as to the ineffectiveness of drill-and-practice software. The U.S. Department of Education recently contracted a national experimental study to analyze the effects of educational software use on reading and mathematics test scores. A total of 16 software products, all of which involved tutorial and practice activities, were carefully selected from recommendations made by expert panels; 12 of the 16 have either received or been nominated to receive awards from trade associations, media, parents, and teachers. The comparative study involved 9,424 students taught by 428 teachers in 132 schools across the country (Dynarski et al., 2007). Teachers were randomly assigned to use 1 of 16 software products designed for teaching reading and math (treatment group) or not (control group) and students were given pre- and posttests during the first year of use. Overall, there was poor classroom implementation by teachers of the

TABLE 10
Links Between Technology Use and Test Scores

Subject: Grade	Test Scores
Math: Fourth grade	
Frequency of school computer use	−.06
Use: games	.03
Student SES	.59
Math: Eighth grade	
Frequency of school computer use	−.06
Use: simulations/applications	.04
Use: drill and practice	−.06
Student SES	.39
Science: Fourth grade	
Frequency of school computer use	−.21
Use: games	.07
Use: simulations	.08
Use: word processing	.09
Student SES	.25
Science: Eighth grade	
Frequency of school computer use	−.12
Use: data analysis	.04
Use: simulations	.07
Student SES	.54
Reading: Eighth grade	
Frequency of school computer use	−.02
Use: writing	.06
Use: grammar/punctuation	−.05
Use: reading	−.05

Source. Wenglinsky (2005).

software (as is apparently often the case with tutorial software; for another example, see Llosa & Slayton, 2009) and no significant effect of the software use on reading or math test scores of treatment students as compared with the control students even when fully implemented.

In contrast, more constructivist uses of technology are often found in one-to-one laptop schools, where students' daily access provides the opportunity for greater mastery of computers and their deployment for writing, research, collaboration, analysis, and publication (see Warschauer, 2006). Students in laptop programs are among the most frequent users of technology, and several recent studies show a positive correlation between laptop program participation and test score outcomes (see, e.g., Suhr, Hernandez, Grimes, & Warschauer, in press; Texas Center for Educational Research,

2008; additional studies reporting positive test score effects, though either without control groups or with self-selection into laptop groups, include Gulek & Demirtas, 2005; Silvernail, 2007; Jeroski, 2008).

Only one of these studies specifically investigated the differential impact of laptop program participation on test scores by SES or race. That study of sixth, seventh, and eighth graders found that being African American, Hispanic, or low-SES negatively affected how much test score benefit in reading and mathematics students received from participating in the laptop program, thus supporting findings from other studies on the differential academic benefits of computer access and use. It should be noted, however, that only in some combinations of grade level, subject, and demographic group did the differential effects rise to the level of statistical significance (Texas Center for Educational Research, 2008). In another study that looked at test score outcomes in both a high- and low-SES school, scores for laptop students actually fell in both schools during the first year of the laptop program implementation (compared with scores for non-laptop students elsewhere in the district), and then bounced back to equivalency with non-laptop students by the end of the second year (Grimes & Warschauer, 2008). The first-year dip was greater in the low-SES school compared with the high-SES school—consistent with the finding discussed earlier that laptop programs are more challenging in low-SES schools—but, at least in this study, the second-year test score rebound in the low-SES school was also greater.

The lack of positive results may be possibly explained by poor implementation of the programs, likely heightened by the fact that teachers were assigned to use a program rather than empowered to choose one themselves, as well as too early testing; technology-enhanced reform is somewhat disruptive (involving new equipment, new ways of teaching, etc.) and thus positive test score results may not appear until the second or subsequent year (see, e.g., Grimes & Warschauer, 2008).

Twenty-First Century Learning Skills

The types of standardized educational tests cited in the above section cover only a small fraction of the knowledge, skills, and attitudes youth need to learn to be successful in today's information society (see, e.g., Gee, 2003, 2004; Jenkins, 2009; Levy & Murnane, 2004, 2005). This suggests the limitations of overly emphasizing basic standards and standardized tests. In an era where everything standardized can be outsourced to another country, and the real premium thus comes from creativity and innovation (see, e.g., Levy & Murnane, 2004), it is counterproductive to focus all our educational efforts on teaching to basic standards.

The broader set of knowledge, skills, and attitudes that are needed for success in today's world are typically labeled *21st century skills*. A number of efforts have been made to define and categorize these skills (for an example, see North Central Regional Educational Laboratory & the Metiri Group, 2003; for an overview of international efforts, see Leu, Kinzer, Coiro, & Cammack, 2004), with the most widely recognized that of the Partnership for 21st Century Skills. The Partnership—a

FIGURE 3
Twenty-First Century Skills

Information, Media, and Technology Skills	• Information Literacy • Media Literacy • ICT Literacy
Learning and Innovation Skills	• Creativity and Innovation • Critical Thinking and Problem Solving • Communication and Collaboration
Life and Career Skills	• Flexibility and Adaptability • Initiative and Self-Direction • Social and Cross-Cultural Skills • Productivity and Accountability • Leadership and Responsibility

Source. Partnership for 21st Century Skills (2009).

broad coalition of educational groups (e.g., National Educational Association, the Association for Supervision and Curriculum Development, the American Association of School Librarians, Educational Testing Service), technology firms (e.g., Apple, Adobe, Cisco, Dell, Intel, Microsoft), and content/media providers (e.g., McGraw-Hill, Pearson, Scholastic, Lego, Blackboard, Sesame Workshop)—describes three sets of skills that are viewed as built on a foundation of core subjects (e.g., English, arts, mathematics, science, history) and interdisciplinary themes (e.g., global awareness, civic literacy). These three skills sets—in information, media, and technology; learning and innovation; and life and career areas (see Figure 3)—are intimately tied up with sophisticated uses of new digital media.

Though there is widespread agreement on the value of these types of skills in today's world, the lack of commonly accepted metrics for measuring achievement of these skills makes it difficult to assess the extent to which they are being mastered in diverse settings. Case study data provide some evidence, though they do not allow for quantifiable comparison.

In school settings, discussion of such skills frequently arises in research on one-to-one laptop schools. Many school laptop programs were established specifically with such skills in mind, and a substantive body of research suggests that well-implemented laptop programs facilitate acquisition of such skills. In Maine, for example, where there is a statewide middle school one-to-one program, more than one-third of students report using laptops from once a week to several times daily to gather data from multiple sources to solve problems, gather data about real-life problems, evaluate information obtained on the Internet, critically analyze data or graphs, solve complex problems by analyzing and evaluating information, explain problem-solving processes and thinking, and visually represent or investigate concepts (Silvernail, 2007). Interviews with teachers, students, and parents; observations of classrooms; and analysis of student work suggest that these kind of activities are yielding positive results for acquisition of 21st century learning skills in Maine and elsewhere (Warschauer, 2006).

There is insufficient data to assess any differential learning of 21st century skills in schools by race, SES, or gender, but the information discussed above about stratified uses of educational technology is worrisome in this regard. The types of drill and practice programs that are disproportionately used with low-SES students are generally geared narrowly on acquisition of academic content or basic literacy and numeracy skills, so it is unrealistic to assume that they would contribute much to broader 21st century skill development. In contrast, the simulations and applications used disproportionately by high-SES students are often deployed with precisely those skill sets in mind.

In addition, the general academic climate in schools substantially shapes how media are used, with technology serving to amplify schools' abilities to achieve their preexisting goals rather than to transform the goals themselves (see, e.g., Warschauer, 1999, 2000). Therefore, schools that are already focused on the kinds of information literacy, critical thinking, and self-direction associated with 21st century learning skills will find new media a powerful way to achieve these, whereas schools that do not have such a focus will not likely suddenly discover it through a diffusion of computers. Warschauer's (2006, 2007b) comparative study of information literacy practices in diverse schools in Maine provides a stark example of this. In a high-SES suburban school (grades 5–8), sophisticated information literacy practices are begun in the fifth grade, a year before students receive their laptops. Students attend library workshops where they learn to access diverse sources of information, critically evaluate them, and integrate the information appropriately into a variety of products. They are later taught to use computers to access information from online reference works and primary source documents. These skills are eventually put to use in challenging interdisciplinary research projects. In contrast, in a low-SES school in an impoverished rural community, no special training in information literacy is provided. Though the school subscribes to the same online database of reference works and primary sources, neither students nor teachers exhibit any awareness of it. Most typically, students grab the first source that comes up in a Google search, without much critical thought, and several of the schools' teachers expect little more. Students are observed spending substantial time cutting and pasting images and texts into low-level PowerPoint presentations. The study is careful to point out that these kinds of practices are not found at all low-SES schools, presenting a counterexample with more positive practices and results. However, based on analysis of data from 10 elementary and secondary schools in California and Maine, the study concluded that "teachers in high-income communities were more likely to expect and promote critical inquiry and information literacy than were teachers in low-income areas" (Warschauer, 2007b, p. 2537).

Out-of-School Development of 21st Century Skills

There is little doubt that intensive use of digital media in out-of-school environments can contribute to the development of 21st century learning skills. As at school, access to and use of new media are necessary but insufficient conditions for the development of such skills. But at least some youth, such as those that Ito and her colleagues found are "geeking out" in interest-driven activities, are undoubtedly mastering sophisticated skills in each of the three areas delineated in Figure 3. Consider the example of Max, a 14-year-old boy who hopes to be a director or filmmaker, and thus decides to set up a video-production company. Max and his friend produce humorous and dramatic videos that they post on YouTube, at least one of which has received 2 million views and more than 5,000 text comments and has been aired on ABC's *Good Morning America*. Max also regularly receives fan mail and has received offers to purchase some of his videos for online advertisements. Who would doubt that Max's use of digital media has enhanced the development of his media literacy, creativity and innovation, communication and collaboration, and initiative and self-direction?

One controversial area of home media use is game playing, with some concerned that it diverts time from more productive pursuits, and others arguing that such play is productive for learning new skills. One study attempted to assess the attitudes developed through game play via a survey of 2,500 Americans, principally business professionals, who included nongamers, moderate gamers, and frequent gamers (Beck & Wade, 2004). The survey methodology simply shows correlations without the power to demonstrate causation; nevertheless, the findings reveal some interesting differences. Among the young people surveyed, frequent gamers are more likely than nongamers to value risk taking, pay for performance, and connecting with the right people to get things done; they are also more likely to value the fate of the organization they work for (see Table 11).

There has long been a concern that girls are not gaining the same knowledge, skills, and attitudes about technology that boys are, because of differential uses of new media at home (see, e.g., AAUW Educational Foundation, 2000). The most recent research suggests that boys and girls spend about the same time on computers at home, but that boys spend substantially more time than girls playing computer games (Roberts et al., 2005). Boys may also be engaged more frequently in certain types of "geeking out" activities described by Ito et al. (2008) such as media production, though girls appear to be more engaged in other types of geeking out, such as those involving creative writing (M. Ito, personal communication). There are still substantial differences at the far end of the pipeline, both by gender and race, as measured by numbers of people who enter advanced study and careers in computer science, engineering, and related fields, to be discussed below.

Finally, we note that classes and informal instruction at computer media centers have been shown to be a particularly effective way of developing youth's 21st century learning skills. Hull and Katz (2006), for example, describe the case of Dara, a 13-year-old girl of Guatemalan heritage who attended an after-school media program

TABLE 11
Percentage of Young Nongamers, Moderate Gamers,
and Frequent Gamers Who Agree With Statements

	Nongamers	Moderate Gamers	Frequent Gamers
The best rewards come to those that take risks	45.7	50.1	60.7
Taking measured risks is the best way to get ahead	52.9	54.6	59.7
I prefer pay and bonuses based on actual performance rather than a set salary	34.6	36.5	47.1
The best way to get things done is to connect with the right people	72.1	70.6	77.5
I really care about the fate of the organization I work for	39.4	41.0	44.0

Source. Beck and Wade (2004).

called DUSTY (Digital Underground Storytelling for Youth). Their article, based on field notes of Dara's participation at the center and at school over 2½ years and story scripts and digital stories created by Dara during this same time period, documents the changes that Dara experienced through participation at the center, both in terms of media skills mastered and in her sense of self and relationship to the world. As the authors explain,

Not only did both Dara and Randy [a young adult at the school] master the technological skills necessary to create digital stories, but they also paid increasingly close attention to the technical aspects of language—to its sound, to genre, to its poetic dimensions, and to textual images as messages of another sort. And they masterfully combined image, sound, and text into powerful and personally meaningful multimedia narratives that also clearly and movingly spoke to others. These others included their DUSTY peers and friends as well as a larger social world that might not otherwise have listened to what they had to say; the fresh nature of the multimodality and multimedia itself appeared to lend their ideas both currency and urgency. (p. 70)

As a result of these new skills, Dara "found ways to reposition herself through digital storytelling both in relation to the people she loved and admired, and in relation to institutions, like school." She accomplished this "not only through her digital stories" but also through her "social relationships with DUSTY peers, mentors, and facilitators who helped build Dara's perception of herself as an expert digital storyteller and a skilled writer possessing technological savvy who could assist her friends in creating digital stories." In the end, a young girl who had a "meek and discontented school identity" thus became a "confident author and active community participant" (p. 61).

This is only one person, in one program, but it is illustrative of the changes that youth can experience when they master powerful symbolic systems to express themselves on issues of high personal and social relevance (see, e.g., Ito et al., 2008; Kafai et al., 2009). It also helps illuminate what agency vis-à-vis new media entails, and why community centers can be such important sites in the development of such agency. As discussed by Baumman and Briggs (1990, and cited in Hull & Katz, 2006), the "construction and assumption of authority" (p. 77) with use of texts rests on four factors: access, legitimacy, competence, and value. Community media centers can provide (a) access to the requisite technology and cultural artifacts for production of multimodal texts; (b) legitimization of learners' entry into the world of new media through the support of a community; (c) the means to acquire knowledge and competence with new media through instruction, apprenticeship, and practice; and (d) the valuing of youth's multimodal products by mentors, peers, and community members in everyday interaction and in special displays or performances. Although some youth are able to find this access, legitimacy, competence, and value through online activity in home environments, not all will be able to, and community centers thus provide a potentially rich alternative venue for the development of authority through media use and mastery.

FROM ACCESS TO OUTCOMES: THE COMPUTER SCIENCE PIPELINE

Although, for the purposes of this broad review, we have divided access, use, and outcomes into three sections, they are, of course, closely intertwined. To illustrate this interconnection we take, as an example, the *computer science pipeline*, that is, the long-term process through which children learn about computer science and pursue advanced study and careers in the field.

A fascinating examination of this pipeline comes from the Los Angeles Unified School District, where a research team at UCLA carried out an ethnographic study of computer science instruction at three Los Angeles area high schools from about 2001 to 2004 (Goode, Estrella, & Margolis, 2006; Margolis et al., 2008). The sites included a 98% Latino school in East Los Angeles, a magnet science school in a mostly White neighborhood but with 64% African American students, and a school in the wealthy hills near the Pacific Ocean with a mix of White (43%), African American (24%), Latino (24%), and Asian American students (8%). Many of the African American and Latino students at the two latter schools traveled long distances by bus to attend.

At the first two schools, which were predominately Latino and African American, no Advanced Placement (AP) classes in computer science were offered. The few computing courses that were offered focused principally on computer literacy and basic applications. A single exception was a programming class at the mostly Latino school taught by an instructor without formal training in the subject. The researchers noted that assignments focused on narrow input–output problems and trivia games, and that "none . . . features the problem solving and scientific reasoning that is the foundational knowledge of computer science" (Margolis et al., 2008, p. 32).

In contrast, the school in the wealthy neighborhood had an extensive computer curriculum, leading up to AP Computer Science. Nevertheless, the advanced computer classes, and especially the AP class, were themselves highly segregated, with the majority of students in them White males. The researchers noted that it was predominately White males who had the extensive experience with computers at home that gave them the confidence to take these elective courses, knowing that they would succeed and get good grades in them. These White male youth often owned more than one computer, had the financial resources to buy the latest hardware and software, and had extensive home experience in programming and gaming, supported by a network of friends and by their parents, many of whom worked in technology industries. These students were able to "play with their own computers, take them apart, put them back together, try out different software, and learn from friends who were doing the same." Many of them were "fully capable not of not only troubleshooting their computers but also building computers 'from scratch'" (Margolis et al., 2008, p. 80).

Few minorities or females at the school had had such extensive experience with computers at home and many were reluctant to take challenging computer science elective courses that could bring down their grade-point average and thus harm their chances at college admission. The handful of females and minority students who took advanced computer science courses often felt intimidated in class when White male "techies" (Margolis et al., p. 83) dominated discussions and made fun of the work of other students. As a result, very few females or minorities at any of three schools got the types of experiences that would lead them to careers in computer science.

These patterns are common beyond these three schools. In California, for example, though African Americans and Latinos made up 49% of the school population in 2004, they represented only 9% of those taking the AP computer science examination that year. Females, who similarly made up 49% of the California school population, represented only 18% of those taking the exam (Margolis et al., 2008). High achieving high school females are much less likely to have computer programming experience than are high achieving high school males (Barron, 2004).

Not surprisingly, women and minorities are underrepresented in college study of computer science and in careers in the field. And for women, the situation is steadily worsening over time. In 1985, women made up 49% of U.S. students receiving associate degrees in computer science and 37% of those receiving bachelor's degrees. By 2005, the percentages had dropped to 30% of associate degrees and only 22% of bachelor's degrees (National Science Foundation, 2008; see Figure 4).

As for race/ethnicity, the precipitous fall off is not so much over time, but rather according to degree level. African Americans received 14.4% of their associate's degrees in computer science, thus reflecting a strong interest among that population in pursuing this field. But they were only able to receive 11.6% of the bachelor's degrees, 7.7% of the master's degrees, and 2.6% of the doctoral degrees (National Science Foundation, 2009; see Table 12). For Latinos, the numbers are even worse. Thus Blacks and Latinos, who made up a total of more than a quarter of the U.S.

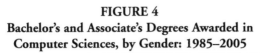

FIGURE 4
Bachelor's and Associate's Degrees Awarded in Computer Sciences, by Gender: 1985–2005

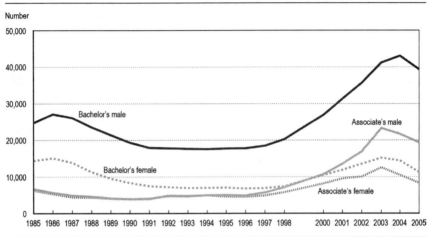

Source. National Science Foundation (2008).

population in 2006, received combined just 3.8% of the doctoral degrees awarded in computer science.

DISCUSSION: OVERCOMING THE NEW DIVIDE

Nearly all youth access computers and the Internet somewhere. Thus, what was considered the original *digital divide* is largely resolved, at least in the United States. Today the digital divide resides in differential ability to use new media to critically evaluate information, analyze, and interpret data, attack complex problems, test innovative solutions, manage multifaceted projects, collaborate with others in knowledge production, and communicate effectively to diverse audiences—in essence, to carry out the kinds of expert thinking and complex communication that are at the heart of the new economy (Levy & Murnane, 2004).

Whereas the first digital divide could be solved simply by providing a computer and an Internet connection, this digital divide presents a greater challenge. The above review suggests five steps that we can take to help meet this challenge, related to individual access, curriculum and instruction, standardized assessment, out-of-school media programs, and research.

Ensuring Regular and Flexible Access

First, we need to provide school-aged youth with individual access to computers with broadband Internet connections. Whereas a weekly trip to a school computer

Table 12
Degrees Received by U.S. Citizens and Permanent Residents
in Computer Science by Race/Ethnicity in 2006

	Percentage			
	Whites	Blacks	Latinos	Asian
U.S. population age 18–24 years	61.4	14.2	17.5	4.3
Associate's degrees	63.1	14.4	9.8	5.0
Bachelor's degrees	60.7	11.6	7.2	11.0
Master's degrees	55.0	7.7	4.8	18.4
Doctoral degrees	70.3	2.6	1.2	21.8

Source. National Science Foundation (2009).

lab will suffice for learning basic computer literacy or for doing reading or math drills, regular and flexible access is required to facilitate the development of advanced knowledge production skills using technology—and, as this review has shown, such regular, flexible access is far from being achieved by many of today's youth, especially those who are already most at risk for failure at school. There are a variety of ways to increase individual access to computers, such as by providing tax credits to families who buy computers for school children at home. However, the simplest and most direct way is through one-to-one laptop programs at school. When such programs also allow students to bring laptops back and forth from home, the programs simultaneously address problems related to school access, home access, and school–home connections.

Until now, the large costs involved—for hardware, insurance, software, technical support, Internet connections, and professional development—made such programs very difficult to implement for financially strapped school districts. However, the continuing fall of laptop prices—with some small "netbook" computers already dropping near $200—will bring down hardware and insurance prices considerably, and the light weight of netbooks will increase their portability both from home to school and within the school environment. At the same time, the growth of free open source software and educational resources can facilitate the use of less powerful and inexpensive netbooks, while also substantially reducing the costs of both software and technical support. Finally, the generational shift of teachers, with more people now entering teaching careers with substantial computing experience, can result in improved pedagogical use of computers and thus further improve the cost–benefit ratio.

A crucial advantage of one-to-one laptop programs is that they potentially allow all students to work on technology-based research assignments and projects at home, thus helping extend learning time for all beyond the 30-hour school week, a major goal for educational improvement (Time, Learning, and Afterschool Task Force,

2007). However, this will be difficult to achieve if students lack broadband Internet access at home. A second policy implication then is the need for universal broadband. School districts and educational policymakers can consider a number of models for expanding home broadband access, from municipal wireless plans (for public access) to school district–private provider partnerships (for subsidized individual household access).

Teaching the Word and the World

Second, as shown throughout this review, access alone will not overcome inequity in use and outcomes. A critical step toward that end will be transforming teaching and learning in schools. Among school laptop programs, for example, the most successful in achieving positive outcomes for all students have clear and well-designed learning and literacy objectives; they are educational reform programs involving laptops, rather than technology programs per se (see discussion in Warschauer, 2006).

Whether in laptop programs or other instructional environments, schools need to move away from a narrow focus on teaching the basics to a broader approach that emphasizes *both* basic and 21st century skills, with the latter including the kinds of expert thinking and complex communication noted by Levy and Murnane (2004). Fortunately, excellent models exist on how to promote these broader skill sets in technology-intensive classrooms, whether in general (e.g., Kozma, 2003; Means, Penuel, & Padilla, 2001; Sandholtz, Ringstaff, & Dwyer, 1997; Wenglinsky, 2005) or in particular ways that address the needs of English language learners and at-risk students (e.g., Brown, Cummins, & Sayers, 2007; Cummins, 2008; Warschauer, 2006, 2007a; Warschauer, Grant, Del Real, & Rousseau, 2004).

Studies of highly successful instruction of at-risk learners in technology-intensive environments have led the first author of this chapter to summarize such a dual approach on basic and advanced skills as *teaching the word and the world* (Warschauer, 2006, 2007a). These studies revealed how Internet-connected computers can become powerful tools for helping learners understand and manipulate text, that is, to grasp the *word*. With appropriate instructional approaches, images and video can scaffold texts and provide clues for developing readers. Hypertext annotations can offer further scaffolding and encourage appropriate reading strategies. Graphic organizing software can help students analyze texts or plan their own writing. Word-processing software allows students to achieve a more iterative writing process. Computer-mediated classroom discussion provides students a way to communicate in written form, thus providing further opportunities for learners to notice others' written language and hone their own writing.

The same studies have shown Internet-connected computers to be a potent tool for bringing the wider *world* into the classroom and thus for both motivating and contextualizing literacy practices. Students can use the Internet to discover authentic reading material on almost any topic and be introduced to up-to-date information and perspectives from peoples and cultures across the globe. They can gather the resources needed to critically consider diverse social issues confronting their community, nation, or world. Students can then develop and publish high-quality products about these issues that can be shared with interlocutors or the public, whether in their community or internationally. And, through these products, students can not only learn about the world, but can also leave their mark on it.

One potent example of teaching both the word and the world is *Project Fresa* (the Strawberry Project), carried out among Spanish bilingual elementary school students in California (Warschauer, 2007a, Warschauer & Ware, 2008). Through conducting technology-enhanced research on the conditions of farm workers in neighboring strawberry fields, and assessing and acting on their findings in light of state and global contexts, Latino children involved in the project worked toward meeting basic standards while flexing their critical thinking and communication skills. Unfortunately, though, when one of the main teachers involved became an administrator, she was unsuccessful in getting other teachers to continue Project Fresa due to their fears that such theme-based projects would distract from their efforts to raise test scores (Warschauer & Ware, 2008).

Measuring What We Value

As seen from the above example, the main impediment to improving teaching with technology may not be lack of ideas on how to reform curriculum and instruction, but rather lack of incentive to do so, because of testing regimes that reward the achievement of only basic and not advanced skills. As Levy and Murnane (2005) explain,

Perhaps the biggest potential obstacle to increasing students' mastery of Expert Thinking and Complex Communication are mandatory state tests (assessments) that emphasize recall of facts rather than these critical skills. Most states now require all students to complete mandatory assessments as part of programs to increase educational accountability. In many states, these assessments have been designed toward minimizing costs while producing numerical scores that can be compared across districts or over time. In a subject like history, a multiple-choice test is more likely to meet these criteria than an essay needed to demonstrate Complex Communication. In an area like math, a multiple-choice test is much less expensive to grade than an exam with open-ended responses that asks students to describe their thought processes— and to demonstrate the nature of their Expert Thinking. In the drive for educational accountability, teachers have strong incentives to teach to the test and so it is particularly important that we get the tests right. (p. 23)

If this is the case, how then can we begin "measuring what we value" rather than simply "valuing what we measure" (Hersh, 2006)? The answer is through an increase in performance assessment, including both the highly interpretive kinds performed by teachers at the class or school level (e.g., portfolio assessment) and the more standardized kinds that will entail development of new large-scale tests. An increase in the use of *classroom performance assessment* will necessitate providing teachers with the training, resources, administrative support, and incentives to reorient their instruction and evaluation of students to focus on the development of expert thinking.

An increase in the use of *standardized performance assessment* will require the funding and commitment to develop and deploy new tests that more accurately measure the kind of skills needed for the 21st century. And assessments of both types will need to involve use of digital media because paper-based examinations cannot accurately capture the learning that occurs through use of digital media (see a study by Russell & Plati, 2002, analysis of the issue by Silvernail, 2005, and discussion of *modal validity* by Luke, 2009).

A number of recent developments related to assessing 21st century skills are worth noting. First, Educational Testing Service (2009) has developed an information and communication technology literacy test called iSkills, which claims to assess "critical thinking in the digital environment" (para 3). Second, the Council for Aid to Education (2009), a nonprofit offshoot of Rand Corporation, has developed a College and Work Readiness Assessment that requires open-ended responses to constructed tasks to purportedly measure "an integrated set of critical thinking, analytic reasoning, problem solving, and written communication skills" (Council for Aid to Education, 2009, fourth paragraph). Third, the National Assessment Governing Board (2008), which sets policy for the NAEP, has contracted with WestEd to recommend the framework and test specifications for a Technological Literacy Assessment that will combine with the current tests of reading, writing, mathematics, and science to become part of the Nation's Report Card beginning in 2012. Fourth, the Programme for International Student Assessment has developed an Electronic Reading Assessment as part of its new battery of tests (Haldane, 2009). And, fifth, Cisco, Intel, and Microsoft have recently funded a team of researchers in Australia, the United States, and Hungary to develop and pilot ICT-based assessments of 21st century skills (Kozma, 2009).

Though none of these initiatives have resulted in replacement for the state-specific tests that carry so much weight under the No Child Left Behind Act, they are welcome efforts toward developing both the intellectual and policy framework for a new orientation toward standardized assessment. Without reform of assessment, teachers and administrators in public schools—and especially in low-SES schools that are so frequently subject to test score pressure—are unlikely to focus on the broad communication and thinking skills required for success in today's world.

Expanding Out-of-School Media Learning

Improved and more equal resources, instruction, and assessment in school cannot in and of themselves completely overcome unequal amounts of physical, human, and social capital in youths' out-of-school environments. This is especially so in relationship to learning of and with technology, so much of which occurs outside of school time. Providing more equal home access to individual computers and broadband Internet, as discussed above, will be one important step toward this end. Yet without enhancing social support for learning to use these resources, the mere provision of equipment could amplify the "Sesame Street effect" discussed earlier.

Initial evidence indicates that community technology centers and youth media programs can provide advanced technology learning experiences for youth. In particular, such centers and programs can help low-income youth transition from being passive consumers of media to more active and critical producers of digital content. Key to this transition is the social support found in such centers, where low-SES youth can gain access to the kinds of mentors, exemplars, peers with common interests, and pro-media production norms that many high-SES youth experience in their home environments. Yet only a small fraction of youth attends these programs. The expansion of funding for youth media programs and the enhanced integration of technology into extant after-school programs should thus be on the agenda of educational policymakers.

Unfortunately, the current economic climate may lead state or private funders to turn away from financing youth media centers. With home access to computers and the Internet slowly but steadily increasing, policymakers may also believe that youth will learn whatever they need to know about technology in home environments, under the myth that all youth are *digital natives* (see Prensky, 2001) who can effortlessly absorb advanced media skills on their own or from friends, thus making community centers redundant. We hope that this review has demonstrated the naïveté of such beliefs and the necessity of providing enhanced social support, such as that offered in youth media programs, if we are to seriously tackle inequity in use of technology and the outcomes associated with such use.

Researching Technology and Equity

Finally, what kind of research is required to increase our understanding of technology and equity? At a national level, the most thorough sources of statistical data on computer and Internet access and use have come from the federal government, either via the Current Population Surveys of the U.S. Census Bureau or from the National Center for Education Statistics of the Institute of Education Sciences (IES). Yet the gathering of data on this topic by both the Census Bureau and IES slowed down during the Bush administration, which downplayed the importance of the issue, and, as of this writing, has yet to be resumed by the Obama administration, which has had other pressing economic matters to address. A resumption of regular federal data gathering on this issue is vital.

Second, scholars addressing the relationship of technology and learning need to continue to include issues of equity, both in quantitative and qualitative studies. In quantitative research, the most widely cited studies on differential technology use in schools are now a decade old (e.g., Becker, 2000c; Wenglinsky, 1998). Quantitative research using more recent data sets can reveal how earlier trends may have persisted or changed course. In qualitative research, there has been a tendency by many scholars of technology and new literacies to examine model rather than typical practices, with the resultant publications presenting an idealized notion of how diverse groups might experience new technologies (see discussion in Warschauer, in press). Ethnographers would do well to replicate in the digital realm Heath's (1983) study of typical communication patterns and literacy practices in two diverse neighboring communities, as such comparative ethnography can richly portray the social contexts that shape inequity.

CONCLUSION

There is a widespread belief that the falling cost of computers and Internet access is rapidly narrowing a digital divide in U.S. society. However, as this review shows, gaps in home access to digital media are still substantial, and inequalities in technology usage and outcomes are even greater. Unfortunately, many of the measures most frequently used for analyzing technology-related access, use, and outcomes are insufficient. For example, phone-based surveys investigating home access disproportionately exclude marginalized groups, such as those who do not speak English or those who cannot afford phone service. And, most important, standardized tests, which have become the sine qua non for measuring school-based outcomes, do not even attempt to assess the broad thinking and learning skills associated with advanced uses of digital media.

Though technology-related access, use, and outcomes are difficult to measure, all available evidence suggests they are critically important factors in shaping social futures. As we rethink how to measure evidence of equitable resources, conditions, and outcomes of student learning, continued close attention to the role of technology in both school and out-of-school environments is urgently needed.

NOTES

Although technology and equity is an important issue facing youth throughout the world, space limitations prevent us from analyzing research on this issue from countries other than the United States. Those interested in international perspectives on technology access and use may wish to consult Warschauer (2003), Matuchniak and Warschauer (2010), Hull, Zacher, and Hibbert (2009), Plomp, Anderson, and Law (2009), or the Centre for Educational Research and Innovation (2009).

ACKNOWLEDGMENTS

We are grateful to Robert Fairlie of the University of California, Santa Cruz for sharing with us his recent analyses of home access to computers and assisting us with interpretation of CPS data. We are also grateful to the editors of *Review of Research in Education*, Allan Luke, Judith Green, and Gregory J. Kelly, and developmental editors, Nichole Pinkard and Vivian Gadsden, for their extremely helpful guidance and feedback on our outline and multiple drafts of this chapter.

REFERENCES

AAUW Educational Foundation. (2000). *Tech-savvy: Educating girls in the new computer age.* Washington, DC: AAUW.

Andrews, G. G. (2007). *A tale of two game worlds: Comparing the literacy practices of low- and high-socioeconomic status (SES) students surrounding video games.* Unpublished master's thesis, Teachers College, Columbia University, New York.

Andrews, G. G. (2008a, June). *Baby games, boy games, games for nerds: Class and gender gaming disparities among U.S. youth.* Paper presented at the Under the Mask: Perspectives on the Gamer Conference, Luton, UK. Retrieved January 29, 2009, from http://underthemask. wikidot.com/gusandrews

Andrews, G. G. (2008b). Gameplay, gender, and socioeconomic status in two American high schools. *E-Learning, 5,* 199-213.

Attewell, P., & Battle, J. (1999). Home computers and school performance. *The Information Society, 15,* 1-10.

Attewell, P., & Winston, H. (2003). Children of the digital divide. In P. Attewell, & N. M. Seel (Eds.), *Disadvantaged teens and computer technologies* (pp. 117-136). Münster, Germany: Waxmann.

Autor, D. H., Levy, F., & Murnane, R. J. (2003). The skill content of recent technological change: An empirical exploration. *Quarterly Journal of Economics, 118,* 1279-1333.

Baumman, R., & Briggs, C. L. (1990). Poetics and performance as critical perspectives on language and social life. *Annual Review of Anthropology, 19,* 59-88.

Barron, B. (2004). Learning ecologies for technological fluency: Gender and experiential differences. *Journal of Educational Computing Research, 31,* 1-36.

Barron, B., Martin, C. K., Takeuchi, L., & Fithian, R. (2009). Parents as learning partners in the development of technological fluency. *International Journal of Learning and Media, 1*(2), 55-77.

Barron, B., Walter, S., Martin, C. K., & Schatz, C. (in press). Predictors of creative computing participation and profiles of experience in two Silicon Valley middle schools. *Computers & Education.*

Beck, J. C., & Wade, M. W. (2004). *Got game: How the gamer generation is reshaping business forever.* Boston: Harvard Business School Press.

Becker, H. J. (2000a). Findings from the teaching, learning, and computing survey: Is Larry Cuban right? *Educational Policy Analysis Archives, 8*(51). Retrieved August 19, 2009, from http://epaa.asu.edu/epaa/v8n51/

Becker, H. J. (2000b). *Snapshot #7: Subject and teacher objectives for computer-using classes by school socio-economic status.* Retrieved January 30, 2009, from http://www.crito.uci.edu/tlc/findings/snapshot7/

Becker, H. J. (2000c). Who's wired and who's not: Children's access to and use of computer technology. *Future of Children, 10*(2), 44-75.

Beltran, D. O., Das, K. K., & Fairlie, R. W. (in press). Are computers good for children? The effects of home computers on educational outcomes. *Economic Inquiry.*

Brown, K. R., Cummins, J., & Sayers, D. (2007). *Literacy, technology, and diversity: Teaching for success in changing times.* Boston: Allyn & Bacon.

Castells, M. (1996). *The rise of the network society.* Malden, MA: Blackwell.

Castells, M. (1998). *End of millennium.* Malden, MA: Blackwell.

Centre for Educational Research and Innovation. (2009). *Digital learning resources as systemic innovation.* Retrieved July 23, 2009 from http://www.oecd.org/document/47/0,3343 ,en_2649_35845581_38777391_1_1_1_1,00.html

Clotfelter, C. T., Ladd, H. F., & Vigdor, J. L. (2008, December). *Scaling the digital divide: Home computer technology and student achievement.* Paper presented at the Education Policy Colloquia Series, Harvard University, Cambridge, MA. Retrieved August 19, 2009, from http://www.hks.harvard.edu/pepg/colloquia.htm

Council for Aid to Education. (2009). *College and work readiness assessment.* Retrieved February 15, 2009, from http://www.cae.org/content/pro_collegework.htm

Cummins, J. (2008). Technology, literacy, and young second language learners: Designing educational futures. In L. L. Parker (Ed.), *Technology-mediated learning environments for young English learners: Connections in and out of school* (pp. 61-98). New York: Lawrence Erlbaum.

DeBell, M., & Chapman, C. (2006). *Computer and Internet use by students in 2003*. Washington, DC: National Center for Education Statistics.

Dede, C. (1995). *Testimony to the US Congress, House of Representatives, Joint hearing on educational technology in the 21st century*. Retrieved February 2, 2006, from http://www.virtual. gmu.edu/SS_research/cdpapers/congrpdf.htm

DeVane, B., & Squire, K. (2008). The meaning of race and violence in Grand Theft Auto. *Games and Culture, 3*, 264-285.

Dimaggio, P. J., Hargittai, E., Celeste, C., & Shafer, S. (2004). Digital inequality: From unequal access to differentiated use. In K. Neckerman (Ed.), *Social inequality* (pp. 355-400). New York: Russell Sage Foundation.

Dynarski, M., Agodini, R., Heaviside, S., Novak, T., Carey, N., & Campuzano, L. (2007). *Effectiveness of reading and mathematics software products: Findings from the first student cohort*. Washington, DC: U.S. Department of Education.

Educational Testing Service (2009). *iSkills overview*. Retrieved February 15, 2009, from www. ets.org/iskills/

Eisenstein, E. L. (1979). *The printing press as an agent of change: Communications and cultural transformations in early-modern Europe*. Cambridge, UK: Cambridge University Press.

Fairlie, R. W. (2007). Explaining differences in access to home computers and the Internet: A comparison of Latino groups to other ethnic and racial groups. *Journal of Electronic Commerce Research, 7*, 265-291.

Fairlie, R. W. (2008, November). *The educational consequences of the digital divide*. Annual Lecture on Science, Technology & Society at the Center for Human Potential and Public Policy, Chicago, IL.

Fairlie, R. W., & London, R. A. (2009, January). *The effects of home computers on educational outcomes: Evidence from a field experiment with community college students*. Paper presented at the Applied Microeconomics Seminar, University of California, Irvine.

Fox, S., & Livingston, G. (2007). *Latinos online*. Retrieved January 20, 2009, from http:// www.pewinternet.org/PPF/r/204/report_display.asp

Gee, J. P. (2003). *What video games have to teach us about learning and literacy*. New York: Palgrave Macmillan.

Gee, J. P. (2004). *Situated language and learning: A critique of traditional schooling*. New York: Routledge.

Giacquinta, J. B., Bauer, J. A., & Levin, J. E. (1993). *Beyond technology's promise: An examination of children's educational computing at home*. Cambridge, UK: Cambridge University Press.

Goode, J., Estrella, R., & Margolis, J. (2006). Lost in translation: Gender and high school computer science. In J. M. Cohoon, & W. Apray (Eds.), *Women and information technology: Research on underrepresentation* (pp. 89-114). Cambridge: MIT Press.

Grimes, D., & Warschauer, M. (2008). Learning with laptops: A multi-method case study. *Journal of Educational Computing Research, 38*, 305-332.

Gulek, J. C., & Demirtas, H. (2005). Learning with technology: The impact of laptop use on student achievement. *Journal of Technology, Learning, and Assessment, 3*(2). Retrieved August 19, 2009, from http://escholarship.bc.edu/jtla/vol3/2/

Haldane, S. (2009). Delivery platforms for national and international computer-based surveys: History, issues and current status. In F. Scheuermann, & J. Bjjörnsson (Eds.), *The transition to computer-based assessment: New approaches to skills assessment and implications for large-scale testing* (pp. 63-67). Luxembourg: European Commission Joint Research Centre.

Harnad, S. (1991). Post-Gutenberg galaxy: The fourth revolution in the means of production and knowledge. *Public-Access Computer Systems Review, 2*, 39-53.

Heath, S. B. (1983). *Ways with words: Language, life, and work in communities and classrooms*. Cambridge, UK: Cambridge University Press.

Hersh, R. H. (2006). *Life is not a standardized test.* Retrieved February 14, 2009, from http://www.educationevolving.org/pdf/Life_not_a_standardized_test.pdf

Horrigan, J. (2008). *Home broadband 2008.* Retrieved January 20, 2009, from http://www.pewinternet.org/PPF/r/257/report_display.asp

Hull, G. A., & Katz, M.-L. (2006). Crafting an agentive self: Case studies on digital storytelling. *Research in the Teaching of English, 41,* 43-81.

Hull, G. A., & Nelson, M. E. (2005). Locating the semiotic power of multimodality. *Written Communication, 22,* 224-261.

Hull, G. A., Zacher, J., & Hibbert, L. (2009). Youth, risk, and equity in a global world. *Review of Research in Education, 33,* 117-159.

Ito, M., Baumer, S., Bittanti, M., Boyd, D., Cody, R., & Herr, B. (in press). *Hanging out, messing around, geeking out: Living and learning with new media.* Cambridge: MIT Press.

Ito, M., Horst, H., Bittanti, M., Boyd, D., Herr-Stephenson, B., & Lange, P. G. (2008). *Living and learning with new media: Summary of findings from the digital youth project.* Retrieved December 22, 2008, from http://digitalyouth.ischool.berkeley.edu/files/report/digitalyouth-WhitePaper.pdf

Jenkins, H. (2009). *Confronting the challenges of participatory culture: Media education for the 21st century.* Cambridge: MIT Press. Retrieved July 1, 2009, from http://mitpress.mit.edu/books/chapters/Confronting_the_Challenges.pdf

Jeroski, S. (2008). *Wireless Writing Program (WWP): Peace River North, summary report on grade 6 achievement, 2008.* Retrieved February 2, 2008, from http://www.prn.bc.ca/wp-content/wwp2008grade6.pdf

Jewitt, C. (2008). Multimodality and literacy in school classrooms. *Review of Research in Education, 32,* 241-267.

Kafai, Y. B., Heeter, C., Denner, J., & Sun, J. Y. (Eds.). (2008). *Beyond Barbie & Mortal Kombat: New perspectives on gender and gaming.* Cambridge: MIT Press.

Kafai, Y. B., Peppler, K., & Chapman, R. (2009). *The computer clubhouse: Constructionism and creativity in youth communities.* New York: Teachers College Press.

Kozma, R. (2003). *Technology, innovation, and educational change: A global perspective.* Eugene, OR: International Society for Technology in Education.

Kozma, R. (2009). Transforming education: Assessing and teaching 21st century skills. In F. Scheuermann, & J. Bjjörnsson (Eds.), *The transition to computer-based assessment: New approaches to skills assessment and implications for large-scale testing* (pp. 13-23). Luxembourg: European Commission Joint Research Centre.

Kulik, J. A. (2003). *Effects of using instructional technology in elementary and secondary schools: What controlled evaluation studies say.* Arlington, VA: SRI International.

Lenhart, A., Arafeh, S., Smith, A., & Macgill, A. R. (2008). *Writing, technology and teens.* Retrieved August 25, 2008, from http://www.pewinternet.org/PPF/r/247/report_display.asp

Lenhart, A., Kahne, J., Middaugh, E., Macgill, A. R., Evans, C., & Vitak, J. (2008). *Teens, video games, and civics.* Retrieved December, 2008, from http://www.pewinternet.org/PPF/r/263/report_display.asp

Lenhart, A., Madden, M., & Hitlin, P. (2005). *Teens and technology.* Retrieved August 25, 2008, from http://www.pewinternet.org/PPF/r/162/report_display.asp

Leu, D. J., Jr., , Kinzer, C. K., Coiro, J. L., & Cammack, D. M. (2004). Toward a theory of new literacies emerging from the Internet and other information and communication technologies. In R. B. Ruddell, & N. Unrau (Eds.), *Theoretical models and processes of reading* (pp. 1570-1613). Newark, DE: International Reading Association.

Levy, F., & Murnane, R. J. (2004). *The new division of labor: How computers are creating the next job market.* Princeton, NJ: Princeton University Press.

Levy, F., & Murnane, R. J. (2005, October). *How computerized work and globalization shape human skill demands.* Paper presented at the Planning Meeting on 21st Century Skills, National Academy of Sciences, Washington, DC.

Llosa, L., & Slayton, J. (2009). Using program evaluation to improve the education of young English language learners in US schools. *Language Teaching Research, 13*, 35-54.

Luke, A. (2009). Critical realism, policy, and educational research. In K. Ercikan, & W.-M. Roth (Eds.), *Generalizing from educational research: Beyond qualitative and quantitative polarization* (pp. 173-200). New York: Routledge.

Margolis, J., Estrella, R., Goode, J., Holme, J. J., & Nao, K. (2008). *Stuck in the shallow end: Education, race, and computing.* Cambridge: MIT Press.

Matuchniak, T., & Warschauer, M. (in press). Equity in technology access and opportunities. In B. McGaw, E. B. Baker, & P. Peterson (Eds.), *International encyclopedia of education.* New York: Elsevier.

Means, B., Penuel, W. R., & Padilla, C. (2001). *The connected school: Technology and learning in high school.* San Francisco: Jossey-Bass.

National Assessment Governing Board. (2008). *Governing board awards WestEd $1.86 million contract to develop first-ever technological literacy framework.* Retrieved February 15, 2009, from http://www.nagb.org/newsroom/release/tech-literacy-100608.pdf

National Science Foundation. (2008). *Bachelor's and associate's degrees awarded in computer sciences, by sex, 1985-2005.* http://www.nsf.gov/statistics/wmpd/2008-05/figc-2.htm

National Science Foundation. (2009). *Women, minorities, and persons with disabilities in science and engineering* (F. 15, Trans.). Arlington, VA: National Science Foundation Division of Science Resource Statistics.

National Telecommunications and Information Administration. (1995). *Falling through the net: A survey of the "Have Nots" in rural and urban America.* Washington, DC: Author.

National Telecommunications and Information Administration. (1998). *Falling through the net II: New data on the digital divide.* Washington, DC: Author.

National Telecommunications and Information Administration. (1999). *Falling through the net: Defining the digital divide.* Washington, DC: Author.

National Telecommunications and Information Administration. (2000). *Falling through the net: Toward digital inclusion.* Washington, DC: Author.

National Telecommunications and Information Administration. (2002). *A nation online: How Americans are expanding their use of the Internet.* Washington, DC: Author.

National Telecommunications and Information Administration. (2004). *A nation online: Entering the broadband age.* Washington, DC: Author.

National Telecommunications and Information Administration. (2008a). *Networked nation: Broadband in America 2007.* Washington, DC: Author.

National Telecommunications and Information Administration. (2008b). *Households using the Internet in and outside the home, by selected characteristics: Total, urban, rural, principal city, 2007.* Retrieved January 20, 2009, from http://www.ntia.doc.gov/reports/2008/Table_HouseholdInternet2007.pdf

Neuman, S. B., & Celano, D. (2006). The knowledge gap: Implications of leveling the playing field for low-income and middle-income children. *Reading Research Quarterly, 41*, 176-201.

North Central Regional Educational Laboratory & the Metiri Group. (2003). *enGauge 21st century skills: Literacy in the digital age.* Naperville, IL: Authors.

Partnership for 21st Century Skills. (2009). *Framework for 21st century learning.* Retrieved February 10, 2009, from http://www.21stcenturyskills.org/documents/framework_flyer_updated_jan_09_final-1.pdf

Peppler, K., & Kafai, Y. (2007). From SuperGoo to Scratch: Exploring digital media production in informal learning. *Learning, Media, and Technology, 32*, 149-166.

Plomp, T., Anderson, R. E., & Law, N. (Eds.). (2009). *Cross-national information and communication: Technology policies and practices in education* (rev. 2nd ed.). Charlotte, NC: Information Age.

Poster, M. (1990). *The mode of information: Poststructuralism and social context.* Chicago: University of Chicago Press.

Prensky, M. (2001). Digital natives, digital immigrants. *On the Horizon, 9*(5), 1-6.

Regional Technology Alliance. (2001). *Mapping a future for digital connections: A study of the digital divide in San Diego County.* Retrieved February 2, 2006, from http://www.sandiego.gov/science-tech/pdf/mapfuturedigitalconnect.pdf

Reich, R. (1991). *The work of nations: Preparing ourselves for 21st century capitalism.* New York: Knopf.

Roberts, D. F., Foehr, U. G., & Rideout, V. I. (2005). *Generation M: Media in the lives of 8-18 year-olds.* Menlo Park, CA: Kaiser Family Foundation.

Russell, M., & Plati, T. (2002). Does it matter with what I write?: Comparing performance on paper, computer and portable writing devices. *Current Issues in Education, 5*(4). Retrieved August 19, 2009, from http://cie.asu.edu/volume5/number4/index.html

Sandholtz, J. H., Ringstaff, C., & Dwyer, D. C. (1997). *Teaching with technology: Creating student-centered classrooms.* New York: Teachers College Press.

Scardamalia, M., & Bereiter, C. (2003). Knowledge building. In *Encyclopedia of education* (pp. 1370-1373). New York: Macmillan Reference.

Silvernail, D. L. (2005). *Does Maine's middle school laptop program improve learning? A review of evidence to date.* Retrieved August 19, 2009, from http://www.usm.maine.edu/cepare/pdf/MLTI705.pdf

Silvernail, D. L. (2007). *The impact of the Maine Learning Technology initiative on teachers, students, and learning.* Retrieved August 8, 2008, from http://www.usm.maine.edu/cepare/mlti.htm

Steinkuehler, C. (2007). Massively multiplayer online gaming as a constellation of literacy practices. *E-Learning, 4*, 297-318.

Suhr, K., Hernandez, D., Grimes, D., & Warschauer, M. (in press). Laptops and fourth grade literacy: Assisting the jump over the fourth grade slump. *Journal of Technology, Learning, and Assessment.*

Texas Center for Educational Research. (2008). *Evaluation of the Texas Technology Immersion Pilot: Outcomes for the third year (2006-2007).* Retrieved August 6, 2008, from http://www.tcer.org/research/etxtip/documents/y3_etxtip_quan.pdf

Time, Learning, and Afterschool Task Force. (2007). *A new day for learning.* Retrieved February 15, 2009, from http://www.newdayforlearning.org/docs/NDL_Jan07.pdf

Tukey, J. W. (1962). The future of data analysis. *Annals of Mathematical Statistics, 33*, 1-67.

U.S. Bureau of Labor Statistics. (2007). *The 30 fastest growing occupations covered in the 2008-2009 Occupational Outlook Handbook.* Retrieved January 13, 2009, from http://www.bls.gov/news.release/ooh.t01.htm

U.S. Census Bureau. (2006). *Current population survey: Design and methodology* (Technical Paper 66). Washington, DC: Author.

Warschauer, M. (1999). *Electronic literacies: Language, culture, and power in online education.* Mahwah, NJ: Lawrence Erlbaum.

Warschauer, M. (2000). Technology and school reform: A view from both sides of the track. *Education Policy Analysis Archives, 8*(4). Retrieved August 19, 2009, from http://epaa.asu.edu/epaa/v8n4.html

Warschauer, M. (2003). *Technology and social inclusion: Rethinking the digital divide.* Cambridge: MIT Press.

Warschauer, M. (2006). *Laptops and literacy: Learning in the wireless classroom.* New York: Teachers College Press.

Warschauer, M. (2007a). A teacher's place in the digital divide. *Yearbook of the National Society for the Study of Education, 106*(2), 147-166.

Warschauer, M. (2007b). Information literacy in the laptop classroom. *Teachers College Record, 109*, 2511-2540.

Warschauer, M. (in press). Digital literacy studies: Progress and prospects. In M. Baynham, & M. Prinsloo (Eds.), *The future of literacy studies*. Basingstoke, UK: Palgrave Macmillan.

Warschauer, M., Grant, D., Del Real, G., & Rousseau, M. (2004). Promoting academic literacy with technology: Successful laptop programs in K-12 schools. *System, 32*, 525-537.

Warschauer, M., Knobel, M., & Stone, L. (2004). Technology and equity in schooling: Deconstructing the digital divide. *Educational Policy, 18*, 562-588.

Warschauer, M., & Ware, P. (2008). Learning, change, and power: Competing frames of technology and literacy. In J. Coiro, M. Knobel, C. Lankshear, & D. J. Leu (Eds.), *Handbook of research on new literacies* (pp. 215-240). New York: Lawrence Erlbaum.

Wells, J., Lewis, L., & Greene, B. (2006). *Internet access in U.S. public schools and classrooms: 1994-2005*. Washington, DC: National Center for Educational Statistics.

Wenglinsky, H. (1998). *Does it compute? The relationship between educational technology and student achievement in mathematics*. Retrieved February 2, 2006, from ftp://ftp.ets.org/pub/res/technolog.pdf

Wenglinsky, H. (2005). *Using technology wisely: The keys to success in schools*. New York: Teachers College Press.

Chapter 7

Evidence of the Impact of School Reform on Systems Governance and Educational Bureaucracies in the United States

GAIL L. SUNDERMAN

George Washington University

The latter half of the 20th century saw an array of reform efforts designed to improve the educational system and achieve other, often ideological goals. These reforms operate within a system that is highly institutionalized, in both its structures and functions, which by design both limit and facilitate particular courses of action. At the same time, reforms often introduce contradictory goals, as is the case with those leading to greater centralization of the system versus those intended to weaken the bureaucracy and inject market principles into schooling. These tendencies give rise to the perception that things rarely change or that reforms have little impact on either school governance or the bureaucracy. Although there is some international convergence of these trends, this chapter examines recent trends in school reform and their impact on school governance and educational bureaucracies in the United States. It takes an institutional perspective, allowing us to examine how the educational system has evolved and understand the implications of particular reforms for educational governance.[1] It argues that reform has expanded the federal and state role in education, transformed the organization of interests, and created a national political culture where educational policy priorities increasingly are established nationally. The result has been greater bureaucratization of the educational system and a more formalized and standardized system reflective of a national political culture. However, because these mostly top-down reforms fail to specify the mechanism by which they will transform education, their impact varies widely depending on local conditions and implementation, allowing local districts to retain considerable power within an increasingly bureaucratic system.

Review of Research in Education
March 2010, Vol. 34, pp. 226-253
DOI: 10.3102/0091732X09349796
© 2010 AERA. http://rre.aera.net

This chapter is organized as follows. The first section examines the evolving state and federal role in education and the implications of an expanded federal role on the structure of the educational system. It pays particular attention to how the debate on the causes and solutions to school reform has shifted and the impact this has had on school governance and on how educational policy priorities are defined and established. It then examines the transformation of institutional relationships, focusing on changes in the organization of interests. The second section takes up the role of the courts and the impact of court decisions on how schools are governed and the reform strategies available to schools and districts. It examines rulings on civil rights, NCLB, and school finance. The third section examines the rise of the market and educational privatization, and the fourth, changes in the governance structure at the district level (mayoral control). The chapter concludes by discussing the implications of these reforms on governance and school reform and the opportunities they generate for the future direction of educational reform.

THE U.S. EDUCATION SYSTEM IN
HISTORICAL PERSPECTIVE

Although the structure of the U.S. educational system is quite familiar to those of us educated here, it is unique among governance systems internationally (Glenn, 2007). In important respects, we have 50 independent state educational systems with 15,700 local variations at the district level that are loosely regulated by the states (U.S. Census Bureau, 2006, p. 155). This variety is related to how different regions of the country developed historically, the demographic makeup of a state's population and its ideas about how to provide for schooling, and the resources available to support public education in each state (Wirt & Kirst, 1982). It is reflected in differences in how state superintendents are selected and in their authority and responsibilities vis-à-vis the other state officials and agencies. Because legal authority for education policymaking is vested with the legislature and governor, the system is highly political. States' historical experiences affected the varied institutional forms the state education systems took. For example, New England states developed highly decentralized systems rooted in their opposition to state-center control that dates to before the Revolutionary War, whereas southern states developed highly centralized systems following the Civil War, which devastated the ability of counties to fund or manage education (Wirt & Kirst, 1982).

Regardless of this variation, state leaders were crucial in establishing and expanding public education. Early in the nation's history, state governments gave public funds to support both public and private education, and state constitutions recognized education as a public interest (Tyack & Hansot, 1982). Both the common school movement in the 1800s and the Progressive movement in the early 1900s relied on state reformers to advance first the expansion of public schools and later the professionalization of the education. States have legal authority over education because state policies determine who can teach, what must be included in children's education, and in most states, what must be learned to graduate and how it will be assessed. States sought to standardize education by passing compulsory attendance laws, lengthening the school term, introducing the graded school, and using standardized textbooks to improve the curriculum (Tyack & Hansot, 1982). They regulate who can teach through state certification requirements and setting standards for teacher training programs. States also pay for a large share of the education bill, often larger than local taxpayers' share and many times larger than the federal government's.

Whereas legal authority over education resided with the states, operational responsibilities rested with local units of government. The system was decentralized and neither the federal nor state government exercised much control over many kinds of education decisions at the local level. By the 1950s, local school boards and superintendents, particularly in large districts, held considerable decision-making authority and operated relatively autonomously from state or federal control. This began to change when the civil rights movement focused attention on achieving equity through improvements in the schooling opportunities for low-income and minority students (Orfield, 1969). For the first time, the federal government became a significant player in education, largely through increased federal aid to public schools. With the increased federal role, a larger role for state departments of education developed, as a way both to funnel money to local districts and to enforce and monitor the emerging federal requirements.

An Evolving State Role

In response to the expansion of the federal role into education, dating to the enactment of the Elementary and Secondary Education Act of 1965 (ESEA), the role of state education agencies changed. The passage of ESEA strengthened the notion of "marble cake" federalism, whereby the national and subnational governments share responsibilities in the domestic policy arena (Wong & Sunderman, 2007). To avoid criticisms of federal control of education, federal officials relied on state education agencies to administer federal funds and monitor compliance with the law's requirements. This act was the catalyst for other federal legislation that followed, including the All Handicapped Children Act of 1975 (now the Individuals with Disabilities Act [IDEA]), the Bilingual Education Act (Title VII under ESEA and Title III under the No Child Left Behind Act [NCLB]) and subsequent reauthorizations of ESEA. Prior to 1965, state education agencies were small agencies that performed a limited range of functions administering some federal grant programs, distributing funds, and collecting statistics. With the passage of ESEA, federal officials needed an organizational structure to administer the federal funds and monitor implementation of the law's requirements, so the act provided modest resources to expand and professionalize state agencies. To receive federal funds under these statutes, states had to develop and implement policies consistent with the requirements of the law. The Education Consolidation and Improvement Act of 1981 (ECIA), which reauthorized ESEA under President Reagan, gave states a larger role in decisions about the allocation of funds than they had in the past (Darling-Hammond & Marks, 1983), again requiring states to take on new responsibilities.

The reform movements during the latter half of the 20th century strengthened the state role in funding and regulating education. States responded to the school finance movement of the 1960s and 1970s and the standards movement of the 1980s and 1990s by introducing laws and regulations designed to monitor local compliance with federal and state requirements. By focusing on funding disparities between districts, states moved toward a more comprehensive approach to funding education (Wong, 1999). At the same time that states were, in many cases, ordered by their state supreme courts to equalize funding across districts, many states also adopted compensatory education programs as a means to provide additional resources for at-risk students, thus reinforcing federal efforts.

In the 1980s and 1990s, when both federal and state legislation embraced standards-based reform, more responsibilities were added to state education agencies. Under these reforms, states extended the scope of regulations to include curriculum standards and expanded state testing. These regulations were more demanding but left districts with considerable discretion to implement the curriculum standards and align them with instruction. At the federal level, the Improving America's Schools Act of 1994 (IASA) provided support for the standards movement by requiring that the same standards apply to all students but left it to the states to develop and implement curriculum standards and assessments. Progress among states varied and weak enforcement of IASA allowed the federal government to avoid state and local opposition to an expanded federal role in education and permitted states to mold the requirements to fit their local policy priorities and the capacity of their state agencies. For example, in 2002, only 21 states were fully in compliance with the IASA (Sunderman & Kim, 2004a). Even fewer had complied with the assessment requirements: 17 states were in compliance whereas 35 were not (General Accounting Office, 2002).[2] As chronicled by *Education Week* yearly report *Quality Counts* by 2001 (the year NCLB was enacted), adoption of strong standards and accountability systems and the extent of state testing varied widely across the nation (Boser, 2001; Otlofshy & Olson, 2001). When states did adopt these reforms, they looked quite different from one state to another and reflected differences in state fiscal capacity, local political culture, and governance structures (Knapp, Stearns, Turnbull, David, & Peterson, 1991; Liu, 2006; Sunderman, 1995). Local districts, particularly, large urban districts, often adopted their own standards and assessments that competed with the state ones.

By developing expertise in particular areas that allowed them to enforce the federal requirements, enact the state policies, and act as a conduit for the flow of federal and state money to school districts, state agencies defined their role largely in traditional bureaucratic and regulatory terms (Elmore & Fuhrman, 1995). However, this bureaucratic structure and reliance on regulatory processes to control education limited their authority over local educational systems and meant that they performed some functions better than others. State agencies' reliance on regulatory processes to control education is further limited by the loose coupling of the education system in which other levels of the education system have considerable autonomy and authority to affect how teachers organize the curriculum and deliver instruction (Rowan, 1990). The educational system is institutionally complex, and state education agencies are limited by a much wider system of organizational relationships that operate within the education system (Meyer, Scott, Strang, & Creighton, 1994). There is a whole network of organized interests, professional groups, the courts, business, and elected state and local officials that affects education that is not easily controlled by the state education bureaucracy.

The 2001 NCLB furthered the trend of making states central to implementing school reform efforts (Center on Education Policy, 2007; Sunderman & Kim, 2007; Sunderman & Orfield, 2006; Wong & Sunderman, 2007). Three noteworthy changes to NCLB altered the state role by placing added demands and new responsibilities on state departments of education. First, requirements that all students, including all subgroups, must reach a state's proficiency goals by 2014 raises the expectations and goals of Title I by requiring that states bring all schools and all subgroups to the same level of performance within a relatively short period of time. Second, NCLB gave states a role in helping schools and districts improve, a requirement that traditionally had not been a state function. Third, the inclusion of timelines for when states must meet the NCLB requirements meant that all states must be at the same place regardless of where they start. Under NCLB, states must adhere to federally determined timelines for establishing an accountability system and having assessments in place, identifying failing schools and improving student achievement, establishing adequate yearly progress goals, and ensuring teacher quality. These new responsibilities, even when states lacked the capacity to meet them, coupled with the power of sanctions to force districts and schools to take the law seriously, gave states greater authority over local districts (Mintrop & Sunderman, 2009; Sunderman & Orfield, 2006).

Impact of an Expanded Federal Role in Education on National Policy Priorities

Although the increased federal role in education strengthened state education agencies as regulatory and monitoring agencies, the result has been greater bureaucratization of the educational system rather than greater centralization where an organizational center dominates the system (Meyer et al., 1994; Rowan, 1990). Indeed, the expansion of the educational bureaucracy created a more formalized and standardized system that reflects a national educational culture (Meyer et al., 1994). In this system, the federal government has become an important arbitrator in establishing the contours of the educational debate and setting national educational policy priorities.

This national educational culture is evident in how federal education policy has shaped the education agenda. The ESEA and other federal education policies that followed in the 1960s and 1970s were important in expanding the federal government's provision of sustained categorical aid to elementary and secondary education, but they also addressed national policy priorities that, for the most part, were neglected at the local level. These policies sought to equalize educational opportunity through integration and compensatory education and to redistribute resources to students who were deprived or who had been discriminated against under a system financed and controlled by state and local governments.

These federal education programs were based on New Deal assumptions that the great majority of the unemployed or impoverished were not personally to blame. Instead, structural inequalities, resulting from racial discrimination, unemployment or underemployment, low wages, lack of education, and inadequate transfer payments were considered to contribute to the high unemployment and poverty of a particular group of people (Kaestle & Smith, 1982; Kantor, 1991; Levin, 1982; Thomas, 1983). Differences between the educational experiences of Black urban students and their White counterparts, for example, were seen to derive from the racial isolation of Black students in urban schools and from the unequal resources available to students in urban schools, which contributed to high dropout rates, low achievement, and unemployment among Black students (Carson, 1962; Council of Economic Advisors, 1964; Harrington, 1962). ESEA in particular was intended to be redistributive by providing additional resources to the poorest schools.

Many of the Great Society programs, enacted in the 1960s, relied heavily on educational strategies to reduce poverty and equalize economic opportunity and advanced the idea that education was the route out of poverty. These programs emphasized the provision of resources and skills through education and training programs that would allow low-income individuals to compete more effectively for jobs. The 1964 *Economic Report of the President* states this view emphatically: "If children of poor families can be given skills and motivation, they will not become poor adults" (U.S. President, 1964).

Under this paradigm, the federal government was considered essential in addressing these problems. The use of federal authority to remedy social and economic problems gained saliency in the 1960s as policies were adopted to address a number of national problems. Through a combination of federal grants-in-aid to assist in the financing and provision of educational programs considered to be in the national interest, national commissions, and media campaigns, the federal government sought to persuade state and local governments to address these national concerns. Major interest groups and the responsible state and local officials were actively involved in shaping federal grant programs and in determining how they were implemented (Feingold, 2007; Peterson, Rabe, & Wong, 1986; Ripley & Franklin, 1991). A rare exception to this collaborative approach was the use of federal power to advance civil rights in the 1960s (Orfield, 1969).

The symbolic significance of ESEA for national education policy was that it cemented an important federal role in education policy (McGuinn, 2006). McGuinn (2006) refers to this as an "equity policy regime." Under this regime, the policy paradigm was that the majority of schools were doing fine, federal education reform efforts should target schools with high concentrations of poor and minority students, and the primary problem facing these schools was segregated schools and/or a lack of adequate funding (McGuinn, 2006, p. 33). This policy paradigm influenced state education policy as states adopted funding programs targeted on disadvantaged students (Wong, 1999).

The Reagan administration challenged both the workings of the intergovernmental system and the prevailing federal ideology (McGuinn, 2006; Sunderman, 1995). Consistent with conservative principles of a limited federal government, the administration sought to reduce the size of government by curtailing entitlement spending and devolving responsibility for service delivery to state and local governments. Called "new federalism," the administration policy sought to replace categorical aid—under which the federal government determined the way funds should be spent—with block grants, which gave state and local governments more responsibility for the use of federal funds. There was an emphasis on deregulation and on weakening guidelines that restricted state and local discretion over program implementation. Decentralization was coupled with efforts to reduce federal aid, eliminate national programs, and cut the rate of growth in education and social spending (D. Walker, 1986). Through these actions, the Reagan administration sought to decrease the federal role in education policy and programs and establish a clear division of intergovernmental responsibility. The commitment, however, was to a shift in authority rather than a release of it (Lowi, 1984) and reinforced the trend toward greater state-level activity in the governance of education.

At the same time, the administration challenged the assumption that structural inequalities contributed to social and economic problems. The administration diagnosed the problem as the low overall performance of the schools rather than focusing on the needs of particular types of students. Low morale, bureaucratization and centralization of the public school system, and politicization of educational issues were identified as major causes of educational deficiencies. Under this orientation, structural causes of educational inequality (i.e., concentration of poverty, racial segregation) were replaced with an emphasis on individual and cultural deficiencies and the failure of educational bureaucracies. Two themes—moral conduct and the intrusion of government bureaucracy in the lives of Americans—were consistent throughout the administration. For example, Reagan's discourse on the problems plaguing the schools concerned the morality of conduct, whereby "learning has been crowded out by alcohol, drugs, and crime" (Reagan, 1985).

The belief that the market, rather than government, was the solution to education problems also gained ground under the Reagan administration. Under this paradigm, the administration considered the market as more efficient than the public sector and believed it would produce better outcomes than would federal policy or spending. This led the administration to favor educational market–based reforms over equity reforms. If vouchers were adopted, for example, Reagan argued, "the potential for competition for enrollment and resources will raise the quality of both public and private education" (Reagan, 1983, p. 716). This message appealed to a political culture and rhetoric that assumed the superiority of private-sector solutions to public solutions. By privatizing education decisions, vouchers lessen public control of schools and separate policy decisions from public input, making it easier for public officials to advance ideas that might not have widespread public support (Crenson & Ginsberg, 2002).

Education gained greater national visibility after the release of the *A Nation at Risk* (NAR) report in 1983, which provided momentum for shifting the education debate from equity to a focus on excellence (National Commission on Excellence in Education, 1983). This report linked the nation's economic problems to the poor performance of the schools and argued that education played a crucial role in preparing students for the workplace. It recommended a broad set of policies to improve the school system that were aimed at enhancing educational productivity and efficiency. These reforms emphasized increasing achievement testing to measure student progress and the adoption of rigorous standards for all students, coupled with increasing the teaching of basic skills and improving the teaching profession by requiring higher teacher standards and competency testing. Consistent with conservative views of federalism, it identified state and local officials as having the primary responsibility for financing and governing the schools and called on local government to "incorporate the reforms we propose in their educational policies and fiscal planning" (National Commission on Excellence in Education, 1983).

The NAR is significant for its sweeping critique of the nation's education system and for the excellence reforms it proposed as remedies. It was the first time in American history that the president used his bully pulpit to define the problems in the nation's public education (Wong, Guthrie, & Harris, 2004). The NAR is also significant for changing the direction of education policy and ushering in a new policy paradigm that is with us today. By offering an alternative to the equity policy paradigm (McGuinn, 2006; Sunderman, 1995; Wong & Nicotera, 2004), the NAR hastened the standards movement that would follow (Viteritti, 2004) and shaped the development of federal education policy, including NCLB of 2001 (Dreeben, 1996; Wong & Nicotera, 2004). Manna (2006) argues that it increased the visibility of education as an issue in national politics and contributed to building public and elite consensus around standards-based reform. By successfully challenging the effectiveness of the equity regime, Reagan discredited the New Deal and Great Society welfare state more generally (McGuinn, 2006).

The impact of the NAR on school governance was no less dramatic. Even though the locus of reform activity was in the states, a national discussion shaped how the problem was framed and advocated specific solutions that were quickly and uniformly adopted by states throughout the 1980s and 1990s (Cibulka, 2001; Sunderman, 1995). Typically, the federal government achieves its policy goals through a system of grants-in-aid to states, where incentives or sanctions are used to accomplish federal policy goals. Policy diffusion across states was a slow and deliberate process, with each state responding to the local context (Gray, 1973; J. L. Walker, 1969). With the reforms advocated by the NAR, states responded by adopting a set of policies advocated by the federal government but not accompanied by federal dollars. This reinforced both the increasing role of the state in education governance and the ascendancy of the new paradigm in education policy. Although it was the states that implemented the reforms, it was the national movement that shaped the way the problem was defined and the specific reforms advocated as solutions.

The latest reauthorization of ESEA, NCLB, represents a major *programmatic* expansion of federal authority over education, thereby extending national policy priorities to cover program aspects of education (Sunderman & Kim, 2007; Sunderman, Kim, & Orfield, 2005; Wong & Sunderman, 2007). Although many of the NCLB concepts were present in IASA in 1994, they were less developed, the mechanisms to hold states accountable for meeting the law's requirements were weak, and few states had made substantial progress in meeting its requirements. Under NCLB, federal law determines what constitutes a failing school, what should be done about it, and by setting timelines for school improvement, what the pace of change should be. NCLB extends the idea of performance-based, or more specially, test-based, accountability nationally to all schools (Mintrop & Sunderman, 2009; Sunderman & Kim, 2007; Wong & Sunderman, 2007). By linking the progress of schools and teachers to a nationally specified rate of progress on state tests, federal education policy drives curriculum and instruction.

Changes in Institutional Relationships and Impacts on School Governance

The Progressive movement sought to insulate school governance from the influence of politics and interest groups as much as possible by placing the governance of public education under professional control (Tyack, 2000). It institutionalized the premise that the only legitimate interest groups were those that advanced professional autonomy and supported the school system rather than any particular interest (Cibulka, 2001). The prevailing model of school governance was one of local control in which school professionals were the primary actors, interests and coalitions were fairly stable, and conflict was contained. Greater state regulation of education and the increased reliance on state funding did not lead to an expansion of education interest groups at the state level or to a fundamental realignment in the organization of interests. For the most part, local interests (business groups, school boards, and professional organizations) organized at the state level to influence funding and policy issues (Cibulka, 2001). These groups focused on advancing material interests, such as insuring low taxes, obtaining favorable salaries and job conditions, or protecting particular programs (Cibulka, 2001).

However, with the growth of a national dialogue on education and the expansion of federal power, the organization of interests was transformed as well. Groups organized at the national level and think tanks emerged and became significant players in public policy. As national groups, they defined issues in national terms rather than those specific to a state or locality and advanced largely symbolic or ideological interests rather than material ones (Cibulka, 2001). These groups were both more numerous and more ideologically diverse than previously, with differing funding sources, affiliations, and missions. At the same time, the Republicans under the Reagan administration learned to use federal power to advance socially conservative agendas (i.e., school prayer, vouchers), while at the same advocating for smaller government. These shifts paved the way for the Bush administration to embark on the largest expansion of the federal government in education since ESEA was passed in 1965.

As education policy was nationalized, the traditional "iron triangle" of special interest groups, federal agencies, and the Congress that had dominated federal education policymaking since the 1960s was dissolved (DeBray-Pelot, 2007). In its place, a network of think tanks, business interests, and governors gained access to legislators, replacing the former network of teacher unions and other groups representing educational professionals. These new actors brought with them a new set of issues focusing on symbolic rather than material issues (Cibulka, 1996). During the 2001 reauthorization of ESEA, this new cadre of interests had extraordinary access to the policymaking process, while educational interests were marginalized (DeBray, 2006).

ROLE OF THE COURTS

Advocates and reformers turned to the courts to achieve their goals when other avenues (i.e., federal, state, and local governments) failed to address their issues. The courts were important in extending the rights of previously excluded groups of students, but they also have played an increasingly important role in setting educational policy and governance. At the same time, the introduction of additional actors—the courts—into the governance arena raised the potential for fragmentation and conflict when there were overlapping responsibilities or competing agendas. This section examines the impact of the courts on school governance, and in particular, on the school reform strategies available to schools and districts. It focuses on rulings in three areas: (a) rulings in civil rights cases that reinforced the use of compensatory funding and standards and accountability as school reform remedies, (b) court decisions on NCLB that furthered the ability of the federal government to control aspects of public education historically under state control, and (c) school finance rulings that supported the expansion of state control of education, but contributed to fragmentation of the funding system.[3]

Civil Rights Cases

We often think of civil rights laws and court decisions such as the 1954 landmark, *Brown v. Board of Education*, which said the system of "separate-but-equal" schools must end, as important in ending mandated racial segregation of the schools. The 1954 Supreme Court decision did set in motion the dismantling of racially segregated school systems in the southern and border states, and some court decisions in the 1960s and 1970s helped to address segregation in the northern and western cities (Boger & Orfield, 2005; Orfield, 1969). Particularly in the South, these decisions were important in expanding the opportunities available to minority students and enabled them to attend better schools. But since 1974, the prevailing legacy of the courts has been to set limits on the tools available to school districts for addressing segregation and inequality and, by the 1990s, to retreat from supporting school desegregation at all

(Boger & Orfield, 2005; Chemerinsky, 2005; Orfield, 2005; Orfield & Eaton, 1996; Orfield & Lee, 2007). The Supreme Court decision in 2007 (*Parents Involved in Community Schools v. Seattle School District No. 1* and *Meredith v. Jefferson County Board of Education*, June 28, 2007) that ended the voluntary use of race to desegregate schools further limited the options available to school districts for pursuing diversity as a school reform strategy (Frankenberg, 2008; Orfield & Lee, 2007).

The rejection by the courts of accepting desegregation as a solution to improving the schools has meant that reformers now focus on improving schools for minority students, a strategy that has yielded little in way of school improvement for impoverished schools serving minority students (Lee, 2007; Natriello, McDill, & Pallas, 1990). It has reinforced a focus on providing compensatory funding and adopting standards-based and accountability reforms as remedies for improving racially isolated, high-poverty schools. The idea, most forcibly articulated by the *all students can learn* formula, is that with additional funding tied to clearly articulated performance standards that are the same for all students, schools can ameliorate disadvantages attributable to social background and poverty (Orfield & Eaton, 1996). In light of the limitations of litigation focused on state or district practices, Lucas and Beresford (2010 [in this volume]) argues for a classroom-based litigation strategy as a means of advancing equity.

The courts also were crucial in establishing the rights of students with disabilities and expanding their access to education, including the right to be educated in the "regular" classroom (Losen & Welner, 2002). Although these decisions increased protections for students with disabilities, they introduced additional institutional actors into the system. The court became an important decision maker and, because of the duration of many of the special education cases, remained involved with school districts for decades. At the same time, the requirements for implementing IDEA created a bureaucracy within a bureaucracy where special education departments operated relatively autonomously from the central administration (Wong & Sunderman, 2000). When there are competing authorities, the potential for a fragmented governance system increases, particularly when there are conflicts over responsibilities (Wong & Sunderman, 2000).

Rulings on NCLB

Other court rulings, such as challenges to the funding mandates of NCLB have further established federal educational control of state systems (Temkin & Roellke, 2009). Following the passage of NCLB, lawsuits challenged the federal government's use of educational funding to mandate that states adopt specific curricular and assessment approaches (e.g., *Reading School District v. Pennsylvania Department of Education*; *Pontiac v. Spellings*, 2005; *Connecticut v. Spellings*, 2005). In these rulings, the courts dismissed the challenge that the federal government failed to provide the funding necessary for states to comply with NCLB and that the Unfunded Mandate Provision of the law did not preclude states from using their own funds to comply with the law's requirements. Temkin and Roellke (2009) argue that the outcome of these cases was to grant the federal government the ability to specify and control several aspects of education that historically were under the control of state education agencies. For example, because state law prohibits Connecticut from spending additional state money to meet the NCLB testing requirements, the ruling meant the state must change its testing system from a costly, free-response test that the state had in place (and preferred) to a less expensive, multiple-choice format (advocated by Secretary Spellings and her staff) or risk losing federal funding. The court rulings also upheld the law's requirements for limiting testing accommodations to just 2% of a school's special education population, thus precluding the state from developing its own requirements for accommodating special education students. The rulings also established federal law as preeminent in deciding when limited-English-proficient students should be tested.

The potential impact of these court rulings is far-reaching:

> By essentially usurping control of states' procedures and assessment formats through these court rulings, and through the coercion of withholding necessary and pre-established funding, the federal government could potentially have the grounds to start implementing stricter and more widespread standards. (Temkin & Roellke, 2009, p. 246)

Essentially, the court rulings upheld federal authority over programmatic aspects of education and thereby prevented states from rejecting the procedures or reform strategies outlined in NCLB regardless of whether they are grounded in research, run counter to state law, or undermine a preferred approach. Although civil rights advocates and others argued for a stronger federal role to counter state resistance to expanding access to education in the 1960s, the expansion of federal control of state curriculum and assessment procedures under NCLB represents a fundamental shift in the federal role. Challenging student assignment plans is a different order of magnitude than mandating particular approaches to assessment and curriculum.

Funding Reform

Relying on property taxes to fund education placed control of education on local authorities. As states assumed greater fiscal responsibility for the public schools, states responded by promulgating and enforcing guidelines and requirements local districts must meet to acquire the funds. The impetus for creating more equitable distribution of school resources benefited from court decisions finding state funding systems unconstitutional (Wong, 1999). Beginning in the 1970s, school finance litigation focused on fiscal disparities caused by the unequal distribution of the local property tax base and on ameliorating these inequities. The success of these lawsuits brought a leveling up of resources to low-spending districts and schools, with states addressing inequities with a higher level of funding from the state and the targeting of resources on disadvantaged students (Wong, 1999). Wong (1999) found that these additional dollars did contribute to improving the schooling opportunities of disadvantaged students, but these improvements depended on both the level of state targeted funding and the ways schools used their resources. Most importantly, adopting interdistrict equity reform allowed states to address inequities without challenging local autonomy in instructional and curricular matters (Wong, 1999).

By the 1990s, the focus of school finance reform, and school finance litigation, shifted from inequities in the tax base to whether school funding was "adequate," that is, sufficient to ensure a quality education (Minorini & Sugarman, 1999a, 1999b). This shift was driven in part by the "Does Money Matter" debate on whether differences in per-pupil spending produced substantive differences in educational opportunities or student learning (Hannushek, 1994; Hedges & Greenwald, 1996; Hedges, Laine, & Greenwald, 1994) and by the standards-based reform movement and whether school finance systems provided sufficient, or adequate, revenues per pupil for districts and schools to deploy educational strategies that are successful in educating students to high standards (Odden, 2003). It also took its impetus from the persistence of the spending gap between districts, the widening disparity in local taxable wealth, and the structural limitations of state efforts to level the differences between lower- and higher-spending districts (Wong, 1999).

But whether the adequacy lawsuits and court decisions actually altered state authority over the schools or resulted in broad changes in school funding is unclear, although it appears they have accelerated the centralization of school funding at the state level (Berry, 2007) and contributed to policy fragmentation in school governance (Wong, 1999). Because the court has no spending authority, the success of court decisions in changing school funding practices is dependent on the political process and the role of the state legislatures in finding a policy solution. Furthermore, litigation is directed solely at the state level, leaving intact the funding strategies and distinct decision rules that govern how funding is allocated at other levels of the school system (Wong, 1999). Any additional state aid goes directly to the districts, which usually decide how to use the funds. Local autonomy is largely unchallenged.

The limited impact of the adequacy court decisions derives in part from the complexity of the school funding system, the layers of decision rules that emanate from different levels of the educational system, and the institutional stability of the system that is in place. Each level pursues different funding strategies and has distinct decision rules that govern how funding is allocated (Wong, 1999). At the federal level, the government actively has pursued social targeting strategies as a means to promote additional services for disadvantaged students. States have taken on greater responsibility for funding education, in part to address social inequities and as a means to address funding disparities across districts. Indeed, the early equity finance litigation directed public and policymakers' attention to interdistrict inequities and promoted state action in states where lawsuits were successful as well as in states where there was no judicial action. This impact almost exclusively was directed at interdistrict inequalities in the local tax base and involved a leveling-up strategy in which the state provided additional resources to poor districts without reducing support for more affluent districts (Wong, 1999). Local allocative decision rules are distinct from those adopted at the federal and state levels and are shaped primarily by the number of students assigned to each teacher for instructional purposes (Wong, 1999). These rules have become institutionalized and are remarkably stable over time, having adapted to these legal challenges.

In response to the limited progress states have made in equalizing and augmenting educational funding, courts have responded by requiring the implementation of particular educational programs or systems of governance (Superfine & Goddard, 2009). In at least eight states, courts have ordered states to implement a variety of specific educational reforms, including whole-school reform, standards-based accountability systems, class size reduction programs, and the adoption of preschool programs (see Superfine & Goddard, 2009, for more information on state-specific court actions).

PRIVATIZATION OF EDUCATION: THE RISE OF THE MARKET METAPHOR

Whereas the federal education reforms and court rulings strengthened the state in bureaucratic and regulatory terms, market-based reforms aimed to weaken educational bureaucracies, particularly, district offices. The idea that the market can provide educational services better and cheaper than the public schools has gained currency, for different reasons, on both the left and the right (Hochschild & Scovronick, 2003). Educational privatization encompasses a broad range of activities, initiatives, and policies, including charter schools, vouchers, the contracting out of instructional and noninstructional services, and the managerial takeover of entire school districts (Burch, 2006). Although educational privatization is not new to the United States (Murphy, Glimer, Weise, & Page, 1998; Rowan, 2002), the current policy debate—and much of the scholarly research on privatization—has polarized around broader ideological arguments about the role of the market and the government in the provision of public services. Proponents argue that contracting out of public services to nongovernmental organizations is a means to control costs while improving the quality of educational services (Hess, 2002; Hill, Pierce, Lawrence, & Guthrie, 1997). Those opposed view privatization as diverting resources from the public schools and contributing to inequities by race, class, and geographic location (Bracey, 2002; Fiske & Ladd, 2000; Ladd & Fiske, 2003). The intensity of this debate, the high visibility of these reforms, the huge attention they have received in the policy literature, and the extraordinary level of support they have received from government officials at all levels have tended to overshadow the rather limited impact of market-based reforms on school reform and school governance.

The argument for school choice and deregulation derives primarily from the idea that consumer choice should shape the market for educational services (Chubb & Moe, 1990; Coons & Sugarman, 1978; Friedman, 1955). Advocates argue that the schools are failing and that radical reform is necessary to prevent economic stagnation and mediocrity (Henig, 1994). This argument links the economic well-being of our nation to the performance of the public schools and advances the notion that consumer choice becomes a means to improve schools. It is important to point out that the market rationalization for school choice, so common in the United States, is less frequently made in European countries, particularly on the continent, where parental choice is commonly thought of as based on the right to educational freedom (Glenn, 2007). Thus, many European constitutions guarantee the right to establish private schools, and the government provides financial support for such schools, including support for religious schools. The idea that parental choice will improve the effectiveness of schools is seldom heard in policy debates in Europe (Glenn, 2007), except in England, where it is frequently used as a rhetorical and policy device (Ball, 2008).

A second claim, most forcibly articulated by Chubb and Moe (1990), is that the academic deficiencies of the public school system are the product of "the very institutions that are supposed to be solving the problem: the institutions of direct democratic control" (Chubb & Moe, 1990, p. 2). They argue that the institutions designed to govern education—the school board (the legislative or policymaking body), superintendent (the administrative head of the system), and the district office (the bureaucratic organization responsible for carrying out the policies of the board and superintendent)—are incompatible with effective schooling and cannot bring about better schooling outcomes because they are the problem. Having made an argument that the schools are failing, an entrenched bureaucracy and the teacher unions are perceived as resistant to institutional change and as obstacles to school reform. The key to better schools, in their view, is institutional reform. These arguments benefit from the nationalization of the education debate and expansion of issue-oriented interest groups.

Evidence that school choice, either vouchers or charter schools, has improved student achievement or resulted in school improvement is mixed and inconclusive, depending on the data sources, research design (e.g., lack of adequate controls), and statistical techniques used. For the most part, charter schools perform no better than public schools (Center for Research on Education Outcomes, 2009). The research base on the effectiveness of other forms of educational privatization (including the NCLB supplemental educational services program), where it exists at all, is equally mixed and inconclusive (Burch, 2009; Chicago Public Schools, 2007; Heinrich, Meyer, & Whitten, 2008; Heistad, 2006; Potter et al., 2007; Rickles, Barnhart, & Gualpa, 2008; Zimmer, Gill, Razquin, Booker, & Lockwood, 2007).

Although there is limited evidence that school choice has improved student achievement or resulted in school improvement, the arguments for school choice and deregulation represent a shift in the norms and values that underpin the organization of schooling. Cuban and Shipps (2000), for example, argue that choice represents a shift from an ideal of the common school to a focus on parents as consumers. Henig (1994) argues that the reliance on market forces to direct educational decisions shifts the focus from a vision of school governance as the pursuit of collective interests of the public to an emphasis on personal self-interest and a retreat from responsibility to a broader collectivity. Similarly, Ball (2008) argues that privatization is not simply a technical change in the delivery of educational services but represents a social transformation in the relationships and values that govern education. For Crenson and Ginsburg (2002), substituting market control for democratic control of the public schools raises issues of how school politics fit within a larger political and social context, given that it means that citizens with no children in the schools would have no voice in school policy even though they would continue to be taxed to pay for education.

By framing the debate around the failings of the public schools, advocates of school choice focus on the strengths and weaknesses of private versus public schools rather than on how decisions are made and to whom schools are responsive (Crenson & Ginsberg, 2002; Gordon, 2008; Henig, 1994). This approach elevates individual concerns above those of broader, collective concerns and erodes forums for public debate. The movement for school choice gains strength from individuals or groups that reject the market metaphor but favor choice, because, in their view, it holds the potential to advance their interests or values, as seen in the expansion of alternative schools, the establishment of private or religious schools that emphasize distinct cultural or intellectual traditions, or community empowerment.

The goal of replacing educational bureaucracies with market mechanisms has not necessarily liberated education from a centrally controlled bureaucracy. Because vouchers and charter schools represent public money, another type of public regulatory system has arisen. States have largely rejected adopting vouchers, and where charter school laws have been passed, they are accompanied by regulations (e.g., caps on the number of schools, preferences for low-income students) that have constrained their growth. To retain political viability, school vouchers, originally intended as universally available to all citizens, have evolved into an educational policy option designed almost exclusively for low-income, urban families (Crenson & Ginsberg, 2002). Other forms of privatization, such as the NCLB supplemental educational services provisions, have expanded the administrative and managerial oversight responsibilities of district officials in the development and implementation of the program (Sunderman & Kim, 2006). Privatization of educational services and products, rather than creating new markets or alternatives to government-provided services, has spurred a greater federal role in education and increased private firms' dependence on the federal government for resources (Burch, 2006).

Some of the most significant developments in educational privatization have been the increasing prominence of private firms in providing an array of educational services and products, including test development, test score data storage, and other test-related services; remedial instruction for low-income students and contracting out for instructional services; and the takeover and management of school districts and schools (Burch, 2006, 2009). In this type of privatization, local school districts contract with private or nonprofit organizations to provide both instructional and noninstructional services. The development of this market has taken place largely outside the view of the public, which remained focused on the voucher and charter school debate, and has been funded by federal, state, and local dollars (Burch, 2009). These new forms of educational contracting are transferring more activities and roles from the public to the private sector. Schools and local governments are estimated to spend approximately $4.8 billion per year purchasing products and services from the private sector, up from about $2.5 billon in 2000 (Burch, 2009).

Although contracting for services has a long history in the United States, historically, the most common types of contracting have been for noninstructional services, such as transportation, food services, and custodial services. In the 1990s, privatization saw the rise of educational management organizations that were brought in to manage entire schools or school systems. These organizations assumed control of all aspects of school operations, including administration, teaching, building maintenance, food services, and clerical support (Burch, 2009). NCLB intensified the emphasis on privatization by making the market model explicit, encouraging greater investment in testing and related products and expanding the market for educational instructional services and products. Because many states and districts lacked the capacity to meet NCLB requirements, (Sunderman & Orfield, 2006), they relied on private firms for assistance with test development and preparation, data analysis and management, the provision of remedial services, and content area programming (Burch, 2006, 2009).

Burch (2006, 2009) argues that these forms of educational privatization affect school governance by introducing new forms of collaboration between school districts and private organizations and by giving private contractors more decision-making authority over regular district functions. For example, private firms that once simply developed tests now assist districts with the overall design and operation of accountability systems. These firms often have a role in making critical decisions about what educational outcomes matter, how to track outcomes, and how to design interventions based on these outcomes (Burch, 2009). The district role becomes highly technical and organized around managing contracts, and the private contractor shapes the substance of the accountability system. A second effect is the growth in the actors and interests supporting privatization. A national lobbying organization—the Education Industry Association—was founded to advance the interests of private firms specializing in educational contracting and to influence the debate on educational privatization.

Supplemental educational services (SES), mandated under NCLB and consequently widely implemented by school districts, offer clues to the validity of the market metaphor for both expanding the educational market and bringing innovation to the schools. Statements and guidance from the U.S. Department of Education characterized the SES market as an open market, where all interested parties could compete for market share, and suggested that by requiring districts to offer SES, the program would expand parental choice and improve student achievement. But rather than expanding the provider market, research suggests that large national firms are capturing a larger share of the market than smaller, local firms through aggressive marketing, acquisition of smaller firms, and the targeting of a few states where the potential for greater revenues is largest (Burch, Steinberg, & Donovan, 2007). This gives a handful of national firms a competitive advantage in the marketplace and positions them to exert a significant influence on industry practices (Burch et al., 2007). As noted earlier, there is little evidence that SES has significantly improved student achievement for those participating in the program.

Evidence is beginning to emerge on the impact of SES on decision-making structures in education. In her study of SES, Burch (2009) found the emergence of new governance structures, such as advisory councils, and structural arrangements (e.g., a system for alerting vendors of schools with eligible students) that were established with the explicit purpose of serving the financial interests of private firms. These new governance structures not only gave private vendors a role in policy decisions, but they also became an important vehicle through which larger firms could lobby for their interests. For example, in one school district studied, both large firms and smaller, local providers served on the district's advisory council. But because of power differentials between small and large firms—the large national firms served the bulk of the students and had a national presence—the concerns of the small firms received far less attention. At the same time, research suggests that market-based education, rather than bringing something new to public education, imitated standard schooling practices (Burch, 2009; Heinrich et al., 2008). Although some SES vendors develop innovative approaches to instruction, most tutoring practices provided "more of the same" and relied on instructional practices prevalent in the regular classroom—worksheets, instruction in large groups, and desk work. There was little communication across instructors, and the curriculum was pulled from many different sources, resulting in little attention devoted to building in-depth understanding.

Other evidence suggests that local districts have retained a key role in managing the SES providers. The inclusion of SES in NCLB was less the result of an overarching theory of how children learn or how reforms take root and succeed than it was a last-minute inclusion that represented a political compromise between supporters and opponents of vouchers (DeBray, 2006; Henig, 2007). Henig (2007) argues that although SES served different purposes for Republican and Democratic proponents, they converged on one key point: "The role of conventional local school districts . . . would be less central and more circumscribed" (Henig, 2007, p. 66). He argues that thinking about SES was guided less by developed theory than by broad symbols and images that simplified the issues. The image of "obsolescent localism" provided a simple definition of the problem—"past efforts at school reform have failed because local school governance is encrusted by parochial values, interest group politics, overbureaucratization, and reflexive loyalty to the status quo" (Henig, 2007, pp. 75-76)—and made it easier for both Republicans and Democrats to accommodate a policy that reduced the authority of local school districts. But rather than being marginalized in the SES market, local districts retained key roles as gatekeepers in determining how the SES market unfolds locally and which SES providers thrive (Henig, 2007). Because they control key resources and points of access that the providers want, districts retained considerable leverage over how the program was implemented. For example, providers must bargain with schools for contracts and access to schools, and local officials are responsible for notifying parents about the availability of supplemental services and processing applications.

Finally, SES has implications for how instruction is organized. One of the criticisms of the early categorical Title I program was that the delivery of instruction was characterized by curricular and instructional fragmentation and that there was little coordination between the Title I program and the regular curriculum (Jeffrey, 1978; Johnston, Allington, & Walker, 1985; Kaestle & Smith, 1982; Kirst, 1988; Kirst & Jung, 1982; Martin & McClure, 1969). Recognizing this as a problem, federal officials began to soften requirements that program services be distinct and easily identifiable in several ways. First, the 1988 Hawkins-Stafford Amendments to the ESEA and, later, the 1994 IASA gave local school districts and schools greater flexibility to decide where and how to use the federal Title I resources and encouraged the adoption of schoolwide programs. As further encouragement, the federal law successively lowered the poverty cutoff point required for schools to qualify for these programs. Although not a panacea, schoolwide programs eliminated some of the major obstacles to integrating Title I services with the school curriculum.

Under NCLB, the supplemental service requirements reversed the direction of earlier Title I legislation that moved the program in the direction of establishing schoolwide programs coordinated with the regular curriculum. By directing resources to outside service providers, SES reversed earlier attempts to provide additional resources to needy schools and limited the school's ability to develop comprehensive strategies to help disadvantaged students (Sunderman & Kim, 2004b). It reduced a school's Title I allocation, because Title I funds must be "set aside" to pay the providers. And it decreased accountability by emphasizing short-term accountability for individual student achievement. Rather than a focus on a broad range of school level outcomes tied to state standards and the development of school improvement plans to meet those standards, it focused on improving individual student achievement but only for those requesting services (Sunderman & Kim, 2006).

INSTITUTIONAL CHANGES IN GOVERNANCE STRUCTURE AT THE DISTRICT LEVEL

In contrast to reforms seeking to replace democratic forms of governance, mayoral control of schools represents changes in the formal structure of governance that locates responsibility for the schools on elected leaders and traditional institutions of local democracy (Henig & Rich, 2004). Akin to the Progressive era reformers, advocates for mayoral control of the schools have confidence that formal governance structure matters and share a belief that authority and accountability should run through electoral politics, with bureaucracy implementing democratically defined policies (Henig & Rich, 2004). Proponents argue that mayoral control promotes efficiency, comprehensive rationality, accountability, and democratic participation and that it can create the institutional pressure and support necessary to promote academic improvement systemwide (Wong, Shen, Anagnostopoulos, & Rutledge, 2007). Wong et al. (2007) contend that mayoral control is a means to integrate school governance with city government and is characterized by a strong political will to improve the operations of the city's school system through partnerships between city hall, the schools, teachers' unions, and civic groups dedicated to systemwide improvements. It has reinforced a focus on systemwide standards and performance outcomes and strengthened district leadership of reform processes and strategies.

In many places in the world, education is part of municipal-level government. Canada and the United States are unusual in having locally elected (or appointed) boards that are separate from municipal government. Thus, the trend toward mayoral control of schools in the United States represents a historical shift in how schools are governed (Wong et al., 2007). Several trends converged that may have allowed the public to accept fundamental change in the way schools are governed, including increasing public criticism of the schools in the 1980s and 1990s, financial mismanagement, poor performance on achievement tests, and a perceived increase in school violence (Henig & Rich, 2004). Other origins of the shift in governance control may lie equally with state legislative-driven reforms intended to undermine minority control of big city schools (Henig & Rich, 2004). Wong et al. (2007) identified a number of factors dating to the 1960s, 1970s, and 1980s that challenged the capacity of independent schools boards: racial tensions over the pace of school desegregation, dissatisfaction with the local property tax burden, the readiness of teachers' unions to strike when collective bargaining stalled, and the declining influence of urban cities in the state legislature (related to population shifts to the suburbs). These challenges gave mayors a new role as crisis managers, who were well situated to manage conflicting interests. In addition, by the 1990s, mayors began to view education as a means to improve the city's overall social and economic conditions (Wong et al., 2007).

Although mayoral control can look quite different across districts and so far has been limited to large, urban districts, research suggests that granting mayors a stronger and more formal role has some objective consequences on school governance. Structural changes in school governance affect how the policy agenda is shaped and how power is allocated to various constituencies with competing values, visions, and concerns (Henig & Rich, 2004). In some communities, for example, Chicago, New York, and Philadelphia, the business community played a critical role in establishing mayoral control, resulting in a corporate model of governance with a CEO and trustees. Interests of minority stakeholders often are marginalized while these new constituencies are empowered. Mayoral control in Chicago, for example, has firmly placed the city's corporate leadership and the mayor's political allies on the school board, displacing representatives from the organized civic sectors of the city (Shipps, 2004). Because the mayor was determined to attract middle-class families back to the school system and to maintain the support of corporate executives who might otherwise relocate their companies, education reform was tied to an economic development agenda. However, this approach did little to benefit low-income schools and communities (Lipman, 2004; Shipps, 2004).

A case study of the evolution of mayoral control in Chicago from 1857 to 1987 reached a similar conclusion—that mayoral control did little to improve schools for the majority of urban students (Carl, 2009). Mayors used their authority as an electoral strategy to maintain political power and, with the exception of Mayor Harold Washington (1983–1987), win the support of the business sector. Concerns about improving the public schools were secondary to electoral considerations—as they were for elected boards previously. In Washington, D.C., Henig (2004) found that shifting power from ward-based elected school boards toward at-large and mayorally appointed boards reconstituted constituencies in ways that affected the racial distribution of power, with the near-term result that the mayor's political base eroded both among grassroots elements that opposed the change and among elite interests concerned that the mayor had not used his new powers quickly, surely, or effectively enough.

The impact of mayoral control on educational issues varies widely, depending on local context, capacity, constraints, and the political will of mayors. Mayors have been most successful at improving the fiscal management and stability of school districts by using their power to address fiscal crises, to launch capital improvement efforts, and if they choose, to buy labor peace through favorable labor contracts (Wong et al., 2007). In some instances, mayors were successful in reorganizing central office administration and improving public confidence in the public schools, actions that helped school leaders develop and implement ambitious educational agendas. For example, in a study of mayoral control in 15 districts, Wong et al. (2007) found that over time, mayors were strategic in prioritizing how resources were allocated, resulting in a shift in priorities and some improvements in efficiency. This strategic agenda brought a stronger focus on the instructional core of education, investments in long-range improvement, and labor cost containment. Although the level of funding for education was largely outside the control of mayors, mayoral control increased the percentage allocation spent on instruction by shifting resources from administration toward instruction. Mayoral control also brought greater emphasis on districtwide standards tied to outcome-based accountability policies that placed low-performing schools under district intervention.

CONCLUSION: IMPLICATIONS FOR GOVERNANCE AND SCHOOL REFORM

The reform movements of the past 40 years have created an elaborate, intergovernmental system in which the federal and state levels of government share responsibilities and have gained power and influence relative to local school districts. This educational system is highly bureaucratic, relying primarily on regulatory process to control education. Even market-based reforms, ostensibly designed to curtail the role of educational bureaucracies, have brought another type of regulatory system and increased private firms' dependence on federal resources. At the same time, we have seen the ascendancy of a national political culture where the federal government plays an important role in setting national priorities and defining the parameters of the educational debate. This has resulted in much more uniform and rapid—but rarely universal—policy diffusion across states, whereby states play an increasing role in implementing the federal policy objectives. The organization of educational interest groups has been realigned as well, with significant new players entering the policy arena and supporting a set of issues defined largely in national rather than local terms. Educational interests no longer dominate, as a network of business interests, governors, and Washington-based think tanks have gained access to policymakers. These changes converge to reinforce standards, assessments, and accountability reforms as remedies for improving schools and the idea that the nation can improve schools without addressing the social and economic conditions that affect them (Mintrop & Sunderman, 2009).

The assumption behind these mostly top-down regulatory reforms is that they will transform instruction and improve student achievement. However, by failing to specify the mechanism by which they will transform education, their impact varies widely depending on local conditions and implementation. Research has shed light on how these mechanisms might work. For example, governance arrangements provide the context within which resources are more—or less—effectively brought to bear in support of student learning (Barr & Dreeben, 1983; Wong et al., 2007). But beyond their impact on improving schooling outcomes, political processes have focused our attention on some reforms rather than others, often without evidence of their effectiveness. As Raudenbush (2009) argues, the dominant school policy paradigm includes tools that policymakers can use to influence schooling "within the received notion of privatized, idiosyncratic practice," that is, within a system that is loosely coupled and where teachers operate with high autonomy (Bidwell, 1965; Lortie, 1975). Reforms designed to operate within this system often lack a clear conception of teaching practice, making it difficult to judge whether they move the system in the right direction (Raudenbush, 2009).

This highly political system, operating within a national educational culture, does hold out opportunities to shift the national debate, albeit within the prevailing economic and political conditions. Political factors can generate a range of policy alternatives, which can gain legitimacy through support from political and policy leaders. For example, the emergence of educational excellence in the 1980s and standards-based reforms in the 1990s as national issues are striking examples of how educational policy is structured to meet political and economic objectives. More recently, research has demonstrated the impact of early education on student achievement, and policymakers are beginning to make this a policy priority by tying it to concerns about the economic competitiveness of the United States. Thus, reforms that promise to address economic concerns and are consistent with beliefs about the functions of education—that is, that education can solve contemporary problems and help the country realize economic goals—can gain legitimacy and move onto the policy agenda. However, it is important to keep in mind that within a highly political system where actors at various levels of government and the school system have a role, policymakers respond to constituency concerns and partisan positions more often than to a careful understanding of particular educational problems and specific, research-based responses to these problems.

ACKNOWLEDGMENTS

I am grateful to Ben Levin and Roger Slee for their very helpful comments on drafts of this chapter as well as the volume editors, Allan Luke, Judith Green, and Gregory Kelly, for their feedback and support throughout the writing process.

NOTES

[1]For an analysis on how evidence is used for educational policymaking, see Wiseman (2010 [in this volume]). For an examination of the role of changing demographics on educational policy, see Lucas and Beresford (2010 [in this volume]).

[2]This includes the District of Columbia and Puerto Rico.

[3]For an analysis of the legal bases for challenging ability grouping and state-mandated high school exit exams, see Welner (2010 [in this volume]).

REFERENCES

All Handicapped Children Act of 1975, Pub. L. 95-561, Nov. 29, 1975, 89 Stat. 773 (1975).

Ball, S. J. (2008). *The education debate*. Bristol, UK: Policy.

Barr, R., & Dreeben, R. (1983). *How schools work*. Chicago: University of Chicago Press.

Berry, C. (2007). The impact of school finance judgements on state fiscal policy. In M. R. West & P. E. Peterson (Eds.), *School money trials: The legal pursuit of educational adequacy* (pp. 213–240). Washington, DC: Brookings Institution.

Bidwell, C. E. (1965). The school as formal organization. In J. G. March (Ed.), *Handbook of organizations* (pp. 972–1022). Chicago: Rand McNally.

Boger, J. C., & Orfield, G. (2005). *School resegregation: Must the South turn back?* Chapel Hill: University of North Carolina Press.

Boser, U. (2001). Pressure without support. *Education Week, 20,* 68–84.

Bracey, G. W. (2002). *The war against America's public school: Privatizing schools, commericializing education*. Boston: Allyn and Bacon.

Burch, P. (2006). The new educational privatization: Educational contracting and high stakes accountability *Teachers College Record, 108*(12), 2582–2610.

Burch, P. (2009). *Hidden markets: The new education privatization*. New York: Routledge/Taylor and Francis.

Burch, P., Steinberg, M., & Donovan, J. (2007). Supplemental educational services and NCLB: Policy assumptions, market practices, emerging issues. *Educational Evaluation and Policy Analysis, 29*(2), 115–133.

Carl, J. (2009). "Good politics is good government": The troubling history of mayoral control of public schools in twentieth-century Chicago. *American Journal of Education, 115*(2), 305–336.

Carson, R. (1962). *Silent spring*. Greenwich, CT: Fawcett.

Center for Research on Education Outcomes. (2009). *Multiple choice: Charter school performance in 16 states*. Stanford, CA: Stanford University.

Center on Education Policy. (2007). *Educational architects: Do state educatoin agencies have the tools necessary to implement NCLB?* Washington, DC: Author.

Chemerinsky, E. (2005). The segregation and resegregation of American public education: The court's role. In J. C. Boger & G. Orfield (Eds.), *School resegregation: Must the South turn back?* (pp. 29–47). Chapel Hill: University of North Caroline Press.

Chicago Public Schools. (2007). *SES tutoring programs: An evaluation of Year 3 in the Chicago Public Schools*. Chicago: Author.

Chubb, J. E., & Moe, T. M. (1990). *Politics, markets, and America's schools*. Washington, DC: Brookings Institution.

Cibulka, J. G. (1996). *The reform and survival of American public school: An institutional perspective*. Washington, DC: Falmer.

Cibulka, J. G. (2001). The changing role of interest groups in education: Nationalization and the new politics of education productivity. *Educational Policy, 15*(1), 12–40.

Coons, J. E., & Sugarman, S. D. (1978). *Education by choice: The case for family control*. Berkeley: University of California Press.

Council of Economic Advisors. (1964). *The annual report of the Council of Economic Advisors.* Washington, DC: U.S. Government Printing Office.

Crenson, M. A., & Ginsberg, B. (2002). *Downsizing democracy: How America sidelined its citizens and privatized its public.* Baltimore: Johns Hopkins University Press.

Cuban, L., & Shipps, D. (2000). *Reconstructing the common good in education: Coping with the intractable American dilemmas.* Stanford, CA: Stanford University Press.

Darling-Hammond, L., & Marks, E. L. (1983). *The new federalism in education: State responses to the 1981 Education Consolidation and Improvement Act.* Santa Monica, CA: RAND.

DeBray, E. H. (2006). *Politics, ideology, and Congress: The formation of federal education policy during the Clinton and Bush administrations.* New York: Teachers College Press.

DeBray-Pelot, E. (2007). Dismantling education's "iron triangle": Institutional relationships in the formation of federal education policy between 1998 and 2001. In C. F. Kaestle & A. Lodewick (Eds.), *To educate a nation: Federal and national strategies of school reform* (pp. 64–89). Lawrence: University Press of Kansas.

Dreeben, R. (Ed.). (1996). *The occupation of teaching and educational reform* (Vol. 2). Greenwich, CT: JAI.

Education Consolidation and Improvement Act of 1981, 20 U.S.C. § 3801 et seq. (1981).

Elementary and Secondary Education Act, 20 U.S.C. § 6651 (1965).

Elmore, R. F., & Fuhrman, S. H. (1995). Opportunity-to-learn standards and the state role in education. *Teachers College Record, 96*(3), 432–457.

ESEA, Title VII—Bilingual Education, Language Enhancement, and Language Acquisition Programs (Bilingual Education Act), 20 U.S.C. § 7101 (1968).

Feingold, R. D. (2007, February 15). *Feingold part of Senate coalition calling for improvements to NCLB testing mandates.* Retrieved March 26, 2007, from http://feingold.senate .gov/~feingold/releases/07/02/20070215nclb.html

Fiske, E. B., & Ladd, H. F. (2000). *When schools compete: A cautionary tale.* Washington, DC: Brookings Institution.

Frankenberg, E. (2008). School segregation, desegregation, and integration: What do these terms mean in a post-Parents Involved in Community Schools, racially transitioning society? *Seattle Journal for Social Justice, 6*(2), 533–590.

Friedman, M. (1955). The role of government in education. In R. A. Solo (Ed.), *Economics and the public interest* (pp. 123–144). New Brunswick, NJ: Rutgers University Press.

General Accounting Office. (2002). *Title I: Education needs to monitor states' scoring of assessments* (No. GAO-02-393). Washington, DC: Author.

Glenn, C. L. (2007). Common problems, different solutions. *Peabody Journal of Education, 82*(2), 530–548.

Gordon, L. (Ed.). (2008). *Where does the power lie now? Devoluion, choice, and democracy in schooling.* Albany: State University of New York Press.

Gray, V. (1973). Innovation in the states: A diffusion study. *American Political Science Review, 67*(4), 1174–1185.

Hannushek, E. (1994). *Making schools work.* Washington, DC: Brookings Institution.

Harrington, M. (1962). *The other America.* New York: Macmillan.

Hedges, L. V., & Greenwald, R. (1996). Have times changed? The relation between school resources and student performance. In G. Burtless (Ed.), *Does money matter?* (pp. 74–92). Washington, DC: Brookings Institution.

Hedges, L. V., Laine, R. D., & Greenwald, R. (1994). Does money matter? A meta-analysis of studies of the effects of differential school inputs on student outcomes. *Educational Researcher, 23*, 5–14.

Heinrich, C. J., Meyer, R. H., & Whitten, G. (2008, March). *Supplemental educational services under No Child Left Behind: Who signs up, and what do they gain?* Paper presented at the American Education Research Association, New York.

Heistad, D. (2006). *Analysis of 2005 supplemental educational services in Minneapolis Public Schools: An application of matched sample statistical design.* Minneapolis, MN: Minneapolis Public Schools; Research, Evaluation, and Assessment Department.

Henig, J. R. (1994). *Rethinking school choice: Limits of the market metaphor.* Princeton, NJ: Princeton University Press.

Henig, J. R. (2004). Washington D.C.: Race, issue definition, and school board restructuring. In J. R. Henig & W. C. Rich (Eds.), *Mayors in the middle: Politics, race, and mayoral control of urban schools* (pp. 191-218). Princeton, NJ: Princeton University Press.

Henig, J. R. (2007). *The political economy of supplemental educational services.* In F. M. Hess & C. E. Finn Jr. (Eds.), *No remedy left behind: Lessons from a half-decade of NCLB* (pp. 66-95). Washington, DC: American Enterprise Institute.

Henig, J. R., & Rich, W. C. (2004). *Mayors in the middle: Politics, race, and mayoral control of urban schools.* Princeton, NJ: Princeton University Press.

Hess, F. M. (2002). *Revolution at the margins: The impact of competition on urban school systems.* Washington, DC: Brookings Institution.

Hill, P. T., Pierce, J., Lawrence, C., & Guthrie, J. W. (1997). *Reinventing public education: How contracting can transform America's schools.* Chicago: University of Chicago Press.

Hochschild, J., & Scovronick, N. (2003). *The American dream and the public schools.* New York: Oxford University Press.

Improving America's Schools Act of 1994, 20 U.S.C. § 8902 (1994).

Jeffrey, J. R. (1978). *Education for children of the poor: A study of the origins and implementation of the Elementary and Secondary Education Act of 1965.* Columbus: Ohio State University Press.

Johnston, P., Allington, R., & Walker, D. (1985). Curriculum confluence in classroom and clinic. *Elementary School Journal, 85,* 465–477.

Kaestle, C. F., & Smith, M. S. (1982). The federal role in elementary and secondary education, 1940–1980. *Harvard Educational Review, 52*(4), 384–408.

Kantor, H. (1991). Education, social reform, and the state: ESEA and federal education policy in the 1960s. *American Journal of Education, 100*(1), 47–83.

Kirst, M. (1988). The federal role and Chapter 1: Rethinking some basic assumptions. In D. Doyle & C. Cooper (Eds.), *Federal aid to the disadvantaged: What future for Chapter 1?* (pp. 97–115). London: Falmer.

Kirst, M., & Jung, R. (1982). The utility of a longitudinal approach in assessing implementation: A thirteen-year review of Title I, ESEA. In W. Williams, R. F. Elmore, J. S. Hall, R. Jung, M. Kirst, S. A. MacManus, B. J. Narver, R. P. Nathan & R. K. Yin (Eds.), *Studying implementation: Methodological and administrative issues* (pp. 119–148). Chatham, NJ: Chatham House.

Knapp, M. S., Stearns, M. S., Turnbull, B. J., David, J. L., & Peterson, S. M. (1991). Cumulative effects of federal education policies at the local level. In A. R. Odden (Ed.), *Education policy implementation* (pp. 105–124). New York: State University of New York Press.

Ladd, H. F., & Fiske, E. B. (2003). Does competition improve teaching and learning? Evidence from New Zealand. *Education Evaluation and Policy Analysis, 25*(1), 97–112.

Lee, J. (2007). *The testing gap: Scientific trials of test-driven school accountability systems for excellence and equity.* Charlotte, NC: Information Age.

Levin, H. M. (1982). Federal grants and educational equity. *Harvard Educational Review, 52*(4), 444–460.

Lipman, P. (2004). *High stakes education: Inequality, globalization, and urban school reform.* New York: RoutledgeFalmer.

Liu, G. (2006). Interstate inequality in educational opportunity. *New York University Law Review, 81,* 2044–2128.

Lortie, D. (1975). *Schoolteacher.* Chicago: University of Chicago Press.

Losen, D. J., & Welner, K. G. (2002). Legal challenges to inappropriate and inadequate special education for minority children. In D. J. Losen & G. Orfield (Eds.), *Racial inequity in special education* (pp. 167–194). Cambridge, MA: Harvard Education Press.

Lowi, T. J. (1984). Ronald Reagan: Revolutionary? In L. M. Salamon & M. S. Lund (Eds.), *The Reagan presidency and the governing of America* (pp. 29–56). Washington, DC: Urban Institute.

Lucas, S. R., & Beresford, L. (2010). Naming and classifying: Theory, evidence, and equity in education. *Review of Research in Education, 34*(1), 25–84.

Manna, P. (2006). *School's in: Federalism and the national education agenda.* Washington, DC: Georgetown University Press.

Martin, R., & McClure, P. (1969). *Title I of ESEA: Is it helping poor children?* Washington, DC: Washington Research Project and NAACP Legal Defense and Educational Fund.

McGuinn, P. (2006). *No Child Left Behind and the transformation of federal education policy, 1965–2005.* Lawrence: University Press of Kansas.

Meredith, Custodial Parent and Next Friend of McDonald v. Jefferson County Bd. of Ed et al., 551 U.S. 701 (2007)

Meyer, J. W., Scott, W. R., Strang, D., & Creighton, A. L. (1994). Bureaucratization without centralization: Changes in the organizational system of U.S. public education, 1940–1980. In W. R. Scott & J. W. Meyer (Eds.), *Institutional environments and organizations: Structural complexity and individualism* (pp. 179–205). Thousand Oaks, CA: Sage.

Minorini, P., & Sugarman, S. D. (1999a). Educational adequacy and the courts: The promise and problems of moving to a new paradigm. In H. Ladd, R. Chalk, & J. Hansen (Eds.), *Equity and adequacy in education finance: Issues and perspectives* (pp. 175–208). Washington, DC: National Academy Press.

Minorini, P., & Sugarman, S. D. (1999b). School finance litiation in the name of educational equity: Its evoluation, impact and future. In H. Ladd, R. Chalk, & J. Hansen (Eds.), *Equity and adequacty in educational finance: Issues and perspectives* (pp. 34–71). Washington, DC: National Academy Press.

Mintrop, H., & Sunderman, G. L. (2009). Predictable failure of federal sanctions-driven accountability for school improvement—And why we may retain it anyway. *Educational Researcher, 38*(5), 353–364.

Murphy, J., Glimer, S. W., Weise, R., & Page, A. (1998). *Pathways to privatization in education.* Greenwich, CT: Ablex.

National Commission on Excellence in Education. (1983). *At nation at risk: The imperative for educational reform.* Washington, DC: U.S Department of Education.

Natriello, G., McDill, E. L., & Pallas, A. M. (1990). *Schooling disadvantaged children: Racing against catastrophe.* New York: Teachers College Press.

No Child Left Behind Act of 2001, 20 U.S.C. § 6301et seq. (2002).

Odden, A. (2003). Equity and adequacy in school finance today. *Phi Delta Kappan, 85*(2), 120–125.

Orfield, G. (1969). *The reconstruction of Southern education: The schools and the 1964 Civil Rights Act.* New York: Wiley-Interscience.

Orfield, G. (2005). The Southern dilemma: Losing *Brown,* fearing *Plessy.* In J. C. Boger & G. Orfield (Eds.), *School resegregation: Must the South turn back?* (pp. 1–25). Chapel Hill: University of North Carolina Press.

Orfield, G., & Eaton, S. E. (Eds.). (1996). *Dismantling desegregation: A quiet reversal of Brown v. Board of Education.* New York: New Press.

Orfield, G., & Lee, C. (2007). *Historic reversals, accelerating resegregation, and the need for new integration strategies.* Los Angeles: University of California, Los Angeles; Civil Rights Project.

Otlofshy, G. F., & Olson, L. (2001). The state of the states. *Education Week, 20,* 86–106.

Parents Involved in Community Schools v. Seattle School District No. 1 et al., 551 U.S. 701 (2007).

Peterson, P. E., Rabe, B. G., & Wong, K. K. (1986). *When federalism works.* Washington, DC: Brookings Institution.

Potter, A., Ross, S. M., Paek, J., McKay, D., Ashton, J., & Sanders, W. L. (2007). *Supplemental educational services in the state of Tennessee: 2005–06 (2004–2005 student achievement results).* Memphis, TN: University of Memphis, Center for Research in Education Policy.

Raudenbush, S. W. (2009). The Brown legacy and the O'Connor challenge: Transforming schools in the images of children's potential. *Educational Researcher, 38,* 169–180.

Reagan, R. (1983). Message to the Congress of the United States, March 17, 1993. *Congressional Quarterly, 9,* 715–716.

Reading School District v. Department of Education, 855 A.2d 166 (Pa. Cmwlth. 2004).

Reagan, R. (1985). *Remarks at the National Association of Independent Schools annual meeting, February 28, 1985* (Weekly Compilation of Presidential Documents 21, No. 9). Washington, DC: U.S. Government Printing Office.

Rickles, J. H., Barnhart, M. K., & Gualpa, A. S. (2008, April). *Supplemental educational services participation and impact on student achievement: The case of one urban district over five years.* Paper presented at the American Education Research Association, New York, NY.

Ripley, R. B., & Franklin, G. A. (1991). *Congress, the bureaucracy, and public policy* (5th ed.). Belmont, CA: Wadsworth.

Rowan, B. (1990). Commitment and control: Alternative strategies for the organizational design of schools. *Review of Educational Research, 16,* 353–389.

Rowan, B. (2002). The ecology of school improvement: Notes on the school improvement industry in the United States. *Journal of Educational Change, 3,* 283–314.

School District of the City of Pontiac, et al. v. Margaret Spellings, 05-2708 (United States Court of Appeals for the Sixth Circuit, 2008).

School District of the City of Pontiac, et al. v. Margaret Spellings, 05 CV 71535-DT (United States District Court Eastern District of Michigan Southern Division 2005).

Shipps, D. (2004). Chicago: The national "model" reexamined. In J. R. Henig & W. C. Rich (Eds.), *Mayors in the middle: Politics, race, and mayoral control of urban schools* (pp. 59–95). Princeton, NJ: Princeton University Press.

State of Connecticut v. Spellings, 3:05 CV 1330 (D. Conn. 2006).

Sunderman, G. L. (1995). *The politics of school reform: The educational excellence movement and state policymaking.* Unpublished dissertation, University of Chicago.

Sunderman, G. L., & Kim, J. (2004a). *Expansion of federal power in American education: Federal-state relationships under the No Child Left Behind Act, year one.* Cambridge, MA: Civil Rights Project at Harvard University.

Sunderman, G. L., & Kim, J. (2004b). *Increasing bureaucracy or increasing opportunities? School district experience with supplemental educational services.* Cambridge, MA: Civil Rights Project at Harvard University.

Sunderman, G. L., & Kim, J. S. (2006). Implementing supplemental educational services: Implications for school districts and educational opportunity. In K. K. Wong & S. Rutledge (Eds.), *System-wide efforts to improve student achievement* (pp. 63–91). Greenwich, CT: Information Age.

Sunderman, G. L., & Kim, J. S. (2007). The expansion of federal power and the politics of implementing the No Child Left Behind Act. *Teachers College Record, 109*(5), 1057–1085.

Sunderman, G. L., Kim, J. S., & Orfield, G. (2005). *NCLB meets school realities: Lessons from the field.* Thousand Oaks, CA: Corwin.

Sunderman, G. L., & Orfield, G. (2006). Domesticating a revolution: No Child Left Behind and state administrative response. *Harvard Educational Review, 76*(4), 526–556.

Superfine, B. M., & Goddard, R. D. (2009). The expanding role of the courts in educational policy: The preschool remedy and an adequate education. *Teachers College Record, 111*(7), 1796–1833.

Temkin, D., & Roellke, C. (2009). Federal educational control in No Child Left Behind: Implications of two court challenges. In J. King Rice & C. Roellke (Eds.), *High stakes accountability: Implications for resources and capacity* (pp. 225–249). Charlotte, NC: Information Age.

Thomas, N. C. (1983). The development of federal activism in education: A contemporary perspective. *Education and Urban Society, 15*(3), 271–290.

Tyack, D. (2000). *The one best system: A history of American urban education.* Cambridge, MA: Harvard University Press.

Tyack, D., & Hansot, E. (1982). *Managers of virtue: Public school leadership in America, 1820–1980.* New York: Basic Books.

U.S. Census Bureau. (2006). *Statistical abstract of the United States.* Washington, DC: Author.

U.S. President. (1964). *Economic report of the president together with the annual report of the Council of Economic Advisors.* Washington, DC: U.S. Government Printing Office.

Viteritti, J. P. (2004). From excellence to equity: Observations on politics, history, and policy. *Peabody Journal of Education, 74*(1), 64–86.

Walker, D. (1986). The nature and systemic impact of "creative federalism." In M. Kaplan & P. Cuciti (Eds.), *The Great Society and its legacy: Twenty years of U.S. social policy.* Durham, NC: Duke University Press.

Walker, J. L. (1969). The diffusion of innovation among the American states. *American Political Science Review, 63*, 880–899.

Welner, K. G. (2010). Education rights and classroom-based litigation: Shifting the boundaries of evidence. *Review of Research in Education, 34*(1), 85–112.

Wirt, F. M., & Kirst, M. W. (1982). *The politics of education: Schools in conflict.* Berkeley, CA: McCutchan.

Wiseman, A. W. (2010). The uses of evidence for educational policymaking: Global contexts and international trends. *Review of Research in Education, 34*(1), 1–24.

Wong, K. K. (1999). *Funding public schools: Politics and policies.* Lawrence: University Press of Kansas.

Wong, K. K., Guthrie, J. W., & Harris, D. N. (2004). A Nation at Risk: A twenty-year reappraisal. *Peabody Journal of Education, 79*(1), 1–6.

Wong, K. K., & Nicotera, A. C. (2004). Educational quality and policy redesign: Reconsidering the NAR and federal Title I policy. *Peabody Journal of Education, 79*(1), 87–104.

Wong, K. K., Shen, F. X., Anagnostopoulos, D., & Rutledge, S. (2007). *The education mayor: Improving America's schools.* Washington, DC: Georgetown University Press.

Wong, K. K., & Sunderman, G. L. (2000). Implementing districtwide reform in schools with Title I schoolwide programs: The first 2 years of Children Achieving in Philadelphia. *Journal of Education for Students Placed At-Risk, 5*(4), 355–381.

Wong, K. K., & Sunderman, G. L. (2007). Education accountability as a presidential priority: No Child Left Behind and the Bush presidency. *Publius: The Journal of Federalism.* doi:10.1093/publius/pjm1011

Zimmer, R., Gill, B., Razquin, P., Booker, K., & Lockwood, J. R. (2007). *State and local implementation of the No Child Left Behind Act: Volume I. Title I school choice, supplemental educational services, and student achievement.* Washington, DC: RAND.

Chapter 8

What Counts as Evidence of Educational Achievement? The Role of Constructs in the Pursuit of Equity in Assessment

Dylan Wiliam

Institute of Education, University of London

If what students learned as a result of the instructional practices of teachers were predictable, then all forms of assessment would be unnecessary; student achievement could be determined simply by inventorying their educational experiences. However, because what is learned by students is not related in any simple way to what they have been taught, assessment is a central—perhaps even *the* central—process in education. At the very least, assessment is integral to effective instruction.

At first sight, it appears that assessment should be relatively uncontested. Everyone— parents, teachers, employers, the wider community that supports public education through taxes, and the students themselves—just wants to know what it is that students have learned. However, two difficulties emerge immediately. The first is that by its very nature assessment *reduces ambiguity*. The fifth-grade mathematics standard for many states requires students to be able to compare two fractions to find the larger, but when we assess, we have to decide which pairs of fractions should be included and which should not. This may be done explicitly, through a formal process of construct definition (see below), which lays out clearly what should be included and what should be excluded from the assessment, or more commonly, it may be done through some less formal process, involving a judgment of what is appropriate, given that this standard is intended for fifth-grade students—as William Angoff (1974) remarked, "lurking behind the criterion-referenced evaluation, perhaps even responsible for it, is the norm-referenced evaluation" (p. 4).

In fact, the choice of the fractions to be compared makes a huge difference to the rate of student success, even if we restrict the domain to fractions where both numerator and denominator are less than 10. In fifth grade, where the fractions have equal

Review of Research in Education
March 2010, Vol. 34, pp. 254-284
DOI: 10.3102/0091732X09351544
© 2010 AERA. http://rre.aera.net

denominators, more than 90% of students are likely to be able to succeed, although fractions with unequal denominators are likely to present more of a challenge (Hart, 1981; Vinner, 1997). However, where the fractions have unequal denominators but equal numerators (e.g., $\frac{5}{7}$ and $\frac{5}{9}$), then fewer than one student in five is able to answer correctly (Hart, 1981). If a requirement to assess something as apparently precise as "can compare two fractions to identify the larger" can produce such different interpretations, even where the domain is restricted to single-digit numbers, then it is hardly surprising that even when different stakeholders agree about the importance of the material to be assessed, the assessments themselves become vigorously contested.

The second difficulty arises because assessments are *representational* rather than *literal* technologies (Hanson, 1993). When we assess students, we are never interested in how well they do on the actual items on which they were assessed; we are interested in how we can generalize beyond the behaviors observed on the assessment (Nuttall, 1987). The desired generalizations may be in terms of future performance in higher education, as is the case with the College Board's SAT; items similar to the ones on which the students were assessed, as in the case of the fractions example above; or even, in the case of a spelling test, whether the students will recall correctly tomorrow what they could do today. Calfee, Lau, and Sutter (1983) suggest that the ability of a soldier to strip down and reassemble a rifle may be a valuable skill in its own right, but as they acknowledge, even here, the reason for practicing the drill is that the skills become so automated that they can be executed in less ideal settings (e.g., at night, knee-deep in a swamp, under fire).

As Nuttall (1987) suggests, "The fidelity of the inference drawn from the responses to the assessment is what is usually called the *validity* of the assessment" (p. 110), and in this chapter, I will trace one strand in the development of the theory of validity—the increasing importance attached to the role of constructs in validating educational assessments—and show how, ensuring that the primary focus is on the construct of interest, rather than the assessment itself, can bring some greater clarity to a number of debates, especially in the area of equity in assessment. To illustrate how a focus on the construct of interest can clarify the debate, I discuss, in some detail, three particular arenas of assessment:

- Testing for admission to higher education
- The rise, and fall, of measures involving constructed-response items
- The assessment of students with special educational needs

Within each of these areas, I explore the interplay of issues of technical adequacy with equity and show how attention that has in the past been directed at the adequacy of the assessments might be more fruitfully directed toward the construct of interest. In other words, I argue that attention should be shifted from how well we measure something to what it is that we are measuring. By clearly separating the values issues—what we should be assessing—from the technical issues—how well we are assessing—we allow greater public engagement in the debate about what should be assessed (because those lacking the necessary technical expertise are not excluded from the debate). Although this is not, in itself, a guarantee of equity, it does, I believe, create the possibility for a wider debate in which previously underrepresented voices can be heard. Greater clarification about the construct of interest may also increase the technical quality of the assessments themselves.

THE ROLE OF CONSTRUCTS IN VALIDITY THEORY

The idea that validity should be considered a property of inferences, rather than of assessments, has developed slowly over the past century. In early writings about the validity of educational assessments, validity was defined as a property of an assessment. The most common definition was that an assessment was valid to the extent that it assessed what it purported to assess (Garrett, 1937) and this definition is still in widespread use (Brasel, Bragg, Simpson, & Weigelt, 2004; Cohen, Mannion, & Morrison, 2004). The problem with such a definition is that an assessment does not actually purport to do anything—the purporting is done by those who claim that a specific assessment outcome has a specific meaning—a test tests just what a test tests. Of course, tests come with labels, which convey implicit or explicit claims about what the test does, in fact, test, but, as Kelley (1927) pointed out, this can be highly misleading. Two tests with very different labels may be assessing very similar things, and two tests with the same label may be assessing very different things. Hence, as Nuttall (1987) points out, "In practice, an assessment does not have a single validity; it can have many according to its different uses and the different kinds of inference made, in other words, according to the universe of generalization" (p. 110). A test can be valid for some purposes, but not others. Performance in mathematics tests at age 16 can be shown to be good predictors of mathematical performance at age 18 (Wiliam, Brown, Kerslake, Martin, & Neill, 1999) but can at the same time be quite poor indicators of performance in specific areas of mathematics (Pirie, 1987). Furthermore, a test can be valid for some students but not others. For example, a test of mathematics with a high reading demand may support valid inferences about mathematical ability for fluent readers, but when students with less developed reading skills perform poorly on the test, we cannot know whether their poor performance was due to an inability to read the items or to their weaknesses in mathematics.

Moss, Girard, and Haniford (2006), in their extensive review of the development of theories in validity, point out that the development of the concept of validity in educational assessment can be traced through successive editions of two key publications. The first originally appeared as the "Technical Recommendations for Psychological Tests and Diagnostic Techniques" in a supplement to *Psychological Bulletin* (American Psychological Association [APA], American Educational Research Association [AERA], & National Council on Measurement Used in Education [NCME], 1954), with new editions appearing in each subsequent decade (APA, AERA & NCME, 1966, 1974, 1985; AERA, APA, & NCME, 1999). The second is the book

Educational Measurement, first published almost 60 years ago (Lindquist, 1951) and its three subsequent editions (Thorndike, 1971; R. L. Linn, 1989; Brennan, 2006). Tracing the development of the concept of validity through these nine publications is beyond the scope of this chapter. Here, I focus specifically on the growing acceptance of the role of constructs as being at the heart of validity argument.

In the first edition of *Educational Measurement*, published by the American Council on Education, Cureton (1951) clarified that validity could not be an inherent property of an assessment, even taking into account the different possible universes of generalization. Rather, validity involves consideration of both the assessment and how it is used:

The essential question of test validity is how well a test does the job it is employed to do. The same test may be used for several different purposes, and its validity may be high for one, moderate for another, and low for a third. (p. 621)

In the early days of the development of the theory of assessment in the first half of the 20th century, the mechanism for generalization was generally assumed to be from a sample of a well-defined domain to the remainder of the domain. So, for example, a test of multiplication facts would define a universe of multiplication facts, such as the 81 multiplication facts from 2×2 to 10×10, and the test would sample randomly from these 81 elements in the domain. If a student scored 50% on a test made up of 10 randomly sampled items from the domain, then the best estimate we can make is that the student knows half of the 81 multiplication facts, and furthermore, we can use the laws of statistical inference to generate confidence intervals about how accurate our estimate is likely to be.

Within such a view of validity—which Cronbach and Meehl (1955, p. 282) point out involves "acceptance of the universe of content as defining the variable to be measured"—verifying the validity of an assessment is a relatively straightforward process. It requires establishing that the items selected are *relevant* to the domain, that the collection of items included in the test is *representative* of the domain, and that enough items are included to provide an *adequate* sample.

However, this content-based approach, although being straightforward, is of very limited applicability, because most assessments are designed to assess domains far more complex than multiplication facts, so that the universe of generalization could not be defined in such a precise manner. Other approaches to the design of assessments avoided the issue of the definition of the domain entirely and instead focused on the extent to which the results of an assessment correlated with other outcomes, so that the assessment could be used to predict future performance or performance on another assessment at the same time. Thus, an assessment such as the College Board's SAT would be validated simply by the extent to which it predicted performance in higher education, for example, by examining the correlation between SAT scores and college freshman grade point average (GPA). A group-administered test of dyslexia that provided similar results to an individually administered 3-hour clinical interview undertaken by an educational psychologist (Miles, 1998) would be validated by examining the correlation between the outcomes on the two assessments. As Bechtoldt (1951) noted, acceptance of criterion-related approaches to validity "involves the acceptance of a set of operations as an adequate definition of whatever is to be measured" (p. 1245), a view encapsulated in Guilford's (1946) observation that "in a very general sense, a test is valid for anything with which it correlates" (p. 429).

These two approaches to validation were termed *predictive validity* and *concurrent validity* and, because both approaches relied on the examination of the relationship between a predictor and a criterion variable, were often grouped together under the heading of *criterion*-related validity.

The problem with these *content-* and *criterion*-related approaches to validity is that there are many things that we might want to assess for which there is no clear definition of the domain nor is there an obvious correlate that we could use to check that the assessment is doing what it is meant to do. To address this, a joint committee of the American Psychological Association, the American Educational Research Association, and the National Council on Measurement Used in Education (which later became the National Council on Measurement in Education) proposed an alternative method of validation—termed *construct* validation—that could be used where "the tester has no definitive criterion measure of the quality with which he [sic] is concerned and must use indirect measures to validate the theory" (APA, AERA & NCME, 1954, p. 14).

The idea of construct validity was further elaborated by Cronbach and Meehl (1955), who suggested that it was involved "whenever a test is to be interpreted as a measure of some attribute which is not 'operationally defined.' The problem faced by the investigator is, 'What constructs account for the variance in test performance?'" (p. 282).

Cronbach and Meehl defined a construct as

some postulated attribute of people, assumed to be reflected in test performance. In test validation the attribute about which we make statements in interpreting a test is a construct. We expect a person at any time to possess or not possess a qualitative attribute (amnesia) or structure, or to possess some degree of a quantitative attribute (cheerfulness). A construct has certain associated meanings carried in statements of this general character: Persons who possess this attribute will, in situation X, act in manner Y (with a stated probability). The logic of construct validation is invoked whether the construct is highly systematized or loose, used in ramified theory or a few simple propositions, used in absolute propositions or probability statements. (pp. 283–284)

As Bechtoldt (1959) points out, this definition involves (at least) three characteristics:

First, it is a *postulated attribute* assumed to be reflected in test performances; second, it has *predictive* properties; and third, the *meaning* of a construct is given by the laws in which it occurs with the result that clarity of knowledge of the construct is a positive function of the completeness of that set of laws, termed the nomological net. (p. 623)

Given the breadth of this definition of the term *construct*, it is not surprising that two years later Jane Loevinger (1957) suggested that construct validity was in fact "the whole of validity from a scientific point of view" (p. 636), not least because Cronbach and Meehl's definition explicitly included criterion-related aspects of validity and implicitly included content considerations as well. Although there were critiques of the notion of construct validity at the time (e.g., Bechtoldt, 1959), Angoff (1988) notes that by the late 1970s, Loevinger's view "became more generally accepted" (p. 28) and there is today a broad agreement that "construct validity is indeed the unifying concept of validity" (Messick, 1980, p. 1015).

Wiley (2001) points out that, in fact, the term *construct* has been used in the psychometric literature in two ways and for two distinct purposes. The first is "to name the psychological characteristics actually estimated by an existing test score or other measurement" and the second is "to name the psychological characteristics that a test score or other measurement is intended ('designed') to measure" (p. 212).

One consequence of this consensus about the central role of construct validity is that there is substantial agreement that construct interpretations should be at the heart of all assessments. This is made clear in the latest version of the *Standards for Educational and Psychological Testing* (AERA, APA, & NCME, 1999):

> Evolving conceptualizations of the concept of validity no longer speak of different kinds of validity but speak instead of different lines of validity evidence, all in the service of providing information relevant to a specific intended interpretation of test scores. Thus many lines of evidence can contribute to an understanding of the construct meaning of test scores. (p. 5)

More recently, Wiley (2001) defined a construct as follows:

> A construct, here, is an ability (i.e., is a human characteristic required for successful task performance). At the simplest level, these constructs can be identified with capacities to perform classes of tasks defined by task specifications. Because they must enable more than a single task performance, the concept implicitly follows from the formulation of an equivalence class of task implementations or realizations, all of which require possession of the same ability construct for successful performance. However, in order to be an ability, a human characteristic must not only differentiate successful from unsuccessful task performance, but must also apply to some tasks and not to others. That is, every ability must be defined so that it subdivides tasks into two groups: those to which that ability applies and those to which it does not. (p. 208)

Assessment is contentious, therefore, because when we assess we go beyond the construct and claim that certain tasks, if performed successfully, indicate the presence of the ability in the individual, although if the individual does not perform the task successfully, this is taken as evidence that the individual does not have the ability in question. In other words, *assessments operationalize constructs*. It is often the case that there is broad agreement on the matter of curriculum, although there is considerable disagreement about the associated assessment because it removes the ambiguity about the construct being assessed. These disagreements frequently manifest themselves as debates about assessments. However, the argument of this chapter is that these disagreements are in general better thought of as differences in what should be the construct of interest, and it is solely because the construct is made manifest only in the assessment does it appear that the validity of the assessment is a matter of opinion. This idea can be illustrated by looking at the issue of gender bias in the assessment of history in secondary school.

AN INTRODUCTORY EXAMPLE: THE ASSESSMENT OF HISTORY

Breland (1991) found that males outperformed females when achievement in history was assessed with multiple-choice tests but that females outperformed males when achievement in history was assessed with constructed-response items. One (quite common) interpretation of this is that multiple-choice tests are biased against female students, and the differential performance of males and female students is therefore a question of the validity of the assessments used. However, such debates can also be examined as debates over construct definition; in other words, when we assess history, what, in fact, are we really assessing? One view is that achievement in history is primarily about "facts and dates." For adherents to this view (see, e.g., McGovern, 1994), multiple-choice tests are highly appropriate ways to measure achievement in history, because they allow a wide range of knowledge to be assessed quickly and efficiently, and they have the additional advantage that the scoring is objective (apart from issues related to erasures, ambiguous marks, etc.). Another view is that history is primarily about the integration of partial (in both senses: partisan and incomplete) and sometimes conflicting sources of evidence to assemble a descriptive, and ideally explanatory, account of historical events (Wineburg & Fournier, 1994). For adherents to this second view, multiple-choice tests are likely to be inadequate as measures of achievement in history because it is extremely difficult, if not impossible, to assess such thinking through multiple-choice tests. Debates between adherents to these differing views of history often manifest themselves as apparently technical discussions about the validity of particular approaches to assessment, but the argument of this chapter is that they are more productively viewed as arguments about construct definition. Like this debate about history, many debates about the adequacy and appropriateness of assessments appear, on the surface, to be debates about technical issues, but they are, in fact, debates about construct definition. The reason that this observation is important is that debates about construct definition cannot be resolved by those with expertise only in assessment. They are debates outside assessment that should be settled before the assessment is designed. Otherwise, what is easy to assess, what is practicable to assess, and what is inexpensive to assess will be unduly influential in the determination of the assessment. This is not to say that these questions are unimportant; only that they must not be allowed to predominate, or prejudice, discussion of other aspects of the quality of assessment. The case of the assessment of history discussed above can be used to illustrate the two main threats to the validity of construct interpretations of assessment outcomes: *construct underrepresentation* and *construct-irrelevant variance* (Messick, 1989)—in other words, whether the assessment is too narrow to support the intended construct interpretations or whether the assessment systematically introduces extraneous information into the scores (McCallin, 2006).

Proponents of the view of history as "facts and dates" may well view multiple-choice assessments as entirely appropriate because they are able to assess all of what they believe history to be through such tests. Proponents of the view of history as "interpreting evidence" will, however, regard such tests as underrepresenting the construct of history; in other words, they argue that inferences one might make about a student's knowledge of facts and dates on the basis of a multiple-choice test may well be valid, but inferences about the ability to assemble historical arguments are much less likely to be warranted, because important aspects of the construct of interest were not assessed. Adherents to the "interpreting history" view would regard that multiple-choice test as suffering from *construct underrepresentation*.

Conversely, proponents of the view of history as "facts and dates" are likely to view assessments that involve items that require extended constructed responses as equally flawed. This is because although such assessments may assess aspects of the construct of interest, they are also assessing other capabilities, such as the ability to convey meaning in writing. All assessment users want the differences in students' scores to reflect differences in the construct of interest, but if the differences in scores are also, in part, attributable to factors unrelated to the construct of interest, then construct interpretations of students' scores are problematic. Advocates of the "facts and dates" view of history observe that although variation in students' outcomes on constructed-response tests of history do, in part, measure knowledge of history, differences in scores also represent differences in the ability of students to write well and even, perhaps, skill in handwriting. In other words, the students' scores would suffer from *construct-irrelevant variance*.

So while the "interpreting evidence" lobby would regard scores on multiple-choice tests as underrepresenting the construct of interest, the "facts and dates" lobby would regard scores on extended constructed response assessments as introducing a degree of construct-irrelevant variance.

Returning to the issue of gender bias, it can be seen from the above argument that the original question about whether multiple-choice tests of history are biased against females resolves into two separate issues, which need to be addressed in different ways. The first is, "What is the construct of history to be assessed?" This is not a technical issue. It is essentially a philosophical issue about the nature of history as an academic discipline (and therefore a specific version of the question, "What is knowledge?"). This is a matter on which individuals can legitimately disagree. The second question is, once a particular view of the construct of history has been agreed, whether a particular set of assessment arrangements adequately addresses the construct.

The advantage of such a formulation is that it clarifies the nature and the origin of any gender difference. If particular assessments show markedly superior performance for boys than for girls, is this because the assessment arrangements have introduced a degree of construct-irrelevant variance into the scores, for example, by choosing historical topics that are of greater interest to boys than girls? Or was the construct of interest defined in such a way that it is intrinsically something at which boys are better than girls?

Similar issues arise in the case of the mental rotation of three-dimensional objects. The ability to determine whether two three-dimensional objects are the same shape but oriented differently, or whether they are different objects, has been extensively studied, and this ability shows marked sex differences, with males outperforming females (often by as much as one standard deviation) in almost all cultures (Voyer, Voyer, & Bryden, 1995). This has led some to suggest that tests of this ability are biased against females. But this is to locate the problem in the wrong place. A test tests only what a test tests, and in this example, males really are better than females at this particular skill. The bias is not in the test but might be present in the inferences based on its outcomes. So whether such items should be included in a mathematics test is an issue of construct definition. The inclusion of items on mental rotation of three-dimensional objects will, for some, introduce a degree of construct irrelevant variance, whereas for others, the exclusion of such items would introduce construct underrepresentation. The important point is that the debate should be focused on the issue of construct definition, and the consequences of the definition, rather than on the technical issues of the extent of construct-irrelevant variance and construct underrepresentation. The ability to rotate three-dimensional objects mentally clearly seems related to mathematics, so the definition of the construct of mathematics in such a way as to include this topic would appear to be justified in terms of an appropriate philosophical imperative for the discipline of mathematics. On the other hand, including in the definition aspects of mathematics at which males are known to be better than females, with a corresponding set of messages about who can and cannot succeed in mathematics, would appear to run counter to a moral imperative about equity. Assessments of mathematics that include mental rotation are not biased, because it ascribes to an assessment a property it cannot have—what Ryle (1949) called a "category error."

There is one more important aspect of the relationship between constructs and the assessments that are intended to assess them, and that is that these relationships can change over time. One common response to the suggestion that a particular assessment suffers from construct underrepresentation is to point out that although the assessment itself might not adequately represent the whole of the construct of interest, the items actually assessed do in fact function as an adequate proxy for those aspects of the construct not assessed (in essence an argument for concurrent validity). For example, the "facts and dates" community might retort that an individual's performance on the multiple-choice test turns out to be quite a good proxy for performance on other aspects of history, such as those assessed with constructed-response tasks. However, the fact that such correlations are observed does not mean that such correlations are likely to be the same in the future. For example, in England, the most commonly used measure of school performance is the proportion of students from that school achieving one of the four highest (of nine) grades in at least five school subjects in the national school leaving examination (the General Certificate of Secondary Education or GCSE). For many years, the percentage of students achieving this benchmark including passes in English and Mathematics was around 10 percentage points lower than if the benchmark included any five school subjects. However, from 2001, as pressure to increase results from government increased, schools increasingly looked for ways to increase student success by matching the choice of subjects taken to the specific aptitudes of the students. By 2008, the effect of this was to increase the "gap" between the two indices (i.e., success rates including, and not including, passes in English and Mathematics) from 10 percentage points to 16 (Department for Children, Schools and Families, 2008). In other words, the relationship between the two measures of success and, in particular, the ability to predict one from the other had changed as a result of the social processes in play. This is, of course, just another example of Campbell's (1976) law:

The more any quantitative social indicator is used for social decision-making, the more subject it will be to corruption pressures and the more apt it will be to distort and corrupt the social processes it is intended to monitor. (p. 49)

The fact that the relationship between assessment outcomes can change over time was one of the reasons that Messick (1989) introduced the idea that the validity argument should include a consideration of the consequences of result interpretation and use, although this has been widely misunderstood and misapplied. Messick was not suggesting that all social consequences of test interpretation and use should be considered part of validity, but only those that were attributable to weaknesses in the test.

As has been stressed several times already, it is not that adverse social consequences of test use render the use invalid, but, rather, that adverse social consequences should not be attributable to any source of test invalidity such as construct-irrelevant variance. If the adverse social consequences are empirically traceable to sources of test invalidity, then the validity of the test use is jeopardized. If the social consequences cannot be so traced—or if the validation process can discount sources of test invalidity as the likely determinants, or at least render them less plausible—then the validity of the test use is not overturned. Adverse social consequences associated with valid test interpretation and use may implicate the attributes validly assessed, to be sure, as they function under the existing social conditions of the applied setting, but they are not in themselves indicative of invalidity. (pp. 88–89)

To see how this formulation of validity works in practice, let us return to the example of history in secondary schools discussed above. Suppose that a state defines the construct of competence at a particular grade in history much along the lines of those advocated by proponents of the "interpreting evidence" view of history, but finds that the costs of constructed response tests to assess this are too great, and therefore decide to rely on multiple-choice tests. The state then defends this course of action on the grounds that concurrent validity studies have shown that scores of students on constructed-response assessments of history are highly correlated with those on the multiple-choice tests. If teachers in the state subsequently change the way that they teach history and focus on the "facts and dates" that are the focus of the test, then the test will support less adequately inferences about aspects of history related to "interpreting evidence," and it may also be the case that female students enjoy history less because the subject is less connected to their existing knowledge

(Belenky, Clinchy, Goldberger, & Tarule, 1986; Gilligan, 1982). In this example, the undesirable consequences were at least in part caused by the fact that the test in use underrepresented the construct of history defined by the state, and so the validity of the state-mandated test is in question. On the other hand, had the state *defined* history as facts and dates, then the fact that such a definition—even though validly assessed with multiple-choice tests—resulted in the marginalization of female students would not compromise the validity of the assessment. It would, however, bring into question the ethical defensibility of defining history in a way that was likely to exclude female students. This might in turn generate debate related to "objectivist" versus "constructivist" views of knowledge (von Glasersfeld, 1995), but it is the thesis of this chapter that it would be more productive to have the debate in these terms rather than in terms of the assessment. Of course, where knowledge is defined as socially constructed, rather than being objectively defined, then construct definition may become more difficult—or at least less straightforward—but unless assessment design begins with construct definition, then establishing the inferences that may validly be drawn from the assessment outcomes becomes difficult, if not impossible.

In the remainder of this chapter, I explore the interplay of constructs and assessment in three broad areas of current interest in assessment. These specific areas have been chosen because they are areas of significant current debate, are areas where there is significant potential for inequity, and, perhaps unsurprisingly, are areas where the particular focus of this chapter provides a useful perspective. Another potential area for such an analysis—that of the testing of English language learners—has been the subject of a thorough review in a previous issue of *Review of Research in Education* (Durán, 2008). As noted in the introduction to this chapter, the three areas are

- Testing for admission to higher education, focusing specifically on impact on people of color
- The rise, and fall, of measures involving constructed-response items (including portfolio assessment, authentic assessment, and performance assessment) in large-scale achievement testing within statewide accountability systems
- The issue of accommodations in mandated assessment for students with special educational needs, especially within the context of the No Child Left Behind Act

Within each of these areas, the chapter explores the interplay of issues of technical adequacy with equity and suggests that a focus on the consequences of particular choices of constructs, rather than on the assessments, will lead to more helpful descriptions of what is happening and what can be done to improve equity in education.

EQUITY IN HIGHER EDUCATION
ADMISSIONS TESTING

Recruiting and selecting students for higher education is a global challenge (Kellaghan, 1996). In many—and perhaps most—countries, this is achieved through the provision of a set of examinations of academic achievement that are either set by higher education institutions (HEIs) or over which HEIs exert a considerable influence (Eckstein & Noah, 1993). Providing a set of standardized procedures for assessing the suitability of students for admission to university has had the effect, in most countries, of establishing a common curriculum for the period of upper secondary schooling (typically the last 2 or 3 years of secondary school). Although such systems may allow for different pathways (e.g., Sweden), constrained choice (e.g., Germany), or even unrestricted choice of subjects (e.g., England), such systems typically share a common "tariff" that allows the results of different students to be placed—more or less meaningfully—on a single scale.

A major factor in the evolution of these assessment systems was that in these countries upper secondary education had been designed from the outset primarily as a preparation for higher education and therefore intended only for the educational "elites" (for most of the 20th century less than 10% of the population). In the United States, however, between 1910 and 1940, there was a massive expansion in the provision of upper secondary education for all students, as a preparation for citizenship. It is notable that in many states in the United States the rate of participation of 18 year olds in education achieved in the 1930s has still not been reached in many rich European countries (Goldin & Katz, 2008; Organisation for Economic Cooperation and Development, 2008).

The fact that upper secondary education was, in the United States, primarily a local matter created few difficulties during much of the 19th century for three main reasons. First, many universities appeared to be recruiting rather than selecting students, so the criteria for entry were as much financial as academic (Levine, 1986). Second, students tended to apply to universities in the same state as the high school they had attended, which made it possible for the universities to assure the quality of entrants, either by accrediting the high schools and their grading standards (as piloted by the University of Michigan) or to set a statewide university entrance examination, such as those instituted by the Board of Regents of the State of New York in 1878. Third, those universities that did draw significant numbers of students from outside the state had their own entrance examinations; Harvard and Yale, for example, had introduced entrance examinations in 1851 (Broome, 1903).

As applications for university places grew in number, and the pattern of applications increased in complexity, a group of eight elite universities now known as the "Ivy League" (Brown, Columbia, Cornell, Dartmouth, Harvard, Pennsylvania, Princeton, and Yale) proposed the establishment of a set of common entrance examinations and established the College Entrance Examinations Board to take this work forward.

For the first four decades of its existence, the College Board relied primarily on written examinations of scholastic achievement based on the traditional school subjects. However, in 1934, Harvard had started using the Scholastic Aptitude Test (SAT), which had been developed by Carl Campbell Brigham from the intelligence tests administered to army recruits during the First World War (Zenderland, 1998), for its national scholarship awards. The early success of the SAT in this context—students who had scored highly on the SAT did well at Harvard—led, in 1937, to the adoption of the SAT for all scholarship decisions at 14 of the universities that were then members of the College Board (Hubin, 1988). In 1941, the "College Boards"—the traditional written examinations that had been in use since 1901—were withdrawn, leaving the SAT as the dominant university entrance test in the United States. A detailed discussion of the development of the SAT is beyond the scope of this chapter. A good account of the early development can be found in Hubin (1988), and Lemann (1999) provides details of the more recent history. Here, I focus, in particular, on issues of construct definition and equity.

The SAT is probably "the most researched test in the world" (College Board, 2009). A review of more than 3,000 studies of the validity of the SAT as a predictor of performance in the early years of college (Hezlett et al., 2001) found coefficients ranging from .44 to .62 and also predicted a range of measures of performance later in college such as likelihood of graduation and cumulative GPA, although the values of the coefficients were lower (ranging from approximately mid-30s to mid-40s). Although high school grade point average (HSGPA) appears to be the best single predictor of a student's GPA in their first year at college, using the SAT in addition does improve the prediction. A study of around 20,000 students who took the SAT in 1995 (Kobrin, Camara, & Milewski, 2002) found values of the correlation coefficients, corrected for attenuation of range (Thorndike, 1949) and shrinkage (Vogt, 1999), ranging from .30 for Hispanic students to .41 for Asian American students for the HSGPA and from .31 for Hispanic students to .44 for Asian American students for the SAT. The combination of HSGPA and SAT, however, does considerably better, ranging from .42 for Hispanic students to .55 for Asian American students (.48 for White and .50 for African American students).

The SAT has been widely attacked on a number of grounds. Some criticisms point out that although the SAT does increase the accuracy of prediction, the increases are marginal. For example, Crouse and Trusheim (1988) used a sample of 2,470 students from the National Longitudinal Study (NLS) of the class of 1972 to examine the utility of the SAT in predicting which students will earn a first-year college GPA of 2.5 or better. They found that forecasts made without the use of high school rank were accurate in 53% of the cases, and those made with high school rank had an accuracy of 62.2%, an increase of 9.2 percentage points. The use of the SAT in addition to high school class rank improves the accuracy by a further 2.7 percentage points. Although this is a proportional increase of almost 30%, Crouse and Trusheim suggest that such a small absolute increase in the accuracy of the prediction would not be noticed by most colleges. They also suggest that achievement tests, rather that tests of so-called aptitude, would have more beneficial social consequences, although the correlation between the SAT and the best-known national achievement test—the ACT—at .92 is comparable to the test–retest reliability of the SAT itself (Dorans, 1999).

Other concerns focus on the fact that scores for most minority students are lower—and in the case of some students, much lower—than for White students, with differences of as much as one standard deviation. The study by Kobrin et al. (2002), discussed above, found that African American and Hispanic students scored, respectively, 1.19 and 0.98 standard deviations below White students. Perhaps the best known of recent attacks has been that by Freedle (2003), wherein he states that "the SAT has been shown to be both culturally and statistically biased against African Americans, Hispanic Americans, and Asian Americans" (p. 1). This statement is inaccurate and misleading in several ways. First, the statistical arguments made by Freedle have been shown to contain important errors. Freedle's analysis focuses on specific types of items and attempts to show that they are more difficult for educationally disadvantaged students and proposes a way of rescoring the SAT (essentially placing greater weight on more difficult items) that raises the score of many minority students (by more than two standard deviations for some minority students on the verbal section of the SAT). Dorans (2004) points out several problems in Freedle's analysis. First, the version of the SAT analyzed by Freedle dated from 1980, before the routine screening of items for "differential item functioning" (Holland & Wainer, 1993)—the idea that an item might function differently for different groups of students of the same overall proficiency—was introduced.

The most significant problem, however, is that for each item a different group of students is used in comparing the success rate of Black and White students, and "the groups used to study a question vary from question to question in a systematic way related to the difficulty of the question and the proficiency of the examinees answering the question" (Dorans, 2004, p. 65). When the items are compared on the same basis, the effects found by Freedle disappear almost entirely (the remaining effect is of the order of one twentieth of a standard deviation). The cause of the small differences that remain are not fully understood but are possibly related to the fact that Black students are less likely to attempt the harder items on the test and are therefore less likely to be penalized for incorrect responses.

Second, and more important in terms of the arguments presented in this chapter, the statement by Freedle is a form of category error, because bias is not a property of assessments but of the inferences that are made on the basis of their outcomes. Even if Freedle's argument is reframed in terms of inferences rather than a statement about the SAT itself, it is incorrect, because the SAT actually *over*predicts performance at college for most minority students on average (Kobrin et al., 2002). This is where the importance of adequate construct definition is most clearly demonstrated. Minority students do less well on the SAT because they do less well in college, and the SAT is designed to predict performance in college. The SAT does underpredict college performance for females, but so does HSGPA (Kobrin et al., 2003). The extent to which HSGPA, SAT, and a composite of the two overpredict and underpredict first-year college GPA at 23 higher education institutions for males and females of different minorities is shown in Table 1 (based on data from Kobrin et al., 2003).

Perhaps the most remarkable feature of the data in Table 1 is that for every group apart from "Other" the SAT either overpredicts or provides a more accurate prediction of first-year college GPA. The broad picture is that the SAT does improve the

TABLE 1
Overprediction and Underprediction of First-Year
College GPA in 23 Institutions

	HSGPA		SAT		HSGPA + SAT	
	Female	Male	Female	Male	Female	Male
African American	.09	.20	.01	.22	−.01	.16
Native American	.13	.24	.06	.32	.07	.28
Asian American	.03	.08	−.01	.15	−.03	.07
Hispanic	.23	.31	.03	.20	.04	.20
White	−.11	−.03	−.11	.06	−.09	.05
Other	−.09	.04	−.13	.03	−.12	.04

Source. Derived from Kobrin et al. (2003).
Note. GPA = grade point average; HSGPA = high school grade point average; SAT = Scholastic Aptitude Test.

accuracy of prediction of performance in the first-year performance at college when compared with HSGPA alone (although not by very much).

The central thesis of this chapter is that many debates in education present themselves as debates about the validity of assessments but are more productively conceptualized as issues of construct definition and construct choice. The SAT is not biased against, for example, African American students not only because bias is not a property of tests but also because for both males and females the SAT actually overpredicts college performance. The purpose of this argument is not to defend the SAT but to frame the debate in a way that is more likely to lead to productive action.

If we read the evidence about the differential impact about the SAT on minorities as being caused by the SAT, then that will focus our attention on measures such as those proposed by Freedle, aimed at reducing Black–White score differences. Although increasing the degree of randomness in a selection procedure may serve to reduce adverse impact on minorities, selecting students for programs on which they are likely to be unsuccessful would seem to do little to advance the cause of equity (Wiliam, 2003).

The argument of this chapter is that a more productive way of reading the evidence from the predictive validity studies of the SAT is in terms of the construct being assessed. In other words, the main reason that many minority groups do less well on the SAT (as well as having lower HSGPA) is because they are less prepared for college, and indeed, scores on the National Assessment of Educational Progress show differences of approximately the same magnitude between White students, on one hand, and African American or Hispanic students on the other, as are found on the SAT—approximately one standard deviation (although the gap between White and minority students has been closing). Such a large gap is not surprising given the fact that minority students tend, on average, to be resourced less advantageously than White students (Piché & Taylor, 1991), are less likely to be taught by well-qualified teachers (Ferguson, 1991), and are more likely to live in conditions that affect cognitive development (Hackman & Farah, 2009; Kishiyama, Boyce, Knight, Jimenez, & Perry, 2009).

However, as David Hume (1973/1896) pointed out in his *Treatise on Human Nature*, one cannot deduce an "ought" from an "is." The fact that the SAT currently does predict reasonably who will, and who will not, do well at college does not mean that we should accept this uncritically. Clearly, it *is* currently the case that levels of school achievement, whether measured by HSGPA or the SAT, predict college achievement well, but this is not in itself evidence of equity when the opportunities for high-quality instruction and support are themselves not equitably distributed. No test is perfect, and indeed, it could be argued that the SAT has more than its share of faults, but blaming the SAT for the failure of students of color to gain admission to, and to thrive in, the most selective colleges is unlikely to do anything to improve the situation. The SAT works as well as it does because it is exquisitely tuned to the system in which it operates. Lowering admissions requirements for college while leaving the educational systems in the college unchanged is likely to do little except increase the number of students failing to complete their studies. Instead, because this is a system problem, systemic approaches are likely to be more successful (O'Day & Smith, 1993). An example of such a systemic approach is provided by the *Access to Medicine* program offered at King's College London (Access to Medicine, 2009).

The medical program at King's College London (part of the University of London) is one of the largest in Europe, graduating approximately 350 doctors every year. The campuses of the College are located in some of the most ethnically diverse parts of London, but prior to the introduction of the Access to Medicine program very few students attending local schools were admitted, and those that were admitted were more likely to be of Asian descent rather than the most common minorities in the area—those of African heritage. As well as raising the issue of equity, such selection policies were unlikely to result in culturally competent health services (Council of Heads of Medical Schools, 1998).

To address this, the Access to Medicine program addressed simultaneously the three issues of *recruitment, selection*, and *retention* (Wiliam, Millar, & Bartholomew, 2004). Recruitment was addressed through intervention programs implemented in local schools with students at the beginning of secondary school (age 11) to raise aspirations and to ensure that curricular choices made by students at the ages of 14 and 16 did not "close off" particular routes into medical education. This was particularly important because informal contacts with schools had suggested that many students aspiring to be doctors thought that the most important subject to study in upper secondary school was biology, whereas, in fact, the only subject required for admission to a medical program by the General Medical Council of the United Kingdom is chemistry.

At the time of the inception of the Access to Medicine program, selection to most medical schools in the United Kingdom was based principally on the grades achieved by students at the Advanced level of the General Certificate of Education examination (usually abbreviated to "A-level"). Students in the local schools rarely achieved the grades required for admission, but lowering the entry requirements for students from local schools would be likely to admit students who were not well prepared, or indeed well suited, to the intense study required in the medical degree program at King's College London.

Because a great deal of the curriculum for the first 2 years of the medical program at King's focuses on basic medical sciences, it was felt that assessing the ability to reason scientifically and specifically the ability to integrate new ideas into existing scientific schema might provide a way of identifying aptitude for medical education even where students had not been well taught. A number of science reasoning tasks, developed by Shayer and Adey (1981), had proved to be very successful at predicting later science learning, and so these tests were used to identify students from local schools who did not meet the traditional criteria for admission to a medical degree program but who did show the ability to learn science quickly. To counter charges of "dumbing down," cut-scores on the science reasoning tasks were established by reference to the cohort of medical students admitted on the traditional basis.

Although the students selected on such a basis were likely to have scientific reasoning skills on par with traditional students, they were much less likely to have a secure grounding in basic scientific knowledge, particularly in chemistry. The students selected for the Access to Medicine program were also less well prepared for higher education in general. To address this it was decided that the Access to Medicine students would be allowed 3 years to cover the same curriculum followed by traditional students in the first 2 years of the 5-year medical degree program. Philanthropic sources of funding were secured to pay for the cost of the extra year (both tuition and living expenses), and the students were given additional support in the form of a part-time tutor.

The first students admitted under the Access to Medicine program graduated in 2007. Although the early cohorts are too small to generate any robust findings, initial outcomes are encouraging: the final scores of the Access to Medicine students are indistinguishable from those of the "traditional students" (Garlick & Brown, 2008).

For the purpose of this chapter, the most important feature of the Access to Medicine program is that instead of focusing on the assessment instrument used in selecting students for admission to medical programs (the A-level), the program used a systemic approach, involving recruitment, selection, and retention. Rather than blaming the instrument for the low scores achieved by minority students, the A-level was accepted as an adequate basis for recruiting and selecting students who had been well prepared for higher education and thus would do well in the traditional medical program. To increase equity in the outcomes for minority students, the program looked for different constructs that might be used in predicting success for nonstandard students, in the context of a nonstandard program.

In the same way, it seems likely that the advancement of underrepresented minorities in American higher education will be better secured by a search for new ways of raising aspirations for students and through new kinds of higher education curricula, supported by new forms of assessment, thus acknowledging the diversity of students' previous experiences, rather than further efforts attempting to show that one particular instrument is biased against minority students.

THE RISE AND FALL OF AUTHENTIC ASSESSMENT IN THE UNITED STATES

Although the provision of education has always been regarded as an essentially "local" matter in the United States, over the last 50 years, state and federal sources have become greater and greater net contributors (Corbett & Wilson, 1991). Despite the fact that the annual polls conducted by the *Phi Delta Kappan* organization have indicated that most parents are happy with their local schools, many states felt the need to make school districts accountable beyond the local community, through the introduction of statewide testing programs. For example, in 1961 California introduced a program of achievement testing in all its schools. Although the nature of the tests was at first left to the districts, in 1972, the California Assessment Program was introduced, mandating multiple-choice tests in English language, arts, and mathematics in Grades 2, 3, 6, and 12 (tests for Grade 8 were added in 1983). Subsequent legislation in 1991, 1994, and 1995 enacted new statewide testing initiatives that were only partly implemented. However, in 1997, new legal requirements for curriculum standards were passed, which, in 1998, led to the Standardized Testing and Reporting program. Under this program, all students in Grades 2 to 11 take the Stanford Achievement Test—a battery of standardized tests—every year. Those in Grades 2 to 8 are tested in reading, writing, spelling, and mathematics, and those in Grades 9, 10, and 11 are tested in reading, writing, mathematics, science, and social studies. In 1999, further legislation introduced the Academic Performance Index—a weighted index of scores on the Stanford Achievement Tests, with awards for high-performing schools, and a combination of sanctions and additional resources for schools with poor performance. The same legislation also introduced requirements for passing scores on the tests for entry into high school and for the award of a high school diploma.

There were some legal challenges to the notion of "minimum competency" testing, most notably in Florida, where in 1978, a student, named Debra P, brought a case against the state commissioner of education, Ralph Turlington, and others because she had been denied a high school diploma on the grounds that she had failed to pass a minimum-competency test required by the state (United States District Court 474 F. Supp. 244 M.D. FL, 1979). The key point in the case was that Debra P was Black, and when she began her education in 1967 she had attended a segregated elementary school, which had been resourced less favorably than the schools attended by Whites. In its final judgment, the court decided that the requirement to pass a minimum-competency test placed a greater burden on a Black student than a White student and was therefore unfair. The court decided that the State of Florida could not deny students high school diplomas for another 4 years from the date of the judgment, by which time the court believed all students would have had adequate opportunity to learn the material on which the test was based. Provided states were prepared to be able to show that all students did have the opportunity to learn the material covered in the tests, minimum-competency requirements for high school diplomas were fair.

At the same time, many states were experimenting with alternatives to standardized tests for monitoring the quality of education and for attesting to the achievements of individual students. In 1974, the National Writing Project (NWP) had been established at the University of California, Berkeley (Lieberman & Wood, 2002). Drawing inspiration from the practices of professional writers, NWP emphasized the importance of repeated redrafting in the writing process, and to assess the writing process properly, one needed to see the development of the final piece through several drafts. In judging the quality of the work, the degree of improvement across the drafts was as important as the quality of the final draft.

The emphasis on the process by which a piece of work was created, rather than the resulting product, was also a key feature of the Arts-PROPEL project—a collaboration between the Project Zero research group at Harvard University (Gardner, 1989) and Educational Testing Service. The idea was that students would "write poems, compose their own songs, paint portraits, and tackle other 'real-life' projects as the starting point for exploring the works of practicing artists" (Project Zero, 2005). Originally, it appears that the interest in portfolios was intended to be primarily formative, but many writers also called for performance or authentic assessments to be used instead of standardized tests (Berlak, 1992; Gardner, 1992).

Two states in particular, Vermont and Kentucky, did explore whether portfolios could be used in place of standardized tests to provide evidence for accountability purposes, and some states also developed systems in which portfolios were used for summative assessments of individual students. However, the use of portfolios was attacked on several grounds. Chester Finn, President of the Thomas B. Fordham Foundation, said that portfolio assessment was "costly [. . .] slow and cumbersome" and went on to say "its biggest flaw as an external assessment is its subjectivity and unreliability" (Mathews, 2004, p. 75).

In 1994, the RAND Corporation released a report on the use of portfolios in Vermont (Koretz, Stecher, Klein, McCaffrey, & Deibert, 1994), which is regarded by many as a turning point in the use of portfolios (Mathews, 2004). Koretz et al. (1994) found that the meanings of grades or scores on portfolios were rarely comparable from school to school because there was little agreement about what sorts of elements should be included. During the short time the portfolios had been in use, the standards for reliability that had been set by standardized tests such as the SAT simply could not be matched. Although advocates might claim that portfolios were more valid measures of learning, the fact that the same portfolio would get different scores according to who did the scoring made their use for summative purposes difficult to sustain in the U.S. context.

In fact, even if portfolios had been able to attain high levels of reliability, it is doubtful that they would have gained acceptance. Teachers did feel that the use of portfolios was valuable, although the time needed to produce worthwhile portfolios detracted from other priorities. Mathematics teachers in particular complained that "the mathematics portfolios required a significant amount of class time, which had to be taken from other activities" (Koretz et al., 1994, p. 26). Furthermore, even before the RAND report, the portfolio movement was being eclipsed by the push for "standards-based" education and assessment (Mathews, 2004).

For the purposes of this chapter, one of the most interesting features of the decline of performance assessment is that construct considerations played a much smaller part in the discussion than technical considerations (such as reliability) or issues of manageability. Even on narrow technical considerations, the widespread rejection of portfolios for high stakes accountability testing in the United States would appear to have been premature, for two reasons.

First, the experiences of many other countries are that, with appropriate sources of support, and given sufficient time, portfolio assessment can attain similar levels of reliability to those achieved in standardized tests. One unpublished investigation into the assessment of portfolios of work in English language arts for 16-year-old students in England found levels of classification accuracy on a 9-point scale of approximately 70% (exact match). Although this was considered rather unsatisfactory (and may have contributed to the decision not to publish), it corresponds to a classical reliability of approximately .92 (Wiliam, 2001)—higher than is achieved on many—if not most—accountability tests.

Second, the experience of other countries is that, given time, teachers are also able to integrate the portfolio work into their ongoing instruction, so that, instead of being seen as an unmanageable addition to the curriculum, portfolios come to be seen as a vehicle for delivering that curriculum as well as a valuable focus for teacher professional development (Maxwell, 2004).

The rejection of portfolios and other forms of assessment requiring students to construct, rather than select, responses for high stakes accountability assessment appears to have profound consequences for overall levels of educational achievement in the United States. E-portfolios are changing from being simply digital repositories to being learning environments that support a range of pedagogical practices and afford novel kinds of collaborative learning (Abrami & Barrett, 2005), which are likely to be increasingly important in the future (Jewitt, 2006).

Moreover, as Newmann, Bryk, and Nagaoka (2001) have shown, accountability systems that rely on what they term *authentic intellectual work* assessed through constructed response items are associated with higher levels of student achievement. Comparative studies suggest that whereas factors such as teacher quality appear to be the most important predictors of high scores in international comparisons of student achievement (Barber & Mourshed, 2007), the use of accountability measures based on constructed-response items measuring higher order knowledge appears to be an important additional factor (Bishop, 2001a, 2001b), although in this context it is worth noting that poorly designed performance measures, combined with very high stakes for teachers and schools, can result in undesirable outcomes (Wiliam, under review).

It would be naive to assume that a focus on constructs, rather than assessments, would have led to the retention of portfolios and other forms of authentic assessment in high stakes accountability testing. However, it seems plausible that an increased focus on what the assessments were supposed to be measuring, rather than on the assessments themselves, would have contributed to the debate and might have made stakeholders more willing to consider alternatives to standardized multiple-choice testing.

In the remainder of this section, I review briefly how issues of construct definition have interacted with equity in the case of the learning of mathematics.

For many years, the fact that the performance of males in mathematics was superior to that of girls attracted little attention, as if somehow this was the natural order of things. Maccoby and Jacklin (1974), in their monumental work *The Psychology of Sex Differences*, reviewed more than a thousand research studies and concluded that it was "fairly well established" that boys outperformed girls in terms of visuospatial ability and mathematics, whereas girls had more developed verbal abilities (pp. 351–352). Although many authors challenged both the methodology and the conclusions (see, e.g., Block, 1976), there can be little doubt that the work served as a significant impetus for further work in this field.

Although Maccoby and Jacklin (1974) made clear that their view was that these differences were caused by a range of factors, including biological predispositions, social shaping, and cognitive self-actualization processes (O'Connell, 1990), much of the subsequent work on sex differences, particularly in mathematics achievement, focused on genetic factors, often with speculations about how the environment of evolutionary adaptedness (Bowlby, 1969) might have contributed to the development of more advanced spatial skills in males. However, in recent years, the extraordinary decline in the size of sex differences in mathematics performance has provided strong evidence that observed sex differences are primarily of environmental, rather than genetic, origin.

Feingold (1988) examined the performance of males and females on the SAT from 1947 to 1983, and although there was evidence of female superiority in language and male superiority in mathematics, the magnitude of the difference declined markedly over the period studied. In fact, current estimates suggest that the magnitude of sex differences has halved over the second half of the 20th century (Hyde, Fennema, & Lamon, 1990; M. C. Linn, 1992), and a meta-analysis of 98 studies from 1974 to 1987 on sex differences in mathematics concluded that a 95% confidence interval for the effect size included zero (Friedman, 1989). Most recently, Hyde, Lindberg, Linn, Ellis, and Williams (2008) found that the mean sex difference on state assessment in mathematics across 10 states in the United States (California, Connecticut, Indiana, Kentucky, Minnesota, Missouri, New Jersey, New Mexico, West Virginia, and Wyoming) was .0065 (not significantly different from zero). There is also increasing evidence that male superiority in mathematics is most marked in countries with the greatest gender inequality (Hyde & Mertz, 2009).

These analyses of the magnitude of sex difference have tended to treat measures of mathematics achievement as interchangeable. A complementary strand of research studies, arguably begun by Carol Gilligan's (1982) landmark book *In a Different Voice* has sought to look at how school subjects are defined and the extent to which they are resonant with the modes of thinking that are preferred by different individuals. In particular, work by Boaler (1997) has shown that while both males and females prefer to make connections between their existing and new knowledge in mathematics, doing so appears to be more important for females. Where mathematics is defined as a series of disembodied facts with no relationship to the world outside the mathematics classroom, then making such connections is difficult and available to only a few students. Where, however, mathematics is presented as being a way of thinking about real issues in a disciplined way, then mathematical thinking is available to all (Boaler, 2008).

This is, of course, an issue of construct definition, analogous to the example of history discussed previously. Absent adequate definitions of the construct of school mathematics, all assessments can be regarded as measuring the same construct. Performance assessments come to be seen as expensive, unreliable, and time-consuming measures of student achievement. It is hardly surprising, therefore, that their use has been radically curtailed in all the statewide assessments mandated by the No Child Left Behind Act of 2001 in the United States, to be replaced by multiple-choice tests.

The argument of this chapter is that had the focus been first on the construct to be assessed, and only second on the technical adequacy of the assessments developed to assess the construct, then the construct of mathematics being assessed in schools in the United States might be very different. A focus on mathematics as inquiry would produce more equal outcomes between males and females (Willingham & Cole, 1997) and between different minorities (Boaler, 2008)—and, as Burton (2004) has shown, closer to the conception of mathematics held by professional mathematicians.

ACCOMMODATIONS FOR SPECIAL POPULATIONS

As Koretz (2008) notes, "Few issues in measurement raise such intense emotions as the assessment of students with special needs: those with disabilities or those with limited proficiency in English" (p. 281). In this chapter, I will not deal with the difficulties of identification and classification of disabilities and special needs nor with general issues of assessments for such students; an excellent summary of the current "state of the art" in this area can be found in Pullin (2008). Here, in keeping with the rest of the chapter, I focus on the importance of construct definition in the design of educational assessments for such students.

The most important pieces of legislation in the United States in this area are the Individuals with Disabilities Education Act (IDEA) 1990, its predecessors (the 1969 Children with Specific Learning Disabilities Act, which was included in the Education of the Handicapped Act 1970, and the Education for All Handicapped Children Act 1975) and its subsequent reauthorizations, particularly those of 1997 and 2004. The 1997 revision, in particular, required all states that choose to accept IDEA funding (all, in fact, have) to arrange for the participation of students with disabilities in state and local accountability systems, with details of how each student will participate and the support needed for such participation being specified in the student's Individualized Education Program (IEP).

The primary ways in which the participation of students with disabilities in large-scale testing programs has been arranged are through *test accommodations* and *alternative assessments*. Test accommodations are defined in the *Standards for Educational and Psychological Testing* (AERA, APA, & NCME, 1999) as variations in the specified procedures for test administration in response to a student's disability. The National Center on Educational Outcomes classifies these accommodations under the headings of (a) presentation, (b) equipment and materials, (c) response, (d) scheduling and timing, and (e) settings (National Center on Educational Outcomes, 2008).

The most common accommodations for test presentation are large-print versions of the test for students with visual impairments; versions of the test in Braille; the use of a scribe or sign interpreter; the opportunity for the student to have instructions repeated, reread, or clarified; and translation of the directions into the student's native language. Equipment and materials accommodations include magnification and amplification equipment, special acoustic conditions, and the use of a calculator. Accommodations for responding to the test items include the provision of a scribe, a computer keyboard, a brailler, or allowing the student to write rather than bubble in an item response. Most states also allow extended time to take the test, allowing the student to take breaks; scheduling the test over multiple sessions, or even over multiple days; and scheduling test times to suit the student. Finally, many states allow students with disabilities to take the tests in a room on their own, in a carrel, in a small group, or even outside the school (e.g., at home or in a hospital).

Where students with disabilities are not able to participate in mandated tests even with test accommodations, *alternative assessments* may be offered. As Pullin (2008) notes, these *alternative* assessments frequently address different standards from the tests taken by students without disabilities and can take very different forms, including out-of-grade testing and portfolios of work that are assessed either by reference to the grade-level expectations and achievement level descriptors specified for all students in that grade or relative to the student's IEP rather than to the relevant state standards (Pullin, 2008).

There is little doubt that accommodations and alternative assessments have in many cases had the effect "of altering the content of special education away from the low-level functional-life-skills approaches traditional for students with more severe disabilities in favor of more academic content associated with the curricular standards articulated for general education" (Pullin, 2008, p. 123). Furthermore, in states that link the award of high school diplomas to performance on standardized tests, such accommodations and alternative assessments have undoubtedly increased the number of students with disabilities who are able to receive high school diplomas (Ysseldyke, Dennison, & Nelson, 2003). However, although the efforts to allow students with disabilities to access a richer curriculum must be applauded, it must also be acknowledged that they take us into unfamiliar territory, particularly in terms of the arguments made in this chapter regarding the centrality of constructs.

It is clear that alternative assessments almost invariably assess different constructs from the assessments administered to students without disabilities, but it is also important to note that even apparently quite minor test accommodations can also affect the construct being assessed.

In the early development of tests, it was common to classify tests as either power tests or speeded tests, depending on whether the primary determinant of a student's score was the accuracy of the answers or the number of items completed. A common definition of speededness is that a test is (at least partially) speeded for a particular group of examinees if any of the examinees fail to complete three fourths of the items in the test and if less than 80% of the candidates complete all the items in the test (Davies, Kaiser, & Boone, 1987), although as Ellerin Rindler (1979) has pointed out, power and speededness interact in ways that are difficult to predict. It has been known for well over half a century that speeded and unspeeded versions of the same test may be measuring different constructs (Davidson & Carroll, 1945) so that even minor accommodations may change the construct addressed by an assessment.

The central argument of this chapter is that because construct interpretations are at the heart of validity argument, the design of assessments should begin by defining the construct to be assessed, and only then designing assessments that will yield evidence that support inferences regarding the construct, as is made manifest in the evidence-centered design paradigm (Mislevy, Almond, & Lukas, 2003). Where the process takes place in reverse, then validation becomes a values-based process rather than the technical process it should be, and in particular, the values of the test designer can feed into test design, resulting in a shift from making the important measurable to making the measurable important, and with test outcomes that are difficult, if not impossible, to interpret. If it is accepted that construct definition should precede assessment design for the general population, then it should also apply to students with disabilities. In other words, the debate should not be about assessments but constructs. The assessment of all students—with and without disabilities—should begin from a consideration of constructs, via a necessarily value-laden debate about whether the constructs should apply to all students or just to some. As the assessment is developed, it may be that accommodations are built in as optional procedures for administration, but these should be such that they do not change the construct being assessed. For example, the provision of large-print test booklets will improve the performance of some students with visual impairments but would not do so for students without visual impairments. As such, the validity of the test would be the same if all students were provided with large-print test booklets—the construct would not have changed—but considerations of efficiency would support the idea that the additional cost of such booklets should be borne only in the cases of students who would benefit from this provision. However, where accommodations would result in a change of construct being addressed, then the reason for this should be examined not in the assessment but in the appropriateness of the construct for the portion of the population in question. In this way, there is at least the prospect of treating all students equitably in terms of their assessment, irrespective of their (dis-)abilities.

CONCLUSION

Over the past century, the notion of validity has developed from a property of assessments, to a property of scores, and finally to a property of "inferences and actions based on test scores or other modes of assessment" (Messick, 1989, p. 13). The idea that construct interpretations are at the heart of validity argument and that therefore construct definition is essential to effective assessment has also now become widely accepted, at least within the measurement community. Such an approach suggests that whereas contestations about the ability of a particular assessment procedure to support valid inferences *may* be related to technical issues about the design and implementation of the procedures, they are more likely to be the result of differences of view about the kinds of construct interpretations that are intended to be made from assessment outcomes. This is important because it separates, to an extent at least, matters of fact from those of value. The extent to which particular assessment procedures support particular kinds of inferences involves the integration of empirical evidence and theoretical rationales and is, therefore, principally, a technical matter. Whether the kinds of inferences that the assessment supports are the right inferences to be drawn is, to a much greater extent, a matter of value.

The argument of this chapter has been that the consequences of this hard-won consensus have not been effectively followed through to the social settings within which assessments are administered. Specifically, I have argued that separating the process of defining the construct to be assessed from the construction of the assessment to assess that construct provides a perspective that is useful in advancing equity.

In the case of assessing history, multiple-choice tests can support reasonably valid inferences about the extent to which examinees know facts and dates, but they are much less able to support inferences about the ability of examinees to weigh evidence and assemble historical arguments. The fact that boys do better on multiple-choice tests of history is often cited as evidence of the bias of multiple-choice tests against female examinees, but in this chapter, I have argued that it is more helpful to locate the inequity in the choice of a definition of construct of history in a way that has differential impact on males and females. In the same way, tests of mental rotation of three-dimensional solids are not biased against females because males really do tend to be better at this particular skill. We could try to find items of mental rotation that minimize the differences between males and females (in a similar way to the approach used by Freedle with the SAT), but surely a more appropriate response is to question whether the construct of mentally rotating three-dimensional solids is important (and if it is, what kinds of educational experiences are helpful in developing this skill).

In the case of admission to higher education, we could blame the SAT for its adverse impact on students of color, but this is likely to be less effective in addressing unequal access to higher education than looking at the experiences of students of color in K–12 education and what kinds of support such students would need to be successful in higher education. In the same way, I have suggested that a greater focus on the construct, rather than the assessment, would frame the debate about the relative merits of performance assessment in a more helpful way.

Finally, in the assessment of students with special educational needs, I have argued that where test accommodations and alternative assessments change the construct of interest, it is essential that this is done through a focus on the construct rather than ad hoc modifications of the assessments, which lead to results that are difficult, if not impossible, to interpret. If a particular construct that is defined for one population is not suitable for another, then it seems to me to be much better to define a construct that *is* appropriate for that second population rather than simply modify the assessment.

In many cases, of course, adverse impact on female students, on students of color, or on students with special needs is the result of deficiencies in the assessment, which thus brings the validity of the assessment for its intended use into question. At other times the assessments will be supporting valid inferences about capabilities that are unequally distributed between different groups of students. Our chances of advancing the cause of equity in education will, I believe, be greatly enhanced if we know which is which.

ACKNOWLEDGMENTS

I would like to thank the developmental reviewers—Val Klenowski and Robert Rueda—and the volume editors—Allan Luke, Judith Green, and Greg Kelly—for helpful comments on earlier drafts of this chapter. Any deficiencies that remain, however, are, of course, entirely mine.

REFERENCES

Abrami, P. C., & Barrett, H. (2005). Directions for research and development on electronic portfolios. *Canadian Journal of Learning and Technology, 31*(3), 1–15.

Access to Medicine. (2009). *Access to medicine.* Retrieved July 31, 2009, from http://www.accesstomedicine.org/

American Educational Research Association, American Psychological Association, & National Council on Measurement in Education. (1999). *Standards for educational and psychological testing* (4th ed.). Washington, DC: American Educational Research Association.

American Psychological Association, American Educational Research Association, & National Council on Measurement Used in Education. (1954). Technical recommendations for psychological tests and diagnostic techniques. *Psychological Bulletin Supplement, 51*(2, Part 2), 1–38.

American Psychological Association, American Educational Research Association, & National Council on Measurement in Education. (1966). *Standards for educational and psychological tests and manuals.* Washington, DC: American Psychological Association.

American Psychological Association, American Educational Research Association, & National Council on Measurement in Education. (1974). *Standards for educational and psychological tests.* Washington, DC: American Psychological Association.

American Psychological Association, American Educational Research Association, & National Council on Measurement in Education. (1985). *Standards for educational and psychological testing* (3rd ed.). Washington, DC: American Psychological Association.

Angoff, W. H. (1974). Criterion-referencing, norm-referencing and the SAT. *College Board Review, 92*(Summer), 2–5, 21.

Angoff, W. H. (1988). Validity: An evolving concept. In H. Wainer & H. I. Braun (Eds.), *Test validity* (pp. 19–32). Hillsdale, NJ: Lawrence Erlbaum.

Barber, M., & Mourshed, M. (2007). *How the world's best-performing school systems come out on top.* London: McKinsey.

Bechtoldt, H. P. (1951). Selection. In S. S. Stevens (Ed.), *Handbook of experimental psychology* (pp. 1237–1267). New York: Wiley.

Bechtoldt, H. P. (1959). Construct validity: A critique. *The American Psychologist, 14,* 619–629.

Belenky, M. F., Clinchy, B. M., Goldberger, N. R., & Tarule, J. M. (1986). *Women's ways of knowing: The development of self, voice, and mind.* New York: Basic Books.

Berlak, H. (1992). Toward the development of a new science of educational testing and assessment. In H. Berlak, F. M. Newmann, E. Adams, D. A. Archbald, T. Burgess, J. Raven, et al. (Eds.), *Towards a new science of educational testing and assessment* (pp. 181–206). Albany: State University of New York Press.

Bishop, J. H. (2001a). A steeper, better road to graduation. *Education Next, 1*(4), 56–61.

Bishop, J. H. (2001b). *Why do students learn more when achievement is examined externally?* Retrieved June 11, 2009, from http://media.hoover.org/documents/ednext20014unabridged _bishop.pdf

Block, J. H. (1976). Issues, problems and pitfalls in assessing sex differences: A critical review of The Psychology of Sex Differences. *Merrill-Palmer Quarterly, 22,* 283–308.

Boaler, J. (1997). *Experiencing school mathematics: Teaching styles, sex and setting.* Buckingham, UK: Open University Press.

Boaler, J. (2008). Promoting "relational equity" and high mathematics achievement through an innovative mixed-ability approach. *British Educational Research Journal, 34,* 167–194.

Bowlby, J. (1969). *Attachment and loss: Vol. 1. Attachment.* New York: Basic Books.

Brasel, K. J., Bragg, D., Simpson, D. E., & Weigelt, J. A. (2004). Meeting the Accreditation Council for Graduate Medical Education competencies using established residency training program assessment tools. *American Journal of Surgery, 188,* 9–12.

Breland, H. M. (1991). *A study of sex differences* (Research Rep. No. RR-91-61). Princeton, NJ: Educational Testing Service.

Brennan, R. L. (Ed.). (2006). *Educational measurement* (4th ed.). Washington, DC: American Council on Education/Praeger.

Broome, E. C. (1903). *A historical and critical discussion of college admission requirements.* New York: Macmillan.

Burton, L. (2004). *Mathematicians as enquirers: Learning about learning mathematics.* Dordrecht, Netherlands: Kluwer Academic.

Calfee, R., Lau, E., & Sutter, L. (1983). Establishing instructional validity for minimum competency programs. In G. F. Madaus (Ed.), *The courts, validity and minimum competency testing* (pp. 95–113). Boston: Kluwer Academic.

Campbell, D. T. (1976). *Assessing the impact of planned social change.* Hanover, NH: Dartmouth College Public Affairs Center.

Cohen, L., Mannion, L., & Morrison, K. (2004). *A guide to teaching practice.* London: Routledge.

College Board. (2009). *New SATs for the press.* Retrieved July 31, 2009, from http://www .collegeboard.com/about/news_info/sat/faqs.html

Corbett, H. D., & Wilson, B. L. (1991). *Testing, reform and rebellion.* Hillsdale, NJ: Ablex.

Council of Heads of Medical Schools. (1998). *Statement of principles.* London: Author.

Cronbach, L. J., & Meehl, P. E. (1955). Construct validity in psychological tests. *Psychological Bulletin, 52,* 281–302.

Crouse, J., & Trusheim, D. (1988). *The case against the SAT.* Chicago: Chicago University Press.

Cureton, E. E. (1951). Validity. In E. F. Lindquist (Ed.), *Educational measurement* (2nd ed., pp. 621–694). Washington, DC: American Council on Education.

Davidson, W. M., & Carroll, J. B. (1945). Speed and level components in time limit scores: A factor analysis. *Educational and Psychological Measurement, 5,* 411–427.

Davies, T., Kaiser, R., & Boone, J. (1987). *Speededness of the Academic Assessment Placement Program (AAPP) reading comprehension test.* Nashville: Board of Regents of the State University and Community College System of Tennessee.

Department for Children, Schools and Families. (2008). *GCSE and equivalent results in England 2007/08 (provisional).* London: Author.

Dorans, N. J. (1999). *Correspondence between ACT and SAT I scores* (Vol. RR 99-2). Princeton, NJ: Educational Testing Service.

Dorans, N. J. (2004). Freedle's table 2: Fact or fiction? *Harvard Educational Review, 74*(1), 62–72.

Durán, R. P. (2008). Assessing English-language learners' achievement. *Review of Research in Education, 32,* 292–327.

Eckstein, M. A., & Noah, H. J. (1993). *Secondary school examinations.* New Haven, CT: Yale University Press.

Ellerin Rindler, S. (1979). Pitfalls in assessing test speededness. *Journal of Educational Measurement, 16,* 261–270.

Feingold, A. (1988). Cognitive gender differences are disappearing. *The American Psychologist, 43,* 95–103.

Ferguson, R. (1991). Paying for public education: New evidence on how and why money matters. *Harvard Journal of Legislation, 28,* 465–498.

Freedle, R. O. (2003). Correcting the SAT's ethnic and social-class bias: A method of reestimating SAT scores. *Harvard Educational Review, 73*(1), 1–43.

Friedman, L. (1989). Mathematics and the gender gap: A meta-analysis of recent studies on sex differences in mathematical tasks. *Review of Educational Research, 59,* 185–213.

Gardner, H. (1989). Zero-based arts education: An introduction to Arts PROPEL. *Studies in Art Education: A Journal of Issues and Research, 30*(2), 71–83.

Gardner, H. (1992). Assessment in context: The alternative to standardised testing. In B. R. Gifford & M. C. O'Connor (Eds.), *Changing assessments: Alternative views of aptitude, achievement and instruction* (pp. 77–117). Boston: Kluwer Academic.

Garlick, P., & Brown, G. (2008, May 17). Widening participation in medicine. *British Medical Journal, 336,* 1111–1113.

Garrett, H. E. (1937). *Statistics in psychology and education.* New York: Longmans, Green.

Gilligan, C. (1982). *In a different voice.* Cambridge, MA: Harvard University Press.

Goldin, C., & Katz, L. F. (2008). *The race between education and technology.* Cambridge, MA: Harvard University Press.

Guilford, J. P. (1946). New standards for test evaluation. *Educational and Psychological Measurement, 6,* 427–438.

Hackman, D. A., & Farah, M. J. (2009). Socioeconomic status and the developing brain. *Trends in Cognitive Science, 13*(2), 65–73.

Hanson, F. A. (1993). *Testing testing: Social consequences of the examined life.* Berkeley: University of California Press.

Hart, K. M. (Ed.). (1981). *Children's understanding of mathematics: 11–16.* London: John Murray.

Hezlett, S. A., Kuncel, N. R., Vey, M. A., Ahart, A. M., Ones, D. S., Campbell, J., et al. (2001). *The effectiveness of the SAT in predicting success early and late in college: A comprehensive meta-analysis.* Paper presented at the annual meeting of the National Council on Measurement in Education, Seattle, WA.

Holland, P., & Wainer, H. (Eds.). (1993). *Differential item functioning: Theory and practice.* Hillsdale, NJ: Lawrence Erlbaum.

Hubin, D. R. (1988). *The Scholastic Aptitude Test: Its development and introduction, 1900–1948.* Unpublished doctoral dissertation, University of Oregon, Eugene.

Hume, D. (1896). *A treatise of human nature: Being an attempt to introduce the experimental method of reasoning into moral subjects.* Oxford, UK: Clarendon Press. (Original work published 1739)

Hyde, J. S., Fennema, E., & Lamon, S. J. (1990). Gender differences in mathematics performance: A meta-analysis. *Psychological Bulletin, 107,* 139–155.

Hyde, J. S., Lindberg, S. M., Linn, M. C., Ellis, A. B., & Williams, C. C. (2008). Gender similarities characterize math performance. *Science, 321,* 494–495.

Hyde, J. S., & Mertz, J. E. (2009). Gender, culture, and mathematics performance. *Proceedings of the National Academy of Sciences, 106,* 8801–8807.

Jewitt, C. (2006). Multimodality and literacy in school classrooms. *Review of Research in Education, 32,* 241–267.

Kellaghan, T. (Ed.). (1996). *Admission to higher education: Issues and practice.* Princeton, NJ: International Association for Educational Assessment.

Kelley, T. L. (1927). *Interpretation of educational measurements.* Yonkers-on-Hudson, NY: World Book.

Kishiyama, M. M., Boyce, W. T., Knight, R. T., Jimenez, A. M., & Perry, L. M. (2009). Socioeconomic disparities affect prefrontal function in children. *Journal of Cognitive Neuroscience, 21,* 1106–1115.

Kobrin, J. L., Camara, W. J., & Milewski, G. B. (2002). *The utility of the SAT-I and SAT-II for admissions decisions in California and the nation* (Report No. 2002-6). New York: College Board.

Koretz, D. M. (2008). *Measuring up: What educational testing really tells us.* Cambridge, MA: Harvard University Press.

Koretz, D. M., Stecher, B. M., Klein, S. P., McCaffrey, D., & Deibert, E. (1994). *Can portfolios assess student performance and influence instruction? The 1991–92 Vermont experience* (Vol. RP-259). Santa Monica, CA: RAND Corporation.

Lemann, N. (1999). *The big test: The secret history of the American meritocracy.* New York: Farrar, Straus & Giroux.

Levine, D. O. (1986). *The American college and the culture of aspiration 1915–1940.* Ithaca, NY: Cornell University Press.

Lieberman, A., & Wood, D. R. (2002). *Inside the National Writing Project: Connecting network learning and classroom teaching.* New York: Teachers College Press.

Lindquist, E. F. (Ed.). (1951). *Educational measurement* (1st ed.). Washington, DC: American Council on Education.

Linn, M. C. (1992). Gender differences in educational achievement. In Educational Testing Service (Ed.), *Sex equity in educational opportunity, achievement, and testing: Proceedings of a 1991 ETS invitational conference* (pp. 11–50). Princeton, NJ: Educational Testing Service.

Linn, R. L. (Ed.). (1989). *Educational measurement* (3rd ed.). Washington, DC: American Council on Education/Macmillan.

Loevinger, J. (1957). Objective tests as instruments of psychological theory. *Psychological Reports, 3*(Suppl. 9), 635–694.

Maccoby, E. E., & Jacklin, C. N. (1974). *The psychology of sex differences.* Stanford, CA: Stanford University Press.

Mathews, J. (2004). Whatever happened to portfolio assessment? *Education Next, 4*(3), 73–75.

Maxwell, G. S. (2004, March). *Progressive assessment for learning and certification: Some lessons from school-based assessment in Queensland.* Paper presented at the third conference of the Association of Commonwealth Examination and Assessment Boards, Nadi, Fiji. Brisbane, Australia: University of Queensland Graduate School of Education.

McCallin, R. C. (2006). Test administration. In S. M. Downing & T. M. Haladyna (Eds.), *Handbook of test development* (pp. 625–652). Mahwah, NJ: Lawrence Erlbaum.

McGovern, C. (1994). *The SCAA Review of National Curriculum History: A minority report.* York, UK: Campaign for Real Education.

Messick, S. (1980). Test validity and the ethics of assessment. *The American Psychologist, 35,* 1012–1027.

Messick, S. (1989). *Validity.* In R. L. Linn (Ed.), *Educational measurement* (3rd ed., pp. 13–103). Washington, DC: American Council on Education/Macmillan.

Miles, E. (1998). *The Bangor dyslexia teaching system.* London: Whurr.

Mislevy, R. J., Almond, R. G., & Lukas, J. F. (2003). *A brief introduction to evidence centered design* (ETS Research Rep. No. RR-03-16). Princeton, NJ: Educational Testing Service.

Moss, P. A., Girard, B. J., & Haniford, L. C. (2006). Validity in educational assessment. *Review of Research in Education, 30,* 109–162.

National Center on Educational Outcomes. (2008). *Participation and accommodation summary reports 2006–2007.* Retrieved June 28, 2009, from http://data.nceo.info/pa-summaries .asp

Newmann, F. M., Bryk, A. S., & Nagaoka, J. K. (2001). *Authentic intellectual work and standardized tests: Conflict or coexistence?* Chicago: Consortium on Chicago School Research.

Nuttall, D. L. (1987). The validity of assessments. *European Journal of Psychology of Education, 2,* 109–118.

O'Connell, A. N. (1990). Eleanor Emmons Maccoby. In A. N. O'Connell & N. F. Russo (Eds.), *Women in psychology: A bio-bibliographic sourcebook* (pp. 231–237). New York: Greenwood.

O'Day, J., & Smith, M. S. (1993). Systemic school reform and educational opportunity. In S. H. Fuhrman (Ed.), *Designing coherent education policy: Improving the system* (pp. 250–312). San Francisco: Jossey-Bass.

Organisation for Economic Cooperation and Development. (2008). *Education at a glance 2008.* Paris: Author.

Piché, D. M., & Taylor, W. L. (Eds.). (1991). *A report on shortchanging children: The impact of fiscal inequity on the education of students at risk* (Prepared for the Committee on Education and Labor, U.S. House of Representatives, One Hundred First Congress, Second Session). Washington, DC: Government Printing Office.

Pirie, S. E. B. (1987). *Nurses and mathematics: Deficiencies in basic mathematical skills among nurses— Development and evaluation of methods of detection and treatment.* London: Royal College of Nursing/Scutari Press.

Project Zero. (2005). *Arts PROPEL.* Retrieved July 31, 2009, from http://pzweb.harvard.edu/ research/propel.htm

Pullin, D. (2008). Individualizing assessment and opportunity to learn: Lessons from the education of students with disabilities. In P. A. Moss, D. C. Pullin, J. P. Gee, E. H. Haertel, & L. J. Young (Eds.), *Assessment, equity, and opportunity to learn* (pp. 109–135). Cambridge, UK: Cambridge University Press.

Ryle, G. (1949). *The concept of mind.* London: Hutchinson.

Shayer, M., & Adey, P. S. (1981). *Towards a science of science teaching: Cognitive development and curriculum demand.* London: Heinemann.

Thorndike, R. L. (1949). *Personnel selection: Test and measurement techniques.* New York: Wiley.

Thorndike, R. L. (Ed.). (1971). *Educational measurement* (2nd ed.). Washington, DC: American Council on Education.

Vinner, S. (1997). From intuition to inhibition—Mathematics, education and other endangered species. In E. Pehkonen (Ed.), *Proceedings of the 21st conference of the International Group for the Psychology of Mathematics Education* (Vol. 1, pp. 63–78). Lahti, Finland: University of Helsinki, Lahti Research and Training Centre.

Vogt, W. P. (1999). *Dictionary of statistics and methodology: A nontechnical guide for the social sciences* (2nd ed.). Thousand Oaks, CA: Sage.

von Glasersfeld, E. (1995). *Radical constructivism: A way of knowing and learning.* London: Falmer Press.

Voyer, D., Voyer, S., & Bryden, M. P. (1995). Magnitude of sex differences in spatial abilities: A meta-analysis and consideration of critical variables. *Psychological Bulletin, 117,* 250–270.

Wiley, D. E. (2001). Validity of constructs versus construct validity. In H. Braun, D. N. Jackson, & D. E. Wiley (Eds.), *The role of constructs in psychological and educational measurement* (pp. 207–227). Mahwah, NJ: Lawrence Erlbaum.

Wiliam, D. (2001). Reliability, validity and all that jazz. *Education 3-13, 29*(3), 17–21.

Wiliam, D. (2003). Constructing difference: Assessment in mathematics education. In L. Burton (Ed.), *Which way social justice in mathematics education?* (pp. 189–207). Westport, CT: Praeger Press.

Wiliam, D. (under review). Standardized student assessment in an age of accountability. *Educational Psychologist.*

Wiliam, D., Brown, M., Kerslake, D., Martin, S., & Neill, H. (1999). The transition from GCSE to A-level in mathematics: A preliminary study. *Advances in Mathematics Education, 1,* 41–56.

Wiliam, D., Millar, M., & Bartholomew, H. (2004). *Selection for medical education: A review of the literature.* Retrieved August 1, 2008, from www.dylanwiliam.net

Willingham, W. S., & Cole, N. S. (Eds.). (1997). *Gender and fair assessment.* Mahwah, NJ: Lawrence Erlbaum.

Wineburg, S. S., & Fournier, J. (1994). Contextualized thinking in history. In M. Carretero & J. F. Voss (Eds.), *Cognitive and instructional processes in history and the social sciences* (pp. 285–308). Hillsdale, NJ: Lawrence Erlbaum.

Ysseldyke, J., Dennison, A., & Nelson, R. (2003). *Large-scale assessment and accountability systems: Positive consequences for students with disabilities* (Synthesis Rep. No. 51). Minneapolis: University of Minnesota, National Center on Educational Outcomes. Retrieved June 28, 2009, from http://education.umn.edu/NCEO/OnlinePubs/Synthesis51.html

Zenderland, L. (1998). *Measuring minds: Henry Herbert Goddard and the origins of American intelligence testing.* Cambridge, UK: Cambridge University Press.

Chapter 9

The Teacher Workforce and Problems of Educational Equity

JUDITH WARREN LITTLE
University of California, Berkeley

LORA BARTLETT
University of California, Santa Cruz

In this chapter, we examine developments in the teacher workforce and in the occupation of teaching across recent generations. We take our point of departure from the perspective of prevailing policy discourse on enduring problems of educational equity, asking not only how teaching has evolved in recent decades but more specifically how that evolution has mattered to the distribution of educational opportunity and the shape of educational outcomes. This terrain is arguably large, and the text necessarily reflects certain choices regarding focus and emphasis. Consistent with the overall volume, we focus principally on conditions in industrialized nations and on teachers as the object of policies intended to remedy problems of persistent inequity. We acknowledge but do not delve into the extensive and complex body of classroom-based research that locates issues of equity in teachers' pedagogical practices, their relationships with students and families, and the expectations they hold of low-income, minority, or special-needs students (Delpit, 1996; Hollins & Guzman, 2005; Ladson-Billings, 1999; C. D. Lee, 1995; Weinstein, 2002).[1]

In characterizing teacher workforce issues, our essay also reflects our deeper familiarity with the policy conditions and research activity in the United States than elsewhere. However, by reviewing international reports and studies, we have made an effort to locate American developments in a complex international landscape that demonstrates a visible institutional isomorphism in education and public policy (Meyer & Ramirez, 2000; Wiseman, 2010 [this volume]) while also preserving significant local variations (Anderson-Levitt, 2003).[2] Our perspective is largely sociological, but

Review of Research in Education
March 2010, Vol. 34, pp. 285-328
DOI: 10.3102/0091732X09356099

we have also benefited from a broader disciplinary reach, with many of the resulting insights derived from the work of anthropologists, economists, historians, and policy researchers.

The discourse on teacher quality takes on particular significance amid the escalating stakes attached to educational achievement and attainment. To an unprecedented degree, an individual's level of formal education matters to his or her life fortunes, and the quality of education systems matters to the viability of communities and nations and to the evolving character of international relationships (Dee, 2003; Murnane & Steele, 2007). The high stakes attendant on educational attainment (with regard to prospects for employment, health, and civic influence, for example) directly implicate the capacity of schools and the quality of teaching—hence the centrality of teacher quality concerns in discussions of educational equity.

Current policy formulations of "teacher quality" reflect a nearly exclusive focus on teachers' academic background and subject specialization as warrants of professional qualification and as anticipated predictors of student achievement and attainment, coupled with a growing concern about the differential distribution of demonstrably qualified or effective teachers. The emphasis on teachers' academic qualifications and the distribution of qualified teachers follows reasonably from equity considerations, bolstered by recent research; nonetheless, we observe that this orientation to teacher quality proves limiting in two respects. First, teacher qualifications (a focus that lends itself most directly to policy intervention) must be distinguished from the quality of teaching, as teachers with equivalent formal qualifications may achieve quite different levels of instructional effectiveness. In addition, the focus on teacher qualifications reflects and reinforces a predominantly individualistic frame of reference that tends to obscure or overlook the role of institutional and organizational processes, including the growing prominence of market-based solutions for reported problems of teacher recruitment and placement. It thus results in systematic inattention to the organizational conditions under which teachers come to develop and demonstrate effective teaching, establish commitments to particular students and schools, and contribute to the collective capacity of schools and school systems.

Following a summary of the prevailing policy discourse and related evidence regarding teacher quality, we argue for a policy and research perspective that more fully integrates individual and collective conceptions of teacher quality and that attends more fully to institutional processes and organizational contexts for teaching. Although a comprehensive review of the relevant research literatures is beyond the scope of this chapter, we signal what we consider to be the contributions and limitations of the extant research.

PURPOSES OF SCHOOLING AND WHAT IT MEANS TO BE A TEACHER

Repeated observations regarding the high stakes attached to education and related assaults on the disparities in educational outcomes necessarily beg the question of what those desired outcomes might be. That is, perspectives on the purposes and goals of education entail notions of what it means to teach and be a teacher. Policy rhetoric for the past several decades has focused most consistently and forcefully on what have been termed "human capital" goals for education (Lingard, 2009). In the United States, as elsewhere, that term is most tightly joined to arguments regarding global economic competitiveness. In certain respects, this is not new. Systems of mass education developed in the context of industrialization and both vocationalism (preparation for work) and social efficiency (sorting for the labor force) have been consistently evident as expressed purposes of education. In *The Struggle for the American Curriculum*, Kliebard (1986) characterized 20th-century struggles among advocates of developmental, humanist, social efficiency, and social meliorist perspectives. In a more recent volume (Kliebard, 2002), he maintains that the social efficiency perspective has prevailed over competing conceptions, arguing that through much of the 20th century, a mood of "hard-edged efficiency" dominated American education as well as a "growing emphasis on the schools as a direct instrument of social control" (p. 94).

Nonetheless, vocational purposes have contended throughout with other avowed purposes, as the title of Kliebard's 1986 volume suggests (Grubb & Lazerson, 2004). Histories of education show the multiple and competing visions of education to be a recurring refrain. Cribb (2009) notes that "there are continuously negotiated tensions between the different conceptions of the goals of education: the correct balance between the pastoral, the academic, the vocational and the civic dimensions of teaching" (p. 40). Labaree (1997) identifies democratic equality (preparing citizens for a democracy), social efficiency (preparation for work), and social mobility (preparing individuals to compete for social positions) as alternative goals over which educational conflicts consistently have been mounted. He maintains that the former two constitute goals focused on the "public good" of education and that the last constructs education as a commodity or "private good"—and that these represent a "fundamental source of strain" in any liberal democratic society between democratic politics (public goods) and capitalist markets (private goods). The conflict among these three goals, Labaree argues, has resulted in a "contradictory structure for the educational system" (p. 39) and, by extension, contradictory expectations for the work of teaching. It has also produced a history of shifting priorities and episodic policy developments as one or another of the goals has gained or lost ascendancy.

Thus, different perspectives on the purposes of schooling orient one to different qualities, qualifications, practices, and accomplishments of teachers. For example, a developmental perspective would seem to require teachers with substantial expertise in child and adolescent development, whereas a humanist perspective would call for a deep understanding and appreciation of various disciplinary and cultural traditions, and the pursuit of democratic equality would require teachers with the dispositions and skills of civic participation. A social justice perspective would require understanding, honoring, and drawing from relevant cultural knowledge in instruction, advocating for disenfranchised students, and adopting an activist stance toward equitable school-ing. A human capital perspective (joining the social efficiency and social mobility purposes described by Labaree, 1997) would presumably emphasize the substantive knowledge, skills, and dispositions valued by labor markets. Although any given teacher or teacher group would likely embrace some combination of these perspectives, and although individual schools, both public and private, are positioned differently in relation to them, it is the last of them that appears most prominent in current discussions and debates regarding qualifications to teach and teaching effectiveness.

EQUITY ISSUES IN THE EVOLUTION OF TEACHING AND THE TEACHER WORKFORCE

In the past century and a half of public schooling, teaching in the United States and in other industrialized nations has evolved as an occupation with a characteristic demographic profile. With a few exceptions, teaching is an occupation of women, especially in elementary schools; it employs the young and the graying, a bimodal age distribution that may reflect a reluctance of "Generation X" (born in the 1960s and 1970s), "Generation Y" (born after 1980), or the current "Millennium Generation" to commit to long-term careers in teaching; and it remains racially, ethnically, cultur-ally, and linguistically homogeneous, even in nations whose school-age populations have become steadily more diverse.[3]

Similarities in the overall demographic profile mask important variations in the localized histories, conceptions, and circumstances of teachers and teaching over time and within and across nations. For example, the widespread feminization of teach-ing developed in different circumstances and at a different pace across regions of the United States (MacDonald, 1999; Perlmann & Margo, 2001; Prentice & Theobald, 1991; Tolley & Beadie, 2006) and today exhibits certain marked variations across countries (McKenzie & Santiago, 2005). Overall, racial and ethnic minorities com-pose a small share of the teacher workforce in the United States (Gay, Dingus, & Jackson, 2003), as do immigrant, refugee, and indigenous minority teachers else-where, but their disproportionately low representation begs explanation best supplied by the kinds of studies emerging in recent years from historians, anthropologists, and sociologists (Cavalcanti, 1996; Fairclough, 2007; M. Foster, 1997; Perkins, 1989; Thiessen, Bascia, & Goodson, 1996; Troyna, 1994). Altogether, attending mainly to demographic patterns and profiles may reify and reinforce largely hegemonic and "generic" conceptions of teachers and teaching.

At issue in this chapter is how the composition of the workforce and develop-ments in the past several decades may equip teachers to embrace and tackle problems of enduring inequity. That is, one might consider how teachers are and have been positioned by biography, training, organizational and community context, and his-torical moment to adopt an orientation toward teaching that is consistent with what might be termed "equity work." Contemporary renderings of the teacher workforce offer something of a mixed picture of dominant orientations toward teaching and the place of equity considerations and social change in conceptions of the teacher's role. Here we highlight four of those renderings: the academic selectivity of the teacher workforce; the inclination of minority individuals to enter and remain in teaching; the likelihood that teachers will be well prepared for work with diverse students and to tackle problems of structural inequity; and teachers' preferences for where and whom they teach.

Academic Selectivity

Policy discourse centers prominently on the intellectual caliber of the teacher workforce: Are teachers up to the task of educating students to the level intended by established standards and narrowing the "achievement gaps" persistently linked to family background? Throughout the history of formal schooling, a teacher's academic background has occupied a central place in the definition of what it means to be qualified to teach, and it has been a perennial touchstone for debates, laments, and defenses centered on the overall quality of the teaching workforce. In recent decades, academic preparation has evolved as perhaps the single most prominent proxy for teacher quality and a necessary (if not sufficient) guarantor of classroom effectiveness—hence widespread interest in the relative attractiveness of teaching as a career to those boasting the highest levels of academic achievement (McKenzie & Santiago, 2005).

A hallmark of national development everywhere has been an escalation in the formal educational attainment of individuals employed as teachers. Fifty years ago in the United States, for example, 15% of teachers surveyed by the National Education Association for its report on the status of teachers still had less than an undergraduate college degree, and only 23% had a master's degree; by the mid-1980s, all teachers surveyed had a BA degree, and more than half held a master's degree (National Education Association, 2003). In an inventory of quality indicators applied to teaching and teachers in the United States, Zumwalt and Craig (2005b) report,

Since 1985, every state has raised the bar for entry into the teaching profession in one or more ways: raising minimum grade point averages (GPAs); requiring majors in content areas; instituting teacher tests; requiring master's degrees for permanent certification; raising standards for program registration; and requiring national accreditation of teacher education programs. (p. 157)

Yet the steady growth in teachers' level of formal education has not protected the occupation in the United States and in other industrialized nations (although not all) from the repeated charge that teachers possess only modest academic qualifications: the problem of "too many lows," as Lanier and Little (1986, p. 540) termed it, noting the disproportionate recruitment of teachers in the United States who were recruited from the lowest quartile of college graduates. Murnane and colleagues (Murnane, Singer, Willet, Kemple, & Olsen, 1991) reported a precipitous decline from the mid-1960s to 1980 in the percentage of "high-IQ" college graduates who entered teaching—a period of time that coincided with opening of labor markets to women and minorities (see also Corcoran, Schwab, & Evans, 2004). Overall, studies in the United States tend to indicate that individuals with higher test scores and grade point averages, or who have attended selective institutions, have been less likely to enter teaching during the past 40 years—a pattern particularly characteristic at the secondary level (Guarino, Santibañez, & Daley, 2006).

A somewhat more encouraging portrait emerges from a recent study conducted by the Educational Testing Service on data collected on Praxis II test takers (a test of content and teaching knowledge required for licensure in 20 states in the United States) from 1994 to 1997 and from 2002 to 2005 (Gitomer, 2007). Data on the test takers included not only their performance on the Praxis II but also their earlier performance on the SAT college admissions test and their college grade point average, or GPA. The analysis shows consistent gains in measures of academic ability among the Praxis II test takers across gender and racial-ethnic categories between the two time periods. Gitomer (2007) reports, "Among prospective teachers, the proportion of those with high GPAs increased while the proportion of those with lower GPAs declined," and determines that "these improvements are not simply artifacts of grade inflation" (p. 13). Furthermore, the analysis shows a consistent gain in SAT Verbal and Math scores that cannot be explained simply by general trends in the population. However, despite relative gains among all groups, some groups of teacher candidates—African Americans and Hispanics, elementary teacher candidates, and those in special education or physical education—still show weaker academic profiles and lower Praxis II passing rates than candidates of other racial and ethnic backgrounds or those in secondary education.

International studies and reports suggest that the challenge of attracting academic high achievers, especially in the fields of mathematics and the sciences, is widespread across countries but not completely uniform; a few countries systematically and successfully recruit prospective teachers from the high-achieving segments of secondary school graduates. According to the 2005 Organisation for Economic Co-operation and Development (OECD) report *Teachers Matter*, "In countries where teaching has high social status—such as Finland, Ireland and Korea—there is strong competition for entry into teacher education" (McKenzie & Santiago, 2005, p. 102).[4]

Assigning priority to teachers' academic preparation, together with concerted efforts to attract well-prepared individuals into teaching, is arguably a reasonable step toward improving the overall quality of educational opportunity. Yet to do so is also to join the shape of the prospective teacher workforce to the dynamics of higher education access. As Reininger (2007) observes regarding workforce supply in the United States, "An important factor contributing to the under-representation of African-Americans and Hispanics in teaching is the general under-representation of African-Americans and Hispanics among college graduates" (p. 6). She reports that minority college attainment has increased in the past three decades but remains proportionately low, with 88% of college graduates in 1976 having been White, compared with 74% in 2003–2004. In the same period, the percentage of graduate

African Americans and Hispanics increased from 6% to 9% and from 2% to 7%, respectively. Using data from the National Education Longitudinal Study (NELS 88), she observes that the percentage of high school students who become teachers from schools enrolling a large share of low-income and minority students is significantly less than the percentage of high school students who become teachers from more advantaged schools. However, among those who do obtain a BA, there are no significant differences by school type in the likelihood that individuals will enter teaching. Reininger concludes, "Because teachers are required to have college degrees, finding ways to improve the college graduation rates of minorities may be a possible solution to the dearth of minorities in teaching" (p. 7). In effect, the press for academic selectivity of teachers, given low levels of postsecondary attainment among low-income and minority students, functions to maintain the relative racial, ethnic, linguistic, and cultural homogeneity of the teacher workforce.

Workforce Diversity

By all accounts, as Gay et al. (2003) sum up, "the school population is becoming more ethnically, racially, and linguistically diverse while teachers remain predominately monoracial, monoethnic, monocultural, and monolingual" (p. 8; see also Guarino et al., 2006; Murnane & Steele, 2007). Although this situation may be most pronounced in the United States, it is by no means confined to the American landscape and now extends to nations that many have long considered relatively homogeneous. The OECD, following a 25-nation study, reports that Norway and the Netherlands are among the countries where "the cultural background of teachers does not reflect the student population" (McKenzie & Santiago, 2005, p. 59). The report goes on to profess "a need to promote the benefits of a teaching career to groups who are often under-represented among teacher ranks, such as males and those from minority cultural backgrounds" (McKenzie & Santiago, 2005, p. 87).[5]

Most explanations for low workforce diversity focus on recruitment and selection problems in the form of weak financial incentives—given expanded career opportunities for college-educated minority individuals—and impediments such as the reliance on standardized testing as a requirement of licensure (Gay et al., 2003; Gitomer, Latham, & Ziomek, 1999). However, recruitment difficulties do not fully account for low numbers, even after acknowledging the relatively small pool of minority graduates and the broader array of occupational choices available to them. Teacher retention may also prove increasingly problematic. Reviews of research conducted in the past two decades or so report proportionately lower attrition by minority teachers (Béteille & Loeb, 2009; Guarino et al., 2006), but there are indications of a recent shift. Drawing on five cycles of data from the National Center for Education Statistics Schools and Staffing Survey (SASS) and Teacher Follow-up Survey (TFS), Ingersoll and Connor (2009) report that by 2004–2005, minority teacher turnover in the United States had become significantly greater than turnover among White teachers—although minority teachers were less likely than White teachers to exit schools in high-poverty areas or with large populations of minority students.

Although survey items like those on the TFS instrument produce similar profiles for White and minority teachers, with working conditions looming large among the reasons both groups leave teaching or move schools, qualitative studies suggest other aspects of minority teachers' experience that seem likely to affect their career decisions. Such studies add needed complexity to the portrayals of the "everyday life" of teachers, portrayals that Troyna (1994) argues have been shaped, normalized, and "globalized" (universalized) in mainstream sociological studies entirely from the perspective of White teachers (see also M. Foster, 1997, on this point). By attending closely to minority teachers' experience with students, colleagues, parents, and administrators in particular circumstances, rather than treating "minority" teachers as a monolithic entity and their teaching contexts as uniform, these studies illuminate what it means to construct one's role as teacher and sustain one's commitment to teaching from a variety of biographical standpoints, in a range of circumstances, and across a span of policy moments.

Perhaps the most sizable body of research revolves around the experience of Black teachers in the United States and the United Kingdom. For example, M. Foster's (1997) oral histories among three generations of Black teachers in the United States chronicle the ways in which the shift from racially segregated to racially integrated schools changed not only the size and concentration of the Black teacher workforce (many Black teachers lost their jobs) but also the ways in which they were able to define their role in schools and communities. In the words of one of the "elders," whose career, remarkably, spanned 70 years from 1921 to 1991, the period of integration "caused many of our black teachers not to be sure of who they are and what they are supposed to stand for" (p. 34).[6] However, an interview-based study of Black women teachers in three intergenerational teaching families (Dingus, 2006) points to the role of family, community connections, and institutional ties (such as those developed by attending historically Black colleges and universities) in cultivating a conception of the teacher's role as "cultural worker" that spans decades. Both the M. Foster (1997) and Dingus (2006) studies are limited by their small, purposive samples, but both also yield insights into (and questions about) the conditions and experiences that shape the identity and commitments of Black teachers.

Rationales for diversifying the teacher workforce typically cite the likely benefits to students—including but not limited to academic benefits—when teachers serve as "role models" whose cultural background matches the students' own (Grant & Agosto, 2008). One line of research, pursued largely by economists working with large-scale quantitative data sets, poses the question of whether race or ethnic matching of teachers and students proves consequential for student outcomes. As Dee (2004) recounts, the findings from that research remain mixed, and the methodological challenges prove substantial. His analysis of data from the Tennessee Project STAR class-size experiment offered an opportunity to investigate the significance of same-race pairing under conditions of reportedly random assignment of teachers to students (a situation not likely to be feasible on any scale or for any sustained period of time). Dee finds that "models of student achievement indicate that assignment to an own-race teacher significantly increased the math and reading achievement of both black and white students" (p. 195) but acknowledges that the available data do not enable one to determine "the exact mechanisms by which own-race teachers influence student achievement (that is, the various types of passive and active teacher effects)" (p. 209; see also Hanushek, Kain, O'Brien, & Rivkin, 2005). Nor do the data permit examination of a broader set of outcomes. The fact that the available large-scale data sets do not afford insight into classroom-level practices, interactions, and relationships makes them of limited utility in guiding the preparation, induction, support, and evaluation of teachers and weakens any warrant they might supply for policymaking.

Recent qualitative studies offer some insight into the complex and problematic aspects of the "role model" rationale. In a recent interview-based study conducted with 60 Afro-Caribbean teachers in England, Maylor (2009) investigated three tenets of the role model argument: that Black teachers regard themselves as role models and embrace that identity in their schools; that Black students also consider their teachers as role models, connecting the teachers' actions, aspirations, and accomplishments with their own; and that Black teachers are necessarily the most appropriate role models for Black students. She found wide variation in teachers' perspectives and priorities, with some embracing and others rejecting the notion of race- and gender-specific role modeling. In addition, teachers produced complex and nuanced accounts of interaction in classrooms and schools, accounts that belie any simplistic chain of influence as a "role model" while also conveying the multiple demands and trade-offs confronting minority teachers in their relationships with students, families, colleagues, and administrators.

Similarly, an interview study of Black teachers working in predominantly White schools in the United States found that the experience of being a "token" minority forced the teachers to consider their personal and professional identity and their relationships with students and colleagues in ways unlikely to confront their White colleagues (Kelly, 2007). Difficulties in navigating the peer culture surface as a dominant theme in a study of African American teachers in predominantly White suburban schools (Mabokela & Madsen, 2007), where teachers felt they were expected to "bear the burden of dispelling myths and representing their race in their exchanges with coworkers" (p. 1171) while at the same time confronting evidence of racial stereotypes (including skepticism about their teaching expertise) and feeling uncertain how to interpret the social and cultural cues that would gain them membership in the school's professional culture. These emerging qualitative studies are limited by their small samples and near-exclusive reliance on interview data. The findings point to complex relationships and career trajectories whose investigation would benefit from both in-depth observational and ethnographic research and from well-designed survey research on larger samples. That said, the existing studies are sufficient to suggest that increased workforce diversity will demand more in the way of both policy formulation and research than a singular focus on recruiting teachers of color.

Teachers Who Are Prepared to Work Effectively With Diverse Students and to Tackle Problems of Inequity

Policy requirements and professional association standards regarding "multicultural" teacher preparation date back in several nations at least as far as the 1970s, but early institutional responses were uneven at best and related research minimal (Verma, 1993). Characterizing the state of affairs through the 1980s and early 1990s, Grant (1993) argued that progress in legitimizing multicultural education was impeded by the relative homogeneity of the teacher educator workforce, the superficial and/ or ambiguous meanings attached to the term *multicultural* or *intercultural,* an ethos of academic ethnocentrism, and the absence of instructional materials and research that could inform curricular choices (see also Tomlinson, 1996, on resistance to the terminology and ideas associated with "antiracist" teacher education).[7]

In the past decade or so, teacher educators have taken steps to make the pursuit of social justice a more compelling value in teacher preparation and a more central aspect of teachers' professional capacity, identity, and commitments (Cochran-Smith, 2004). Experienced teachers and teacher educators, often working within a Freireian tradition, have also emphasized the moral and political dimensions of teaching, sometimes forming local and regional associations to promote systemic, equity-oriented change in schools and support the work of teachers committed to a "critical pedagogy" (e.g., Levine, Lowe, Peterson, & Tenorio, 1995).[8] This set of shifts is evident in the dramatic difference in the contents of two compilations of research on teacher education separated by almost two decades: two iterations of the *Handbook of Research on Teacher Education* (Cochran-Smith, Feiman-Nemser, McIntyre, & Demers, 2008; Houston, 1990). The earlier volume contains one chapter on preparing teachers for diversity (Grant & Secada, 1990)—a chapter attesting to the scarcity of empirical research and a narrow conception of teacher education reform—together with individual chapters focused more specifically on the preparation of teachers for language minority students (Garcia, 1990) and special-needs students (Reynolds, 1990). In reviewing the volume, Goodwin (1992) charges,

Measured against [a] multicultural standard, the handbook comes up exceedingly short and in fact perpetuates the notion of multiculturalism as an add-on concern. . . . While some authors have used multicultural education as one of several constructs to define the field, the majority have not. (p. 415)

In an introductory essay for the later volume, Grant (2008) observes that "while attention to mathematics, science, and technology is often at the forefront in discussions about what teachers need to know, attention to issues of diversity have for the most part been marginalized or omitted from the discourse" (p. 129). Accordingly, that volume contains a combination of framing chapters, commentaries, and artifacts that accord issues of equity and diversity a prominent place and tackle them from a range of perspectives (Grant & Agosto, 2008; Howard & Aleman, 2008; Kumashiro, 2008; Siddle Walker, 2008).

Recent developments in teacher education and among practicing teachers thus suggest heightened sensitivity to problems of enduring inequity in educational opportunity and outcomes together with more vigorous efforts to muster programmatic responses. Research has also multiplied during this period, with studies focused in part on the level and type of institutional investment in multicultural or antiracist teacher preparation (Zeichner, 1996) and more specifically on the effectiveness of selected strategies for cultivating intercultural sensitivity and developing intercultural teaching competence (Ladson-Billings, 1999). Yet the progress in institutional change and the growth in research have both proved markedly uneven. As Hollins and Guzman (2005) sum up in their comprehensive review,

> Basic changes in teacher education for diversity are necessary, but have not occurred despite 25 years of attention; although some studies suggest a positive impact of teacher preparation approaches, the findings about preparing teachers for diversity are generally inconsistent and inconclusive; outcome measures are not well developed; and there are too few longitudinal or large-scale studies, whereas there are many short-term and small-scale studies that have little general application. (p. 479)

The available research has served to identify a small number of programs with ambitious visions and well-developed strategies (Ladson-Billings, 1999) but has also yielded sobering results. First, the scale of effort remains relatively modest, typically taking the form of designated courses that may be elective rather than compulsory and that encapsulate issues of diversity rather than integrating them as a fundamental feature of professional preparation (Ghosh, 1996; Grant, 1993; Hickling-Hudson & McMeniman,1996; Hollins & Guzman, 2005; Zeichner, 1996). Second, programmatic developments are relatively constrained in scope and vision, with the result that many teacher educators and teachers view "multicultural education" as something only for those who will teach in particular kinds of classrooms and schools. Absent is a broader perspective on educating all children for life in plural societies (Craft, 1996) or equipping teachers to perceive and address underlying institutional structures and processes that perpetuate inequity (Cochran-Smith, 2004).

Finally, the empirical research literature that focuses on preparing teachers to work in classrooms with a diverse population of students, or with students whose backgrounds are unlike their own, suggests this to be a task of considerable magnitude. Some progress appears evident, if hard-won, in cases where admission procedures screen candidates on the basis of demonstrated cultural sensitivity and commitments to social justice; where a multicultural, intercultural, or antiracist perspective pervades the program; where field experiences are structured to build the necessary competence and confidence to work in classrooms, schools, and communities; and where prospective teachers are engaged in activity that requires them to delve deeply into their own assumptions and beliefs while also developing orientations and practices that will help them succeed (Cochran-Smith, 2004; Ladson-Billings, 1999; Zeichner, 1996; for an example of research with practicing teachers, see Comber & Kamler, 2004). The available studies offer testimony to the complexities entailed in such preparation, but few go beyond tracing effects on prospective or practicing teachers' awareness and sensitivity to gauge the longer-term benefit to teachers' classroom practices, relationships with students and parents, and disposition toward equity as a fundamental value in teaching (Ladson-Billings, 1999). Furthermore, most have focused on the experience of White teachers in preparing to teach students of color; only recently have studies begun to emerge that chronicle the challenges that may confront teachers of color as well (Achinstein, Ogawa, Sexton, & Freitas, 2009). And finally, the task of preparation is complicated by prospective and practicing teachers' own expectations and preferences for where and whom they will teach.

Teachers' Preferences Regarding Where and Whom They Teach

As student populations diversify, gaps in achievement persist or widen, and school staffing difficulties remain concentrated in urban and poor communities, one issue is where new and practicing teachers seek or accept employment. In numerous studies of teacher employment and mobility, teachers—especially White teachers—opt for schools with low enrollments of poor, minority, or low-performing students. In a review of research on preservice teachers, Gay et al. (2003) report, "Most students in teacher education programs expressed preferences for teaching students like themselves, and in communities similar to their own" (p. 9). In a review of developments in multicultural education, Ladson-Billings (1999) concludes that "teacher education programs are filled with prospective candidates who have no desire to teach in schools where students are from racial, ethnic, or linguistic backgrounds different from their own" (p. 224).

Teachers' preferences also manifest in the career decisions of practicing teachers, characterized more fully below. Researchers engaged in the New York City Pathways Study have produced a series of articles on early-stage career choices and transitions. In an article focused on the career decisions of high-achieving teachers in schools with low-performing students, they reported, "Teachers, especially highly qualified teachers, are more likely to transfer or quit when teaching lower-achieving students, even after accounting for student and teacher race" (Boyd, Lankford, Loeb, & Wyckoff, 2005). Those findings are echoed in recent analyses of state-level data sets in the United States (Hanushek, Kain, & Rivkin, 2004; Scafidi, Sjoquist, & Stinebrickner, 2007).

Each of these four aspects of the teacher workforce—the degree to which teachers are academically equipped for the work of teaching, the correspondence between the demographics of the student population and the teacher workforce, teachers' preparation for work with diverse students and families, and teachers' predilections regarding where and whom they teach—form the backdrop for contemporary debates about teacher quality and the crafting of policy responses.

CONTEMPORARY POLICY PERSPECTIVES
ON TEACHER QUALITY

A comprehensive policy perspective on teacher quality would most certainly encompass the qualifications and dispositions of individual teachers, the collective capacity and commitments of the teacher workforce, and the observable quality and effectiveness of classroom teaching. On the whole, however, contemporary policy discourse has conceived the terrain in more narrowly defined terms. Policy initiatives have tended to emphasize academic background versus other dimensions of teacher quality and to concentrate attention on individual qualifications and incentives rather than on employing organizations and the organizational conditions associated with teacher effectiveness and retention. Policy rationales emphasize current or projected shortages in selected subject areas (math, science, special education) or in euphemistically labeled "hard-to-staff" schools,[9] or they point to a differential distribution of qualified teachers that further disadvantages schools in poor communities. From such rationales flow policy remedies designed to improve teacher supply and bolster the qualifications of staff in schools with chronically low profiles of academic performance.

Qualification to Teach

Recent comparative studies in a range of fields—engineering, medicine, law, social work, and the ministry as well as teaching—focus on the role of formal preparation in cultivating the distinctive knowledge, skills, dispositions, identities, and relationships associated with work in each professional domain (Foster, Dahill, Goleman, & Tolentino, 2006; Sheppard, Macatangay, Colby, & Sullivan, 2009; Sullivan, Colby, Wegner, Bond, & Shulman, 2007). In education, unlike most other fields, contentious debates center on whether and in what way professional education—or more specifically, initial training in both general and subject-specific pedagogy, classroom management, instructional planning, student assessment, child or adolescent development, and theories of learning—should be considered an essential prerequisite for the work of *teaching*.

Of course, fields vary in the extent to which professional preparation actually maps fully onto the professional work itself. Legal education, firmly steeped in the tradition of legal analysis, has long relied on the case method to teach the foundational skills and habits of "thinking like a lawyer" but has devoted little attention to the actual practices of "lawyering" (Sullivan et al., 2007). Similarly, engineers have been required to acquire scientific and mathematical knowledge germane to the field of engineering, but only recently have engineering schools begun to consider various practical contingencies of successful engineering work (Sheppard et al., 2009). That said, there seems no question that legitimate entry into each of these fields requires some capacity that prior professional education is thought to supply.

Policymakers, education leaders, and researchers across a wide spectrum agree that teachers should themselves be well educated and that they should have sufficient depth of knowledge in the subjects they are employed to teach (Zeichner, 2003). However, each group is divided as to the special preparation for teaching that teachers should require prior to taking on the responsibilities of a classroom. A distinctive element in the discourse and debates related to teacher qualifications, therefore, is the increasingly vigorous debate between those who maintain that extended professional preparation for teaching is essential, given the scope and complexity of the work (Darling-Hammond, 2006; Darling-Hammond & Bransford, 2005) and those who assert that the essential skills of teaching will best develop through job experience and through the aid of contextually relevant professional development activity (Hess, 2001).

Not surprisingly, the two groups are divided in their assessment of what preservice preparation has to offer. Critics of the teacher education system contend that the field lacks agreement on an accepted body of practice as well as a body of empirical research that would aid such consensus. Hess (2001) maintains that in education, unlike medicine or law, "there is no canon. While there is some agreement on what teachers should know, there is no consensus on how to train good teachers or ensure that they have mastered essential skills or knowledge" (p. 1). Proponents of teacher education would acknowledge that not all programs are exemplary but would nonetheless assert that a strong knowledge base can be derived from research on teaching and teacher development; in that light, the solution to the uneven quality in professional education would be to strengthen rather than dispense with it. Reflective of this latter perspective is the recent volume *Preparing Teachers for a Changing World* (Darling-Hammond & Bransford, 2005), the result of the Committee on Teacher Education convened by the National Academy of Education in the United States. Its chapters represent an effort to summarize "what teachers know and should be able to do" in domains that include, among others, the teaching of subject matter, teaching diverse students, managing classrooms, and assessing learning. This position gains some reinforcement from international studies indicating that higher-achieving countries tend to invest in teacher education, exerting regulatory control while also supporting coherent programs of induction (McKenzie & Santiago, 2005).

Equity considerations loom large in the justificatory rhetoric employed by *both* the supporters and the critics of preservice professional education. In their introduction to the National Academy of Education volume cited previously, Bransford, Darling-Hammond, and LePage (2005) explain,

In addition to preparing teachers to learn throughout their lifetimes, we seek to describe the initial understandings that teachers need to serve adequately the very *first* students they teach. We believe that these students, like all others, are entitled to sound instruction and cannot afford to lose a year of schooling to a teacher who is ineffective or learning by trial and error on the job. This is especially important since beginning teachers—and those who are unprepared—are disproportionately assigned to teach students in low-income, high-minority schools and students in lower track classes who need skilled teachers in order to succeed. (p. 3)

Similarly, the preface to Hess's (2001) critique orients readers to

> what we must do in order to formulate policies that work for our nation's students, particularly the most disadvantaged amongst them. It is worth noting that our most vulnerable youngsters are most impacted by the quality shortfall in our nation's teaching force. (p. 3)

Hess seeks more flexible recruitment and hiring conditions as an alternative to teacher assignment practices that systematically disadvantage some students: "The situation is even more troubling than it appears, since many large school systems have classrooms filled with uncertified teachers and long-term substitutes" (p. 3).

The Differential Distribution of Qualified and Effective Teachers

Although the composition of the workforce—its academic strength and demographics—has been a repeated focus of historical accounts (Clifford, 1989; Rury, 1989) as well as in research in sociology and economics (Lortie, 1975; Murnane et al., 1991; Waller, 1932), the *distribution* of the teacher workforce has now emerged as an equity issue and a focus of current research and policy attention. Commenting on the situation in the United States, Murnane and Steele (2007) assert,

> The unequal distribution of effective teachers is perhaps the most urgent problem facing American education. Poor children and children of color are disproportionately assigned to teachers who have the least preparation and the weakest academic backgrounds, and this pattern is long-standing. (p. 36)

Public and policy-level concern about the differential distribution of teachers—and the consequences of that distribution along various equity dimensions—is a relatively new development, although the phenomenon itself is not (Becker, 1951). When the commissioned report *A Nation at Risk* was published in the United States in 1983, stimulating a wave of "omnibus" reform initiatives at the state level, its critique of teaching focused on the modest academic qualifications of the existing teacher workforce and the insufficient supply of appropriately qualified teachers in the specialized areas of math, science, foreign languages, and special education.[10] Absent from that report was any explicit concern that qualified teachers might be differentially distributed in ways that systematically advantaged some schools and students and systematically disadvantaged others.

That picture has changed. Evidence of the differential distribution of qualified teachers constitutes a prominent feature of reports issued by or for government agencies, and more equitable distribution has become the focus of academic and policy research. Policy initiatives in some countries (such as No Child Left Behind in the United States) together with the availability of large-scale databases (e.g., the SASS and selected state databases) and the high visibility of international comparative studies (Third International Mathematics and Science Study [TIMSS], Program for International Student Assessment [PISA]) have fueled an interest not only in the relative selectivity of the teacher workforce but also in the distribution of teachers deemed qualified.

Three problematic patterns surface consistently in an array of reports, public presentations, and published research: the high proportion of underqualified and inexperienced teachers employed by schools with the least advantaged students and families; the likelihood of out-of-field teaching by otherwise fully certified teachers in such schools; and the propensity of better-educated and better-qualified teachers to leave such schools rapidly even if hired. The differential distribution of qualified teachers thus presents what Zeichner (2003) terms the "demographic imperative" for teacher education and teacher policy: "The most striking aspect of the current demographic situation in our public schools and teacher education institutions is that the effects of teacher shortages and the provision of qualified teachers have been felt unequally by different groups" (p. 493; see also Cochran-Smith, 2004).

The distribution of the teacher workforce results not only from entering qualifications but also from teachers' decisions to remain in a school, change schools or districts, or leave teaching altogether. The existence of large-scale databases has enabled scholars not only to trace movements in and out of teaching but also to see the extent to which attrition and turnover are localized. These patterns consistently work to the disadvantage of schools enrolling low-income and minority students. Multiple studies report an inverse relationship between teacher qualifications and student poverty, minority enrollment, English language learner status, and school performance (Goe, 2002; Guha, Shields, Tiffany-Morales, Bland, & Campbell, 2008). Citing recent studies in several regions of the United States, Goldhaber, Choi, and Cramer (2007) sum up, "By almost any measure, highly qualified teachers are inequitably distributed across districts, schools, and classrooms" (p. 161).

Among industrial nations, the United States stands out for a persistent "maldistribution" of qualified and experienced teachers. Akiba, LeTendre, and Scribner (2007) employed TIMSS data from 46 countries to examine eighth graders' access to qualified mathematics teachers, defining teacher quality in terms of full certification, an undergraduate degree in mathematics or mathematics education, and 3 years or more of teaching experience. They found that average teacher quality in the United States is comparable to that in other nations but that "the opportunity gap in students' access to qualified teachers between students of high and low socioeconomic status (SES) was among the largest in the world" (p. 369).

An issue, of course, is what propels such an opportunity gap. Evidence suggests that explanations reside both in teacher dispositions and/or career choices and in state and local policies, practices, and workplace conditions. With regard to the former, studies find consistently that teachers elect to teach in schools with relatively advantaged student enrollment and profiles of high achievement and to avoid schools in poverty-stricken areas, especially those with high minority enrollments (Hanushek, Kain, & Rivkin, 2001). Minority enrollment looms especially large as a factor in at least one recent study. By merging three sources of data on all public elementary teachers and elementary schools in the state of Georgia, researchers were able to evaluate school performance, students' economic status, and the percentage of minority enrollment as factors in teacher mobility (Scafidi, Sjoquist, & Stinebrickner, 2007). As in other studies, teachers were found "more likely to change schools—both within and across districts—if they begin their teaching careers in schools with lower student test scores, schools with lower income students, or schools that have higher proportions of minority students" (Scafidi et al., 2007, p. 146), but minority enrollment emerged as the dominant explanatory factor. The authors acknowledge that "there has been substantial reference to a perception that teachers are much more likely to leave high poverty schools" but add,

> Our results indicate that, while this perception is correct, it occurs because teachers are more likely to leave a particular type of poor school—one that has a large proportion of minority students. More generally, the main policy point . . . is very direct—if a policymaker is interested in understanding retention and attrition issues, then it is of importance to gain a better understanding of what is happening at schools with high minority rates. (Scafidi et al., 2007, pp. 152–153)

However, individual predilections and decisions do not fully account for the supply and distribution of well-qualified teachers. Throughout the history of public schooling, hiring and teacher assignment practices have routinely (if selectively) subordinated academic background to other considerations, including judgments regarding a teacher's character, likely skill in "keeping school" or classroom management, general perceived fit with the school and community, or sheer availability (Elsbree, 1939). The result of local hiring practices has been a wide range of academic qualifications and a differential distribution of academically well-prepared teachers.

Although much of the monitoring of teacher workforce distribution focuses on the district or school level, students experience the reality of teacher competence in the more intimate confines of the classroom. Analyses of the SASS data confirm that American schools vary substantially in the incidence of out-of-field teaching, with urban schools having significantly higher rates (Ingersoll, 2002). Again, the United States compares unfavorably with other nations in this respect. As Akiba et al. (2007) report, eighth graders studying mathematics in the United States are as likely as students elsewhere to have "fully certified" teachers but among the least likely (41st out of 46 countries) to have teachers with a major in mathematics or mathematics education. The authors underscore the importance of their finding with regard to students' access to a sound education:

> This research highlights the importance of access to quality public education as one of the few mechanisms available in the United States to counterbalance the transmission of social status and privilege. Access to high-quality teachers, then, appears essential to mitigating long-term social inequality in the absence of other policy levers. Unlike other nations with more developed social welfare or youth ministries, the United States traditionally has relied on school-based measures to ameliorate the effects of poverty. (p. 370)

In their study of teacher assignment in Houston, a large employer of alternatively certified teachers, Darling-Hammond, Holtzman, Gatlin, and Heilig (2005) found that teachers without standard certification . . . were disproportionately likely to be teaching African American and Latino students and low-income students. Although the percentages of Houston students being taught by standard-certified teachers rose substantially over the [6] years covered by this study, the racial/ethnic and economic disparities associated with students' access to certified teachers also increased substantially. . . . This suggests that as Houston hired and retained greater numbers of certified teachers, these teachers were disproportionately distributed to higher-income students and white students. (pp. 13–14)

Another face of the maldistribution of teachers, both within and across schools, centers on students' access to teachers designated as exceptionally well prepared. The relatively large pool of National Board Certified Teachers (NBCTs) in the state of North Carolina—approximately 1 in 17 teachers as of 2003—provided one opportunity to test the idea that identifying and recognizing highly accomplished teachers might in turn create a staffing resource for schools struggling with low performance or enrolling the most disadvantaged students. Employing a state database that tracks the placement and movement of all North Carolina teachers at the district, school, and classroom levels, Goldhaber et al. (2007) found that board-certified teachers were more likely to be teaching in "advantaged" settings at every level (district, school, and classroom). Indeed, the differential distribution became more pronounced with each move closer to actual teacher-student interaction:

The teacher sorting we observe becomes more pronounced as we move from the district to the classroom. . . . Not only are NBCTs unequally distributed across districts, but within districts they are unequally distributed across schools, and within schools they are unequally distributed across classrooms. (p. 166)

Taken together, these two perspectives—a widespread concern for the maldistribution of qualified teachers but deeply divided views regarding the requirements that should be satisfied to enter teaching—manifest in multiple and competing policy solutions to problems of teacher quality.

POLICY DIRECTIONS IN THE PURSUIT OF TEACHER QUALITY

In their account of the "profound institutional change" marking the American health care industry in the second half of the 20th century, Scott, Ruef, Mendel, and Caronna (2000) trace three consequential trajectories: the decline of professional hegemony, the rise of federal responsibility and regulation, and the relatively recent but rapid ascendance of market logics and actors.[11] The current era, they conclude, marks a period in which the "three logics—professional, public, corporate—are all present, active, and contending with one another" (p. 316). It is an era they view as institutionally unstable, one of the simultaneous destructuration and restructuration of the field.[12]

We maintain that the same dynamic contention obtains in education and, more specifically, in discourse and decision making surrounding teachers and teaching. Although education has never enjoyed the level of professional stature and autonomy accorded to medicine, and has generally evolved as a creature of the state, the competing logics of professional autonomy and government control are readily evident in virtually every policy debate and interwoven in policy or reform initiatives.

Professional associations and interest groups, including but not restricted to unions, have proven to be influential actors in shaping government initiatives and regulations (DeBray, 2006). That is, for most of the past century, throughout the rise of mass education systems, the prevailing perspectives and governing mechanisms have been those of the profession and the state.

Yet what education now shares with American medicine is the dramatic rise of market logics and the growing role of corporate entities, think tanks, and other "non-system" actors (Coburn, 2005) in defining teacher quality and influencing education policy. In their review of the literature on alternative certification, Birkeland and Peske (2004) characterize the debate about certification and licensure as one between advocates of regulation and advocates of the market:

Participants in the public and scholarly debate about alternative certification usually identify with one of two positions, often characterized in opposition to each other: a market-based, or anti-regulatory approach, and advocacy for strict regulation of entrants to teaching and their preparation. (p. 10)

As summarized by the authors, the regulatory position "maintains that improving teacher quality by increasing standards of accreditation, licensing, and certification will, in turn, promote a profession that is more appealing to highly-qualified candidates, who will eventually enter teaching, thus increasing the supply" (Birkeland & Peske, 2004, p. 10). In contrast, market-oriented critics argue that such a policy stance

will raise barriers to entry. . . . These market advocates focus on the problem of the shortage, and are primarily concerned with promoting greater access to non-traditional teaching candidates, such as mid-career candidates, whom they contend will improve the quality of the teaching force. (Birkeland & Peske, 2004, pp. 11–12; see also Hess, 2001)

Although the Birkeland and Peske (2004) review focuses specifically on alternative certification, the debates they describe also populate the discourse on teacher quality more broadly. In his essay on contemporary reform orientations in the education of teachers, for example, Zeichner (2003) outlines three reform agendas: professionalization, which relies in part on state legitimation and incorporates state regulation; deregulation and the development of markets; and social justice. The first two parallel the regulatory and market positions outlined by Birkeland and Peske, both linked to the human capital orientation outlined earlier. The third agenda, associated largely with teacher education organizations and with researchers and educators interested in multicultural education, focuses on the recruitment, preparation, and retention of teachers of color (Achinstein et al., 2009; Gay et al., 2003) and on what has been termed culturally responsive teaching (Ladson-Billings, 1999; C. D. Lee, 1995).

Zeichner (2003) maintains that each of the agendas has roots in long-standing traditions of educational debate and reform. Thus, the professionalization agenda

represents the current incarnation of what has been referred to as the social efficiency tradition of reform in teacher education—the quest to establish a profession of teaching through the articulation of a knowledge base for teaching based on educational research and professional judgment. (p. 498)[13]

The market agenda, although linked in contemporary discourse to "the larger neo-liberal and neoconservative agendas to privatize and deregulate K–12 schooling in the United States"—and elsewhere, as Luke (2004) observes—can also be viewed as an outgrowth of the "academic tradition" in the United States, with its long-standing critiques of the teacher education establishment (Zeichner, 2003, p. 502). The social justice agenda finds its roots in what Zeichner (2003) terms the "social reconstructionist" tradition in which "both schooling and teacher education [are seen] as crucial elements in the making of a more just society" (p. 507).

However deep the roots of these three traditions, they have achieved unequal purchase in contemporary policy domains. Policy actors in industrialized nations have employed rationales derived from equity dilemmas but have done so less often to pursue explicit social justice goals than to frame and pursue policy responses consistent with the professionalization and market logics. In the discussion that follows, we highlight four policy responses that in combination have potential to reshape the teacher workforce in communities where the maldistribution of teachers constitutes a particularly pressing problem. In each case, we have characterized the policy response and then taken up the question of the available evidence that might help us gauge its value as a means of strengthening teacher quality.

Financial Incentives

Consistent with the rise of market logics, policy initiatives turn with some regularity to the proposition that financial incentives will stimulate the recruitment and retention of academically well-prepared teachers and supply inducements for individuals to teach in high-shortage subject areas or in schools most in need. There is some evidence that overall levels of compensation are associated with variations in teacher quality. Ladd (2007) reports,

"In high-salary OECD countries such as Germany, Japan, and Korea, the share of [underqualified] teachers in primary and secondary schools is low: less than 4%, as against more than 10% in countries such as Sweden and the United States, where salaries (relative to GDP per capita) are low" (p. 203).

However, countries vary in the extent to which teacher hiring and wage setting are centralized, making national comparisons problematic. In a study focused on local teacher labor markets in the United States, Figlio (1997) drew on SASS data to determine whether the higher-paying districts within 19 large metropolitan areas were able to attract more highly qualified teachers. He found consistently that when controlling for other district factors that might influence teachers' choices, the higher-paying districts were better able to attract teachers from selective undergraduate institutions and teachers who had completed majors in mathematics, science, computer science, or engineering.

After teachers are hired, however, their decisions regarding staying, moving schools or districts, or leaving teaching altogether, although not insensitive to matters of compensation (Loeb & Page, 2000), appear to be shaped heavily by working conditions. Hanushek and Rivkin (2007) found that teachers in Texas who moved from urban to suburban school districts achieved a very small average salary gain (less than half of 1%) but did experience a difference in student population—higher achieving, with fewer minority and low-income families—and in other school-level working conditions. They sum up, "Our analysis of teacher mobility showed that salary affects mobility patterns less than do working conditions, such as facilities, safety, and quality of leadership. Compensation alone, it seems clear, is but a partial measure of the returns to work" (Hanushek & Rivkin, 2007, p. 82; see also Ingersoll, 2001).

Furthermore, although overall level of compensation may be a factor in a district's or school's ability to attract high-quality teachers, it is less clear that incentives targeted specifically at shortages in particular fields, geographic locations, or low-performing schools operate in the intended way. For example, researchers associated with the Harvard Project on the Next Generation of Teachers employ the case of the Massachusetts Signing Bonus program to demonstrate the limitation of this particular policy instrument as a means to achieve intended outcomes, specifically, the recruitment and retention of well-prepared teachers in hard-to-staff schools (Liu, Johnson, & Peske, 2004). Interviews with recipients of the signing bonus—an amount of $20,000 awarded to eligible new hires—revealed flaws in the policy's theory of action: its assumption that the money would constitute a compelling incentive (the associated alternative certification opportunity mattered more), that incremental payments across 4 years would encourage retention (working conditions were more salient in shaping teachers' decisions), and that recipients of the bonus would be streamlined into schools in need (there was no mechanism to orchestrate placement in such schools). Although limited to one case, this study casts doubt on the viability of relatively modest front-end pecuniary incentives for teacher recruitment and hiring, especially in the absence of corresponding nonpecuniary incentives or advantages in the form of favorable working conditions. Similarly, research on performance-based pay plans shows that such plans often yield unintended outcomes that compromise the aims of the program. In a review of research on plans involving both individual- and school-level or group rewards, Lavy (2007) finds evidence that programs in Israel, Kenya, the United Kingdom, and the United States resulted in significant short-term improvements in student outcomes, student learning, and school completion. However, the research also points to demonstrated problems with the implementation and sustainability of such initiatives, including the cost of adequate measurement and monitoring.

The Proliferation of Pathways Into Teaching

Intensified recruitment efforts have spawned a debate about whether academic qualifications are sufficient for entry into teaching or whether teachers require additional professional preparation, a debate that has occurred in the context of a growing market of alternative pathways into teaching, especially in the United States, United Kingdom, Australia, and New Zealand. As Grossman and McDonald (2008) remark, "Alternative routes are now part of the broad landscape of teacher education and are major players in preparing teachers" (p. 194); they also caution that the conventional terminology of *alternative* versus *traditional* has lost meaning, given the wide variation in programs and the fact that many "alternative" programs are located within colleges and universities. Within the United States, Zumwalt and Craig (2005b) identified "some sort of approved alternative certification program" (p. 170) in nearly all of the 50 states and observed that "definitions of 'certification' have been adjusted to widen the teacher supply pool" (p. 181). In a chapter of the recent OECD report that focuses on "making teaching an attractive career choice," McKenzie and Santiago (2005) indicate that 17 of 25 countries surveyed offer alternative pathways into teaching and that "in almost all countries for which information is available . . . it is possible to start working as a teacher before completing the preparation in pedagogy" (p. 84). The report explains,

Countries face difficult challenges in balancing the requirements to increase the supply of prospective teachers while at the same time maintaining or hopefully improving teacher quality. However, most countries are now seeking more flexible approaches to both teacher education and entry into the field. These new approaches are intended to help address teacher shortages, as well as to bring new types of skills and experience into schools. (McKenzie & Santiago, 2005, p. 84)

Alternative route programs target a number of quite different populations, among them graduates of elite colleges who are persuaded to undertake teaching as a form of public service on their way to other lucrative careers; mature individuals who have established careers in industry or the military and who, in making a transition into teaching, bring with them knowledge and experience in specialized fields; and education paraprofessionals who have accumulated classroom experience and demonstrated commitment to students in low-performing schools but who generally lack the formal education necessary to qualify for a teaching credential.

Although not all alternative pathways are intended or designed to enhance the supply of teachers in "hard-to-staff" schools,[14] many of the most widely publicized among them link their recruitment efforts directly to persistent problems of educational disadvantage. Thus, Teach for America (TFA) announces that its central aim is to "end educational inequity."[15] Troops to Teachers (United States) describes one of its major purposes as recruiting teachers for schools that serve low-income families. Teach First (United Kingdom) purports to "address educational disadvantage" by placing top college graduates in "challenged secondary schools." The New York City Teaching Fellows program seeks individuals dedicated to "[raising] student achievement in the New York City classrooms that need them the most." And Teach for Australia recruits "high-achieving graduates" to be one of the "innovative solutions" needed to remedy persistent "pockets of disadvantage" in what is portrayed as an otherwise strong educational system. A few programs specifically embrace the goal of diversifying the teacher workforce by recruiting teachers from ethnic, racial, or cultural minority backgrounds (Humphrey, Wechsler, & Hough, 2008).

The rapid growth of alternative pathways beginning in the mid-1980s provoked a certain degree of controversy but also stimulated a steadily expanding program of research (for reviews of this body of research, see Wilson, Floden, & Ferrini-Mundy, 2002; Zeichner & Conklin, 2005). That research has been organized to pursue three main questions: whether alternative pathways succeed in attracting a more academically well-prepared and more diverse teacher workforce; whether teachers recruited via such pathways prove as effective as conventionally prepared teachers, as measured by gains in students' academic achievement scores; and finally, whether teachers who enter through streamlined pathways then remain in teaching.

The first of those questions proves complicated by the wide variation in the pool of candidates targeted by different programs, from paraprofessionals already working in urban schools to graduates of elite colleges, and in the selectivity of the undergraduate institutions attended by those candidates (Humphrey et al., 2008). Using a measure of self-reported alternative certification in the 1993–1994 SASS data, Shen (1997) found that "the data on both bachelor's degree and highest degree suggested that [alternative certification] failed to attract personnel with higher academic qualifications" (p. 279). However, Gitomer's (2007) more recent analysis of Educational Testing Service data on two cohorts of Praxis II test takers found that individuals in the latter cohort who were designated as pursuing an "alternative route" had somewhat higher college entrance (SAT) examination scores than those pursuing a traditional route, although they did not pass the Praxis II test at a higher rate. There is also evidence that at least some alternative pathways have succeeded in attracting a more diverse group of prospective teachers (Boyd, Grossman, Lankford, Loeb, & Wyckoff, 2005) as well as teachers who may be more willing to teach in urban schools enrolling low-income students (Zeichner & Conklin, 2005).

Variations in legal requirements for certification and in the design of programs also present problems for studies attempting to examine the contribution of alternative pathways to various outcomes of interest, including teacher retention and classroom effectiveness. Researchers have in some instances responded by creating operational definitions that permit more systematic comparisons, for example, definitions centered on the timing and amount of course-based professional preparation prior to assuming a full-time teaching assignment. A further adaptation to wide programmatic and policy variation has been to shift from multiple-site studies to designs centered on particular teacher labor markets, especially those centered on the large cities where teachers from alternative pathways tend to be concentrated. One example is the New York City Pathways Study, a longitudinal study that permits a close examination of the relationships among multiple pathways, individual teacher characteristics, teaching contexts, and various outcomes (Boyd et al., 2006).

Efforts to determine the relative effectiveness of teachers from alternative route programs, many of them focused specifically on comparisons involving TFA recruits, have yielded mixed results. For example, Laczko-Kerr and Berliner's (2002) study of a matched sample of traditionally certified and "undercertified" teachers found that students of fully certified teachers outperformed those of undercertified teachers; similarly, a study of fourth- and fifth-grade student achievement across a 6-year period in Houston (a large employer of alternative route teachers, including TFA recruits) found that certified teachers "consistently produce significantly stronger student achievement gains than do uncertified teachers" (Darling-Hammond et al., 2005, p. 2). Both studies found certification status to be the defining factor but otherwise found no difference in the performance of students assigned to teachers originally recruited by TFA versus other programs or routes. However, Kane, Rockoff, and Staiger (2008), employing 6 years of student test data to gauge the effectiveness of certified, uncertified, and alternatively certified teachers in New York City, found little difference in average effectiveness across those certification categories but substantial variation within each one. Researchers associated with a Mathematica Policy Research study found that students who were randomly assigned to TFA teachers did better in mathematics and about the same in reading when compared to students randomly assigned to other teachers in the same school (Decker, Mayer, & Glazerman, 2004). Citing methodological critiques of the Mathematica study, Glass (2008) observes, "As with so many issues in education research, the relative effectiveness of alternatively certified teachers dissolves into arguments about recondite matters of statistical methods" (p. 14).

Yet the contrasting findings among studies have arguably pushed researchers to sharpen definitions, craft research designs more able to withstand scrutiny, and identify assumptions and limitations more fully. The New York City Pathways Study, although not an experimental design, benefits from its ability to link individual, pathway, and school-level data to investigate the influence of pathway features and teachers' reported preparation experiences on student learning gains and teacher retention. An important advance in the Pathways Study is its ability to remedy the limitations of simple program designations (e.g., TFA) as proxies for program design and teachers' preparation experience by specifying pathway features and surveying teachers' preparation experiences. Boyd and colleagues (Boyd, Grossman, Lankford, Loeb, & Wyckoff, 2008) find that

features of teacher preparation can make a difference in outcomes for students. One factor stands out. Teacher preparation that focuses more on the work of the classroom and provides opportunities for teachers to study what they will be doing produces teachers who are more effective during their first year of teaching. (p. 26)[16]

An analysis of outcomes associated with four pathways—traditional "college recommended," TFA, New York City Teaching Fellows, and an "individual evaluation" option—underscores the complexity of judging the relative value of alternative routes (Boyd et al., 2005). By comparison with teachers from conventional college pathways, TFA recruits did roughly as well in elementary mathematics and better in middle school mathematics but significantly worse at both levels in the area of reading and language arts; Teaching Fellows struggled for effectiveness in both subjects and at both levels. Teaching experience yielded positive gains between the 1st and 2nd year for both groups, especially in mathematics, but attrition rates were also high, especially among TFA recruits: 85% after 4 years, compared with 37% of college recommended teachers and 54% of Teaching Fellows.

Teaching for the Short Term

Some of the most widely publicized recruitment ventures explicitly promote short-term teaching in "hard-to-staff" schools. TFA calls for a 2-year commitment to teach in poor urban or rural schools, as does Teach First (United Kingdom) and the newly formed Teach for Australia; although reliable retention figures are hard to come by, indications are that relatively few of the recruits to these programs intend a career in teaching or remain in classroom teaching beyond the end of the required commitment (Humphrey et al., 2008).[17] In their comparative study of new teachers in New York City who entered teaching via TFA, the New York City Teaching Fellows Program, or traditional college-recommending programs, Boyd et al. (2005) found the highest attrition (more than 80%) among TFA teachers and the lowest among those who had been recruited and prepared through conventional programs. However, among those teachers placed in the most challenging schools, with the highest recorded turnover, the retention rates did not vary greatly between those from conventional programs (45%) and recruits to the New York City Teaching Fellows (55%), suggesting that alternative routes differ in consequential ways in the stance they adopt toward teaching as short-term service.

Long-term careers in teaching evolved from more temporary, part-time work as school systems grew in size, school terms lengthened, and teachers secured more stable salaries and conditions of work (Rury, 1989).[18] Yet as an occupation, school teaching has continued to incorporate part-time positions (McKenzie & Santiago, 2005) and short-term work as well as the kind of "in-and-out" career pattern historically associated with women teachers' taking time away for child rearing (Lortie, 1975).[19] Indeed, some have observed that school teaching, at least in the United States, is structured in ways that readily accommodate high rates of turnover, with relatively easy entry into the occupation (Lortie, 1975) and schools organized to require or support low levels of interdependence among teachers; exacerbating the turnover problem is the financial opportunity cost that escalates steadily for those who remain in teaching past the first year or two (Goldhaber, DeArmond, Liu, & Player, 2008; Johnson & Liu, 2004).

Nonetheless, policy concerns with teacher turnover and attrition have grown, intensified by the observation that classroom effectiveness increases with experience, especially within the first several years (Béteille & Loeb, 2009) and that "high-need" schools and districts are those most likely to be affected by a chronic churn of relatively inexperienced teachers (Allensworth, Ponisciak, & Mazzeo, 2009). What makes "teaching for the short term" particularly interesting in this context, then, is its centrality as a purported boost to teacher quality in poor schools and districts. The underlying premise of programs adopting this strategy is that young, highly educated individuals will stimulate achievement and motivation in low-performing schools, even if they remain only a short period; a corollary but more implicit premise is that high turnover of such teachers will do no harm to students or schools, presuming that programs and schools are able to recruit a steady supply.

To produce such a steady supply of short-term recruits to high-need schools and districts, programs engage in a recruitment strategy that couples elements of high selectivity, altruism, temporary sacrifice, and longer-term career self-interest. Programs recruit candidates from highly regarded colleges and universities, selecting and placing a relatively small proportion of those who apply. The programs appeal to the graduates' political and social idealism while also positioning them to benefit socially and materially from their short-term experience in challenging schools. Teach First and Teach for Australia both incorporate a "partnership and deferred entry" arrangement, by which the program and various corporate employers recruit jointly on campuses; successful candidates teach for 2 years while also receiving various kinds of training that will ease their transition to corporate careers. A recent press release announcing the formation of Teach for Australia highlights this aspect of the program's appeal, subordinating "positive societal impact" to the participants' likely career benefits:

Teach First and Teach For America are considered amongst the most prestigious employers in their respective nations, attracting graduates into teaching who would otherwise have gone into investment banking, consulting, law, engineering, medicine or other careers. These programs are considered launch pads for very successful careers (the list of alumni destinations is diverse and highly prestigious) as well as an opportunity to have a positive societal impact. (press release, Teach for Australia, April 21, 2009)[20]

To our knowledge, no research focuses specifically on assessing the consequences of the short-term recruitment strategy, that is, research that gets directly at the benefits or limitations of programs that promise a steady supply of highly educated, short-term recruits in comparison with other extant strategies for staffing high-need schools—strategies that may range from the fatalistic (accepting involuntary transfers, substitutes, or whomever else the school can get) to the aggressively entrepreneurial (establishing both pecuniary and nonpecuniary incentives and actively recruiting for talent, professional skills, and commitment). It seems likely that schools in a given labor market will vary to some extent along such a dimension, such that judging the short-term recruitment strategy begs the question, "Compared to what?"

Absent such research, existing studies of teacher turnover afford some purchase on the questions surrounding the "teaching for the short term" remedy. Certainly, such studies demonstrate the dismal state of staffing in high-need schools, showing consistently that turnover is higher in schools that enroll low-income students and/or minority students (Dolton & Newson, 2003). However, studies report mixed findings regarding the significance of high turnover for student achievement. Using data from a large Texas school district, Hanushek and Rivkin (2007) compare the relative value of stayers and leavers in terms of students' average test score gains in mathematics; they find that the teachers who remained in a given school were not lower in measured effectiveness than those who left. Kane et al. (2008) examined turnover among certified, uncertified, and alternatively certified teachers in New York City schools and the impact on student achievement of hiring teachers with predictably high turnover; finding that the students of alternatively certified teachers achieve as well as others in mathematics and only modestly worse in reading, they conclude that "even high turnover groups (such as Teach for America participants) would have to be only slightly more effective in each year to offset the negative effects of their high exit rates" (p. 615). A less sanguine view emerges from a recent study in Britain. For a study of 316 primary schools in the London area, Dolton and Newson (2003) assembled a database that combined individual teacher mobility data for the period from 1996 to 1999, information on selected school characteristics (including student demographics), and students' test results in English and mathematics in 2001. Although a school's measure of "social deprivation" (number of pupils eligible for free school lunch) was also a determining factor in achievement profiles, a school's average teacher turnover during the period from 1996 to 1999 was a significant predictor of student achievement in English and mathematics in 2001. None of these studies addresses the question of whether variations in a school's turnover rate over time can be shown to be associated with fluctuations in student achievement. However, as a set, the studies do little to relieve concern for attrition or to settle debates about the worth of the "teach for the short term" remedy.

Capitalizing on a Global Teacher Workforce

Increasingly, industrialized nations are recruiting teachers from developing nations to address labor shortfalls. Transnational teacher migration is evident in the shift of Commonwealth African teachers to England as well as in the growing movement of Filipino teachers to the United States (Bartlett, 2009; Edwards & Spreen, 2007; McNamara, Lewis, & Howson, 2007; Miller, 2007). Generally framed as a short-term solution that shifts teachers on the basis of labor market needs and demands, transnational teacher migration is premised on the notion that teachers' qualifications are readily transferable among countries and cultures. That said, some observers have acknowledged that "irregular recruitment practices associated with teacher migration" (Keevy, 2009, p. 4) may threaten the professional status of teachers and teaching. In an address to a conference of Commonwealth Education Ministers, Keevy (2009) argues for a Commonwealth-wide "standard for the professional registration of teachers" (p. 10)—in effect, a step toward a system of international reciprocity in the expectations for and recognition of teacher credentials (see also Morrow & Keevy, 2006).

The extent of the teacher labor flows between countries is not fully known, as national and international data on migration scope and pattern are not readily available. A 2003 National Education Association report estimated there were 10,000 "foreign" teachers in U.S. public schools on nonimmigrant visas (Barber, 2003), but Bartlett's (2009) analysis of California and a recent report issued by the American Federation of Teachers (2009) suggest this number is much larger today. Certainly, the overall numbers are relatively small as a proportion of the teacher workforce but perhaps no more so (especially in some local labor markets) than the number of those recruited through some of the more highly visible alternative route programs. At issue here is the policy logic associated with this recruitment strategy and its bearing on problems of equity.[21]

From the perspective of the certifying and employing organizations—states, districts, or schools—the hiring of overseas-trained teachers represents a set of trade-offs. Such teachers typically bring strong academic preparation and teaching experience acquired in their home countries, holding credentials that are equivalent to those earned by indigenously educated teachers (Kane et al., 2008); their recruitment thus constitutes one remedy for teacher shortages, especially in the subject areas of math, science, and special education. However, the hiring of overseas-trained teachers also presents certain dilemmas. In effect, the hiring of overseas-trained teachers privileges subject specialization over workforce stability, cultural knowledge, or community connections.

First, the positions of overseas-trained teachers tend to be relatively transient, with employment secured under the terms of work or cultural exchange visas. Teachers employed under such arrangements, although often very experienced in years of teaching and educational preparation, constitute a short-term, high-turnover workforce much like other short-term recruits; schools that rely on them are therefore vulnerable to higher rates of attrition.

Second, teacher migration may move teachers far from their cultural frame of reference. Despite the widespread observation that structural features of schooling have achieved a certain institutional isomorphism (Meyer & Ramirez, 2000), the daily work of teaching also reflects quite localized notions of what teachers and children are expected to do and achieve in classrooms as well as the relationships teachers are expected to form with colleagues, administrators, parents, and the community. For example, Anderson-Levitt's (2002) comparative study of first-grade classrooms in France and the United States shows considerable differences in teachers' ideas regarding the appropriate behavior of 6-year-olds and in the practices the teachers employed in teaching those 6-year-olds to read. In a video-based component of the study, Anderson-Levitt found that teachers from each country recognized similarities in each other's classroom environment but also expressed substantial surprise. For example, American teachers were surprised to see the use of cursive writing in French first-grade classrooms, judging 6-year-olds not "ready" for cursive; French teachers were surprised to see American 6-year-olds grouped together on a rug for reading time, viewing that as a practice to be left behind when children entered the "real work" of first grade. Anderson-Levitt asks, "So, what about the transnational, even universal, knowledge for teaching that many scholars seem to take for granted?"

(Anderson-Levitt, 2002, p. 110). Her answer is to acknowledge parallel aspects of school organization (both countries group 6-year-olds together for instruction in what is termed first grade) and point to certain "professional know-how" that reflects a transnational understanding of classroom culture, but also to argue that "teachers are similar across national boundaries only at a high level of abstraction. Most of the professional knowledge shared across national boundaries remains open-ended, abstract and bland until filled in with nation-specific details" (Anderson-Levitt, 2002, p. 110).

Similarly, Alexander (2001) introduces his five-nation study of primary education by observing, "Though a few comparative studies have ranged convincingly over several countries [such studies] concentrate their attention on the macro or national level and say little about the day-to-day workings of schools, still less hazard analysis of pedagogy" (p. 3). Furthermore, he argues,

> Though there are undoubted cross-cultural continuities and indeed universals in educational thinking and practice, no decision or action which one observes in a particular classroom . . . can be properly understood except by reference to the web of inherited ideas and values, habits and customs, institutions and world views which make one country, or one region, or one group, distinct from another. (p. 5)

Differences in culturally specific frames of reference for teaching, together with the absence of community knowledge and connections, thus seem likely to present challenges to the sense of efficacy experienced by overseas-trained teachers and to their demonstrated effectiveness. Such challenges would seem to require more support than one would ordinarily anticipate for experienced, professionally certified teachers. Research on this matter is scant to date, although Kane et al. (2008) find that the students of "internationally recruited teachers" in New York City scored lower on standardized math and reading tests than traditionally certified U.S. teachers. Although the analysis of international teachers' effectiveness was incidental to the overall focus of that study, and analysis did not extend to retention, it is the only research that documents these teachers' relative effectiveness using a large-scale, longitudinal data set.

These trade-offs acquire particular significance in light of the distribution of overseas-trained teachers in schools and classrooms. In England and in the United States, at least, such teachers are concentrated in certain demographic areas. Low-income communities in California draw disproportionately on the global market to ensure an adequate supply of teachers to meet the highly qualified teacher policy requirements (Bartlett, 2009). Schools in these communities have traded a historic reliance on underqualified teachers (emergency credentialed, out of field, intern, etc.) for professionally qualified teachers recruited from overseas. Yet by comparison with the high visibility of "alternative routes" into education, the hiring of overseas-trained teachers remains what Bartlett describes as a "hidden phenomenon" (Bartlett, 2009), as districts and schools are not required to report on the country of origin, education, or visa status of their workforce.

TOWARD A MORE COMPREHENSIVE MODEL
OF TEACHER QUALITY

The teacher workforce looms large as both a resource and a problem in the policy discourse that surrounds the dilemma of persistent educational inequity. At issue in that discourse have been the academic selectivity of the workforce, the fit between teacher demographics and those of the student population, the degree to which teachers are prepared to teach students with backgrounds unlike their own, and teachers' willingness to accept employment in schools with high proportions of minority, low-income, and low-performing students. Four policy responses—financial incentives, alternative pathways to certification, a reliance on short-term workforce participation, and the use of overseas-trained teachers—are indicative of the ascendance of market logics in the pursuit of teacher quality. These responses tend to demonstrate a greater emphasis on recruitment than on retention and to reflect a conception of workforce quality that centers on individual characteristics and choices.

Consistent with this policy perspective, a growing body of research, much of it conducted by labor economists on large-scale data sets, has focused on the relationship between teachers' backgrounds and characteristics (including the pathway by which they entered teaching) and the academic performance of the students they teach. Results have been mixed, attesting in part to the sheer messiness and complexity of the phenomena under investigation but also suggesting the need for a more elaborated explanatory model. Most studies still focus principally on the individual teacher as the unit of analysis and the focus of research interest; similarly, policy discourse tends to revolve around the qualifications and demonstrated effectiveness of individual teachers. Yet research, even while dominated by individual-level analyses, increasingly implicates institutional and organizational structures and processes in the construction of teacher quality. A prominent example is sociologist Richard Ingersoll's (2002) analyses of out-of-field teaching, teacher turnover (Ingersoll, 2001), and the differential distribution of qualified teachers (Ingersoll, 2004), each of which points to features of school-level working conditions and to local practices of hiring and teacher assignment in accounting for identified problems of teacher supply. One relatively recent advance has been the development of longitudinal studies situated in local and regional teacher labor markets and organized around questions that begin to take account of contextual variation. For example, researchers affiliated with the New York City Pathways Study explain,

> Our central question concerns the effects that pathway characteristics have on student outcomes and on teacher labor market dynamics. However, to assess accurately such effects, we also need to understand something about how teacher background characteristics affect the selection of pathways, how individual characteristics of teachers influence student outcomes, how pathways influence prospective teachers' opportunities to learn, how pathways influence teachers' matching to schools, and how characteristics of teachers and their pathways interact with features of school context to influence student outcomes. (Boyd et al., 2006, p. 158)

By extending our conceptual scope to encompass the institutional and organizational aspects of teaching, we entertain a broader set of explanations for problems of teacher quality and teaching effectiveness. Such a conceptual frame would necessarily preserve attention to individual characteristics, career choices, and effects but would also take account of the ways in which teachers and teaching reside in complex organizations and systems and in community contexts that vary in consequential ways. Furthermore, it would go beyond the additional specification of organizational variables in accounting for individual outcomes and posit teacher quality to be both an individual and a collective characteristic, simultaneously a property (the acquired knowledge, skill, and experience of individuals and groups) and an ongoing accomplishment, manifest in what teachers do, individually and together, and in institutional- and organizational-level developments. Those latter developments encompass a broad terrain of institutional arrangements for teacher recruitment, preparation, hiring, assignment, compensation, evaluation, and retention. In the space available, we make our case by attending specifically to the school-level organizational conditions that are most proximal to the work of teaching.

Research dating back to the 1970s and spanning several decades points squarely at organizational features as factors in teachers' effectiveness and the improvement capacity of schools (arrayed chronologically, examples include Little, 1982; Rosenholtz, 1989; Newmann & Wehlage, 1995; McLaughlin & Talbert, 2001; and Bryk, Sebring, Allensworth, Luppescu, & Easton, 2010). Research conducted during the 1990s coincided with a large number of publicly and privately funded school restructuring initiatives, many of which invoked "education for all" as a rallying cry for whole-school changes that included new leadership roles for teachers in addition to proposed changes in curriculum, instruction, assessment, parents' roles and relationships, and community ties (Little & Dorph, 1998; Peterson, McCarthey, & Elmore, 1996).[22]

Among the most ambitious of these studies, both conceptually and methodologically, is the longitudinal, mixed-method study of school reform in the Chicago Public Schools conducted from 1990 to 1997 by researchers affiliated with the Consortium on Chicago School Research. As a site for investigating persistent problems of educational disadvantage, Chicago stood out even among large urban centers: "The CPS was plagued by astronomically high dropout rates, extremely low student achievement, constant labor strife, unstable leadership, and a wholesale lack of political and public support" (Bryk et al., 2010, p. 13).

The researchers took as their principal concern the quality of instruction in the classroom and their principal task "an explanation of how the *organization of a school* and its day-to-day operations, including the connections out to parents and community, *interact with work inside its classrooms* to advance student learning" (Bryk et al., 2010, p. 48; emphasis in original). Drawing on prior studies of school reform, they conceived of the school in terms of five "essential supports" that they posited would bear directly or indirectly on classroom experience and would differentiate between improving and stagnating (or declining) schools. They theorized that these measured aspects of the school—leadership, instructional guidance, professional capacity, ties with parents and community, and a climate conducive to learning within the school—would not merely prove helpful in boosting improvement but would in fact prove to be "essential" in determining school outcomes, a premise subsequently borne out in analysis.

In effect, Bryk and colleagues (2010) framed the problem of teacher quality and its relationship to desired student outcomes in organizational and collective terms.[23] In this model, professional capacity comprises four elements: (a) the *quality of staff* that flows not only from recruitment and hiring of knowledgeable and skillful individuals but also from the school's response to poor performance and incompetence;[24] (b) *professional development opportunity*, conceived both as external resources and internal supports for teacher learning; (c) *work orientation*, or teachers' collective dispositions toward continuous improvement; and (d) *professional community*, through which teachers make their classroom teaching public for examination by colleagues and others, engage in critical dialogue about classroom practices, and collaborate to strengthen the school's instructional guidance system.

These elements of professional capacity proved to be consistently and significantly related to improvements in student achievement. To test the conceptual model, Bryk and colleagues (2010) employed extensive longitudinal data on students, teachers, principals, and schools, creating a database on more than 200 schools coupled with case study data on a smaller subset. The overall sample size, longitudinal mixed-method design, and tested measures overcome some of the serious methodological limitations of most earlier studies.[25]

The Chicago study offers compelling evidence that the collective capacity of a school matters in charting trajectories of improvement or decline and is consistent in this respect with findings from other longitudinal studies (V. E. Lee, Smith, & Croninger, 1997; Newmann & Wehlage, 1995). A daunting implication of the Chicago findings is the level of shared perspective, interdependence, and coordinated action that appear to be required if low-performing schools are to improve; the image is rather like that of a symphony orchestra or surgical team in which the accomplishments of the whole are simply not possible on the basis of individuals acting alone.

The Chicago study thus suggests that such capacity requires both the presence of well-prepared teachers and their collective and effective pursuit of the five essential supports.[26] Indeed, the researchers report that a "particularly disabling combination was detected . . . when teachers with weak educational backgrounds clustered in schools with weak work orientation and professional community" (Bryk et al., 2010, p. 119). Approximately half the schools with this profile stagnated in both subjects, and less than 5% improved in either math or reading. Such a "disabling combination" was particularly problematic for those schools that Bryk and colleagues (2010) label "truly disadvantaged." Although improving schools could be found in virtually every neighborhood in the city without regard to race or social class, . . . the most negative reports about the progress of reform tended to cluster in schools whose enrollments were predominately African-American and where 90-plus percent of the students were low income. A distinct and troubling pattern of inequity in school improvement had emerged. . . . Within an overall school system where disadvantage is normative, these places stood out as truly extreme. (Bryk et al., 2010, pp. 22, 23-24).

The story of enduring failure and stagnation in such schools cannot be confined to—or altered by—a narrative regarding teacher quality; it reaches more broadly and deeply into the dynamics of poverty and race, in neighborhoods where social institutions (including schools but also churches, employers, community-based organizations, and families) struggle for viability. As depicted by Bryk and colleagues (2010), such neighborhoods lack both "bonding social capital" based on trust among residents and "bridging social capital" that supplies connections to outside information and resources (a distinction credited to Saegert, Thompson, & Warren, 2001). Schools in such neighborhoods prove particularly hard-pressed to recruit and retain well-prepared teachers or to engage in the work of constituting the five essential supports for improvement, including productive ties to parents and community. They may also be the schools most dependent on the short-term staffing strategies described earlier and least well organized to make sound choices among such strategies, even as research offers testimony to the long-term work required to build the conditions of improvement.

Although this short summary cannot do justice to the complexity of the essential-supports model or to the sophistication of the analysis undertaken by Bryk and colleagues (2010), we offer it to underscore our main argument: that both policy discourse and research contributions would be strengthened by pursuing a more comprehensive and integrated model of teacher quality. To pursue research in this vein will require continued investment in longitudinal, mixed-method studies; the design of methods and measures adequate to the added complexity of the questions, including better measures of what teachers do to achieve results with students; and the availability of state or national data sets that enable more sophisticated linking of student-, teacher-, school-, and classroom-level data. (The last of these propositions, of course, introduces familiar tensions between the advantage to research and the threat to individual privacy.) Elaborating such a comprehensive and integrated model would also benefit from well-conceived ethnographic and case study research (for example, research that examines more closely the experience of teachers and students in schools that rely on short-term hiring). Finally, making good on the promise of such a conceptual model would require that researchers acquire greater facility in conveying its logic and related research in policy and professional venues in ways that transform the complexity of teacher quality into viable policy and practice alternatives. The research we envision would benefit, as the Pathways Study and the Chicago Consortium Study both have benefited, from assembling a team of researchers who command a range of disciplinary perspectives and training and who enter into sustained working relationships with professional and policy actors. Such a model would facilitate tackling the equity agenda on multiple fronts, joining a focus on the characteristics and demonstrated accomplishments of individual teachers to a complementary focus on the organizational structures, resources, and processes through which teacher effectiveness is forged and through which schools, like orchestras or surgical teams, may accomplish more than the sum of their parts.

ACKNOWLEDGMENTS

We wish to acknowledge Nicole Jackson, Anthony Kim, and Jessica Koistinen for their valuable contributions to the background research for this chapter as well as Geraldine Joncich Clifford for fruitful conversation regarding the history of teachers and teaching. We thank Diane Mayer, Rodney T. Ogawa, Allan Luke, and Judith Green for their helpful comments on earlier drafts.

NOTES

[1]This essay speaks only to problems of equity facing students. A separate line of research attends to issues of equity pertaining to teachers themselves, encompassing the history of teacher activism (Urban, 1989) as well as studies of specific problems of discrimination related to gender (Leroux, 2006), race (Fairclough, 2007; Shircliffe, 2008), and sexual orientation (Blount, 2004).

[2]Although the United States is not the only nation in the Americas, we use the term American periodically to designate the United States, as that term has the virtue of being usable as an adjective.

[3]For a comprehensive demographic profile of American teachers, see Zumwalt and Craig (2005a); see also Gay, Dingus, and Jackson (2003); Murnane, Singer, Willet, Kemple, and Olsen (1991); and National Education Association (2003). Béteille and Loeb (2009) provide a thorough review of research on teacher quality and teacher labor markets in the United States. For what has been described by Ladd (2007) as "the most comprehensive analysis to date of teacher policies at the international level" (p. 215), see the Organisation for Economic Co-operation and Development (OECD) report *Teachers Matter: Attracting, Developing and Retaining Effective Teachers* (McKenzie & Santiago, 2005).

[4]The OECD authors add a cautionary note: "Setting tighter entrance criteria for teacher education is difficult in countries with a tradition of largely unrestricted entrance to higher education" or, they continue, in countries with well-diversified and lucrative labor market opportunities (McKenzie & Santiago, 2005, p. 102).

[5]There is an extensive literature, both empirical and hortatory, that also attends to issues of gender representation and to a combination of gender and race or ethnic matching of teachers with students. In this text, we have concentrated on racial, ethnic, and cultural diversity.

[6]This sense of career dislocation parallels that observed in other periods of large-scale external change, for example, among teachers in largely working-class "secondary modern schools" in the United Kingdom when those schools merged with the more selective "grammar schools" in the 1960s (Beynon, 1985).

[7]Our focus on industrialized nations in this review leads us to exclude an increasing volume of research on the recruitment and preparation of indigenous teachers in developing countries as well as research on policy developments in teacher education, some of which reflects tensions in the relationship of economic growth to issues of equity (for example, Cavalcanti, 1996; Ludke & Moreira, 1999).

[8]There is an emerging body of research on the development of multicultural (and to a lesser extent, antiracist) emphases in teacher education but no research that we are aware of on the equity-oriented, teacher-driven professional associations. Tomlinson (1996) briefly recounts the role of the National Union of Teachers and the teacher-initiated National Association for Multiracial Education in promoting antiracist teacher education in Britain prior to the Education Reform Act of 1988, but we do not find any indication of a line of research focused on the role of such groups.

[9]Stein (2004), in the introduction to her book *The Culture of Education Policy*, observes that the accountability movements of the past decade, at least in the United States, mark a shift from a policy logic in which poor and minority children and families were cast as the problems to which schools were the solution (as embodied in the original Elementary and Secondary Education Act) to a logic in which low-performing schools and ineffective teachers have been cast as a problem to be remedied through more tightly specified standards, accountability measures, and sanctions (embodied in No Child Left Behind).

[10]The report located its explanation in part in the system of teacher preparation, faulting programs of teacher education for mediocre preparation offered to prospective teachers, and in part in the career disincentives presented by uncompetitive salaries and by working conditions that tended to undermine professional judgment and erode professional commitment.

[11]On developments in federal regulation, see Sunderman (2010 [this volume]).

[12]Scott, Ruef, Mendel, and Caronna (2000) detail what they summarize as multilevel change away from professional dominance and in the direction of managed care, entailing shifts in employment (individuals more likely to be employed in managed care organizations), the development of new organizational forms and roles, the emergence of cultural beliefs defining health care as a consumer–supplier relationship (and an escalation in demands for equitable access), and an increase in bureaucratization with an emphasis on efficiency.

[13]The professionalization strategy relies on state governance mechanisms of certification and licensure. Zeichner (2003) reports on a set of developments that are consistent with a professionalization (regulation) stance and supported by government and policy actions, among them the shift to performance assessment of prospective teachers enrolled in university- or college-based teacher education programs. But governments in the United States and elsewhere have also been important proponents and facilitators of market-oriented strategies. And because certification remains a requirement for entry into teaching, the development of markets cannot be fully considered as "deregulation." In addition, policy initiatives demonstrate the ongoing implication of government in both the professionalization and market perspectives. For example, policymakers have responded to projected teacher shortages and to public criticisms of teacher quality by simultaneously intensifying controls on traditional teacher education programs and by opening up the marketplace to alternative routes to certification.

[14]Programs may be portrayed primarily as a means of streamlining entry into teaching or may be targeted specifically at subject areas experiencing shortages, without reference to "high-need" schools or districts. Glass (2008) observes,

> The growth in alternatively certified teachers is spurred on by both exigency (a shortage of teachers in poor urban and rural schools) and ideology (a political opposition to regulation by government agencies and to university-based pre-service teacher education programs that are perceived as too progressive). (p. 1)

[15]All direct quotations in this paragraph were taken from official program websites.

[16]One example of an opportunity "to study what they will be doing" is the opportunity to examine curriculum used in New York City schools.

[17]Teach First, founded in 2002, maintains on its website that 55% of its recruits had remained in teaching by 2009 but provides no cohort-level detail. Documents available from Troops to Teachers, dated 2007, report a retention rate of more than 75% but also lack detail

regarding whether teachers have been retained in the low-income schools or districts in which they were initially placed.

[18]Historian Geraldine Joncich Clifford (personal communication, February 23, 2009) observes that historians typically portray teaching as short-term, temporary work prior to the formalization of large school systems and beset by high turnover since. She makes the point, however, that there have also been "career" teachers from the very early days of public education (Clifford, personal communication, February 23, 2009; see also Clifford, 1989). Our main point here is that short-term and part-time work, together with long-term careers, remain among the occupational possibilities associated with teaching.

[19]The 2005 OECD report, based on a 25-nation study, reports

> a range of teaching employment conditions in public schools. . . . Part-time teaching is possible in almost all countries; only in Greece, Japan and Korea are "regular" teachers unable to work part-time. . . . The country average of part-time teaching is 19% in primary education and 24% in secondary education. The incidence of part-time teaching is more common in secondary education in 16 of the 21 countries for which data for both levels of education are available. Countries vary widely in the extent to which part-time teaching is used. In Israeli primary schools and Mexican secondary schools about 80% of the teachers are classified as part-time, as are approximately 50% of the primary teachers in Germany and the Netherlands. On the other hand, less than 5% of primary teachers in Finland, Greece, Ireland and Japan work part-time, and there are very few part-time primary or secondary teachers in Italy and Korea. (McKenzie & Santiago, 2005, p. 78)

[20]Based on a 2009 survey of employers, career service advisors in U.S. colleges, and undergraduate students, *Business Week* magazine listed Teach for America seventh among the "best places to launch a career" (http://bwnt.businessweek.com/interactive_reports/career_launch_2009/). To realize the career opportunities touted by any of these organizations, it seems likely that individuals must demonstrate their capacity for innovation, leadership, and initiative in ways that most novice teachers might feel reluctant to do for fear of running afoul of administrators who control tenure decisions.

[21]Although this chapter focuses on industrialized nations, we note that the flow of overseas-trained teachers from developing nations to industrialized nations implicates equity dynamics in the former. For example, England has been asked to regulate its recruitment more stringently lest it undermine the development of South Africa and other developing countries from which it attracts teachers (Commonwealth Secretariat, 2003).

[22]Teddlie and Stringfield (2007) characterize this period as reflecting a shift from the equity concerns that had developed in the 1960s and 1970s to a preoccupation with national competitiveness in a global economy. They assert, "Reformers' emphasis was no longer aimed at schools serving the disadvantaged, but instead was oriented toward creating schools that would generate a competent workforce for a competitive global economy" (Teddlie and Stringfield, 2007, p. 149). Our own reading of the reform rhetoric suggests less of a clearly demarcated shift than a steady redefinition of equity in human capital and social efficiency terms, such that "closing the achievement gap" has come to be measured almost exclusively by student performance on standardized tests in a small set of academic domains. In one recent panel discussion among prominent sociologists, David Labaree (2009) characterized both the standards and school choice movements as having embraced the equity language associated with civil rights campaigns to boost their political appeal, thus marrying the language of equity to the logic of social efficiency and economic growth.

[23]The framing of teacher quality in terms of collective capacity and disposition is not unique to Bryk, Sebring, Allensworth, Luppescu, and Easton (2010); for example, see Johnson (2009), Little (1999), and Newmann, King, and Youngs (2000).

[24]The element of "staff quality" in this model maps most directly on to the conventional definitions of teacher quality but is given a distinctly organizational bent here by considering the school's capacity for effective recruitment, hiring, assignment, and evaluation.

[25]Individual-level student achievement data (standardized test scores in reading and mathematics), demographic information, and school registration data made it possible to track student achievement and mobility from 1990 to 1996. A series of surveys from 1991 to 1997 generated high response rates and provided extensive information on the experiences and perceptions of teachers, principals, and students. In particular, teacher surveys examined teachers' professional work orientations, their self-reported instructional practices, opportunities for professional development, participation in professional collaboration, experience of professional community, and felt obligations toward students. Surveys also tapped teachers' perception of the school environment, participation in school governance, and perceived involvement of parents and community in school life. Missing from the teacher database were independent measures of teachers' academic background and performance, such as undergraduate grade point average. Rather, the study employed two background measures. Teachers' undergraduate institution served as a general proxy for academic background. A second "cosmopolitan" measure was based on whether teachers acquired any part of their education outside Chicago. As the researchers explain, "Its formation was motivated by earlier research that described a troublesome phenomenon in Chicago, in which poorly educated CPS graduates attended weak undergraduate institutions in Chicago and then return to teach in the CPS" (Bryk et al., 2010, p. 73).

[26]In this regard, some limitations of the study are its incomplete measures of individual teachers' academic and professional qualifications and its reliance on undergraduate institution as a proxy for selectivity combined with a "cosmopolitanism" measure indicating whether the teacher acquired any of his or her education outside Chicago. A stronger set of individual measures might have yielded evidence of an independent relationship between teacher background and student achievement. The question arises here of how much of a gain in organizational capacity might be made through hiring practices alone and how much is dependent on the cultivation of other enabling conditions.

REFERENCES

Achinstein, B., Ogawa, R., Sexton, D., & Freitas, C. (2009, April). *The socialization and retention of new teachers of color: Promises and challenges.* Paper presented at the annual meeting of the American Educational Research Association.

Akiba, M., LeTendre, G., & Scribner, J. P. (2007). Teacher quality, opportunity gap, and national achievement in 46 countries. *Educational Researcher, 36,* 369–387.

Alexander, R. (2001). *Culture and pedagogy: International comparisons in primary education.* Oxford, UK: Blackwell.

Allensworth, E., Ponisciak, S., & Mazzeo, C. (2009). *The schools teachers leave: Teacher mobility in Chicago public schools.* Chicago: University of Chicago, Consortium on Chicago School Research.

American Federation of Teachers. (2009). *Importing educators: Causes and consequences of international teacher recruitment.* Washington, DC: American Federation of Teachers.

Anderson-Levitt, K. (2002). *Teaching cultures: Knowledge for teaching first grade in France and the United States.* Cresskill, NJ: Hampton.

Anderson-Levitt, K. (Ed.). (2003). *Local meanings, global schooling: Anthropology and world culture theory.* New York: Palgrave Macmillan.

Barber, R. (2003). *Report to the National Education Association on trends in foreign teacher recruitment.* Washington, DC: Center for Economic Organizing.

Bartlett, L. (2009, April). *The global migration of teachers: The scope and pattern of overseas-trained teachers in California public schools.* Paper presented at the annual meeting of the American Educational Research Association.

Becker, H. (1951). *Role and career problems of the Chicago public school teacher.* Chicago: University of Chicago Press.

Béteille, T., & Loeb, S. (2009). Teacher quality and teacher labor markets. In G. Sykes, B. Schneider, & D. Plank (Eds.), *Handbook of education policy research* (pp. 596–612). New York: Routledge.

Beynon, J. (1985). Institutional change and career histories in a comprehensive school. In S. J. Ball & I. F. Goodson (Eds.), *Teachers' lives and careers* (pp. 158–179.). London: Falmer.

Birkeland, S. E., & Peske, H. G. (2004). *Literature review of research on alternative certification.* Washington, DC: National Education Association.

Blount, J. M. (2004). *Fit to teach: Same-sex desire, gender, and school-work in the twentieth century.* Albany: State University of New York Press.

Boyd, D., Grossman, P., Lankford, H., Loeb, S., Michelli, N. M., & Wyckoff, J. (2006). Complex by design: Investigating pathways into teaching in New York City schools. *Journal of Teacher Education, 57,* 155–166.

Boyd, D., Grossman, P., Lankford, H., Loeb, S., & Wyckoff, J. (2005). *How changes in entry requirements alter the teacher workforce and affect student achievement* (NBER Working Paper 11844). Cambridge, MA: National Bureau of Economic Research.

Boyd, D., Grossman, P., Lankford, H., Loeb, S., & Wyckoff, J. (2008). *Teacher preparation and student achievement* (NBER Working Paper 14314). Cambridge, MA: National Bureau of Economic Research.

Boyd, D., Lankford, H., Loeb, S., & Wyckoff, J. (2005). Explaining the short careers of high-achieving teachers in schools with low-performing students. *American Economic Review, 95*(2), 166–171.

Bransford, J., Darling-Hammond, L., & LePage, P. (2005). Introduction. In L. Darling-Hammond & J. Bransford (Eds.), *Preparing teachers for a changing world: What teachers should learn and be able to do* (pp. 1–39). San Francisco: Jossey-Bass.

Bryk, A. S., Sebring, P. B., Allensworth, E., Luppescu, S., & Easton, J. Q. (2010). *Organizing schools for improvement.* Chicago: University of Chicago Press.

Cavalcanti, M. C. (1996). Collusion, resistance, and reflexivity: Indigenous teacher education in Brazil. *Linguistics and Education, 8,* 175–188.

Clifford, G. J. (1989). Man/Woman/Teacher: Gender, family, and career in American educational history. In D. Warren (Ed.), *American teachers: Histories of a profession at work* (pp. 293–343). New York: Macmillan.

Coburn, C. E. (2005). The role of nonsystem actors in the relationship between policy and practice: The case of reading instruction in California. *Educational Evaluation and Policy Analysis, 27*(1), 23–52.

Cochran-Smith, M. (2004). *Walking the road: Race, diversity and social justice in teacher education.* New York: Teachers College Press.

Cochran-Smith, M., Feiman-Nemser, S., McIntyre, D. J., & Demers, K. E. (Eds.). (2008). *Handbook of research on teacher educaiton: Enduring questions in changing contexts.* New York: Routledge.

Comber, B., & Kamler, B. (2004). Getting out of deficit: Pedagogies of reconnection. *Teaching Education, 15*(3), 293–310.

Commonwealth Secretariat. (2003). *Teachers: Recruitment, retention and development issues.* Paper presented at the 15th Conference of Commonwealth Education Ministers, Edinburgh, UK.

Corcoran, S., Schwab, R., & Evans, W. (2004). Women, the labor market and the declining relative quality of teachers. *Journal of Policy Analysis and Management, 23,* 449–470.

Craft, M. (1996). Cultural diversity and teacher education. In M. Craft (Ed.), *Teacher education in plural societies: An international review* (pp. 1–15). London: Falmer.

Cribb, A. (2009). Professional ethics: Whose responsibility? In S. Gewirtz, P. Mahony, I. Hextall, & A. Cribb (Eds.), *Changing teacher professionalism: International trends, challenges and ways forward* (pp. 31–42). London: Routledge.

Darling-Hammond, L. (2006). Why teacher education is important—And difficult. In L. Darling-Hammond (Ed.), *Powerful teacher education: Lessons from exemplary programs* (pp. 19–41). San Francisco: Jossey-Bass.

Darling-Hammond, L., & Bransford, J. (Eds.). (2005). *Preparing teachers for a changing world: What teachers should learn and be able to do.* San Francisco: Jossey-Bass.

Darling-Hammond, L., Holtzman, D. J., Gatlin, S. J., & Heilig, J. V. (2005). Does teacher preparation matter? Evidence about teacher certification, Teach for America, and teacher effectiveness. *Education Policy Analysis Archives, 13*(42), 1–48.

DeBray, E. (2006). *Politics, ideology and education: Federal policy during the Clinton and Bush administrations.* New York: Teachers College Press.

Decker, P. T., Mayer, D. P., & Glazerman, S. (2004). *The effects of Teach for America on students: Findings from a national evaluation.* Princeton, NJ: Mathematica Policy Research.

Dee, T. S. (2003). *Are there civic returns to education?* Cambridge, MA: National Bureau of Economic Research.

Dee, T. S. (2004). Teachers, race, and student achievement in a randomized experiment. *Review of Economics and Statistics, 86*(1), 195–210.

Delpit, L. (1996). *Other people's children: Cultural conflict in the classroom.* New York: New Press.

Dingus, J. E. (2006). Community reciprocity in the work of African-American teachers. *Teaching Education, 17*(3), 195–206.

Dolton, P., & Newson, D. (2003). The relationship between teacher turnover and school performance. *London Review of Education, 1*(2), 131–140.

Edwards, D., & Spreen, C. A. (2007). Teachers and the global knowledge economy. *Perspectives in Education, 25*(2), 1–14.

Elsbree, W. S. (1939). *The American teacher: Evolution of a profession in a democracy.* Westport, CT: Greenwood.

Fairclough, A. (2007). *A class of their own: Black teachers in the segregated South.* Cambridge, MA: Harvard University Press.

Figlio, D. N. (1997). Teacher salaries and teacher quality. *Economic Letters, 55*, 267–271.

Foster, C. R., Dahill, L. E., Goleman, L. A., & Tolentino, B. W. (2006). *Educating clergy: Teaching practices and pastoral imagination.* San Francisco: Jossey-Bass.

Foster, M. (1997). *Black teachers on teaching.* New York: New Press.

Garcia, E. F. (1990). Educating teachers for language minority students. In R. W. Houston (Ed.), *Handbook of research on teacher education* (pp. 717–729). New York: Macmillan.

Gay, G., Dingus, J. E., & Jackson, C. W. (2003). *The presence and performance of teachers of color in the profession.* Washington, DC: National Education Association.

Ghosh, R. (1996). Multicultural teacher education in Canada. In M. Craft (Ed.), *Teacher education in plural societies: An international review* (pp. 45–56). London: Falmer.

Gitomer, D. (2007). *Teacher quality in a changing policy landscape: Improvements in the teacher pool.* Princeton, NJ: Educational Testing Service.

Gitomer, D., Latham, A. S., & Ziomek, R. (1999). *The academic quality of prospective teachers: The impact of admissions and licensure testing.* Princeton, NJ: Educational Testing Service.

Glass, G. V. (2008). *Alternative certification of teachers.* East Lansing, MI: Great Lakes Center for Education Research and Practice.

Goe, L. (2002). Legislating equity: The distribution of emergency permit teachers in California. *Educational Policy Analysis Archives, 10*(42). Available from http://epaa.asu.edu/epaa/v10n42/

Goldhaber, D., Choi, H.-J., & Cramer, L. (2007). A descriptive analysis of the distribution of NBPTS-certified teachers in North Carolina. *Economics of Education Review, 26,* 160–172.

Goldhaber, D., DeArmond, M., Liu, A. Y.-H., & Player, D. W. (2008). *Returns to skill and teacher wage premiums: What can we learn by comparing the teacher and private sector labor markets?* (Working Paper 8). Seattle: University of Washington, School Finance Redesign Project.

Goodwin, A. L. (1992). Review of The Handbook of Research on Teacher Education. *Teachers College Record, 94*(2), 414–417.

Grant, C. A. (1993). The multicultural preparation of US teachers: Some hard truths. In G. K. Verma (Ed.), *Inequality and teacher education: An international perspective* (pp. 41–57). London: Falmer.

Grant, C. A. (2008). Teacher capacity: Introduction to the section. In M. Cochran-Smith, S. Feiman-Nemser, D. J. McIntyre, & K. E. Demers (Eds.), *Handbook of research on teacher education: Enduring questions in changing contexts* (pp. 127–133). New York: Routledge.

Grant, C. A., & Agosto, V. (2008). Teacher capacity and social justice in teacher education. In M. Cochran-Smith, S. Feiman-Nemser, D. J. McIntyre, & K. E. Demers (Eds.), *Handbook of research on teacher education: Enduring questions in changing contexts* (pp. 175–200). New York: Routledge.

Grant, C. A., & Secada, W. G. (1990). Preparing teachers for diversity. In R. W. Houston (Ed.), *Handbook of research on teacher education* (pp. 403–422). New York: Macmillan.

Grossman, P., & McDonald, M. (2008). Back to the future: Directions for research in teaching and teacher education. *American Educational Research Journal, 45*(1), 184–205.

Grubb, W. N., & Lazerson, M. (2004). *The education gospel: The economic power of schooling.* Cambridge, MA: Harvard University Press.

Guarino, C. M., Santibañez, L., & Daley, G. A. (2006). Teacher recruitment and retention: A review of the recent empirical literature. *Review of Educational Research, 76*(2), 173–208.

Guha, R., Shields, P., Tiffany-Morales, J., Bland, J., & Campbell, A. (2008). *California's teaching force 2008: Key issues and trends.* Santa Cruz, CA: Center for the Future of Teaching and Learning.

Hanushek, E., Kain, J. F., O'Brien, D. M., & Rivkin, S. G. (2005). *The market for teacher quality.* Cambridge, MA: National Bureau of Economic Research.

Hanushek, E. A., Kain, J. F., & Rivkin, S. G. (2001). *Why public schools lose teachers.* Cambridge, MA: National Bureau of Educational Research.

Hanushek, E. A., Kain, J. F., & Rivkin, S. G. (2004). Why public schools lose teachers. *Journal of Human Resources, 39*(2), 326–354.

Hanushek, E. A., & Rivkin, S. G. (2007). Pay, working conditions, and teacher quality. *Future of Children, 17*(1), 69–86.

Hess, F. M. (2001). *Tear down this wall: The case for a radical overhaul of teacher certification.* Washington, DC: Progressive Policy Institute.

Hickling-Hudson, A., & McMeniman, M. (1996). Pluralism and Australian teacher education. In M. Craft (Ed.), *Teacher education in plural societies: An international review* (pp. 16–26). London: Falmer.

Hollins, E., & Guzman, M. T. (2005). Research on preparing teachers for diverse populations. In M. Cochran-Smith & K. Zeichner (Eds.), *Studying teacher education: The report of the AERA panel on research and teacher education* (pp. 477–548). Mahwah, NJ: Lawrence Erlbaum.

Houston, R. W. (Ed.). (1990). *Handbook of research on teacher education: A project of the Association of Teacher Educators.* New York: Macmillan.

Howard, T. C., & Aleman, G. R. (2008). Teacher capacity for diverse learners: What do teachers need to know? In M. Cochran-Smith, S. Feiman-Nemser, D. J. McIntyre, & K. E. Demers (Eds.), *Handbook of research on teacher education: Enduring questions in changing contexts* (pp. 157–174). New York: Routledge.

Humphrey, D. C., Wechsler, M. E., & Hough, H. J. (2008). Characteristics of effective alternative teacher certification programs. *Teachers College Record, 110*(1), 1–63.

Ingersoll, R. (2001). Teacher turnover and teacher shortages: An organizational analysis. *American Educational Research Journal, 38*(3), 499–534.

Ingersoll, R. M. (2002). *Out-of-field teaching, educational inequality, and the organization of schools: An exploratory analysis.* Seattle: University of Washington, Center for Teaching and Policy.

Ingersoll, R. M. (2004). Why some schools have more underqualified teachers than others. In D. Ravitch (Ed.), *Brookings papers on education policy* (pp. 45–88). Washington, DC: Brookings Institution.

Ingersoll, R., & Connor, R. L. (2009, April). *What the national data tell us about minority and Black teacher turnover.* Paper presented at the annual meeting of the American Educational Research Association, San Diego.

Johnson, S. M. (2009). *How best to add value? Strike a balance between the individual and the organization in school reform* (Briefing Paper No. 249). Washington, DC: Economic Policy Institute.

Johnson, S. M., & Liu, E. (2004). What teaching pays, what teaching costs. In S. M. Johnson (Ed.), *Finders and keepers: Helping new teachers survive and thrive in our schools* (pp. 49–68). San Francisco: Jossey-Bass.

Kane, T. J., Rockoff, J. E., & Staiger, D. O. (2008). What does certification tell us about teacher effectiveness? Evidence from New York City. *Economics of Education Review, 27*(6), 615–631.

Keevy, J. (2009, June). *The status of teaching in the Commonwealth: Noble, but not always professional.* Paper presented at the Teachers Forum of the 17th Conference of Commonwealth Education Ministers, Kuala Lumpur, Malaysia.

Kelly, H. (2007). Racial tokenism in the school workplace: An exploratory study of Black teachers in overwhelmingly White schools. *Educational Studies, 41*(3), 230–254.

Kliebard, H. M. (1986). *The struggle for the American curriculum 1893–1958.* New York: Routledge.

Kliebard, H. M. (2002). *Changing course: American curriculum reform in the 20th century.* New York: Teachers College Press.

Kumashiro, K. K. (2008). Partial movements toward teacher quality . . . and their potential for advancing social justice. In M. Cochran-Smith, S. Feiman-Nemser, D. J. McIntyre, & K. E. Demers (Eds.), *Handbook of research on teacher education: Enduring questions in changing contexts* (pp. 238–242). New York: Routledge.

Labaree, D. F. (1997). Public goods, private goods: The American struggle over educational goals. *American Educational Research Journal, 34*(1), 39–81.

Labaree, D. F. (2009, August). *Education: Whither the common school?* Panel held at the annual meeting of the American Sociological Association, San Francisco.

Laczko-Kerr, I., & Berliner, D. C. (2002). The effectiveness of "Teach for America" and other undercertified teachers on student academic achievement: A case of harmful public policy. *Education Policy Analysis Archives, 10*(37). Available from http://epaa.asu.edu/epaa/v10n37/

Ladd, H. F. (2007). Teacher labor markets in developed countries. *Future of Children, 17*(1), 201–217.

Ladson-Billings, G. (1999). Preparing teachers for diverse student populations: A critical race theory perspective. *Review of Research in Education, 24*, 211–247.

Lanier, J. E., & Little, J. W. (1986). Research on teacher education. In M. Wittrock (Ed.), *Handbook of research on teaching* (3rd ed., pp. 527–569). New York: Macmillan.

Lavy, V. (2007). Using performance-based pay to improve the quality of teachers. *Future of Children, 17*(1), 87–109.

Lee, C. D. (1995). A culturally based cognitive apprenticeship: Teaching African American high school students skills in literary interpretation. *Reading Research Quarterly, 30*(4), 608–630.

Lee, V. E., Smith, J. B., & Croninger, R. G. (1997). How high school oganization influences the equitable distribution of learning in mathematics and science. *Sociology of Education, 70*(2), 128–150.

Leroux, K. (2006). "Lady teachers" and the genteel roots of teacher organization in Gilded Age cities. *History of Education Quarterly, 46*(2), 164–191.

Levine, D., Lowe, R., Peterson, B., & Tenorio, R. (Eds.). (1995). *Rethinking schools: An agenda for change.* New York: New Press.

Lingard, B. (2009). Pedagogizing teacher professional identities. In S. Gewirtz, P. Mahony, I. Hextall, & A. Cribb (Eds.), *Changing teacher professionalism: International trends, challenges and ways forward* (pp. 81–93). London: Routledge.

Little, J. W. (1982). Norms of collegiality and experimentation: Workplace conditions of school success. *American Educational Research Journal, 19*(3), 325–340.

Little, J. W. (1999). Organizing schools for teacher learning. In L. Darling-Hammond & G. Sykes (Eds.), *Teaching as the learning profession: Handbook of teaching and policy* (pp. 233–262). San Francisco: Jossey Bass.

Little, J. W., & Dorph, R. (1998). *Lessons about comprehensive school reform: California's School Restructuring Demonstration Program.* Berkeley: University of California, Graduate School of Education.

Liu, E., Johnson, S. M., & Peske, H. G. (2004). New teachers and the Massachusetts Signing Bonus: The limits of inducements. *Educational Analysis and Policy Evaluation, 26*(3), 217–236.

Loeb, S., & Page, M. (2000). Examining the link between teacher wages and student outcomes: The importance of alternative labor market opportunities and non-pecuniary variation. *Review of Economics and Statistics, 82,* 393–408.

Lortie, D. (1975). *Schoolteacher.* Chicago: University of Chicago Press.

Ludke, M., & Moreira, A. F. B. (1999). Recent proposals to reform teacher education in Brazil. *Teaching and Teacher Education, 15,* 169–178.

Luke, A. (2004). Teaching after the market: From commodity to cosmopolitan. *Teachers College Record, 106* (7), 1422–1443.

Mabokela, R. O., & Madsen, J. A. (2007). African American teachers in suburban desegregated schools: Intergroup differences and the impact of performance pressures. *Teachers College Record, 109*(5), 1171–1206.

MacDonald, V.-M. (1999). The paradox of bureaucratization: New views on progressive era teachers and the development of a woman's profession. *History of Education Quarterly, 39*(4), 427–453.

Maylor, U. (2009). "They do not relate to Black people like us": Black teachers as role models for Black pupils. *Journal of Education Policy, 24*(1), 1–21.

McKenzie, P., & Santiago, P. (2005). *Teachers matter: Attracting, developing and retaining effective teachers.* Paris: Organisation for Economic Co-operation and Development.

McLaughlin, M. W., & Talbert, J. E. (2001). *Professional communities and the work of high school teaching.* Chicago: University of Chicago Press.

McNamara, O., Lewis, S., & Howson, J. (2007). "Turning the tap on and off'": The recruitment of overseas trained teachers to the United Kingdom. *Perspectives in Education, 25*(2), 40–54.

Meyer, J. W., & Ramirez, F. O. (2000). The world institutionalization of education. In J. Schriewer (Ed.), *Discourse formation in comparative education* (pp. 111–132). Frankfurt, Germany: Peter Lang.

Miller, P. (2007). "Brain gain" in England: How overseas trained teachers have enriched and sustained English education. *Perspectives in Education, 25*(2), 25–37.

Morrow, W., & Keevy, J. (2006). *The recognition of teacher qualifications and professional registration status across Commonwealth member states: Balancing the rights of teachers to migrate internationally against the need to protect the integrity of national education systems.* London: Commonwealth Secretariat, Education Section.

Murnane, R., Singer, J., Willet, J., Kemple, J., & Olsen, R. (1991). *Who will teach? Policies that matter.* Cambridge, MA: Harvard University Press.

Murnane, R. J., & Steele, J. L. (2007). What is the problem? The challenge of providing effective teachers for all children. *Future of Children, 17*(1), 15–43.

National Education Association. (2003). *Status of the American public school teacher 2000–2001.* Washington, DC: Author.

Newmann, F., & Wehlage, G. (1995). *Successful school restructuring: A report to the public and educators by the Center on Organization and Restructuring of Schools.* Madison, WI: Center on Organization and Restructuring of Schools.

Newmann, F. M., King, M. B., & Youngs, P. (2000). Professional development that addresses school capacity: Lessons from urban elementary schools. *American Journal of Education, 108*(4), 259–299.

Perkins, L. M. (1989). The history of Blacks in teaching: Growth and decine within the profession. In D. Warren (Ed.), *American teachers: Histories of a profession at work* (pp. 344–369). New York: Macmillan.

Perlmann, J., & Margo, R. A. (2001). *Women's work?: American schoolteachers, 1650–1920.* Chicago: University of Chicago Press.

Peterson, P. L., McCarthey, S. J., & Elmore, R. F. (1996). Learning from school restructuring. *American Educational Research Journal, 33*(1), 119–153.

Prentice, A., & Theobald, M. R. (Eds.). (1991). *Women who taught: Perspectives on the history of women and teaching.* Toronto, ON: University of Toronto Press.

Reininger, M. (2007). *Factors influencing the local supply of teachers.* Unpublished PhD, Stanford University.

Reynolds, M. C. (1990). Educating teachers for special education students. In R. W. Houston (Ed.), *Handbook of research on teacher education* (pp. 423–436). New York: Macmillan.

Rosenholtz, S. (1989). *Teachers' workplace.* New York: Longman.

Rury, J. (1989). Who became teachers? The social characteristics of teachers in American history. In D. Warren (Ed.), *American teachers: Histories of a profession at work* (pp. 9–62). New York: Macmillan.

Saegert, S., Thompson, J. P., & Warren, M. R. (Eds.). (2001). *Social capital and poor communities.* New York: Russell Sage Foundation.

Scafidi, B., Sjoquist, D. L., & Stinebrickner, T. R. (2007). Race, poverty, and teacher mobility. *Economics of Education Review, 26*, 145–159.

Scott, W. R., Ruef, M., Mendel, P. J., & Caronna, C. A. (2000). *Institutional change and healthcare organizations: From professional dominance to managed care.* Chicago: University of Chicago Press.

Shen, J. (1997). Teacher retention and attrition in public schools. *Journal of Educational Research, 91*, 81–88.

Sheppard, S. D., Macatangay, K., Colby, A., & Sullivan, W. M. (2009). *Educating engineers: Designing for the future of the field.* San Francisco: Jossey-Bass.

Shircliffe, B. (2008, November). *Teacher salary cases in Florida: Changing race relations among educators in the Deep South.* Paper presented at the Conference of the History of Education Society, St. Petersburg, FL.

Siddle Walker, V. (2008). A thought from another world: The professional education of Black teachers in Georgia, 1930–1965. In M. Cochran-Smith, S. Feiman-Nemser, D. J. McIntyre, & K. E. Demers (Eds.), *Handbook of research on teacher education: Enduring questions in changing contexts* (pp. 117–122). New York: Routledge.

Stein, S. (2004). *The culture of education policy.* New York: Teachers College Press.

Sullivan, W. M., Colby, A., Wegner, J. W., Bond, L., & Shulman, L. S. (2007). *Educating lawyers: Preparation for the profession of law.* San Francisco: Jossey-Bass.

Sunderman, G. (2010). Evidence of the impact of school reform on systems governance and educational bureaucracies. *Review of Research in Education, 34*(1), 226–253.

Teddlie, C., & Stringfield, S. (2007). A history of school effectiveness and improvement research in the USA focusing on the past quarter century. In T. Townsend (Ed.), *International handbook of school effectiveness and improvement* (pp. 131–166). Dordrecht, Netherlands: Springer.

Thiessen, D., Bascia, N., & Goodson, I. (Eds.). (1996). *Making a difference about difference: The lives and careers of racial minority immigrant teachers.* Toronto, ON: Remtel/Garamond.

Tolley, K., & Beadie, N. (2006). Socioeconomic incentives to teach in New York and North Carolina: Toward a more complex model of teacher labor markets, 1800–1850. *History of Education Quarterly, 46*(1), 36–72.

Tomlinson, S. (1996). Teacher education for a multicultural Britain. In M. Craft (Ed.), *Teacher education in plural societies: An international review* (pp. 27–44). London: Falmer.

Troyna, B. (1994). The "everyday world" of teachers? Deracialised discourses in the sociology of teachers and the teaching profession. *British Journal of Sociology of Education, 15*(3), 325–339.

Urban, W. (1989). Teacher activism. In D. Warren (Ed.), *American teachers: Histories of a profession at work* (pp. 190–209). New York: Macmillan.

Verma, G. K. (Ed.). (1993). *Inequality and teacher education: An international perspective.* London: Falmer.

Waller, W. (1932). *The sociology of teaching.* New York: Russell and Russell.

Weinstein, R. (2002). *Reaching higher: The power of expectations in schooling.* Cambridge, MA: Harvard University Press.

Wilson, S. M., Floden, R. E., & Ferrini-Mundy, J. (2002). Teacher preparation research: An insider's view from the outside. *Journal of Teacher Education, 53*(3), 190–204.

Wiseman, A. W. (2010). The uses of evidence for educational policymaking: Global contexts and international trends. *Review of Research in Education, 34*(1), 1–24.

Zeichner, K. (1996). Educating teachers for cultural diversity in the United States. In M. Craft (Ed.), *Teacher education in plural societies: An international review* (pp. 141–158). London: Falmer.

Zeichner, K. M. (2003). The adequacies and inadequacies of three current strategies to recruit, prepare and retain the best teachers for all students. *Teachers College Record, 105*(3), 490–519.

Zeichner, K., & Conklin, H. G. (2005). Teacher education programs. In M. Cochran-Smith & K. M. Zeichner (Eds.), *Studying teacher education: The report of the AERA Panel on Research and Teacher Education* (pp. 645–735). Mahwah, NJ: Lawrence Erlbaum.

Zumwalt, K., & Craig, E. (2005a). Teachers' characteristics: Research on the demographic profile. In M. Cochran-Smith & K. M. Zeichner (Eds.), *Studying teacher education: Report of the AERA Panel on Research and Teacher Education* (pp. 111–156). Mahwah, NJ: Lawrence Erlbaum.

Zumwalt, K., & Craig, E. (2005b). Teachers' characteristics: Research on the indicators of quality. In M. Cochran-Smith & K. M. Zeichner (Eds.), *Studying teacher education: Report of the AERA Panel on Research and Teacher Education* (pp. 157–260). Mahwah, NJ: Lawrence Erlbaum.

Chapter 10

The Changing Social Spaces of Learning: Mapping New Mobilities

KEVIN M. LEANDER
NATHAN C. PHILLIPS
KATHERINE HEADRICK TAYLOR
Vanderbilt University

Writing on contemporary culture and social life, sociologists and cultural theorists have been describing new or changing forms of movement, variously described as cultural "flows" (e.g., Appadurai, 1996), "liquid life" (Bauman, 2005), or a "networked society" (Castells, 1996). The change in such movements or mobilities of people, media, material goods, and other social phenomena, including the reach or extension of such movements, connections between "global" and "local" life, the creation of new spaces and places, and new speeds and rhythms of everyday social practice, is arguably the most important contrast between contemporary social life and that of just a decade or two ago. Despite these changes and longer conversations about their meanings in a range of disciplines, mobilities and their relations to learning within education are still understudied and undertheorized.

The present review maps current and relevant engagements with mobility and learning across conceptual and empirical studies. The first section considers the relationship of learning to space and place in educational research, and focuses in particular on the classroom-as-container as a dominant discourse of the field. By "dominant discourse" we intend that the classroom-as-container constructs not only particular ways of speaking and writing in educational research, but also systems of rules concerning how meaning is made (Foucault, 1972). This discourse functions as an "imagined geography" of education, constituting when and where researchers and teachers should expect learning to "take place." This dominant discourse shapes educational research practice and perspectives, we posit, even when research questions cross "in school" and "out of school" borders. Next, in the second section, we consider disruptions and expansions of the classroom-as-container discourse within

Review of Research in Education
March 2010, Vol. 34, pp. 329-394
DOI: 10.3102/0091732X09358129
© 2010 AERA. http://rre.aera.net

educational research. This section is organized around three expansive metaphors of learning in space–time: learning-in-place, learning trajectories, and learning networks. This critical expansion of boundaries, we argue, involves emerging conceptions and questions concerning learning geographies and mobilities. We consider how the (newly) imagined geographies of place, trajectory, and network critique, interact with, and push open the boundaries of the enclosed classroom as a dominant discourse and historically sedimented geography within education research.

In the third and fourth major sections, we continue to develop these three expansive metaphors of learning and space–time (place, trajectory, and network) as we extend our review into two areas of research that are most often outside of mainstream educational research literature. In the third section, we review empirical work in human and critical geography that examines children's patterns of mobility in different historical periods and in different geographical locations (e.g., Christensen, 2003; Hart, 1977; Karsten, 1998, 2002; 2005; Lareau, 2003; Valentine & McKendrick, 1997). In the fourth section, we examine empirical studies of children's virtual geographies within Internet and media studies (e.g., boyd, 2007; Ito, Okabe, & Matsuda, 2005; Lam, 2000, 2004, 2006, 2009; Skop & Adams, 2009; Thulin & Vilhelmson, 2007; Valentine & S. Holloway, 2001; Valentine & S. L. Holloway, 2002).

In these two sections, our review of research that is typically "extracurricular" to educational studies is aimed at addressing questions we believe are key for understanding children's mobilities across dynamically changing socio-cultural spaces. How, for example, might we reconceive of the relations between physical mobility, virtual mobility, and educational mobility as social phenomena? Further, how does empirical work involving children's movements in physical and virtual spaces extend our understanding and raise questions about learning in place, learning trajectories, and learning networks? With regard to the physical or embodied movements of children, we consider how children's changing practices of moving (and being moved) from place to place, and their changing associations with place, are relevant for theorizing contemporary opportunities to learn.

With regard to virtual mobilities, we consider how children are using new technologies and digital media to build social connections across space–time, produce virtual "places" in online spaces, and otherwise interrupt the spatiotemporal contours of their lives. These two forms of mobility—akin to Appadurai's (1996) "ethnoscapes" and "mediascapes"—shape our binocular vision concerning the contemporary transformation of types of learning, situations for learning, and opportunities to learn. In the fifth section, connections are then built across the empirical studies with an eye toward evidence and equity issues with respect to learning, and possibilities for the study of learning as mobile social practices are discussed.

Prior to exploring the classroom as an imagined and expanding geography, a brief consideration of our perspectives on the relations between learning and mobility is in order. We begin from a sociocultural perspective that takes processes of thinking and learning to be not contained within individual minds, but rather distributed across persons, tools, and learning environments. This perspective, historically and chiefly inspired by the work of Lev Vygotsky (1978), and as extended by Vygotskian scholars (e.g., Cole, 1996; Cole & Engestrom, 1993; Gutierrez, Morales, & Martinez, 2009; Wertsch, 1991, 1998), may be properly described as "mediational" perspectives on learning as it focuses on mediational tools of all types (e.g., language, material tools, other persons) used in the process of learning. Our commitment in this regard aligns with Gee's (2008) description of an expanded notion of "opportunity to learn" (OTL; p. 76), which pushes beyond traditional psychological perspectives of mind and thought and traces the relations between learners and their experiences in the world. From a sociocultural perspective, questions concerning evidence and equity in education are in principle questions about systems and distributions rather than about individuals alone.

Herein lies our concern with mobilities—because evolving social systems and distributions involving resources for learning that are on the move, or constantly configured and reconfigured, and because people are on the move within such social systems and distributions, then the examination of learning involves an expanded series of questions concerning learning, space, and time. An entire category of inquiry concerns the constitution of places for learning. How do people (on the move) build qualitatively distinct relations with different learning "environments." What does it mean to recast the notion of the "learning environment" to "learning-in-place"?

Another category of inquiry concerns the experience of individuals across places, spaces, and times. For example, how do people traverse or otherwise connect one environment with another in their everyday lives? And, how is opportunity to learn organized and accomplished through trajectories connecting multiple places?

Moreover, in addition to questions concerning place and learning trajectories through them, we raise a category of inquiry concerning how resources, people, and places are brought into relationships through networks or circulations. How are the dynamically moving elements of social systems and distributions, including people themselves and all manner of resources for learning as well, configured and reconfigured across space and time to create opportunities to learn? These categories of inquiry and specific questions suggest the terrain of our perspective in this review, which expands the conversation concerning sociocultural "learning environments" and opportunity to learn to one of "geographies of learning" and "mobilities of learning."

THE CLASSROOM AS AN IMAGINED GEOGRAPHY: OPENING UP THE CONTAINER

If mobilities of learning are new in some fashion, then part of this newness is conceived in relation to something familiar and conventional: the classroom. The classroom is significant not just as a material location in which education research is located (along with the laboratory, which it sometimes reproduces), but also as a conceived or imagined space—an imagined geography of a particular kind. Lefebvre (1991) describes a house in a fashion that critiques how people hold container-like perspectives on the material and social locations of everyday life:

Consider a house, and a street, for example. The house has six storeys and an air of stability about it. One might almost see it as the epitome of immobility, with its concrete and its stark, cold and rigid outlines . . . Now, a critical analysis would doubtless destroy the appearance of solidity of this house, stripping it, as it were, of its concrete slabs and its thin non-load-bearing walls, which are really glorified screens, and uncovering a very different picture. In the light of this imaginary analysis, our house would emerge as permeated from every direction by streams of energy which run in and out of it by every imaginable route: water, gas, electricity, telephone lines, radio and television signals, and so on. Its image of immobility would then be replaced by an image of a complex of mobilities, a nexus of in and out conduits. (pp. 92–93)

In Lefevbre's analysis, a radically different image of the house is made possible by stripping off the walls and observing flows of energy of every kind, seeing the house as a "complex of mobilities" or an "active body." The everyday image or imagined geography is defined by the walls, and, failing to see them as screens emphasizes their stability and capacity for creating boundaries. In this container-like perspective, space is perceived of as a location in which activity occurs, while Lefebvre's counter-imagination of in and out conduits is one way of representing (social) space as produced through ongoing movements.

One might almost see the classroom as the epitome of immobility as well, representing not only conventions of material structure but also conventions of teaching practice, of schedule, of seating charts, and seatwork routines. If we deliberately "destroy the appearance of solidity," however, what might we observe? What types of materials (books, clay, earthworms, mounds of trash), energies (electricity, gas), resources (federal money, lottery surplus), information flows (Channel One, Internet, parent phone calls) permeate the classroom from every direction? Moreover, what of the diversity of children and adults entering the classroom doors, with their associated histories and geographies? These two conceptions of classrooms or other settings for learning—a container-like perspective on the one hand and a nexus-like perspective on the other—offer a metaphor for the shape of this review, as it works through a transition from one imagined geography of learning to another. Still, containers and networks are not mutually exclusive; even as we focus on new geographies of learning, we recognize that multiple coeval space–times inform our own and others' visions, with significant implications for evidence and equity.

Perhaps much of what maintains the power of the classroom-as-container as the key imagined geography of education is how this conception is highly mobile (somewhat ironically) across teacher, researcher, and policy communities. For teachers, the classroom is the domain of every practice and design—the space within which activity must be managed and the space that can be potentially transformed into a rich place of learning. Researchers create classrooms or classroom-like ensembles: "naturally occurring" groupings for interventions, trials, and controls, or bracket classrooms like small villages for ethnographic work. The microgeography of the contained classroom is reproduced in examinations of classroom conversation and examinations of the small group gathered around the pond. Research and policy work at "larger" scales place the classroom in larger classroom-like containers; the classroom is the fractal of educational research that can be multiplied, expanded, and combined for "larger" images of learning. Moreover, as a dominant discourse, "the classroom" and its pedagogical practices and relations permeate researcher mindsets about learning in the wild beyond the classroom (the classroom-like "locale" or "situation") such that "out of school learning" is often associated with other classroom-like places. Latour (1983) argued that in the case of Pasteur, science was successful to the extent that it disciplined and constructed the world outside of the laboratory to behave like the laboratory, hence his well-known dictum "Give me a laboratory and I will raise the world." In modern educational science, we might claim a parallel dictum, "Give me a classroom and I will raise the world."

We Have Never Been Roadville

We assume from the outset that classrooms are not merely material spaces that are readily perceived but also conceived spaces (Lefebvre, 1991; Soja, 1989)— representations of space that powerfully shape our attempts at new visions and productions of education. By exploring how classroom-like containers are present in research on learning in "out of school" settings, we might tease out the presence of the *implicit*, or imagined, classroom as a powerful imagined geography of educational research. Possibly few locales have shaped our geographic imagination of learning-in-place as much as Heath's (1983) depiction of the communities of Roadville and Trackton in the Piedmont Carolinas, White and Black (respectively) working-class communities that Heath studied with respect to cultural practices of language and literacy. The work has been modeled and cited ubiquitously; through these patterns Roadville and Trackton have come to stand in for the idea of emplaced culture. (Even Heath notes that there were many "Roadvilles" and "Tracktons" throughout the Piedmont Carolinas [p. 7].) As imagined geographies for educational research, Roadville and Trackton function as evidence that cultural patterns are located and can be found in specific communities, even at very small scales (e.g., Roadville consists of nine families), and that located cultural practices (especially language) come into contact with one another in school.

Roadville and Trackton are constructed as sites for educational evidence and equity by interpreting social and cultural practices as bounded by the physical and social community, and by following a tenet of the ethnography of communication to trace the "limits and features of the situations in which such communication occurs" (Heath, 1983, p. 6). Situated historically, Heath's (1983) method of examining culture practices as located in place participates in a long tradition in anthropology of the analysis of culture in place, which came under increasing critique in the 1990s as the ethnographic "place" began to be reconceived as a "nexus of practice" (Olwig & Hastrup, 1997). Heath (1983) states that she reads local cultural practices, and specifically "face to face networks" in which "each child learns the ways of acting, believing, and valuing those about him" (p. 6) over and against sociodemographic, quantitative, input/output business models of research (p. 8), and against deterministic categories of race and class (p. 3). The primary community for the children—and in this geographical imagination—is "geographically and socially their immediate neighborhood" (p. 6).

Heath expands beyond a localist perspective on activity by interpreting the two communities through their social history, and primarily that of labor (e.g., mill work) in the Piedmont. This history reaches back to 18th century slave labor, but focuses primarily on the post–Civil War development of the cotton mill industry, and changes in the labor opportunities and management–labor relations throughout the 20th century. She places the two communities into a long stream of history that courses through them as it moves toward the future. Geographically, however, we might consider multiple relations that this localist and historical vision do not immediately render.

What if we conceived of Roadville and Trackton as not merely locales in time, but—to borrow Massey's (2005) definition of social space—as the "simultaneity of stories-so-far" (p. 9)? What if we loosened their boundaries as "sites" and instead examined their simultaneous relations to other places-in-the-making, and to the movement of culture crisscrossing them (e.g., Clifford, 1992)? What if we critiqued our nostalgic visions and considered the messy ways in which Roadville and Trackton, in Latour's (1993) terms, "have never been modern"?

Some of this simultaneous and mobile geographical imagination is clearly present in Heath. In the case of Roadville, for instance, the movements of the White working-class include young people who have moved just 30 miles away to the nearby big city of "Alberta." Heath notes that Alberta-influenced cultural differences—including differences of clothing, hair styles, dance moves—are "carried into Roadville" at times of visiting relatives. In addition to these occasions of actual travel, the mobility of urban locales through popular media and consumerism seems to be continuously present in Roadville, shaping aspirations for the future, home decor, activities for children, and parenting practices. In this manner, family trips out of Roadville for Alberta can be interpreted as embodied enactments of desires and imaginations produced by the traffic of material culture, media culture, and stories of relocated family that are told and retold.

Situating Learning as a Research Act

Although Heath's (1983) ethnographic work may stand in for the idea of bounding or containing culture in the local, in its own formulation and equally in its use by others, research and writing on "situated learning" (e.g., Lave & Wenger, 1991) have contained learning largely within localist visions. Importantly, Lave and Wenger (1991), in their model of learning as "legitimate peripheral participation" in a "community of practice," critique the association of learning "situation" with a "simple location in space and time" (p. 32). The theorists describe how their perspective on situated learning involves a much more multifaceted and relational perspective in which "agent, activity, and the world mutually constitute one another" (p. 33).

Yet, if we turn from the theory of situated learning in Lave and Wenger (1991) toward the specific forms of activity under analysis, the types of ethnographic work and ethnographic places that come under the lens look quite local: nondrinking alcoholics being apprenticed at Alcoholics Anonymous meetings as studied by Carol Cain, butchers being apprenticed in shops from the research of Marshall (1972), and Lave's own study of Vai and Gola tailors, working with apprentices in small commercial shops. These relatively bounded, small scale, local studies are repeated across the sociocultural tradition in key illustrations of theory and within empirical studies: Classic representations of similar imagined geographies of learning include Wertsch's pole vaulters (1991), Cole's and Olga Vasquez's Fifth Dimension sites for after-school learning (Cole, 1996; Vasquez, 2002), and Engestrom's (1993) medical clinic studies. While developing an expanded version of mind and learning as distributed and mediated, theories of distribution within this tradition have been packed rather tightly within local containers.

Still, for conceptualizing learning and mobility, Lave and Wenger (1991) raise a critically significant point concerning the relations between the production of the community and the production of the learner's identity, noting that such community/individual relations raise questions about the "sociocultural organization of spaces into places of activity and the circulation of knowledgeable skill . . ." (p. 55). In empirical work leading to theory building, a more fully relational perspective on mobility and learning will only come into being to the extent that specific relations are followed, traced, and analyzed; the "social" will be lost or epiphenomenal to activity when less visible movements of people, texts, tools, and other cultural resources are bracketed out of activity or assumed to exist through only local visibility.

This brief consideration about the classroom-as-container deliberately stepped well outside of traditional classroom studies in order to show how this dominant discourse and imagined geography organizes and informs contemporary understandings of learning. That is, even in the move outward from the classroom to the ethnographic field, and in the concurrent movements in learning from psychology to anthropology and sociology, classroom activity containers continue their lives without much disruption (although perhaps at a higher level of abstraction). Classrooms, or classroom-like situations, maintain their abilities to corral and organize the local in our analyses of learning. The cultural artifacts and social practices of research in education continually evoke the figured world (Holland, Lachicotte, Skinner, & Cain, 1998) of the classroom. Hence, the possible "selves" or identities of learners are cast in relation to the classroom—their possible and likely activities, their motivations, and their positions with respect to one another. Container-like visions of social spaces of learning—perspectives emphasizing categories, stasis, structures, and located representations over the mobilities of practices—are often recreated, despite attempts to disrupt them. Nevertheless, messy circulations and plural geographies—complex mobilities of practices—have always been on the move, however domesticated by our mappings of locales. Such are the geographies that increasingly haunt our past and current imagination.

RESEARCHING MOBILITIES IN EDUCATIONAL RESEARCH:
PLACE, TRAJECTORY, AND NETWORK

If we set about "interpreting beyond the appearance of solidity" (Lefebvre, 1991, p. 92) of the classroom or any other learning "situation," what types of questions might guide our inquiry? How might we reframe evidence? Following, we review three approaches to this larger concern, beginning with learning in place. A perspective on place enables us to consider how a particular locale—a classroom, community, town, after school club, or website—is not an isolated container, but positioned in a *nexus of relations* to other such locales. The simultaneity of multiple locales, and the contact zones between them, become an expanded terrain of examination and evidence concerning learning and place. Additionally, places for learning have distinctive qualities about them that "recruit" or draw learners to them. What are such qualities and how does a perspective on place help us conceive of engagement for learning? How are spaces of resource distribution made into *affectively charged places of learning*?

Second, as classrooms or other sites of learning are seen less as parking lots and more as intersections, then the particular mobilities of people moving through them become a key issue for evidence and equity. How are social groups of people afforded access to *trajectories* across resources for learning, including physical landscapes, discourses and forms of representation, and other tools? How do individuals create their own trajectories or pathways given such affordances?

Third, how are participants in activity not merely "situated" in spaces and times, but rather actively *"networking" learning resources* across space–time in the course of their activity (Nespor, 1994, 1997; Leander, 2001, 2002b)? What are the speeds, rhythms, and frequencies of movements within these networks? How are movements qualitatively different among distinct forms of mobile culture—people, policies, pieces of paper, and megabytes of Internet-transmitted video? Such questions about *learning in place, learning trajectories*, and *learning networks* have significant implications for research evidence and equity. They guide our thinking as we review how strains of educational research are increasingly unsettling the relations between learning and the classroom-as-container.

New Directions for Learning-in-Place in Educational Research

Research and experimentation that unsettle notions of "place" in education—that intentionally disrupt the classroom as a bounded space either materially or discursively—have a varied history. To a certain extent, the first (and last) problem of "place" in learning is to understand how to think about place as a multiplicity, a product of interrelations, and thus, as constantly opened up to interactions with other places. Nespor (1997), for instance, argues that to understand the individual fourth graders he studied at "Thurber Elementary," one must also take into account the histories of their neighborhoods, the fragmentation of the African American community in their city, the creation of expressways and railways, public housing, magnet schools, and the children's "lived spaces" that "took their meanings from the ways people did things in them, from the smells and noises and routines of everyday life" (p. 94).

How might we think of place, and especially places of learning, as multiplicities? Discourse analytic work has for some time interpreted the spaces of the classroom in relation to other discourses and texts located "beyond" it, and especially to those of the state, institution, or orders of discourse involving gender, race, culture, sexuality, and others. Such work most often involves reading texts from multiple sites or scales of activity, such as Lee's (1996) interpretations of curriculum alongside and in relation to student–student interactions and student writing, as she analyzes gender production as an outcome of student writing in an Australian secondary geography classroom (see also Anagnostopoulos, 2003). However, for the most part, discourse analytic work has been developed from a logocentric, aspatial perspective; although such work has greatly enriched our critical perspectives on making meaning and the social world, it has had relatively little to offer concerning space, place, or mobility.

Current approaches to social action that include but are not limited to the analysis of discourse are beginning to produce promising frameworks for thinking beyond linguistic theories and texts and toward the interaction of multiple sign systems, bodies, and the material world (Norris, 2004; Norris & Jones, 2004; Scollon & Scollon, 2003). Scollon and Scollon's (2003) approach critiques "placeless" or nonmaterial conceptions of discourse and discursive activity by examining how discourses are located in and indexical to specific material contexts. A key example in their analysis is the street sign. The sign on the street does not offer meaning on its own; rather, it enters into intertextual and dialogic relations with a whole range of other signs, including other actual street signs and other multimodal and linguistic signs in the social world (Bakhtin, 1981). Simultaneously, the sign on the street is indexical to a specific material "place." The material place helps to give meaning and significance to the discourse, just as the (material and discursive) sign serves to give meaning and significance to the place. This notion of how the signs and the material world operate relationally, dialogically, and indexically—termed the *semiotic aggregate* by Scollon and Scollon (2003)—is central to their project of "geosemiotics" and signals one important shift in discourse analysis across the material and discursive hybridity of place-making.

Prior to his untimely death on the first day of 2009, Ron Scollon was taking up mobilities more directly, moving from his earlier considerations of place (Scollon & Scollon, 2003) to questions concerning discourses and material bodies connected across expansive social spaces. In a late, unpublished paper, Scollon (2008) considers the "geography of discourse" of Mt. Ripinsk. The mountain is not merely a material location in Alaska, but is also, for example, a brand image that is pasted onto bottles of micro-brewed beer, which circulate in new material/sign combinations, and become transported by human bodies (e.g., as tee-shirt slogans). From the semiotic aggregate (drawing on Goffman's, 1981, interaction order), Scollon's later (2008) work began to sound nearly Latourian, perhaps reaching for a new ontological ordering of signs and objects on the move. Scollon (2008) expressed the desire to develop the "conceptual software," which he imagined would be geographic information systems (GIS)-like or GIS-enabled, which would "allow us to see directly how someone can go from action to action to get from here to there in this discursive world" (p. 14).

While geosemiotics situates discourse in (material) place, other work in education (e.g., Hirst, 2004; Nespor, 1994, 1997; Willis, 1977) reads the location, control, and regionalization of (children's) bodies in school as discursive ordering (Foucault, 1979). In Nespor's (1997) ethnography of fourth graders at an urban elementary school in Roanoke, Virginia, he offers a critically complex assessment of children's bodies in school spaces. Much of the ethnography disrupts the notion of field "site"; hence, giving site-based "background" information to the study is problematic at best. Yet, across two years of ethnographic work, Nespor describes how "Thurber Elementary" was located and constituted at an intersection of community and city politics, how neighborhoods regionalized children's experiences, offering children in the "same" school very different experiences of the school, and how flows of popular culture and commercialism were powerfully present in children's experiences of social space. Nespor (1997) considers how schooling is involved in the process of abstracting children from social space and from their own bodies. Drawing from Lefebvre (1991), he traces how "people's actual ways of moving through the world" (Lefebvre's "spaces of the body") are replaced through schooling with "the body rendered as a visual display or text readable to an outsider's gaze" (Lefebvre's "body in space"; p. 121). Through control and disciplining of the body in classroom management and other school practices (e.g., single file lines, sitting quietly for long periods of time without moving, regulating the bowels and bladders, p. 128), children undergo a transformation through which "the body ceases to be acknowledged as a tool for mediating relations with the world" (p. 122). The emphasis on the abstracted body is also supported, Nespor argues, through school practices that emphasize written texts and media representations (p. 122). Because of such regulation and abstraction, children's bodies become all the more salient for both teachers and children to interpret in raced, classed, and gendered ways, and exuberant childlike activity (e.g., chase games) become all the more marked as unschooled through social identity construction.

Nespor (1997) raised a number of issues concerning the schooled body and learning in place that are still largely untapped in educational research. In particular, for questions of equity and learning, we might consider how the abstraction of the body in schooled practices and discourses is not "applied" evenly across children: When the body becomes an abstracted site of display over and against a living, engaging body, then dominant power relations and identities of gender, race, class, and other forms of identity have occasion to be reinstantiated. In this manner, conventional practices of abstraction involving bodies are not merely a question of the development of mind, as strong-text theorists (e.g., where literacy is associated with the unique demands of alphabetical writing and the learning of forms of abstraction) such as Ong (1982) would argue, but may well be productive of inequitable opportunities to learn for schooled bodies-in-place (cf. Leander, 2002a).

Although schooled place-making may be evident in the disciplining and abstraction of children's bodies in classrooms, the specific economies of classroom circulations have also been examined as (re)producing stabilities of place. Why is it, despite teachers' best intentions and student participation, that teacher-centered practice is so intransigent? In order to offer a response, Sheehy (2004) directly associates place-making with the particular economies of ideas and texts in the classroom. In this manner, Sheehy's and others' (discussed in the following text) perspectives on place may be properly considered "network" analyses, drawing on various theories to formulate ideas around networks, which are conceived of as producing "place." The typical classroom economy, which Sheehy terms, after Sack (1997), a "thick place," involves teacher–student–teacher (e.g., initiation–response–evaluation) flows of information and texts, and docile, subdued, and disengaged student bodies. The thick place was defined by stasis and an inward-focus of both bodies and ideas, along narrow pathways. In a "thin place," on the other hand, students were more actively involved in determining the direction of their study as well as the distribution of texts, ideas, and bodies.

Objects in new space followed numerous paths. Students situated objects with actual towns and an actual school board . . . the boundary made in their typical school practices thinned out; the membrane between their bodies and ideas became permeable, because ideas moved into networks of relations that mattered to them. (Sheehy, 2004, p. 102)

Although the account of "new space" or a "thin place" may feel familiar to those invested in new forms of learning in school, significant in this case is that Sheehy offers an account of stability that is not based on teacher agency and knowledge, policy, student resistance, or other common tropes. Rather, her analysis is based on the notion that new forms of circulation—new movements of ideas, objects, and bodies—are especially difficult to sustain as they come into contact with old space/"thick place." Hence, educational experiments become located in "in-between spaces" until they fall back into common forms of power/knowledge—circulations with deeper space–time grooves in the routines and resources of schooling.

Critical assessments of the disciplining of the body as a feature of schooled practices of the classroom-as-place also raise the question of how freedom of movement for the child—embodied mobility—is associated with the production of positively associated "place." Nespor's ethnography provides a compelling illustration of how experiences of place, and therefore attachments to place, are widely various, embodied through activities, and largely perspectival. For example, although White middle-class teachers may see children's bodies as problems for management and control, positioning their own bodies and viewpoints with this regard (Nespor, 1997), children seem most exuberant and alive outside in the boundary zones beyond the classroom. Drawing on work on "affective filters" (Dulay, Burt, & Krashen, 1982), Gee (2008) notes that learners whose "affective filters" (e.g., a negative response to perceived threat) are high do not have the same opportunity to learn as those whose filters have not been raised, even though, technically speaking, both groups of learning might be said to be in the "same" environment.

How discursive affective "filters" and embodied affective engagements are articulated, and may be understood through new research methodologies, is a complex and pressing concern in education research. Affectively charged immobilities constraining learning opportunities as well as affectively charged mobilities providing them could permit significant insights into learning-in-place. How do children enter into positive emotional relationships with places of learning? How might we move beyond folk theories emphasizing surface features alone (e.g., classroom decor) or human-centered theories only (e.g., student–teacher relations)? How could school places be made more affectively malleable to become more equitable? Powerful affective relations of place are indicated more broadly in the emerging study of "geographies of fear" in human geography, where specific places are associated in participants' minds with fear or danger. For instance, Kwan's (2008) study of Moslem women in the city can be read as a significant critique of simplistic views on "access" to resources based on material or institutional proximity and circulations alone. Kwan (2008) shows how fear—intensely emotional responses to dynamic cityscapes in post-9/11 U.S. cities—has significantly reduced and constrained Moslem women's circulations, even though their physical accessibility to places may be said to be unchanged.

Others in educational research have also been relatively considering affect and embodiment through the philosophy of Gilles Deleuze and Félix Guattari (1980/1987), and especially their considerations of affective intensities as established through "lines of flight," or unpredictable directions taken in relations among social and affective associations of all kinds. Such associations are arrayed like "rhizomes" (Deleuze & Guattari, 1980/1987), root-like arrangements that extend in multiple directions, and break off. Empirically speaking, Eakle's (2007) object of analysis is the literacy practices of a faith-based school, as such practices move from the classroom to an assembly, and to field trips and a popular motion picture. Eakle studies how texts, spaces, and social practices made available and possible the distances or "ruptures" between particular content and given expressions.

Perhaps more significant than his empirical "results" in this study is Eakle's creative appropriation of Deleuze and Guattari (1980/1987) to establish a spatial research methodology. This methodology, a type of nomadology (Deleuze & Guattari, 1980/1987), works at the interplay between conventions and resisting conserving forces in research—explicitly finding ways to follow "lines of flight" or escape routes in data collection and data analysis. Analytically, for example, Eakle engages in methodologies such as "data walking" (an exploration of data "similar to strolling in physical space," examining the "data traces as a whole" [p. 483]), mapping ("multidirectional free play" [p. 485], but structured by their relation to ethnographic traces), and dramatization (creatively analyzing by setting certain participant perspectives in dramatic form).

Leander and Rowe (2006) also engage with Deleuze and Guattari (1980/1987) to shift an analysis of a literacy performance away from an examination of representations and their meanings and toward the emergence of relations and differences by mapping a performance-in-motion. This "rhizomatic analysis" shifts attention away from fixed meanings and toward action and the new "becomings" that are an important part of literacy performances. The authors argue that the risk of conventional interpretations is such that, due to their own manipulations of space and time, they can miss or entirely erase the notion that literacy performances are often about creating differences, including differences in the moving, shifting relations of semiotic resources and differences in the performed identities of participants.

Although such Deleuzian or rhizoanalytic work in education (Alvermann, 2000; Hagood, 2004; Kamberelis, 2004; St. Pierre, 1997) is in its early stages and is chiefly concerned with methodological issues, it raises a number of possibilities and key questions for the analysis of learning-in-place (and space). First, such theories and developing methodologies challenge difficult-to-overcome notions of places-as-containers by emphasizing the continual movements and transformations within places. Second, movements are associated with the moment-by-moment affective intensities of a vast range of bodies-in-interaction, including human bodies. As such, the theory nudges us toward an appreciation of engagement as ongoing forms of affective energy rather than merely a gateway to learning. Third, and highly important for rethinking learning-in-place, rhizoanalytic approaches eschew decomposing the notion of "learning environment" a priori into components, such as is common in sociocultural or activity system accounts, and instead treats the "environment" as an assemblage or set of assemblages that is composed in unfolding activity. The spatiotemporal contours of the emergent assemblage are interpreted as critically significant for multiple readings of its effects and emergent possibilities.

New Directions for Learning Trajectories in Educational Research

Relatively recent case studies of identity trajectories imply a critique of studies of identity in classrooms or other settings that rely only on single-event analyses. As an alternative, such studies build up histories of identification and/or learning processes over multiple events. Stanton Wortham's (2004) research perhaps best represents this type of case development of tracing, for example, the production of "Tyisha's" social identity as a "disruptive student." Wortham's cases show the effort and ingenuity that go into the identification process on the parts of all classroom participants, and not just the student who is successfully positioned. The way in which repetition works to stabilize identity over time is perhaps best captured at what Wortham terms an *intermediate timescale* of development (months-long development of categories and identities within a classroom). Tyisha's social identity as a disruptive student is achieved through repeatedly correcting her for being such and through her own repeated and responsive uptake of this position. However, Wortham reminds us that the particularities of the events and settings of repetition matter, and not just repetition as an abstract process. The association (discussed elsewhere as a "lamination," Holland & Leander, 2004) appears to have a particular holding power not merely because it is repeated, but because the repetition happens on a particular sort of occasion when being positioned just so is especially marked or re-markable. The repetition, therefore, is not simply an effect of being located in numerous time–spaces, but an effect of the accrual or accumulation of particularly marked time–spaces that are collected and organized.

Wortham's approach to analyzing how identities are stabilized or objectified across events is further fleshed out in a case concerning "Philip," who after 2 months of interaction in a new middle school science lab group would seemingly become established as a good student who would be in charge of lab processes, but have low social status (2008). Wortham compares entextualization (the process by which signs come to presuppose one another, such that meanings for signs are built up interactionally and not given in advance) as a process descriptive of event-based objectification with "interdiscursive" objectification (Agha, 2007; Wortham, 2006), whereby signs and meanings are connected and reconfigured across events. The interdiscursive relation is clearly the more difficult movement to theorize. Wortham (2008) makes the broader conceptual argument that identity research should consider processes at several relevant timescales (rather than, for instance, just "micro" and "macro" timescales [p. 310]) and that research should also consider how a multiplicity of resources, including social interactions but also curricula, classroom organization, materials, and other academic and nonacademic resources, are involved in processes of objectification. This latter point concerning co-present multiple resources pushes on what could be considered the spatial distribution of identity resources, although the analysis in Wortham is primarily temporal.

Erstad, Øystein, Sefton-Green, and Vasbø (2009) also feature cross-site identity processes prominently in their emerging work in the TransActions research group at the University of Oslo. They currently focus on key resources for identity work that travel across contexts, including "personal histories" and "future orientations," used to create "narratives of the self." The Oslo group argues that such narratives are "central to productive learning" (Erstad et al., 2009, p. 100). This learning, which occurs across the permeable boundaries of formal and informal, school and out-of-school, is posited as a connective, in between process; narrativization is a key means of stitching a life trajectory across time. Zacher (2009) presents a nuanced spatiotemporal account of the identity practices of one fifth-grade child, "Christina," who often constructed her own identity as Latina, even though, according to her parents, she was White. Through school-based ethnography and interview analysis, Zacher shows how Christina uses the classroom (and its social justice curriculum), as well as social spaces outside the school, as resources: "Christina redrew her racial identity map every day, adding new locations, new people, new supporting characters and threads" (p. 275). For instance, Zacher examines how Christina's decision to ride the city bus to school allowed her to construct an identity as "more urban, grown up, and independent in her peers' eyes, especially compared to the other White girls" (p. 275). Zacher reads the interactions between Christina and social spaces as a type of dialectic—she is both shaped by these spaces and uses them to shape herself. In contrast to the accounts in Wortham, who emphasizes the social construction of a stable identity position, Zacher proposes that children attend to power dynamics and consciously use social spaces to negotiate their life situations and provide proof for their flexible identity claims (cf. Hull, Zacher, & Hibbert, 2009).

Wortham (2004, 2008), Erstad et al. (2009), and Zacher (2009) make evident the great complexity of resources used in identity and learning processes, and, reflexively, how resources and processes we fix on indicate as much about our own (developing) methods as they do about the social. Interactions and narratives, for instance, are not simply key resources for mobilizing identity and learning in the naked world, but are made to be so by researchers. What "moves" in these cases is a multitude of potential resources, practices or actors, but also of course researchers, who collect data associated with specific space–time assumptions (e.g., the classroom interaction or the interview) and move and organize that data in particular space–time configurations. For example, longitudinal analyses may be said to have already addressed significant problems around learning across time, but are often heavily cloaked in a particular version of developmentalism that overwrites lived spaces and times with its own spatiotemporal narrative. Hence, a key challenge in researching mobilities involves a critical reassessment of the space–time shape and assumptions of research methods, assumptions, and modes of analysis.

An obvious methodological problem for trajectories work, as it strives to disrupt accounts that focus on single events to record evidence of learning and/or identity production, is how to operationalize the study of youth across events and contexts. Lemke (2000), among others, considers how historical and contemporary methods of research very often index what is reachable by a single researcher (in place and time), and how it may well "take a village" to study a village (p. 275), or ecological system of learning. An additional research problem, perhaps not nearly so evident, is how to understand time itself. In querying learning "across time," what understanding of time do we bring to the table? "Time" may appear to be an immutable construct, or one might even argue that we must naturalize our assumptions about time in order to move on with the real work concerning evidence and equity for learning. Yet time, as it is lived and experienced socially and culturally, is constructed in specific and diverse ways; time is "made" rather than simply given in advance and filled up (Dubinskas, 1988). Time as "kairos," or our experience of time, is markedly different than time as "chronos," or clock and calendar time. And yet clock and calendar time—whether truncated at the event or extended and divided up into units at greater "scale"—is what orders and structures research and guides our notions of "development."

To a certain extent, Lemke's (2000) work on timescales, highly influential in sociocultural theory (including in Wortham's 2006 and 2008 studies), upholds conceptions of timescales and their necessary constraints. This perspective on temporality builds its case from timescale hierarchies in complex systems theories and the "adiabatic principle" from physics, which describes why very fast and much slower processes cannot interact efficiently with one another. Although it seems worth raising critical questions on the degree of suitability of these biological and physical processes and rules as metaphors for social system analysis, we presently follow Lemke's own thinking concerning a remarkable characteristic of time in social systems. One of Lemke's (2000) key points is that, in human activity, processes from one "time scale" routinely interact with processes from a completely different "time scale." Social time, in other words, routinely breaks rules from biological time (e.g., the adiabatic principle). In particular, through "semiotically mediated heterochrony" (p. 279), long timescale processes are brought to bear on and interact with processes in very short timescales, which Lemke notes as "the basis for human social interaction across timescales."

A textbook in a classroom is a clear example of heterochrony, as the years-long process of writing and publishing the textbook (and perhaps, for the teacher, of using it) are brought into the student's lesson-long interaction with it. Lemke associates his concern for heterochrony with Star and Griesemer's (1989) concept of the "boundary object" from science studies—objects that circulate through networks and serve roles of coordinating different institutions, social spaces, fields of study, or projects. One can read Lemke (2000) as signaling how temporalities (including time scales) do not merely exist in the world, but are rather semiotically performed, made significant, and coordinated. Such is evident, for instance, in Erstad et al.'s (2009) concern with narratives and their uses across situations that compose a life. In such a reading, trajectories are not merely wooden movements forward through time, where temporal separations are linked through some linear social process; they also describe the social semiotics of making particular forms of time visible and relevant (e.g., this class period, this textbook history, the presence of African American children in this school), building (or breaking) connective relationships between forms of time.

A second critical point concerning Lemke (2000), and trajectory work following how particular learners develop across time, concerns the relative emphasis on time over space. In the case of Lemke's (2000) work, although he eschews *some* spatial perspectives in his movements across timescales, what he primarily rejects is spatiality as static slices of the social, including "lines of connectivity," "horizontal layers," and "flat views" of human interactions that travel only to very local interactions, where immediate human scales of activity are most visible (p. 274). In brief, what is rejected are a-temporal perspectives on space. This type of critique—essentially the separation of space from time, resulting in static spatiality—is often also found within contemporary theories of social space (e.g., Lefebvre, 1991; Massey, 2005; Soja, 1989; Thrift & Dewsbury, 2000), and is the central reason why many theorists coin and prefer combined terms (i.e., "space–time," "time–space," "social space"). Turning this critique the other way around, we might consider the relative absence of dynamic simultaneity and moving distributions in the trajectories work. The trajectory itself creates its own thin slice, not across space, but through multiple spaces, dropping coeval spatial extension and spatial plurality to the cutting room floor. We might consider how spatial–social learning and identity networks interact with temporal–individual trajectories or pathways, toward a richer interpretation of spatiotemporal mobility. We turn next to some key formulations of learning networks.

New Directions for Learning Networks in Educational Research

Along with newly developing conceptions of place and the formulation of learning trajectories across space and time, educational research is beginning to open up new conceptions of networks for learning. Such networks for learning may be accompanied by the rise of new technical networks (e.g., the Internet), but the idea of dynamic conception of "networking" cannot be replaced by the static human or technical map of distributions. Hence, following Latour (1999), this section could perhaps be more productively titled "New Directions in Learning Networking." Presently, we discuss networking as a mode of conceiving social spaces dynamically and relationally, where objects of all variety are moving and undergoing transformation. After considering networking in educational research, we return to a three-part review of place, trajectory, and network in studies of children's learning-relevant activity outside of school.

The spatiotemporal notion of networking within actor network theory (ANT; Callon, 1986; Latour, 1987, 1999, 2005; Law, 1994) has many dimensions, and is not a unified theory. Presently, we will consider some of these dimensions in the development and use of ANT for considerations of evidence and equity in educational research. Although ANT is not the only theoretical approach to studying networks for learning, it is a highly promising and emerging body of work that seems especially suited for considering mobilities of various kinds, for reconceiving of learning "environment," for challenging current perspectives on agency as a quality unique to individual humans, for considering how power is enacted through particular network formations and flows, and for challenging current perspectives on the relations between humans, tools, and signs.

However, one of the difficult problems with ANT is that it directly offers little on the analysis of learning or change of individuals. It is not a theory or set of orientations "designed" to understand learning. Scientists, who feature prominently in the work as individuals, are generally treated as givens in ANT rather than as actively produced or transformed (critiqued by Nespor, 1994, p. 15). Thus, although this problem and others make ANT a novel and potentially productive approach for rethinking access to learning, learning–identity relations, and other aforementioned problems and issues, the relationship of ANT to problems of learning is an indirect and uncertain one. The task of translating this "theory of translation" (Latour, 1996b) for productive use in conceiving of evidence for learning or problems of equity is indeed promising, but still only emerging.

ANT has introduced a wide range of constructs for thinking about networking, most of which have only begun to be deployed in education research. A recent analysis (Stevens, O'Connor, Garrison, Jocuns, & Amos, 2008) that spans trajectory and network approaches to learning takes up an approach to movements and connections across time and space that is characteristic of ANT and operationalizes the construct of "obligatory passage points" (Latour, 1987)—officially designed gateways through which one must pass to be recognized (in this case) as a particular kind of person. Using longitudinal data and focusing on engineering education, the researchers create "person centered ethnographies" (Hollan & Wellencamp, 1993) of students who become (or do not become) engineers across 4 years of undergraduate education. Although it is somewhat common to associate knowledge (here, "accountable disciplinary knowledge" or ADK) with development of identity work in studies of

disciplinary learning, Stevens et al. (2008) bring "navigating" in as a critical third relational construct. As an illustration of what Stevens et al. intend by "navigation," they
discuss among other cases that of "Simon," who did not do well enough on early college
coursework to be admitted to the engineering program at "Large Public University."
From the perspective of disciplinary knowledge and institutional requirements, Simon's
trajectory toward engineering was doubtful. However, a professor father of a childhood
friend, who was a frequent mentor in Simon's childhood learning experiences, wrote
him a strong letter of recommendation that helped him secure a job in a mechani-
cal stress testing facility. Simon's experiences in the testing facility—as an opening or
form of navigation—were pivotal for his institutional acceptance into an engineering
program, for later success in coursework, and importantly, for the development of his
identity as an engineer (p. 362). In the last 2 years of his undergraduate degree, the
"noncurricular" forms of learning that Simon had accrued through the testing facility
began to become increasingly significant to his (classroom) disciplinary learning.

Obligatory passage points exemplify, in the analysis of networked approaches to
learning, how new (and old) mobilities of learning are not distributed over nude and
abstract landscapes, but rather over complex institutional and political spaces that
predefine necessary routes and transitions for continual movement through them.
Given these necessary mobility practices across powerful boundaries and through
deep institutional grooves, one's "individual ability" or presumed lack thereof is a
poor explanation for disciplinary success (Stevens et al., 2008, p. 364). To concep-
tualize navigation work from the perspective of the person, we might consider his or
her unofficial strategies (e.g., Simon's letter of recommendation) and unofficial routes
(his work in the testing facility; p. 361). Moreover, and an important contribution of
this analysis as it formulates an account of learning and mobility, institutions show
marked differences in the degree to which they provide "navigational flexibility" for
students. Unsurprisingly, "Suburban Private University" provided more of such flexibility than did "Large Public University" or "Urban Private University" (p. 361).
Stevens et al. (2008) suggest that navigational flexibility—as materially and discursively structured into the buildings, policies, and pathways of institutions, and also as
practiced within the strategies of individuals—is deeply entwined with what we have
come to associate with higher learning in the disciplines. Hence, issues of access and
equity are fundamentally framed spatially in the study, and associated with both the
built environment and the material and discursive navigation practices of individuals.

Whereas Latour (1996b) argues that the split between the political world and
the material world is characteristic of the modern period, in ANT the work of the
material, technical world of the network is brought to the fore and given its due—the
image of the world becomes one in which technologies are active agents, recruiting and "enrolling" humans (Latour, 1996a). A priori distinctions between humans
and nonhumans are not made, indexing a tenet of ANT known as "generalized
symmetry" (Callon, 1986; Pardoe, 2000). Rather than purifying categories, Latour
(1993) calls for a "new anthropological matrix" in which notions such as "subject"
and "agency" are replaced by "variable geometry entities" (p. 11). The extension of

agency across humans and nonhumans is central to Brandt and Clinton's (2002) theoretical critique of social practice theories of literacy, where the authors address, among other issues, the ways in which material objects "act," along with humans, to carry literacy into social spaces. The notion of agency distributed among humans and nonhuman actors is related to a larger body of work developing the idea of "sponsors" of literacy—"agents who enable or induce literacy and gain advantage by it in some way" (p. 349). The idea of sponsorship, further developed elsewhere for literacy studies (Brandt, 2001), could potentially be a rich lens through which to conceive of access to a broad range of social practice associated with schooling (e.g., mathematics), particularly were this distributed yet personalized account of agency expanded through an explicit analysis of sponsorship and mobility.

The Latourian "anthropological matrix" is highly relevant to inquiry into "environments" or spaces for learning and what they afford learning, as well as for understanding how learning within a disciplinary field involves ways of seeing, doing, and thinking and interacting that are coordinated and achieved by moving the "world" of that discipline across tools, representations, and persons. Nespor draws heavily on the ANT concept of "mobilization" as developed by Callon (1986), which refers to a particular form of movement or "translation" (Latour, 1987)—where two things that are not the same are taken as equivalent. In a common form of translation, a "spokesman" or representative (human or nonhuman) speaks for or represents an entity that has been recruited or "enrolled" in a relationship with it (Nespor, 1994, p. 15). Nespor compares how resources were mobilized in an undergraduate physics program at a public university with how resources were mobilized for learning management in a business program. In physics, Nespor traces chains of mobilization across sequences of activity and ways of seeing inside and outside of the classroom, including textbooks, which take physics from everyday life and represent it such that references to individual actors and their agency are stripped away, producing "context-independent universals" (p. 55) through books that are widely disseminated. Textbooks are then mobilized by physics professors, who reconstruct the textbook "facts" into a collection of brief narratives, restoring some of the context-dependence to the text, in their own fashion. A further chain is then student note-taking practices, which mobilize professor lectures as a means of interacting with the professor's performances, not merely as a way of recording them, but as a means of concurrently enacting them on paper (p. 69). Importantly, as students move along into higher level physics, the transformations from world and experience to page shift as well, as students increasingly learn to see things that they cannot observe in the everyday world.

Mobility studies inspired by ANT are directed toward describing and understanding the specific qualities of circulation among participants, including orientation, directionality, proximity, and others (Bingham & Thrift, 2000, p. 290). These relations are not merely of theoretical interest, but may also guide empirical work as researchers enrich ways of moving beyond claims that learning is distributed or mobilized and analyze how specific qualities of distributed networks afford and constrain learning opportunities, and for whom. For example, in a research study that analyzed one youth's engagement across school contexts and contrasted it with his engagement in a massively multiplayer online game (Leander & Lovvorn, 2006), ANT was marshaled as a conceptual resource to contrast types of activity in schooling and gaming. One highly contrastive quality of networking in the two environments was difference of activity. In contrast to schooling, gaming rhythms for "Brian" were highly regular, and were partially structured by circulations of the game environment that required his ongoing engagement—movements that effectively inserted him as having a purpose for returning to play. A further contrast, which also indexes the specific relationships between networked entities as paramount, was that in the game, Brian was provided representations of his own activity that afforded him both local and more global (larger scale) perspectives on his own activity, in rapid circulation with one another. Yet, in his school practices Brian seemed often unaware of a perspective on his activity beyond the immediate and more-or-less pressing task.

Finally, beyond the reinterpretation of learning "environments" as learning networks, ANT is also being taken up to a limited degree in researching educational policy and its relation to practice (e.g., Clarke, 2002; Hamilton, 2001). Such approaches draw again on the generalized symmetry and mobilization of humans (e.g., policy authors, state officials, organizational heads) and objects (texts of all types, tests, devices). Hamilton (2001), for example, examined how the International Adult Literacy Survey (IALS) was turned into commonsense knowledge for a broad public, even while it left the history of that translation obscured. The author traces how the survey organized knowledge about literacy and the literate subject by translating its findings into a "simplified, received wisdom about what counts as literacy, who has and has not got it" (p. 192). This form of language translation, together with enrolling powerful institutional agents and achieving a very large number of enrolled texts, media sources, and human participants, permitted the IALS to achieve the status, functionally, as a social fact sheet about literacy.

The use of ANT in policy study, or policy to classroom-connection studies, provides one means of addressing matters of scale in other approaches, including discursive approaches to "place" discussed previously. The tendency in many multilevel or multiscale approaches, which use a more or less implicit embedded approach to contexts, e.g., Bronfenbrenner's (1979) "ecological model," is to place oneself in the center (or at the periphery) and to point in the other direction, abstracting the "global" or "local" or merely asserting their "influence" rather than empirically demonstrating such relations. Through an actor network, localities and globalities are achievements of network nodes, expansions and compressions, and translations, and are not given in advance as matters of social scale. Particularly in an era of increasing standardization, when policies are not only being increasingly mobilized but also taken up in multifarious ways, a studied examination of the chains of mobilization from policy to practice and back would seem a significant contribution with respect to opportunity to learn (e.g., how knowledge and being a knower become defined within subjects and disciplines) and with respect to evidence (e.g., how the complex effects of policy to practice and back are analyzed).

RESEARCHING MOBILITIES IN CHILDREN'S GEOGRAPHIES

This and the following section reach into bodies of literature that, for the most part, are beyond or outside mainstream education research. In many if not most cases, the interest of the researchers in these sections is not learning per se, but on the geographical, cultural, and social dimensions of children's lives. In the present section we review work from the developing area of "children's geographies," which, as presented here, is primarily comprised of human and cultural geographies of children. We have selected studies that are representative of key issues in this area of work, and have primarily focused on work with empirical data.

As opportunities for child engagement increase, with technological advancements and densifying and diversifying communities, so too does the gap between an adult's understanding of childhood and the actual day-to-day experience of being one. Matthews and Limb (1999) write,

Assumptions are made by adults about what it means to be a child and therefore what environments they need. In so doing they fail to recognize that children differ from adults in terms of their "ways of seeing." What goes on during the day of an average young person is different in rhythm, scale and content from that of adults. Understanding of these differences needs to be rooted in the life worlds of children. (p. 66)

Therefore, stepping outside the educational literature and looking primarily at studies that describe the everyday lives of children should be a priority for practitioners and researchers wanting to educate learners in a culturally relevant and responsive way.

"Place" in Children's Geographies

We first engage with the idea of children's everyday lives by examining the changing nature of places of learning. Treated as a nexus of social, political, institutional, and cultural flows, places serve as methodologically significant nodes of analysis. Place may be defined as ". . . a space which people in a given locality understand as having a particular history and as arousing emotion identifications, and which is associated with particular groups and activities" (Watt & Stenson, 1998, pp. 252–253). In the following section, human and children's geographers locate their vision in outdoor, indoor, liminal, adult-controlled, commercialized, and coproduced places that shed light on and raise questions for children's learning and identity formation.

Indoor and Outdoor Spaces

Using methodologies that place the childhood experience and their construction of reality front and center (Holloway & Valentine, 2000), studies from children's geographies demonstrate that the childhood experience of and in space has changed dramatically between generations. The first change in absolute space, or how children from two generations experience their built/material environments, is the shift from spending leisure time outdoors to indoor play. To understand this phenomenon, an intergenerational approach is necessary (Karsten, 2005).

Through the comparison of oral histories of parents to the mobility patterns of their children, the radical shift from time spent outdoors to time spent indoors for today's children is apparent (Karsten, 2005; Pooley, Turnbull, & Adams, 2005). Research in Amsterdam has shown that children of the 1950s through the 1960s enjoyed extensive outdoor playtime without a lot of adult supervision. This freedom of movement was demonstrated in the journey to school and youth patronizing local shops. Furthermore, children were urged to play outside due to a lack of indoor space for urban families. Regardless of neighborhood, age, or class, leisure time meant playing out-of-doors, in streets, yards, and sometimes parks (Karsten, 2005). For children between the ages of 8 and 13 years in a New York City working-class neighborhood in the 1950s, 42 different sites were reported as places visited independent of adults. Adjacent woods, caves, the movie theater, and the park were local hot spots for children to enjoy without their parents (Gaster, 1991).

But as the years progressed, and the urban society and environment changed, so too did the ways in which children used time and space after school. Whereas in the 1950s when neighborhood streets were filled with playing children, many streetscapes of today allocate more land use to parking, have more traffic, and are void of youth. Gaster (1991) found that children of today's generation in one New York City housing development have fewer community settings to visit because of changes in the built environment and increasing restrictions placed on them by parents. Rather than roaming around neighboring environs, such as caves and parks, children spent almost all of their free time on the grounds of their housing development. This finding is consistent with Valentine and McKendrick's (1997) analysis of data collected from parents who have children between 8 and 11 years old in Northwest England. These authors write,

The children who are most restricted, both in terms of spatial range and the activities they have the opportunity to pursue, are those who live in high-rise apartments. Unlike children living at ground level, children who live several storeys up are a long way from the "street" which means that when on the street they are a long way from parental surveillance. (p. 222)

So as our communities urbanize with more offices, stores, apartment complexes, and parking garages, children's outdoor play space diminishes (Aitken, 1994; C. Katz, 1994). But if children are not outside, what are they doing indoors, and how do these spaces of activity provide opportunities to learn?

Street as Place and Home

Another research area pertinent to new understandings of place in children's geography involves studies of the street as place. Studies of streetscapes elucidate how particular outdoor spaces continue to be adopted and transformed by youth as significant places of learning and identity formation. Many of these urban streetscapes have "liminal place" qualities that make them exceptional sites of research for people on the threshold between childhood and adulthood.

Describing the importance of streets to Amsterdam children from the 1950s and 1960s, Karsten (2005) writes,

Children used the outdoor space of the street for many different activities, and urban public space was regularly appropriated for their own games. They built tents and even huts on the pavements and defended these against intruders of all ages. Playing in the street with few toys or other means generally demanded a high level of creativity. (p. 281)

Adult expectations have changed from the 1950s and 1960s—children should be off the streets, indoors. But while it may not be as socially acceptable, teenagers continue to "post-up" or hang-out at particular spots on street corners or sidewalks. The practice is more common among working-class youth living in densely urban areas. In their study of working-class, White adolescents living in areas of high unemployment and crime in the United Kingdom, Matthews, Limb, and Taylor (2000) describe teenagers using streetscapes to meet-up with friends, to avoid judging adult glances, and to create deeply personal spaces of identity. These youth find safety and solidarity in the intermediary space of the street that is neither public nor private. Matthews et al. write, "Streets comprised (semi) autonomous space or the 'stage' where young people were able to play out their social life, largely unfettered by adults" (p. 76). In Table 1, Matthews (2003) gives a sample of what adolescents in an impoverished Scottish community actually report doing on the street (p. 105).

This table shows how participation in informal sports on the street remains frequent throughout adolescence. Looking at the "hang-out" and "get away from it" categories simultaneously, one can see that as children get older, streetscapes primarily become a gathering place where teens can be with peers and away from adults and the pressures they represent. Reporting that "I'm doing nothing" becomes more acceptable with age, whereas reporting that "I'm just playing" becomes much less so.

In her study of "risk and risk anxiety . . . and its consequences for children's everyday lives" in Scotland, Harden (2000, p. 45) calls the familiar boundary of street space, where children are close to home and still have access to friends and community, the "local sphere." Although not inside the home, children tend to perceive the local sphere as a safe haven. To one teenager named Anthony, in Seyer-Ochi's (2006) study of the Fillmore in Los Angeles, one street corner is the cornerstone to his understanding of community, neighborhood, identity, and social life. This realization becomes painfully obvious to the young man when the street corner was "renovated" because of crime. Here on the street, the intersections of politics, economics, racism, and culture are not as easily ignored as they can be inside the home.

But what can the everyday experiences of those children who call the streets their home tell us about the experience of childhood? Children's geographers explicate the need for all youth to identify with and in place through studies of street children. These youth, who have fled abusive relationships with adults, have been nefariously misunderstood, or have suffered familial economic hardship in a changing global economy (Beazley, 2000), live in the interstitial space of streets at all times, trying to

TABLE 1
Most Popular Activities Carried Out on the Street by Age Group

Activity	Percentage (Frequency)			
	9–10 Years Old	11–12 Years Old	13–14 Years Old	15–16 Years Old
Informal sport	31 (8)	29 (8)	27 (12)	21 (9)
Just play	23 (6)	21 (6)	7 (3)	1 (1)
Meet/hang about with friends	19 (5)	25 (7)	30 (13)	38 (16)
"Get away from it"	—	7 (2)	11 (5)	24 (10)
Do nothing	8 (2)	7 (2)	18 (8)	12 (4)
Other activities	19 (5)	11 (3)	7 (3)	4 (2)

carve out particular niches to call their own. In this way, street children could epitomize what it means to be modern, surviving in spaces that are constantly destroyed, then renewed, revitalized, then updated (Ruddick, 1998). For homeless youth in Uganda, Van Blerk (2005) illustrates how episodic mobility and nomadic mobility are fundamentally different, afford different possibilities for producing identities, and can be understood by studying the time frames and patterns through which youth access multiple spaces and places. Van Blerk emphasizes that the proliferation of technology and place exponentially increases the mobility for some children while simultaneously restricts it for others. This finding is complementary to Young's (2003) study of full-time street children in Kampala, Uganda. She found that socially and spatially marginalized youth claim "untouchable" spaces—those areas that are too rancid, detestable, or isolated for adults. However, laying claim to and keeping rooftop, underground, or trash-ridden spaces comes with its share of negotiations with adult street-dwellers. She writes,

Their acceptance . . . is based on them renouncing their subcultural behaviours and work in harmony with society to be allowed to engage in desired activity. In other cases they are driven by a money incentive to behave according to the social rules that govern their working activity. (p. 624)

Regardless of the motive, street children build connections throughout their local sphere for survival.

Adults and Place-Shaping Power, Supervision, Fear

Yet another area of research relevant to a new conceptualization of place in children's geography is studies of how adult authority and fear powerfully shape and control children's spaces. Studies of place-shaping power show how the movement from outdoor to indoor spaces described previously is further complicated by how "public" spaces are becoming increasingly adult-controlled and supervised, raising tensions between older and younger generations. Those adolescents who take to the streets by choice or out of necessity experience the most intense version of marginalization as they are constantly under the watchful eye of disapproving adults, vying for space that others feel they do not deserve. Exclusion from public spaces may prove extraordinarily challenging for street children; however, some still manage to find acceptance and make a new family, as Beazley (2000) found in her observations and interviews of street children in Java, Indonesia.

The punk squatters in Hollywood during the mid-1970s and early 1980s, for instance, faced intense resistance to their practice of inhabiting condemned buildings. As the group gained a reputation for being violent, marginalized spaces in which they lived, such as abandoned apartments and warehouses, were demolished. Frank, a former punk and participant of Ruddick's (1998) study, is quoted, "We're talking about the erosion of free space. You know, not just open space in the sense of, 'oh yeah, nice parks.' We're talking about space with any kind of latitude for independent action" (p. 350). Eventually, the mainstream, adult-led dissolution of space resulted in the decimation of the punk scene, but not before these adolescents changed the meaning and identity of "homeless youth" in Los Angeles. According to Ruddick, social workers and other professionals working with street kids had to "change their understanding and mode of treatment of youth in this act of suturing the positive identities that the youth chose for themselves and the images they (the service providers) had of runaways in a new space within Hollywood" (p. 359). At least in this example from northwest Los Angeles, adults were forced to examine and understand the everyday reality of youth in order to live harmoniously and provide a service in a relevant way.

Today, however, many adults characterize youth seen on the street as loiterers and "up-to-no-good." Valentine (1996) sketches how an "angel"/"devil" dichotomy shapes conceptions of children in space, such that the concept of danger runs parallel to the concept of dangerous children. Adolescents' time in public spaces is limited and often reprimanded. In one specific case, two adolescent girls in Wales were ticketed by police officers for drawing with chalk on a neighborhood sidewalk. The police claimed it was "graffiti" (Gill, 2007). Skelton (2000) ethnographically traced how deprived adolescent girls in a depressed urban area in the Rhondda Valleys in South Wales were frequently threatened and chased off by adults.

Even though spending time on the streets continues to be snubbed by adults, children continue to resist being compressed into indoor spaces. Rather than remaining idle or under constant supervision of adults, children "resist, oppose and find gaps in adult restrictions," Valentine (1997) writes. Streets of today serve as an intermediary space between private and public realms, especially neighborhood streets. Perhaps more important, streets act as a zone of development and transition, whereupon children gradually move away from home and the comfortable confines of family life to a more "adult" existence of peers and the tensions and pressures of the outside world (Matthews, 2003).

Institutional and Commercial Sponsors of Learning Places

Research from children's geography regarding the institutionalization and commercialization of learning places enhances our understanding of the current state of children's places. Examining how new urban developments affect children in the Netherlands, Karsten (2002) argues that along with child safety, a focus on personal achievement and changing ideas about motherhood is a dominant discourse that is changing the spatialization of children in the city. But the shift has occurred differently for children from disparate socioeconomic backgrounds. Although on average, children spend much more time indoors than their parents' generation, some youth experience the daily routine under constant adult supervision. Others have more autonomy, either indoors or outdoors. These distinctive experiences are delineated across social and economic class (Karsten, 2005; Lareau, 2003).

Children from poor or working-class families have more opportunities for outdoor and autonomous play because parents have fewer resources (money and time) to provide youth with organized activities (Valentine & McKendrick, 1997). In her study with Turkish/Moroccan, Surinamese/Antillean, and Dutch-born children living in Amsterdam, Karsten (1998) found that a child's class (i.e., working class, middle class) is a better predictor of how she spends her leisure time than her ethnicity. Although children from working-class or poor families may have more opportunities to be independently out of doors, the discussion above has shown that outdoor spaces are being eliminated.

Children from middle- and upper-class families have alternative places within which to spend time—institutionalized spaces. Middle- and upper-class families in the United States dedicate a lot of time and money to the "cultivation" of their children—providing opportunities that will perhaps look good on a resume (Lareau, 2003). In a cross-cultural study of children from Kenya, Brazil, and the United States, Tudge et al. (2006) discovered that, regardless of geographic location, "children from middle-class families were more likely than their working-class peers to be involved in academic lessons and were more likely to play with academic objects" (pp. 1462-1463). Rather than informally playing outdoors, these children experience "leisure time," or after school time, engaged in a formal activity supervised by an adult (Lareau, 2003), such as a piano lesson, soccer practice, or chess club. In this way, the daily life of middle- and upper-class children has been insularized; increasing money flows and markets for afterschool "child care" in this capitalist market have minimized the amount of outdoor space available to youth. Many of today's children spend their leisure time within walls, fences, or behind hedges, creating a continuum of traveling from one "contained" space to the next (Zeiher, 2003). Fuller, Bridges, and Pai (2007) found that even in United States preschool classrooms, where the curriculum may be "emergent," these government-sanctioned institutions are standardizing the ways in which very young people from culturally diverse backgrounds learn and develop. Pre-K teachers and administrators pressure parents to prepare their children for school in a very particular way.

Analyzing adult attitudes toward children and childhood in the United Kingdom, Gill (2007) argues that adult supervision and contestation over space has pushed adolescents into the house to fully explore virtual space—begging the question of what children without computers in the home do with their free time. In her study involving a questionnaire of 1,600 children and young people in the United Kingdom and fewer in-depth interviews, McNamee (1998) found that the containment of both genders inside the home (not just the girls, anymore) has created a more competitive atmosphere over resources, like the remote and computer games. "Young men are controlling and policing their sisters' access to computer and video games in the expression of their masculine identity" (p. 204). Some of these contained "play" spaces are even commercialized, connected to restaurants, malls, and shopping centers. Their use requires money, necessitating a parent that patronizes the establishment (McKendrick, Bradford, & Fielder, 2000).

However, the play spaces designed and built for children do not necessarily match what children actually want in a play environment. Studies in the United Kingdom and the United States found that children between 8 and 13 years old prefer the outdoors, or open spaces, utility sites, and home spaces for play more than any others (Moore, 1976). Therefore, perhaps parental desires are considered more than those of children when designing commercialized play centers. Busy, working mothers and fathers can use these facilities as a way to relax, have a drink at the adjoining bar, and let someone else (an employee) watch their children. McKendrick et al. (2000) write, "These centres serve a useful function for adults, undoubtedly centres pander to parents' often irrational concerns for children's safety" (p. 113). Insular spaces, such as indoor play grounds, fenced yards, and hedged-in soccer fields, are characteristically supervised by an adult, the ongoing activity is organized, and rules are adult-negotiated and enforced.

So with few opportunities to negotiate time and space independently, these children are missing out on a developmental experience had by their parents, and some children from poor and working-class families (Valentine & McKendrick, 1997). Middle class children's lack of independence and participation in shaping their daily time schedule brings up the question of whether some of today's youth experience a lack of agency in decisions made about the spaces within which they function (Zeiher, 2003). Having the opportunity to call a particular chosen space a "place" may be absent for some children.

Coproduction of Social, Critical, and Physical Dimensions of Learning Places

Another research area important to new understandings of place in children's geography are studies of places as social, critical, and physical coproductions of learning. These studies of places as sites of coproduction illuminate how the commercialization of spaces described earlier is complicated by how children view and categorize these places as either spaces of exclusion, marginalization, structure, etc. Therefore, asking children how they would envision and change the places through which they travel and participate, such as their own school grounds, allows learners to engage in the spatial arrangement of their own lives. Rather than living, working, and playing in a space configured by others, learners engage with their surroundings in a way that is empowered with possibility and agency. In their study of the ethnically and culturally diverse suburbs of Adelaide, South Australia, Comber, Nixon, Ashmore, Loo, and Cook (2006) write, "Many school projects strip out the richness of everyday life and the complexity of getting things done in the real world" (p. 243). In this "urban renewal" activity, children possess the authority and power to map their own spaces. Harvey (1996) describes mapping when he writes,

Mapping is a discursive activity that incorporates power. The power to map the world in one way rather than another is a crucial tool in political struggles. Power struggles over mapping . . . are fundamental moments in the production of discourses. (pp. 111–112)

A sense of agency and appropriation over lived spaces can be the result of children drawing maps of envisioned or re-imagined (Comber et al., 2006) school grounds and communities. To Harvey (1996), they become active participants and creators of the discourse used in that space.

As many children grow up, they watch their neighborhoods, streets, and houses deteriorate. These deteriorating spaces only add to feelings of exclusion for children in that facilities once appropriate for use are now in ruins (Morrow, 2003). In Detroit, Michigan, for example, Breitbart (1998) discovered just how affected young people are by their surroundings. She writes,

Young people who live in declining parts of the city are profoundly aware of the influence that their local environments exert. They can literally see and feel the constraints that dangerous and/or inadequately provisioned neighborhoods place upon them, and they can appreciate the opportunities that safe places, with ample resources provide. . . . These spaces send messages to young people about how an external world values or fails to value the quality of their lives. (p. 308)

In this project, adolescent volunteers who engaged in a community revisioning initiative made astute observations of the bleak urban conditions, and set out on a course to change them. By creating new public art installations, usually in the form of gardens or murals, youth actively changed their community, participated in intergenerational projects, and came to a better understanding of the political, social, and economic forces that make cities dynamic, for better or worse (Breitbart, 1998). Presumably, gaining an understanding about where you are in the world promotes realizations of where others are in relation. Targeting the spatial aspect of learning is thus an important way of promoting democratic values and citizenship.

"Trajectories" Across Children's Geographies

Historically, the ways in which children have traveled between places have been understudied and undertheorized. Even today, little is known about the salient qualities of one's pathway from place to place, or what happens in those transitional periods at all. However, if we compare the mobility of children from previous generations to that of present-day children, the contrast between the two prompts a reconceptualization of "learning on the move." The lack of self-directed mobility and the immense amount of time children spend in transit problematizes the notion of rides in automobiles as mundane, unthinking routines. Research from the United Kingdom has shown that there has been a substantial increase in the proportion of children riding in a car to school and a decrease in children arriving to school on foot with an adult (Pooley et al., 2005). Hillman, Adams, and Whitelegg's (1990) study, in response to an increase in car use patterns and child fatalities in traffic accidents in Britain, correlated a significant decrease in children's independent mobility with an increase in traffic congestion. In 1971, 80% of 7- and 8-year-old children went to school on their own, by 1990 only 9% were making the journey unaccompanied, with more than four times as many being driven than 20 years earlier. The study, based on an historical analysis of survey data in the United Kingdom and Germany, illustrated how children's discretionary space has undergone an inversion in the past 40 years, from independent mobility in outside spaces to sequestered play inside homes or other adult-monitored spaces. Movements between these places are determined by adults. Adult accounts of their mobility as children contrast starkly to today's image of "contained" children. One particularly idyllic report highlights the incredible independence of a 4-year-old boy as retold by Ward (1978):

Not as a chore, but as an eagerly desired pleasure, I was fairly often entrusted with the task of buying fish and bringing it home alone. This involved the following: walking to the station in five to ten minutes; buying a ticket; watching train with coal-burning steam locomotive pull in; boarding train; riding across long bridge over shallows separating small-boat harbor (on the right) from ship's harbor (on the left), including small naval base with torpedo boats; continuing through a tunnel; leaving train terminal, sometimes dawdling to look at railroad equipment, walking by and sometimes entering fisheries museum; passing central town park where military band played . . . selection of fish; haggling about price; purchase and return home. (pp. 10–11)

Compared with this account of a fish-buying errand, there are very few everyday activities of today's children that demonstrate so much responsibility, independent mobility, and agency within our own communities (Ward, 1978).

Constricted Mobilities of Today's Children

Research concerning constricted mobilities of today's children from children's geography elucidates the changing nature and importance of trajectory. Today, more family time and resources in the United States suburbs are dedicated to driving children around the adjacent community and beyond (Lareau, 2003). Nespor (1997) demonstrates that some children in suburban/urban environments in the United States recount their daily travel trajectories around the corporate, commercialized places they pass, such as grocery stores, mega-churches, and fast food chains. These establishments become the easily identifiable landmarks of modern daily life. Such mobility patterns draw a clear picture of where and what resources children notice, recognize, and access within a community. Pia Christensen (2003) describes an 11-year-old girl's experience of her community in Copenhagen:

[Mie] knew her local neighborhood only through the particular routes she used. She knew the route from home to school and also the route from her house to the local cinema but she did not know the route from school to the cinema. This became an issue for her when a children's film club started up at the cinema. (p. 22)

For Mie, her unique and constricted trajectory through space and time both illuminated certain parts and pathways of her community and hid others.

Although today's middle-class youth travel over greater physical distances, their degree of self-directed mobility appears to be much smaller than the prior generation. When a child is ferried around town in the backseat of a car, from one organized activity to another, there is little environmental understanding or community participation required (Valentine & McKendrick, 1997). Whereas independent mobility affords collective interactions with neighborhood peers, shopkeepers, and other community stakeholders (Christensen, 2003), rides in the backseat of a car usually do not. Older adolescents who would be more likely to travel around without an adult present, on foot, on bikes, or in cars, are having their mobility restricted by policymakers. Breitbart (1998) writes, "Middle class suburbs [in the United States] with exceedingly low crime rates now join cities in the use of legal time curbs on the free access of citizens below the age of 18 to the out-of-doors. Indeed, President Clinton has come out publicly in support of curfews for *all* cities and towns in the U.S." (p. 307). Therefore, children's "home ranges" are not just restricted by overprotective and fearful parents. Structural limitations, laws, and urban plans are built into the terrain over which children travel.

Obviously, children's mobility increases with age, but is also highly dependent on gender. In a rural Vermont community, Hart (1977) found that boys enjoy an increased range of movement away from the home as they mature, but girls are kept close to the hearth. Whereas boys are encouraged to exercise their independence out in "the wild," girls are taught domestic skills in the confines of the house. This disparity may be even greater in rural landscapes where adolescent girls struggle to find any space outside their own homes with which to identify—to call a "place" (Dunkley, 2004). In urban and suburban areas, especially in the United States and Europe, adolescent girls have enclosed malls, town centers, and restaurants that provide more security than the open streets where unwanted male attention is feared (Watt & Stenson, 1998). These establishments become places of socialization and identity formation for young girls. But by the time their children are 8 years old, parents stipulate gender-specific rules regarding locations that can be visited, mode of transportation, and time allowances, limiting the diversity of places in which girls can associate. Additionally, in his study of Coventry schoolchildren in the United Kingdom, Matthews (1987) found that a more restricted "home range" is detrimental to girls' understanding of spatial tasks such as mapping or making graphical representations.

Track Data Studies

Another research area relevant to new understandings of changing trajectories in children's geography is studies that use new technologies such as geographic information systems (GIS) and global positioning system (GPS) to study the everyday movements and activities of children. These studies, using geospatially referenced data, further illuminate how the increasingly restricted mobilities of today's children exhibit structural constraints that directly affect opportunities for elective learning. After strapping GPS devices to the wrists of schoolchildren in Cheshunt in Hertfordshire in the United Kingdom, and accelerometers to their waists, Mackett, Gong, Kitazawa, and Paskins (2007) reify the finding that just having an adult present changes the nature of a child's mobility. They write,

[children] tend to walk faster, more energetically and straighter when with an adult. Without an adult they tend to "potter about" in a much more exploratory way. Whilst speed has its benefits, there is a need for children to explore the environment at their own pace, gaining experience and learning about the world. (p. 15)

Boys, especially, seem to be fond of meandering around the open spaces they might encounter on the journey between home and school.

Another GPS track data study in the southern United States (Headrick Taylor, 2008) has shown that some upper middle-class adolescents have an expansive range of mobility that spans upward of 15 miles and through diverse communities in terms of race and income. However, in a time-density surface (where time-in-place rises on the z-axis above the surface of the map created in GIS software, the analysis demonstrates that these adolescent participants do not spend any time at all in these "diverse" locations, but are instead just passing through. In this regard, one's home range or trajectory is divided into places with high or low relevance for elective learning.

Using GIS/GPS methods along with some form of time-diary to capture daily accounts of activities is participatory for children in that they are building their own biographical record. With children from an academically nonselective school in northern England, Walker et al. (2009) viewed track data together with the participant/producer to once again move the research perspective from the researcher to the child. Interviews about the track data and the accompanying photo-journals permitted children to generate their own categories of places. Comparing points in the track data that were *not* elaborated by accompanying photos also helped researchers to understand places in a child's daily round that are distasteful, scary, or even too mundane to take special notice.

Learning as Mobility

Researchers in human and children's geography and elsewhere have been using innovative methods to ascertain a person's learning and identification related to particular spaces throughout one's surroundings that explicate the changing nature of trajectory. Taking the importance of traveling between places very seriously, Laurier et al. (2008) equip car dashboards with cameras to understand how the small interior of an automobile reconfigures discourse and relationships. The car is a *"translation and displacement* of the office or the domestic spaces which the drivers and passengers also shared" (p. 26). For parents and their children, especially, the car is a place of sharing and learning about one another, where the day's events are shared and time and attention can be largely undivided. Learning here, occurring throughout one's trajectory, is not at all trivial or mundane.

Another way of ascertaining nodes of salience for a learner is free recall maps, or having study participants draw maps of their communities. This task allows researchers to see what places along the complicated daily pathway are important and actively mediating environmental cognition (Hart, 1977). Free recall maps are also countertexts, or another version of the participant's biography, that clearly identify structures of salience. Places that are mapped, and therefore have relevance, are interpreted as spaces of deep engagement where some type of learning is taking place. Those places that are absent (but exist in "reality") have no relevance to the participant (Seyer-Ochi, 2006), and are therefore, not part of the cognitive map.

Lehrer, Jacobson, Kemeny, and Strom (1999) demonstrate that an everyday understanding of space can be used as the groundwork for mathematically thinking about coordinate systems, for example, but explicit facilitation by a pedagogue is necessary for children to "see" mathematical properties in our everyday surroundings (p. 79). However, children's everyday spatial awareness seems like an untapped and underutilized resource in the classroom. Could this be because of a disconnect between adults' and children's experience of space? Whereas one generation never "toured" World of Warcraft, or built complex environments in SIMs, the other generation spends countless leisure hours traveling through all kinds of virtual worlds. Therefore, how can educators "spatially connect" to the learners they teach? One place to start, perhaps, is to first understand today's teen experiences of space *outside* of school.

"Networks" Across Children's Geographies

How do embodied movements and technology fit together to make a sustainable network, and what role do these tools play in mediating where we go and how space is produced? The social studies of science have contributed research to a new understanding of space–time that elucidates the nature of maps as a kind of discursive technology that mediates human travel. Maps do not merely *show* us how people understand and reason about space. Just like any other piece of technology in the Latourian sense, maps are one example of an "immutable mobile," instantiating durability (Latour, 1991). Vertesi (2008) demonstrates how the London Tube map, with its iconic status, acts as "an essential visual technology that stands as an interface between the city and its user, presenting and structuring the points of access and possibilities for interaction within the urban space." Based on what the map shows as possible, in terms of routes, connections, and distance within a certain time constraint, exploration and an experience of space are produced. Although mass-produced maps are not generally intended to do so, they oftentimes come to serve as a general representation of the city in the user's mind. Although facilitating wayfinding and route-planning are still seen as an important function of these graphical representations, scientists are now starting to recognize the cognitive influence of maps.

Lammes (2008) points out that mapping practices in the cyber/gaming world, one in which more and more people interact, are much more flexible and dependent on the user's needs at any given time.

In *Age of Empires*, for example, the player is in a constant flux of moving through territory, which is translated into an expansion (filling-in) of the mini map. Conversely, one can click on the mini map to move to an area on the big screen. It is even possible to click on an explorer on the main screen, go back to the mini map, click on the area you want to send her or him to, and subsequently move her or him to that chosen spot on the main screen. Hence, mapping and touring entertain a highly dynamic relationship. The player indeed becomes a mapmaker, but this cannot be described as a straightforward depersonalized endeavor. It would be more precise to call the player a cartographer on tour. (p. 267)

In the virtual world, people have rich opportunities to make their own maps, both onscreen and mentally. New practices of virtual navigation and movement present challenges for human geographers studying trajectories and networks.

Social Network Studies

Another research area relevant to new understandings of network is studies of children's social networks. Sociology and psychology have contributed a massive body of empirical research on the role of parent social networks in either affording or constraining learning and development opportunities for children (e.g., Crockenberg, 1981; Homel, Burns, & Goodnow, 1987; Tietjen, 1985). These studies that find some way of measuring social cohesion, or the layout of a network, usually use a common instrument in which respondents are interviewed on the following concepts: "name generation" or asking for a list of people with whom the respondent comes in contact, "characteristics of network members and their relationships to respondents," "exchange content" or the type of interaction the named network member has with the respondent, and "intensity of relations" or how frequently a name is generated (Cochran & Niego, 2002, p. 128). Many of these studies, conducted all over the world, found that adults outside the home, but part of parents' social networks, provide children with access to more resources, more support, and differing perspectives than what is dominant in the home culture (Cochran & Niego, 2002).

Children are not merely accessing adult networks for support, however, but also create multi-tiered peer-to-peer networks, especially in places like school. Younnis (1994) asked children between the ages of 6 and 12 years to recount stories of being kind and unkind to a friend and/or peer. As is typical, the material focus of the stories changed as the children aged, but all children in this age range alluded to the notion of interdependence and past and future consequences of one's actions. In this way, learning reciprocity is one way in which peer-to-peer networks socialize children. Younnis writes,

Visiting a sick friend can be understood as part of a continuing series of actions in which the roles of being in need and being able to help were previously reversed and are potentially reversed in the unstated future. At any moment, circumstances might place one or the other friend in either role. What distinguishes friends from peers in general, therefore, is mutual obligation and interdependence, which develop through reciprocity. (p. 78)

Children, too, have a sophisticated sense of the importance of relationships with people. For psychologists studying young people, social networks are not just a way to learn culture and become socialized into a particular world, but networks reify the scientific claim that we are all social from the very beginning of our lives and need personal interaction on a deep level.

THE CHANGING VIRTUAL GEOGRAPHIES OF CHILDREN

In describing the way Hong Kong youth use ICQ, a popular chat and instant messaging (IM) software, Jones (2001) writes, "If you were to ask the question 'what are you doing' to most secondary or university students in Hong Kong when they are 'playing ICQ,' chances are the reply would be something like 'homework'." Jones goes on to explain that this would not be a deceptive answer. Rather, the Hong Kong youth in his study fully integrated their use of ICQ with other online and offline activities. While "playing ICQ," which could involve IM sessions with more than one person, they interacted in the offline world, chatting with siblings, parents, and friends. They also surfed the Internet, watched music videos online, played computer games, and emailed. One might ask not only what these youth are doing, but also *where* are they doing it? Although a young person may be physically located in an apartment in Hong Kong, sitting on the couch with a laptop on her lap, she may be virtually located in other cyberspaces: in a chat session with a friend next door, in an online computer game environment with others from across the city, or watching videos produced by youth from another country. Jones (2001) argues that these movements across virtual space are "really more like *navigation* than 'communication,' more like 'walking' than 'talking'." He also points out that "the interface [for their online communications] is not the screen; it's the world." Virtual mobilities, then, must be seen as movements across and through physical and virtual spaces made possible by Internet and other technologies (e.g., cell phones and video game systems).

We open this section of the chapter, our review of empirical studies of children's virtual geographies, with the above scene as a way of introducing the landscape of virtual geographies. What the scene makes clear is that young people who spend time on the Internet are living and learning and moving in and through places and in ways that were not possible only two decades ago. How do researchers come to understand these new mobilities (to gather evidence about them)? And what are the implications for equitable learning opportunities for students moving across the virtual landscape?

The scene of students "playing ICQ" in Hong Kong can also set the stage for the three-part framework of this section, wherein we consider studies that offer perspectives on place, trajectories, and networks. Consider the ways in which each of these perspectives might offer a distinct look at the student in her Hong Kong apartment. First, a focus on place in the Hong Kong scene might consider how particular locales—the chat room or the apartment—are constructed of and through a nexus of multiple relations (e.g., in the chat room, the various participants, the software and hardware that form ICQ technology, the positioning of the laptop on the lap, parents or siblings in the apartment looking into the chat room). Second, a focus on trajectory might consider this particular student's history of conversations online and offline with others throughout the days and weeks leading up to this afternoon or evening in the apartment. We might also think about the homework the student is doing as contributing to a trajectory of assignments and learning that has occurred over time and space. Third, a focus on network might consider the interconnectedness of this student's learning and homework production. Does she seek advice from friends online, go to Internet sites with helpful tips for a particular assignment posted by other students, or work collaboratively with others?

We move away from this scene as one example of the virtual geographies of children to a broader description of the virtual landscape and an explanation of our methodologies in considering studies for this section. Extensive reviews of the rise of Internet use from the early 1990s to the present in the United States (Tapscott, 1998; Warschauer & Matuchniak, 2010) and other countries (Haythornthwaite & Wellman, 2002; Thulin & Vilhelmson, 2005) show both rapid increases in Internet access, at home and in public and work settings, and nearly ubiquitous Internet use among youth in developed countries (Lenhart, Arafeh, Smith, & Macgill, 2008; Thulin & Vilhelmson, 2005). As for the developing world, "community centers and cybercafés are helping the Internet move from an elite preserve to a way in which ordinary people can do business and chat with friends, quickly and cheaply" (Haythornthwaite & Wellman, 2002, p. 7).

Now that the Internet is a part of the lives of so many young people across the globe, what do we know about how they travel across it? We follow from recent calls for research that take into account the everyday ways that youth use the Internet (e.g., Bennet, 2004; Bingham, Valentine, & Holloway, 1999; Haythornthwaite & Wellman, 2002; Hine, 2000; Ito et al., 2008; Leander, 2008; Leander & McKim, 2003; Thulin & Vilhelmson, 2005; Valentine, S. L. Holloway, & Bingham, 2000) and also adopt a geographical, spatial, and mobility frame in regards to studies of everyday Internet use (Hine, 2000; Jones, 2005; Leander & Lovvorn, 2006; Lemke, 2006) in reviewing empirical studies that investigate the virtual geographies of children and youth. We focus on empirical studies that consider the everyday travels of youth and children across virtual landscapes in the context of the rest of their lives. We eschew technological determinism for context, believing, with Skop and Adams (2009) that the medium has no particular essence; instead, diverse Internet users invest multiple cyberspaces with varied meanings. Thus it is necessary to study the uses of the Internet in a careful, empirical fashion in order to make sense of the role this new medium plays in geographical processes of particular user groups. (Skop & Adams, 2009, p. 128; see also Holloway & Valentine, 2001; Valentine & Holloway, 2002)

We have not considered studies in which educators have made efforts to introduce new technologies into formal or informal pedagogical environments. Rather, our interest is in the ways that children and youth live and learn across the many virtual geographies available to them. In particular, we are interested in what is new, changed, or changing in regards to the ways that youth and children live and learn today, what evidence there is for these shifts, and how our understanding of inequalities and equalities are framed by changes in virtual geographies. Because they focus in detail on the context of everyday travels across virtual geographies, most of these studies are, at least in part, methodologically qualitative and ethnographic. Such research "looks down and discovers limitless internal complexity within, which is materially heterogeneous, specific, and sensuous" (Law, 2004, p. 13). The following section proceeds in three subsections; each subsection includes discussion of representative studies rather than a comprehensive consideration of all available studies.

"Place" in Virtual Geographies

Kitchin (1998) carefully considers the issues and arguments surrounding the spatial nature of cyberspace. It can be seen as transformative space, shifting space–time relations and creating new social spaces and places. But the nature of these transformations is debated. On one side, arguments exist for the compression of space–time such that cyberspace becomes spaceless and placeless, a nowhere and everywhere, where geographic and temporal boundaries no longer matter. Or, others argue that space and time maintain their significance: For example, Internet connections and bandwidth capabilities very much depend on one's place in the world, while using information from the Internet also depends largely on where one is bodily located (Kitchin, 1998).

It is also argued that space and time maintain significance as humans seek community connections in virtual space: "these [community] ties have transformed cyber*space* into cyber*places*, as people connect online with kindred spirits, engage in supportive and sociable relationships with them, and imbue their activity online with meaning, belonging and identity" (Wellman, 2001, p. 229). These arguments also frame thinking about inequalities and equalities perpetuated by or produced through cyberspace. It is either an equalizing and globalizing force, compressing inequities prevalent in the physical structures and allowing access to all children to learn; or, cyberspace excludes outsiders without technical savvy to participate, neglects those without access, and otherwise perpetuates existing barriers to equality (Hargreaves, 2002; Holloway, Valentine, & Bingham, 2000).

In considering virtual geographies from the perspective of "place," we take Massey's (2005) conception of places as formed in *negotiations* "within and between both human and nonhuman" (p. 140). Here, we consider empirical studies that report on the construction of places created through particular negotiations of humans and nonhumans in online and offline spaces. As children and youth traverse virtual geographies, new places are constructed or reconstructed through negotiations in virtual and in physical spaces.

The construction of these places depends on the interactions and negotiations of both humans and machines across the physical and virtual world. To illustrate the way that virtual places are differently constructed depending on social negotiations around them, consider the placeness of cyberspace. In case studies of family Internet use (Facer, Furlong, Furlong, & Sutherland, 2001; Valentine & S. Holloway, 2001), the way cyberspace was constructed by parents and families as a particular kind of place had impacts for parents and children on traversals into and through the virtual, thereby affecting the learning opportunities afforded children and youth in cyberplaces. Parents who interpreted Internet sites such as chat rooms as places akin to the physical street, where there is a perceived danger of abduction by strangers and other safety concerns, heavily restricted children's unsupervised use of the Internet. Facer et al. (2001) found that families restricted access in varying ways (e.g., not allowing Internet access at all in the home, requiring parent-held passwords for access, only allowing access with supervision). These restrictions, all coming out of the construction of home and certain online places (e.g., chat rooms) as dangerous, have obvious effects on children's equitable access to learning opportunities online. But other parents, although still making this comparison of the physical street and the cyber street, saw Internet use as apart from the physical street and, therefore, more safe: "two sets of parents explain that they would rather that their children were indoors using the PC where they could see them than on the street where they did not know where they were or what they were doing" (Valentine & S. Holloway, 2001, p. 76). Other parents recognized the co-constitutive nature of places virtual and physical and believed that cyberplaces were no more or no less dangerous than physical places.

These alternative possibilities as conceptions of place-making in the virtual and physical world serve to introduce the next section of the review, which considers place as constructed through negotiations of humans and nonhumans. In the first part of this section, *physical* places were found to be in flux as a result of these negotiations between the virtual and physical. In the second part, the construction of *virtual* places is at play for children simultaneously constructing identities in the physical world.

Physical (Re)Constructions of Place for Online/Offline Lives

Holloway and Valentine (2001) drew on their research with 30 British families with children aged 11 to 16 years to examine physical changes in space because of the introduction of new technologies. They investigated households that represented a variety of home computing and Internet use arrangements, believing that the implications of introducing new technologies "emerge as people and objects come together in communities of practice and different households domesticate technologies in different ways (Wenger, 1987; Silverstone et al., 1992)" (p. 569).

Families materially structure the lived space differently when introducing technology into the home (Holloway & Valentine, 2001). These decisions are in part based on broader social processes including the family's socioeconomic status. Also important were the ways in which families viewed the social processes surrounding activities associated with the computer: Are computer users viewed as isolated or involved in larger social processes that connect to other family activities and structures? The answer to this question affected whether or not the computer would be placed in public or private space. Learning also played an important role in decisions about structuring the lived space as a particular kind of place. Children's educational needs were often placed ahead of all other types of computer use (e.g., adult use and children's recreational use) such that the nexus of relations surrounding the computer in the home create the location of the computer as a place for learning.

Like Holloway and Valentine (2001), Facer et al. (2001) found that

> a reconfiguring of domestic space can be seen in the arrangements that are made within families to incorporate these newer technologies, arrangements that both alter and draw upon the existing geography of the family space and indicate the functions constructed for this technology within the family system. (p. 17)

The material changes in home spaces differed depending on the families' visions of computer use—whether or not, for example, time on the computer should be spent in private or in public spaces in the home. The researchers argue that these differing spatial formations "impact on the ways in which young people negotiate the relationship between their physical and 'virtual' existences" (p. 18). "Screen space" (Jones, 2005) was another site of material change brought about by the domestic settings and relationship structures: Individual computer users would "inscribe their identities and ownership by leaving traces of themselves and eradicating traces of others' occupation" (Facer et al., 2001, p. 20)—e.g., by changing settings on the computer: altering the desktop layout to include bright colors, relocating menu bars, or changing the screensaver. The construction of home and computer as places was, then, continually in flux.

Of particular import for children's learning in place afforded by new technologies, Facer, Furlong, Furlong, and Sutherland (2003) focused a section of their monograph devoted to understanding home computer use in the United Kingdom on "how and what young people are learning when they use computers at home" (p. 185). Home, here, was constructed as a learning place by the intersections of resources that support learning. Young people participated in "knowledge-creating communities" made up of members of their families and groups of friends that, together, co-constructed knowledge at the site of the home computer by sharing expertise gained in the home and elsewhere (e.g., at school or from friends or relatives outside the home). Other resources that youth drew on while learning in the home were texts (both digital and paper-based) and a method of "creatively copying" resources that further enabled learning (e.g., copying a basic program from a book to get started with computer programming, copying clipart and transforming the image, or copying templates for Web page design).

Like the home, the classroom was found to be a place constructed through negotiations among the physical, virtual, and social. Valentine, S. Holloway, and Bingham (2002) considered whether or not students had access to technology that was materially available in the classroom. In their analysis, they followed Latour (1996b) and Law (1994) in arguing that the "technical and the social codevelop" (p. 308). The analyzed place of the classroom included technically savvy boys who were socially shunned. Some of the girls in the class refused to become familiar with the technology, even though it was readily available, because they did not want to be associated with this particular group of boys. The machine itself carried an identity, then, of social exclusion and some students' technophobia resulted from the computer's identification. In discussing equitable access to technologies at the scale of policy, Valentine, S. Holloway, et al. (2002) argue that "we cannot focus on the provision of the technology alone. Rather, we need to understand how children and technology come together and how they are transformed by and transforming of each other" (p. 310).

Lægran (2002) described such places—where human interaction and technology intersect—as "technospaces" (p. 158). She investigated two particular technospaces frequented by youth in two rural Norwegian villages: the petrol station and the Internet café. Lægran was able to contrast the two Internet cafés and show that the new material spatial and social formations that accompany changes in technology are tied to local and global context in the construction of an Internet café as a certain kind of place. Although each Internet café was physically constructed in an existing space in a small rural village in Norway, the difference in the material structure of these places (i.e., a purposefully "urban" interior design and Italian coffee machine in one place and worn out couches and instant coffee in the other) made for very different social formations and uses of the Internet. In the "urban" café, the Internet was symbolic of urban culture and was used to reach out to the world. In the other café, which came to be thought of more as a youth center, patrons used the Internet to "extend their repertoire of identities as well as their network in the local community, with less interest in 'going global'" (p. 166). As with other offline places we discuss that were changed by the introduction of virtual geographies, Lægran argues that "this study suggests that youth make use of the Internet . . . in different ways to construct spaces suited to their lifestyles and orientations, and to communicate and mediate meanings within the village as well as the wider world" (p. 166).

Local area network (LAN) cafés, which offer LAN gaming (game play only with onsite players) for café goers as well connections to the Internet, in Australia, were also found to be formed as hybrid places through the complex intersections of the physical, social, and virtual:

Their licensing requirements, their location in the city, their relationship to schools and the street, their connection to and disconnection from online global culture, and the mix of online and offline social interaction that goes on inside, give LAN cafés what we have described as a "liminal" quality, a refusal to be readily fixed and labeled. (Beavis, Nixon, & Atkinson, 2005, p. 58)

Beavis et al. (2005) also found that these cafés were important places of learning—"where people both learn and are taught computer-based skills, as well as social 'lessons' about how to act and be in the world" (p. 58).

A final example of physical place-making was the Deaf club in the United Kingdom. Valentine and Skelton (2008) describe the history of Deaf clubs, established throughout the United Kingdom in the 19th century as places where deaf people "could escape the oppressive oralism of hearing society (Stevens 2001) and develop an active sense of identity, culture and belonging predicated on their shared language—sign language (Padden and Humphries 1998)" (p. 472). With the more widespread use of the Internet, however, there is no longer a need to gather at Deaf clubs to communicate or receive information. Deaf people can access information online and communicate with each other in sign language without being in the same physical place. Valentine and Skelton present evidence that attendance at Deaf clubs is decreasing and that young deaf people, in particular, are organizing to meet at other offline places (e.g., pubs) in smaller groups. Some older people have expressed mixed feelings about the lack of younger people in the clubs: satisfaction at having the place to themselves, but sadness at the possibility that Deaf clubs will not survive into the next generation. These changes in physical places, the Deaf clubs, are accompanied by changes in online places for deaf people to gather, as they are now able to communicate via webcams with sign language-speaking people around the world because of the similarities among the world's 200 sign languages.

Immigrant Youth and Hybrid Places

We move now away from the construction and reconstruction of physical places to the formation of new virtual places. Several studies (Brouwer, 2006a, 2006b; Lam, 2000, 2004, 2006; Lam & Rosario-Ramos, 2009; Lee, 2006; Skop & Adams, 2009) considered the virtual places created and inhabited by immigrant youth (i.e., youth who are either immigrants themselves or the children of immigrant parents). These diasporas, formulated from negotiations and hybridizations among cultural identities, languages, and geopolitical distinctions represent sites of new possibilities for children's learning.

Skop and Adams (2009) surveyed Indian immigrants to the United States and their American-born children to consider how they used the Internet. They found that the Internet is a resource used by these immigrants "for overcoming separation at intra- and international scales, for creating a variety of connections across space and for constructing a sense of identity" (p. 128). New conceptions of identity and hybridized forms of community that are neither concurrent with "old" Indian culture nor, necessarily, the expectations of the host country are created—that is, new virtual places—as these diasporic people interact in virtual spaces. But the virtual places within which they interact are created, formed, and reformed, as they network among information and people grounded both in India as it is now and in dynamic relationship with elements of American culture. "Identities are forged across space as well as in places, and through both direct and indirect (mediated) communications" (p. 143).

This dynamic identity formation was not evident in Lee's (2006) study of Tongan immigrants on the Internet, which, as best we can tell, included textual analysis of the websites as artifacts and did not include interactions with the participants on the site. Still, she claims that many of the participants are youth and children of immigrants born outside of Tonga (particularly in the United States, New Zealand, and Australia). Lee's focus in this study was on the ways that language use is contested in cultural identity negotiations, especially as these negotiations take place across time and space on websites (i.e., particular online places) for and about Tongan culture. Although we can read these sites as places of hybridized cultural identity formulations, they were still highly contested places of ongoing negotiations, where some voices were silenced by an inability to speak certain languages (sometimes Tongan, sometimes English). Still, participants reported the value of the sites as places they could learn from others about Tongan culture and also speak freely and openly (because of the anonymity of participating) in a way that was not approved of in Tongan culture outside of these virtual places.

Like the Tongan youth who felt open to discuss issues and topics that they would not have been able to discuss in the physical presence of other Tongans—particularly adults—Moroccan Muslim immigrants in the Netherlands appropriated a website discussion forum for their needs, creating a new virtual place. Girls, in particular, focused the online discussion on issues of importance to them (e.g., religion, relationships, and marriage). Like the Tongan website, participants were anonymous, and this allowed them the possibility of openly discussing topics that would be prohibited in offline spaces.

In another analysis of Dutch Moroccan websites, Brouwer (2006a) outlines the construction of a new place for second-generation immigrants (Dutch-born children of Moroccan-born parents): an imagined Morocco. Brouwer argues that these second-generation children have no physical attachments to Morocco and so they create a place of imagined relationships to their parents' homeland by forming social relationships on the Internet with other second-generation Dutch Moroccan youth. At the intersections of these social relationships, and at the specific locales of these websites, these youth create a new place for learning and being.

Over the past 10 years, Lam (2000, 2004, 2006, 2009) has focused research on immigrant youth on the Internet, particularly in the context of language and literacy. Lam's work stands out among the other studies we review in this section for her explicit attention to learning. In all of these pieces, learning and identity work are explicitly tied together. Immigrant youth learn second-language literacy skills by interacting in cyberspace with other youth around the globe. But they also form identities as learners and English speakers that are hybridized—both local and global, and particular to the setting—the place—in which they perform.

In the earliest piece, Lam (2000) presents a case study of a Chinese immigrant teenager corresponding on the Internet with a transnational group of peers. Here, she explicitly calls on educators to reconsider the significance of identity formation in learning to become literate in a second language, as her focal participant gained confidence in a variety of English language uses on the Internet while previously feeling alienated from native-born Americans offline. Later, Lam (2004) studied two Chinese immigrant girls participating in a bilingual chat room. Again, she focuses on the role of identity construction and language use for the focal participants and their friends around the globe in a hybridized space: "a mixed-code variety of English is adopted and developed among Yu Qing, Tsu Ying, and their friends to construct their relationships as bilingual speakers of English and Cantonese" (p. 59). Spending time in the chatroom gave the girls the confidence to speak English to others, but it also created a new place of identity for Chinese immigrants around the globe—the kinds of place formations that would not have been possible prior to the spread of the Internet.

In Lam (2006), the contextual elements at play in hybridized place construction are expanded to include the flow of cultural materials "that provide new avenues for people to construct social relationships and identities beyond a bounded notion of national belonging" (p. 172). Lam focuses on two case studies: The first includes the same focal participants from the previously discussed study, whereas the second involves a Chinese immigrant boy creating and maintaining an anime website. Lam's analysis centers on transnational identity making among these youth and others online in a way that recognizes the flow of cultural influences in their online activities and calls on educators to consider ways that children and youth could be given tools to critique, analyze, and reflect "on the relationships they were developing with their peers around the globe and how these relationships were constructed and represented through the use of language, symbolic media, and forms of communication" (p. 189).

Lam's (2009) final study under consideration expands the scope of her previous studies, using interview data with 35 adolescents of diverse national origins along with survey data from 262 foreign-born high school students in the United States to explore "the ways in which young migrants of diverse national origins in the United States are utilising digital media to organise social relationships with friends and families, and engage with news and media products across the United States and their native countries" (p. 174). Again, learning plays an important role in Lam's findings. For example, she points out that IM and email are ideal ways for these immigrant youth to maintain proficiency in their home languages as well as to learn English. When IMing in English, participants are able to look up unfamiliar words in an online dictionary and learn the word's definition, synonyms, and antonyms. As with the other studies, identity making across national borders and home- and host-country languages play out with these students. Lam argues that the experiences of these youth online require a reconsideration of multilingualism such that we "grapple with how multilingual literacies can be fostered and used to build connections and develop knowledge across cultural and geopolitical territories" (p. 187).

"Trajectories" Across Virtual Geographies

As our review of studies from the perspective of "place" has shown, the in-placeness of locations for learning and living made possible by new technologies requires an understanding of place as negotiated space, as locations in a nexus of relations. We move now to the second section of this review of virtual geographies, where we consider the ways that children and youth move across and through such physical and virtual places in life trajectories. These trajectories are formed as individuals move through online and offline spaces and across time and distance. Life trajectories also come in contact with and are affected by the trajectories of technological advancement. That is, there are trajectories to the developments of technologies as there are to the developments of humans and that these trajectories intersect and interact in ways that have import for children and their learning. Learning along pathways of trajectory from place to place (including places physical and virtual) is afforded not only by pausing in those places along the way but also by and through tools that make learning and connecting on the move a possibility (e.g., cell phones). This section reviews empirical studies that approach trajectories from two vantage points: First, we review studies that show the mutually constitutive nature of trajectories through online and offline places—that is, the ways in which the social landscapes of the virtual and physical worlds form and reform each other as children and youth move across them; second, we review studies that examine mobile technologies (i.e., the mobile phone) as key tools in the trajectories of children and youth through and across virtual and physical geographies.

Social Formations Mutually Constituted Through Online/Offline Trajectories

Insofar as the life trajectories of children and youth include the increasing capacity for online interactions as technologies become available and as children mature, researchers have found that these changing capacities tend to enhance current social formations rather than significantly alter them (Thulin & Vilhelmson, 2005, 2006; Valentine, S. L. Holloway, et al., 2000). This is not to downplay changes in social formations afforded by the Internet but rather to point to the way that online and offline behavior are mutually constituted (Holloway et al., 2000; Holloway & Valentine, 2001). In considering changes in social formations brought about by changes in virtual mobilities, Thulin and Vilhelmson (2006) started by asking about time displacement. They argue that time spent on the Internet necessarily involves time taken away from other activities and wondered what would happen as time spent on "virtual mobility" (p. 29) increased. This issue of time displacement is important to establishing changes in social formations brought on by the widespread use of the Internet because new activities on the Net imply changes in social activity patterns elsewhere. Specifically, Thulin and Vilhelmson point to the stationary, place-bound nature of online activities conducted from a computer fixed in geographical space and ask

> how this tension between spatially exploding networks characterized by flexible use of place, on one hand, and imploding, place-bound privatization of solitary activities, on the other, actually affects everyday life—i.e. local communities and people's use of place. (Thulin & Vilhelmson, 2006, p. 30)

They found, in a study that included data from nationally distributed surveys of Swedish youth as well as in-depth interviews and time-use diaries from a smaller group of participants, that time spent with information and communication technologies (ICTs) decreased personal time spent with other media (e.g., television, music, DVDs) but did not take away from social time spent in offline relationships. Also, they found that the Swedish youth in their study used ICTs to sustain and reinforce local contacts and seldom established completely new contacts as a substitute for their existing local social relationships. The key here is that existing relationships were not displaced as these youth moved across new virtual geographies. Instead, ICT use "generally enhances rather than undermines children's friendships" (Valentine, S. L. Holloway, et al., 2000, p. 163).

Further, new technologies become integrated into old ways of life (Valentine, S. L. Holloway, et al., 2000). As evidence of this, playing computer games and surfing the Internet became new ways of sharing time with friends rather than replacing that time or those friendships. Using the Internet even improved the ability to maintain contact with offline friends through the ability of rural school children to meet online when meeting face-to-face would have been prohibitive because of distance. Chat features also improved communications among friends who could previously only interact individually with different members of the group over the phone. Now, an entire group of friends could gather in one virtual locale. Local social relationships maintained their importance despite the desires of adults for rural children to expand their global and educational horizons via the Internet (Valentine & S. L. Holloway, 2001). While adults hoped that their children would develop characteristics of global citizens by engaging with others in virtual space, children interacted with their offline peers or added new friendships.

Although children's "virtual activities are not, in practice, disconnected from their off-line identities and relationships" (Valentine & S. L. Holloway, 2002, p. 316), the extensibility afforded by the Internet did enable children to reconfigure, realign, and extend their social relationships and identities. This contrasts somewhat with previous findings (Valentine & S. L. Holloway, 2001), in which adults hoped that extensibility would enable global relationships and learning. Here, the researchers do not necessarily find that children are cultivating global friendships (in contrast, cf. Leander & Mills, 2007) but that they do extend beyond the local in the establishment of new social relationships.

As social trajectories move across physical and virtual geographies, the online and offline are mutually constituted. Specifically, Valentine and S. L. Holloway (2002) found four different processes through which children's offline worlds were incorporated into their online worlds

through direct (re)presentations of their off-line identities and activities; through the production of alternative identities contingent upon their off-line identities; through the reproduction on-line of off-line class and gender inequalities; and through the ways in which everyday material realities limit the scope of their on-line activities. (p. 316)

They also identified four different processes through which children's online worlds were incorporated into their offline worlds, including incorporating online information into their offline activities, maintaining relationships, changing offline social networks with online friendships, and recontextualizing activities and identities (p. 316).

Trajectories Involving Mobile Technologies

Thus far, we have mostly focused on studies that document changes in children's virtual geographies brought about by and through interactions on the Internet. But perhaps even more revolutionary than the technologies associated with the Internet are mobile technologies, primarily cell phones (J. E. Katz, 2006; Sheller, 2004). Although both Internet use and mobile technology use have been shown to co-constitute the virtual and the physical, Ito (2005) argues that the trajectories across virtual and physical are different with Internet and mobile technologies:

> Internet studies have been tracing the increasing colonization by real-life identity and politics of the hitherto "free" domain of the Net; *ketai* [mobile phones in Japan] represent the opposite motion of the virtual colonizing more and more settings of everyday life. (p. 8)

Mobile devices are used on a broader global scale than ICTs: By 2005, one in three humans on the planet were mobile phone users (J. E. Katz, 2006), and the rates of mobile phone adoption among people in developing countries were staggering (Sheller, 2004), including the expansive use of cell phones "in the squatter communities that surround the cities of developing countries, places where conventional wired phones have never existed" (Townsend, 2000, p. 86). Youth in many countries have nearly ubiquitous access to mobile phones (see Matsuda, 2005a; Thulin & Vilhelmson, 2007). As Ling and Campbell (2009) have argued, "the proliferation of wireless and mobile communication technologies gives rise to important changes in how people experience space and time" (p. 1). "Phone-space" has become each individual's node of connection to "the temporally, spatially fragmented network of friends and colleagues they have constructed for themselves" (Townsend, 2000, p. 94). In this section devoted to "trajectories" and in the final section of the review of virtual geographies devoted to "networks," we review studies that consider some of these important changes in experiences of time and space—for example, the maintenance of complex and spatially distributed social networks, the changing nature of private and public space (see Wellman, 2001), and new practices of coordination—among children and youth brought about by the increasing use of mobile technologies. Here, the focus is on the ways that children and youth move across the physical and virtual landscape while nearly always connected to "phone-space" (Townsend, 2000, p. 94).

Although Thulin and Vilhelmson (2007) found access to mobile phones in Sweden to have nearly reached the saturation level by 2002, they found lower levels of use: the youth in their study averaged 2.5 contacts per day (SMS text messages and voice calls). This study included time-use diaries and in-depth interviews with 43 high school students living in a medium-sized city in western Sweden. The researchers followed up their initial contact with another wave of interviews and time-use data 2 years later, when the students were out of high school. They found that social contacts and interactions increased with increasing use of the mobile phone and that the role of physical proximity in maintaining social relationships was diminished. As has been shown in studies throughout our review, the technology, in this case the mobile phone, complemented rather than replaced existing social networks. One way it complements existing social networks is to allow the possibility of more impulsive gathering. The researchers also found that the social practices of scheduling and coordinating face-to-face meetings and joint activities have changed significantly with an increasing use of mobile phones: "A more *impulsive and hasty practice of decision-making* has evolved, characterized by continuous negotiation and re-negotiation, a preference for retaining freedom of action as long as possible, and last-minute choices" (Thulin & Vilhelmson, 2007, p. 249). Because leisure time is no longer scheduled ahead of time and fixed to specific times and places, youth were more careless about timekeeping.

One element of Thulin and Vilhelmson's (2007) study points to issues in our using empirical studies published in academic journals to gauge the current usage of mobile technologies. They report, for example, that by 2002 phone applications such as Internet browsing, email, digital media players, and built-in cameras were not yet available and "when asked about such upcoming features, the interviewees showed a rather shallow interest" (p. 241). In a third wave of research with this same set of participants (Thulin & Vilhelmson, 2009), conducted in 2005, Thulin and Vilhelmson still found little adoption of new cell phone features (but contrast this with the early adoption and heavy use of these features, i.e., Internet browsing, email, cameras) among youth in Japan (see Matsuda, 2005a, 2005b; Okada, 2005). Surely this has changed over the last few years. And yet these studies were published within the past 2 years. Thus the ability of our empirical work to keep up with rapid changes in technology and, in particular, to account for the effects of these changes in the everyday lives of children and youth through ethnographic studies is called into question. Smartphones (e.g., the iPhone and the Blackberry) are continuously upgraded, increasingly giving youth access to computer and Internet applications at all times and in all places. Additionally, applications that have not been typically associated with laptops and the Internet (e.g., GPS technologies) are now available on phones. We would expect to see studies in the future that document, for example, the ways that children and youth are afforded new opportunities for learning across their life trajectories through the use of iPhone applications.

Youth not only use their phones to communicate across spatial distance but also use them for particular symbolic purposes in negotiating on-the-ground social relationships (J. E. Katz, 2006). Students in Katz's small study would pretend to talk on the phone if walking home late at night as a signal to would-be attackers that they were in contact with someone who could help immediately. They would also use their phones as symbols in other social relationships: pretending to be having a mobile phone conversation as a way of avoiding talking face-to-face with someone, or pretending to get a call as a way of getting out of an embarrassing social situation. Katz argues that "there is a large world of communication usage having little to do with those who are distant or virtual and everything to do with those who are co-located, socially and physically with the user" (p. 11).

Ito et al. (2005) edited a collection of studies that investigated mobile phones in Japanese life. Mobile phones in Japan are called *ketai*, which roughly translates to "something you carry with you" (Ito, 2005, p. 1). Ito (2005) differentiates the relationships suggested by the term *ketai* as opposed to the American "cellular phone" or the British "mobile": "A *ketai* is not so much about a new technical capability or freedom of motion but about a snug and intimate technosocial tethering, a personal device supporting communications that are a constant, lightweight, and mundane presence in everyday life" (p. 1). This "intimate technosocial tethering" suggests the relationships between social life and technology that we have seen across the studies in this section: Through life trajectories, the virtual and the physical and the social and the technological are mutually incorporated.

In one of the studies in the Ito et al. (2005) collection, Okada (2005) followed from theories of social construction of technologies in showing how youth culture influenced the developmental trajectory of mobile phone technology in Japan. He has been conducting research on mobile media use in Japan over the past 15 years, and he uses surveys, statistical data, and on-the-street interviews to capture and describe the historical development of technologies. As one example of the social construction of mobile technologies in Japan, Okada describes the trajectory of pager development. Pagers were initially designed to allow a person receiving the page to call the phone number on the pager. But Japanese youth began using the pager as a way of exchanging short messages with words being assigned to sequences of numbers and codes. Seeing how youth were using the pagers, pager manufacturers added a new function to the pager that converted certain number combinations into letters or phonetic symbols that could be read by all. These developments, of course, eventually led to text messaging. The interrelated development of youth life trajectories and technologies is also evident in other examples that Okada describes (e.g., ring tones and camera phones).

Young people across the globe (specifically in Europe, the Americas, Africa, and the Asian Pacific) have been quick to adopt new mobile technologies and integrate these technologies into their everyday lives, finding new purposes and uses for devices beyond those intended by designers (Castells, Fernández-Ardèvol, Qiu, & Sey, 2007). As studies of Internet usage have also shown, the mobile technologies used by these youth across international contexts help maintain traditional social institutions (e.g., school and family) despite the fact that the phone offers new autonomies. One key factor in the availability of mobile technology and the uses of new technologies was the purchasing power of the youth. Differences were found, for example, in the uses of mobile phones by American children for game playing as compared with young Chinese migrant workers who do not download games.

In addition to studies that have shown the repurposing of mobile communication devices (i.e., pagers and cell phones) along the development of people and technologies, there is evidence that youth repurpose other mobile technologies for learning and identity construction across their life trajectories. In the context of their broader case for considering how multimodal analytic frameworks can be used for studies of mobility, Leander and Vasudevan (2009) include a brief case description of Joey, a 19-year-old man who produces and displays multiple texts using a PlayStation portable (PSP) gaming device. Joey used the camera features and an image-editing program built into the PSP to document his movements and time with friends in a variety of settings across an urban landscape. The affordances of the device and Joey's social purposes for using it to create images and videos that he can subsequently display on his MySpace profile and other places mutually shaped one another.

"Networks" Across Virtual Geographies

New changes in the virtual geographies of children and youth not only allow them to move in trajectories and pathways of learning like the ones we have shown, but they also make it possible at any point along these trajectories to connect across vast social networks (e.g., via the Internet or mobile technologies). Social networks may not be new, but the possibilities for engaging them has changed with the advent and spread of digital technologies: Wellman (2001) writes that "complex social networks have always existed, but recent technological developments in communication have afforded their emergence as a dominant form of social organization" (p. 228). (For further historical context regarding networked communities, see Wellman & Gulia, 1999.) This dominance extends around the globe (Castells, 2000) and has implications for the ways in which children and youth live and learn across time and space:

Contemporary life is dominated by the pervasiveness of the network. With the worldwide spread of the mobile phone and the growth of broadband in the developed world, technological networks are more accessible, more ubiquitous, and more mobile every day. The always-on, always-accessible network produces a broad set of changes to our concept of place, linking specific locales to a global continuum and thereby transforming our sense of proximity and distance. (Varnelis & Friedberg, 2008, p. 15)

In this final section of the review of changes in children's virtual geographies, we consider studies from the perspective of the network. We focus on two key areas of work: The first is studies of youth social networking via the Internet and other mobile technologies; the second is networking through gaming.

Social Networking Through the Internet and Other Mobile Technologies

boyd (in press) and her colleagues found that during the course of their landmark study (Ito et al., in press) aimed at documenting the new media practices of youth in the United States from 2005 to 2008, they "watched as a new genre of social media— social network sites—gained traction among U.S. teenagers." (For a comprehensive introduction to social network sites, see boyd & Ellison, 2007.) A social network site is an Internet site that allows users to "(1) construct a public or semi-public profile within a bounded system, (2) articulate a list of other users with whom they share a connection, and (3) view and traverse their list of connections and those made by others within the system" (boyd & Ellison, 2007). Although boyd (in press) admits that not every teen frequents social network sites, she argues that from the years 2004 to 2007 "social network sites became central to many teens' practices." Despite this centrality, research into youth social networking via social network sites is sparse because of the relative newness of these sites and of youth engagement with them. Still, boyd has published two studies (boyd, 2007, in press) that investigate the everyday uses of social network sites by young people.

boyd (2007) spent 2 years observing and interviewing U.S.-based youth as they engaged with MySpace (a social network site), following them across online and offline spaces, and systematically documenting their practices with MySpace. She found that MySpace and other social network sites act as networked publics, "spaces and audiences that are bound together through technological networks (i.e. the Internet, mobile networks, etc.)" (p. 125). boyd documented the ways that the networked public nature of MySpace came into conflict with young people's desire for MySpace to be "my space," a place "for teenagers to be teenagers" (p. 132) and with their identity work in perceived local settings when viewed more globally. As an example of the latter, boyd describes a call she received from an admissions officer at a prestigious college who was shocked to find that a student to whom they were planning on offering a scholarship had a MySpace profile "full of hip-hop imagery, urban ghetto slang, and hints of gang participation" (p. 133), all of which seemed to counter his admissions essay about the problems of gang violence in his community. What boyd makes clear is that young people's movements across networks afforded by new technologies are not without consequences for their accesses to learning—although the possibilities for increased connectivity on a broader scale—with attendant increases in opportunities to learn—are possible, the ecology of the networked public can also be perilous.

Presenting one slice of the much larger corpus of data from the Digital Youth research project (see Ito et al., in press), boyd (in press) focuses on the role of social media in young people's friendship practices. She argues that learning to socialize with peers and make friendships "is a key component of growing up as a competent social being, and that young people need to be immersed in peer cultures from an early age." Viewed from this perspective, networked social media (social networking sites, mobile technologies) play a key role in youth learning to become adults. boyd found that virtual networks available via social media are not viewed as separated from the rest of young people's lives. Rather, social media are another way to connect with peers "that feels seamless with their everyday lives." These youth did not use social media as a networking tool to make contact with new people; instead, they maintained existing relationships with friends they knew mostly from school. But their networking with these friends, especially with a small-scale group of intimate friends, is maintained in "'always-on' networked publics inhabited by their peers."

This always-on network is kept up via mobile phones, IM, and social network sites. boyd found that the affordances of networked social media make it possible for social relations to be maintained beyond the constraints of physical space.

Youth are not only connected in networks via social network sites. They also participate in networks via other Internet technologies like IM and through mobile technologies. Kasesniemi and Rautiainen (2002) focused their study of Finnish youth, aged 13 to 18 years, on one particular aspect of mobile communication—the text message—and showed that the text message as a form of communication is able to overcome constraints of time and space that would otherwise inhibit communication and has a particular role in sustaining social relationships at all times (see also Johnsen, 2003): "Teenagers send messages during class in school, a text message unites two young lovers in the middle of the night, and a message sent by mom discreetly instructs the teen to come home from a party" (p. 171). Text messaging also allows for identity play, with some youth enacting brash personas via their text messages while exhibiting public shyness.

Internet-based IM is another method youth use in the construction of social networks. Networks constructed and maintained via IM by one immigrant youth (Lam, 2009) were found to be much more wide-reaching and complex than those reported in the other studies in this section. Lam reports on the case of Kaiyee, a 17-year-old recent Chinese immigrant to the United States, using data taken from a larger comparative study. Lam observed Kaiyee's online activities at her home over an 8-month period, conducted interviews, recorded Kaiyee's screen during IM exchanges, and engaged Kaiyee in a retrospective reflection on the IM exchanges. Lam also observed Kaiyee at school and interacting in the local Chinese immigrant community. Lam found that Kaiyee constructed—via IM and other social media—social networks that included the local (her peer group in the Chinese immigrant community), translocal (English-speaking Asian American youths in the United States who she had met while gaming online), and transnational (her peers in China). Kaiyee deployed various linguistic resources across these groups: "standard American English, hip-hop English, the Shanghainese dialect that she used in her family, Cantonese and Mandarin that predominated in her immigrant community, and both Mandarin and Shanghainese that connected her to people and events in China" (p. 393), often mixing her language. Kaiyee's maintenance of multiple identities and a rich linguistic repertoire via IM points to the affordances of new technologies to allow for networking across large gaps in space and time through which migratory youth can form and reform identities old and new.

Social Networking Through Gaming

In addition to the social networks constructed via the Internet and mobile technologies, gaming also presents an opportunity for children and youth to build networks. Although nearly all children aged 12 to 17 years in the United States have been found to play games online, on a console, or on their phones, only 21% of them play massively multiplayer online games (MMOGs; Lenhart, Kahne, et al., 2008).

In one survey of children's online activities in the United Kingdom, 70% of children aged 9 to 19 years reported playing games online, but MMOGs were not addressed specifically (Livingstone & Bober, 2005). Although playing MMOGs is clearly not an activity that all (or even most) children participate in, these games are played by millions of young people (Crowe & Bradford, 2006) and represent a significant change in the kinds of virtual spaces available to children. Studies of children playing these games describe their interactions in and with new virtual spatial formations and across new networks, navigating through these particular kinds of virtual geographies as part of their everyday movements.

In choosing to study the virtual world of Runescape, a free MMOG developed in the United Kingdom with an estimated 5 million young players, Crowe and Bradford (2006) argue that "virtual spaces must be understood as social contexts (in principle, like any other) where young people spend parts of their leisure lives" (p. 331). As with other network construction we have discussed, the new networks of MMOG geography extend from and are influenced and mediated by the material world. Geographically, Runescape "takes the form of a Tolkeinesque quasi-medieval environment incorporating towns, buildings, dungeons, forests, landscapes and seascapes within which gamers live their virtual lives" (Crowe & Bradford, 2006, p. 335).

In living out these virtual lives, Crowe and Bradford (2006) found that virtual spaces such as Runescape gave youth opportunities to make and remake identities both in and through the game space by, for example, creating avatars as public identity markers. Although there were significant findings here in regards to the possibilities of new networks afforded by such identity play and interactions in virtual worlds, Runescape also exemplified new alternative places where youth spend their time. In other words, Runescape was not only a new social space, but a new geographical place:

> In a world in which material public space (the street or the town centre) has become inaccessible to many young people or is considered risky or unsafe by them or their parents, it is not surprising that virtual public space has become attractive as a leisure setting. (Crowe & Bradford, 2006, p. 337)

For some youth, Runescape's virtual geography offered them a chance to spend time in relaxing "tourist locations" or "special spaces" (e.g., a waterfall or ocean beach), places where they could relax not only from the demands of their lives offline but also from the demands of work within the virtual environment.

Learning was also important for Runescape players. Working in the game world was necessary to develop a character within the game, and players "gain[ed] experience through in-game tasks or challenges: fighting, fishing, mining or cooking, for example" (p. 336). Although not all players strived to make a living in the virtual space—some were content to just hang out—gaining experience at a trade was valued and players were aware of the mistakes that new players (noobs) were making.

Networked possibilities are sometimes mitigated by social, physical, and virtual constraints. In three distinct social settings for gaming in Taiwan—at home, in cybercafés, and in college dormitories—Taiwanese youth are subjected to regulating forces (Lin, 2008). This was especially true for young females. In examining the barriers to females who wanted to participate in games in each of these three settings, Lin considered both the social relations in the game world as well as those in the physical spaces wherein the game is played. Although Lin found significant barriers to female gamers in Taiwan participating in game play (e.g., sharing access to the home computer with family members, the design of cybercafés such that female players have to walk past pool-playing males that they view as threatening, or the perception that female players should not be disruptive roommates in college dormitories), he also found that MMOGs open up "new virtual spaces for girls to experiment with exploratory behaviors without worrying about physical danger or other consequences" (p. 79). The networks that female gamers participated in across the physical and virtual space had varying effects on their ability to comfortably play games.

Similar to MMOGs, online virtual worlds are spaces where thousands (or even millions) of players can interact, using an avatar to move from place to place across varied virtual landscapes. Unlike MMOGs, however, virtual worlds have less structure and allow for more choice in player mobility. Fields and Kafai (2009) focused on the in-game practice of teleporting in a virtual world called Whyville.net. At the time of this study, Whyville featured more than 1.5 million registered players aged 9 to 16 years. Fields and Kafai used a connective ethnographic approach (Leander, 2008; Leander & McKim, 2003) to follow a group of 21 players, aged 9 to 12 years, learning and sharing the practice of teleporting as they traveled across their virtual and physical geographies in and out of an after school club. Through their detailed efforts to follow the practice of teleporting across the entire group of participants, Fields and Kafai capture the networked nature of Whyville play. Participants moved in and out of many virtual and physical spaces available to them in order to learn a particular practice in the game. Collaborative learning and teaching were found to be occurring outside of the physical space of the club and across virtual terrain as well.

CONCLUDING (AND FUTURE) PROVOCATIONS: REMAPPING EVIDENCE AND EQUITY WHILE RESEARCHING LEARNING ON THE MOVE

Our subtitle for this review chapter is the phrase "mapping new mobilities," which we intended to move in two different directions and involve two different meanings of the "new." First, reviewing research within and beyond the education tent we have considered ways in which the social practices of youth involve forms of movement that are undergoing change. This perspective borrows from and extends research and discourses on social change, globalization, technology, and flows and, theoretically and empirically considering such changes, asks what relation these may have for the opportunities and environments for children's learning. From the research we have reviewed, it is clear that the new mobilities of youth are not merely a broader and faster version of "old" mobilities—that opportunities to become physically or virtually mobile are simply expanding for children everywhere. A second and equally important perspective on the "new" reflexively engages theory and method with respect to methodology in educational research. Here, we ask what it would mean for education researchers to shift their historical vision of the classroom as a container for learning. What if the classroom were unsettled as a place, or were considered as a dynamic place-in-the-making? What if the classroom were considered as a point along a complex learning trajectory, or as a node in a network? At the base of this critical questioning is an assumption that theories of knowledge and learning—behaviorism, information processing, situated cognition, sociocultural theory, and others—always involve more or less explicit geographies or space–times of the individual in (or out of) a social "environment." Studying learning has always involved a notion of "where" and "when" learning is happening, whether that version involve studies of child development in psychological labs, classroom design experiments, or virtual ethnographies.

Making explicit and unsettling our assumptions about the when and where of learning is thus not simply making a repeated claim for the ubiquity of learning out of school, but rather, calling for the development of a learning theory that is expansive enough to fill the geographies and mobilities of children's actual lives. It is a push to move conversation from where we expect or desire learning to happen to where it does happen. The conversation on learning in this review focuses primarily on access and opportunity to learn at empirical and theoretical levels. However, a more intensive reappraisal of learning theories through a mobilities or geographical perspective pushes the field in a number of compelling directions: It moves us to reconsider fundamental assumptions about the role of the body in learning, about places of engagement and affect, about learning "transfer" as a psychological and social process of mobility, about development as distributed over social spaces and time, and about disciplinary ways of thinking as fundamentally "scaled" and shaped through particular forms, perspectives, and distributions of resources and people.

Although we have attempted to review complex and sometimes competing accounts, and although we have traversed literatures in human geography, critical geography, new literacy studies, media studies, sociocultural theories of learning, and others, the perspective on "mobilities" we have pursued is obviously incomplete and shaped by our own investments. For instance, we have largely shortchanged cultural studies analyses of youth identity construction amid globalization, including diaspora studies (e.g., Dolby & Rizvi, 2008). Such bracketing is not a critical assessment of this important work, but is chiefly strategic—a struggle with our own limitations to corral a very broad and diverse conversation with an eye toward rethinking issues of learning. In this sense, we have favored a consideration of the "how" of mobilities more than the "what," we have asked how youth (and learning resources) move, how these movements are changing, and how they might be studied in relation to learning. Somewhat implicit in our analysis is the notion that the mobilities of people and objects—whether on the ground or in the virtual—open up opportunity to learn and transform dead learning places into living ones. Problems of equity, then, can be framed as problems of immobility versus mobility. Although we generally assume this orientation, we recognize a number of problems with it, including the fact that the associations between human and virtual mobility on the one hand and social mobility or economic mobility on the other are vastly understudied. Although it seems plausible that children who are moving through extensive online/offline networks, or are situated in engaging places, would at the same time be socially or economically "mobilized," the history of educational research suggests that social mobility cannot merely be read off of schooled or unschooled forms of learning (e.g., Graff, 1979).

Traversing research and theory-building within and beyond educational studies, we have organized our review through the constructs of place, trajectory, and network. These constructs were selected because of their current use as dominant metaphors and modes for reconsidering learning as it relates to "situation" or "environment." Moreover, the differences between and relations among "place" with "network" reflect contemporary conversations in geographic thought, where traditional notions of "place" are under challenge and the dynamisms of "place" relative to "networks" is being theorized (Massey, 2005; McDowell, 1997). In this manner and others, place, trajectory, and network are intended as orientations toward space–time that are mutually informing rather than mutually exclusive. We consider them different entrée points or perspectives that have different theoretical and methodological capacities for critiquing and recasting container-like notions of learning "contexts." Across these perspectives, within our partial mapping of theory-building and research in education, we raise the following key questions. Although issues of evidence and equity are fundamentally intertwined, we have separated them as a matter of emphasis:

Evidence
- What imagined geographies of learning are enacted in our historical or present research methodologies?
- How do our research methods actively construct space–times of learning through the types of data we collect, our perspectives on the data, our levels of abstraction, and our representational practices?
- To what degree do "scales" of activity exist in the world, and to what degree is "scale" a socially constructed abstraction for "distant" discourse and activity that we argue into existence?
- What methods or models might researchers develop to account for the dynamic simultaneity of multiple social spaces as well as movement across periods of time?
- What role is the moving, active body given in current research on learning? How is the body disciplined or made docile not only in school but also through research evidence?
- How would our current perspectives on causal relations and agency change if we seriously engaged not only how people use things, but also how things "use" people? What would it mean to give nonhuman actors their "due" in educational research—to consider how policies, material objects, technologies, and texts are on the move, translating people and entering into dynamic configurations with them?

- What are the specific spatiotemporal dynamics of a particular learning "environment"—its rhythms, tempos, extensibilities, connections to other social spaces, durations, internal divisions, accelerations, fluidities, and other qualities? What would accounting for these spatiotemporal dynamics tell us about a learning environment that simply considering it as a resource cache—a box for learning "affordances"—would leave out?

Questions of evidence in educational research pertaining to imagined geographies, circulations of people and things, research "scale," and other issues are simultaneously questions of equity, as these methodological issues involve critical perspectives on what the "social world" is and how social goods are distributed within it. Extending these issues, the following questions more explicitly consider equity in educational research, calling for a spatiotemporal reappraisal of place, access, recruitment, and difference:

Equity
- How do children differentially experience school as related to other places in their everyday geographies, and in their geographical histories?
- For children who have few opportunities to build associations and attachments to places, including school-as-place, how can school places be made more open, accessible, and engaging?
- How is access to schools and learning institutions spatiotemporally structured into everyday life, including bodily as well as information navigation? How is learning to use these navigational forms made available to all students?
- Who is recruited by particular networks of education, including classrooms and schools, but also literacy, mathematics, magnet schooling, enrichment programs, summer programs, and so on? What passage points do children encounter to move through these networks, and which children are not permitted access through these passage points?
- What social and cultural differences become marked and identified in schools, or in places of learning outside of school? By what processes of mobility are such identity differences either disrupted or solidified? What are the consequences for opportunity to learn of these mobile identity processes?

To these questions for further theory-development and research from the educational research literature, we add additional questions synthesized from the literature on children's (human) geographies and virtual geographies. The questions raised by these bodies of work, for evidence and equity, serve to expand and challenge an emergent agenda in educational studies for studying children's learning across space and time.

Evidence
- To what degree do present studies of children's mobilities and learning account for their routine and constant traversals across material and virtual spaces, or the "always-on" presence of the virtual during face-to-face engagements?

- How do present accounts of learning and development take into account socio-technical co-development, or the reciprocal and continual transformation of children and machines? Further, from this perspective do learning and development have spatial extension as well as temporal duration?
- To what degree are liminal places and spaces, such as physical street scenes and virtual streets, key sites for learning and identity work?
- What do social networks reveal about children's opportunities to learn, and how might such networks be considered in relation to actor networks?
- How might current methods of studying children in situ be complemented by methodologies of understanding their movements across space time and their interpretations of social spaces, including GPS/GIS technologies for mapping embodied movements, time diaries, and free recall maps?

These methodological questions gleaned from the human and virtual geographies of children are expanded by a large range of considerations of how learning opportunities are shaped and constrained by marked inequalities of mobility for different groups of children, by new geographies of fear, by the commercialization of the social world, and by other critical issues.

Equity
- To what extent do children of different cultures and backgrounds, and different geographical locations, experience self-directed mobility in physical and virtual spaces?
- Is the move indoors for children, over historical time, articulated with the move to the screen? To what extent has virtual mobility and play substituted for outdoor mobility and play of a generation or two ago, and what are key differences for learning in these forms of activity? How are the consequences different for different age groups?
- How are physical and virtual "home ranges" for children's mobility structured by adult fear, but also by social or virtual structures within particular communities and homes, financially supported access to institutional environments, the built environment of neighborhoods, transportation networks, and other phenomena?
- How is adult fear and surveillance of children, which appears to have increased historically, expressed in different cultural communities and how does this fear (unequally) constrain opportunities to learn?
- What types of learning about space and time are embedded into physical and virtual daily rounds? If children are becoming increasingly constructed as "immobile subjects" in embodied form, what consequences does this immobility have for (embodied) learning?
- In what ways does the institutional and commercial sponsorship and absorption of "public" spaces for children shape the opportunities to learn in these spaces, the identities of children learning in them, and the discourses and content embedded in them?

- Do children with robust online networks accelerate their means of acquiring and maintaining face-to-face social networks; is there a "Matthew Effect" of social networking and potential learning such that the rich get richer?
- How is the large amount of research on children's identity construction and identity geographies in digital practices research potentially relevant for understanding learning?

Our hope is that these questions, developed from our mapping of the field, serve to engage "futures conversations" concerning possible directions for research, including our own. With the expansion of new mobilities, the expansion of interdisciplinary relations, and the needed expansion of methodologies and theory, there is certainly plenty of work to discuss and set about doing. The latter questions emerging from human and virtual geographies make evident that when we engage with "new" youth practices of mobility that such practices and geographies present complicated and sometimes contradictory images. While children are experiencing new and rapid movements and new opportunities to learn, they are not simply caught up in an idealized version of global life that includes rapid and unfettered travel, continual technologies of instantaneity, and the compression of space by time. Rather, their learning lives are located, positioned, and emplaced in relations of power, politics, and culture. However, the locations of children, in and through which they learn, are not simple containers, are not bounded, and will not hold still.

REFERENCES

Agha, A. (2007). *Language and social relations*. New York: Cambridge University Press.

Aitken, S. (1994). *Putting children in their place*. Washington, DC: Association of American Geographers.

Alvermann, D. E. (2000). Researching libraries, literacies, and lives: A rhizoanalysis. In E. A. S. Pierre & W. Pillow (Eds.), *Working the ruins: Feminist poststructural theory and methods in education* (pp. 114–129). New York: Routledge.

Anagnostopoulos, D. (2003). Testing and student engagement with literature in urban classrooms: A multi-layered perspective. *Research in the Teaching of English, 38,* 177–212.

Appadurai, A. (1996). *Modernity at large: Cultural dimensions of globalization.* Minneapolis: University of Minnesota Press.

Bakhtin, M. M. (1981). *The dialogic imagination: Four essays by M. M. Bakhtin.* (C. Emerson & M. Holquist Trans.). Austin: University of Texas Press.

Bauman, Z. (2005). *Liquid life.* Cambridge, UK: Polity Press.

Beavis, C., Nixon, H., & Atkinson, S. (2005). LAN cafés: Cafés, places of gathering, or sites of informal teaching and learning? *Education, Communication & Information, 5,* 41–60.

Beazley, H. (2000). Home sweet home? Street children's sites of belonging. In S. Holloway & G. Valentine (Eds.) *Children's geographies: Playing, living, learning* (pp. 194–210). New York: Routledge.

Bennet, A. (2004). Virtual subculture? Youth, identity and the Internet. In A. Bennett & K. Kahn-Harris (Eds.), *After subculture: Critical studies in contemporary youth culture* (pp. 162–172). New York: Palgrave Macmillan.

Bingham, N., & Thrift, N. (2000). Some new instructions for travelers: The geography of Bruno Latour and Michel Serres. In M. Crang & N. Thrift (Eds.), *Thinking space* (pp. 281–301). New York: Routledge.

Bingham, N., Valentine, G., & Holloway, S. (1999). Bodies in the midst of things: Re-locating children's use of the internet. In S. Ralph, J. L. Brown, & T. Lees (Eds.), *Youth and the global media: Papers from the 29th University of Manchester Broadcasting Symposium, 1998* (pp. 24–33). Luton, UK: University of Luton Press.

boyd, d. (2007). Why youth (heart) social network sites: The role of networked publics in teenage social life. In D. Buckingham (Ed.), *Youth, identity, and digital media* (pp. 119–142). Cambridge: MIT Press.

boyd, d. (in press). Friendship. In M. Ito, S. Baumer, M. Bittanti, d. boyd, R. Cody, B. Herr-Stephenson, et al. (with Antin, J., Finn, M., Law, A., Manion, A., Mitnick, S., Scholssberg, D., & Yardi, S.). *Hanging out, messing around, and geeking out*. Retrieved November 24, 2009, from http://digitalyouth.ischool.berkeley.edu/book-friendship

boyd, d. m., & Ellison, N. B. (2007). Social network sites: Definition, history, and scholarship. *Journal of Computer-Mediated Communication, 13*(1). Retrieved November 24, 2009, from http://jcmc.indiana.edu/vol13/issue1/boyd.ellison.html

Brandt, D. (2001). *Literacy in American lives*. New York: Cambridge University Press.

Brandt, D., & Clinton, K. (2002). Limits of the local: Expanding perspectives on literacy as a social practice. *Journal of Literacy Research, 34*, 337–356.

Breitbart, M. M. (1998). "Dana's mystical tunnel," Young people's designs for survival and change in the city. In T. Skelton & G. Valentine (Eds.) *Cool places: Geographies of youth cultures* (pp. 305–327). New York: Routledge.

Bronfenbrenner, U. (1979). *The ecology of human development*. Cambridge, MA: Harvard University Press.

Brouwer, L. (2006a). Dutch Moroccan websites: A transnational imagery? *Journal of Ethnic and Migration Studies, 32*, 1153–1168.

Brouwer, L. (2006b). Giving voice to Dutch Moroccan girls on the Internet. *Global Media Journal, 5*(9), Article 3. Retrieved July 3, 2009, from http://lass.calumet.purdue.edu/cca/gmj/fa06/gmj_fa06_brouwer.htm

Callon, M. (1986). Some elements of a sociology of translation: Domestication of the scallops and the fishermen of St. Brieuc Bay. In J. Law (Ed.), *Power, action, and belief* (pp. 196–233). London: Routledge.

Castells, M. (1996). *The rise of the network society*. Cambridge, MA: Blackwell.

Castells, M. (2000). Materials for an exploratory theory of the network society. *British Journal of Sociology, 51*, 5–24.

Castells, M., Fernández-Ardèvol, M., Qiu, J. L., & Sey, A. (2007). *Mobile communication and society: A global perspective*. Cambridge: MIT Press.

Christensen, P. (2003). Place, space and knowledge: Children in the village and the city. In P. Christensen & M. O'Brien (Eds.), *Children in the city: Home, neighbourhood and community* (pp. 13–28). London: RoutledgeFalmer.

Clarke, J. (2002). A new kind of symmetry: Actor-network theories and the new literacy studies. *Studies in the Education of Adults, 34*, 107–122.

Clifford, J. (1992). Traveling cultures. In L. Grossberg, C. Nelson, & P. A. Treichler (Eds.), *Cultural studies* (pp. 96–116). London: Routledge.

Cochran, M., & Niego, S. (2002). Parenting and social networks. In M. H. Bornstein (Ed.), *Handbook of parenting: Social conditions and applied parenting* (pp. 123–148). Mahwah, NJ: Lawrence Erlbaum.

Cole, M. (1996). *Cultural psychology: A once and future discipline*. Cambridge, MA: Belknap Press of Harvard University Press.

Cole, M., & Engestrom, Y. (1993). A cultural-historical approach to distributed cognition. In G. Salomon (Ed.), (Ed.), *Distributed cognitions: Psychological and educational considerations* (pp. 1–46). Cambridge, UK: Cambridge University Press.

Comber, B., Nixon, H., Ashmore, L., Loo, S., & Cook, J. (2006). Urban renewal from the inside out: Spatial and critical literacies in a low socioeconomic school. *Mind, Culture and Activity, 13*, 228–246.

Crockenberg, S. (1981). Infant irritability, mother responsiveness, and social support influences on the security of infant-mother attachment. *Child Development, 52*, 857–865.

Crowe, N., & Bradford, S. (2006). "Hanging out in Runescape": Identity, work and leisure in the virtual playground. *Children's Geographies, 4*, 331–346.

Deleuze, G., & Guattari, F. (1987). *A thousand plateaus: Capitalism and schizophrenia* (B. Massumi, Trans.). Minneapolis: University of Minnesota Press. (Original work published 1980).

Dolby, N., & Rizvi, F. (Eds.). (2008). *Youth moves: Identities and education in global perspective.* New York: Routledge.

Dubinskas, F. A. (Ed.). (1988). *Making time: Ethnographies of high-technology organizations.* Philadelphia: Temple University Press.

Dulay, H., Burt, M., & Krashen, S. (1982). *Language two.* Oxford, UK: Oxford University Press.

Dunkley, C. M. (2004). Risky geographies: Teens, gender, and rural landscape in North America. *Gender, Place and Culture, 11*, 559–579.

Eakle, J. (2007). Literacy spaces of a Christian faith-based school. *Reading Research Quarterly, 42*, 472–510.

Engestrom, Y. (1993). Developmental studies of work as a testbench of activity theory: The case of primary care medical practice. In S. Chaiklin & J. Lave (Eds.), *Understanding practice* (pp. 64–103). Cambridge, UK: Cambridge University Press.

Erstad, O., Øystein, G., Sefton-Green, J., & Vasbø, K. (2009). Exploring "learning lives": Community, identity, literacy and meaning. *Literacy, 43*, 100–106.

Facer, K., Furlong, J., Furlong, R., & Sutherland, R. (2001). Home is where the hardware is: Young people, the domestic environment and "access" to new technologies. In I. Hutchby & J. Moran-Ellis (Eds.), *Children, technology and culture: The impacts of technologies in children's everyday lives* (pp. 13–27). London: RoutledgeFalmer.

Facer, K., Furlong, J., Furlong, R., & Sutherland, R. (2003). *ScreenPlay: Children and computing in the home.* London, UK: RoutledgeFalmer.

Fields, D. A., & Kafai, Y. B. (2009). A connective ethnography of peer knowledge sharing and diffusion in a tween virtual world. *Computer-Supported Collaborative Learning, 4*, 47–68.

Foucault, M. (1972). *The archaeology of knowledge.* (Trans. A. M. Sheridan Smith). New York: Pantheon Books.

Foucault, M. (1979). Discipline and punish: The birth of the prison. New York: Vintage Books.

Fuller, B., Bridges, M., & Pai, S. (2007). *Standardized childhood: The political and cultural struggle over early education.* Palo Alto, CA: Stanford University Press.

Gaster, S. (1991). Urban children's access to their neighborhoods: Changes over three generations. *Environment and Behavior, 23*, 70–85.

Gee, J. P. (2008). A sociocultural perspective on opportunity to learn. In P. A. Moss, D. C. Pullin, J. P. Gee, E. H. Haertel, & L. J. Young (Eds.), *Assessment, equity, and opportunity to learn* (pp. 76–108). New York: Cambridge University Press.

Gill, T. (2007). *No fear: Growing-up in a risk adverse society.* London: Calouste.

Goffman, E. (1981). *Forms of talk.* Philadelphia: University of Pennsylvania Press.

Graff, H. (1979). *The literacy myth: Literacy and social structure in the nineteenth-century city.* New York: Academic Press.

Gutierrez, K., Morales, P. Z., & Martinez, D. C. (2009). Remediating literacy: Culture, difference, and learning for students from nondominant communities. *Review of Research in Education, 33*, 212–245.

Hagood, M. (2004). A rhizomatic cartography of adolescents, popular culture, and constructions of self. In K. M. Leander & M. Sheehy (Eds.), *Spatializing literacy research and practice* (pp. 143–160). New York: Peter Lang.

Hamilton, M. (2001). Privileged literacies: Policy, institutional process and the life of the IALS. *Language and Education, 15*, 178–196.

Harden, J. (2000). There's no place like home: The public/private distinction in children's theorizing of risk and safety. *Childhood, 7*, 43–59.

Hargreaves, A. (2002). Sustainability of educational change: The role of social geographies. *Journal of Educational Change, 3*, 189–214.

Hart, R. (1977). *Children's experience of place.* New York: Irvington.

Harvey, D. (1996). *Social justice and the geography of difference.* London: Blackwell.

Haythornthwaite, C., & Wellman, B. (2002). The Internet in everyday life: An introduction. In B. Wellman & C. Haythornthwaite (Eds.), *The Internet in everyday life* (pp. 3–41). Malden, MA: Blackwell.

Headrick Taylor, K. (2008, September). *Examining changes in adolescent mobility and leisure time across two generations.* Paper presented at the 2nd International Society for Cultural and Activity Research Congress, San Diego, CA.

Heath, S. B. (1983). *Ways with words: Language, life, and work in communities and classrooms.* New York: Cambridge University Press.

Hillman, M., Adams, J., & Whitelegg, J. (1990). *One false move . . . A study of children's independent mobility.* London: Policy Studies Institute.

Hine, C. (2000). *Virtual ethnography.* London: Sage.

Hirst, E. (2004). Diverse social contexts of a second-language classroom and the construction of identity. In K. M. Leander & M. Sheehy (Eds.), *Spatializing literacy research and practice* (pp. 39–66). New York: Peter Lang.

Hollan, D. W., & Wellencamp, J. C. (1993). *Contentment and suffering: Culture and experience in Toraja.* New York: Columbia University Press.

Holland, D., Lachicotte, W., Skinner, D., & Cain, C. (1998). *Identity and agency in cultural worlds.* Cambridge, MA: Harvard University Press.

Holland, D., & Leander, K. M. (2004). Ethnographic studies of positioning and subjectivity: An introduction. *Ethos: Journal of the Society for Psychological Anthropology, 32*, 127–139.

Holloway, S., & Valentine, G. (2000). Children's geographies and the new social studies of childhood. In S. Holloway & G. Valentine (Eds.), *Children's geographies: Playing, living, learning* (pp. 1–26). New York: Routledge.

Holloway, S. L., & Valentine, G. (2001). Children at home in the wired world: Reshaping and rethinking home in urban geography. *Urban Geography, 22*, 562–583.

Holloway, S. L., Valentine, G., & Bingham, N. (2000). Institutionalising technologies: Masculinities, femininities, and the heterosexual economy of the IT classroom. *Environment and Planning A, 32*, 617–633.

Homel, R., Burns, A., & Goodnow, J. (1987). Parental social networks and child development. *Journal of Social and Personal Relationships, 4*, 159–177.

Hull, G., Zacher, J., & Hibbert, L. (2009). Youth, risk, and equity in a global world. *Review of Research in Education, 33*, 117–159.

Ito, M. (2005). Introduction: Personal, portable, pedestrian. In M. Ito, D. Okabe, & M. Matsuda (Eds.), *Personal, portable, pedestrian: Mobile phones in Japanese life* (pp. 1–16). Cambridge: MIT Press.

Ito, M., Baumer, S., Bittanti, M., boyd, d., Cody, R., & Herr-Stephenson, B., et al. (with Antin, J., Finn, M., Law, A., Manion, A., Mitnick, S., Scholssberg, D., & Yardi, S.). (in press).

Hanging out, messing around, and geeking out. Retrieved November 24, 2009, from http://digitalyouth.ischool.berkeley.edu/report

Ito, M., Horst, H., Bittanti, M., boyd, d., Herr-Stephenson, B., & Lange, P., et al. (2008, November). *Living and learning with new media: Summary of findings from the Digital Youth Project* (MacArthur Foundation Reports on Digital Media and Learning). Retrieved November 24, 2009, from http://digitalyouth.ischool.berkeley.edu/report

Ito, M., Okabe, D., & Matsuda, M. (Eds.). (2005). *Personal, portable, pedestrian: Mobile phones in Japanese life.* Cambridge: MIT Press.

Johnsen, T. E. (2003). The social context of the mobile phone use of Norwegian teens. In J. E. Katz (Ed.), *Machines that become use: The social context of personal communication technology* (pp. 161–169). New Brunswick, NJ: Transaction.

Jones, R. H. (with Lou, J., Yeung, L., Leung, V., Lai, I., Man, C., & Woo, B.). (2001, November-December). *Beyond the screen: A participatory study of computer mediated communication among Hong Kong youth.* Paper presented at the meeting of the American Anthropological Association, Washington, DC.

Jones, R. H. (2005). Sites of engagement as sites of attention: Time, space and culture in electronic discourse. In S. Norris & R. H. Jones (Eds.), *Discourse in action: Introducing mediated discourse analysis* (pp. 141–154). London: Routledge.

Kamberelis, G. (2004). A rhizome and the pack: Liminal literacy formations with political teeth. In C. Lankshear, M. Peters, M. Knobel, & C. Bigum (Eds.), *New literacies and digital epistemologies* (pp. 161–197). New York: Peter Lang.

Karsten, L. (1998). Growing-up in Amsterdam: Differentiation and segregation in children's daily lives. *Urban Studies, 35,* 565–581.

Karsten, L. (2002). Mapping childhood in Amsterdam: Spatial and social construction of children's domains in the city. *TESG/Journal of Economic and Social Geography, 93,* 231–241.

Karsten, L. (2005). It all used to be better? Different generations on continuity and change in urban children's daily use of space. *Children's Geographies, 3,* 275–290.

Kasesniemi, E.-L., & Rautiainen, P. (2002). Mobile culture of children and teenagers in Finland. In J. E. Katz & M. A. Aakhus (Eds.), *Perpetual contact: Mobile communication, private talk, public performance* (pp. 301–317). Cambridge, UK: Cambridge University Press.

Katz, C. (1994). Textures of global change: Eroding ecologies of childhood in New York and Sudan. *Childhood, 2,* 103–110.

Katz, J. E. (2006). *Magic in the air: Mobile communication and the transformation of social life.* New Brunswick, NJ: Transaction.

Kitchin, R. M. (1998). Towards geographies of cyberspace. *Progress in Human Geography, 22,* 385–406.

Kwan, M.-P. (2008). From oral histories to visual narratives: Re-presenting the post-September 11 experiences of the Muslim women in the United States. *Social and Cultural Geography, 9,* 653–669.

Lægran, A. S. (2002). The petrol station and the Internet café: Rural technospaces for youth. *Journal of Rural Studies, 18,* 157–168.

Lam, W. S. E. (2000). L2 literacy and the design of the self: A case study of a teenager writing on the Internet. *TESOL Quarterly, 34,* 457–482.

Lam, W. S. E. (2004). Second language socialization in a bilingual chat room: Global and local considerations. *Language Learning and Technology, 8*(3), 44–65.

Lam, W. S. E. (2006). Re-envisioning language, literacy, and the immigrant subject in new mediascapes. *Pedagogies, 1,* 171–195.

Lam, W. S. E. (2009). Multiliteracies on instant messaging in negotiating local, translocal, and transnational affiliations: A case of an adolescent immigrant. *Reading Research Quarterly, 44,* 377–397.

Lam, W. S. E., & Rosario-Ramos, E. (2009). Multilingual literacies in transnational digitally mediated contexts: An exploratory study of immigrant teens in the United States. *Language and Education, 23,* 171–190.

Lammes, S. (2008). Spatial regimes of the digital playground: Cultural functions of spatial practices in computer games. *Space and Culture, 11,* 260–272.

Lareau, A. (2003). *Unequal childhoods: Class, race, and family life.* Los Angeles: University of California Press.

Latour, B. (1983). Give me a laboratory and I will raise the world. In K. Knorr-Cetina & M. Mulkay (Eds.), *Science observed: Perspectives on the social study of science* (pp. 141–170). London: Sage.

Latour, B. (1987). *Science in action.* Cambridge, MA: Harvard University Press.

Latour, B. (1991). Technology is society made durable. In J. Law (Ed.), *A sociology of monsters: Essays on power, technology, and domination* (pp. 103–131). London: Routledge.

Latour, B. (1993). *We have never been modern.* Hemel Hempstead, UK: Harvester Wheatsheaf.

Latour, B. (1996a). *Aramis, or the love of technology.* Cambridge, MA: Harvard University Press.

Latour, B. (1996b). On interobjectivity. Symposium on "the lessons of simian society." *Mind, Culture, and Activity, 3,* 228–245.

Latour, B. (1999). On recalling ANT. In J. Law & J. Hassard (Eds.), *Actor network theory and after* (pp. 15–25). Oxford, UK: Blackwell/The Sociological Review.

Latour, B. (2005). Reassembling the social: An introduction to actor-network-theory. Oxford, UK: Oxford University Press.

Laurier, E., Hayden, L., Brown, B., Jones, O., Juhlin, O., & Noble, A., et al. (2008). Driving and "passengering": Notes on the ordinary organization of car travel. *Mobilities, 3,* 1–23.

Lave, J., & Wenger, E. (1991). *Situated learning: Legitimate peripheral participation.* New York: Cambridge University Press.

Law, J. (1994). *Organising modernity.* Oxford, UK: Blackwell.

Law, J. (2004). And if the global were small and noncoherent? Method, complexity, and the baroque. *Environment and Planning D, 22,* 13–26.

Leander, K. M. (2001). "This is our freedom bus going home right now": Producing and hybridizing space-time contexts in pedagogical discourse. *Journal of Literacy Research, 33,* 637–679.

Leander, K. M. (2002a). Locating Latanya: The situated production of identity artifacts in classroom interaction. *Research in the Teaching of English, 37,* 198–250.

Leander, K. M. (2002b). Polycontextual construction zones: Mapping the expansion of schooled space and identity. *Mind, Culture, and Activity, 9,* 211–237.

Leander, K. M. (2008). Toward a connective ethnography of online/offline literacy networks. In J. Coiro, M. Knobel, C. Lankshear, & D. J. Leu (Eds.), *Handbook of research on new literacies* (pp. 33–65). New York: Lawrence Erlbaum.

Leander, K. M., & Lovvorn, J. F. (2006). Literacy networks: Following the circulation of texts, bodies, and objects in the schooling and online gaming of one youth. *Cognition and Instruction, 24,* 291–340.

Leander, K. M., & McKim, K. K. (2003). Tracing the everyday "sitings" of adolescents on the Internet: A strategic adaptation of ethnography across online and offline spaces. *Education, Communication and Information, 3,* 211–240.

Leander, K. M., & Mills, S. (2007). The transnational development of an online role player game by youth: Tracing the flows of literacy, an online game imaginary, and digital resources. In C. Clark & M. Blackburn (Eds.), *Literacy research for political action and social change* (pp. 177–198). New York: Peter Lang.

Leander, K., & Rowe, D. W. (2006). Mapping literacy spaces in motion: A rhizomatic analysis of a classroom literacy performance. *Reading Research Quarterly, 41,* 428–460.

Leander, K. M., & Vasudevan, L. (2009). Multimodality and mobile culture. In C. Jewitt (Ed.), *The Routledge handbook of multimodal analysis* (pp. 127–139). London: Routledge.

Lee, A. (1996). *Gender, literacy, curriculum: Re-writing school geography*. Bristol, PA: Taylor & Francis.

Lee, H. (2006). Debating language and identity online: Tongans on the net. In K. Landzelius (Ed.), *Native on the Net: Indigenous and diasporic peoples in the virtual age* (pp. 152–168). London: Routledge.

Lefebvre, H. (1991). *The production of space* (D. Nicholson-Smith, Trans.). Cambridge, MA: Blackwell.

Lehrer, R., Jacobson, C., Kemeny, V., & Strom, D. (1999). Building on children's intuitions to develop mathematical understanding of space. In E. Fennema & T. A. Romberg (Eds.), *Mathematics classrooms that promote understanding* (pp. 63–87). Mahwah, NJ: Lawrence Erlbaum.

Lemke, J. (2006). Toward critical multimedia literacy: Technology, research, and politics. In M. C. McKenna, L. D. Labbo, R. D. Kieffer, & D. Reinking (Eds.), *International handbook of literacy and technology* (Vol. 2. pp. 3–14). Mahwah, NJ: Lawrence Erlbaum.

Lemke, J. L. (2000). Across the scales of time: Artifacts, activities, and meanings in ecosocial systems. *Mind, Culture, and Activity, 7*, 273–292.

Lenhart, A., Arafeh, S., Smith, A., & Macgill, A. R. (2008). *Writing, technology and teens*. Retrieved July 24, 2009, from http://www.pewinternet.org/Reports/2008/Writing-Technology-and-Teens.aspx

Lenhart, A., Kahne, J., Middaugh, E., Macgill, A. R., Evans, C., & Vitak, J. (2008). *Teens, video games, and civics*. Retrieved July 29, 2009, from http://www.pewinternet.org/Reports/2008/Teens-Video-Games-and-Civics.aspx

Lin, H. (2008). Body, space, and gendered gaming experiences: A cultural geography of homes, cybercafés, and dormitories. In Y. B. Kafai, C. Heeter, J. Denner, & J. Y. Sun (Eds.), *Beyond Barbie and Mortal Kombat: New perspectives on gender and gaming* (pp. 67–81). Cambridge: MIT Press.

Ling, R., & Campbell, S. W. (2009). Introduction: The reconstruction of space and time through mobile communication practices. In R. Ling & S. W. Campbell (Eds.), *The reconstruction of space and time: Mobile communication practices* (pp. 1–15). New Brunswick, NJ: Transaction.

Livingstone, S., & Bober, M. (2005). *UK children go online: Final report of key project findings*. London: Economic and Social Research Council.

Mackett, R. L., Gong, Y., Kitazawa, K., & Paskins, J. (2007). *Children's local travel behavior: How the environment influences, controls and facilitates it*. Paper presented at 11th World Conference on Transport Research, University of California, Berkeley, CA.

Marshall, H. (1972). Structural constraints on learning. In B. Geer (Ed.), *Learning to work* (pp. 39–48). Beverly Hills, CA: Sage.

Massey, D. (2005). *For space*. London: Sage.

Matsuda, M. (2005a). Discourse of *ketai* in Japan. In M. Ito, D. Okabe, & M. Matsuda (Eds.), *Personal, portable, pedestrian: Mobile phones in Japanese life* (pp. 19–39). Cambridge: MIT Press.

Matsuda, M. (2005b). Mobile communication and selective sociality. In M. Ito, D. Okabe, & M. Matsuda (Eds.), *Personal, portable, pedestrian: Mobile phones in Japanese life* (pp. 123–142). Cambridge, MA: MIT Press.

Matthews, H. (1987). Gender, home range and environmental cognition. *Transactions of the Institute of British Geographers, 12*, 32–56.

Matthews, H. (2003). The street as a liminal space: The barbed spaces of childhood. In P. Christensen & M. O'Brien (Eds.) *Children in the city: Home, neighbourhood and community* (pp. 101–117). London: RoutledgeFalmer.

Matthews, H., & Limb, M. (1999). Defining an agenda for the geography of children: Review and prospect. *Progress in Human Geography, 23*, 61–90.

Matthews, H., Limb, M., & Taylor, M. (2000). The "street" as thirdspace. In S. Holloway & G. Valentine (Eds.), *Children's geographies: Playing, living, learning* (pp. 63–79). New York: Routledge.

McDowell, L. (Ed.). (1997). *Undoing place? A geographical reader.* New York: Arnold.

McKendrick, J., Bradford, M., & Fielder, A. (2000). Time for a party!: Making sense of the commercialisation of leisure space for children. In S. Holloway & G. Valentine (Eds.), *Children's geographies: Playing, living, learning* (pp. 100–116). New York: Routledge.

McNamee, S. (1998). Youth, gender and video games: Power and control in the home. In T. Skelton & G. Valentine (Eds.), *Cool places: Geographies of youth cultures* (pp. 195–206). London: Routledge.

Moore, R. C. (1976). Theory and research on the development of environmental knowing. In G. Moore & R. Golledge (Eds.), *Environmental knowing* (pp. 83–107). Stroudsburg, PA: Dowden, Hutchinson & Ross.

Morrow, V. (2003). Improving the neighbourhood for children: Possibilities and limitations of "social capital" discourses. In P. Christensen & M. O'Brien (Eds.), *Children in the city: Home, neighbourhood and community* (pp. 162–183). London: RoutledgeFalmer.

Nespor, J. (1994). *Knowledge in motion: Space, time and curriculum in undergraduate physics and management.* London: Falmer Press.

Nespor, J. (1997). *Tangled up in school: Politics, space, bodies and signs in the educational process.* Mahwah, NJ: Lawrence Erlbaum.

Norris, S. (2004). *Analyzing multimodal interaction: A methodological framework.* New York: Routledge.

Norris, S., & Jones, R. H. (Eds). (2004). *Discourse in action: Introducing mediated discourse analysis.* New York: Routledge.

Okada, T. (2005). Youth culture and the shaping of Japanese mobile media: Personalization and the *ketai* Internet as multimedia. In M. Ito, D. Okabe, & M. Matsuda (Eds.), *Personal, portable, pedestrian: Mobile phones in Japanese life* (pp. 41–60). Cambridge: MIT Press.

Olwig, K. F., & Hastrup, K. (Eds.). (1997). *Siting culture.* New York: Routledge.

Ong, W. J. (1982). *Orality and literacy: The technologizing of the word.* New York: Methuen.

Pardoe, S. (2000). Respect and the pursuit of "symmetry" in researching literacy and student writing. In D. Barton, M. Hamilton, & R. Ivanic (Eds.), *Situated literacies: Reading and writing in context* (pp. 149–166). London: Routledge.

Pooley, C., Turnbull, J., & Adams, M. (2005). The journey to school in Britain since the 1940s: Continuity and change. *Area, 37*, 43–53.

Ruddick, S. (1998). Modernism and resistance: How "homeless" youth sub-cultures make a difference. In T. Skelton & G. Valentine (Eds.), *Cool places: Geographies of youth cultures* (pp. 343–360). London: Routledge.

Sack, R. D. (1997). *Home geographicus: A framework for action awareness, and moral concerns.* Baltimore: Johns Hopkins University Press.

Scollon, R. (2008). *Geographies of discourse: Action across layered spaces.* Unpublished manuscript.

Scollon, R., & Scollon, S. (2003). *Discourses in place: Language in the material world.* New York: Routledge.

Seyer-Ochi, I. (2006). Lived landscapes of the Fillmore. In G. Spindler & L. Hammond (Eds.), *Innovations in educational ethnography: Theory, methods, and results* (pp. 162–232). Mahwah, NJ: Lawrence Erlbaum.

Sheehy, M. (2004). Between a thick and a thin place: Changing literacy practices. In K. M. Leander & M. Sheey (Eds.), *Spatializing literacy research and practice* (pp. 91–114). New York: Peter Lang.

Sheller, M. (2004). Mobile publics: Beyond the network perspective. *Environment and Planning D, 22,* 39–52.

Skelton, T. (2000). "Nothing to do, nowhere to go?" Teenage girls and "public" space in Rhondda Valleys, south Wales. In S. Holloway & G. Valentine (Eds.), *Children's geographies: Playing, living, learning* (pp. 80–99). New York: Routledge.

Skop, E., & Adams, P. C. (2009). Creating and inhabiting virtual places: Indian immigrants in cyberspace. *National Identities, 11,* 127–147.

Soja, E. W. (1989). *Postmodern geographies: The reassertion of space in critical social theory.* London: Verso.

St. Pierre, E. A. (1997). An introduction to figurations: A poststructural practice of inquiry. *Qualitative Studies in Education, 10,* 279–284.

Star, L., & Griesemer, R. J. (1989). Institutional ecology, "translations" and boundary objects: Amateurs and professionals in Berkeley's museum of vertebrate zoology, 1907–39. *Social Studies of Science, 19,* 387–420.

Stevens, R., O'Connor, K., Garrison, L., Jocuns, A., & Amos, D. M. (2008). Becoming an engineer: Toward a three dimensional view of engineering learning. *Journal of Engineering Education, 97,* 355–368.

Tapscott, D. (1998). *Growing up digital: The rise of the net generation.* New York: McGraw-Hill.

Thrift, N., & Dewsbury, J.-D. (2000). Dead geographies—and how to make them live. *Environment and Planning D, 18,* 411–432.

Thulin, E., & Vilhelmson, B. (2005). Virtual mobility of urban youth: ICT-based communication in Sweden. *Tijdschrift voor Economische en Sociale Geografie, 96,* 477–487.

Thulin, E., & Vilhelmson, B. (2006). Virtual mobility and processes of displacement: Young people's changing use of ICT, time, and place. *Networks and Communication Studies, 20*(3/4), 27–39.

Thulin, E., & Vilhelmson, B. (2007). Mobiles everywhere: Youth, the mobile phone, and changes in everyday practice. *Young: Nordic Journal of Youth Research, 15,* 235–253.

Thulin, E., & Vilhelmson, B. (2009). Mobile phones: Transforming the everyday social communication practice of urban youth. In R. Ling & S. W. Campbell (Eds.), *The reconstruction of space and time: Mobile communication practices* (pp. 137–158). New Brunswick, NJ: Transaction.

Tietjen, A. (1985). Relationships between the social networks of Swedish mothers and their children. *International Journal of Behavioral Development, 8,* 195–216.

Townsend, A. M. (2000). Life in the real-time city: Mobile telephones and urban metabolism. *Journal of Urban Technology, 7,* 85–104.

Tudge, R. H., Doucet, F., Odero, D., Sperb, T. N., Piccinni, C., & Lopes, R. S. (2006). A window into different cultural worlds: Young children's everyday activities in the United States, Brazil, and Kenya. *Child Development, 77,* 1446–69.

Valentine, G. (1996). Children should be seen and not heard: The production and transgression of adults' public space. *Urban Geography, 17,* 205–220.

Valentine, G. (1997). A safe place to grow up? Parenting perceptions of children's safety and the rural idyll. *Journal of Rural Studies, 13,* 137–148.

Valentine, G., & Holloway, S. (2001). On-line dangers? Geographies of parents' fears for children's safety in cyberspace. *Professional Geographer, 53,* 71–83.

Valentine, G., & Holloway, S. L. (2001). A window on the wider world? Rural children's use of information and communication technologies. *Journal of Rural Studies, 17,* 383–394.

Valentine, G., & Holloway, S. L. (2002). Cyberkids? Exploring children's identities and social networks in on-line and off-line worlds. *Annals of the Association of American Geographers, 92*(2), 302–319.

Valentine, G., Holloway, S., & Bingham, N. (2002). The digital generation? Children, ICT and the everyday nature of social exclusion. *Antipode, 34,* 296–315.

Valentine, G., Holloway, S. L., & Bingham, N. (2000). Transforming cyberspace: Children's interventions in the new public sphere. In S. L. Holloway & G. Valentine (Eds.), *Children's geographies: Playing, living, learning* (pp. 156–173). London: Routledge.

Valentine, G., & McKendrick, J. (1997). Children's outdoor play: Exploring parental concerns about children's safety and the changing nature of childhood. *Geoforum, 28,* 219–235.

Valentine, G., & Skelton, T. (2008). Changing spaces: The role of the Internet in shaping Deaf geographies. *Social and Cultural Geography, 9,* 469–485.

Van Blerk, L. (2005). Negotiating spatial identities: Mobile perspectives on street life in Uganda. *Children's Geographies, 3,* 5–21.

Varnelis, K., & Friedberg, A. (2008). Place: The networking of public space. In K. Varnelis (Ed.), *Networked publics* (pp. 15–42). Cambridge: MIT Press.

Vasquez, O. (2002). La Clase Magica: Imagining optimal possibilities in a bilingual community of learners. Mahwah, NJ: Lawrence Erlbaum.

Vertesi, J. (2008). Mind the gap: The London Underground map and users' representations of urban space. *Social Studies of Science, 38*(7), 7–33.

Vygotsky, L. S. (1978). *Mind in society: The development of higher psychological processes.* Cambridge, MA: Harvard University Press.

Walker, M., Whyatt, J. D., Pooley, C., Davies, G., Coulton, P., & Bamford, W. (2009). Talk, technologies and teenagers: Understanding the school journey using a mixed-methods approach. *Children's Geographies, 7,* 107–122.

Ward, C. (1978). *The child in the city.* New York: Pantheon.

Warschauer, M., & Matuchniak, T. (2010). New technology and digital worlds: Analyzing evidence in equity of access, use, and outcomes. *Review of Research in Education, 34*(1), 179–225.

Watt, P., & Stenson, K. (1998). The street: "It's a bit dodgy around here": Safety, danger, ethnicity and young people's use of public space. In T. Skelton & G. Valentine (Eds.), *Cool places: Geographies of youth cultures* (pp. 249–265). London: Routledge.

Wellman, B. (2001). Physical place and cyberplace: The rise of personalized networking. *International Journal of Urban and Regional Research, 25,* 227–252.

Wellman, B., & Gulia, M. (1999). Net-Surfers don't ride alone: Virtual communities as communities. In B. Wellman (Ed.), *Networks in the global village: Life in contemporary communities* (pp. 331–366). Boulder, CO: Westview Press.

Wertsch, J. V. (1991). *Voices of the mind: A sociocultural approach to mediated action.* Cambridge, MA: Harvard University Press.

Wertsch, J. V. (1998). *Mind as action.* New York: Oxford University Press.

Willis, P. (1977). *Learning to labor.* New York: Columbia University Press.

Wortham, S. (2004). From good student to outcast: The emergence of a classroom identity. *Ethos: Journal of the Society for Psychological Anthropology, 32,* 164–187.

Wortham, S. (2006). *Learning identity.* New York: Cambridge University Press.

Wortham, S. (2008). The objectification of identity across events. *Linguistics and Education, 19,* 294–311.

Young, L. (2003). The place of street children in Kampala's urban environment: Marginalisation, resistance and acceptance in the urban environment. *Environment and Planning D, 21,* 607–627.

Younnis, J. (1994). Children's friendship and peer culture: Implications for theories of networks and supports. In F. Nestmann & K. Hurrelmann (Eds.), *Social networks and social support in childhood and adolescence* (pp. 75–88). Berlin: Walter de Gruyter.

Zacher, J. C. (2009). Christina's worlds: Negotiating childhood in the city. *Educational Studies, 45,* 262–279.

Zeiher, H. (2003). Shaping daily life in urban environments. In P. Christensen & M. O'Brien (Eds.), *Children in the city: Home, neighbourhood and community* (pp. 66–81). London: RoutledgeFalmer.

About the Editors

Allan Luke is Professor of Education at Queensland University of Technology, Australia, where he teaches language and literacy education, curriculum, and policy studies and sociology. He trained as a primary teacher and completed his graduate studies at Simon Fraser University in Canada. He was Deputy Director General and Ministerial Advisor in Queensland from 1999-2002, working on state curriculum and assessment reforms. From 2002-2005, he was Foundation Dean of the Centre for Research on Pedagogy and Practice, National Institute of Education, Singapore. His most recent books are *Pierre Bourdieu and Literacy Education* (Routledge) and *Curriculum, Syllabus Design and Equity* (Routledge). He currently is working on a longitudinal evaluation of Aboriginal and Torres Strait Islander school networking and reform for the Australian federal government.

Judith Green is currently a professor and emphasis leader in Qualitative & Interpretive Research in the Department of Education in the Gevirtz Graduate School of Education at the University of California, Santa Barbara. She is also director of the Center for Literacy and Inquiry in Networking Communities. She obtained her PhD in education from the University of California, Berkeley, in 1977. Her research interests include the social construction of disciplinary knowledge in classrooms; literacy as a social process; and ethnography, discourse, and video analysis of factors that support and constrain equity of access to disciplinary knowledge, identity potentials, and literacy as a social process in classrooms and other social contexts. Her published books include *Handbook of Complimentary Methods in Education Research* (Green, Camilli, & Elmore, 2006), *Multiple Perspective Analyses of Classroom Discourse* (Green & Harker, 1988), and *Multidisciplinary Perspectives on Literacy Research* (Beach, Green, Kamil, & Shanahan, 2005).

Gregory J. Kelly is currently a professor of science education and head of the Department of Curriculum and Instruction at the Pennsylvania State University. He is a former Peace Corps Volunteer and physics teacher. He received his PhD from Cornell University in 1994. His research focuses on classroom discourse, epistemology, and science learning and has been supported by grants from Spencer Foundation, National Science Foundation, and the National Academy of Education. His recently published chapter, "Epistemology and Educational Research," appears in J. Green, G. Camilli, and P. Elmore (Eds.), *Handbook of Complementary Methods in Education Research*. He teaches courses in science education and qualitative research methods. He serves as editor for the journal *Science Education*.

Review of Research in Education
March 2010, Vol. 34, pp. 395
DOI: 10.3102/0091732X09360896
© 2010 AERA. http://rre.aera.net

About the Contributors

Lora Bartlett is Assistant Professor in the Education Department at the University of California, Santa Cruz. She earned her PhD in education at the University of California, Berkeley. Her research focuses on the composition of the teacher workforce, conceptions of teacher professionalism, and the policy and organizational contexts of teachers' work. Prior to joining the UCSC faculty she was an Atlantic Public Policy Fellow in Britain, where she examined policy responses to problems of teacher recruitment and retention. She is currently conducting research on the global migration of teachers.

Lauren Beresford is a doctoral student in sociology at the University of California, Berkeley. Her areas of interest include labor market stratification, inequality in educational outcomes, and the role of organizational actors in producing and reproducing persistent, structural inequalities. She is currently conducting research which explores how hiring practices diffuse within organizations and produce occupational closure through requirements for credentials and work experience.

Katherine Headrick Taylor is a doctoral student in the Department of Teaching and Learning at Vanderbilt University's Peabody College. Her research concentration is in the area of diversity, learning, and development. She is currently studying learning communities outside of the formal classroom in which adolescents participate. Taylor is also a member of the Space, Learning, and Mobility (SLaM) research team, conducting ethnographic observations of professional work groups.

Will J. Jordan (PhD, Columbia University) is Associate Professor of Educational Leadership and Policy Studies and Director of the Institute for Schools and Society at Temple University. His research focuses on deconstructing social forces within the context of urban schools for the purposes of reform. His broader scholarly interests, informed by a background in sociology, include educational policy and social stratification.

James G. Ladwig is Principal Research Fellow in The Australian Institute for Social Inclusion and Wellbeing at the University of Newcastle, Australia. His research areas

Review of Research in Education
March 2010, Vol. 34, pp. 396-399
DOI: 10.3102/0091732X09360895
© 2010 AERA. http://rre.aera.net

include the sociology of education, school reform, educational policy and the philosophy of education. He has served as Principal Research Fellow for the University of Queensland, visiting Research Professor at the National Institute of Education, Singapore, designed and directed several large national and comparative studies and has acted as a research advisor to several school reform initiatives in Australia.

Kevin M. Leander is an Associate Professor in the Department of Teaching and Learning at Peabody College, Vanderbilt University. Prior to pursuing his PhD at the University of Illinois, he taught high school English and French in California and Italy. His research interests include contemporary social practices with literacy and new media, networked approaches to literacy and learning, spatial and multimodal analyses of human interaction, and embodied practices of learning and identity. He is currently collaborating with Rogers Hall (Vanderbilt) and doctoral students in an NSF-funded research project on embodied mathematics, ethnographically investigating spatial analysis and modeling in professional practices (*Space, Learning, and Mobility, or SLaM*). He is also collaborating in *Wired Up*, a study of new media and migrant networks in The Netherlands, with Mariette de Haan and Sandra Ponzanesi (University of Utrecht). He is currently co-lead Editor of the 58th *Yearbook of the National Reading Conference*.

Judith Warren Little is the Carol Liu Professor of Education Policy at the Graduate School of Education, University of California, Berkeley. She holds a PhD in sociology from the University of Colorado and concentrates her research on teachers' work and careers, the organizational and policy contexts of teaching, and issues in professional education. She has published numerous papers and co-edited two books in the areas of teachers' work, school reform, and teacher policy. She is an elected member of the National Academy of Education, and serves as an advisor to foundations, government agencies, professional associations, university programs, and local education authorities in the US and elsewhere.

Samuel R. Lucas, an Associate Professor of Sociology at the University of California–Berkeley, has research and teaching interests in social stratification, sociology of education, research methods, and statistics. His book, *Tracking Inequality: Stratification and Mobility in American High Schools*, received the Willard Waller Award from the Sociology of Education Section of the American Sociological Association in 2000 for the most outstanding book in the sociology of education for 1997, 1998, and 1999. Publishing multiple articles on education transitions, he recently edited a journal special issue on this approach. His book titled *Theorizing Discrimination in an Era of Contested Prejudice*, the first volume of a three-volume analysis of discrimination, was published in 2008.

Tina Matuchniak is a Lecturer in the Department of English and Faculty Liaison for the Beach Learning Community program at California State University, Long Beach. She is currently also a doctoral student in the Department of Education at the

University of California, Irvine, specializing in Language, Literacy, and Technology. Previously, she has served as the Assistant Director of the Writer's Resource Lab at California State University, Long Beach and has taught writing at several universities (California State University, Monterey Bay) and community colleges (Orange Coast College and Coastline Community College). Her research focuses on technology use and literacies of first-year, under-prepared, under-represented college students.

Nathan C. Phillips is a doctoral student in the Department of Teaching and Learning at Peabody College at Vanderbilt University. Before beginning doctoral studies, Phillips taught high school English and language arts. He is interested in new literacies and, in particular, in the ways that adolescents live and learn across virtual and physical landscapes and among multiple media. Phillips is also a member of the Space, Learning, and Mobility (SLaM) research team at Vanderbilt, and is conducting a workplace ethnography of people performing complex spatial reasoning and analysis as part of their everyday work practices. His present research sometimes involves waiting for helicopter rides.

Gail L. Sunderman is Senior Research Scientist at The George Washington University Center for Equity and Excellence in Education where she directs the Mid-Atlantic Equity Center. Her research focuses on educational policy and politics, and urban school reform. She is a former Fulbright scholar to Afghanistan and received her PhD in political science from the University of Chicago.

Mark Warschauer is Professor of Education and Informatics at the University of California, Irvine and director of the university's Digital Learning Lab. His research focuses on the relationship of digital media use to language and literacy practices of culturally and linguistically diverse learners. His recent books include *Laptops and Literacy: Learning in the Wireless Classroom* (Teachers College Press) and *Technology and Social Inclusion: Rethinking the Digital Divide* (MIT Press). Warschauer also directs the PhD in Education program at UCI, which includes a specialization in Language, Literacy, and Technology. He can be reached via his Website at http://www.gse.uci.edu/markw.

Kevin Welner is professor and director of the University of Colorado at Boulder Education and the Public Interest Center (EPIC). He has received the AERA's Early Career Award and its Palmer O. Johnson Award, the Rockefeller Foundation's Bellagio Residency, and the NAEd/Spencer Post-Doctoral Fellowship. His most recent book is *NeoVouchers: The Emergence of Tuition Tax Credits for Private Schooling* (Rowman & Littlefield, 2008). Other publications include *Legal Rights, Local Wrongs: When Community Control Collides with Educational Equity* (SUNY Press, 2001); and *Education Policy and law: Current issues* (with Wendy Chi, Information Age Publishing, 2008). He received his B.A. in Biological Sciences from UCSB and his J.D. and PhD from UCLA.

Dylan Wiliam is Deputy Director of the Institute of Education, London. In a varied career, he has taught in urban public schools, directed a large-scale testing program, served a number of roles in university administration, including Dean of a School of Education, and Provost, and pursued a research program focused on supporting teachers to develop their use of assessment in support of learning.

Alexander W. Wiseman is Associate Professor of Comparative and International Education in the College of Education at Lehigh University. Dr. Wiseman's interests are in comparing educational policymaking and reform processes among nations as well as investigating and understanding global trends in education. His work specifically focuses on policymaking, cross-national trends and comparative phenomena in three overlapping areas: school organization and management, schooling and the labor market, and schooling as a national project.